6/89
Rev 2016

St. Louis Community College

Forest Park
Florissant Valley
Meramec

Instructional Resources
St. Louis, Missouri

THE
CUBA READER

THE MAKING OF A
REVOLUTIONARY SOCIETY

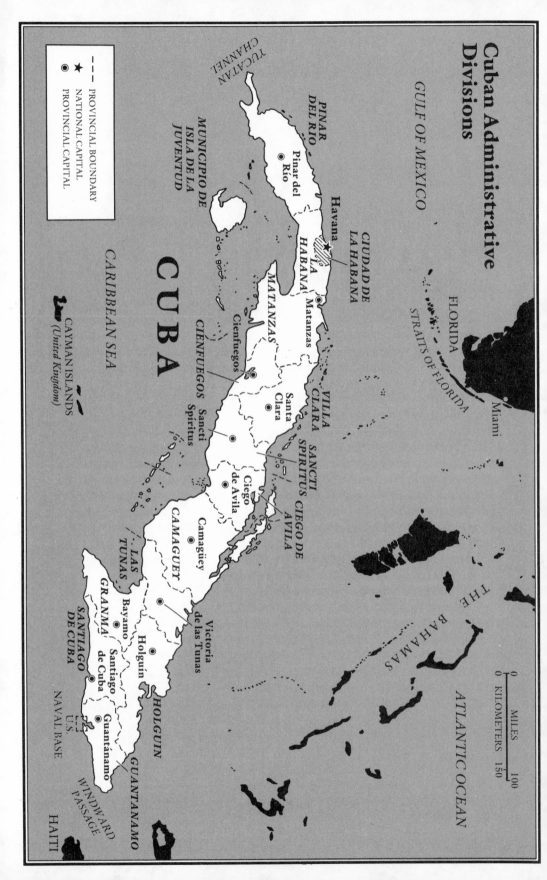

Cuban Administrative Divisions

PROVINCIAL BOUNDARY
NATIONAL CAPITAL
PROVINCIAL CAPITAL

GULF OF MEXICO

YUCATAN CHANNEL

PINAR DEL RIO

Pinar del Río

Havana

LA HABANA

CIUDAD DE LA HABANA

Matanzas

MATANZAS

VILLA CLARA

Santa Clara

Cienfuegos

CIENFUEGOS

Sancti Spíritus

SANCTI SPIRITUS

CIEGO DE AVILA

Ciego de Avila

Camagüey

CAMAGUEY

Victoria de las Tunas

LAS TUNAS

GRANMA

Bayamo

Holguín

HOLGUIN

SANTIAGO DE CUBA

Santiago de Cuba

GUANTANAMO

Guantánamo

U.S. NAVAL BASE

MUNICIPIO DE ISLA DE LA JUVENTUD

CUBA

CARIBBEAN SEA

CAYMAN ISLANDS
(United Kingdom)

FLORIDA

STRAITS OF FLORIDA

Miami

THE BAHAMAS

ATLANTIC OCEAN

MILES
0   100
0   KILOMETERS   150

WINDWARD PASSAGE

HAITI

THE
CUBA READER

THE MAKING OF A
REVOLUTIONARY SOCIETY

EDITED BY

Philip Brenner
William M. LeoGrande
Donna Rich
Daniel Siegel

GROVE PRESS
New York

Published by Grove Press
841 Broadway
New York, N.Y. 10003

Library of Congress Cataloging-in-Publication Data

The Cuba reader:the making of a revolutionary society/edited by
    Philip Brenner . . . [et al.].—1st ed.
        p. cm.
    Bibliography: p.
    Includes index.
    ISBN 0-8021-1010-X ISBN 0-8021-3043-7 (pbk.)
    1. Cuba.   I. Brenner, Philip.
F1758.C975 1988
972.91—dc19   88-11070
                                                          CIP

Manufactured in the United States of America

This book is printed on acid-free paper.

Designed by Irving Perkins Associates

First Edition 1989

10 9 8 7 6 5 4 3 2 1

ACKNOWLEDGMENTS

Several institutions contributed services and resources that greatly facilitated work on this book. We want to thank The American University, Center for Cuban Studies, Centro de Estudios sobre los Estados Unidos at the University of Havana, *Granma,* Institute for Policy Studies, National Security Archive, Policy Alternatives in the Caribbean and Central America (PACCA), and *Prensa Latina.*

We also very much appreciate the generosity of individuals who contributed their ideas and efforts to the development and production of *The Cuba Reader:* Juan Arroyo, Manuel Davis, Naomi Friedman, Sandra Levinson, Rene Mujica, Jerome Nickel, Sarah Peasley, Peter Rosset, Ramon Sanchez-Paródi, Wayne Smith, Margery Tabankin, and John Vandermeer.

Our editors at Grove Press have been a delightful group of people with whom to work. Jennifer E. Atkinson, our copy editor, brilliantly created consistency out of so many disparate and excerpted articles. The book was initially developed under the creative guidance of Lisa Rosset. It has been expertly brought to life by the careful and patient hand of Walt Bode, without whom the book would not have been possible.

Contents

Preface

Every trip each of the editors has taken from the United States to Cuba has been a very long one. Though the distance between the two countries is only 90 miles at the closest point—or about 200 miles from Miami to Havana—the voyage carries with it a sense of having gone far away.

In part, the feeling comes from the regulations involved. Cuba and the United States do not recognize each other diplomatically, and it is rarely easy to obtain a visa to enter Cuba. The United States also maintains an economic embargo against Cuba, and prohibits U.S. citizens from spending any money there. There are exceptions to the rule, but the process of securing a valid Treasury Department license to visit the island, or of arranging charter flight accommodations or travel through another country because of the lack of scheduled direct flights, is enough to remind any visitor that the United States officially characterizes Cuba as an "enemy."

The distance is also cultural. Cuba is a Latin American country with an African heritage; it is a socialist country and has close ties with the Soviet Union. Cuba supports revolution in the Third World, and proclaims that it continues on a revolutionary path internally. All of these aspects of contemporary Cuba are quite foreign to most visitors from the United States; none are easily assimilated into neat categories that might explain what one experiences.

One final element contributes to the sensation of a long voyage. In the United States, knowledge about Cuba is clouded by misinformation and disinformation. Storytellers abound, because there are more than one million people who either have emigrated from Cuba since 1959 or are the children of émigrés. But their stories often distort contemporary Cuba. Limited direct contact between U.S. and Cuban citizens reduces the possibility of corroborating or rejecting their claims. Cold war propaganda often intrudes ill-conceived impressions about the country. Cuba arouses passions and has generated devoted antagonists and apologists. As a consequence, what often passes for "the facts about Cuba" is little more than myth. Like most myths, those about Cuba have taken on larger-than-life qualities; their Cuba is a fantasy that seems out of this world. Hence, the feeling that a trip there is a long one indeed.

Our view is that this set of circumstances is undesirable and potentially dangerous. The purpose of *The Cuba Reader* is to provide information that addresses prevailing myths about Cuba—myths about its economy, politics, foreign policy, and culture—in the hope of reducing Cuba's phantasmagoric proportions. To be sure, the articles here only begin the process. They provide basic information about Cuba. They also offer a way of asking questions that can help you extract accurate perceptions about the country from the large number of in-depth, scholarly studies on Cuba that are available. Several of the articles in the collection are drawn from such studies. Others were written for this volume, or are journalistic accounts that have stood the test of time. We have also included official Cuban documents and statements by government officials that provide a clear exposition of key positions.

We begin with two essays that capture the basic outlook of this book, that Cuba is a sovereign country struggling with its fundamental nature as a nation. Saul Landau has been one of the leading U.S. experts on Cuba since he first visited the island in 1960, and he is known widely for his films and articles about the country. Perhaps equally important, his private briefings have taught a large number of journalists and scholars the right questions to ask about the Cuban Revolution. He focuses on the historical context of the revolution and the way in which the larger Cuban drive for independence has interacted with particular conditions inherited and subsequently shaped by the revolutionary process. Carlos Franqui was a leader in the July 26th Movement that spearheaded the drive to overthrow the brutal dictatorship of Fulgencio Batista in 1959. He was editor of the movement's newspaper and later became editor of the main newspaper in Cuba, although he went into exile in the late 1960s. The essay is one of his entries in *Diary of the Cuban Revolution*.

The pre-1959 legacy has a great bearing on the course of the Cuban Revolution. To ignore it would be to repeat the most prominent, though often unstated, myth about Cuba—that Cuban history begins in 1959 with the rise to power of Fidel Castro and the July 26th Movement. For many in the United States, Cuba did not exist before then. It was almost an invisible appendage to the United States, a weekend paradise of beautiful beaches, good cigars, rum and gambling, and the cha-cha. Such a U.S.-centered view of the island defines Cuban history and the revolution exclusively in terms of U.S. interests and leads to a distortion of what the revolution meant to Cubans. In Part I we trace the pre-1959 history and examine the sources and continuities of the revolution.

Subsequent chapters describe the unfolding of the Cuban Revolution since 1959. Part II, on the economy, details the process of development through each decade, highlighting important debates and decisions. It is important to appreciate that most economic decisions also serve political purposes. This is seen best in the reading by Che Guevara (Reading 10), in which he links the economic development of Cuba to the political development of a so-called "new Cuban man." Similarly, the major political institutions that are described in Part III have significant economic functions. Many are directly responsible for organizing the economy, and others provide ways for Cuban citizens to participate in economic decision making.

Cuban leaders see a successful foreign policy as the sine qua non for a successful revolution, because Cuba is a small country and its relations with other countries determine its ability to survive. The two superpowers loom most directly over Cuba in this regard, and much of Part IV is devoted to Cuba's relations with the United States and the Soviet Union since 1959. Yet the Cuban Revolution is also defined by its internationalism and commitment to revolution in other Third World countries, and Cuba's relations with these countries are also given attention in Part IV.

By way of conclusion in Part V, we attempt to capture the significance of the revolution on the life of Cuba: How people live each day; how the revolution has affected enduring social problems such as sexism and racism, and what its impact on Cuban culture has been. These are snapshots of a dynamic process. They do not capture the extraordinary energy and flux Cubans experience as they have been engaged in the revolutionary transformation of their society. Still, they convey the sense, important to all Cubans, of the revolution as an unfinished effort and an ongoing struggle.

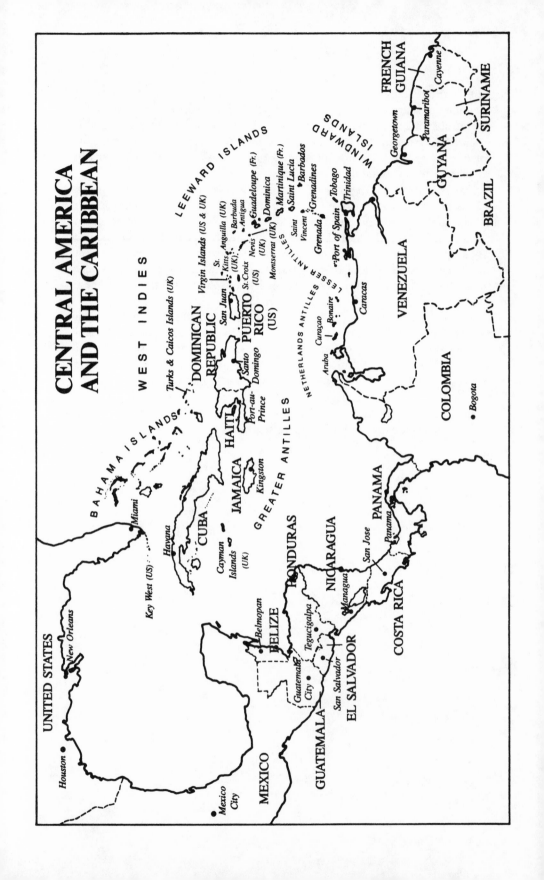

Introduction

*Asking the Right Questions About Cuba**

By Saul Landau

The closer one is to an issue the more difficult it is to gain objectivity. Cuba is so close to the United States that U.S. policymakers, like a physician trying to diagnose a family member's ailment, have been unable to see it objectively. They have asked the wrong questions and inevitably have come up with faulty diagnoses of the problem.

Instead of adopting an unemotional and even scientific approach to a process of change in the island neighbor, U.S. officials have tried to destroy the Cuban Revolution and have declared it a failure—or worse. Yet, the revolution holds a strange aura of success for much of the Third World. Countless visitors to Cuba from Latin America, Africa, and Asia see one of their own kind succeeding in the face of an almost thirty-year campaign by the world's mightiest power and Cuba's closest neighbor to obliterate the experiment.

These visitors from distant places see the Cuban Revolution as an attempt to come to grips with and overcome its past of underdevelopment, the colonial legacy imposed first by Spain and then by the United States. Unlike the Third World view, U.S. officials and some prestigious scholars look at the revolution through an ahistorical lens, one that focuses on Cuba only as a threat to U.S. security. Thus, in response to their misguided questions, they adopt methods that do not promote healthy inquiry or learning.

The first wrong questions concern Fidel and his ideology: Was Castro a Marxist from his student days on, a fact that he concealed from his own movement and non-Marxist well-wishers around the world? Did the Cuban leader secretly believe in a Leninist party and state model while still a university student?

*This essay was written for this volume. Copyright 1988 by Saul Landau.

A second sterile issue is: Who lost Cuba? Several books postulate that Cuba's revolutionary trajectory into the Soviet orbit would have, and indeed should have, been avoided if only U.S. policymakers had removed their blinders. The debate over how to treat revolutions in general, and Cuba's specifically, continues to this day.

A third misleading query was posed by journalist Tad Szulc. "The fundamental question concerning Fidel Castro, the 1959 revolution, and Cuba's transformation into a Communist state," he states, "is naturally whether this whole experience was logically dictated by Cuban history or represents an extraordinary political aberration primarily instigated by his own overwhelming personality."[1] Revolutions are by definition aberrations, and the Cuban Revolution could not have occurred without the unique character of Fidel Castro.

The questions Szulc and other scholars have avoided are: Did there exist in the 1950s genuine revolutionary thought in Third World countries that was not connected to Marxism-Leninism? Is there today a material road that would allow small groups of Third World peoples to enter the course of history—other than receiving direct Soviet aid and the influence that inevitably comes with it? Indeed, is there a language, a vocabulary available for revolutionaries that is not Marxist-Leninist in derivation? In the 1980s can revolution, seen as gaining independence or a homeland, be separated from the question of economic transformation?[2] This alternative set of questions goes to the heart of the reality faced by Cuba's revolutionary leaders. It also allows scholars to consider Cuba in terms larger than ideology.

FIDEL'S IDEOLOGY

In 1968 Fidel Castro explained to me that as a university student his first reading of the *Communist Manifesto* deeply impressed him, and that he first read and understood Lenin's genius while in prison at the Isle of Pines in 1954. But Fidel was also somewhat of a Jeffersonian who believed in the moral right of an oppressed people to make revolution,[3] a *Martiano* who saw that only revolution could open Cuba's path to the mainstream of the historical process, as well as a fan of C. Wright Mills, whose *Power Elite* provided him with immense insight into the nature of U.S. politics.

Castro also read Freud and Jean-Paul Sartre, whom he found illuminating. He studied the lives of Martí and Bolívar, the men with whom he most directly linked his own life. Castro devoured the writings of Martí and the Cuban historians who wrote of the independence wars of the 1860s and 1890s, from whom he sought insight into the nature of the political and military mistakes of de Cespedes, Agramonte, Maceo and Máximo Gómez—in other words, Cuban history became a guide for Castro for his own successful revolution.[4]

The key to victory, he understood from his reading of history, was national unity, a formula that coincided with Marxism-Leninism as practiced by the Soviet leaders. The fact that he was a Marxist and a Leninist, however, did not make him different from most other Third World nationalist revolutionaries. Mao Zedong, Ho Chi Minh, and the leaders of many of the African revolutions were also Marxist-Leninists.[5] This revolutionary ideology offered not only the mobilizing rhetoric for anti-imperial campaigns, but a language for achieving social and economic justice within the emerging new nation.

How can a revolution occur in contemporary Latin America, Africa, or Asia that does not address the need to transform the economy, the issues of class structure, and the distribution of wealth? Indeed, José Martí had confronted these issues in the 1890s, and, along with them, strategies for how to realize revolutionary change. Martí, however, did not have the communist issue to contend with, but, like Fidel, had to confront the anti-revolutionary colossus of the North, and therefore had to proceed covertly both in terms of forging a revolutionary organization and in only partly revealing his substantive agenda.

Fidel has often quoted Martí that "to achieve certain things they must be kept concealed; to proclaim what they are would raise difficulties too great to attain them in the end." Castro knew from the late 1940s what kind of changes he thought Cuba needed—even though he continued to work through the traditional political party structure until Batista's 1952 coup made it impossible to do so, and thus freed him to begin his revolutionary career.

A revolutionary is a driven person, one whose need is transformed into a way of life, an all-consuming energy to play a key role in the alteration of his or her people's destiny. The successful revolutionary cannot afford to be dogmatic, inflexible; he must be, at times, pragmatic. Success stems from the ability to judge the possibilities of ebbing and flowing class coalitions and thus be able to manipulate them toward the goal. At this Castro was and is a master. However, his political compromises during and immediately after the insurrection led to the charge that he had betrayed the revolution because, at different stages he had agreed to concessions that he deemed useful to furthering the struggle against Batista.

Castro made pacts with elements that he knew were his enemies as well as with some that developed into foes of the revolution as he took it into the Soviet orbit. The basic fact about Fidel Castro was his determination to carry out a social revolution. This prescribed who would be friends and enemies. Castro knew that the old and corrupt politicians like Carlos Prío and members of the old political parties had no interest in pursuing transformations of economic and political life inside Cuba. His political alliances with such people were necessarily temporary. Likewise, other propertied groups would inevitably charge Fidel with betrayal, for he was determined to change the property system.

According to James O'Connor, Cuban capitalism was underdeveloped and overdeveloped. Underdeveloped, in that it could not employ modern technology, nor free itself from the U.S. fetters; overdeveloped, in that it had used up the investment possibilities on the island itself, and had rationalized the island economy so as to create a permanent dependency relationship.[6]

Castro's father, Angel, provided Fidel with the most immediate experience of Cuban dependency. A *colono,* or peasant landowner with holdings between the size of the *latifundistas* and small proprietors, Angel Castro had his own sugar quota, which was determined by the association of *colonos,* which had struck an agreement with the large and small-sized sugar growers, who, in turn, had received their authorization from the Cuban legislature and president, but only after the U.S. Congress had set forth the yearly Cuban sugar quota.[7] Other sectors of Cuban agriculture were also rationalized to remove any vestige of Adam Smith's invisible hand, because the visible hand of the outsider, the United States, determined the options for Cuban capital and thereby for labor as well. Cubans could not invest in productive enterprises that might compete with U.S. imports.

The point that is missed when writers refer to the natural or aberrational courses of Cuban history is that for Cubans to reenter history with some semblance of national identity, they could not continue in the same relationship with the United States. The question for Cuba was not capitalism or socialism, but how to forge its own economy.

Nor was sugar land a source for surplus capital. The quota was artificially set, and should the Cubans sell "too much" on the international market, they would both drive the price down and anger the U.S. growers who also had to sell on that market. So the Cuban investor put capital into nonproductive sectors—real estate and tourism. Tourism, replete with gambling, meant heavy Mafia influence. Havana in 1958 was not only the largest Latin American market for Cadillacs, but the sex and abortion capital of the Western Hemisphere. No wonder so many Americans remember the "good old days when Cubans were happy and carefree."[8] This was not an economic route to healthy nation building, since it insured that future Cuban generations would work either as cane cutters or servants, but it was the one that existed when Fidel's forces marched triumphantly into Havana on January 2, 1959. Cuba had no national economy—a key fact that its critics ignore. Rather, Cuba was an extension of the U.S. economy, without the privileges attached to statehood.[9]

Castro knew that he would have to face the power of the United States. He had removed the Batista violence machine, which, like other dictatorships in the Caribbean and Central America, had stood as a sort of U.S.-backed Cuban Maginot line against revolution. But behind that buffer was the U.S. government, the traditional peacekeeper in the Caribbean and Central America.

As the United States became the seat of world counterrevolution, in the post-World War II era, responding in hostile Pavlovian fashion to the ringing of the revolutionary bell, what power could respond to the needs of fledgling revolutionary states so as to assure them minimal security?

In 1959, the USSR stood as the only veritable insurance company for those viable Third World revolutions that needed fuel supply, weapons, and basic survival aid. As Latin American revolutionaries and reformers have learned for a century or more, there is no possibility of achieving national independence without cutting dependency ties to the United States. Not only did U.S. companies own the best sugar-growing and cattle-grazing land in Cuba, they also owned goodly shares of the mines, utilities, hotels and casinos, real estate, TV and newspapers, and, most important, the lines of credit that controlled Cuban foreign trade. Cuban spare parts came from U.S. factories, Cuba's railroads were gauged to U.S. standards. In the United Nations and the Organization of American States, Cuba voted 100 percent with the United States. Cuba was an informal colony of the United States. President Batista, the story is often told, was referred to as "the second-most important man in Cuba, behind the U.S. Ambassador."

The U.S. government does not make it easy to break such a dependency relationship, and it forced upon Cuban leaders, and subsequently on Nicaraguans as well, a limited set of options: Surrender to U.S. demands or turn to the Soviets.

Castro was familiar with the noble arguments of the 1776 Declaration of Independence, but Jefferson's pronouncement about the inalienable rights, including the right to revolt, did not apply in practice in Latin America. Genuine revolution below the Rio Grande has been historically accompanied by a U.S.-backed counterrevolution. Recognition of this oft-repeated phenomenon should end the sterile argument about whether or not the U.S. reaction to the Cuban Revolution in 1959 and 1960 drove Castro into the arms of the Soviets, or whether Castro had always intended to go in that direction.

The United States had destroyed the Cuban Revolution of 1898, and had intervened several times afterwards to prevent Cuban self-determination. One could argue that the political character of Fidel Castro and many of the revolutionaries who joined him was determined by a series of U.S.-sponsored acts, some of which occurred before Castro was born. These events range in time and breadth from passage of the 1901 Platt Amendment, which gave the U.S. the right to send troops to Cuba, to the spectacle of American sailors urinating on the statue of Martí in 1949; from the the CIA-sponsored coup to overthrow a reformist Arbenz regime in Guatemala in 1954, to the exclusion by wealthy Americans of Cubans from their private beaches in Cuba.

The betrayer of the Cuban Revolution has historically been U.S. government power, not a Cuban. To the extent that the United States intervened in Cuban affairs, from the 1890s through Batista's regimes and into the post-1959 Cuban scene, it was the element that forced internal decisions. By carrying out Cuban revolutionary policies, Castro brought about the response of the United

States, which in turn led to the chain of events that forced Cuba to turn to the Soviets. By 1960 Castro, the determined revolutionary, had no other options.

The so-called capitalist alternative, the multinational corporate creations like South Korea or Taiwan, do not fulfill rudimentary demands for national identity or economic justice. It offers neither democracy nor the satisfaction of popular needs for a sense of national self-realization. U.S.-based multinational corporations invested capital in places where large and docile labor forces would be assured by repressive and often military-run governments. These firms pay little or no taxes, have no environmental responsibilities nor are they contractually obligated to maintain their factories on health and safety standards set in the United States or Europe.

The Soviet model, however, allows for the development of nationalist thought and culture, but directs the economic and political course of socialism around the only paradigm known by Soviet leaders—their own. The revolutionary leaders who decide on policies that then affect their nation for many decades must do so on the basis of a class loyalty, not on fidelity to forms of government. The decision to make the revolution for the majority, the poor, meant that the power, wealth and privileges of the wealthy and the middle class would be severely restricted. To those in the middle class who supported the anti-Batista revolution and assumed that the new order would benefit them, directly or indirectly, Castro's policies were a betrayal.

The betrayal theory assumes that the Cuban revolution was a middle-class revolution designed to bring about the restoration of property-based liberty, not one-party socialism. First put forth in articulate fashion by Theodore Draper,[10] the betrayal argument assumes that a Third World revolutionary leadership can and should adhere to ideal U.S. standards of civil liberties, even when it is attacked by the U.S. government with force and violence. The betrayal focus omits or plays down internal class struggle and the role of the United States in that internal battle for both control of social wealth and cultural hegemony.

Castro's goals were the restructuring of the Cuban social and economic order so that the structural poverty that engulfed the majority could be eliminated. To accomplish that, a Cuban nation had to be built, based on real sovereignty and national unity. To the revolutionary leaders, democratic forms had long obscured the substance of democracy, or real equality. Such a transformation of the economy would not only strip wealth and power from an owning class, but would necessarily entail extreme hardship for the working and peasant classes as well.

Castro insisted on unity because that was the sine qua non for the kind of political faith required to endure the difficult transition period. To allow for the democratic forms to operate as they had at certain points in the Cuban past would have necessarily meant that the Cuban people would have been subjected to a torrent of conflicting, confusing, and indeed obfuscating information, images, and rhetoric from the media and the rhetoric of traditional political campaigns. In addition, the political faith required to make the leap toward a new system would have been further undermined by CIA-directed propaganda efforts, which, Castro believed, would become a front for a U.S.-backed covert war.

The small Cuban class that owned great estates and productive property derived their power from the assumption that the United States would not permit a genuine revolution to take place. They had assurance of this from the past interventions or threats of sending troops every time a Cuban leader even hinted at plans to redistribute wealth. And U.S. entrepreneurs, ranging from close advisers to presidents to mafia leaders,[11] could be expected to fight with any means at their disposal to retain their holdings.

U.S. and Cuban businessmen used their substantial control over Cuban newspapers to attack the revolutionary government. They used civil liberties arguments, about which they had cared little in the past, to cover their true concerns about property. Democracy, for the Cuban and U.S. owning groups, meant the opportunity to challenge the revolution in order to preserve their way of life, not to better the lives of the vast majority.

By preserving the forms of democracy, Castro would have in effect vitiated the substance. Those who held power from the 1890s through the Batista years had little interest in ending the state of dependency with the United States, and absolutely no inclination to channel their wealth to the services of the majority. This was the essence of the class war that confronted Castro and the revolutionaries by spring 1959. It cast its shadow over their way of thinking about democratic forms, a shadow that has remained into 1988.

Those who espouse the betrayal theory argue that the revolution was first and foremost about democratic forms of government and guarantees of rights and liberties, but they do not see as primary the issue of property ownership and its relation to political power. Huber Matos, a guerrilla commander who was subsequently jailed for twenty years, represented certain propertied interests. (Carlos Franqui, the exiled former editor of *Revolución,* appears to be more a victim of internal power struggles than a man who stood for property. Franqui did not defect until the late 1960s.)

Some of the participants obviously believed that a social revolution that redistributed property and social wealth could coexist with the kinds of political freedoms and democratic forms that characterized capitalist societies in which wealth and social property are unequally distributed. Castro, as Szulc makes clear, had few illusions about the compatibility of bourgeois democracy with egalitarian socialism. Like the economic and political system, the system of political epistemology also had to be taken on, and destroyed by the revolution. Some of the left-wing critics ask whether or not Castro did not destroy socialist freedoms as well.[12]

Such betrayal arguments downplay class struggle and often ignore the question of options open for revolutionary leaders. The critics often see revolutionary power only in terms of possibilities, not limits. Can a revolutionary leadership insure the survival of nation and revolution without Soviet aid? Is there a realistic scenario in which the United States would allow revolution for genuine independence and sovereignty to develop in the Caribbean or Central America? Could a European Social Democratic consortium provide the economic stake and the professional expertise to a revolution that would allow it to escape from the narrow choices? These are the questions with which the people in power have to deal. In order to revise their Leninism, to modify notions of international class struggle, to actually make a revolution that is not caught directly in the East versus West conflict, some alternate route for development must be made available.[13]

The betrayal theorists do not address these issues. Nor do they analyze the nature of the Third World state in the transition period from colonial to post-colonial status. The fragility of a Cuban economy, without the United States as supplier, banker, provider, marketer, and owner, meant that Cuba would have to look elsewhere for support.[14]

Historically, the United States, by virtue of its power and aggressiveness, has pushed much of its political and commercial culture onto Cuba. The Soviets, on the other hand, have never invaded Cuba to prevent political changes, nor do Soviet troops occupy the island. Soviet companies have not made vast profits from the Cuban labor force or resources. The United States still claims that Cuba owes several billion dollars to its companies. The Soviets, should Castro order them out tomorrow, would have no claim, since they own not an inch of Cuban territory, nor any enterprises in Cuba.

To understand the nature of Third World revolution one must begin with the material realities, just as revolutionary ideology is based on materialism. The old colonizers have fashioned skillful writers to present what sound like reasonable humanitarian cases against besieged Third World revolutions.

How, then, to judge historical processes that are ongoing? What criteria to apply to the Cuban revolution that would allow us objectively to say success or failure?

JUDGING THE CUBAN REVOLUTION AND FIDEL CASTRO

In 1987 Fidel Castro inaugurated a revolutionary health plan that allows each Cuban to have a family doctor located in his neighborhood and willing to make house calls. In addition, Cubans have access to high-quality hospital care and advanced methods of preventive medicine. Cuba has fashioned an educational system that encourages all students to finish at least ninth grade and has increased its higher education potential by immense proportion. Cuban doctors not only dot their national landscape, but act as a kind of Peace Corps for countries throughout the Third World. Advances made in housing—more than one million new units built over the past 15 years—match the achievements of infant and preschool care institutions. Although still insufficient to provide adequate housing and child care for the growing population, the increases in these areas are objects of envy for most of the Third World.

The Cuban Revolution has met the basic substantive rights outlined in the United Nations Human Rights Covenant. The dicey area for Cuba, and all socialist revolutions, is in the procedural arena, which also effects the quality of life. Cuban apologists have argued that the counterrevolution has forced this behavior on the revolution. Like all clichés, this has some basis in fact, but leaves the debate in limbo. The substantive accomplishments have come at great sacrifice, but the procedural stagnation has not balanced those gains; rather it has produced institutional sickness in Cuba's socialism.

The origin of socialist repression derives from the counterrevolutionary process. The very instrument designed initially to protect the revolution transforms itself into the fetter on revolutionary progress. Once forming and empowering a secret police—the red terror to stop the white—the people of a socialist nation lose their rights as individuals. Revolutions, thus, look wonderful for the masses, and, indeed, the masses of Cuba enjoy Fidel's speeches to this day, but individuals' rights remain in a gray area, and law bends itself to national security notions, much as it does in the capitalist democracies when state prerogatives are challenged.

The Cuban security apparatus has insured the survival of the revolution, but Fidel himself has declared that he is dissatisfied with the quality of the process that he has nurtured from its outset. His critique of the revolution, made at the last Party Congress in 1986, focused on bureaucracy, absenteeism, shoddy work habits, corruption, the lack of democracy—the quality of life that state institutions dictate for the society. The capitalist ethic, fought by revolutionary ideology for 25 years, surfaced in rampant form when the state permitted a parallel market for consumer goods. Some Cubans became millionaires in a short time by charging exorbitant prices for scarce goods. The revolution's aim, to create a society based on equality, was thus seriously undermined by the relaxation of economic rules, and Castro took steps to restore guidelines of equality—to try to insure that the revolution would maintain the standards that he outlined in its earliest days.

The Cuban Revolution promised a new society of equality, social justice, and intellectual freedom. Cuban socialism would differ from the East European and Chinese models by allowing freedom of speech and would not allow the state security people to determine the limits of expression. That was what Fidel told Jean-Paul Sartre and C. Wright Mills in 1960.[15] Throughout the mid-1960s Castro promised to strive for exciting, albeit utopian, goals: a society without money, a place where the university was everywhere and where each citizen was a student and a professor. And, miraculously, the Soviets continued to provide the material aid to such a heretically led society. Few probed beneath the surface and asked why the Soviets felt obliged to support Cuba so generously throughout the 1960s when its leader advocated armed struggle as the only road to genuine political change in the Third World, a strategy the Soviets denounced as infantile. Anti-Communist intellectuals accepted that the Soviets would behave like an insurance company for Cuba, without questioning the cost of the premium. Through 1968 it appeared that Fidel somehow maintained his independence.

European and U.S. intellectuals who visited Cuba in the early years of the revolution quoted Fidel's statement about culture in the early 1960s: "Within the revolution, everything; outside the revolution, nothing." And Cuban culture did develop inside that simple yet enigmatic formulation. A formidable film industry grew, producing movies exciting in form and content. Barely known poets, novelists and playwrights became world famous; painters, dancers, and composers had state subsidies for their work, which was shown in Cuba and throughout the Western and Eastern worlds.

By early 1968 Havana had become the literary capital of the Spanish-speaking world. And Fidel himself greeted intellectuals and artists from all over the world on the celebration of the ninth anniversary of the revolution's triumph. European, North and South American literati wined and dined and rode in chauffeur-driven limousines, opining on all subjects. The infatuation did not derive from an understanding of the dynamics of Cuban politics, but from a naive sense that Fidel had finally produced a picture-book revolution, egalitarian and romantic internally, as well as anti-American and implicitly anti-Soviet.

Then, in August 1968, the Soviets invaded Czechoslovakia. In July, as we had ridden through bumpy dirt roads in the Sierra Maestra, Fidel had talked about the "deformations" of Soviet socialism. He spoke angrily about the Soviet leadership's conservatism, their fear of revolution abroad, their heavy bureaucracy, their lack of democracy, the divorce of the party from the masses. He cited Herbert Marcuse's critique of Soviet socialism as insightful and swore that Cuba would never travel that road. He even attributed some of the blame for Che Guevara's death in Bolivia, some eight months before, on the Moscow line as carried out by the "traitorous Communist Party of Bolivia."[16]

One month later, Fidel delivered his speech supporting the Soviet action. Although he denied that any legal or moral reasons could justify the Soviet invasion, he nevertheless backed the move on the grounds that the imperialists would have taken control had Brezhnev not acted, and that not one inch of socialist territory could be allowed to return into imperialist hands. He argued the point toughly and passionately, but the facts of the case did not support his conclusion. In the test case of the decade, Fidel had sided with the corrupt, bureaucratic, even antirevolutionary Soviet leadership, not with the Czech rebels that the anguished Western radical intelligentsia had embraced. The non-Communist intellectuals supported the Prague uprising against the established Communist party; the rebels held out hope that there could develop a scenario that would lead to the growth of a decent and democratic socialism in Eastern Europe.

The support that Castro had won from non-Communist European intellectuals and from some American ones as well dissipated. How could he have betrayed them by siding with the Soviets? They attacked him in print. Castro angrily and rhetorically asked me: "How much wheat, oil, arms have they ever given to Cuba? How many of them have mobilized masses to support the revolution on the streets of Paris, Rome, London and New York?" The Soviets, according to him, for all of their deficiencies, had never denied nor even threatened Cuba with the denial of survival materials.

Ironically, some of the very intellectuals who had considered Castro's Czechoslovakia speech a betrayal continued to offer full support to Ho Chi Minh, whose reaction to the invasion of Czechoslovakia echoed the Brezhnev line and did not even offer the modifiers Fidel put forth. Somehow it was not expected of Ho; he had not raised high their hopes that a Western intellectual paradise could be built in Vietnam.

Indeed, Fidel did raise those hopes, and he, therefore, had to pay the price for dashing them against the rocks. He encouraged or at least allowed state security to lock up a poet[17] and, by so doing, to define revolutionary law. Since then some of the jailings of intellectuals and homosexuals have been reversed, presumably by Fidel's order. But this kind of *personalismo* hardly assures a citizenry. Cuba has a constitution and a code of law, which conforms 100 percent to the U.N. Human Rights standards. Yet, 28 years after the revolution established itself, the argument that permitting free speech and assembly would allow the counterrevolutionaries a forum that would work against the interests of the majority does not ring with compelling truth. There is no viable alternative to the present government inside Cuba. The bourgeoisie who returned to Cuba for family visits, beginning in the late 1970s, showed their affluence, proselytized for their way of life under capitalism, and even brought with them large amounts of consumer goods that were new to Cubans, like VCRs and other electronic gadgets. The exposure to a more affluent life did have an impact on a segment of the society, but the vast majority showed little interest in emigrating to the United States.[18]

By the mid-1970s Cubans had debated and adopted a criminal and civil law code and a constitution that proclaims that citizens have rights. The problem with socialism everywhere is precisely over this issue—the enshrined freedoms and the practice of repression.

The Cuban population is aware of its basic rights and freedoms and even those born after the triumph of the revolution are conscious of the long years of sacrifice required to get them. But do the much-discussed constitution and codified laws offer real protection for the citizenry if state security agents were to decide that an individual is counterrevolutionary? The law has not been tested against the unofficial powers of state security and some of the old *guerrilleros* who still retain power in and around the official agencies of repression. In some cases, however, the law has prevailed over the unofficial policies set by the police. Recently, a lesbian couple was granted custody of an orphan, and homosexuals won a case in court over their rights to keep jobs.[19]

In Cuba today a recognized artist can announce that he is a homosexual without fearing that he will lose his job or become a pariah. Yet, there is no public forum for opposition to national economic and foreign policy. And there is no path open to create political space.

This is not to accept the Armando Valladares line, that Cuba is a dungeon with systematic torture of political dissidents,[20] nor the fashionable negativism that intellectual life in Cuba is dead as a result. Cuba produces more intellectual creativity than most of the Spanish-speaking countries and infinitely more than the U.S. models like South Korea or Taiwan. Despite this intellectual accomplishment there is less than the ideal atmosphere for the exercise of political imagination. However, the editors of literary magazines no longer submit stories, poems or essays to a censor.[21]

After almost 30 years of revolution, Third World visitors see Cuba as exemplary. Not to see barefoot children with bloated bellies, not to see parasite-infested beggars and waifs in the cities and countryside is a rarity in much of the Third World. Cuba can boast that its kids now finish ninth grade, have low infant-mortality rates, good teeth, long life expectancy, etc. Life in Havana is still full of inconvenience, including rationing of scarce goods and the need to line up to buy them. But Cubans are quick to compare their situation with the neighboring Dominican Republic, where, they say, money is rationed, which effectively denies the poor their most elementary needs. Cuban distribution problems are minimal compared to their Third World neighbors, and most Cubans appear to appreciate the good fortune of having had a revolution whose primary mission has been to meet their basic needs.

Why then is there no serious political discussion in Cuba's press or television on issues of economic and foreign policy? The Cuban media remain narrow and inflexible in their political line. Why cannot *Granma* or *Juventud Rebelde* publish the Central Committee debates? In lieu of opposition parties, this appears to be one way to open Cuban political discussion to the wider public. Ironically, Cubans listen to Radio Martí, the Voice of America, and Spanish-language news broadcasts from Florida, all of which include analysis and opinion about what is happening in Cuba. Only Fidel throughout the years has patiently explained, analyzed and offered lengthy rationales for policy. Lee Lockwood called him "Cuba's living newspaper."[22]

What keeps the society closed to political discussion about foreign and national economic policy? Is it part and parcel of the dynamic of the Soviet model that was chosen in the early 1960s, when it offered salvation from U.S. attack? The Soviet-style Communist party model was the metaphorical premium paid for the insurance policy, and today that imported model—not necessarily Lenin's—is institutionalized in Cuba as it is being reformed in the USSR. The model came under the rule of Leonid Brezhnev, whose regime was characterized by bureaucracy, rigidity, and corruption. The Communist party model that Cuba imported was a far cry from Lenin's notion of a party, and even from Nikita Khrushchev's. Nevertheless, it has served Cuba during the difficult transition from a dependency on the U.S. economy into its current stage of developing partner inside the socialist bloc economy.

It would take all of the monumental will that Tad Szulc and all others who have known Fidel attribute to him to undo the negative features of this model, which have been both caricatured and portrayed accurately *ad nauseam* in the Western media. Fidel would, however, have ample support from those Cubans who feel the stultified climate in their everyday life and work and are sick and tired of the already crusty bureaucracy and the petty corruption. These new citizens are products of the revolution, eager members of the militia, people who are not vulnerable to whatever counterrevolutionary messages would surface in a freer atmosphere.

Fidel, the greatest figure in Latin American history since Bolívar, possesses the courage to make a major effort to open a society that he helped to close as a means for revolutionary survival. "Courage," Fidel told me in 1974, "is changing your mind, reversing your policy after you've made a real investment in it." He was talking about John F. Kennedy, and his belief that the young president had changed his mind shortly before his death about the issues of the Cold War, and was about to pursue a peace policy. Indeed, Castro believed that Kennedy was assassinated because of his courage.[23]

The revolutionary heritage that begat the Cuban Revolution and formed the thought of Fidel Castro is also a democratic heritage. There is no necessary contradiction between socialism and democracy, either in the Soviet Union or in Cuba. It has been the structures of their Communist parties, their inflexible understanding of democratic centralism and the refusal to drop the cultural legacies of paternalism that have brought Cuban society into its present condition: a model welfare state for the Third World, including a large educated population, without the compatible condition of full political participation. Just as the United States postures with a Cold War rhetoric that no longer coincides with reality, so too Cuba's national security apparatus, built to defend the revolution against the mighty Yankees, reflects an elitism and rigidity of more fragile times. The Cubans are now a smart and healthy people; they have grown up and can be "trusted" by their leaders.

Castro has been in power more than nine times longer than Kennedy, more than enough time for a judgment. Yet policymakers and scholars alike continue to ask the wrong questions and thus to measure the Cuban Revolution by a rod that doesn't read its features. The United States did not have the power to "keep" Cuba. Nor do U.S. politicians have viable alternatives or models to guide any Third World nations in their transition from colonial to sovereign status. The United States government provides models only for counterrevolution and repression in the Third World.

The judgments on Castro will take into account his ability to survive the terrible wrath of the United States. His revolutionary test may well be not only the material quality of life the Cuban citizen enjoys, but the extent to which real democracy can overcome the paternal tradition, which clung to the Cuban Communist party in the transition from a U.S. colony to a member of the Soviet Bloc economy.

Ideological posturing about moral incentives played a role in the early stages of the Cuban revolution, when the image of Che Guevara as a romantic "new man" motivated people to work harder, sacrifice, and struggle. The Cuban Revolution is now almost 30 years old, and its leaders still appeal to the workers to give more. Such exhortation can only succeed if the workers themselves become meaningful participants in all levels of the society they are making. The paternalism of the party elite, with their relative material wealth, provides poor motivation for the Cuban worker to sacrifice more. Will Castro make the move that Gorbachev made in the Soviet Union and, instead of pushing only the ideology of sacrifice, turn to genuine democracy as well?

After almost 30 years there is a valid question: Why hasn't Cuba achieved meaningful democratic forms? That question—not whether Fidel was or wasn't a secret Marxist-Leninist—must engage socialists in Cuba and elsewhere. What is there about the model of government then that prevents the ruling circles from extending political trust? On May Day 1987, more than half-a-million *Habaneros* marched enthusiastically in support of the values of international proletarianism and to greet Fidel and the members of the Politburo, who returned their salutes from the tribunal. As soon as this trust is fully reciprocated, Cuba may emerge as the first genuine socialist democracy.

NOTES

1. Tad Szulc, *Fidel: A Critical Portrait* (New York: Morrow, 1986), p. 25.

2. The Iranian Revolution might be seen as an exception in that it seeks a restoration of an ancient order. Movements like the mainstream PLO or IRA have remained more narrowly nationalist in orientation, but have openly Marxist wings that address the class issues as well.

3. To the extent that Jefferson was the first modern nationalist revolutionary, Castro like his African, Asian, and Latin American contemporaries believed in the right, indeed duty of the

people to revolt, so as to establish independence—a basic route with which to enter the course of history.

4. In 1974 Castro told Frank Mankiewicz, Kirby Jones, and me that he was also a sea story aficionado, and that he had just read *Jaws*. "Quite a thriller," said Mankiewicz. "More than that," Castro added, "it is an excellent critique of capitalism." He then explained to us how *Jaws* illustrated capitalism's values, in that the town merchants prevented the honest police chief from closing the beaches. My experience with Castro in the course of making three films with him confirms the view that he integrates all his experiences into a revolutionary Weltanschaaung, one that always affirms a positive view of human nature.

5. The exceptions, like Gandhi for example who combined his principles of national unity with nonviolence, did not offer a viable route for most nations to get out of colonial or dependent status. World War II became a crucial factor for Indian independence, since Great Britain was so depleted by it and could hardly afford to maintain a colonial government in territories as large and populous as India.

Nationalists like Nasser of Egypt and Jomo Kenyatta of Kenya were anti-imperialists, like Castro, but precisely because their ideology stopped short of the class analysis, they could not promote lasting social revolutions. They were independence leaders, in the Jeffersonian tradition, rather than revolutionaries.

6. Two works, Robin Blackburn's essay in *New Left Review* (1963) and the deeper study by James O'Connor, *The Origins of Cuban Socialism* (Ithaca, N.Y.: Cornell University, 1970), deal with the hidden dynamics of Cuban history—the legacies of dependency that went beyond sugar quotas and, in fact, determined the life-styles and possibilities of the Cuban people.

7. Each year the U.S. Congress agreed to buy a specified quantity of Cuban sugar at a fixed price. This meant that Cuba would have a guaranteed market for half or more of its sugar crop. The remaining could be sold to the world market at a fluctuating price. The arrangement appeared beneficial to Cuba, but in fact, it was a deal that put the island into bondage. Cuba could not risk selling too much sugar abroad and thus lowering the price since this would anger Florida and Louisiana growers whose congressional representatives could reduce the amount and price by threatening to filibuster the quota bill. The yearly quota also put the rest of the Cuban economy into a straitjacket since no sector of the Cuban society could afford to alienate any U.S. interest for fear that the sugar quota would be reduced.

8. A popular Cuban saying in 1968 was "Como quiera que te pongas, tienes que llorar." No matter what you do, you end up crying.

9. J. O'Connor, *The Origins of Cuban Socialism*.

10. Theodore Draper, *Castroism: Theory and Practice* (New York: Praeger, 1965).

11. Adolph A. Berle, for example, was a member of FDR's "Brain Trust" and served President Kennedy as an adviser. He was also a major shareholder and executive in the American Sugar Company, which was expropriated in 1960. The organized crime syndicates owned hotels and gambling casinos in Cuba, which were used both to make immense profits and to launder other dirty money.

12. Socialist literature makes clear that freedom of debate is vital to the existence of just order, and Stalinism, as practiced in the USSR during the Stalin and post-Stalin periods until recently, does not meet the most rudimentary criteria for socialist freedom. But, on the other side, counter-revolutionary or previously passive elements become active partisans for free speech and press when the issue of property redistribution begins to take place. While civil liberties are a co-equal partner with substantive human rights, they should not become a façade to mask the issues of class struggle that take place in revolutionary times, like those in Cuba in 1959–60, or in Nicaragua today.

13. Given the lessons of Cuba, the results of adopting Soviet-style models and fitting them together with Cuban conditions, can the Sandinistas reroute their revolution? The Soviets also have learned from the past and may also be more flexible. The question is whether or not the European Social Democrats can muster the will and courage to help defuse the Cold War in the Third World.

14. China, with whom the Cubans flirted briefly after the disillusionment with Khrushchev following the 1962 Missile Crisis, proved to be unreliable and far more bossy than the Soviets. The European Social Democratic leaders became prisoners of their own central banks, usually right after their electoral victories, and have not acted in concert to help Third World revolutionaries or even reformers.

15. C. Wright Mills wrote *Listen Yankee* (New York: Ballantine Books, 1960), and Jean-Paul Sartre wrote *Sartre on Cuba* (New York: Ballantine Books, 1960), two polemics defending the Cuban Revolution.

16. The Bolivian party had not only been ideologically opposed to Che's revolutionary guerrilla mission but had also taken steps to thwart his recruitment of Bolivian combatants and supply needs.

17. In 1971 the poet Heberto Padilla was arrested and held without charges for some 38 days. Upon his release Padilla spoke to the Cuban Writers' Union. He denounced himself and a few other Cuban writers as counterrevolutionary, heaping upon them phrases used in the Soviet purge trials of the 1930s. Either Padilla was presenting a farce in bad taste, or he was acting as a voice for Stalinist elements of state security. Charges made by Padilla's friends abroad that he had been tortured appear to be untrue, but nevertheless, the arrest of the poet and the subsequent spectacle at the Writers' Union further damaged the already bad image of Fidel in non-Communist intellectual circles.

18. In 1980 some 125,000 Cubans left in small boats for Florida. Castro allowed them to leave after President Carter declared them welcome. Castro shut down the exodus before all those who desired to leave had done so, mainly because Carter began to complain that among the refugees were recently released prison and insane asylum inmates. The CIA estimated that perhaps as many as another 250,000 Cubans would have left had the door remained open. This estimate contrasts with a Cuban calculation of about another 50,000.

19. Several hundred Cuban gays had been fired by a Cultural Ministry official and were reinstated after a judge declared that firing based on sexual preference was unconstitutional.

20. Amnesty International and Americas Watch do not have any certain cases of human rights violations, that is imprisonment for political ideas, imprisonment without trial, or systematic or routine torture. The OAS Human Rights Committee also has not documented any such cases. All three complain that Cuba does not allow systematic monitoring. The Cubans claim that the OAS expelled them in 1962, but have not ruled out inviting observers and investigators from Amnesty and Americas Watch.

The claims by former prisoners, such as former Batista policeman Armando Valladares, that they were imprisoned because of their ideas and were systematically brutalized in prison have not been substantiated. The Cuban government did demonstrate, for example, that Valladares simulated paralysis while he was in prison. Notably, when Valladares was freed, TV news cameras showed him walking normally and even running as he disembarked from the airplane.

21. The long-time cultural commissar and keeper of the party line, Antonio (Tony) Perez, and his minions were ousted along with some of the original *guerrilleros* including Ramiro Valdés, who held the post of Minister of the Interior and a seat on the Politburo. This led to a definite opening in the arts, and an atmosphere of freedom for intellectuals and artists both to pursue their imaginations and to control their own professional organizations—like the Writers' Union.

22. Lee Lockwood, *Castro's Cuba; Cuba's Fidel* (New York: Vintage, 1969).

23. Castro quoted from Kennedy's May 15, 1963, American University speech to illustrate the point, but offered nothing beyond that. He said he was convinced that Kennedy had decided to reverse the bellicose posture of his early years and pursue a more mature foreign policy. "The Kennedy that was assassinated in Dallas in 1963," he said, "was a much more mature man than the one who was inaugurated in 1961."

The Island of Cuba*

BY CARLOS FRANQUI

The brief but intense history of Cuba presents two constants and a single movement.

There was the world's invasion of the island and the island's struggle to repel it, to know and project itself on the world, to re-create itself at home and abroad.

The constant is movement. The island is a dance, a cyclone.

Its character and destiny are those of an island crossroads: a ship. It looks toward its neighboring or distant continental shores, a tradition inherited from its founders, who never stayed long in port.

Cuba is an adventure without fear of the unexpected, the magical, the impossible, or the unknown.

Cuba is not Indian. Cuba is not white. It is neither black nor yellow. Cuba is mulatto, mixed, whitish black, and tobacco-hued. Together with Brazil, it is one of the blackest countries in white America. One of the whitest of black countries as well.

Cuba, like the United States—which is geographically so near and yet so remote and different in everything else—is one of the newest nations of the world. One is a continent, the other is an island. One is Anglo-Saxon Protestant in character, and based on the industrial revolution, power, and wealth. The other is Latin, Spanish, black, and Chinese.

If Venice was Europe's door to the Orient and Florence symbolized the end of antiquity and the coming of the Renaissance, Cuba is the beginning of America's new world, yesterday embodied in today. There, everything began. All travelers paused there. The island was a bridge, a crossroads, and a base for continental expeditions in the New World.

The Spanish presence in America lasted from 1492 to 1899—four centuries in which Spain remained untouched by the Reformation, the industrial revolution, and the bourgeois upsurge.

And so there remained the prehistoric and the feudal establishments: adven-

*From Carlos Franqui, *Diary of the Cuban Revolution* (New York: Viking, 1980), pp. vii–ix.

ture, religion, absurdity, dreams of grandeur, madness, impracticality, genius, caudillismo, militarism, and the lack of laws and institutions and other establishments which accompanied the development of the bourgeois world. What did remain were the features of a world which preceded the industrial, machine civilization. And that ancient world was merged with what was left of the Indian world and the black world.

The slow-going, predominantly Spanish population of Cuba was engaged mostly in agriculture and in cattle raising until the industrial development of sugarcane and the gigantic slave trade it generated upset the balance of a more developed agricultural economy—cattle, coffee, cocoa, minor products—and created a violent shock in the colonial community.

Thousands of Chinese and Canary Islanders arrived later, most of them expert farmers, artisans, and merchants.

In the first half of the nineteenth century, an educated class, the Creoles, began emerging in Cuba. Its members studied in France and England, or in the fine schools of Havana founded by Varela and Luz y Caballero.

Cuba's Wars of Independence—1868 and 1895—were caused fundamentally by the development of nationality, the economic and political clashes with Spanish colonialism, the great English, French, and American revolutions, and the impact of the struggles of Simón Bolívar and others inspired in Latin America to achieve liberation from Spain.

The first books, printing press, and newsprint to reach Spanish America came in through Cuba. Later, José Martí, the liberator, poet, and first antiimperialist known in America, initiated the revolution known in literature as *modernismo.*

Thus mulattoes and mestizos, burghers, peasants, workers, intellectuals, and revolutionaries began appearing in that exuberant island paradise, "the most beautiful land that human eyes have ever beheld," as Columbus called it, a violent island with a rebellious Caribbean to the south and a placid lazy shore on the north, an island without frost and seasons, abounding in lush greenery, in sugarcane and tobacco but lacking in great wealth.

A good Cuban is one who possesses the rhythm of the black, who dances well, and is as delirious as a Spaniard but a bit more graceful; one who thinks like a Frenchman, believes in gambling luck as the Chinese, is as much of a Don Juan as if he were an Italian, does not like the gringos, is a chatterbox, and is also capable of embarking on *anything,* be it a ship, a plank, a rubber tire, a war, a fiesta, a ball, a love affair, a drinking spree, or a scientific experiment (the first rocket was invented by a Cuban—only on a postage stamp); capable of embarking even on a revolution against the Yankees or on socialism.

The Cuban always has time for anything. Nothing is impossible to him. He is always on the move; "the only thing one must not do is die," he says. Child or adult, he emphatically dislikes being ordered about.

The Cuban says no, and means it, to all authority; to bosses, kings, generals, presidents, colonels, commanders, doctors. And no to empires, too. Spanish, American, or Russian. He wants none of them.

Sí, señor, that's how it is.

Cuba has everything; there everything starts and nothing is finished.

And so . . .

In that world without norms, without logic, without classicism, bourgeois culture or an industrial world, all myths are real. Things exist before they are invented. The only requirement is to search for the origin of things—the real, not the supernatural—learn, and then re-create them.

Therein lies the story of the men who represent our Latin American world. Where did Bolívar learn the art of war and the philosophy of revolution he needed to launch Latin American independence? In Europe, of course.

And José Martí, how did he discover that the problem was the United States, not Spain, and then start the anti-imperialist war right within the monster itself, while living in the United States?

Bolívar and Martí balance Marx. To his revolutionary analysis of the German capitalist world, Bolívar and Martí added the continental unity needed in our feudal world and gave it a permanent anti-imperialist outlook. And that unity and that outlook still constitute the revolutionary political thought of our Latin American world.

Cuba could be called the Island of Beginnings. The Spanish conquest began there. The Indian rebellion began there.

Cuba was the beginning of the end of Spain's power.

The rebellion against the United States began in Cuba.

Three rebellions are struggling simultaneously in Cuba: the anticolonialist, the anticapitalist, and the antibureaucratic.

Cuba is an island of immigrants and émigrés. In constant movement and danger. Coveted by the great powers. Invaded by buccaneers and pirates. Occupied by Spaniards, Britons, North Americans. An island of sugar and tobacco, of misery and slavery: rebellion itself.

PART I

The Setting of the Cuban Revolution

Introduction

The Cuban Revolution is often viewed as an event that took place on the first of January 1959, rather than as a process encompassing Cuba's fight against four hundred years of Spanish colonial occupation and 60 years of United States domination. What lies at the core of the Cuban Revolution, as Carlos Franqui characterized it, is the dynamic between "the world's invasion of the island and the island's struggle to repel it." It was a revolution fought in the 19th century by Creole landowners and black slaves, in the 1930s by student radicals and urban and rural workers, and in the 1950s by a multiclass coalition. Inspired by Simón Bolívar's struggle for national liberation throughout the hemisphere, and by José Martí's later vision (Reading 3), the causes and origins of the Cuban Revolution cannot be reduced to a single and often superficial factor—such as Castro's charisma, Communist plotting, or U.S. hostility. It is rooted in a long historical process that Cubans believe continues to unfold today.

In the Manifesto of the 26th of July Movement (Reading 6), the organization which began the modern Cuban Revolution in the 1950s, the drafters self-consciously saw the movement as "resuming the unfinished Cuban Revolution." The manifesto begins with the promise "to take up the unfulfilled ideals of the Cuban nation and to realize them." It continues:

1

The Revolution is not precisely a war or an isolated episode, but the continuities of an historic process which presents different movements and stages. The landings of Narcizo Lopez in the middle of the nineteenth century, the 1868 and 1895 wars, the movement of the 1930s, and today the struggle against Batista's banditry are all parts of the same and only national Revolution.[1]

Each stage of the Cuban Revolution was confronted by different material conditions and thus shaped by different understandings of what needed to be done. The wars of independence in 1868 and 1895 were initiated by Cuba's landowning aristocracy—particularly ranchers, coffee and sugar planters—who opposed Spain's political control and mercantilist economic policies. Although Martí addressed questions internal to Cuba such as racism and the need for a new national culture and identity, the First and Second Wars of Independence were primarily aimed at freeing Cuba from the grip of Spanish colonialism.

Cubans won their long and bloody war against Spain, but lost their struggle for nationhood when the United States transformed the island from a colony to a protectorate. After occupying the island from 1898 to 1901, the U.S. intervened (1906–1909, 1912, 1917) to protect economic interests and restore "political stability." When Cuba's political elite shifted loyalties from Madrid to Washington, the island's landed aristocracy became tightly integrated into the U.S. economy: Between 1909 and 1929, U.S. capital investments in Cuba increased 700 percent. The sugar slump after World War I saw the island's monoculture economy virtually taken over by foreign-based companies, a process that drove small and independent farmers into sugar cultivation, making the island a virtual plantation for U.S. business.

Declining economic conditions in the 1920s, corruption and repression by the local government, and recurring U.S. intervention spawned the new generation of reformers and revolutionaries in the revolution of 1933. Unlike those of 1868 and 1895, this movement combined rejection of foreign domination with demands to transform the local political economy by ending large landholdings, nationalizing public services, regulating foreign investment, and protecting the rights of workers. Some of these fundamental reforms were carried out in 1933 and later written into the 1940 Constitution. However, the revolutionary government backed by radicalized students and workers was short-lived, undercut by Cuban army officers, traditional politicians, the U.S. Embassy, and by the revolutionaries' own ideological divisions and tactical blunders.

Twenty years later, on March 10, 1952, Fulgencio Batista abrogated the constitution and staged a military coup, prompting a new generation of Cubans to take up arms. The rebels' failed attack at the Moncada Barracks on July 26, 1953, inaugurated the most recent phase of the Cuban Revolution. In his defense of the Moncada attack, "History Will Absolve Me" (Reading 5),

Fidel Castro cataloged the many ills that had turned Cuba into a "defenseless colony," unable to feed and house its people, educate its young, or control its politics, economy and culture. By the 1950s, the complete loss of nationhood and personal dignity was readily apparent as the island had become a brothel for North American businessmen and a casino for the mafia.

What followed the trial was jail and later exile for the small band of survivors who had attacked the Moncada Barracks. But they inspired a broad movement with cadres among the peasantry, professionals, white collar urban workers, and the dispossessed. Returning from Mexico in 1956, Castro and the other leaders of the July 26th movement announced their intentions in the manifesto:

> Let it be clear, that we are thinking about a true revolution. We are not fighting to simply oust a gang of thieves from power, nor are we going to substitute some bosses for others. . . . We are working on a program of serious political, economic, agrarian, and educational transformations. We move resolutely towards the roots of Cuba's problems.[2]

These roots, they believed, were imbedded in the unequal relationship between the United States and Cuba, and in the class structure that left most Cubans impoverished. To overcome these intertwined circumstances, the young revolutionaries proclaimed that armed insurrection was the only viable path towards full national and social liberation.

Their triumph in 1959 did not end the Cuban revolutionary process. While the victory allowed a popular majority of Cubans to arrange their own affairs at home and abroad, it also intensified the conflicts between the classes in Cuba and between Cuba and the United States. (Indeed, U.S. antagonism contributed to the world-threatening confrontation of the Cuban Missile Crisis. See Reading 38.) Underdevelopment and a stultifying sugar monoculture faced Castro and his triumphant revolutionaries as they attempted to transform the island's economy from capitalism to socialism. Inertia weighed on those who worked vigilantly to transcend the heritage of ignorance, racism, sexism, and corruption. The articles in this Part make clear that contemporary Cuban decisions cannot be understood without a recognition of the legacy from which they emerge.

Robin Blackburn's "Prologue to the Cuban Revolution" (Reading 7) shows why the fight to overcome the Batista dictatorship could develop into a revolution: He notes, "The social structure of pre-revolutionary Cuba provide[s] a key to an understanding of the nature and development of the Revolution," and explains how no landed oligarchy or Cuban bourgeoisie ever "established stable domination of the Cuban Republic." The weak Cuban ruling class—lacking class institutions and ideology because of its dependence on the United

States—was thus unable to defeat the rebel army or, later, to forge a counter-revolution capable of toppling the revolutionary government.

The struggle against Batista was also propelled by his abuses of basic human rights and the disparities of wealth in Cuba in the 1950s, as described by Leo Huberman and Paul M. Sweezy in their pre-1959 history (Reading 1). The long shadow cast on Cuba by the United States was most clearly articulated in the infamous Platt Amendment (Reading 4). Named after U.S. Senator Orville Platt, this 1901 U.S. law specified that the United States could inter-vene in Cuban affairs wholly at its own discretion. Cuba was forced to include the amendment in its 1901 Constitution as a condition for the departure of U.S. troops from the island. That amendment officially governed relations between the two countries until it was abrogated in 1934.

Luis E. Aguilar reflects on the failed 1933 Revolution as a crucial prologue to the revolutionary victory of 1959 (Reading 2). He examines the successes and setbacks of this period which "open[ed] the way for remarkable economic and social progress" and "gave the Cubans a taste of nationalism and a new sense of sovereignty."

"History Will Absolve Me" by Fidel Castro (Reading 5) was the rebel leader's defense statement at his trial for the attack on Moncada Barracks. Trained as a lawyer, Castro created a defense that justified not only his own actions but also, in a manner reminiscent of the U.S. Declaration of Indepen-dence, the revolution itself.

The "Manifesto of the 26th of July Movement" (Reading 6) was written in November 1956. Some might discount how accurately it reflects the move-ment's goals, because one of the manifesto's purposes was to bring divergent groups into a broad coalition against Batista. Thus, it may not include the views of the July 26th Movement leaders that would have antagonized moder-ates. Nonetheless, the manifesto indicates the values on which the revolution rested, and it reveals a commitment to change Cuba fundamentally. In this regard, the July 26th Movement leaders did not obscure their intentions, as some critics claim.

In the last reading (Reading 8), Richard Fagen identifies the major charac-teristics of what may be deemed the political style of the Cuban Revolution. The continuities he identifies 12 years after the revolution's triumph extend long before and after 1959. Indeed, they still serve as important elements that explain the island's current revolutionary political culture.

NOTES

1. "Program Manifesto of the 26th of July Movement," in Rolando E. Bonachea and Nelson P. Valdés, ed., *Cuba in Revolution* (Garden City, N.Y.: Anchor Books, 1972), pp. 126–27.

2. *Ibid,* p. 115.

CHAPTER 1

The Revolutionary Heritage

1. Background of the Revolution*

BY LEO HUBERMAN AND PAUL M. SWEEZY

When Columbus discovered Cuba on Sunday, October 28, 1492, he was so struck with its charm that he called it "the most beautiful land human eyes have ever seen." If he had had time to explore the island he would have learned it was much more than that—Cuba is a rich as well as a beautiful land.

It is the largest island in the West Indies with a total area of 44,218 square miles. Long and narrow, it stretches 745 miles from its western to its eastern tip; in width, it ranges from 125 miles to 22 miles with an average of about 60 miles. It is only 90 miles south of Key West, 112 miles from the continental United States, and about 130 miles from Mexico across the Yucatan Channel.

Cuba lies just south of the Tropic of Cancer but its climate is more semitropical than tropical with the temperature averaging 75° F. for the year, ranging normally from 70° in the winter to 81° in the summer. Though the humidity is fairly high in both winter and summer, cooling breezes help to make even unpleasantly hot summer days bearable, and at no time is the weather extremely cold. . . .

Given an equable climate and adequate rainfall, only fertile soil is needed to raise an abundance of crops. Cuba's soil is extremely fertile. More than half of its area is arable land, suitable for growing a diversity of crops. Compared to most other countries this is a very high ratio, and Cuba's land is good not only in terms of its fertility but also in terms of its being level—about three

*From Leo Huberman and Paul Sweezy, *Cuba: Anatomy of a Revolution* (New York: Monthly Review Press, 1962). Edited for this volume.

fifths of the island is either flat or gently rolling. The rest is mountains and hills. Much of the nonarable land is suitable for grazing.

The highest and most rugged mountains are the Sierra Maestra, in the easternmost province of Oriente. The Pico Real de Turquino, the highest mountain in this range, rises to a height of 6,496 feet. On the south coast of the province of Las Villas, in the center of the island, are the Trinidad-Sancti Spíritus Highlands which reach a maximum elevation of 3,792 feet; and in Pinar del Río, the westernmost province, lies the Sierra de los Organos, a range of highlands paralleling the northern coast for about 112 miles and reaching a maximum elevation of 2,532 feet. The short narrow rivers that flow down from these mountain ranges are generally too shallow to be navigated. But Cuba has 2,175 miles of coastline along which are found excellent fishing grounds and many large pouch-shaped bays forming superb well-protected harbors.

The island has no coal and, to date, very little oil has been discovered. But extensive deposits of iron and nickel exist—so large as to be considered among the most important potential sources in the world. Chrome, manganese, and copper are also found in large quantities.

Four and a half centuries after Columbus, a different type of explorer, after a year's intensive study of Cuba, wrote that it is "without question one of the most favorable spots for human existence on the earth's surface." So it is. The "Pearl of the Antilles," as the island has been known since the time of Columbus, could have become a paradise.

But Cuba in the middle of the 20th century was not a paradise. Far from it. . . .

POOR PEOPLE

There were, in 1957, only about 6.4 million Cubans—less than the population of New York City—in an area larger than Denmark, Belgium, and the Netherlands combined. With so few people in a country so rich in natural resources, you would expect them to be well off. But they weren't. Most of the people of Cuba were desperately poor.

In the United States, the section of the country where living conditions are most miserable is the South. And the poorest state in the South is Mississippi. In the years 1950–1954, while the average per capita income for Delaware, the richest state in the nation, was $2,279 it was only $829 for Mississippi. But average per capita income for Cuba, in those same years, was not nearly half as much as Mississippi's—only 312 pesos. (The exchange rate between the peso and the dollar is one-for-one, and the two are used interchangeably throughout this work.)

Three hundred twelve pesos means $6 a week. That's what the average person had to live on in Cuba in those years. It wasn't enough. Actually, most of the people of Cuba got less than that—and their way of living showed it.

The 1953 census divided the population of Cuba into 57 percent urban, 43 percent rural. Housing in the cities was generally much better than in the country districts. In fact, the most common rural dwelling unit is not a house at all but a hut, called a bohío, generally made in whole or part from material obtained from the royal palm tree. The roof is usually thatched, the floor is most often the earth itself. Sometimes there are interior partitions, sometimes not. One of the bohíos we visited in the tobacco district of Pinar del Río had a single partition which separated the small kitchen from the rest of the hut. Wood chips were used for fuel for cooking. There was no running water, no electric light, no toilet. This was "home" for 12 people.

The extent of sanitary and other conveniences—or rather the appalling lack of them, particularly in the rural districts—is shown in the table below from the 1953 census:

Houses having:	All Cuba %	Urban %	Rural %
Lights:			
Electric	58.2	87.0	9.1
Acetylene	.9	.3	1.9
Kerosene	40.1	12.3	87.6
Other	.8	.4	1.4
Water:			
Inside piping	35.2	54.6	2.3
Cistern	5.0	5.2	4.6
Outside piping	16.8	22.0	8.1
River, well, or spring	43.0	18.2	85.0
Toilets:			
Water closet, inside	28.0	42.8	3.1
Water closet, outside	13.7	18.9	4.8
Privy	35.1	33.3	38.0
None	23.2	5.0	54.1
Baths:			
Tub or shower	44.4	64.9	9.5
None	55.6	35.1	90.5
Refrigeration:			
Mechanical	17.5	26.5	2.4
Ice	7.3	11.0	1.1
None	75.2	62.5	96.5

Two figures in the above table are of special importance because of their relation to the health of the Cuban people. Note that in all of Cuba, both in the urban and rural areas, only 35.2 percent of the dwelling units have running water, and only 28 percent have inside flush toilets. Note that 54.1 percent, more than half the people in the rural areas, have no toilets at all—not even a privy. With the lack of proper water and sewage systems, with so many Cubans having not enough food or the wrong kind of food because they are poor, with the almost total absence of teaching of the fundamentals of good hygiene, with medical care for the rural masses often unobtainable, it is easy to understand why health conditions in Cuba have been deplorably bad. Though the plagues of yellow fever and typhus which half a century ago took an enormous toll have been eliminated, malaria, tuberculosis, and syphilis have still not been brought fully under control. And malnutrition and parasitic infestation continue to be major health problems. In rural areas, particularly, a large number of children get infected with parasitic worms, suffer miserably, and die a painful death. . . .

One of the things that might have been done over the years was to teach the children and their parents simple elementary facts about the causes and cure of the diseases that plagued them. Dietary deficiency was one of the causes. It came from not enough food and from the wrong kinds of food. Many rural families just did not have enough money to buy all the food they needed, but others spent most of what little money they had on starchy foods instead of on green vegetables which contained the vitamins they needed. They could have been taught the right things to eat—but there weren't enough schools to do the teaching. Professor Lowry Nelson, in his excellent study entitled *Rural Cuba,* summarizes the rural school problem in these words:

> The most obvious fact about Cuban education is the lack of opportunity for rural children to attend school. In some places there are school buildings, but no teachers, in other places there are teachers, but no school buildings. There has been no systematic plan of school-building construction for rural areas. . . .

The extent and quality of education are a key index of the state of a society. By that standard, Cuba was a miserable failure. Cuban law made eight years of school attendance compulsory, but government officials did not supply the teachers, schools, and equipment to make enforcement of the law possible. (For the children of the rich, of course, there were adequate private schools.) The census of 1943 showed that only 35.1 percent of the children in the required age group were attending school. . . . And those who did attend did not go all the way. The figures for the drop in enrollment were appallingly large. The statistics for 1949–1950, gathered by the Economic and Technical Mission of the International Bank for Reconstruction and Development for its 1950 *Report on Cuba,* showed that "while 180,370 children start the first grade, only 4,852 enter the eighth grade."

Those who did not drop out generally went to school only a few hours a day, and they were taught by teachers whose training consisted of just a four-year course in a normal school upon completion of only eight years of elementary school training.

The census-takers in 1953 gave a "literacy test" to the persons they interviewed which consisted of asking whether they could read and write in any language. They found that 23.6 percent could not pass the test. . . .

That one-out-of-four figure is important to remember in another connection. A careful analysis of employment figures from the 1953 census showed that on an annual basis only about 75 percent of the Cuban labor force was employed. This meant that on an average day one out of four Cubans who were able to work and wanted to work could not find a job. Nor was 1953 a specially bad year. On the contrary, it was a pretty good year: It is safe to say that this one-out-of-four unemployment figure was normal in prerevolutionary Cuba.

The full significance of this startling—and tragic—fact can be grasped if you remember that in the worst year of the worst depression in United States history there were about 25 percent unemployed. *For Cuba, in respect to unemployment, every year was like the worst year of our worst depression.* And there was no system of unemployment insurance or unemployment relief.

When a country has a "normal" unemployment rate of 25 percent, it is a sure sign that something is wrong with the economic system. So great an imbalance in the economy is found in most nations of the world only rarely, in periods of deep crisis. Cuba's phenomenally large rate of unemployment, year in and year out, was a reflection of the fact that its economy was in a permanent state of crisis.

The trouble was sugar.

Good soil, a warm climate, and considerable moisture are necessary for the growing of sugar cane. Cuba has what is needed. It can produce sugar more cheaply than any country in the world, and over the years it became the world's largest producer and exporter of sugar. Its entire economy came to revolve around the amount and the value of the sugar crop.

The quantity of sugar produced determined how many workers would have jobs and for how long they would work, the traffic on the railroads, the activity in the harbors, the sales in the stores, the attendance at the movies.

The trouble was that the economy of Cuba came to center almost exclusively on this single crop; a crop that had to be sold in foreign markets unable to absorb all that could be produced.

The trouble was also that the sugar industry around which the economic life of Cuba revolves is a seasonal industry. If the season of work were long and the season of no work short, then that wouldn't matter too much. But it's exactly the other way around. During the time of the *zafra,* the period when the cane is harvested and brought to the mills, hundreds of thousands of field workers, swinging their machetes, cut down millions of tons of cane stalks, trim off the leaves, and throw the stalks into piles which are loaded into carts to be carried to the mills, or to the railroad cars which run to the mills. The *zafra* is a period of great activity—but it lasts only three or four months. Then comes the *tiempo muerto*—the dead season—when the field workers and most of the mill hands are idle—and hungry.

The *zafra*'s short period of plenty followed by the dead season's long period of want affected directly a large proportion of the workers of Cuba. The Census of 1953 showed that the sugar industry employed 474,053 workers or 23 percent of the total labor force.

Though the workers in the sugar industry had a miserable life, lots of money was being made by the owners (they had good and not-so-good years but over the long period they did very well), and those who were in a position to do so increased their acreage of land and installed bigger and better machinery in their mills. The little fellows found it harder to compete and were bought up by big corporations headed by capitalists whose only concern was greater profits, not the welfare of the people of Cuba.

By purchase, or by fraud, or by economic pressure, small farms were added to the acreage of big corporations, and Cuban land which had once been distributed widely became concentrated in fewer and fewer hands.

Virgin lands were added, too. Did it matter that the new tracts of land were covered with forests of good timber? Not at all. Forest lands were a treasure of great value to the nation as a whole, but that made no difference to profit-seeking sugar capitalists. So millions of feet of fine mahogany and cedar were cut down and as soon as the trees were dried, the entire area was set ablaze. Thus the land was cleared for more cane. And thus a great natural resource was sacrificed to sugar.

From the beginning of Cuban history there had been, in cattle ranching, enormous tracts of land called *latifundia,* owned by single individuals or groups. Now sugar *latifundia* came into being when the giant sugar corporations acquired large blocks of land, often holding large parts of it as reserves, idle, unutilized.

The extent of the concentration of agricultural land in the hands of the large corporations was revealed in the Agricultural Census of 1946:

One hundred and fourteen farms, or fewer than 0.1 percent of the total number, encompassed 20.1 percent of the land.

Eight percent of the total number encompassed 71.1 percent of the land.

At the other end of the scale, the small farms of less than one acre to under 25 acres, were 39 percent of the total number but they encompassed only 3.3 percent of the land.

By this time, more than half the cultivated area of Cuba was devoted to sugar cane. The constantly growing acreage in cane made heavy inroads into the amount of land in food crops. So great was the subordination of the entire national economy to the production of sugar that Cuba, one of the richest agricultural countries in the world, was not able to feed itself! Only about 70 percent of what Cubans ate was produced in Cuba. One of the principal items in the diet of the people was rice—yet rice had to be imported along with such other staples as lard, pulses, wheat flour, and canned goods.

Attention of the people with capital to invest was so focused on sugar that opportunities for making money in other ways were neglected. Thus the economy tended to get more and more lopsided. In its *Report on Cuba* the World Bank gave some striking examples:

> Numerous available Cuban raw materials are not adequately utilized at home, and some are even exported instead, while the finished products made from identical materials are imported. Though seasonal prices may have something to do with it, the fact is that out of 11,000,000 kilos of tomatoes *exported* annually, an estimated equivalent of 9,000,000 kilos *return to Cuba* in various forms such as tomato sauce, paste, ketchup, etc.

The trouble with the economy was sugar.

A warning of the danger of monoculture, of the trend toward a one-crop economy, had been given as far back as 1883 by the greatest of Cuba's heroes. In that year José Martí, revolutionist, orator, poet, philosopher, sounded the alarm: "A people commits suicide the day on which it bases its existence on a single crop."

The warning was justified—death to the economic welfare of the country, death to its national aspirations, were certain to follow if the trend toward monoculture continued.

But in Cuba's case it wasn't suicide. It was murder. In 1883 Cuba was on the road to the top of the cliff, but it was the United States that pushed it over the top. . . .

FOREIGN DOMINATION

From the beginning of its history as a nation, the United States was always interested in Cuba. Its closeness to our shores, the possibility that its fine harbors might be used by enemy navies to threaten our Atlantic seaboard or our commerce—this was the reason for our early interest in the island. In later years our interest was renewed as we developed a considerable trade with Cuba, and its strategic military importance in respect to the Panama Canal impelled us to secure a naval base there.

In the early 19th century the United States government felt that one day Cuba would become a part of the United States. Until it did, it was better, American statesmen thought, that it remain a colony of Spain. If, like the other colonies of Spain in Latin America, it won its independence, then there was danger that England might seize it—and England's power was something to be feared, Spain's was not. (England had the same attitude vis-à-vis the United States—better that Cuba remain a colony of Spain than win its independence and be annexed by the United States.)

So, though Cubans chafed under Spanish misrule, the United States was happy with the situation. We had only to bide our time and Cuba would be

ours. That's precisely what Secretary of State John Quincy Adams wrote to
the American Minister of Spain on April 28, 1823:

> There are laws of political as well as of physical gravitation; and if an apple,
> severed by the tempest from its native tree, can not choose but fall to the ground,
> Cuba, forcibly disjoined from its unnatural connection with Spain and incapable
> of self-support, can gravitate only toward the North American Union, which, by
> the same law of nature can not cast her off from its bosom.

A generation later, we were inclined to give nature a shove and push the
gravitation process along by buying Cuba from Spain. The United States
Minister in Madrid made a secret offer of $100 million for the island, but Spain
turned it down. The fact was that though Cuba was still politically dependent
on Spain, it had become commercially more attached to the United States. By
the 1850's our exports of $8 million and imports of $12 million represented
about one third of Cuba's entire foreign trade. She was doing more trading
with us than with Spain. Senator Stephen A. Douglas was roundly applauded
when he said, in a speech in New Orleans, on December 6, 1858: "It is our
destiny to have Cuba and it is folly to debate the question. It naturally belongs
to the American continent."

The Cubans, however, had a different idea of their own destiny. They had
the curious notion that Cuba "naturally belonged" to the Cubans. In 1868 they
rose in armed rebellion to fight for their independence. The depth of their
desire to be free and the intensity of their unsuccessful struggle can be gauged
from the fact that the war lasted for ten years, 80,000 Spanish soldiers died,
and half a billion dollars were spent by the mother country.

A large part of the Cuban countryside was laid waste, the farmers suffered
terrible losses, and some American merchants who had financed Cuban sugar
estates were now able to pick up good sugar properties at bargain-basement
prices.

The drop in sugar prices which resulted meant that the old Cuban mills,
some still grinding by ox-power, would have to be made more efficient or go
out of business. New machinery had to be installed, new lands had to be
planted, railroads had to take the place of ox-carts in hauling the cane to the
mills. Many Cuban millowners did not have the capital that was necessary—
but some Americans did. In the 1880's and 1890's, American capitalists began
to invest in sugar plantations in a big way. By 1896, they had about $30 million
worth of sugar properties—and 10 percent of Cuba's total production came
from American-owned mills.

American capitalists bought mining properties too. Iron ore, manganese,
and nickel mines were acquired by Bethlehem Steel and Rockefeller interests.
By 1896, American mining properties were worth about $15 million. With
another $5 million of American money in tobacco plantations, American
investments in Cuba totaled $50 million in 1896.

The Cubans meanwhile were still pursuing their goal of independence from Spain. Spurred on by the writings of Martí, they rose up in arms a second time in 1895. In 1898 they were still waging a successful but as yet undecided war, and their bloody struggle for freedom from Spain won the sympathy of the American people.

In the debates that followed the blowing up of the U.S.S. *Maine* in the harbor of Havana on the evening of February 15, 1898, the position of those who wanted the United States to intervene in the Cuban-Spanish War because it was our "destiny" to control Cuba was stated again and again. So, too, was the position of those who wanted to intervene for humanitarian reasons, to stop the bloodshed and cruelties going on in Cuba. And there were those who argued for intervention to win independence for the Cuban Republic. In his message to Congress on April 11 advocating "the forcible intervention of the United States as a neutral to stop the war," President McKinley argued that the state of affairs in Cuba was "a constant menace to our peace," that intervention was justified "by the very serious injury to the commerce, trade, and business of our people and by the wanton destruction of property and devastation of the island." He made only a slight reference to the fact that the day before he delivered his message to Congress he had received a cable from the American Minister at Madrid advising that immediate peace in Cuba could be secured by negotiations, that a final settlement could be obtained in which Spain would grant the rebels autonomy, or independence, or cede the island to the United States! . . . .

The war was over in less than four months, with the United States the victor in both the Caribbean and the Pacific. The treaty of peace signed in Paris on December 10, 1898, provided for the independence of Cuba and the cession to the United States of Puerto Rico, Guam, and the Philippines (we were to pay Spain $20 million for the Philippines); it provided also for the protection of private property and the pacification of Cuba by the United States.

On January 1, 1899, the Spanish troops evacuated the island, and American military occupation under General Leonard Wood began the job of pacification. We were pledged, by the fourth clause of the war resolution, to get out of Cuba when that job was completed and "leave the government and control of the island to its people."

That was the promise. Now came a maneuver which made the promise hollow.

On November 5, 1900, General Wood, the American military governor, called a constitutional convention in Havana. The delegates were instructed to write a constitution and frame a treaty outlining the future relations between Cuba and the United States. They wrote the constitution and were working on the treaty when that task was taken from them. On March 3, 1901, the Cuban constitutional convention was handed a set of articles, known as the Platt Amendment, which the United States Congress had passed into law and which were now to be incorporated into the new constitution. The Platt Amendment defined Cuba's relations to the United States. The convention could add its provisions to their constitution—or else. Or else what? Or else the American army of occupation would remain in Cuba.

All the articles in the Platt Amendment were restrictions on the sovereignty of Cuba; the two which were of especial importance are quoted in full:

> Article III. The Government of Cuba consents that the United States may exercise the right to intervene for the preservation of Cuban independence, the maintenance of a government adequate for the protection of life, property, and individual liberty, and for discharging the obligation with respect to Cuba imposed by the Treaty of Paris on the United States, now to be assumed and undertaken by the Government of Cuba.
>
> Article VII. To enable the United States to maintain the independence of Cuba, and to protect the people thereof, as well as for its own defense, the Cuban Government will sell or lease to the United States the land necessary for coaling or naval stations, at certain specified points, to be agreed upon with the President of the United States.

Confronted with this ultimatum from the United States what were the Cubans to do? They recognized that the Platt Amendment was a menace to their sovereignty. They protested that real independence for Cuba meant being "independent of every other nation, the great and noble American nation included." They were assured by Secretary of State Root that Article III of the Platt Amendment was not "synonymous with intermeddling or interference in the affairs of the Cuban government."

They didn't believe him, but still they had no choice. On June 12, 1901, by a vote of 17 to 11, the Platt Amendment was added to the Cuban constitution (two years later it was written into a permanent treaty between the two countries), and on May 20, 1902, American military occupation of the island was ended.

But as the Cubans had feared, in spite of the pious assurances of Secretary Root, that was not the end of meddling in Cuban affairs, or even of further military occupation of the island. American troops intervened for the first time under the Platt Amendment in 1906, a second time in 1912, and a third time in 1917. In 1920 the United States sent a series of political and financial advisors who controlled the Cuban government without benefit of troops. . . .

The United States did, indeed, have the key to the Cuban house; it did, indeed, enter at will; and the Cuban governments which it supported had, in the nature of the setup, to be run by politicians who could be relied on to do Washington's bidding.

Of politicians who bend the knee not much can be expected in the way of honest, efficient, or democratic government. Following Tomás Estrada Palma, elected the first President of the Republic of Cuba in 1902, came a succession of Presidents whose terms were characterized by venality, nepotism, incompetence, graft, and despotism. Some were elected to office by ballots, others seized or held power by bullets. Two of the better of a thoroughly bad lot were Dr. Ramón Grau San Martín and Dr. Carlos Prío Socarrás; two of the worst, General Gerardo Machado and Sergeant Fulgencio Batista. Machado, who held power from 1924 to 1933, and Batista, who seized control of the army in September 1933 and of the government the following year, were bloody dictators whose regimes were nightmares of repression, assassination, gangsterism, bribery, and corruption.

The Cuban people, led by brave students of the University of Havana, revolted against Machado, "The Butcher," and he fled the country in August 1933. In the turmoil that followed, Grau became president for a brief period of four months. He introduced a series of necessary reform measures designed to alleviate the miserable conditions of the poor, made worse than ever by the Great Depression. Such reforms were what the island needed— but they were not what the privileged upper class of Cubans or American interests wanted. So the administration of Franklin D. Roosevelt which, to its credit, abrogated the Platt Amendment, withheld recognition from the Grau government and Grau was ousted from office. The recognition that was denied Grau was granted to Batista when he became the "strong man" of Cuba in 1934, and he stayed in power, to the further debasement of Cuban life, for another ten years. Whether the administration in Washington was reactionary or liberal, whether the Platt Amendment was on the books or not, the long arm of United States power was never absent from Cuba. And the results were always the same—good for North American capitalists, bad for the Cuban people.

There was in Cuba a group of people who had thought through to the answer to Mr. Jenks' [Leland Jenks, a social scientist—eds.] question of "whether a country can long endure on the basis of one-crop latifundia managed by absentee proprietors." Their answer to the question was a firm *no*.

They had an answer to another question that had long plagued their country—what to do about the succession of corrupt politicians who were lackeys of the foreign investors and who ran the government not in the interest of the people of Cuba but for their own enrichment. Their answer was: *Get rid of them.*

They were convinced that the land of Cuba should belong to the people who inhabit it; that, rationally managed in the interest of all the people, their rich island could become what Columbus saw, "the most beautiful land human eyes have ever seen."

In 1952 they dedicated themselves to the task of making their dream come true.

THE ASSAULT ON MONCADA

A Cuban presidential election was scheduled for June 1, 1952. A public opinion poll taken on March 1 showed that of the three candidates, Fulgencio Batista was running last. Ten days later, at 2:43 A.M., Batista walked into Camp Columbia, the largest military fortress in Cuba, and took over the armed forces. If he couldn't win at the polls, he could do what he had done in 1934—take over the government by force.

A few weeks after the *coup d'état,* a young, 25-year-old lawyer who had received his doctorate degree at the University of Havana just two years before, appeared before the Urgency Court in Havana. He submitted a brief showing that Batista and his accomplices had violated six articles of the Code of Social Defense for which the prescribed sentence was 108 years in jail. He demanded that the judges do their duty:

> Logic tells me that if there exist courts in Cuba Batista should be punished, and if Batista is not punished and continues as master of the State, President, Prime Minister, senator, Major General, civil and military chief, executive power and legislative power, owner of lives and farms, then there do not exist courts, they have been suppressed. Terrible reality?
>
> If that is so, say so as soon as possible, hang up your robe, resign your post.

Who was this foolhardy Cuban citizen who alone had the audacity to challenge the army cutthroat who had seized power a second time? What manner of man was he?

His name was Fidel Castro.

He was born in Oriente Province on August 13, 1926, on his father's sugar plantation at Mayarí, 50 miles from Santiago de Cuba. His father, Angel Castro, had emigrated to Cuba from Galicia, in northwestern Spain, and had prospered in sugar and lumber. The Castro family was rich but everywhere about them, in the foothills and the mountains, the boys learned to know what poverty means; they saw the neighboring farmers living on the borderline of starvation in miserable hovels without electric light or running water or plumbing facilities of any kind.

Coming from a Roman Catholic family, Fidel was sent to parochial schools. In the elementary grades he was a boarding student in Santiago; for his high school education he went to the Belén Jesuit school in Havana. He did well in high school, both in his studies and in extracurricular activities. He was on the debating team, played basketball and baseball, and graduated in the top third of his class.

. . . Fidel entered the University of Havana in 1945. Students in Latin American universities, and particularly those in Havana, have always been politically active and Fidel was no exception. He jumped into politics with both feet, and his astounding oratorical gift marked him early as a campus leader in the fight for honest government and for better conditions for the poor of Cuba.

He took time out in 1947 to join an expeditionary force of 3,000 men whose objective was to invade the Dominican Republic and overthrow its dictator, Trujillo. When the invasion fleet was intercepted by Cuban naval vessels, Fidel and two companions, determined that they would not be caught and put under arrest, swam three miles to shore.

Back at law school, Fidel pitched into political life again by helping to organize a committee to fight racial discrimination at the university where Negro students were barred from official representation on athletic teams. In his junior year he ran for the vice-presidency of the student governing body and was elected. Later, when the president resigned, he became president.

On October 12, 1948, Fidel married Mirtha Díaz Balart, a philosophy student at the university. A son was born to them 11 months later. The bride's conservative family kept hoping that their son-in-law's interest in politics was merely youthful idealism which would soon pass. But that didn't happen— Fidel was arrested again and again for his active participation in mass meetings and student protests against corruption in Cuba and other Latin American countries. The marriage ended in divorce in 1955.

The year of his marriage marked the first time Fidel voted in a presidential election. He voted for Eduardo Chibás, candidate of the newly formed Ortodoxo party, running on a platform of clean government and social reform. Chibás was a remarkably able, intelligent, and courageous fighter against the corruption which he saw everywhere in government. He had served in both the House and Senate so he knew Cuban politics from the inside. What he had learned he told the people in Sunday night radio broadcasts so filled with a consuming hatred for the plunderers and so daring as to hold his immense audience spellbound. He exposed the crooked schemes of grafting officials, named names, and called for their removal from office. Though he lost the election, he had a profound influence on the thinking of young people. Chibás became one of Fidel's heroes—along with the great patriot José Martí, whose every word on independence for Cuba he had studied and learned to treasure.

On graduation from the university in 1950, Fidel hung out his shingle as a lawyer in Havana. He had a busy practice, with most of his time spent in defending workers, farmers, and political prisoners. He continued his own activity in politics and was a candidate for Congress on what would have been the winning ticket in the 1952 election—the election that never came off because of Batista's *coup.*

When his petition for the imprisonment of Batista was rejected by the court, Fidel decided that there was only one way in which the usurper could be overthrown—revolution. Only one way to put into power an honest government dedicated to the establishment of economic reform—revolution. Only one way to make real Martí's dream of a truly sovereign Cuba—revolution.

Having decided that revolution was necessary, Fidel, with characteristic energy and singleness of purpose, now devoted himself to the task of preparing it. To round up a group of volunteers who burned with a desire to overthrow the tyrant was not enough; only those would qualify who were still willing to join in the struggle after they were made to understand that the odds against their success were tremendous and the penalty for failure was horrible— torture and death. They must be trained in the use of arms, and money for guns and ammunition must be obtained. All preparations had to be made secretly, for Batista's spies were everywhere.

After a year of recruiting, training, plotting, and planning, Fidel was ready. His rebel "army" consisted of some 200 men, and two women. Most of them were students or graduates, and nearly all of them were young people like himself, aged 26, and his brother, Raúl, aged 22.

On the outskirts of Santiago in Fidel's native province of Oriente stood Fort Moncada, second largest of the country's military fortresses. The plan was to attack Moncada at dawn—to take by surprise the 1,000 soldiers quartered there, capture their machine guns, tanks, armored trucks, up-to-date rifles and ammunition; then seize the radio stations and call upon the people of Cuba to support the rebel force against the dictator.

On July 26, 1953, the attack was made. In part it was successful—according to plan; in part it was a failure due to errors in the plan as well as some unlucky breaks. Some of the attackers were killed on the spot; others were captured, horribly tortured, then put in jail to wait trial, or murdered in cold blood; still others, including Fidel and Raúl, got away, pursued by Batista's army. . . .

By far the largest number of rebels who lost their lives were murdered after the assault was over. But the story of the butchery that followed the rebel assault on Moncada could not be suppressed. Too many families in Santiago had seen or heard about the killings of their loved ones, or friends, and they protested. Monsignor Pérez Serantes, Archbishop of Santiago, intervened. He secured a promise from the army commanding officer in the city that the lives of the rebels still at large would be spared if they gave themselves up; they would be brought to trial, not murdered.

. . . The army patrol that discovered Fidel and two companions exhausted and asleep in a shack in the foothills of the Sierra Maestra, was headed by Lieutenant Pedro Sarría who had been a student at the university while Fidel was active there. None of the other soldiers in the patrol recognized the prisoner. As he bent over Fidel, ostensibly searching him for arms, Lieutenant Sarría whispered in his ear: "Don't give your right name or you will be shot."

With Fidel in prison Raúl Castro, with his men, came down from their hideout in the mountains and surrendered.

The assault on Moncada had ended in defeat. But this first battle, the opening chapter of the Revolution, was not entirely a failure. For though the fort had not been captured, the attention of the people had been won. Fidel Castro and the July 26th Movement had become known. In Oriente, if nowhere else, the spirit of resistance to Batista tyranny was aroused.

2. The Revolution of 1933*

By Luis E. Aguilar

For those who have "discovered" Cuba and Cuban history only after, and under, the impact of Castro's revolution, it is easy to dismiss as unimportant the revolutionary episode of 1933—and, for that matter, all Cuban history before Castro. On the other hand, the similarities between the earlier episode and the later revolution are so obvious that they suggest a point-by-point historical comparison which could be as dangerous as ignoring the 1930's altogether. After all, the same Fulgencio Batista whom Guiteras failed to defeat in 1934 was defeated by Castro in 1958; a student leader of 1933, Eduardo Chibás, sponsored Fidel Castro at the beginning of his political career in 1951; the same Blas Roca who justified the "opportunistic" mistake of the Communist party in 1933 is now a full-fledged, though not very influential, member of the Executive Committee of the Cuban Communist Party, which, at least theoretically, rules the island. As in 1961, so also in 1933, Cuba was diplomatically isolated, surrounded by American warships, and fighting at Montevideo's Pan-American Conference for her right to develop her revolutionary programs. And was not Raúl Roa, for a time the most important spokesman of Castro's government, one of the members of the Student Left Wing of 1933?

Yes, the links are obvious. They could be further dramatized by remembering the chilling prediction of Rubén Martínez Villena in 1933, when Fidel Castro was only six years old: "The red flags hoisted in the silence of dark night upon the factory chimneys of the Armour Company sugar mills herald the raising of those other red banners which will float in the glare of the sunlight over all the factories of the whole sugar industry. . . . *Eyes that are young today will not yet have grown old when they look upon this marvel.*"[1] Or one could ponder the conclusion of Ezequiel Ramírez Novoa: "If the United States in 1933 had respected the decision of the Cuban people, the process of independence would have been freely carried out, and there would have been no need for the sacrifices which the present generation of Cubans have had to make."[2]

*From Luis E. Aguilar, *Cuba 1933: Prologue to Revolution* (New York: W. W. Norton, 1974), pp. 230–47. Edited for this volume.

Perhaps, perhaps if what we have called "the Right" had not frustrated the revolution of 1933—and killed the attendant reforms—then the Left in 1959 would not have needed extreme radical measures, or perhaps there would have been no need for revolution. But let us avoid the game of conjecture to dwell upon the actual reasons and results that make 1933–1934 a crucial time in Cuban history. One fact at least appears certain: the Cuban society that Castro found in 1959 was basically forged by the forces that emerged and grew out of the revolutionary episode of 1933.

The long struggle against Machado and the turbulent period following his downfall have characteristics usually attributed to true revolutionary phenomena: violence, participation of the masses, radical programs, and some basic changes in the social and political structure of the nation. By profoundly shaking the political order in Cuba, by defying with a measure of success the hitherto unchallenged position of the United States, and by partially applying some of the radical ideas and programs that had been gaining ground since the 1920's, revolutionary groups of 1933 effected a profound change in Cuba. The revitalization of nationalism, the opening of new economic opportunities for several national sectors, and the weakening of foreign dominance in Cuba were some of the consequences of their actions. The vanguard of the 1933 revolutionary forces—the students, Grau, Guiteras—did fail to remain in power for long and, as a consequence, were able only to "offer" the nation their ideas and projects. But the mere realization of the necessity and possibilities for change created a new national conscience and initiated a trend that was afterward almost impossible to reverse. As early as August 1933, when the real revolutionary period was about to begin, an alert Spanish writer had already noticed the new dimension of events in Cuba: "In comparison with the usual Latin American revolution—which seldom is anything more than a *pronunciamiento*[3]—the fall of Machado offers a new aspect: the weapon with which he was defeated. That weapon was a general strike, that is, the none-too-frequent intervention of the masses in the fight for their claims."[4] The awakening and politization of the Cuban masses was indeed one important result of the conflict but, as we have already seen, there were many others.

Of the three political parties of the prerevolutionary era, Liberal, Conservative, and Popular, only the Liberals reappeared later to play a role, a minor one, in Cuban politics. New parties, more or less imbued with the ideas of 1933, dominated the scene after the revolution.[5] The Congress, the courts, the bureaucracy, and the university were purged of corrupt elements. The feeble labor unions of the 1920s evolved into the powerful CTC (Confederation of Cuban Workers), the only central labor organization of Cuba, bringing together all organized workers. In 1942, four years after its founding, the CTC had a membership of more than 400,000 workers.[6] Under the growing power and pressure of the CTC, which was dominated by communists from 1939 to 1946, labor legislation was augmented steadily before and after the promulgation of the Constitution of 1940. Simultaneously the *colonos* [sugar plantation owners], who were almost defenseless before the revolution, joined forces in the Cane Growers Association of Cuba (created by the revolutionary government in January 1934) and fought successfully for their economic security and for a more just distribution of sugar profits between them and the *hacendados*. . . .

The Revolution of 1933, while opening the way for remarkable economic and social progress and increasing the role of the state in economic affairs, also gave the Cubans a taste of nationalism and a new sense of sovereignty. The Platt Amendment was officially abrogated in 1934, and Cuban politics gained a visible measure of independence. No one doubted the still enormous weight and importance of American influence in Cuba, but in comparison with a very recent past— . . . when almost all eyes were fixed on the American ambassador as the supreme political arbiter—the new period brought a refreshing sensation of liberation and the feeling that Cuba was beginning to be the master of her own destiny.[7] Protected by an expanding web of nationalistic legislation, the Cubans ceased to be pariahs in their own land, squeezed by the double pressure of American companies and Spanish commercial interests. . . .

Politically, the period 1933–1952 represents a general progress toward democracy. Batista's ten years in power (1934–1944) after the collapse of Grau's government should not be viewed simply as a period of counterrevolution and military oppression. Batista was too smart and too realistic not to try to use in his favor the popular energies liberated by the revolutionary government of 1933. He never hesitated to use force when necessary—the ruthless methods employed to prevent a general strike in 1935 were proof enough[8]—but force and brutality were not his natural tendencies. In power, as when he was struggling to reach it, he relied more on his political skill, maneuverability, and cunning. In 1936, when President-elect Miguel Mariano Gómez refused to act like a puppet and tried to oppose Batista's dominance, the former sergeant did not resort to the usual method of deposing the president and establishing a military dictatorship; instead he used all his political influence to force the Congress to depose the president and call for new elections. . . .

In 1944, Cuba offered the refreshing, and in Latin America, infrequent, spectacle of a strong man abandoning the presidency to a democratically elected rival. From 1944 to 1952, the Cuban Revolutionary party (the "Auténticos"), a political organization created by the principal revolutionary leaders of 1933, ruled Cuba, first under Ramón Grau San Martín (1944–1948), and then under Carlos Prío Socarrás (1948–1952). Under the Auténticos, Cuba enjoyed the prosperity brought about by the high price of sugar after the Second World War, and a remarkable period of political freedom and democracy. Social and economic legislation continued to expand, the army lost its preeminence, the Communists were forced out of the leadership of the CTC, and freedom of expression reached a very high level.

How can we explain, then, that after such remarkable progress brought about by a revolutionary process, a nation considered prosperous by Latin American standards—where the middle class was expanding, labor legislation was advanced, and the most dramatic aspect of the usual Latin American spectacle, a miserable and defenseless mass and a handful of rich people, was absent—was to enter after a few years into the terrible throes of a socialist revolution?

There is no easy answer. Even after considering all the factors involved—including the most decisive and elusive, the character and personality of Fidel Castro—there is still wide margin for uncertainty and doubt. That is why, when reflecting upon this entire period, one must consider inadequate the usual leftist simplification of gathering some figures about the imperialist exploitation of Cuba, and about the famous and favorite "corruption" of Havana, to conclude that in 1959 Cuba was ripe for a socialist revolution. That ripeness as late as 1958 no Marxist in or out of Cuba had foreseen or predicted. The easy anti-Marxist explanation (so dear to many Cuban exiles) which presents a paradisaical Cuba falling through deceit and betrayal into the grip of a group of international Communist conspirators also misses the mark.

Where then is the answer? Who knows it? Historical causes are always difficult to discover, and sometimes it appears that, as in Plotinus' theory of beauty, they exist primarily in the eyes of the observer. After revolutions, theories multiply. Impressed by the spectacular explosion, investigators scrutinize the past, searching for clues and portents of the impending revolution, and in their eagerness they transform any suitable episode, no matter how trivial, into a significant event. This entire prerevolutionary period, then, acquires a new, and largely artificial, dimension: Its events were only the prelude to the revolution. What seems evident is that in the period following the revolution of 1933 a series of events occurred in Cuba that created a national crisis and produced a situation for favorable exploitation by anyone capable of confronting the crisis. Surely those events do not explain the emergence of Fidel Castro or the decisions he made (or was forced to make) radically to alter the course of Cuban history, but they do help us to understand the historical moment in which Castro appeared and some of the actions and reactions of the Cuban people when he became the new champion of a national cause.

But before we consider those significant developments of the postrevolutionary period, it is essential to emphasize the obvious: The revolutionary episode of 1933 was for Cuba a step forward, but only one step, and a step fraught with frustration and disillusion. The relative progress that Cuba enjoyed from 1933 to 1952 did not solve many of her problems, nor did it change many unjust conditions. The existence of *latifundia,* the periodical unemployment of thousands of cane-cutters, the basic dependence on one product (sugar) and one market (the U.S.A.) were still dramatic and at times agonizing problems for thousands of Cubans.[9] And there were many others: public corruption, an absurd concentration of political power in the city of Havana (a Cuban minister of education once said "Havana is Cuba, all the rest is landscape"), some vestiges of racial discrimination, and the poor conditions of Cuban rural population were some of the most evident.[10] But these were old problems that Cuba shared in a greater or lesser degree with the rest of Latin America and should be considered only as the background for some important specific developments that give the period we are dealing with its special characteristics. These developments are keys to understanding the Cuban situation in 1959.

. . . Faith is something that is regained slowly, if at all. But the atmosphere [in the 1950s] was open and propitious for a new voice to remake the broken dream, for a young figure to replace the worn-out leaders of the 1930s and give fresh meaning to unfulfilled aspirations.

From the very beginning the new champion interpreted correctly the signs of the times: He spoke the language that the people wanted to hear. He mentioned Chibás, Guiteras, and Martínez Villena; he spoke against Batista and militarism; he promised to restore the constitution of 1940, to call for elections, and to move the republic forward with an honest government and a true social democracy. Who this new champion was, how he succeeded in embodying the general aspirations of the Cuban people, and how he drastically changed his course and the course of Cuban history toward an unexpected, formidable, tragic, and still unreached objective is quite another story. But this story cannot be understood if one ignores the historical current that emerged from the violent episode of 1933—the accomplishments and failures, the hopes and despairs, that preceded Castro and, to a certain extent, formed the essential prologue for the new situation.

NOTES

1. Rubén Martínez Villena, "The Rise of the Revolutionary Movement in Cuba," *The Communist,* Vol. 12 (1933), p. 569 (italics mine).

2. Ezequiel Ramírez Novoa, *Historia de una gran epopeya: Cuba y el imperialismo yanky* (Lima: Ediciones 28 de Julio, 1960), p. 108.

3. *Pronunciamiento* is a word used mainly in Spain to indicate an act of rebellion of an individual, or some small group, usually of the armed forces, who generally represent no interest other than their own.

4. Quoted in Ramón Vasconcelos, *Dos años bajo el terror* (Havana: Cultural, 1935), p. 20.

5. "It is axiomatic among Cubans," wrote William S. Stokes some years later, "that the only parties capable of winning a national campaign are those which opposed the dictator Machado in the 30s." See his penetrating article, "The Cuban Revolution and the Presidential Elections of 1948," *Hispanic-American Historical Review* (February 1951), p. 38.

6. José R. Alvarez Díaz *et al., A Study on Cuba* (Miami: University of Miami Press, 1963), p. 584.

7. While interpreting it according to Marxist ideas, Castro's historians and economists do recognize this decline of American influence in Cuba during this period. One of them, Oscar Pino

Santos, described this as the moment when American imperialism "sort of silenced itself" ("Historiografía y Revolución," *Casa de las Américas* [special issue of the 10th anniversary of the Cuban Revolution], Vol. 9, Nos. 51–52 [November 1968–February 1969], p. 105).

8. In March 1935 almost all revolutionary groups—the Auténticos, Guiteras' Joven Cuba, the ABC, and the Communists—joined forces to topple Batista through a general strike. The loyalty of the army, severe methods of repression, and the usual division among revolutionary groups saved the government. After that failure, the majority of the groups decided to abandon violent tactics and organized themselves as political parties. Antonio Guiteras was killed while trying to escape into exile to continue the fight against Batista.

9. After reading some of the most recent studies of Cuba's economic problems (for example, René Dumont, *Cuba: Est'il Socialist* [Paris: Gallimard, 1970]), and after witnessing the tremendous and not quite successful effort to produce 10 million tons of sugar—pushing Cuba back to the state of a sugar factory—plus the undeniable economic dependence on Soviet aid, which is always accompanied by growing political pressure, one feels compelled to ask a somber but realistic question: To what extent is it possible for a small, nonindustrialized nation really to free herself from foreign influence?

10. "How can we fail to tremble for the future of our political institutions," I wrote in 1954, "and of our nation, if a large section of our rural population is illiterate, reduced to support 'rights' they do not understand and 'liberties' that have no meaning, . . . an easy prey for the demagogue or the Marxist of the future, capable always of using for his own benefit this kind of tragic situation" (Luis E. Aguilar, "La Verdadera Tragedia," *Bohemia* [November 15, 1954], p. 76).

3. *Our America**

BY JOSÉ MARTÍ   *Translated by Eliana Loveluck*

TO THE *NEW YORK HERALD*

To the Editor:**

The New York Herald has nobly offered the publicity of its newspaper to the Cuban Revolution waged on behalf of the island's independence and the creation of a stable Republic. As representatives-elect of the Revolution, empowered until such time as this revolution chooses leaders befitting its new form, it is our duty to explain as clearly as possible to the people of the United States and the world, the reasons, composition and purposes of the revolution fought in Cuba since the beginning of this century. The revolution has been waged heroically from 1868 to 1878, and today is revitalized through the organized efforts of this nation's sons, both within the island and abroad. Through these efforts we wish to establish an independent nation worthy of the government that releases the wealth of the island of Cuba, thus far stag-

*From José Martí, *Obras Completas* (Havana: Editorial Nacional de Cuba, 1963). Vols. 3 and 4.
**The *New York Herald* apparently did not publish Martí's letter.—eds.

nated. We wish to live in the peace which can assure man's dignity, freedom to work for its citizens, and free access by the entire world.

Cuba has taken up arms with the joy of sacrifice and the solemn determination of possible death. It has not done this to interrupt the development of a people who would have been able to obtain maturity peacefully with fanatical patriotism over the incomplete goal of political independence from Spain. Nor has our purpose been to hinder the accelerated course of the world which at the closing years of this century is widening and renewing itself. Rather, our purpose has been the emancipation from Spain of an intelligent and generous people with a universal spirit but special responsibilities in America. Spain is inferior to Cuba in her abilities to adapt to the modern world with a free government. Spain wants to shut off the island—so exuberant with native strength and the native character to unleash it—from the productivity of great nations by violently oppressing a useful American nation. Cuba is the only market for Spain's industrial production, and these Cuban revenues pay for Spain's debts on the continent. In this manner Spain maintains the unproductive and wealthy class in leisure and power, a class which does not seek in manly effort the rapidly gained and plentiful fortunes which they have been expecting day after day from Spain's conquests in America and which they are obtaining from the colony's venal occupations and iniquitous taxes.

Only superficial thinking, or a certain kind of brutal disdain can, by overlooking Cuba's armed and intellectual struggle for freedom throughout this century, claim that the Cuban Revolution is the insignificant desire of an exclusive class of poor Cubans living abroad, or an uprising of the majority of blacks in Cuba, or the country's sacrifice to a dream of independence unsustainable by those who achieve it. The son of Cuba, raised to such moral, industrial, and political abundance during a quarter of a century of war and migrant work, that he does not take second place to the finest human product of any other nation, is suffering in unspeakable bitterness to see his productive soil—and upon it his strangled human dignity—chained to the obligation of paying, with his free American hands, almost the entire proceeds of his productivity, and the daily and most painful proceeds of his honor, to the needs and vices of the monarchy. The Spanish government's bureaucratic composition and its constant protection of worthless and perverse elements of society, emanating from gifts and land grants in America, prevent it from ever allowing the tormented island of Cuba (that at the historic moment when the world opens itself to her and the oceans hug her shores) to spread wide her ports and her gold-bearing entrails to a world that is replete with unused capital and idle masses who would find the serenity of ownership and a friendly crossroads in the warmth of a strong Republic.

Cubans recognize the urgent duty imposed upon them by their geographical position in the world at the present time of universal gestation; and although childish observers or the vanity of the proud are unaware of it, they are fully capable, through the power of their intelligence and the impetus of their strength, to fulfill that duty. And they want to fulfill it.

At the opening of the oceanic currents where three continents come together, at the moment when humanity's active step stumbles against the useless Spanish colony in Cuba, and at the gates of a nation dismayed by the plethora of products it could produce itself but today buys from its oppressor, Cuba wants to be free so that man can there be fulfilled, so the world can go work there, and so Cuba's hidden riches can be sold in American markets where the Spanish master now prohibits her from buying. Cubans ask nothing more from the world than recognition and respect for their sacrifices, and they are giving the universe their blood. A quick review of the national composition of Spain and Cuba would be enough to convince an honest mind of the need and justice of the revolution, and of the incompatibility of their national characters resulting from diverse origins and different degrees of development. An honest mind is convinced that the two nations' objectives cause them to clash in the modern, hard-working American island's subjection to the backward European fatherland. It is convinced of the loss of modern energy in keeping an agile and good people dependent, during the world's most fraternal and hard-working era. It is convinced that this throne must deny the natural beauty of Cuba, as well as the energetic Cuban character, from working together to resolve her own superficial conflicts and those of other nations, because of the corrupt makeup of her decadent majority.

Allied four hundred years ago against the harsh but effeminate Moor, the Spanish possessions became solidified and unified in the conquest of America's barren lands. Spain became rich with their products, and with permanent possession of the Indies, it quieted down and employed, under the kings, the soldierly and adventurous population with which Spain's nationality was founded. Manual labor on the land and industries was handed over to the more learned, as a minor occupation, because the temptation of America attracted the most daring and capable men in the country, even from the lower and uncultured classes, and created—at first with hope and then with satisfaction—a kind of vast and vagabond order of knighthood. The Spaniard, until recently a sober man, always found love, fighting, and literature sufficient nourishment for his extravagant and exuberant life. America was so wide a haven of solid wealth or temporary gain that Spanish national life and personal character molded themselves to it and to its productivity, and rediscovered in Cuban riches (increased by means of commerce, the privilege of slavery, and Creole industriousness) the sources of which, with the loss of the continental colonies, had seemed shut off to them. In the Spain of recent times, a tenacious imitation of the luxurious ways of modern life—lacking the industry and enterprise which in Europe's brilliant nations create and excuse it—has given the Spanish people more of the necessities of life, without a corresponding increase in the sources of production which in personal affairs continue in very large part to be the revenue from Cuba. This is Spain in relation to Cuba. . . .

[May 2, 1895]

THE THIRD YEAR OF THE CUBAN REVOLUTIONARY PARTY: THE SPIRIT OF THE REVOLUTION AND CUBA'S DUTY TO AMERICA

. . . The sight of our unity, and the meeting of free wills in the Cuban Revolutionary Party, would be worthless—even if the party understood the country's internal problems and the wounds they cause—if it did not take into account the even greater mission called for by the era in which it is born, and by its position at the crossroads of the world. Cuba and Puerto Rico will achieve freedom with very different structures, in very different times, and with far greater responsibilities than other Spanish-American nations. It is necessary to have the courage of greatness, and live up to one's obligations. The world is full of priests who would deny Columbus the possibility of discovering the Western Passage. What is important is not to sit down with the priests, but to embark with Columbus on his caravels. [A caravel is a small sailboat used by the Spanish in the 16th century.—eds.] We know about the man who ran out with his little signal flag to warn people to be afraid of the approaching locomotive; the locomotive arrived and the flag waver remained huffing and puffing in the road, or crushed to a pulp if he stood in the way. We have to foresee the future, and keep pace with the world. Glory belongs to those who look ahead, not back. We have no intention of merely publicizing two flower-decked islands composed of still disparate elements, but of saving them and serving them so that the strong and capable structure of their present components will, when faced with the possible greed of a powerful and perilous neighbor, assure independence to the fortunate archipelago that Nature has placed at the center of the world. History is making freedom possible for them just when the continents are preparing for meeting and embracing through these generous lands. The Antilles [Caribbean islands] lie at a pivotal point in America. If enslaved, they would be nothing more than a bridge for an imperialist republic's war against the suspicious and superior world already preparing to deny it power; nothing more than a fortress for an American Rome. If free—and deservedly so by virtue of equitable and industrious liberty—they would be the guarantors of balance on this continent, of a still threatened Spanish-American independence, and of honor for the great republic of the north. The United States will find more certain greatness in the development of its own land (unfortunately feudal and divided into hostile camps), than in the ignoble conquest of its lesser neighbors, and in the inhumane struggle that achieving possession of them would unleash against world powers for global domination. Not with a light hand but with a consciousness developed over centuries should new life be restored to the liberated Antilles. This great human responsibility should be undertaken with earnest respect. A person reaches tremendous heights through nobility of purpose, or falls to abysmal depths unable to comprehend. It is a world we are holding in balance, not merely a couple of islands we are about to free. How petty everything is, how inconsequential are village gossip, and the pinpricks of feminine vanity, and the worthless intrigue of indicting this work of continental foresight for demagoguery and for crowd flattering when compared to the true greatness of assuring friendship among the opposing sections of a continent. How important it is to strive for the happiness of men working industriously for the independence of their nation, and to avoid, in the liberated life of the prosperous Antilles, unnecessary conflicts between a nation which oppresses America and a world aligned against its greed! Life's difficulties will teach us to build a stairway to the skies. Looking upward, we will mold with healthy blood—our own—this national life composed of the glories of virtue, the resentments of lost privileges and too many just aspirations. The responsibility of our goals will give the Cuban people the stability to achieve freedom without hate, and to direct their enthusiasm with moderation. A mistake in Cuba is a mistake in America, a mistake in present-day humanity. Whoever rebels with Cuba today, rebels for all time. Since Cuba is our sacred homeland, it requires special thought; serving it, in so glorious and difficult a time, fills a man with dignity and nobility. This worthy obligation fortifies us with strength of heart, guides us like a perennial star, and will shine from our graves like a light of eternal warning. We must set our hand to solving a problem of such vast scope and honor with a singular reverence. With this reverence the Cuban Revolutionary Party is entering its third year of life, firm and compassionate, convinced that the independence of Cuba and Puerto Rico is not only the means of assuring both islands of the decent well-being that free men ought to have in their legitimate work, but also that it is the one historic event essential to save the threatened independence of a free Antilles, a free America, and the dignity of the North American republic. Weaklings, show respect! Great men, march on! This is a task for the great.

[April 17, 1894]

TO MANUEL MERCADO*

Now I can write, now I can tell you how tenderly and gratefully and respectfully I love you and that home which I consider my pride and responsibility. I am in daily danger of giving my life for my country and duty, for I understand that duty and have the courage to carry it out—the duty of preventing the United States from spreading through the Antilles as Cuba gains its inde-

*This unfinished letter was written one day before Martí was killed in a skirmish near Dos Rios, Cuba.—eds.

pendence, and from overpowering with that additional strength our American lands. All I have done thus far, and all I will do, is for this purpose. I have had to work quietly and somewhat indirectly, because to achieve certain objectives, they must be kept undercover; to say what they are would raise such difficulties that the objectives could not be achieved.

The same minor and public duties of these nations—nations such as yours and mine that are most vitally concerned with preventing the opening in Cuba (by annexation on the part of the imperialists from there and the Spaniards) of the road that must be closed, and is being closed with our blood, the road leading to the annexation of our American nations to the brutal and turbulent North which despises them—prevented their apparent adherence and obvious assistance to this sacrifice made for their immediate benefit.

I have lived in the monster and I know its entrails; my sling is David's. . . . I am doing my duty here. The Cuban war, a reality of higher priority than the vague and scattered desires of the Cuban and Spanish annexationists, whose alliance with the Spanish government would only give them relative power, has come to America in time to prevent Cuba's annexation to the United States, even against all those freely used forces. . . .

[May 18, 1895]

CHAPTER 2

A Four-Hundred-Year Struggle

4. The Platt Amendment*

That in fulfillment of the declaration contained in the joint resolution approved April twentieth, eighteen hundred and ninety-eight, entitled "For the recognition of the independence of the people of Cuba, demanding that the Government of Spain relinquish its authority and government in the island of Cuba, and to withdraw its land and naval reserve forces from Cuba and Cuban waters, and directing the President of the United States to use the land and naval forces of the United States to carry these resolutions into effect," the President is hereby authorized to "leave the government and control of the island of Cuba to its people" so soon as a government shall have been established in said island under a constitution which, either as a part thereof or in an ordinance appended thereto, shall define the future relations of the United States with Cuba, substantially as follows:

I. That the government of Cuba shall never enter into any treaty or other compact with any foreign power or powers which will impair or tend to impair the independence of Cuba, or in any manner authorize or permit any foreign power or powers to obtain by colonization or, for military or naval purposes or otherwise, lodgment in or control over any portion of said island.

II. That said government shall not assume or contract any public debt, to pay the interest upon which, and to make reasonable sinking fund provision for the ultimate discharge of which, the ordinary revenues of the island, after defraying the current expenses of government shall be inadequate.

III. That the government of Cuba consents that the United States may exercise the right to intervene for the preservation of Cuban independence, the

*From U.S. Statutes at Large, XXI, 897–898; Treaty Between the United States and Cuba, signed in Havana May 22, 1903; proclaimed by President Theodore Roosevelt July 2, 1904.

maintenance of a government adequate for the protection of life, property, and individual liberty, and for discharging the obligations with respect to Cuba imposed by the Treaty of Paris on the United States, now to be assumed and undertaken by the government of Cuba.

IV. That all Acts of the United States in Cuba during its military occupancy thereof are ratified and validated, and all lawful rights acquired thereunder shall be maintained and protected.

V. That the government of Cuba will execute and as far as necessary extend, the plans already devised or other plans to be mutually agreed upon, for the sanitation of the cities of the island, to the end that a recurrence of epidemic and infectious diseases may be prevented, thereby assuring protection to the people and commerce of Cuba, as well as to the commerce of the southern ports of the United States and of the people residing therein.

VI. That the Isle of Pines shall be omitted from the proposed constitutional boundaries of Cuba, the title thereto being left to future adjustment by treaty.

VII. That to enable the United States to maintain the independence of Cuba, and to protect the people thereof, as well as for its own defence, the government of Cuba will sell or lease to the United States land necessary for coaling or naval stations at certain specified points, to be agreed upon with the President of the United States.

VIII. That by way of further assurance the government of Cuba will embody the foregoing provisions in a permanent treaty with the United States.

5. History Will Absolve Me*

By Fidel Castro

> History Will Absolve Me *was Castro's speech in his own defense during his 1953 trial for the assault on Moncada Barracks. It was later distributed as a revolutionary pamphlet.*

Why were we sure of the people's support? When we speak of the people we are not talking about those who live in comfort, the conservative elements of the nation, who welcome any oppressive regime, any dictatorship, any despotism, prostrating themselves before the masters of the moment until they grind their foreheads into the ground. When we speak of struggle and we mention the people we mean the vast unredeemed masses, those to whom everyone makes promises and who are deceived by all; we mean the people who yearn for a better, more dignified and more just nation; who are moved by ancestral aspirations of justice, for they have suffered injustice and mockery generation

*From Fidel Castro, *History Will Absolve Me* (Havana: Editorial de Ciencas Sociales, 1975). Edited for this volume.

after generation; those who long for great and wise changes in all aspects of their life; people who, to attain those changes, are ready to give even the very last breath they have, when they believe in something or in someone, especially when they believe in themselves. The first condition of sincerity and good faith in any endeavor is to do precisely what nobody else ever does, that is, to speak with absolute clarity, without fear.

In terms of struggle, when we talk about people we're talking about the *six hundred thousand* Cubans without work, who want to earn their daily bread honestly without having to emigrate from their homeland in search of a livelihood; the *five hundred thousand* farm laborers who live in miserable shacks, who work four months of the year and starve the rest, sharing their misery with their children, who don't have an inch of land to till and whose existence would move any heart not made of stone; the *four hundred thousand* industrial workers and laborers whose retirement funds have been embezzled, whose benefits are being taken away, whose homes are wretched quarters, whose salaries pass from the hands of the boss to those of the money-lender, whose future is a pay reduction and dismissal, whose life is endless work and whose only rest is the tomb; the *one hundred thousand* small farmers who live and die working land that is not theirs, looking at it with the sadness of Moses gazing at the promised land, to die without ever owning it, who like feudal serfs have to pay for the use of their parcel of land by giving up a portion of its produce, who cannot love it, improve it, beautify it nor plant a cedar or an orange tree on it because they never know when a sheriff will come with the rural guard to evict them from it; the *30 thousand* teachers and professors who are so devoted, dedicated and so necessary to the better destiny of future generations and who are so badly treated and paid; the *20 thousand* small-businessmen weighed down by debts, ruined by the crisis and harangued by a plague of grafting and venal officials; the *ten thousand* young professional people: doctors, engineers, lawyers, veterinarians, school teachers, dentists, pharmacists, newspapermen, painters, sculptors, etc., who finish school with their degrees anxious to work and full of hope, only to find themselves at a dead end, all doors closed to them, and where no ear hears their clamor or supplication. These are the people, the ones who know misfortune and, therefore, are capable of fighting with limitless courage! To these people whose desperate roads through life have been paved with the bricks of betrayal and false promises, we were not going to say: "We will give you . . ." but rather: "Here it is, now fight for it with everything you have, so that liberty and happiness may be yours!"

The problem of the land, the problem of industrialization, the problem of housing, the problem of unemployment, the problem of education and the problem of the people's health: these are the six problems we would take immediate steps to solve, along with restoration of civil liberties and political democracy.

This exposition may seem cold and theoretical if one does not know the shocking and tragic conditions of the country with regard to these six problems, along with the most humiliating political oppression.

Eighty-five per cent of the small farmers in Cuba pay rent and live under the constant threat of being evicted from the land they till. More than half of our most productive land is in the hands of foreigners. In Oriente, the largest province, the lands of the United Fruit Company and the West Indian Company link the northern and southern coasts. There are *two hundred thousand peasant families* who do not have a single acre of land to till to provide food for their starving children. On the other hand, nearly *three hundred thousand caballerías* [One caballería equals 33 acres.—eds.] of cultivable land owned by powerful interests remain uncultivated. If Cuba is above all an agricultural State, if its population is largely rural, if the city depends on these rural areas, if the people from our countryside won our war of independence, if our nation's greatness and prosperity depend on a healthy and vigorous rural population that loves the land and knows how to work it, if this population depends on a State that protects and guides it, then how can the present state of affairs be allowed to continue?

Except for a few food, lumber and textile industries, Cuba continues to be primarily a producer of raw materials. We export sugar to import candy, we export hides to import shoes, we export iron to import plows. . . . Everyone agrees with the urgent need to industrialize the nation, that we need steel industries, paper and chemical industries, that we must improve our cattle and grain production, the technique and the processing in our food industry in order to defend ourselves against the ruinous competition of the Europeans in cheese products, condensed milk, liquors and edible oils, and the United States in canned goods; that we need cargo ships; that tourism should be an enormous source of revenue. But the capitalists insist that the workers remain under the yoke. The State sits back with its arms crossed and industrialization can wait forever.

Just as serious or even worse is the housing problem. There are *two hundred thousand* huts and hovels in Cuba; *four hundred thousand families* in the countryside and in the cities live cramped in huts and tenements without even the minimum sanitary requirements; *two million two hundred thousand* of our urban population pay rents which absorb between one fifth and one third of their incomes; and *two million eight hundred thousand* of our rural and suburban population lack electricity. If the State proposes the lowering of rents, landlords threaten to freeze all construction; if the State does not interfere, construction goes on so long as the landlords get high rents; otherwise they would not lay a single brick even though the rest of the population had to live totally exposed to the elements. The utilities monopoly is no better; they extend lines as far as it is profitable and beyond that point they don't care if people have to live in darkness for the rest of their lives. The State sits back with its arms crossed and the people have neither homes nor electricity.

Our educational system is perfectly compatible with everything I've just mentioned. Where the peasant doesn't own the land, what need is there for agricultural schools? Where there is no industry, what need is there for technological or vocational schools? Everything follows the same absurd logic; if we don't have one thing we can't have the other. . . . The little rural schoolhouses are attended by a mere half of the school age children—barefooted, half-naked and undernourished—and frequently the teacher must buy necessary school materials from his own salary. Is this the way to make a nation great?

Only death can liberate one from so much misery. In this respect, however, the State is most helpful—in providing early death for the people. *Ninety percent* of the children in the countryside are consumed by parasites which filter through their bare feet from the ground they walk on. Society is moved to compassion when it hears of the kidnapping or murder of one child, but it is criminally indifferent to the mass murder of so many thousands of children who die every year from lack of facilities, agonizing with pain. Their innocent eyes, death already shining in them, seem to look into some vague infinity as if entreating forgiveness for human selfishness, as if asking God to stay wrath. And when the head of a family works only four months a year, with what can he purchase clothing and medicine for his children? They will grow up with rickets, with not a single good tooth in their mouths by the time they reach thirty; they will have heard ten million speeches and will finally die of misery and deception. Public hospitals, which are always full, accept only patients recommended by some powerful politician who, in turn, demands the electoral votes of the unfortunate one and his family so that Cuba may continue forever in the same or worse condition.

With this background, is it not understandable that from May to December over a million persons are jobless and that Cuba, with a population of five and a half million, has a greater number of unemployed than France or Italy with a population of 40 million each?

When you try a defendant for robbery, Honorable Judges, do you ask him how long he has been unemployed? Do you ask him how many children he has, which days of the week he ate and which he didn't, do you investigate his social context at all? You just send him to jail without further thought. But those who burn warehouses and stores to collect insurance do not go to jail, even though a few human beings may have gone up in flames. The insured have money to hire lawyers and bribe judges. You imprison the poor wretch who steals because he is hungry; but none of the hundreds who steal millions from the government has ever spent a night in jail. You dine with them at the end of the year in some elegant club and they enjoy your respect. In Cuba, when a government official becomes a millionaire overnight and enters the fraternity of the rich, he could very well be greeted with the words of that opulent character out of Balzac—Taillefer—who in his toast to the young heir to an enormous fortune, said: "Gentlemen, let us drink to the power of gold! Mr. Valentine, a millionaire six times over, has just ascended the throne. He is king, can do everything, is above everyone, as all the rich are. Henceforth, equality before the law, established by the Constitution, will be a myth for him; for he will not be subject to laws: the laws will be subject to him. There are no courts nor are there sentences for millionaires."

Cuba could easily provide for a population three times as great as it has now, so there is no excuse for the abject poverty of a single one of its present inhabitants. The markets should be overflowing with produce, pantries should be full, all hands should be working. This is not an inconceivable thought. What is inconceivable is that anyone should go to bed hungry while there is a single inch of unproductive land; that children should die for lack of medical attention; what is inconceivable is that 30 percent of our farm people cannot write their names and that 99 percent of them know nothing of Cuba's history. What is inconceivable is that the majority of our rural people are now living in worse circumstances than the Indians Columbus discovered in the fairest land that human eyes had ever seen.

To those who would call me a dreamer, I quote the words of Martí: "A true man does not seek the path where advantage lies, but rather the path where duty lies, and this is the only practical man, whose dream of today will be the law of tomorrow, because he who has looked back on the essential course of history and has seen flaming and bleeding peoples seethe in the cauldron of the ages, knows that, without a single exception, the future lies on the side of duty."

I know that imprisonment will be harder for me than it has ever been for anyone, filled with cowardly threats and hideous cruelty. But I do not fear prison, as I do not fear the fury of the miserable tyrant who took the lives of 70 of my comrades. Condemn me. It does not matter. History will absolve me.

6. Program Manifesto of the 26th of July Movement (November 1956)*

Translation by Rolando E. Bonachea and Nelson P. Valdés

THE PRESENT

The 26th of July Movement is resolved to take up the unfulfilled ideals of the Cuban nation and to realize them. To accomplish these aims, the movement counts on its credential and its distinctive feature: the contribution and pres-

*From Rolando E. Bonachea and Nelson P. Valdés, eds., *Cuba in Revolution* (New York: Anchor, 1972), pp. 113–40. Edited for this volume.

ence of the reserves of youth who are anxious for new horizons in the chronic frustration of the Republic.

By declaring itself a continuation of the revolutionary generations of the past, it defines the reason for the present struggle and the direction guiding it toward the future. This is a path of national affirmation, human dignity, and democratic order. Those of us who make up the 26th of July Movement, as free men, are guided solely by a compromise of honor with our consciences. We are not moved by stubbornness or insanity but by a well-thought-out conviction in justice, in the necessity of revolution, and a faith—well proven by blood—in the worthy destiny of Cuba. . . .

We are resuming the unfinished Cuban Revolution. That is why we preach the same "necessary war" of José Martí for exactly the same reasons he proclaimed it: against the regressive ills of the colony, against the sword that shelters tyrants, against corrupt and rapacious politicians, against the merchants of our national economy. We fight against the ills produced by that sorrowful amalgam. . . .

DOCTRINE OF THE REVOLUTION

Ideology

"A Constitution is a lively and practical law that cannot be constructed with ideological precepts."

                                                                                    Martí.

. . . The 26th of July Movement can be defined as guided by the *ideals of democracy, nationalism, and social justice.* . . .

With regard to *democracy,* the 26th of July Movement still considers valid the Jeffersonian philosophy and fully identifies with Lincoln's statement, "government of the people, by the people and for the people." Democracy cannot be the government of a race, class, or religion, it must be the government of *all* the people. . . .

Nationalism is the natural outcome of geographic and historic circumstances which from the outset determined Cuba's independent status. It refers to "wanting to be a nation" of a people that has been capable of conquering its own freedom. Cuba achieved nominal independence in 1902, but it has not yet accomplished its economic independence. . . .

With regard to *social justice,* the 26th of July Movement foresees the establishment of an order in which all the inalienable rights of a *human being—* political, social, economic, and cultural—will be fully met and guaranteed. . . .

In summary, the 26th of July Movement declares that the above-stated principles emanate from the political thought of José Martí, who once stated that the essential principle was that of the *full dignity of man.* All human relations—fatherland, politics, economy, education—converge at that point. In that position, in the following of Martí's ideas, the philosophical base of our struggle must be found.

This ideological position can be divided into the following points. . . .

1) National Sovereignty

"If the family of American republics have a specific function, it is not to be servants of any other."

Martí.

Sovereignty is the right of a nation to orient and shape its own destiny. Without it, everything else—state, government, culture—lacks national meaning; it is false. The first objective of the Revolution, therefore, is to assert the full sovereignty of Cuba.

This condition is officially recognized in terms of international politics, especially since the abrogation of the Platt Amendment in 1934. But Cuba still suffers from a situation which, although not direct political intervention, constitutes essential violations of its sovereignty. The presence of foreign bases and missions in the national territory, the different economic pressures, and the interference of diplomats who publicly take sides and issue declarations about our internal affairs are clear and eloquent examples. . . .

2) Economic Independence

"The only fruitful and lasting peace and freedom are those accomplished by one's own effort."

Martí.

Economic independence is understood as the capacity of a country to take care of itself within the natural system of international relations. This independence is the indispensable foundation for political sovereignty. Cuba possesses sufficient resources to aspire to its economic independence like any other sovereign nation in this world. . . .

With the aim of avoiding such disastrous consequences and assuring a stable economic development which will not be vulnerable to abrupt changes or foreign contingencies, the state will exert a policy of controls over natural resources, public services, banks, insurance, capital investments, and all other forms of production and credit. . . .

3) Work

"The general happiness of a people depends on the individual independence of its inhabitants."

Martí.

Although the 26th of July Movement does not defend the doctrines of economic determinism, it proclaims that there cannot be democracy or social justice if man does not have the means to satisfy in an honorable way his material needs. Consequently, we maintain that the state is obliged to provide those means, principally in the form of adequate production instruments and well-paid opportunities to work.

Hence, work is considered a right and a way to achieve individual progress. . . .

4) Social Order

"We must impede the distortion or exploitation of Cuba's interests by the interests of one group, the excessive authority of a military or civil organization, a given region, or of one race over another."

Martí.

The 26th of July Movement takes its ideas with respect to social problems from Martí. Its ideal about this is the *organic unity of the nation.* According to this concept, no group, class, race, or religion should sacrifice the common good to benefit its particular interest, nor can it remain aloof from the problems of the entire social order or one of its parts.

The concept of organic social order will incorporate all, without privilege or exception, to the advantages and responsibilities of progress. The incorporation will be done through a more just and dynamic conception of property (especially land), capital, and production, and through the elevation of labor to the category of cooperating agent in the direction and profit sharing of the enterprise. In this way the causes that provoke class antagonisms are eliminated or reduced, and the cohesion of all on the basis of the common good is made easier. . . .

5) Education

"The measure of responsibility is related to the extent of one's education."

Martí.

Education is the radical solution to be implemented by the Revolution (the immediate or urgent one is political insurrection). Since we cannot have a fatherland without a national consciousness, nor democracy without citizens, it is necessary to have a thorough and systematic instrument dedicated to provide the people with those indispensable instruments.

. . . In a country like Cuba, still struggling to achieve its *national* fulfillment, education must be aimed toward the achievement of important goals, some of which are *subjective,* while others are *objective.* The subjective goals are the values of freedom and fatherland, both of which are complemented by the basic principle of the *dignity of man.* Among the objective goals can be found, at the forefront, the cultural, vocational, and technical preparation of the citizen which will make him a capable and aggressive instrument in the face of the country's social and economic problems.

All this explains the great revolutionary importance of the educational process. It also shows why the state must pay special attention and interest to the philosophy that will guide this process. . . .

6) Politics

"To govern is to direct the national forces in such a manner as to allow each man to fulfill himself in a dignified way, and to make good use of public prosperity."

                                                                    Martí.

The 26th of July Movement is determined to achieve the ideal of a democratic republic, inspired in the credo of freedom and founded in the character and capacity of its citizens. It aspires to establish in Cuba a form of government and a system of public and individual rights that will be fully practiced in real life and not forgotten in written Constitutions and laws. . . .

The 26th of July Movement will propose a juridical project to guarantee as a fundamental issue the validity of the citizen's vote, providing at the same time the necessary educational means that will secure the certainty that that vote is at all times the spontaneous manifestation of a conscious and constructive public opinion.

This stand by the 26th of July Movement arises from its ideological aim of inaugurating in Cuba the practice of true political democracy, i.e., the competition of ideas between political parties and a representative government based on the genuine expression of the general will.

7) Civil Authority

"Governmental power should be only in the hands of civilian men. . . . A nation is not established as one runs a military camp."

                                                                    Martí.

With the increment of the military-police power as a determining factor in public life (a salient cause and consequence of the March 10 coup),* Cuba has returned to a very primitive political level. So much so that, except for the absolute ideological vacuum that characterizes it, the bandits ruling the country, led by Batista, reproduce one by one all the horrors of totalitarian regimes.

This state of affairs is in direct contradiction to the purest national tradition. The founders of the fatherland always were, by conviction and temperament, profoundly civilian-oriented. Céspedes, Aguilera, Agramonte, Gómez, Maceo,

*Fulgencio Batista seized power in a military coup on March 10, 1952, from the civilian government.—eds.

García, Sanguily, Varona, Martí . . . even those like Gómez and Maceo, who
won innumerable laurels on the battlefront, were men who subordinated their
authority to civilian leaders. But there is more. . . . We also have the Constitutions and other juridical documents of the Revolution expressing its political
thought. The October 10, 1868, Proclamation, the Montecristi Manifesto, the
bases of the Partido Revolucionario Cubano, and the Constitutions of
Guáimaro, Jimaguayú, and La Yaya are filled with the civilian outlook which
shaped the formation of Cuba at every moment. . . .

8) Freedom of Conscience
"Freedom is the right every man has to be honest and to think and speak
without hypocrisy."

Martí.

The Revolution considers as one of the essential elements of democracy the
principle of freedom of conscience. Each citizen will be free to sustain whatever
creed or religion he might want, or none at all, as long as his attitude does not
diminish human dignity or endanger the rights and freedoms of others.
   . . . State secularism suffers constant violations in Cuba, especially in the
form of privileges—many of them economic and granted to religious groups.
Under the banner of charity the unequivocal separation of the state from
religious creeds—so essential to any democratic system—is being undermined
and weakened. . . .
   On this matter, the 26th of July Movement adopts and proclaims the ideas
of Martí, declaring that it will fight at all times for those conditions which
would make the principle of freedom of conscience effective. In political terms
this means a secular state.

9) Public Morality
The Republic was born carrying the colonial germs of political corruption.
At the same time it lacked the moral or philosophical strength to counteract
corruption, and time has done nothing but aggravate the evil. It is not surprising, therefore, that public matters in Cuba constantly fall prey to profi-
teers and thieves for whom the institutions of democracy are only a
profitable market. . . .
   The 26th of July Movement maintains that the problem demands the action of a double program. First, we need a thorough investigation and sanctions that would purify the responsibilities contracted by those in power with
the threat of confiscation, among other things, to those who are guilty of
enriching themselves illegally. Secondly, there must be a joint plan of electoral and administrative reforms that would eliminate, or at least minimize,
the possibilities for crime. The law would point out in due time the details of
the procedure. What is important is to have in mind that the revolutionary

task cannot reach its objectives if it is not accompanied by intense, firm, and systematic action.

10) International Position

The Cuban Revolution is historically situated within the purest American tradition. The common ideals and interests which necessarily unite the republics of the hemisphere—both north and south—are a reality that should be developed and maintained cooperatively by all the nations of the continent. . . .

With regard to the specific matter of the relations between Cuba and the United States, the 26th of July Movement formulates a doctrine of *constructive friendship.* By this we mean mutual respect, particularly in the economic and cultural areas.

In good political terminology, it is improper in America to utilize the word "imperialism"; but forms of economic penetration still persist, accompanied generally by political influence. These cause irreparable damage to the moral, as well as material, well-being of the country that suffers them.

Fortunately, such a situation can be overcome without damage to any legitimate interest. Through *constructive friendship,* Cuba can truly become, as is indicated by a multitude of geographical, economic, and even political factors, a loyal ally of the great country to the north, yet at the same time preserve its ability to control its own destiny. Through new and just agreements, without unnecessary sacrifices or humiliating sellouts, it can multiply the advantages that are derived from our neighborhood.

CHAPTER 3

Themes of the Cuban Revolution

7. Prologue to the Cuban Revolution*

BY ROBIN BLACKBURN

For the first time a socialist revolution has been carried through without the leadership of a Communist party. For the first time one of the nonaligned nations has joined the Communist world. For the first time a socialist revolution has occurred in a relatively developed country. . . .

The Cuban Revolution is now widely recognized as an event of world-historical importance. For the first time there has been a socialist revolution in the Americas. . . . The universal significance of the Cuban Revolution makes it one of the decisive phenomena of our time. Yet this significance can only be properly understood after an exact characterization of its *particular* nature. . . . The study which follows attempts to offer a provisional model of the social structure of prerevolutionary Cuba, and by doing so, to provide a key to an understanding of the nature and development of the revolution.

1. THE ECLIPSE OF THE LANDED ARISTOCRACY

Cuba is strikingly and immediately set apart from the rest of Latin America by its late independence. The whole of the Spanish American mainland was liberated by 1825. In Cuba, Spanish rule lasted a full 73 years longer, till 1898. . . .

*From Robin Blackburn, "Prologue to the Cuban Revolution," *New Left Review* (London) (October 1963). Edited for this volume.

Cuba was discovered by Columbus in 1492. The first Spanish foothold in the Americas was, however, for nearly three centuries one of the least developed. The Indian population of Cuba, the peaceful and primitive Caribs, were virtually wiped out by repression and disease within the first two decades of colonization, leaving a severe labor shortage in the island. The discovery of gold and silver on the Latin American mainland led to prolonged neglect of the immense potentialities of Cuban agriculture. . . .

Cuba's physical isolation from the mainland was, of course, critically important in the success of the Spaniards in maintaining their hold of the island; the purely geographical factor which now impedes U.S. attempts to export counterrevolution blocked the spread of revolution to Cuba in the early 19th century. However, if it was the logistic situation which prevented the kind of military liberation which the Venezuelan armies effected in, say, Bolivia, this does not explain why there was no profound internal upheaval in Cuba for more than 50 years after the Declaration of Venezuelan Independence. The fundamental cause of this paralysis lay not in the geographical position, but in the socioeconomic structure of Cuba. The white population was outnumbered by the black: 291,021 to 339,959 by the census of 1817. By comparison, only 2 percent of the population of mainland Spanish America was African in origin at this date; there were fewer Negroes in all the mainland colonies of Spain put together than in Cuba. At the same time, because of the very belated and rapid rise in population in the late 18th century, the majority of the white population of Cuba itself must have been Spanish-born. This made Cuba a further exception among Spanish American colonies. . . .

The Spanish-American revolutions of the 19th century were made by the white landowning class born in the colonies. . . . Any revolt by the [Cuban] Creole landowners against Spain risked snowballing into a racial and social avalanche which would have buried them. The conflagration in Haiti was close and memorable. Small Negro revolts and conspiracies had already occurred in Cuba in 1792 and 1793; larger uprisings erupted in 1795 and 1814. . . .

The wars for independence in Cuba were clearly qualitatively distinct from the Latin American revolts of the early 19th century. On the threshold of the 20th century, the campaigns in Cuba prefigured the pitiless, total wars of decolonization of this century. [Spanish General Valeriano] Weyler's repression in Cuba can only be compared to the colonial wars of Algeria and Vietnam: The lineage of the Spanish *campos de reconcentracion* in Cuba to the French *regroupements* in Algeria and the American "strategic hamlets" in Vietnam is direct. Cuba's whole social order was shattered. The landowning aristocracy was decimated and demoralized. It had missed its chance: Nerveless before one revolution, blasted by another, it had been ground between its fear of its African slaves and the vengeance of its Spanish overlords.

Its last possibility of assuming the domination of independent Cuba was destroyed by the evolution of the sugar industry. The late 19th century had

seen the rationalization of Cuban sugar cultivation and the emergence of a
colono [sugar planter] system: Production rose from 223,000 tons in 1850 to
over 1,000,000 tons in 1894, while the number of mills was reduced from 2,000
to 207. The sugar latifundists, mainly located in Matanzas and Las Villas
provinces, survived the Wars of Independence more successfully than any
other section of the landowning class. They were the most coherent and stable
power group for the first two decades of the Republic established in 1902.
Although almost each election brought U.S. military intervention or even
outright military administration (1906–1909), the consolidation of a landowning oligarchy of the classic Latin American type still seemed possible. The
catastrophic sugar slump that followed the First World War delivered the
coup de grâce to this hope. The value of the crop fell from 1,022 million dollars
in 1920 to 292 million dollars in 1921 and 56 million dollars in 1932. . . . The
foreign-owned companies survived the slump much more successfully than the
Cuban companies, and by 1929 were milling over 78 percent of the cane. One
quarter of the cane land was owned by four United States companies alone.
. . . Total U.S. investment in Cuba rose from 220 million dollars in 1913 to
1,525 million in 1929, and from 17.7 percent of all U.S. investments in Latin
America to 27.3 percent. The per capita value of the U.S. stake in the Cuban
economy was thus seven times as great as for the continent as a whole. It had
reached dimensions where it no longer supported and secured the local landowning class, as it did everywhere else in Latin America: It had largely
replaced this class. . . .

The land census of 1946 revealed that even the characteristic circular shape
of land-holdings of early 19th century Cuba had disappeared, except in some
small areas of the backward westernmost province, Pinar de Río. First the
social cohesion, then the economic base of the traditional latifundists had been
destroyed. The class was in eclipse. By the 1930s, the Cuban power structure
had decisively diverged from the Latin American norm. The classic regime of
landed oligarchy had failed to crystallize.

2. THE DEBILITY OF THE BOURGEOISIE

The nascent bourgeoisie of the first decades of independence had, along with
all other sections of the Cuban population, suffered catastrophically from the
collapse of the 20s. . . . The recovery and rise of the class began with the
Second World War. High sugar prices refloated the whole economy; profits
once again rapidly accrued to Cuban capitalists. The value of the sugar crop
rose from 110 million dollars in 1940 to 256 million in 1942, and to 677
million in 1947.[1] . . .

However, the absolute—and ostentatious—monetary wealth of this class
concealed its relative economic weakness. The invasion of U.S. capital which
ended the traditional aristocracy in the countryside, shackled and stunted the
bourgeoisie which succeeded it. Simple percentage figures reveal the extent of

U.S. control over the Cuban economy: 40 percent of raw sugar production was U.S. owned, 23 percent of non-sugar industry, 90 percent of telephone and electrical services, 50 percent of public service railways. Moreover, these figures show only the scale of U.S. investment. The *mode* of investment was at least equally important, for it typically took the form of the establishment of subsidiaries by U.S. companies with participation by local Cuban capital or, alternately, participation by U.S. capital in already established Cuban concerns. These industries were dependent on the U.S. parent company for essential supplies, and it was often on the sales between the two that real profits were made. . . .

The result was the structural integration of the Cuban bourgeoisie within the economy of an alien capitalism. . . . The de facto situation was clinched juridically. A reciprocal trade treaty in 1934 guaranteed Cuban sugar a preferential U.S. market and in return secured U.S. manufacturers a privileged entry into the Cuban market. Henceforward it was usually worthwhile for a Cuban industrialist to set up a plant in Cuba only if he could do so under some arrangement with the large U.S. corporations.

The most decisive and glaring result of this integration was that Cuban capitalists had to limit their field of operations to the boundaries set for them by North American neo-colonialism. Only sectors of the Cuban economy complementary to those of the United States could be developed. This confiscation of its economy condemned Cuba to extreme underutilization of its resources, and blocked any real economic growth. . . . The repatriated capital siphoned off to the U.S.A. amounted to 369.1 million dollars net disinvestment between 1952 and 1958.[2] G.N.P. rose by a derisory 1.4 percent per annum between 1951 and 1958, or at a slower rate than the population. In a work force of 2,700,000, unemployment ran at 700,000 men for the greater part of the year.[3]

It is clear then that the Cuban capitalist class could not properly be described as a "national" bourgeoisie. All major sections of Cuban capital were compromised in the exploitation of Cuba by U.S. capital and collaborated as subordinates in prolonging the retardation and stagnation of the economy. The term "national" bourgeoisie is made still more inappropriate by the strikingly deracinate and expatriate composition of the Cuban capitalist class. The island's largest "Cuban-owned" sugar enterprise was the property of Julio Lobo, a naturalized Cuban of German origin (original name Wulf), who owned sugar plantations throughout the Caribbean and a flourishing brokerage business in New York. Cuba's largest native industrialist was Burke Hedges of "Textilera Ariguanabo," a naturalized Cuban of U.S. origin. The largest rum-producing company, Bacardi, was owned by two families, the Espins of French origin, and the Boschs of German origin. . . .

. . . The markedly *parasitic* character of [the Cuban bourgeoisie] could not but have a significant effect on its cohesion and consciousness. Its ignoble role and image within the U.S. economic and socioaffective system made it almost impossible for it to have a *morale* of the kind which is vital to a class's political and social efficacy. A dominant social class must believe in its own necessity. The Cuban bourgeoisie was too compromised: It was never able to achieve real confidence and combativity. . . .

The classic Latin American power structure, from Independence to this day, may be summarily described. Wealth lies in the hands of an oligarchy of landowners and businessmen, more or less aristocratic or *arriviste* according to the country. The property regime remains untouched, no matter what the formal political system. Surface turmoil—electoral campaigns, cabinet intrigues, armed uprisings, military putsches—is directly proportionate to structural stability. The ruling class preserves the status quo indifferently through anarchy, autocracy or "democracy." But of its various institutional instruments, the classic trio have undoubtedly been: the Church, the Army, Political Parties. The character of each of these in Cuba is worth some examination.

Church

The Catholic Church has been a major institutional buttress of the social order everywhere in Latin America. . . .

Cuba, however, was an exception. Churches existed only in the rich suburbs and old city centers. The priesthood was woefully inadequate to its ostensible flock: There were only 725 priests in the whole island, 1 to every 7,850 parishioners (the comparable ratio for Chile is 1 for 2,750, for Venezuela 1 for 4,350, for Colombia 1 for 3,650).[4] Furthermore, the overwhelming majority— 75 per cent—of these priests were not Cubans at all. They were Spaniards dispatched from Spain to maintain the Cuban Church. The hierarchy itself was Hispanized: The Archbishop of Santiago, Enrique Pérez Serantes, who intervened on Fidel Castro's behalf after the Moncada attack in 1953, for example, was a Spaniard.

Thus, when the revolution came, the Church was unable to put up any serious resistance. The comparison with, say, Argentina, is instructive. The social program of Perón was infinitely less radical than that of the Cuban Revolution, yet when the Church joined the opposition a successful uprising was almost immediately precipitated. Faced with a far greater challenge in Cuba, it was helpless. The Church was politically a broken reed in Cuba.

Political Parties

It is an error to imagine that political life in Latin America is, or has been in the past, virtually reducible to personalized military putsches. Parliamentary interludes have, in some countries and in some periods, been reasonably lengthy and relatively orderly. . . .

The typical political formations of 19th and early 20th century Latin America made up an almost indistinguishable dyad, the Liberal and Conservative parties. This couplet was found throughout the continent: in Mexico, in Venezuela, in Colombia, in Ecuador, in Chile. Almost everywhere,

the sole substantial difference between these alternate factions of the oligarchy was their attitude to the Church. The Liberals were anticlerical, the
Conservatives ultramontane. The economic regimes of each were virtually
identical. . . .

It is against this background that the political parties of independent Cuba
should be seen. There, as elsewhere, a Liberal and a Conservative party were
formed, and the two parties furnished the presidents of the initial decades of
the Republic: Estrada Palma, Gómez, Menocal, Zayas. This was also the
period of repeated and regular U.S. intervention: 1906–1909, 1912, 1915, 1917,
1920. The creaking and corrupt parliamentary façade of the Cuban Republic
was successfully sustained by U.S. military presence. This phase came to an
end with the ascension to power of the Liberal Gerardo Machado in 1925, and
the onset of the world depression. The economic and social effects of the sugar
slump has already been noted. Machado installed a sanguinary personal dictatorship which lasted until 1933, when a wave of student attentats, followed by
a general strike, forced him into exile. . . .

The revolution of 1933 was the achievement of a coalition of university
students and army sergeants, which seized power on September 5. Ramón
Grau San Martín, leader of the Student Directorate, became President and
Fulgencio Batista, the stenographer-sergeant leader of the insurgent noncom-
missioned officers, became Chief of Staff. The revolutionary government nationalized the island's U.S.-owned electrical company and promised to
distribute land to the peasants. Four months later Batista, urged on by [U.S.
Ambassador] Sumner Welles, who regarded the revolution as "ultra-radical"
and "frankly communistic," suppressed his student allies, murdered their
left-wing leader Antonio Gutieras, and abandoned their program of reform
and anti-imperialism. A socialist *jacquerie* [peasant uprising] that had broken
out in the countryside was brutally quelled. The United States immediately
recognized the new regime.

Batista ruled as de facto dictator for six years, from 1934 to 1940. In 1940
he was elected president against Grau in a relatively open plebiscitary election.
But effective parliamentary life was suspended for a decade; it was only really
resumed again as the Second World War drew to a close. Batista himself
inaugurated Cuba's second—and last—parliamentary period. Convinced that
he could win an open election, he allowed one. His candidate, Carlos Sala-
drigas, lost, although only by a narrow margin. To general surprise, he accepted the defeat and retired to Miami with the spoils of office.

. . . The victor of the 1944 election was Grau San Martín. Grau was head
of the Auténtico party (Partido Revolucionario Cubano), theoretically left-
wing and faithful to the ideals of the 1933 Revolution. Yet the Auténtico party
won both the 1944 and 1948 elections (when Carlos Prío Socorrás became
President) in coalition with the ultraright Republican party. The Auténtico
government was in alliance with the Communist party from 1945 to 1947; in
1947 it turned on the party and purged the trade unions of Communists; but

the major Auténtico trade unionist, Eusebio Mujal, who became secretary-general of the Cuban Confederation of Labor (CTC) under Prío, himself later defected to Batista—supposedly the sworn enemy of the Auténticos.

. . . Under the Auténtico regimes of the early post-war years, the major opposition party was the newly formed (1947) Ortodoxo Party. This had no independent political or sociological content; it was founded by the Auténtico Senator Eddy Chibás in protest against Auténtico corruption, and its only platform was the "broom." Anarchic violence and terrorism were endemic.

. . . It is certain that if the 1952 election had been held, the candidate of the Ortodoxo party would have won campaigning solely on the issue of Auténtico venality. Grau was reliably believed to have stolen the ceremonial emerald embedded in the Chamber of the Cuban Senate. Prío surpassed his predecessor; the end of his administration saw a frenzied, wholesale plunder of public funds. . . .

The true character of the parliamentary regime was conclusively revealed by the manner of its termination. Just as the interlude had begun at Batista's fiat, so Batista ended it, when he wished and how he wished, without bloodshed. On the night of March 10, 1952, he effortlessly and almost single-handedly reassumed control. There was no resistance, scarcely even token opposition, from the government party, the legislature, the executive, the press or the judiciary. No government was ever more supine; no coup smoother. . . .

Of the classic institutional instruments of rule in Latin America, the Cuban bourgeoisie proved utterly unable to create a lasting or coherent party system. The failure of parliamentarism in Cuba was a common enough phenomenon. But the complete failure to crystallize durable, substantial political parties was exceptional even in Latin America. The debility and disarticulation of the Cuban bourgeoisie were nowhere more evident.

Army

The army has, of course, historically been the prime instrument of oligarchic domination in Latin America. Its officer corps has been overwhelmingly recruited from aristocratic and merchant families. In the 20th century it has provided a certain limited escalator for sons of professional families and white-collar groups. But the attraction of right-militarist ideologies has nearly always neutralized the class origin of these new entrants, and absorbed them into a reactionary and repressive elite. . . .

The Cuban Army of the first decades of the Republic was unmistakably of this kind: It was a small, U.S.-created force, designed by West Point officers to replace the revolutionary armies of the War of Independence which the U.S. expeditionary corps had deliberately disbanded a decade before. Its early history was uneventful. However, with the accession of Machado (himself a general) to power in 1925, the army became directly compromised with the prevailing dictatorship. Then, when Machado was overthrown in 1933 and

[Carlos Manuel de] Céspedes installed as the new president, something unique in Latin American history happened. In alliance with revolutionary student group, the *sergeants* of the Cuban Army led the enlisted men in a revolt against their officers. . . .

The Sergeants' Revolt destroyed the army as an instrument of traditional oligarchic rule. It did not replace [the army] with a stable institution of middle-class character. Here, as elsewhere, the Cuban bourgeoisie failed to create its own institutions. Batista, a man of Afro-Chinese descent and peasant origin, converted the Cuban Army into a personal machine.

. . . The dictatorship remained, of course, the guarantor of the capitalist order in Cuba, but this was because of the context external to it, not because of its class content or ideological orientation. Within the limits of this context, its policy was purely opportunist.

Thus, the distinctive feature of the first Batista dictatorship was its "social" policy. A period of intense labor unrest, rural uprisings and brutal repression, culminating in an unsuccessful general strike in 1935, followed by the installation of the dictatorship. In 1937, however, Batista changed his tactics. Fearing the growing isolation of his regime, he began to make overtures to the trade union movement. In 1939 he allowed the formation of the Cuban Confederation of Labor, of which a Communist (Lazaro Peña) became secretary-general. Thenceforward, the Cuban working class won a number of important concessions. Minimum wage levels, an eight-hour day, a month's paid annual holiday and guarantees against dismissal were secured. Many of these provisions were even, at Communist insistence, written into the new constitution proclaimed in 1940. . . . By the end of the first Batista dictatorship, Cuban labor legislation was among the most advanced in Latin America. It was against this background that Batista was able to win a genuine victory in the elections of July 1940.

When Batista seized power again in 1952, he immediately attempted to recreate the entente which had won him popular support before. Eusebio Mujal, the Auténtico Secretary-General of the CTC, was summoned to the Presidential Palace and a working agreement was arrived at. However, this alliance at the summit failed to "take" at the base of the union movement. The Communist party, which had supported the Batista regime in the 1940s, was now cool. The rank and file of the unions were almost as mistrustful of Mujal as the I.C.F.T.U. was enthusiastic. In 1955, for instance, the sugar workers staged a successful national strike in defiance of Mujal's instructions.

From 1957 onwards, as the revolutionary forces consolidated their position in the Sierra Maestra, while the urban resistance of the 26th of July Movement increased its activity in the towns, the dictatorship became more and more isolated. . . . As students, workers and even naval officers went over to the opposition, the regime struck out blindly in retaliation. The more isolated it became, the more it relied on terror to survive, and the more it increased its isolation. By 1958, it no longer had any support outside itself: it was a pure apparatus of terror and extortion. In its second period, the Batista regime was personified in the international gangsters and adventurers who bedecked it at all echelons.

. . . Meyer Lansky, a Russian-born and U.S.-naturalized gangster identified by the Kefauver Committee as one of the six most powerful racketeers in the United States, controlled Havana's vast gambling concerns and built the last and most lavish of Cuba's luxury hotels, the Riviera. Amadeo Barletta, an Italian who had been a member of Mussolini's General Council, monopolized Cuba's lucrative Cadillac concession and was the island's largest newspaper owner. In men like these, the carrion character of Cuban capital found its last and purest expression. Their predominance marked the impending collapse of the regime.

. . . The preceding analyses explain this crucial facet of Cuban society. A century of successive shocks radically and repeatedly shattered and destructured Cuban society. The bitter wars against Spain, the savage expansion of sugar, the wild cycle of boom and slump, the crushing influx of foreign capital radically smashed Cuban social structure and replaced it only with an inchoate, volcanic magma. No durable social forms coalesced. A proto-bourgeoisie never achieved true consciousness of its interests and identity; lacking elementary class consciousness, it never discovered class solidarity. It produced no institutions. Lumpenized, destructured, disintegrated, it failed to lodge itself lastingly in Cuban history. When the guerrilla troops entered Havana on January 1, 1959, its extinction was close.

. . . The fusion of the rebel leadership and the broadest mass forces in Cuba sealed the revolution. The problem of revolutionary institutions, however, remained. As has been seen, the special nature of prerevolutionary Cuban society made the overthrow of Batista possible without a real political organization or ideology. In a different way, the special nature of Cuban society allowed the creation and consolidation of a mass revolution in an unprecedentedly short period of time, still without a political organization or ideology. But thereafter, in the long-term task of socialist accumulation, and the mortal struggle with the United States, both were inevitably needed. The Cuban road to communism was open. Today, when Cuba has crossed the threshold into a plural Communist world, the tension between the distinctive values of the "uninstitutionalized" character of its revolution, and the imperative needs of its new economy and society, continues. . . .

NOTES

1. *Anuario Azucarero de Cuba* (1957), p. 97. Prosperity led to an extension of Cuban ownership of sugar mills. The proportion of sugar production originating from Cuban-owned mills rose from less than 35 percent in 1926 to 59 percent in 1955. Also see Leo Huberman and Paul Sweezy, *Cuba: Anatomy of a Revolution* (New York: Monthly Review Press, 1962), p. 21.

2. L. Huberman and P. Sweezy, *Cuba: Anatomy of a Revolution,* p. 141.

3. Economist Intelligence Unit, *Cuba: Dominican Republic: Haiti: Puerto Rico,* Three-Monthly Economic Review (May 1960), Annual Supplement, p. 2.

4. William J. Gibbons, S.J., Frank B. Avesing, Raymond Adamek, "Basic Ecclesiastical Statistics for Latin America," World Horizons Report #25 (Maryknoll, N.Y.: Maryknoll Publications, 1960), p. 50.

8. *Continuities in Cuban Revolutionary Politics* *

By Richard R. Fagen

The most obvious continuity in Cuban politics under the revolutionary government is, of course, Fidel Castro himself. A complex and intelligent personality, an event-making man par excellence, and the most commanding figure in 20th century Cuban (and possibly Latin American) history, his centrality to the revolutionary process is undisputed by either his enemies or admirers. But simply to assert Fidel's centrality to revolutionary politics in Cuba is to risk superficiality or tautology in understanding other continuities. In other words, although much of what we see as continuous in the Cuban political style is shaped by the beliefs and temperament of Fidel, the style has a vitality of its own, conditioned by additional aspects of Cuban history, culture, and the revolutionary experience. . . .

What are the general characteristics of the Cuban political style? Although each will subsequently be developed at some length, it is well to have them in mind from the outset: (1) the rebel army and the guerrilla experience; (2) pragmatism, flexibility, and adaptability; (3) the search for a politics of unity and harmony; . . . and (4) human transformation and the search for productivity.

Notice that these characteristics are neither logically exclusive nor all of the same type. If they were, in fact, it would be difficult to justify calling them a style, for the very notion of style suggests an interrelation of different—and sometimes clashing or contradictory—elements. Thus, the rebel army and the guerrilla experience are historical realities supplying the revolution with men, models, and certain ways of viewing the past, present, and future. Pragmatism, flexibility, and adaptability refer to ways of doing political business, making decisions, and ordering priorities. And the final topics may be thought of as problems that have been with the revolution from the outset. . . .

*From Richard Fagen, "Continuities in Cuban Revolutionary Politics," *Monthly Review* (April 1972), pp. 24–48. Edited for this volume.

THE REBEL ARMY AND THE GUERRILLA EXPERIENCE

One of the most enduring features of Cuban revolutionary politics is the continued preeminence of veterans of the Sierra in the ranks of top leadership. Beginning with Fidel, his brother Raúl, the comrades-in-arms like Guillermo García and Juan Almeida, not only the Central Committee of the Communist Party of Cuba but also many other top bureaucratic and party positions have been and continue to be held by charter members of the rebel army. If members of the urban branch of the 26th of July Movement and the several university factions are also considered legitimate children of the glory and tragedy of the struggle against Batista—as they certainly should be—then the first and second levels of revolutionary leadership are overwhelmingly staffed by persons whose credentials were first legitimized in the guerrilla period. . . . The Sierra and the urban resistance of the late 1950s together gave political education to the overwhelming majority of men and women who now exercise power in Cuba. And of these two arenas, it is the Sierra which above all continues to give a special tonality to the Cuban revolutionary style.

What are the ideas of the guerrilla period, the "guerrilla complex," carried by these men and women into the governance of revolutionary Cuba? Most immediate was belief in the viability and propriety of armed struggle as a way to national liberation, and the particular emphasis given to the guerrilla *foco* [center] in the theory subsequently elaborated by Che Guevara and Régis Debray. . . . It was a theory built on an analogy whose primary term was the Sierra Maestra, 1957–1958. Few have violated the rule "thou shalt not generalize from a sample of one" as completely as Guevara, Debray, and their Cuban *compañeros.*

. . . The general and . . . enduring legacies of the period are voluntarism, egalitarianism, and ruralism.[1] Voluntarism is a formal and somewhat colorless word for the expansive sense of efficacy, competence, and personal power generated during the guerrilla period. The struggle against Batista was the stuff of which legends are made. Again and again, Fidel and the tiny band of survivors of the *Granma* [the boat that they used to return from exile in Mexico—eds.] narrowly escaped betrayal, defeat, and death. . . . The rebels marched into Havana, overflowing with the conviction that, having routed Batista, there was no developmental redoubt or political rearguard that they could not handle with facility. . . .

As might be expected, the initial ebullience cooled under the impact of the chilling realities of developmental dilemmas and international relations. For instance, on July 26, 1970, in the wake of the failure to achieve a sugar harvest of ten million tons, Fidel opened his speech by saying, "Today we are going to talk about our problems and difficulties, our setbacks rather than our successes." . . . Yet during the same speech, as he and others have done again and again over the past 12 years, Castro reiterated the basic revolutionary belief that anything is possible, given man's will and man's capacity to make history. . . .

The second important legacy of the guerrilla experience is egalitarianism. As Guevara emphasizes in his writings on the period, and as is evident from frequent references in the speeches of Castro and others, the mountains taught a number of hard and enduring lessons. One, of course, was an understanding of the plight of the Sierra peasant (and by implication, the plight of all *campesinos*), and a determination to do something about it once in power. But more central to the growth of the egalitarian ethic was the rudimentary experience of living, fighting, and surviving in the mountains. . . . The always primitive and at first highly mobile life of the guerrilla troop discouraged the growth of internal differentiation and privilege. Guns, hammocks, assignments, and rank were distributed on the basis of performance in the mountains. . . . Thus, there developed as a natural concomitant of the situation in the mountains not only a strong sense of identification with and respect for the local peasantry but also a basic belief in the rightness of the "career open to talent." . . .

The ramifications and manifestations of this egalitarianism have been considerable in revolutionary Cuba. In the elegant social clubs now open to all, in the performance criteria established for entry into the new Communist party, in the profound attempt to redress cultural and economic imbalances, in the pervasive informality of dress and address, in the spectacle of members of the Central Committee in the fields, sweat-soaked from cutting sugarcane, in numerous other programs and activities of the revolution, this egalitarianism is practiced and enlarged. But it should also be pointed out that it is essentially an egalitarianism of equal opportunity and shared hardship.

. . . Not in the Sierra, however, nor in Cuba today is it a nonhierarchical or fully participant egalitarianism. Just as *comandantes* gave orders in the mountains and the troops obeyed or were summarily punished, so in Cuba since the revolution decisional power has been extremely concentrated and dissent has been rather strictly controlled. The Sierra-born concept of equality does not include a commitment at the national level to participatory and decisional egalitarianism, or even significant sharing. As we shall subsequently see, there *is* in the Cuban Revolution a countertendency of long standing in which participatory forms are sought out and explored; but it is best to consider this apart from the theme of egalitarianism. . . .

Ruralism is a corollary and extension of egalitarianism. The essential tenet of this strain of revolutionary thought is that the countryside is not only where the major developmental struggle must be waged, but also the locus of values and a way of life from which every Cuban has much to learn. Celebrated in this way of life are simplicity, comradeship, loyalty, hard work, tenacity, courage, sharing, and sacrifice—an idealization of the character and behavior

of the *guerrillero-campesino*. The programs and formative experiences that
flow directly from these beliefs are legion: the literacy campaign of 1961 which
brought city youth into contact with *campesinos* for months at a time, the
"schools to the countryside" movement in which entire classrooms move to
rural areas for extended periods, the *cordón* or green belt around Havana
where tens of thousands of urban dwellers have planted and harvested crops,
the annual forays of nonagricultural workers into the canefields at harvest
time, the extensive programs for young adults on the Isle of Pines.

. . . From the very outset there has been a number of constants in the theory
and practice of ruralism. First, ruralism contains an implied and sometimes
explicit critique of urban values, not just a romantic celebration of the countryside for the virtues it engenders. The kind of egalitarianism which is taught
involves a "return to basics," through bringing all Cubans into contact with
an environment in which achievements and skills entitling one to status in the
more "advanced" sectors of society open no doors and lighten no burdens.
Second, ruralism as a way of encouraging individual *formación* and culture
change is very much oriented to direct experience. The lessons of ruralism are
not learned from books or from discussions, but rather are intended to alter
consciousness through extended and profound personal confrontation with
rural life and work.[2] Finally, although it implies a critique of certain urban
values and a celebration of life-styles associated with the countryside, there is
nothing primitivistic about ruralism. That is, the dirt, poor housing, and
general impoverishment that comprise the common lot of many, if not most,
rural residents are considered unacceptable, whatever salutary effect experiencing such conditions might have on the consciousness of urbanites.

PRAGMATISM, FLEXIBILITY, AND ADAPTABILITY

Even those who sympathize fully with the revolution are forced to admit that
Fidel and his lieutenants have taken Cuba—and at times the world—through
a dizzying and often contradictory scenario of promises, programs, alliances,
and adventures. What are we to make of a political system in which the
leadership welcomes Israeli technical aid while outspokenly supporting the
Palestinian guerrillas, first claims that sugarcane cultivation has distorted the
economy and then plants more cane than ever, rehabilitates prostitutes and
moralizes public life but officially acknowledges and runs the *posadas* or hotels
to which men take the women whom they cannot take home? The list could
fill pages and be extended into every domain of government activity. . . .

What explanations can be offered for this complex tangle . . . of Cuban public
policy? One answer is that we are seeing little more than the Cuban variant
of the contradictions and illogic that characterize the public acts of any government. Another easy and frequently expressed hypothesis is that Cuban policy
stems from the projection onto a national and sometimes international stage

of the antic and inconstant (or, in another view, the forceful and fertile) disposition of Fidel Castro. . . .

But closer to the heart of the matter is the fact that with the exception of a few closed or nonnegotiable questions and issues—national sovereignty, public ownership, the right of Castro's group to rule—almost all other aspects of both the theory and practice of revolutionary governance can be considered "up for grabs." . . . Almost the entire institutional and organizational life of the revolutionary government, including such key aspects as the role of the Communist party, is unfettered by conventional constraints of theory or dogma. Similarly, the basic structure of economic relations has been hammered out in practice without either the benefits or the constraints imposed by a theory (much less a detailed plan) of the economic system. A powerful strain of pragmatism and experimentation thus constantly intrudes into public life. The operating rule in many policy areas—touching subject matters as different as hemispheric armed struggle and agricultural policy—seems to be, "try it; if it doesn't work, abandon it and try something else."

The policy consequences of these elements of style are most visible in the large arenas of international and domestic affairs. A foreign policy which embraces diplomatic and commercial exchange with governments and groups as diverse as mainland China, Spain, Britain, the South Vietnamese National Liberation Front, Israel, Egypt, France, the Soviet Union, and the Vatican cannot be accused of dogmatism or inflexibility. . . . Similarly, the gross dimensions of shifts in agricultural and industrial policy during the first decade of the revolution reveal not the implementation of a grand design, but rather the awkward and costly gropings of an inexperienced, antitheoretical, but pragmatic and relatively open-minded group of leaders. . . .

On a smaller but pervasive scale the consequences of these elements of style are manifest in revolutionary attitudes toward the planning and implementation of programs. From the outset of the revolution, extensive developmental programs were launched, without the detailed planning and organizational work that would subsequently be necessary to keep them going. From the revolutionary point of view, the important thing was to begin; the planning and organizational work would come after, not before, this commitment-through-action. It was believed that the act of trying, the struggle itself, would open up possibilities and generate resources that could not have been imagined or counted on before the battle was joined. . . . The ambivalent Cuban posture toward planning and organization, so attractive and liberating at one point in the developmental process, often produces waste and debilitation later on. The Cubans' genius for "inventing" the revolution as they go along has not yet been fully harnessed to the machinery of planning, organization, and management necessitated by the developmental road on which they have set out.

THE SEARCH FOR A POLITICS OF UNITY AND HARMONY

Like many other aspects of the revolutionary style, the search for a politics of unity has roots deep in the prerevolutionary experience. The enduring heroes of the last 100 years of Cuban history, beginning with Maceo and Martí, all preached an inclusivist variety of nationalistic thought. . . . This idealized vision of an inclusive and integrated society nurtured Fidelista formulations of the revolutionary future, giving to them a distinct ring. In fact, from his "History Will Absolve Me" speech through his most recent pronouncements, Fidel's thought has been remarkably free of the rhetoric and the conceptual apparatus of conventional Marxist class analysis.

. . . Cuban leaders believe that social, cultural, organizational, and ethnic schisms are in some basic sense "unnatural," the product of an imperfect past and a still imperfect revolutionary experience. . . . Thus, the egalitarianism and ruralism previously described blur class lines without ever coming to grips theoretically with the "class problem." . . .

Other manifestations of the continuing search for a politics of unity can be seen in areas as diverse as the regime's hemispheric vision, doctrine of mass organizations, relations with artists and intellectuals, and attitudes toward black nationalism. Despite the diplomatic and economic isolation brought about through the U.S.-engineered decisions of the Organization of American States, Cuba has continued to express solidarity with "the people" of the hemisphere.

For obvious reasons, the mass organizations of the revolutionary government provide the most propitious setting for experimenting with and implementing the politics of unity. Whether intended for youth, women, farmers, workers, or the neighborhood in general (Committees for Defense of the Revolution, CDRs), the mass organizations have always been inclusive rather than exclusive. The consequences of this organizational philosophy can be seen most dramatically in the CDRs where by 1965 one out of every two adult Cubans held at least nominal membership. Speaking in 1961, on the first anniversary of the founding of the committees, Castro emphasized that anyone could belong, young and old, men and women, students and housewives, workers and pensioners, intellectuals and peasants. The only test would be one's disposition toward the revolution. . . .

As might be expected, the search for a politics of harmony is put to a special test by the regime's relations with artists and intellectuals. To the extent that the government had an official cultural policy during the 1960s, it was promulgated in 1961 in a speech in which Fidel asked and then answered the following question: "What are the rights of writers and artists, whether revolutionaries or not? Within the Revolution, everything: against the Revolution, nothing." In architecture, graphics, and to a great extent in cinema, this dictum has been interpreted broadly; and the buildings, posters, stamps, and movies done in Cuba are in general colorful, innovative, and tasteful. The visual excesses of socialist realism are pleasantly absent in Cuba—except for the remnants of an earlier period of heroic muralism still evident in and on some public buildings. In literature, however, agreement between the regime and the writers has been achieved much less easily, and in many cases not at all. . . .

Finally, official attitudes toward black nationalism in Cuba illustrate yet another consequence of the search for a politics of unity. Although the socio-cultural and economic place of the black man in both pre- and postrevolution-ary Cuba is a subject of great complexity, at least one aspect of the current situation is clear: After moving with dramatic speed and effectiveness to end institutionalized manifestations of racism (if not prejudice) on the island, the revolutionary government has steadfastly resisted any temptation and all pres-sures to identify blacks as a group warranting special attention or programs. To the extent that blacks are found disproportionately among the most disad-vantaged social sectors, they of course benefit greatly from revolutionary programs designed to bring health, education, employment, and participatory opportunities to those sectors. But the notion of "special" opportunities for blacks in the revolutionary context would strike the Cuban leadership as profoundly violative of norms of egalitarianism and national unity. In related fashion, what murmurings there are of an indigenous (or imported) black cultural nationalism fall on deaf ears in leadership circles. Why should the revolution encourage or support movements, the leadership asks, that tend to re-fragment the population into racial groups when the very purpose of the revolutionary effort is to forge a new Cuban identity and nation that are above distinctions of race, class, and region? . . . Thus, although there are official ethnographic and folkloric programs to discover and preserve Afro-Cuban religious and cultural forms, no encouragement is given to those who would kindle a Cuban movement of Negritude. . . .

HUMAN TRANSFORMATION AND THE SEARCH FOR PRODUCTIVITY

The radicalism of the Cuban leaders is nowhere more in evidence than in their determination to create a new society through transforming the common man into a revolutionary man, a man devoid of *egoismo,* guided by *conciencia,* who puts service to society above service to self. . . .

Whether in educational programs, the work of the mass organizations, the operation of the Communist party, or the controversy over moral versus material incentives, the influence of this vision—however much attenuated—is felt. A massive, societywide, and continuing effort at human transformation dominates the revolutionary tapestry, tying together its disparate elements, tonalities, and textures.

As an integral part of this view of the world and of how change ought to take place, problems of economic development are considered to be—in the first instance—problems of human transformation. . . .

The key operational focus and test of this doctrine of economic development come in the domain of productivity. If the revolutionary vision of the new societal order is to be viable, the ordinary worker must give generously of his energies and talents, even if not motivated by conventional economic insecurities or expectations of personal gain. It is precisely at this critical point that politics and economics come together to define the central questions facing the revolutionary leadership: Is it possible to engage the best and continuing energies of the population in production without resorting to conventional systems of economic incentive, reward, and punishment? . . .

Only the most passionate celebrant of the Cuban Revolution would argue that consistently positive answers can at present be given to these questions. On the contrary, the performance of the Cuban economy has been mixed and erratic, and it would be relatively easy to dismiss the Cuban experiment in development-through-human-transformation as having been tried and proven a failure. . . . The tension and irony that inhere in the clash between the harsh demands of economic development (through high productivity and discipline) and the vision of a society organized around more humane and brotherly principles, thus continue unabated. As Castro commented in response to a series of complaints by a public health worker:

> Perhaps our greatest idealism lies in having believed that a society that had barely begun to live in a world that for thousands of years had lived under the law of "an eye for an eye and a tooth for a tooth," the law of the survival of the fittest, the law of egoism, the law of deceit and the law of exploitation could, all of a sudden, be turned into a society in which everybody behaved in an ethical, moral way.[3]

Not to appreciate the extent to which this idealism continues to fuel the developmental effort in Cuba is to invite misunderstanding. No single aspect of Cuban politics is as important as this commitment to the creation of revolutionary man and the tangled relationship of that commitment to economic development in general. . . .

NOTES

1. Voluntarism is here used in its technical sense, denoting a philosophy which conceives human will to be the dominant factor in experience and thus history. This usage has nothing to do with the notion of voluntary labor as used by the Cubans themselves.

2. For further elaboration of this theme see Richard R. Fagen, *The Transformation of Political Culture in Cuba* (Stanford: Stanford University Press, 1969), especially pp. 148–150, and 169–179.

3. From a speech by Captain Jorge Risquet, Cuban Minister of Labor, reported in *Granma Weekly Review* (September 20, 1970).

PART II

The Cuban Economy

Introduction

Sixty years of a semicolonial relationship with the United States made it clear to most Cubans in 1959 that improvements in basic living standards could be accomplished only if there were a major transformation in the island's economy. Increased housing, improved health care, rural electrification, universal education and literacy, and an end to malnutrition were articulated goals of the revolution. But the dependent, inegalitarian, and stagnant Cuban economy provided little basis from which to achieve these objectives.

Key resources were controlled by foreigners and by a Cuban elite that had shown no inclination to develop the country for the mass of people. Underdevelopment itself was an obstacle. Necessary skills were absent; poor health and illiteracy reduced workers' productivity and capability, and bad roads and communications made the organization and distribution of goods and services difficult. Dependency also had robbed Cuba of its ability to be self-sufficient in basic goods and services. Products that could have been produced easily at home were regularly imported, which absorbed precious hard currency reserves that might have been available for development.

The revolution in the Cuban economy, then, lies at the heart of the Cuban Revolution. Yet a discussion of the Cuban economy requires knocking down the walls that usually segment economics into a cubicle apart from the rest of society. Such a segmentation obscures what building a new society in Cuba meant. To appreciate the nature and goals of Cuban economics is to transcend narrow questions about macroeconomic and microeconomic policy. For Cuba's leaders, economic development has meant a broad transformation of the economy—from production and consumption to the relationship between the individual and society.

The transformation of the Cuban economy had its roots in processes unfolding long before 1959. Cuba's economic class structure underwent two important changes early in this century. First, the 19th-century petty bourgeoisie—independent tobacco farmers and sugar cane growers—lost their farms during the crises of the 1920s and the Great Depression. Large-scale foreign capital—mainly North American—moved into the expanding sugar industry, thus limiting the growth of Cuba's own middle and upper classes. The Cuban bourgeoisie that did exist—weak and demoralized due to their inability to compete with efficient foreign enterprises or privileged imports from the U.S.—lacked, in James O'Connor's words, "a sense of themselves as agents of progress."[1] The weakness of these classes explains why there was no significant social bulwark against revolutionary change in the late 1950s.

The second development was the change in class consciousness. The economic crises that erupted into the 1933 Revolution opened up a new era of worker and peasant agitation in the countryside. Farm laborers' awareness of themselves and their position in the social structure increased, enabling them to cohere and strengthen as a class in the years that followed. Both of these changes, in the class structure and consciousness of Cuba's laboring classes, advanced the island's revolutionary potential.

The leaders of the 1959 Revolution sought to remedy the many ills plaguing the underdeveloped and dependent economy. Their goals included achieving a high rate of economic growth; eliminating sugar monoculture through rapid industrialization and agricultural diversification; reducing economic dependence on the United States by varying trade and capital markets; attaining full employment; and raising the standards of living of the peasants and the unskilled urban workers. The priority given to these goals and the strategy for achieving them was subject to intense debate and tremendous change in the two decades following the triumph. Carmelo Mesa-Lago gives a comprehensive appraisal of the five stages the Revolution's economic policies went through during these years (Reading 9).

The failure of the second stage of economic policy—the two-year effort between 1961 and 1963 to pursue heavy industrialization—sparked a major ideological debate between two alternative paths for Cuban development. The debate turned on issues such as the nature of transition between capitalism and communism, on the role of moral versus material incentives in production, and on centralization versus decentralization in the planning process.

On one side of the debate stood Ernesto "Che" Guevara (Reading 10), who argued that production could be increased primarily through moral persuasion since, in his belief, ideas or consciousness—"subjective conditions"—could change "objective reality" or the material base. This school of thought scorned orthodox Soviet doctrine that relied on the use of material incentives and profit to judge economic performance. Influenced by Mao's Great Leap Forward, the Guevarists believed it was possible for a country to bypass the transition stage between capitalism and communism and thereby avoid reliance on the market, the law of supply and demand, and wage differentials. Only in this way did they believe it possible to create communism's New Man unadulterated by vestiges of the capitalist past.

Opposing the Guevarists was a more pragmatic group identified with economist Carlos Rafael Rodríguez and members of Cuba's prerevolutionary, pro-Soviet Communist party. This group saw the Guevarists as overly idealistic, and believed that some market mechanisms were necessary during the transition to socialism and communism. Rodríguez's group, Mesa-Lago writes in Reading 9, "argued that subjective conditions cannot ignore objective conditions, that a socialist country cannot go farther than its structure allows it to go, that the material base has to be developed first and will, in turn, raise consciousness, and that it is impossible to skip the transitional—socialistic—stage between capitalism and full communism." Nevertheless, the Guevarist line won out, and was implemented in the 1966–1970 period.

The "moral economy" proved to be a failure. The experiment was marked by low productivity and growth rates, inefficient and centralized decision making, and severe declines in output. Wassily Leontief (Reading 12) explains an important reason for the failed economic strategy: "[I]n Cuba as in other socialist countries such moral incentives failed in their effectiveness to measure up to more conventional individualistic self-interest . . . the abolition of the old profit system has not eliminated the driving forces of individualistic interest."

Despite the unevenness of Cuba's development strategy, the revolution's leadership can claim success for their goal of redistributing land, wealth, and social services. In the early years of the revolution, the government instituted two land reforms that left the state in control of 63 percent of the island's cultivated land. The creation of state farms and cooperatives immediately improved the job security, working conditions, and standard of living of farm workers. The government also distributed 110,000 land titles to former tenants, sharecroppers, and squatters, tripling the number of small private farmers. As Medea Benjamin, Joseph Collins, and Michael Scott explain in their discussion of Cuba's agrarian reform (Reading 11), the existence of this private farm sector—while still essential for agrarian production—creates inequalities often deemed intolerable by government leaders.

Claes Brundenius (Reading 13) documents the equity gains of the revolution, which remain a model for many Latin American and Third World countries: the eradication of open unemployment; the satisfaction of basic needs such as food, health care, education, and social security; and the redistribution of wealth and income. He argues that this basic needs approach to development spurred rather than hindered economic growth in the 1970s.

In his main report to the Third Congress of the Cuban Communist Party in February 1986 (Reading 14), Fidel Castro laid out a litany of problems plaguing the Cuban economy between 1981 and 85. Castro criticized, among other things, weak management, sloppy planning and administration, poor worker discipline and attitudes, excessive and bureaucratic procedures, and shortcomings in accounting. These problems created sluggish growth in the "exports of goods and services and import substitution," resulting in the deepening of the hard currency debt and the failure to meet "some delivery commitments to the socialist countries." Castro declared that "there will be no tolerance whatsoever for laziness, negligence, incompetence, or irresponsibility. The apprentice stage must be left behind once and for all."

Andrew Zimbalist and Susan Eckstein acknowledge that the continuing "key role" played by sugar in the Cuban economy harmed the country's external development strategy. But in their overview of 25 years of Cuba's economic development (Reading 15), they emphasize that apparent problems should not obscure the sustained growth that has occurred. The internal development strategy, they contend, contributed to an average annual 7 percent rate of growth in the first half of the 1980s. This contrasts to negative rates experienced by most Latin American countries.

In Reading 16, Marifeli Perez-Stable explains that the leadership's self-criticisms are part of a larger effort to rectify shortcomings that resulted from the introduction of market mechanisms, decentralization, and material incentives early in the decade. Those changes had been similar to the proposed restructuring of the Soviet economy called *perestroika*. But Cuba encountered difficulties with them that were heightened by its particular circumstances: The U.S. embargo meant that Cuba could not take advantage of goods made cheaper by a devalued dollar; the drop in the world price of sugar and oil reduced its hard currency; natural disasters hurt its agricultural output. Above all, Perez-Stable observes, Castro was critical of the changes because they had not contributed to the socialist development of the country. She concludes that Cuba "once again staked a claim to its own road to socialism."

NOTES

1. James O'Connor, "Cuba: Its Political Economy," in Rolando E. Bonchea and Nelson P. Valdés (eds.), *Cuba in Revolution* (N.Y.: Anchor, 1972), pp. 52–81.

CHAPTER 4

The Prerevolutionary Economy and an Overview of Policy

9. *Revolutionary Economic Policies in Cuba**

BY CARMELO MESA-LAGO

THE STATE OF THE CUBAN ECONOMY AT THE EVE OF THE REVOLUTION

The five crucial socioeconomic problems existing in Cuba in 1958 were the slow rate of economic growth, sugar monoculture or the excessive significance of this product in the generation of GNP and exports, the overwhelming dependence on the United States in regard to investment and trade, the high rates of unemployment and underemployment, and the significant inequalities in living standards, particularly between urban and rural areas.

Slow Economic Growth. Some economists have claimed that the Cuban economy was stagnant either since the 1920s or throughout the republican periods beginning in 1902. Informed estimates are difficult to make because of the lack of data. National accounts began to be computed by the newly established National Bank of Cuba in the 1940s, and prior to that no reliable statistics existed in this field.

According to the National Bank, in 1950–58 the Cuban GNP estimated at

*From Carmelo Mesa-Lago, *The Economy of Socialist Cuba: A Two-Decade Appraisal* (Albuquerque, N.M.: Univ. of New Mexico Press, 1981), pp. 7–32.

current prices (not correcting for inflation) grew at an average rate of 4.6 percent annually. But taking population growth and inflation into account, the increase of real GNP per capita in 1950–58 was about 1 percent. Cuba's GNP devoted to investment in 1950–58 reached an average of 18 percent, and showed a steady tendency to climb, creating some hope that the rate of growth would rise in the 1960s. Hence, the Cuban economy was not stationary in the decade before the revolution; indeed, it grew, but at a very slow rate, with some expectations for a higher rate in the future.

Sugar Monoculture. In the period 1949–58, an average of from 28 to 29 percent of GNP was generated by the sugar sector. However, a tendency toward the lessening of the importance of sugar was noticeable, not only during that period, but in comparison to the 1940s. Thus in the years 1957–58, sugar originated only 25 percent of GNP. On the other hand, nonsugar industrial output grew 47 percent between 1947 and 1958. As a typical export economy, Cuba depended heavily on foreign trade; thus, in 1949–58, some 36 percent of its GNP was generated by exports. Sugar and its by-products represented an average of 84 percent of the total exports, and the remaining ones were mainly tobacco and minerals. The price fluctuations of sugar on the international market, as well as the varying sugar quota policies and prices fixed by the United States, were exogenous factors that Cuba found impossible to control. As a result of the excessive importance of sugar, these fluctuations had a serious impact on GNP, provoking a situation of instability and uncertainty.

Economic Dependence. United States investment in Cuba by 1958 was possibly the second largest in Latin America, and in the period 1949–58, an average of two thirds of Cuba's foreign trade was with the United States. This commercial dependence invariably resulted in a negative balance of trade for Cuba, building up a cumulative deficit of almost $350 million during that period. Some scholars argue that the proximity of Cuba to the United States, the world's most powerful economy, resulted in a total integration of the Cuban economy into the American economy; moreover, because Cuba was tied to the U.S. economy, the former could not achieve a satisfactory degree of independence or domestic integration. Others contend that heavy U.S. investment and transfer of technology to Cuba were largely responsible for the development achieved by the country in 1958, placing it among the top three or four nations in Latin America.

Unemployment and Underemployment. Between 1919 and 1957, the labor force employed in agriculture fell from 49 percent to 39 percent. The principal increases in employment were found in construction, commerce, and industry, in that order, but such increases were not high enough to absorb both the rapidly growing labor force and rural-to-urban migration. On the eve of the

[1959] Revolution, 16 percent of the labor force was totally unemployed, and approximately 14 percent found itself in various forms of underemployment.

These figures represent annual averages, and they therefore do not reveal the fluctuations of unemployment during the year. From 20 to 25 percent of the labor force found work in the sugar sector, but due to the seasonal character of the sugar crop and its processing, this portion of the work force had stable work for only four months out of the year. During the so-called dead season (May to December), the proportion of employment in the sugar sector fell to 4 or 5 percent. It is difficult to determine what percentage of the temporarily unemployed sugar workers worked on their own land or on other crop harvests during the dead season, although it is known that about one third of the sugar workers found employment for another three months in the harvesting of the coffee crop. Statistics on total unemployment in 1956–57 recorded an increase from 200,000 workers during the period of greatest activity in the sugar harvest (February to April) to 457,000 workers during the period of least activity (August to October). Although strict comparisons are not possible, a review of statistics from the years 1943, 1953, and 1956–57 suggest that unemployment was worsening.

Inequality in Distribution. An accurate study of income distribution in Cuba is impossible due to the absence of figures. Only a general index exists, indicating how the national income was distributed within two large categories: remuneration for labor (wages, fringe benefits, pensions), and remuneration for capital (rent, interest, dividends). Between 1949 and 1958, the average labor share was 65 percent, a figure surpassed in 1958 by only three developed Western countries: Great Britain, the United States, and Canada. Moreover, this percentage showed a noticeable tendency to increase. Employed labor had sufficient political and economic power to capture and increase its share of the national income, but those gains were obtained in large measure at the expense of the unemployed and the peasants.

In 1953, 44 percent of the Cuban population lived in rural areas, compared with 55 percent in 1919. During those years, legislation was enacted to better protect the peasants. Nevertheless, urbanization was accompanied by preferential state expenditures—especially to Havana and other large cities. In 1957–58, national averages in education, public health, and social security placed Cuba among the top three Latin American countries in delivery of social services: Its literacy rate was the fourth highest; its percentage of the labor force covered by old age, invalidity, and survivors social insurance was the second highest; its indices of number of inhabitants per doctor and hospital bed were the third lowest; its morbidity index was the second lowest; and its death rate and infant mortality rate were the lowest. But social-service facilities were mainly concentrated in the capital city and urban areas, whereas their availability and quality declined sharply in the rural areas. Results of a survey taken in 1956–57 revealed the disparity between urban and rural conditions. The caloric intake, diet, health, medical attention, housing, and income of peasants were very much below the national averages for 1953. The migratory movement from the countryside to the city was accentuated by the impoverished condition of the rural population, which made itself visible in Havana's shantytowns. A large number of these rural migrants found low paying work in the tertiary sector (for example, domestic services and peddling) or they simply became beggars. The high and growing percentage of the work force engaged in tertiary activities was a clear symptom of underemployment in Cuba.

In summary, during the decade prior to the revolution, the Cuban economy showed a small rate of real growth; however, the rate of investment was increasing. Even though development in the nonsugar sector occurred, sugar monoculture still dominated the economy. Cuba was heavily dependent on the United States for capital and trade, and the latter resulted in a deficit against Cuba. Both unemployment and underemployment were high and apparently worsening. The economic growth that occurred largely benefited capital and employed labor, as well as the urban sector, at the expense of the unemployed and the rural sector, all of which resulted in significant inequalities in living standards.

THE CHANGING ECONOMIC POLICIES OF THE REVOLUTION

The most important developmental goals announced by the triumphant revolution were aimed at correcting the socioeconomic problems summarized above: to achieve high rates of economic growth; to eliminate sugar monoculture through rapid industrialization and agricultural diversification; to reduce economic dependence on the United States by varying trade and capital markets; to attain full employment; and to improve the standards of living of the peasants and the unskilled urban workers. But the economic policies used to achieve those goals were modified several times in the course of the first two decades of the revolution. Furthermore, priorities among goals also changed. Hence, a discussion of such policies must identify five stages of the revolution: (1) 1959–60, liquidation of capitalism and erosion of the market; (2) 1961–63, attempt to introduce the Soviet pre-economic reform model of command economy; (3) 1964–66, debate over and test of alternative socialist economic models; (4) 1966–70, adoption and radicalization of the Mao-Guevarist model; and (5) 1971 on, shift to the current Soviet model of economic reform.

The Liquidation of the Capitalist System and Erosion of the Market, 1959–60

The first stage of the revolution lacked a clearly defined ideology. Some scholars have indicated that the "structuralist" philosophy of the Economic

Commission for Latin America (which favors a mixed economy, decentral-ized-indicative planning, import substitution, industrialization, agrarian re-form, and tax reform) exerted influence in the guerrilla period of the revolution as well as in the early years in power. Others have attempted to prove that Marxism was the prevalent ideology of the revolutionaries. Whether there was an underlying ideology or not, the new leaders soon showed nationalist, statist, antimarket, antibureaucratic, and consumptionist attitudes. Fidel Castro and his close associates did not have any knowledge of economics (most of them were lawyers), and the few economists occupy-ing government posts were soon dismissed and their jobs passed to enthusias-tic but inexperienced revolutionaries. For example, Ernesto Guevara, a physician, first became the head of the Industrialization Department of the National Institute of Agrarian Reform (INRA), then president of the Na-tional Bank, and finally the Minister of Industry. Bureaucrats and techni-cians were viewed as opportunists who deliberately complicated economic and administrative matters in hope of making themselves indispensable. Partly due to their ignorance in economic matters and partly because they were captivated by the revolution's almost magical success against the sup-posedly technical army of Batista's dictatorship, the revolutionary leaders proposed the application of guerrilla techniques to the Cuban economy. It was widely believed that the nation's five major socioeconomic problems would be rapidly and simultaneously resolved by the power of the revolu-tion, the zeal and hard work of the leaders, the audacity of the improvisa-tion, and the enthusiasm and support of the people. In summary, willingness, consciousness, morale, austerity, and loyalty were emphasized over material and human resources, technology, and knowledge and expertise.

. . . Collectivization of the means of production gradually increased and gained momentum in the second half of 1960. This occurred either because the leadership believed it was a necessary step to achieve their developmental goals or because they were forced to do it by domestic and international events or by a combination of both. In 1959 several means were used in the collectiviza-tion process: confiscation of property and assets embezzled by officials of the overthrown dictatorship; expropriation of latifundia (farms exceeding a ceiling of 400 hectares) through the first Agrarian Reform Law; expropriation of rental housing; state intervention in enterprises (factories, warehouses, trans-portation) abandoned by their owners or in which labor conflicts disrupted production; confiscation of assets of those who failed to pay due taxes; and confiscation of all property belonging to those convicted of counterrevolution-ary crimes or who had become political exiles. In successive waves between June and October 1960, the collectivization process was rapidly extended. Involved were all foreign-owned oil refineries, U.S.-owned sugar mills, banks, telephone and electricity corporations, and all remaining U.S. properties as well as most domestically owned major industries, banks, and transportation business. By the end of 1960 all domestic wholesale and foreign trade and banking, and most transportation, industry, construction and retail trade, as well as more than one third of agriculture was in state hands. This swift transfer of ownership liquidated the capitalist system and brought about the erosion of the automatic mechanisms of the market; as a result, production and distribution of goods and services partly ceased to be determined by the laws of supply and demand.

In the meantime several government agencies had been created to direct state domination over the economy. The first was INRA, which gradually grew to become a bureaucratic monster controlling one third of agriculture and a good part of industry, and which developed the first experiments with central planning. The Central Planning Board (JUCEPLAN) was initially established to coordinate government policies and to guide the private sector through indicative planning; however, these functions were never exercised, and JUCEPLAN eventually became the agency for state central planning. Financing of the economy was increasingly done by the state, with private financing largely restricted to agriculture. The Ministry of Finance began to control the financing process through the state budget, while the National Bank expanded its command over credit and foreign exchange. The Ministry of Labor played an increasingly active role as labor arbiter and fixer of labor conditions as a step toward mastering trade unions. The collectivization process and the dissatisfaction of managers and technicians induced the exodus of this vital group. Their jobs were promptly filled with loyal but inexperienced revolutionaries, the cadres that eventually became responsible for the implementation of central planning as a substitute for the market forces.

. . . Apparently economic growth continued at the same time the liquidation of the capitalist system occurred. This was accomplished mainly by full utilization of equipment, accumulated stocks and inventories, and foreign exchange reserves. Besides, confidence in the government was very high in 1959, and revenue from delinquent taxes flowed to the state. Much of that money was invested in a dynamic program of public works and housing construction. To reduce dependency on sugar, a program of agrarian diversification was launched in 1960, and large estates producing sugarcane began to be cleared off and replanted with rice, fruits or vegetables. However, this cut in the size of cane was not yet important enough to affect sugar output, and the nationalization of sugar plantations and mills did not occur until the end of 1960. Hence, the first two sugar harvests under the revolution were fairly good and generated badly needed foreign exchange, while output of most agricultural products increased slightly. In 1960, a Soviet industrial fair was held in Havana, and Cuba began to sign contracts for the purchase of manufacturing equipment from the USSR, German Democratic Republic (GDR), and Czechoslovakia. The movement to cut economic dependence on the United States was accelerated in July 1960 when the U.S. quota to buy Cuban sugar was suspended. The USSR and China then made commitments to buy most of that sugar. Cuba started to import Soviet oil in early 1960 and by the end of the year was receiving most of its needed oil from the USSR. Trade with the United States began to decline in 1960 and shifted to socialist countries with whom Cuba signed commercial and economic aid agreements. In October 1960 all U.S. investment in Cuba had been nationalized; to retaliate, the United States imposed an economic embargo on Cuba, which would eventually terminate trade between the two nations.

In spite of the stated goal of full employment, the rate of unemployment increased in 1959–60. The government tried to cope with this problem by impeding job dismissals, by absorbing part of the unemployed in state agriculture, the growing armed forces, and social services, and by extending education thus keeping young people from entering into the labor market. The collectivization of most means of production, real estate, and banking practically eliminated nonwage income (that is dividends, rent, and interest) except in agriculture. On the other hand, raises were enacted for overall monetary wages, the minimum wage in agriculture, and minimum pensions. The net results of these two actions was a decrease in extreme income differentials. Moreover, the disposable income of the poorest sector was augmented as a result of the reduction of housing rent and electricity rates, subsidized public housing, and the expansion of free education and medical care. Most of the expansion in social services took place in rural areas, which helped begin to close the gap of living standards with urban areas. The consumptionist policy, however, sharply reduced the proportion of GNP devoted to investment. Also consumption increased faster than production and imports, rapidly depleting existing stocks.

In this stage of the revolution the leaders tried to achieve all the five goals at the same time but with divergent results. Although a clear policy to promote growth did not exist, moderate growth was achieved by taking advantage of underutilized equipment, stocks, and reserves and by being aided by fair sugar crops and an active government expenditures policy. Little of significance was done to reduce sugar monoculture, and unemployment grew worse in spite of some government measures to stop it. On the other hand, economic dependence on the United States was substantially reduced, and distribution in favor of rural areas and low-income urban groups was improved.

The Attempt to Introduce the Soviet Pre-Economic-Reform Model, 1961–63

The year 1961 brought the break of diplomatic relations with the United States, the defeat of the Bay of Pigs invasion which consolidated the revolution, and the declaration that the revolution was socialist and that its leader was a Marxist. Facing the collapse of the market mechanisms and having established a survival pipeline with the Soviet Union, the revolutionary leadership attempted to apply to Cuba the model of economic organization prevalent in the

USSR and the strategy of development of heavy industrialization successively tried by the Soviets in the 1930s.

. . . The process of state collectivization continued in this stage but at a slower rate than in the previous one: in 1961 all private educational institutions were nationalized; in 1962, private agricultural cooperatives established since 1959 in nationalized latifundia were transformed into state farms; in 1963 the second Agrarian Reform Law expropriated land of farms having more than 67 hectares, hence eliminating the middle-sized farmer; finally, the state exerted control of private agriculture through INRA introducing compulsory procurement quotas (*acopio*, that is, the sale of part of the crop to the state at prices set below the market price).

The Cubans tried rapidly to convert an economy in chaos into a command economy through highly centralized physical planning for which the island lacked the needed infrastructure. The novel economic organization began to be introduced in early 1961 with the creation of a new administrative structure. JUCEPLAN was charged with formulating annual and medium-range macro development plans to be submitted for consideration of the political leadership. A network of central ministries and agencies was created or modified to take charge of the various economic sectors, mostly as state monopolies dealing with foreign trade, industry and mining, domestic trade, finance, labor, and banking. State enterprises producing the same type of goods were merged into trusts (*consolidados*) controlled by the proper central ministry. Financing of the economy was done in all state enterprises through budgetary allocations; annual state budgets were prepared but applied using primitive accounting techniques. Most prices began to be centrally fixed and, in 1962, physical allocation of consumer goods through rationing began. The 1962 annual plan was prepared with the aid of Czech planners. Their efforts, though, were hamstrung by lack of both accurate statistics and trained cadres and because the Czech model was inappropriate. It was too centralized, shaped by a developed, industrialized economy, and was rigidly applied with no effort to adapt it to Cuba's insular, monoculture, developing economy. Figures were grossly estimated or invented, there was no real input and feedback from lower echelons, and hence production goals were too optimistic with no basis in reality. When the final version of the plan was ready, its gross miscalculations made it practically useless. Apparently other plans were elaborated from 1963 and 1964 but never really enforced. A medium-range plan for 1962–65 was also drawn up with the aid of Polish and Soviet planners, but the lack of sophisticated knowledge of the economy and of clear economic directives from the leadership made that plan a theoretical study divorced from reality and impeded its practical usage. Other reasons contributed to the failure of planning in this stage. The collectivization was too wide and rapid; hence, millions of economic microrelations were destroyed at once, breaking the automatic mechanisms of the market when the state was not ready to take over these functions. The new central ministries and agencies lacked coordination among themselves, were hastily organized and staffed with inexperienced personnel, and operated in a freewheeling manner with no control procedures. Economic decisions were taken by the political leadership without consultation with JUCEPLAN, which resulted in serious inconsistencies. No investment plan existed, investment decisions were not coordinated but made in an arbitrary manner lacking mechanisms to assure their efficiency; the result was poor capital productivity. Land collectivization and the *acopio* system dislocated the flow of supplies from the countryside to the towns. Due to lack of information or managerial control, agricultural products badly needed in the cities were lost in the ground or, after being harvested, spoiled because of unavailability of transportation. Because of price rigidity, many state stores did not reduce prices and lost perishable goods. Moreover, irrational prices discouraged private farmers from producing the badly needed crops.

. . . In view of the above explained problems, it was a miracle that economic growth continued in 1961. The main reason behind this success was an exceptionally good sugar harvest, conducted in the first four months of the year, when the full impact of collectivization and administrative reform had not taken place. But in the next two years, the situation rapidly deteriorated, resulting in one of the worst recessions of the revolution. In the sugar sector, reduction of the cultivated area of sugarcane (down 25 percent over 1958), scarcity of professional sugarcane cutters (who had shifted to easier jobs), and disorganization created by administrative changes and the new state farm structure had a heavy toll on sugar output, which in 1963 reached the lowest level under the revolution. At the same time several key agricultural products (for example, tobacco, coffee, beans, and tubers) suffered output declines; hence, in 1963 agricultural output was 23 percent below 1959. Cuban officials had predicted that by 1965 Cuba would lead Latin America in per capita output of steel, cement, tractors, electricity, and refined petroleum. By 1963 Cuba was neither producing steel nor tractors, and its overall output of cement, electricity, and most important manufactures (such as cigars and beer) was below the 1961 level. Furthermore, the output of minerals (except for nickel) in 1963 was below the 1957 level. Contributing to this economic failure were lack of spare parts—most Cuban factories were still U.S. made—the exodus of U.S. and Cuban industrial managers and technicians, and the poor planning for the installment and integration of the newly bought factories.

Decreasing revenues from the sugar sector created a bottleneck in the ambitious program of industrialization. The decline of production of the principal exports (sugar, minerals, and tobacco) induced a cumulative trade deficit of more than half a billion pesos in 1962–63. The USSR provided credits to back up the deficits, but this aid rapidly increased Cuba's foreign debt. In 1962 almost 83 percent of Cuban trade was with socialist countries—almost one half with the USSR, which held 80 percent of the island's trade deficit. Cuba achieved full economic independence from the United States only to become dependent on the USSR. It is true that the latter did not have direct investment in Cuba, but still the island could not survive without the vital Soviet pipeline of oil, credit, weapons, and a myriad of other imports.

By 1963 open unemployment in Cuba had probably been cut to one half the prerevolutionary rate, but this was achieved by transforming most of the open unemployment into underemployment. Such a shift meant solving in the short run the social problem but spreading the economic costs to all the population and negatively affecting growth. In state farms, workers enjoyed guaranteed jobs and minimum wages the year around, but their productivity was one half that of the private farmers. Industrial mergers and shutdowns should have generated unemployment but instead of being dismissed, unnecessary workers remained on the enterprise payroll waiting for retraining. The tertiary sector became hypertrophied with the expansion of the bureaucracy, social services, the armed forces, and internal security. An artificial manpower deficit appeared in 1962 in the main crops, particularly sugar. To cope with it, the government resorted to mobilization of "voluntary" unpaid labor trying to transfer the urban labor surplus to the countryside. In many cases, however, the cost of mobilizing the inexperienced volunteers was higher than the value of the product created by them. The hope was to employ productively the urban sector in the new industries, but in spite of overstaffing, not much of the force was absorbed because the industrial sector was small.

The increase in demand for consumer goods and the stagnation or decline in their supply resulted in a widening gap. In a market economy, such an unbalance would have corrected itself automatically through inflationary price increases; the Cuban government, however, chose the egalitarian path and, trying to protect the poorest sector of the population, froze prices and imposed rationing. The black market soon appeared, and the resulting high prices served to discriminate against the lowest income brackets, who could not afford the high prices that realistically reflected the underlying forces of supply and demand. Income distribution probably became more equal with the elimination of the middle-sized private farmer and the introduction of *acopio*, which operated like a tax on private farmers most of which had an income above the national average. On the other hand, the deterioration of the economy impeded the expansion of social services (particularly housing), which received lower proportions of both state investment and the budget than in the early years of the revolution. The quality of educational and medical services suffered because of the emigration of about one half of the physicians and the majority of university professors.

In this stage, the decline in sugar revenue provoked a serious economic crisis in 1962–63. Priority was given to diversification but without significant increases in nonsugar output and with the negative result of expanding trade deficits and declining growth rates. Economic independence from the United States was consolidated at the cost of worsening dependence on the USSR.

Open unemployment was significantly cut and the emphasis in equality in distribution continued, but these achievements had an adverse effect on productivity and growth.

The Debate over and Test of Alternative Socialist Economic Models, 1964–66

The failure of the Stalinist model of economic organization and development strategy in Cuba prompted that country's leadership to question whether another model was more appropriate for an insular, plantation economy. As a result, it was decided to postpone heavy industrialization and return to sugar as the engine for development. Accompanying this change in development strategy was a lively ideological debate between two alternative models of economic organization: Mao-Guevarism and Libermanism.

Ernesto "Che" Guevara and a group of devoted followers, indirectly influenced by War Communism (tried in the USSR in 1918–20) and more directly by the Maoist Great Leap Forward (applied in China in 1958–60), endorsed an idealistic line of thought contrary to the conventional Soviet doctrine of the 1960s. Guevara believed that "subjective conditions" (ideas, consciousness, willingness; all belonging to the superstructure in Marxist terms) could decisively influence "objective conditions," that is, the material base, the forces of production, the structure which in the conventional interpretation of Marxism determines the superstructure. Guevara and others argued that the successful development of consciousness ahead of the material-base development could enable a country to skip the transitional, socialist stage between capitalism and communism or to build socialism and communism simultaneously. Two sets of actions were proposed to achieve that end: In the material realm the basic objective was the total elimination of the market or the law of supply and demand. This was to be achieved through the following measures: full collectivization of all means of production; a highly centralized mathematical-physical planning apparatus; the organization of state enterprises as simple branches of a central enterprise (agency, ministry); central financing of all state enterprises through the state budget (the so-called budgetary financing based on nonrepayable, interest-free grants with transfer of all enterprise profits to the state, cancellation of any resulting deficits, and allocation of state investment disregarding enterprise profitability); elimination of mercantile relations among state enterprises (selling and buying using money were substituted by simple accounting transactions); gradual eradication of money (limited only as a unit for accounting purposes but not as a means for assessing profitability); steady downplaying of economic or material incentives (for example, wage differentials, production bonuses, overtime payments, awards in kind); and state physical allocation and pricing of consumer goods to substitute for the law of supply and demand. In the ideal realm, economic incentives to assure productivity, quality, investment efficiency, and reduction in costs should be largely replaced by raising the consciousness of managers and workers. Therefore, Guevara's model, to be successful, had to create a New Man who, contrary to the economic man, would be unselfish, frugal, egalitarian, motivated not by greed but by patriotism and solidarity, and who would give his maximum labor effort to the collective and receive from it the basics to satisfy his needs. This ideal human being would be the product of mass consciousness-raising through education, mobilization, unpaid voluntary labor, moral incentives (for example, banners, medals won in fraternal competition), and the gradual expansion of state-provided free social services. If conducted simultaneously, the two sets of actions (in the material and ideal realms) would be reinforcing rather than conflicting and result in economic and consciousness development.

Confronting Guevara was a moderate, pragmatist group led by the economist Carlos Rafael Rodríguez (then Director of INRA) and composed mostly of members of the prerevolutionary pro-Soviet Communist party. This group was indirectly influenced by "market socialism"—the application of selected market mechanisms within the framework of a socialist economy. That model had influenced economic reform in Eastern Europe and eventually the Russian economist E. G. Liberman's program of economic reform, which had been experimented with in the USSR by Khrushchev in the early 1960s and moderately implemented by Brezhnev-Kosygin since 1965 to revive the sluggish Soviet economy. Rodríguez's group, sticking to the Soviet interpretation of Marxism, argued that subjective conditions cannot ignore objective conditions, that a socialist country cannot go farther than its structure allows it to go, that the material base has to be developed first and will, in turn, raise consciousness, and that it is impossible to skip the transitional—socialistic—stage between capitalism and full communism. In the necessary transitional stage, there will be traits of the capitalist past and some features of the communist future. It would not be possible in this stage to eliminate the law of supply and demand and hence some market mechanisms should be used (for example, money, profit, interest, and differential rent). Foreign supporters of this group, including René Dumont and Charles Bettelheim, were against excessive collectivization, particularly in agriculture, small retail trade, and personal services, and in favor of small individual farms and middle-sized private cooperatives rather than gigantic state farms. The Cuban group endorsed central planning but coupled it with cybernetic and input-output techniques, economic accounting, and market mechanisms. Local enterprises would have much more autonomy than in the Guevarist approach in hiring and dismissing labor, making investment decisions, and so forth, and they could buy and sell among themselves using money as a means of exchange. This group was against budgetary financing and instead advocated "self-financing": State enterprises would be responsible for their profits and losses; receive repayable loans with due interest from the banking system, which would exert supervision through monetary calculation; enterprises would retain part of their profit for reinvestment and distribution and would face closing if incapable of eliminating persistent deficits. Finally, to foster labor productivity, the group advocated material rather than moral incentives in the transitional stage and the need of work quotas connected with wages. The work quotas would fix the output to be produced by a worker in a given time period and fulfillment of it would result in a full wage, but nonfulfillment meant a proportional wage cut. This group believed that to ignore the law of supply and demand and cut down material incentives would have a negative effect on production and the development of the material base.

. . . The two models operated at the same time in different sectors of the Cuban economy, although the Libermanist model was adulterated with such features of the Mao-Guevarist model as covering enterprise deficits with budgetary grants. The Libermanist model was tried in one third of Cuban enterprises, mostly agriculture and domestic and foreign trade; the Mao-Guevarist model operated in two thirds of the state sector, primarily in industry. Guevara's centralistic model could work in the concentrated small industrial sector in which labor is skilled and its output relatively easy to check. But in agriculture, there are natural factors impossible to predict and control, and production is dispersed and in the hands of hundreds of thousands of unskilled workers and peasants whose output is difficult to monitor. The Cuban economy is essentially agrarian and depends heavily on foreign trade. Market mechanisms seemed more appropriate to agriculture and foreign trade, and in the latter sector Cuban officials faced the real outside world of internationally set market prices, tough competition based on costs, and the need for foreign exchange. Each of the two groups also controlled the key financing institution akin to its respective model; the Guevarists had the Ministry of Finance, which was in charge of the budget and capital grants; Rodríguez's group had the National Bank, the traditional dispenser of loans to be repaid with interest.

This stage of the revolution seemed to be mainly concerned with the shift in development strategy, and few significant decisions were made on national economic organization. Collectivization did not advance. While both sides in the debate advocated a central plan, no annual plans were enforced nor was there discussion or preparation for a 1966–70 medium-range plan. Instead, sectorial plans began to proliferate, the first and most important one in the sugar industry. Capital accumulation increased moderately. Budgetary finance ruled in two thirds of the economy and self-finance (often adulterated) prevailed in the rest. Perhaps the only nationally important step was the introduction of the Soviet system of work quotas and wage scales, which was quite advanced by the end of 1965.

. . . Economic growth resumed in 1964–65 mainly as a result of fair sugar harvests and higher sugar prices in the international market, but also probably helped by better incentives in agriculture, increases in labor productivity through work quotas and economic incentives, and pay-off of capital accumulation with slightly improved efficiency in investment allocation and use. The goal of diversification suffered a severe blow with the return to sugar. The leadership attempted to justify and embellish that development strategy with the following rationale: The return to sugar was temporary and eventually would generate the necessary impetus for industrialization; sugar output would increase gradually in the 1960s to reach record crops that would allow a significant improvement in living standards in the 1970s; Cuba was suited to produce sugar cheaper than the USSR and other developed socialist countries, which in turn could produce machinery cheaper than Cuba; exchange of sugar for machinery and manufactures would result in mutual benefit because the USSR and other socialist countries would not take advantage of their privileged position in their trade with Cuba. In this spirit Cuba and the USSR signed a five-year economic and trade agreement (1965–70) in which the latter committed to increase imports of Cuban sugar by 150 percent and at a higher price than the Soviets had paid before. Just prior to that trade pact, though, market conditions favored trade with nonsocialist countries. The increase in sugar prices in the international market augmented the value of Cuban exports, particularly in 1964, but imports escalated reaching new records and trade deficits continued. Interestingly in this stage Cuba had a valued product (sugar) to trade with market economies, and as a result trade with socialist countries declined, reaching a low ebb in 1964 when the sugar price was high. This economic development seemed to call into question the assumption that trade with socialist countries was more advantageous than trade with market countries. In mid-1964 the Organization of American States imposed a collective embargo on Cuba applied by all members except Mexico; hence, most Cuban trade with market economies in this stage was with Europe and Japan.

Open unemployment was further reduced in this stage using the same approach as in the previous stage. But postponement of the industrialization plan ended the expectation that the urban labor surplus would become productively employed in the industrial sector. On the other hand, the return to agriculture boosted the demand for manpower in the countryside. The government attempted to detect the labor surplus through the application of work quotas, to cut down the surplus with a campaign to reduce the bureaucracy by relocating redundant workers, and to transfer the urban surplus to the countryside by compulsory military service, mobilization of voluntary labor, restrictions of labor mobility, and selective incentives in the countryside rather than in the cities. Concerning distribution, the national establishment of wage scales set the basis for equal wage for equal work within the state sector. But the resilient forces of the market impeded the total elimination of old wages when they were higher than the new wages and were needed to keep technicians in vital sectors of the economy. Those who performed well or gave an extra effort were rewarded with production bonuses and overtime payments. The rising income of private farmers also contributed to some income inequalities.

In this stage, to save the economy from the 1962–63 crises, growth was emphasized with fair results, particularly in 1964 with the aid of higher sugar prices. This was achieved, however, at the cost of sacrificing industrialization and returning to sugar, a shift in strategy justified on theoretical and long-term grounds. Dependence on the USSR continued, and yet trade partner concentration diminished somewhat, aided by higher sugar prices. Full employment and distribution continued to be emphasized but slightly subordinated to productivity and growth.

The Adoption and Radicalization of the Mao-Guevarist Model, 1966–70

The discussion and confrontation between two competing economic ideologies and organization models could not last too long. For three years, Fidel Castro abstained from open participation in the controversy, but by the end of 1965 the leaders of the two groups were no longer in command. Guevara resigned as minister of industry and left Cuba to lead the revolution in South America, where he eventually met death; Rodríguez resigned as director of INRA but cleverly stayed in Cuba as a minister without portfolio. In the summer of 1966, Fidel Castro announced the new directions in economic organization—the Mao-Guevarist approach embellished with Fidelista features.

. . . Collectivization was reactivated in agriculture by taking family plots away from state farmers, state buying of private farms, expansion of the *acopio,* and banning sales from the farmers to individuals. In the spring of 1968 collectivization climaxed with the launching of the "Revolutionary Offensive." The remainder of the nonagricultural private sector passed to state control— 56,000 small businesses such as street food outlets, consumer service shops, restaurants and bars, repair outfits, handicraft shops, even street vendors. The most important economic decisions were not grounded in a "scientific and objective" central planning apparatus capable of achieving some kind of optimality in resource allocation or development, rather those decisions were made by the political leadership. By the end of 1966, the annual plan lost its directive nature and was reduced to a tool for internal calculation (actually the plan was probably dropped altogether in the second half of the 1960s) and JUCEPLAN was limited to research and the logistic functions of assuring the needed inputs to meet the output targets fixed by the political leadership and of solving eventual discrepancies. In place of medium-range and annual macroplans, medium-range miniplans were developed for specific sectors (for example, sugar, cattle raising, fishing, and electricity). The official reason for such an approach to planning was that Cuba lacked both statistics and cadres for highly abstract exercises and was better off concentrating its scarce resources on the vital sectors of the economy. Furthermore, special and extra plans were also introduced in a case-by-case manner by the leadership to tackle urgent economic problems. The administration of those plans was usually entrusted to loyal revolutionaries and the allocation of resources to the plans done by "superior order," outside of JUCEPLAN. This resulted in the reduction of resource allocation made to central projects already in operation but ranked lower in priority than the special or extra plans. Incompatibilities between central and special plans were resolved in an arbitrary manner by the political leadership as conflicts arose. . . .

Capital accumulation was emphasized over consumption, which resulted in increasing investment ratios and stagnating or declining consumption per capita. But capital productivity sharply declined because neither the interest rate nor the Soviet "coefficient of relative effectiveness"—a formula to evaluate efficiency among alternative investment projects based on the time required to pay them off—were used. Labor productivity also fell due to the negligence of work quotas, its disconnection with wage scales, the suppression of production bonuses, and the gigantic labor mobilization that disregarded costs. Interest charges on loans to private farmers and all personal taxes were eliminated. Monetary currency was not reduced but substantially increased; hence, with fewer consumer goods available, money began to lose value as a means of exchange and incentive for the labor force. Material incentives were dramatically curtailed or eliminated. The ultimate goal was proclaimed: Eradication of wage differentials (thus an engineer and a sugarcane cutter would eventually earn the same wage) and gradual application of the communist principle of distribution according to needs instead of the socialist principle of distribution according to work. In theory, the so-called New Man was supposed to substitute for both automatic market mechanisms and central planning commands. Contrary to expectations, the old "economic man" was not transformed and economic chaos ensued.

The absence of a central plan and of coordination among special plans provoked shortages in inputs, bottlenecks, shutdowns, and proliferation of uncompleted projects. Advances in certain sectors were offset by declines in others. . . . The lack of maintenance and the rejection of depreciation costs resulted in the deterioration of installation and equipment, with eventual slowdown or shutdown, for example, electricity blackouts and water supply shortages. Finally, relaxed maintenance controls and standards plus either the lack of labor or its deficiencies in knowledge and expertise resulted in breakdowns of costly equipment.

. . . The absence of mechanisms to use efficiently the significant increase in capital investment and labor mobilization resulted in significant waste of material and human resources. Hence, the economy deteriorated, declining in terms of per capita growth rates. Grandiose plans in the sugar sector set increasing output targets in 1965–70 to reach 10 million tons of sugar at the end of the period and twice that target for the 1970s. But the sugar plan was fulfilled only in its first year; total accumulated output during the six years was 25 percent below the goal. The 1970 sugar harvest set a historical output record, but it still was 15 percent short of the target. Furthermore, this was a Pyrrhic victory achieved by depleting resources from other sectors of the economy, which in turn suffered output declines offsetting the increase in sugar output. The fiasco of the sugar plan brought failure to both the developing strategy and model of organization nurtured in the second half of the 1960s. Huge sugar crops in the 1970s were expected to generate the necessary resources to reanudate the industrialization effort, repay the enormous debt to the USSR, and substantially increase the standards of living of the population. Actually, industrial production with few exceptions peaked in 1965-67 and thereafter declined. Trade with the USSR set a record of 56 percent in 1967, and trade deficits also increased setting a record of more than half a billion pesos in 1969. The USSR held 80 percent of such deficit, and the main cause was that Cuba failed to deliver the committed sugar exports to the USSR. From 1966 to 1969, the cumulative deficit in sugar deliveries was about 10 million tons. In spite of the increasing dependency upon the Soviet Union in this stage, Cuba confronted the latter in several crucial areas, including an opposite model of economic organization and the claim that the island was ahead of the USSR in approaching full communism. The Soviets attempted to retaliate against the irritant and costly Cuban economic experiment by reducing the supply of oil to the island in 1968. The Cubans initially responded with open criticism of this move and put several members of the prerevolutionary Communist party on trial; soon, however, they had to accept economic reality and endorsed the Soviet invasion of Czechoslovakia in the summer of 1968.

Full employment was practically achieved in 1970, but studies conducted in 1968 in state enterprises showed that in many of them from one fourth to one half of the workday was wasted. Unemployment had been disguised but not significantly reduced. To harvest the gigantic sugar crop in 1970, the government stepped up labor mobilization; however, the inefficiency and high economic cost of the volunteers actually contributed to the failure of the crop. Labor absenteeism increased sharply in this stage—reaching 20 percent of the labor force after the 1970 harvest was over—because of lack of incentives, disenchantment over the failure of the sugar crop, and ability to stay home and still be able to buy the scarce goods available with money already earned. Egalitarianism was advanced by the reduction in wage differentials, the elimination of production bonuses and overtime payments, the selective expansion of free social services (to burials, public phone calls, sports), and the decline in value of money. But the black market boomed in 1969-70 in spite of government restrictions.

Although growth was a priority goal in this stage—as the policy in favor of investment at the cost of consumption testified—in practice inefficiency and mismanagement provoked grave economic decline and dislocation. Diversification continued to be sacrificed and greater emphasis put on sugar, with the hope of generating the resources for both economic independence and industrialization in the long run, but the failure of the sugar plan destroyed those expectations. Economic dependency persisted, while full employment and egalitarianism were pushed forward at a significant economic cost for the nation.

The Shift to the Soviet Economic Reform Model, 1971 on

The failure of both the development strategy and model of economic organization tried in 1966–70, along with the subsequent economic dislocation, labor absenteeism, and spiraling foreign debt (combined with other political and international factors), forced the Cuban leadership to a significant shift in the 1970s. They entered into a new mature and pragmatic stage usually referred to as the "Institutionalization of the Revolution." In several speeches delivered in the 1970s, Castro criticized the previous stage as idealistic, utopian, and unreal. He explained the mistakes committed in the following manner: Although the Cubans lacked good economists, scientists, and theoreticians to make a significant contribution to the construction of socialism, they tried to invent a new approach. In doing so they showed contempt for the experiences of other more advanced socialist countries, experience which could have helped them considerably. The Cuban approach (Mao-Guevarism) was highly idealistic, minimized actual serious difficulties, and pretended that willingness could overcome the lack of objective conditions. The leadership was guilty of idealism in assuming that the attitude of a conscious minority was typical of the overall society, and this misconception proved detrimental to the economy. Now it is realized that it is easier to change the economic structure than man's consciousness, that the latter has a long way to go, and that material-base development should precede efforts to raise the consciousness of society. It is also currently accepted that the transitional stage between capitalism and communism cannot be skipped: It was folly to believe that the Cuban society could leave capitalism and enter into, in one bound, a society in which everyone would behave in an ethical and moral manner. It is hence accepted that currently Cuba is only building the foundations of socialism while the USSR has gone beyond full socialism and is building the foundations of communism. In the future Cuba should advance slowly, carefully, and realistically; if it tries to go farther than possible, it will soon be forced to retreat. Measures of a Communist character that were previously put into effect should be reconsidered: When it might have seemed as though we were drawing nearer to communistic forms of production and distribution, we were actually pulling away from the methods proper to the stage of building the foundations of socialism.

. . . In the new stage, Cubans have gradually introduced the model of economic reform currently in force in the USSR. Collectivization has slowly advanced in agriculture through gradual transformation of private farms into cooperatives (like Soviet *kolkhoz*) and to a lesser extent into state farms.

On the other hand, private farmers have been authorized to sell their surplus to individuals in free peasant markets, at prices set by supply and demand. State prices for *acopio* have been increased also. In addition, there is a trend to decollectivize such individual services as repairs and minor construction; these services have to be provided under state license and usually are performed outside the regular work schedule and without paid employees.

Central planning has been reinstated as the main tool in the economy, and lower-level plans like mini, sectorial, and special are subordinated to the former. The 1970s saw annual macro plans since 1973; a global economic model for 1973–75; the first five-year plan (1976–80); and the preparation of the second five-year plan (1981–85) and a twenty-year development and forecast plan (1980–2000). . . . A new Soviet-style System of Economic Management and Planning (SDPE) was gradually introduced in the second half of the 1970s, should be completed in 1980, and is expected to be in full operation in the mid-1980s. The SDPE takes into account the law of supply and demand and the need of monetary and mercantile relations in the transitional stage. To improve efficiency in the allocation and utilization of capital and human and material resources, the new economic system uses market instruments such as credit, interest, rational prices, budgets, monetary controls, and taxes. State enterprises have been decentralized—from 300 in 1968 to less than 3,000 in 1979—and enjoy more independence to hire and dismiss labor, request loans, and make investment decisions. Along with this they are held responsible to balance revenue with expenses and generate a profit. The efficiency of Cuban enterprises is measured by a set of indicators with profit as the main one and including others such as output, quality, cost, and productivity. The price fixed for enterprises and wholesalers includes production costs (labor, capital amortization and interest, and depreciation) and a profit, out of which the enterprise has to pay a sort of corporation tax and a social security tax and develop an economic incentive fund for workers. Retail prices are expected to include, in addition, a sales tax which will be aimed at balancing supply and demand as well as generating revenue for the state. In the initial model, part of the enterprise revenue went to a development fund for self-expansion, but this has been temporarily discarded and expansion is to be decided centrally. The state budget was reintroduced in 1978, after being discarded for almost a decade, and economic calculation began also in that year. The budgetary system of finance has been largely substituted by self-finance: the state provides to its enterprises and farms, and to private cooperatives and farms, repayable loans with interest ranging from 4 to 12 percent.

The Soviet system of work quotas and wage scales, briefly tried in 1964–65, has been gradually reintroduced to control and foster labor productivity. Material incentives have also been reintroduced, including wage differentials which take skills and special effort into account, bonuses for fulfilling and

over-fulfilling work quotas, payments for overtime, priorities in the allocation of
housing and durable consumer goods, and vacations according to certain skills
and productivity. The size of the economic incentive fund, introduced in 1979 in
7 percent of the enterprises, is determined by enterprise profitability. It is partly
used to provide economic rewards for its workers—both collectively (for example, enterprise restaurants and day-care centers) and to individuals (for example, cash bonuses). In order for these new incentives to be effective, "socialist
inflation," which is monetary surplus, has been reduced by curtailing demand
through higher prices and increasing supply of consumer goods.

    . . . Economic growth, so neglected in 1966–70, took first priority in the
1970s. The measures introduced to strengthen capital and labor productivity,
as well as the more rational approach in planning and financing, combined
with booming sugar prices in the international market resulted in impressive
rates of growth in 1971–75. But the decline in sugar prices, compounded by
difficulties in implementing the new model of economic organization and by
agricultural plagues and other problems, provoked a slowdown in economic
growth in 1976–80. The economic strategy of the 1970s continued to be
fundamentally based on sugar but with a more balanced and rational approach. The government sought to produce as much sugar as possible with the
material and human resources allocated to the sugar sector without depleting
resources from other economic sectors and by relying on technology—including mechanization of cane cutting and modernization of mills—rather than on
labor mobilization. Sugar harvests declined in 1971–75, but this loss was more
than compensated by the booming sugar prices; the latter resulted in increased
value of exports which, paradoxically, worsened the dependency on sugar with
a record high in 1975. Harvests in 1976–79 increased in volume although not
in value. Industrial output rapidly recuperated in the first half of the 1970s,
although it leveled off in the second half of the decade. Performance of nonsugar agriculture, with some exceptions, was not as good as in industry but
certainly better than during the Mao-Guevarist experiment. Helped by the
favorable conditions in the sugar market, Cuba gradually reversed her balance
of trade from a deficit of half a billion pesos in 1971 to a small surplus in
1974—the first in 15 years. Yet decaying sugar prices built up the deficit again
in 1975–78. With high sugar prices in the international market, Cuban trade
moved away from socialist to market economies in 1974–75, but declining
international sugar prices and Soviet subsidies to Cuban sugar reversed the
trend again since 1976. Cuba entered COMECON in 1972 and signed trade
agreements with the USSR for 1973–75 and 1976–80, actions which reinforced
her dependency with the socialist camp. In 1972 the enormous debt with the
USSR was postponed (and interest cancelled) until 1986 thus giving Cuba a
most needed break. But new Soviet credits both to cover trade deficits and for
development kept building up the debt in the 1970s reaching probably more
than six billion pesos in 1975, for the highest per capita debt in Latin America.

With the shift in economic model in the 1970s, both employment and distribution were negatively affected. It was officially accepted that the previous policy of subsidized employment and labor mobilization had resulted in low labor productivity and a burden for the economy. The new model of economic organization stresses efficiency and gives more power to enterprise managers for dismissals, while the application of work quotas releases surplus labor from state enterprises, hence unemployment pockets have appeared. Voluntary labor is now only used when its net productivity can be proved beforehand. Previous emphasis on egalitarianism came also under official criticism as an idealistic mistake. The reintroduction of material incentives, the increasing use of prices, the halt or curtailment of some free social services, and the restoration of the value of money as a buying tool resulted in a retrenchment in egalitarianism and some stratification.

Facing economic chaos and danger to the survival of the revolution at the end of the 1960s, the Cuban leadership dramatically rearranged goal priorities in the 1970s. Economic growth became the most important goal to which the others were subordinated. Diversification continued to be sacrificed and external economic dependence increased. The most significant change, though, was that adoption of policies which stressed efficiency and growth resulted in the downgrading of full employment and egalitarianism.

10. Man and Socialism in Cuba*

BY ERNESTO "CHE" GUEVARA
Translated by Margarita Zimmerman

> *Ernesto "Che" Guevara was born in Argentina and joined Fidel Castro's guerrilla army in Mexico in 1955. He was one of the foremost leaders of the revolutionary government until 1965, when he left Cuba to carry on armed struggle first in Africa and later in Bolivia. He was captured and killed by the Bolivian army in 1967.*

I shall now attempt to define the individual, the actor in this strange and moving drama that is the building of socialism, in his twofold existence as a unique being and a member of the community.

I believe that the simplest approach is to recognize his unmade quality. He is an unfinished product. The flaws of the past are translated into the present in the individual consciousness, and constant efforts must be made to eradicate

*Excerpted from Ernesto "Che" Guevara, "Man and Socialism in Cuba," in Bertram Silverman, ed., *Man and Socialism in Cuba: The Great Debate* (New York: Atheneum, 1973), pp. 337–54. Letter to Carlos Quijano, editor-publisher of the Uruguayan weekly *Marcha*, written early in 1965, then published in Cuba as "El Socialismo y el Hombre en Cuba" (Havana, Ediciones R.). Official government translation.

them. The process is twofold: On the one hand, society acts on the individual by means of direct and indirect education, while on the other hand, the individual undergoes a conscious phase of self-education.

The new society in process of formation has to compete very hard with the past. This makes itself not only in the individual consciousness, weighed down by the residues of an education and an upbringing systematically oriented toward the isolation of the individual, but also by the very nature of this transition period, with the persistence of commodity relations. The commodity is the economic cell of capitalist society: As long as it exists, its effects will make themselves felt in the organization of production and therefore in man's consciousness.

Marx's scheme conceived of the transition period as the result of the explosive transformation of the capitalist system torn apart by its inner contradictions: Subsequent reality has shown how some countries, the weak limbs, detach themselves from the imperialist tree, a phenomenon foreseen by Lenin. In those countries, capitalism has developed sufficiently to make its effects felt on the people in one way or another, but it is not its own inner contradictions that explode the system after exhausting all of its possibilities. The struggle for liberation against an external oppressor, the misery that has its origin in foreign causes such as war, whose consequences make the privileged classes fall upon the exploited, the liberation movements aimed at overthrowing neocolonial regimes, are the customary factors in this process. Conscious action does the rest.

In these countries, there still has not been achieved a complete education for the work of society, and wealth is far from being within the reach of the masses through the simple process of appropriation. Underdevelopment and the customary flight of capital to "civilized" countries make impossible a rapid change without sacrifices. There still remains a long stretch to be covered in the building of the economic base, and the temptation to follow the beaten paths of material interest as the lever of speedy development is very great.

There is a danger of not seeing the forest because of the trees. Pursuing the chimera of achieving socialism with the aid of the blunted weapons left to us by capitalism (the commodity as the economic cell, profitability, and individual material interest as levers, etc.), it is possible to come to a blind alley. And the arrival there comes about after covering a long distance where there are many crossroads and where it is difficult to realize just when the wrong turn was taken. Meanwhile, the adapted economic base has undermined the development of consciousness. To build communism, a new man must be created simultaneously with the material base.

That is why it is so important to choose correctly the instrument of mass mobilization. That instrument must be fundamentally of a moral character, without forgetting the correct use of material incentives, especially those of a social nature.

As I already said, in moments of extreme danger it is easy to activate moral incentives: To maintain their effectiveness, it is necessary to develop a consciousness in which values acquire new categories. Society as a whole must become a huge school. . . .

We can see the new man who begins to emerge in this period of the building of socialism. His image is as yet unfinished. In fact, it will never be finished, since the process advances parallel to the development of new economic forms. Discounting those whose lack of education makes them tend toward the solitary road, toward the satisfaction of their ambitions, there are others who, even within this new picture of overall advances, tend to march in isolation from the accompanying mass. What is important is that people become more aware every day of the need to incorporate themselves into society and of their own importance as motors of that society.

They no longer march in complete solitude along lost roads toward far-off longings. They follow their vanguard, composed of the party, of the most advanced workers, of the advanced men who move along bound to the masses and in close communion with them. The vanguards have their eyes on the future and its recompenses, but the latter are not envisioned as something individual; the reward is the new society in which human beings will have different characteristics: the society of Communist man.

The road is long and full of difficulties. At times the route strays off course, and it is necessary to retreat; at times a too rapid pace separates us from the masses; and on occasion the pace is slow, and we feel on our necks the breath of those who follow at our heels. Our ambition as revolutionaries makes us try to move forward as far as possible, opening up the way before us, but we know that must be reinforced by the mass, while the mass will be able to advance more rapidly if we encourage it by our example.

. . . To achieve total success, all of this involves the necessity of a series of mechanisms, the revolutionary institutions. The concept of institutionalization fits in with the images of the multitudes marching toward the future as that of a harmonic unit of canals, steps, and well-oiled apparatuses that make the march possible, that permit the natural selection of those who are destined to march in the vanguard and who dispense rewards and punishments to those who fulfill their duty or act against the society under construction.

The institutionality of the revolution has still not been achieved. We are seeking something new that will allow a perfect identification between the government and the community as a whole, adapted to the special conditions of the building of socialism and avoiding to the utmost the commonplaces of bourgeois democracy transplanted to the society in formation (such as legislative houses, for example). Some experiments have been carried out with the aim of gradually creating the institutionalization of the revolution, but without too much hurry. We have been greatly restrained by the fear that any formal aspect might make us lose sight of the ultimate and most important revolutionary aspiration: to see man freed from alienation.

Notwithstanding the lack of institutions, which must be overcome gradually, the masses now make history as a conscious aggregate of individuals who struggle for the same cause. In spite of the apparent standardization of man in socialism, he is more complete; his possibilities for expressing himself and making himself heard in the social apparatus are infinitely greater in spite of the lack of a perfect mechanism to do so.

It is still necessary to accentuate his conscious—individual and collective—participation in all the mechanisms of direction and production, and associate it with the idea of the need for technical and ideological education so that the individual will realize that these processes are closely interdependent and their advances are parallel. He will thus achieve total awareness of his social being, which is equivalent to his full realization as a human being, having broken the chains of alienation.

This will be translated concretely into the reappropriation of his nature through freed work and the expression of his own human condition in culture and art.

In order for it to develop in culture, work must acquire a new condition; man as commodity ceases to exist, and a system is established that grants a quota for the fulfillment of social duty. The means of production belong to society, and the machine is only the front line where duty is performed. Man begins to free his thought from the bothersome fact that presupposed the need to satisfy his animal needs by working. He begins to see himself portrayed in his work and to understand its human magnitude through the created object, through the work carried out. This no longer involves leaving a part of his being in the form of labor power sold, which no longer belongs to him; rather it signifies an emanation from himself, a contribution to the life of society in which he is reflected, the fulfillment of his social duty.

We are doing everything possible to give work this new category of social duty and to join it to the development of technology, on the one hand, which will provide the conditions for greater freedom, and to voluntary work on the other, based on the Marxist concept that man truly achieves his full human condition when he produces without being compelled by the physical necessity of selling himself as a commodity.

It is clear that work still has coercive aspects even when it is voluntary: Man has still not transformed all the coercion surrounding him into conditioned reflexes of a social nature, and in many cases he still produces under the pressure of the environment. (Fidel calls this moral compulsion.) He is still to achieve complete spiritual recreation in the presence of his own work—without the direct pressure of the social environment but bound to it by new habits. That will be communism.

. . . I should now like to explain the role played by the personality, the man as the individual who leads the masses that make history. This is our experience and not a recipe.

Fidel gave impulse to the revolution in its first years. He has always given it leadership and set the tone, but there is a good group of revolutionaries developing in the same direction as Fidel and a large mass that follows its leaders because it has faith in them. It has faith in them because these leaders have known how to interpret the longings of the masses.

It is not a question of how many kilograms of meat are eaten or how many pretty imported things can be bought with present wages. It is rather that the individual feels greater fulfillment, that he has greater inner wealth and many more responsibilities. In our country, the individual knows that the glorious period in which it has fallen to him to live is one of sacrifice; he is familiar with sacrifice.

. . . Let me say, with the risk of appearing ridiculous, that the true revolutionary is guided by strong feelings of love. It is impossible to think of an authentic revolutionary without this quality. This is perhaps one of the great dramas of a leader; he must combine an impassioned spirit with a cold mind and make painful decisions without flinching. Our vanguard revolutionaries must idealize their love for the people, for the most hallowed causes, and make it one and indivisible. They cannot descend, with small doses of daily affection, to the terrain where ordinary men put their love into practice.

The leaders of the revolution have children who do not learn to call their father with their first faltering words; they have wives who must be part of the general sacrifice of their lives to carry the revolution to its destination; their friends are strictly limited to their comrades in revolution. There is no life outside the revolution.

In these conditions the revolutionary leaders must have a large dose of humanity, a large dose of a sense of justice and truth, to avoid falling into dogmatic extremes, into cold scholasticism, into isolation from the masses. They must struggle every day so that their love of living humanity is transformed into concrete deeds, into acts that will serve as an example, as a mobilizing factor.

. . . Thus we go forward. Fidel is at the head of the immense column—we are neither ashamed nor afraid to say so—followed by the best party cadres, and right after them, so close that their great strength is felt, come the people as a whole, a solid bulk of individualities moving toward a common aim—individuals who have achieved the awareness of what must be done; men who struggle to leave the domain of necessity and enter that of freedom.

That immense multitude is ordering itself; its order responds to an awareness of the need for order; it is no longer a dispersed force, divisible in thousands of fractions shot into space like the fragments of a grenade, trying by any and all means, in a fierce struggle with their equals, to achieve a position that would give them support in the face of an uncertain future.

. . . Each and every one of us punctually pays his share of sacrifice, aware of being rewarded by the satisfaction of fulfilling our duty, aware of advancing with everyone toward the new human being who is to be glimpsed on the horizon.

Allow me to attempt to come to some conclusions:

We socialists are more free because we are more fulfilled. We are more fulfilled because we are more free.

The skeleton of our complete freedom is formed, but it lacks the protean substance and the draperies. We will create them.

Our freedom and its daily sustenance are the color of blood and swollen with sacrifice. . . .

Economic Transformation in the 1960s and 1970s

11. The Agrarian Revolution*

BY MEDEA BENJAMIN, JOSEPH COLLINS, AND MICHAEL SCOTT

> *Editors' Note: The Cuban government ended its experiment with free peasant markets in May 1986 on the grounds that it was producing serious social inequalities.*

During the days of the guerrilla war in the Sierra Maestra mountains, Fidel Castro and his rebel army gradually won the hearts and minds of the peasants. The rebels treated the peasants with respect and, unlike most armed groups, paid for all the food and supplies they used. Gradually the guerrilla army was transformed into a peasant army—by 1959, three fourths or more of the soldiers were peasants.[1]

Having lived among the peasants, the revolution's leaders were vividly aware of the enormous disparity between city and countryside. They knew that the majority of Cuba's peasants lived in isolated thatched-roof shacks with no electricity or running water, no land security, no schools, no medical facilities. They also knew that the average farmworker earned only 91 pesos a year, in contrast with the nationwide average income of 374 pesos.[2]

Once in power, the revolutionary government instituted a series of reforms designed to improve life in the countryside. All land rents were abolished.

*From Medea Benjamin, Joseph Collins, and Michael Scott, *No Free Lunch: Food and Revolution in Cuba Today* (San Francisco, CA: Institute for Food and Development Policy, 1984), pp. 150–65.

Tenant farmers, sharecroppers, and squatters were given title to the land they worked, along with guaranteed fixed prices for their produce and low-interest loans. Many seasonal workers were given full-time employment. Rural salaries were raised. People's stores were created to bring cheap consumer goods to the countryside. In 1961, the government initiated a massive literacy campaign, sending urban students to the countryside not only to teach reading and writing, but to gain an understanding and appreciation of rural life. For the first time, rural communities were provided with schools, clinics, and recreational and cultural activities. Teams of projectionists traveled to remote villages showing movies, free of charge, to people who had never seen a film. The documentary "Por Primera Vez" (For the First Time), which captured the faces of villagers watching their first movies, is vivid testimony to the revolution's efforts at improving the quality of rural life.

The Cuban peasant, previously downtrodden and abused, acquired a new status after the revolution. As Fidel said in a speech just after the promulgation of the agrarian reform, "From now on when a peasant goes to the city . . . no one will laugh at him, no one will make jokes about him, for the peasant is now a hero and will be treated with respect. From now on when a peasant goes to the city, no one will watch to see how he walks, how he eats, how he picks up a knife, what he buys, what color his wife's dress is. . . . Why? Because now that feeling of hostility against the peasant, . . . that timidity of the peasant who was always mistreated by the Rural Guard, by the big landowners, by the politicians . . . is gone forever."[3]

The revolution's leadership assumed that private individual farming would eventually disappear.[4] Many farmers, perhaps most, would move out of agriculture altogether. Others would join agricultural cooperatives, or sell their land to the state and take jobs on state farms. Both state farms and cooperatives (in that order) were thought to be superior to small private farms in terms of both productivity and the social benefits they could offer their workers. Ideologically, state farms were considered superior to cooperatives, since they were not privately owned and the wealth they generated benefited the public at large.

But paradoxically, by giving land titles to tenants, squatters, and sharecroppers, the agrarian reforms helped make small farmers more secure. Small farming represents virtually the only private sector that still exists in Cuba. Since Fidel Castro has personally and categorically promised that small farmers will never be forced to give up their land, the state finds itself in the awkward position of having to guarantee the existence of islands of small farmers in a sea of large state farms. A look at the evolution of state versus private agriculture should give us a better understanding of how this relationship stands today.

THE FIRST AGRARIAN REFORM

The revolutionary government instituted its far-reaching land reform law just five months after taking power. Symbolically, it was signed at the former headquarters of the rebel army in the Sierra Maestra. The maximum land area one person could own was set at 1,000 acres, with exceptions made for particularly productive farms. Land ownership was so concentrated that by expropriating twelve thousand large farms, the government gained control of 44 percent of farm and ranch land.[5] State farms became key to Cuban agriculture for both domestic and export production.

For those with too little land to make a living, a "vital minimum," defined as the amount of land needed to support a family of five, was set at 67 acres. Peasants with less were given that amount free, plus the right to buy another 100 acres.[6]

Whether they owned the land or not, farmers were still a minority of the rural population. Wage-earning farmworkers on large estates outnumbered them four to one. Most observers, both foreign and Cuban, assumed the government would divide the large estates among the laborers who had worked them. Traditional wisdom among socialist thinkers was that even if the eventual goal was to collectivize agriculture, the first step was to divide up the land among the workers, then at some later point encourage them to pool their resources and work together. In the Soviet Union, China, and all of Eastern Europe, land reform programs were all based on this principle of "land to the tiller."[7]

But the Cuban land reform did not divide up the large estates among the workers, converting them instead into state farms and cooperatives. Why? "I found upon the victory of the Revolution that the idea of land division still had a lot of currency," Fidel explained years later. "But I already understood by then that if you take, for example, a sugar plantation of 2,500 acres . . . and you divide it into 200 portions of 12.5 acres each, what will inevitably happen is that right away the new owners will cut the production of sugarcane in half in each plot, and they will begin to raise for their own consumption a whole series of crops for which in many cases the soil will not be adequate."[8] Castro believed dividing the land would lead to a decline in production, which would be disastrous for the whole country.

Castro offered the same explanation for not dividing up the large cattle ranches. During the guerrilla war, the rebels had confiscated herds and distributed them among the peasants. Within a few months, practically all the animals had been eaten. "The majority of the *campesinos* had killed their cows because they preferred the immediate benefit of being able to eat them to the longer-range value of having the milk," Castro explained. "This naturally fortified my conviction that the land of the *latifundistas* should not be divided."[9]

Cuba's leaders understood that circumstances in Cuba were different from those of other countries which carried out significant land-reform programs. The workers on large estates in Cuba were not small farmers who aspired to own their own land, but rather a rural proletariat whose main concerns were job security, better working conditions, and a higher standard of living. Thus the decision to create cooperatives rather than divide up the land did not encounter resistance from the farm workers.[10]

HOW WAS THE LAW IMPLEMENTED?

Even with the exemptions for particularly productive land, the agrarian reform law still called for the expropriation of half of Cuba's cultivated land. The National Agrarian Reform Institute (INRA) was to determine where to start and how fast to move.

INRA had to walk a thin line. If it moved too slowly, it would alienate the poor peasants and allow the rural elite more time to react—perhaps by sabotaging production. If INRA moved too fast, it would take on more land than it could administer properly and production would fall.

INRA's first moves were timid. In ten months, only six thousand small farmers received redistributed land. French agricultural economist Michel Gutelman noted that, with 150,000 small farmers to be dealt with, "At this rate, it would have taken twenty years" to complete the redistribution.[11] But as the large owners (both Cuban and American) began to actively oppose the reforms, INRA was forced to adopt a more radical position.

Since one fourth of the best land in Cuba was owned by U.S. companies, agrarian reform placed the Cuban government in direct conflict with U.S. interests and set into motion a series of moves and countermoves that eventually led to the Bay of Pigs invasion in April 1961. (Cubans themselves see the passage of the agrarian-reform law as "the beginning of the end" of Cuba-U.S. relations.)[12] With history moving at lightning speed, the legal text of the agrarian reform law was soon left behind. In fact, only one quarter of the land taken over was actually taken under the terms of the law itself. The majority came from the nationalization of U.S.-owned sugar mills and agricultural enterprises after the U.S. cut its sugar quota and from the confiscation of land owned by persons who left the country or engaged in efforts to bring down the revolutionary government after the Bay of Pigs invasion.[13]

Two years into the reform, nearly half Cuba's total land area had been affected.[14] More than 100,000 peasants—mostly tenants, sharecroppers, and squatters—had gained title to the land they worked. But having made the decision to keep the large estates intact, the big winner was the state, which now controlled 44 percent of the land.[15]

THE STATE SECTOR

Apart from the ranches, the rest of the state's land was converted into "cooperatives." The cooperatives set up by the first agrarian reform were more akin to state farms than to traditional self-administered cooperatives whose members receive a share of the profits. Cooperatives were accountable to INRA and had little autonomy. Production targets were set by INRA and produce was sold to the state purchasing agencies. The cooperatives selected their own coordinator, but the administrator was appointed by INRA, creating a two-tier power structure in which the appointed administrator had the upper hand over the elected coordinator.

Workers reportedly were not enthusiastic about the creation of cooperatives. Their experience as farmworkers left them ill-equipped to take on administrative responsibilities.[16] While their monthly wage was theoretically an advance on their share in the year's profits, in practice it was simply a wage. (Since no accounts were kept, it was never known if there was anything left at the end of the year to distribute.)

The cooperatives also posed two challenges to the government's commitment to equality. One was the increasing difference between rich and poor cooperatives. Some co-ops had advantages—in particular, fertile land and high value crops such as tobacco—that gave them higher revenues independent of the work of the members. The other problem was the friction between cooperative members and temporary workers. Temporary workers received higher wages than members (3.00 pesos a day vs. 2.50), since cooperative wages were supposed to have been supplemented by yearly dividends. Cooperative members, though, had a host of other advantages, such as free health care, housing, schools, sick leave, and accident insurance. Temporary workers became, in the words of Fidel Castro, "second-class citizens."[17]

By 1962, the cooperatives were converted into state farms. Like the cattle ranches, they were called *granjas del pueblo*. In part, this move was merely an acknowledgment of existing reality. But there were some important differences. Workers no longer even theoretically shared the farm's profit but received a fixed wage. All workers received the same wage. Planning and investments were made more centralized than before. Since state farms were often formed by combining cooperatives, purportedly to take advantage of economies of scale, the average size was larger.

From the start, state farms received priority over private farms. Besides taking advantage of economies of scale, the government wanted direct control over rural investments and agricultural production. Vice-President Carlos Rafael Rodríguez, formerly the head of INRA, saw the existence of state-controlled agriculture as "a guarantee that, unlike the situation that prevailed for a time in a number of socialist countries, Cuba's economy will not be dependent on the will and actions of the individual peasants."[18] Fidel Castro held that the state farms were superior in both economic and social terms: "You can utilize the land in an optimum way . . . determining at each moment that whatever crop benefits the nation shall be produced. And you guarantee the workers a satisfactory income, housing, schools, roads—all those social benefits that are needed as much by the man who is planting sugarcane as by the man who is planting tobacco or tomatoes or sisal grass."[19]

In a short period of time, the life of the farm workers vastly improved. On a 3,000-acre former cattle estate in Pinar del Río province, just a few months after it became a state farm, 200 families moved in to work the land, and a new town was built with modern concrete housing, a school, a "people's store," a clinic, and a cafeteria. School children were given clothing, free lunch, and free transportation. A visiting Chilean economist observed, "Of course, it was not possible to multiply this experience in each of the People's Farms across the country. There simply were not enough resources to do so. But the importance of this experience is that it reveals the ambitious ideas of the revolutionary leadership."[20]

THE PRIVATE SECTOR

While the state sector was being created, the private sector was being transformed. By giving titles to former tenants, sharecroppers, and squatters, the agrarian reform added about 110,000 peasants to the already existing 45,000 small farmer-owners. Thus two thirds of Cuba's small farmers became farm owners thanks to the revolution.[21]

The private sector included both small and large farmers. Defined as those with under 165 acres, the small farmers constituted 94 percent of the private farmers. Large farmers, while in the minority, still held 42 percent of the land in the private sector.[22] Together they were important producers not only of food but also of foreign exchange, accounting for 85 percent of tobacco production, 80 percent of coffee, and 33 percent of sugarcane.[23]

The small private farmers reaped the benefits of the government's first agrarian reform. With land rents abolished, their incomes grew dramatically. They were given low-interest loans, guaranteed fixed prices for their crops, access to low-priced "people's stores," schools for their children, free medical care, and more. Freed from exploitative intermediaries and price fluctuations—harvest prices were now fixed and guaranteed before planting—small farmers improved their material conditions considerably.[24]

In May 1961, on the second anniversary of the agrarian reform law, the National Association of Small Farmers (ANAP) was formed. Membership was voluntary and restricted to farmers with fewer than 165 acres and larger farmers who had proven allegiance to the revolution. ANAP was to coordinate small farm production, mainly through the allocation of credit. Before the revolution, government credit was largely confined to the estates and large farms. Many small farmers were forced into the hands of loan sharks charging up to 30 percent interest. Now small farmers were given credit at 4 percent annual interest. (From 1967 to 1978, no interest at all was charged on loans.)[25]

Excluding the larger farmers from membership in ANAP represented a critical step in differentiating the remaining large farmers from the small ones. Rich farmers were few in number; two years after the first agrarian reform law, only 592 farms over 1,000 acres remained. (The number of holdings between 165 and 1,000 acres had grown from 9,752 to 10,623, their ranks swelled by former large owners.) While small farmers received special support from the state, large private farmers were excluded from the mainstream of agricultural planning.[26] With the nationalization of the banking, transport, and distribution systems, it became increasingly difficult for these farmers to obtain supplies and deliver their goods to urban markets. "Discrimination against this group of farmers was apparently official policy of the revolutionary leadership that wished eventually to nationalize these properties," according to Canadian economist Archibald Ritter. "It refrained from doing so immediately due to a scarcity of INRA administrators and to political factors, i.e., the wish to avoid creating another body of opponents to the regime."[27]

But while the government made it difficult for large farmers both to produce and sell their goods, the increase in national consumption coupled with the inexperience of the newly created state sector made these farmers more important than ever in supplying the nation's food. Rather than sell to the state at fixed prices, these farmers preferred selling their produce privately to the highest bidder.

In an effort to force the farmers to sell to the state, serious errors were committed. A number of farms were illegally expropriated. The large farmers used these errors to make even small farmers fear expropriation. To quell the fears of the small farmers, the government was forced to hand back lands taken illegally. Fidel said at the time, "If the return of illegally confiscated farms is going to restore peace and quiet to thousands of people who must go along with the revolution, then they will have to be given back."[28]

Although the government considered the remaining rich farmers incompatible with the revolution, it did not want to precipitate their downfall and affect the economy adversely. The idea was to organize the state sector for several years and then deal the death blow to the remaining large farmers. But once again, the course of events forced the revolution to speed up its plans. Many rich farmers sabotaged production. Others, particularly in the Escambray mountain region, were directly involved in counterrevolutionary activities. Perhaps even more critical were their efforts to convince small farmers that the government was out to do away with all private farmers, big and small alike. These problems, coupled with the need to control food supplies in the face of ever-growing demand and shortages, led the government to promulgate a second agrarian reform.

THE SECOND AGRARIAN REFORM

In October 1963, the second agrarian reform was instituted, expropriating the land of all farmers with more than 165 acres. The government believed that state farms would guarantee food for everyone as well increased exports. They would make resurgence of capitalism in the Cuban countryside impossible. INRA took over about 10,000 farms, comprising approximately 20 percent of the nation's farmland.[29] This left the state in control of about 63 percent of the cultivated land,[30] as well as all agricultural credit, inputs, and marketing facilities.

Now the small farmers were the only significant private sector remaining in the entire economy. The government went to considerable lengths to reassure them there would be no "third agrarian reform" and that all future steps at collectivization would be strictly voluntary. Fidel Castro himself made a strong and highly visible political commitment toward the small farmers and their style of production. Not until a small farmer personally believed it was advantageous to farm collectively would his farm be joined with others in a cooperative, Fidel promised. If a farmer chose to live out his years as an individual farmer, this was fine. Fidel even promised that the farmer could be buried on his individual plot of land. "It is better to be patient as long as is necessary rather than have it be said in the future that our revolution forced a peasant to join a cooperative," Castro told the farmers. "We must be patient. If we have endured the ranches, the corrals, the *latifundia* and the *minifundia* all these centuries, what does it matter if we wait ten, fifteen, twenty, thirty, or fifty years for isolated cases? And if the owner of a *minifundium* wants to have it become a museum piece, then let him."[31]

When the government offered to buy out small farmers in the early 1960s, four thousand immediately rushed forward to sell, and the government was forced to retract its offer. It decided to purchase land only from those farmers who were old or unable to work. "If a young able-bodied farmer wants to sell, we'll have to tell him no. We need him to stay on the land and keep producing," Fidel later said.[32]

During the late 1960s, however, there was a big push to persuade farmers to sell or lease their land to the government for its ambitious agricultural projects. (Undoubtedly the deal was attractive to some; others, we have been told, felt forced more than persuaded.) Between 1967 and 1970, the government purchased about 20,000 farms, then slowed down to buying fewer than 1,500 a year.[33]

Land in Cuba cannot be privately sold; it can only be sold to the government or to cooperatives. Land can be inherited, if the heir is within the family and personally willing to continue farming it. The law is enforced flexibly to keep people on the land, the head of ANAP's legal department told us. For example, a farmer's daughter can inherit the land if her husband agrees to farm it.[34] If a farmer dies or retires without heirs who want to work the farm, the farmer's family must sell the land to the government. In the 20 years following the second agrarian reform in 1963, the percentage of land in the private sector diminished from 37 to 20 percent.[35]

Private farmers are private only in the sense that they own their land and live mainly off the sale of their produce. But unlike private farmers in capitalist countries, they cannot freely sell their land, they must respond to the government's request as to what to grow, they are dependent on the government for inputs, and they must sell part of their produce to the government at prices the government sets.

While there are no statistics available on private farmers' incomes and there are still poor private farmers, farmers seem to enjoy higher incomes and better standards of living than most other Cubans. Indeed many would say they are pampered. A private tobacco farmer we met in Pinar del Río in 1978 said he earned 10,000 pesos that year—five times the national average and considerably more than the salary of the minister of agriculture. "You know some farmers are millionaires," Castro said in 1982. "In keeping with the measures taken by the revolution, the prices set by the revolution and the markets and opportunities it has provided, some farmers have hundreds of thousands of pesos."[36]

Virtually all private farm families are better off in food terms than other Cubans. Not only are small farmers able to grow much of their own food, but along with all other Cubans they purchase foods inexpensively through the ration system. In addition to receiving guaranteed prices for their crops and low-interest credits from the government, private farmers can take advantage of food shortages to sell part of their produce through nongovernment channels (mainly the black market) at high profits. Many farmers also have leased part of their land to the government in return for a lifetime monthly "rent check"—often higher than the average monthly wage. And all farmers and their families reap government benefits from free education and free health care. Little wonder that many joked that Cuba's small capitalist farmers were exploiting the socialist state.

THE SMALL FARMER DILEMMA

Though individual farmers can make lots of money from their farming, they have not necessarily produced up to capacity. While they are required to produce certain quantities for sale to the government, these contracted amounts have apparently been based on state-farm yields, which tend to be low; most private-farm families could easily fulfill them. Farmers who have failed to fulfill the contract have seldom been penalized. At a certain point the revolution had provided so much for the farmer that "he did what any normal human being would do: relax and take life easy," Vice-President Rodríguez told us.

As we have previously noted, it is impossible to determine how much the private farmers really produce because official statistics only take into account sales to the government. If private consumption, barter, black-market, and free-market sales were recorded, the picture could change considerably. When the farmers' markets were created in 1981 and suddenly much more food was legally available for sale, it was obvious that black-market sales had been substantial and that probably, given the right incentives, private farmers could produce more.

Why weren't the farmers producing more? In part, it was because private farmers had the lowest priority for buying scarce agricultural inputs, such as fertilizers, irrigation equipment, and farm machinery and vehicles, that would have enabled them to produce more. During our visits to the countryside, we met farmers who could not buy even such a commonplace implement as a hose for watering vegetable crops.

Why weren't the farmers selling more to the government? Private farmers could make far more money selling their extra production directly to consumers. To control these sales without formally restricting the farmers, the government limited buyers to purchases of 25 pounds or less.[37] But this restriction has been hard to enforce.

The existence of the private farmers continues to pose a dilemma for the Cuban leaders. The private farmers' production is still essential. Twenty years ago officials predicted that private production would be insignificant by now. But in 1982 it still accounted for 25 percent of Cuban-grown beans, 28 percent of the taro, 42 percent of the onions, 92 percent of the peppers, 52 percent of the coffee, and 18 percent of the sugar. (These official statistics, for the reason already noted, underestimate private production, perhaps considerably.) Given incentives—as the farmers' market experience demonstrated—they could produce even more. But the more they produced, the richer they became, and the greater the inequality—among the private farmers, between the private farmers, the cooperatives, and the state farms, and in the Cuban population as a whole.

In the 1980s, a series of measures were taken to encourage private farmers to produce more and sell more to the government, while at the same time curbing their incomes. The government raised the prices it pays for contracted production. Anything sold to the state above and beyond contracted amounts is now purchased at a higher price. Farmers' contracts with the government are enforced, with penalties for nonfulfillment. Private farmers must now honor their government contracts before selling either on the private market or to the government at the higher price. Furthermore, contracts are to be reevaluated each year in view of the amount of surplus sold the previous year. The idea seems to be that if records show a farmer met his contract and was able to sell an additional sizeable amount on the private market, the next year the amount he is contracted to sell to the government should be raised accordingly.[38]

DISTRIBUTION OF LAND: PRIVATE VS. STATE SECTOR*
100 percent = total cultivated land

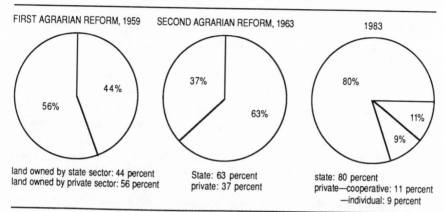

FIRST AGRARIAN REFORM, 1959

56% · 44%

land owned by state sector: 44 percent
land owned by private sector: 56 percent

SECOND AGRARIAN REFORM, 1963

37% · 63%

State: 63 percent
private: 37 percent

1983

80% · 11% · 9%

state: 80 percent
private—cooperative: 11 percent
—individual: 9 percent

*Varying figures appear in both official and secondary sources. Land surveys, especially before the revolution, were far from accurate. Another problem is that some figures refer to total land area, others to cultivated land.

To make private-market sales less tempting, taxes on these sales were raised to 20 percent for individual farmers. There is also, as of 1983, a progressive tax (5 to 20 percent) on the private farmer's gross income. Farmers will now have to pay for their own crop insurance (previously the government picked up the tab). And those who want to sell their land to the state will no longer be offered generous lifetime monthly payments but one lump sum.

NOTES

1. Leo Huberman and Paul Sweezy, *Cuba: Anatomy of a Revolution* (New York: Monthly Review Press, 1960), p. 78.

2. David Barkin, "La redistribución del consumo," in David Barkin and Nita R. Manitzas, eds., *Cuba: Camino abierto* (Mexico City: Siglo XXI, 1973), p. 193.

3. Fidel Castro, speech in Santa Clara, July 26, 1959, as cited in Antonio Nuñez Jimenez, *En marcha con Fidel* (Havana: Editorial Letters, 1982), p. 201.

4. Personal communication, Solon Barraclough, March 3, 1984.

5. Jacques Chonchol, "El primer bienio de reforma agraria (1959–1961)," in Oscar Delgado, ed., *Reformas agrarias en America Latina* (Mexico City: Fondo de Cultura Economica, 1965), pp. 483 and 509. Chonchol cites the legal department of INRA. We advisedly use the word *control* since the government turned over part (the estimates range as high as 60 percent) of the expropriated land to land-poor peasants.

6. Michel Gutelman, "The Socialization of the Means of Production in Cuba," in Rolando E. Bonachea and Nelson P. Valdés, eds., *Cuba in Revolution* (New York: Anchor Books, 1972), p. 255.

7. Carlos Rafael Rodríguez, *Cuba en el tránsito al socialismo: 1959–1963* (Mexico City: Siglo XXI, 1978), p. 143.

8. Lee Lockwood, *Castro's Cuba, Cuba's Fidel* (New York: Vintage Books, 1969), p. 96.

9. Ibid., p. 97.

10. Arthur MacEwan, *Revolution and Economic Development in Cuba* (New York: St. Martin's Press, 1981), pp. 50ff.

11. M. Gutelman, "The Socialization of the Means of Production in Cuba," p. 242.

12. See, for example, Fidel Castro's speech of May 17, 1974, marking the 15th anniversary of the reform.

13. For a comprehensive breakdown, see M. Gutelman in *Cuba in Revolution.*

14. J. Chonchol, "El primer bienio de reforma agraria (1959–1961)," p. 483.

15. M. Gutelman, "The Socialization of the Means of Production in Cuba," p. 247.

16. James O'Connor, *The Origins of Socialism in Cuba,* (Ithaca, N.Y.: Cornell University Press, 1970), p. 109.

17. "Conversion de las cooperatives en granjas del pueblo caneras," *Trimestre* (April–June 1962), p. 111. Cited in J. O'Connor, *The Origins of Socialism in Cuba,* (Ithaca, N.Y.: Cornell University Press, 1970), p. 110.

18. Andrew Pearse, *The Latin American Peasant* (London: Frank Cass, 1975), pp. 249–50.

19. L. Lockwood, *Castro's Cuba, Cuba's Fidel,* p. 98.

20. Sergio Aranda, *La revolución agraria en Cuba* (Mexico City: Siglo XXI, 1968), p. 184.

21. A. MacEwan, *Revolution and Economic Development in Cuba,* p. 56.

22. Figures calculated from table in C. R. Rodríguez, *Cuba en el transito al socialismo: 1959–1963,* p. 137.

23. S. Aranda, *La revolución agraria en Cuba,* p. 32.

24. A. Pearse, *The Latin American Peasant,* p. 245.

25. S. Aranda, *La revolución agraria en Cuba,* p. 144.

26. Andrés Bianchi, "Agriculture—The Post-Revolutionary Development," in Dudly Seers, ed., *Cuba: The Economic and Social Revolution* (Chapel Hill, N.C.: Univ. of North Carolina Press, 1964), p. 140.

27. Archibald R. M. Ritter, *The Economic Development of Revolutionary Cuba* (New York: Praeger, 1974), pp. 102–3.

28. Fidel Castro, speech to the Provincial Committee of the ORI in Matanzas, April 10, 1962, in *Revolución* (Havana), May 10, 1962.

29. J. O'Connor, *The Origins of Socialism in Cuba,* (Ithaca, N.Y.: Cornell University Press, 1970), p. 130.

30. A. MacEwan, *Revolution and Economic Development in Cuba,* p. 73.

31. Fidel Castro, "Speech at the Fifth ANAP Congress," *Granma Weekly Review* (Havana), May 29, 1977.

32. Fidel Castro, "Sixth Congress of the ANAP," *Speeches at Three Congresses* (Havana: Editora Politica, 1982), pp. 145–201.

33. Personal interview with Rogelio Garayta, an official at ANAP, January 22, 1982.

34. Ibid.

35. The decline in the private sector is largely due to the retirement or death of small farmowners without heirs willing to farm and from the sales of farmland to the government. The reduced percentage of land in private hands may also reflect an increase in the total amount of land under cultivation. In 1983 an ANAP official told us that the farmers' market experience led them to

believe that official figures underestimate the amount of private farmland. A new survey is now being undertaken to ensure that all land is accounted for. Personal interview with Rogelio Garayta, November 1983.

36. F. Castro, *Speeches at Three Congresses,* p. 187.

37. Ibid., p. 34.

38. Interview with Rogelio Garayta, November 1983.

12. 1970 and the Trouble with Cuban Socialism*

By Wassily Leontief

Last July 26, on the day that marked the 11th anniversary of the Cuban Revolution, addressing hundreds of thousands of citizens on the same rostrum from which he was accustomed to hail his victories, Fidel analyzed in detail the failure of the great ten-million-ton harvest. To critical observers who followed from within or looked on from the outside the struggles and stresses that marked the attempt to lay the economic foundations of a new socialist society, this failure had not come as a surprise when it was first announced on May 11. What must have been surprising to those accustomed to the ways of politicians, on the right as well as on the left, was the resounding candor of the speech.

Under conditions normally prevailing in a free-enterprise economy like our own, the failure of one of the major industries to reach an anticipated output level, even by as much as 15 percent, would hardly be considered a national tragedy. In a centrally guided (socialist) economy, the failure to reach a production target which has been officially proclaimed the national goal must, indeed, be interpreted as a sign of a major breakdown.

Whatever its weaknesses may be—and as we shall see presently there are many—a strong socialist regime should be capable of concentrating ruthlessly all the economic and spiritual resources it commands on that single goal. The fact that, despite such capability and the obvious determination to make the greatest possible sacrifices, Cuba nevertheless harvested fewer than ten million tons of sugar leads one to conclude that these sacrifices must have been pushed to the extreme. . . .

Indeed, the list of subsidiary failures—subsidiary, that is, to the ten-million-ton sugar harvest—itemized in Castro's speech is distressingly impressive.

*From Wassily Leontief, "The Trouble with Cuban Socialism," *The New York Review of Books* (January 7, 1971), pp. 19–23.

Milk production fell 25 percent in one year, delivery of steel 38 percent, the output of cement 23 percent, and so on, and so on. The proportion of normal working time spent by thousands of highly trained technicians away from their real jobs, and the portion of the normal school year which both students and teachers devoted to swinging the machete and loading the cut cane, must have, in many instances, approached 100 percent.

The poor performance by industry, agriculture, transportation, and distribution predicted by all of Fidel's hostile as well as many of his friendly critics is now confirmed by the official figures. If before July 26 two different interpretations of the state of the Cuban economy were possible, a distressing unanimity now prevails: The high hopes for rapid growth have been disappointed; the situation is desperate, although, one must hasten to add, still far from hopeless. It is not surprising, however, that in the explanation of how all this came about, no such unanimity exists.

Though one is tempted to ask what "the cause" of the debacle was, to yield to this temptation would be to oversimplify the issue. A national economy, even the national economy of a small country like Cuba, is a complicated system. Fidel is, of course, the big wheel in it. He would be, however, the first to admit that his effectiveness depends to a great extent on a large number of other wheels and gears.

Whenever many different experts set out to explain a development as complex as the economic difficulties in Cuba, the dispute about its true cause can safely be assumed to reflect a disagreement about appropriate remedies. . . .

The economic difficulties confronting Cuba are fundamentally the same as those that plagued the Soviet Union and other socialist countries after the overthrow of their capitalist semifeudal regimes. In the Cuban case there was, of course, no physical devastation from a prolonged civil war such as accompanied the Russian Revolution, although the blockade imposed by the United States, in cutting off the flow of indispensable replacement parts for American machinery unobtainable from any other source, caused great and lasting damage to the economy. On the other hand, Cuba received extensive economic aid from the Soviet Union as well as modest, but not negligible, trade credits from other parts of eastern and western Europe and from China.

In the same July 26 speech, Fidel blames the plight in which his country finds itself on bad planning. All available evidence seems to indicate that the low and apparently steadily falling efficiency of labor is another, probably more important, factor responsible for this trouble. It is my contention that the second problem—the characteristically low productivity of labor, rooted in the basic difference between a socialistic and an individualistic society—will moreover prove to be particularly difficult, perhaps even impossible, to overcome.

The first two years after the overthrow of the old regime were a glorious revolutionary honeymoon. The immediate political and social objectives of the victorious popular movement were attained. The standard of living of large masses of the population shot up. This increased rate of consumption was, however, maintained only through the depletion of existing stocks. The sharp rise in the per capita meat consumption, for example, was sustained by the abnormally high rate of animal slaughter, which always in all countries accompanies the nationalization of private herds. After all, the social upheaval at the outset could only have had a negative effect on the organization of production and, consequently, on the flow of current output.

By 1962 reserves were used up, shortages began to be felt, and rationing of food and clothing was inaugurated. In 1959 the National Agrarian Reform Institute had been organized to carry out agrarian reforms; and in 1960 the Central Planning Office—the JUCEPLAN—was established to guide the overall economic growth. . . .

The original idea of transforming the predominantly agricultural economy into an industrial one was given up after two frustrating years. The decision to base plans for further economic growth on a diversified agriculture with particular emphasis on sugar production and cattle raising appears to have been quite sound, since next to rich deposits of nickel and a few other minerals the main natural resources of the island are its agricultural land and propitious climate. Another aspect of Cuban economic strategy—the exceptionally high rate of saving and investment—is characteristic of all modern socialist countries. In this, Marxist practice is in keeping with the precepts of orthodox economic thought that are preached, but not practiced to the same extent, by capitalist societies. . . .

In a socialist country where the government takes over the responsibility for all the large and small decisions involved in the operations of the national economy, the function of a plan or rather the responsibilities of the central planning organs are very great and very grave indeed.

Since Lenin inaugurated the first socialist five-year plan nearly half a century ago, problems of central planning have become a favorite subject of theoretical analysis both in the East and in the West; originally, in fact, more in the West than in the East. . . .

With one or two exceptions the revolutionary leaders who found themselves responsible for managing all the nationalist branches of the Cuban economy were even less well prepared for their task than the men who came to power in Russia in 1917. . . .

Large-scale economic planning, so long as it has not yet become an applied science, remains, to a large extent, an art that cannot be taught but rather must be learned through painful practical experience. In the Cuban case the difficulties are aggravated by the loss, through officially permitted emigration to the United States, of many thousands of skilled workers, foremen, managers, and engineers.

A typical pitfall of beginning socialist planners is a fascination with technological innovation combined with supreme disdain for cost-accounting and all other kinds of economic calculations. This fault has often been described as a bias in favor of technological as against economic considerations. From the point of view of modern economic theory such a distinction is fundamentally misleading.

The price of any particular product reflects in a concentrated manner—as the round curved mirror hanging over the mantelpiece in an old-fashioned parlor reflects in miniature the entire room—the structural, i.e., technological, characteristics of the entire economy of which that product is but a small component part. The market price of a ton of steel or of a kilowatt-hour of electric energy communicates to the buyer of these products how the available supply of various primary resources and the production methods used in all the different branches of the particular economy affect the physical availability of one ton of steel or, respectively, of one kilowatt-hour of electric energy. In order to make possible the computation of the "correct" accounting prices of steel and electric energy in an ideal centrally planned economy, the central technological data bank would have to provide the central planning office with tapes carrying a detailed quantitative description of the technical "cooking recipe" of each and every sector of the national economy that contributes directly or indirectly to the production of these goods.

In choosing between two or more possible methods of production, one, for example, requiring more steel and the other more electric power, the planner must take into account the prices of these as well as those of all the other inputs. In insisting on this we really are saying that the acceptance or rejection of a technological innovation in one particular industry cannot be rationally decided upon without knowledge of the technologies, that is of the methods of production, that are or could be used in all the other industries. . . .

In promulgating many of the spectacular technological changes and economic shifts introduced in recent years, the Cuban planners have based their decisions on distorted prices or, to judge by reports of such experienced observers as René Dumont, they have more probably arrived at them without the benefit of price or cost computations of any kind.

There could be hardly any doubt that the Cuban economists are fully aware of these problems and that they do all they can to replace what might be called impulsive planning by rational economic calculations. The choice of correct prices is facilitated in the Cuban case by the fact that, as a small, primarily agricultural economy depending largely on a single crop (sugar), it exports a very large proportion of its total output, and imports most of the domestically used tools, raw materials, machinery, and even food. The correct accounting prices for these goods are, of course, those quoted on the world market or agreed upon in the special purchase and delivery contracts with foreign buyers or suppliers.

After some years of additional experience Cuban planners can be expected to learn to use conventional planning routines with effectiveness comparable to that of their colleagues in older socialist countries. It will take much longer to put into practice the sophisticated mathematical techniques proposed by both socialist and capitalist theorists. As things stand now, many economic decisions involving the expenditure of hundreds of thousands of dollars are still being made without any systematic justification.

As I said before, bad planning is only one of the factors contributing to the economic difficulties in which this socialist island finds itself; the other— possibly the more important—is the low productivity of labor. This seems to be lower now than it was before the revolution. With the same equipment and under otherwise identical physical conditions the same worker, or the same group of workers, seems to produce in all branches of industry and agriculture smaller amounts of goods, or goods of lower quality, or both, than would have been produced before the revolution.

The so-called moral incentives on which so much emphasis is placed now seem ineffective as a means of inducing laborers, white-collar workers, managerial and supervisory personnel to perform their respective jobs as well as they did before the revolution. The material threat of joblessness and hunger, combined with the often inequitable but nevertheless tangible and potent material rewards of higher wages, salaries, and profits, unfortunately works incomparably better. . . .

Persistent, albeit unsuccessful, experimentation with mechanical cane cutters seems to have been prompted by the belief that the low efficiency of labor could be compensated for by large-scale use of sophisticated automatic equipment. For reasons that I have presented above, such hope is hardly justified. Careless handling and poor maintenance of machinery, buildings, and all other kinds of fixed capital goods is one of the surest signs of an insufficiently motivated labor force. So long as moral incentives continue to work as badly as they apparently have up to now, large-scale introduction of costly new equipment might aggravate the economic difficulties of Cuba instead of alleviating them.

The struggle between the advocates of material incentives and the proponents of so-called moral ones has marked the ideological development of the Cuban Revolution throughout its course. . . . In the early years this struggle went on in the open, then it became less visible, but still continued. As late as 1965 the wage of the lowest agricultural worker was 63.80 pesos per month, while the salary of a top-level executive or technician was 938.05 pesos per month. As shortages led to more and more stringent rationing of most consumer goods the differences in monetary earnings became less and less meaningful.

With increasing emphasis on the creation of a truly socialist society and with the progress of a powerful educational effort aimed at transforming the old narrow individualist attitude into a community-oriented equalitarian one, the doctrine of moral incentives, as contrasted with material incentives, gained the upper hand. The trial and condemnation of Aníbal Escalante and his "microfaction of rightist deviationists" in 1968 marked the decision to accept the elimination of material incentives and replace them by incentives of a purely moral kind—the immediate objective of social and economic policies. . . .

The New Man is now defined by the Cubans as a member of an equalitarian society who is expected to exert himself for the benefit of the entire community to the utmost limits of his physical and mental capabilities. While ultimately he is supposed to do this out of deep inner conviction, unmindful of any personal advantages or rewards, at the present time much emphasis is laid on public encouragement and recognition of creditable efforts. There is also public celebration of the outstanding individual or group performance. A negligent attitude, absenteeism, and poor work elicit public exposure and criticism from officials and fellow workers. Moral incentives, then, depend to a great extent on the reactions of the group one belongs to.

All available evidence, of which I spoke before, indicates that in Cuba as in other socialist countries such moral incentives failed in their effectiveness to measure up to more conventional individualistic self-interest. Moreover, material self-interest continues to persist, and, in cases of conflict, to weaken and distort the hoped-for effect of moral motivation.

Below the surface of the new morality and the idealistic attitude, pursuit of private gain goes on. The outward show of great and even supreme efforts in the interest of the public good is combined with apathy and downright sloppy performance in those areas and in the type of work that, by its very nature, cannot be easily assessed from the outside. In his remarkable speech of last July 26 Fidel declares, again and again, that while much attention is being paid to the quantity of the product, its quality tends to deteriorate to such an extent that it becomes practically useless.

The explanation of this phenomenon, again common to all socialist countries, is of course that a worker's peers (on whose acclaim or approbation a man or woman moved by moral incentives primarily depends) can more easily observe the quantity of the output than judge its quality. Poor maintenance of equipment and the shortage of "small work tools and measuring instruments," which Fidel laments, must also be explained in the same way. Most readers of these lines will remember occasions when the taxicab they rode in seemed about to fall apart: The driver, when queried, explained that neither he nor any of the other cabbies who drive the car for the company is interested in its proper care and upkeep. How different the attitude, and consequently the appearance of the vehicle, when the cab he drives happens to be his own.

In a system in which the motive of profit or material gain has been effectively excluded, the only workable alternative for maintenance of efficient performance is internal dedication that functions independently even of the popular approval on which the moral incentives, as introduced now in Cuba, so heavily depend. There can be no doubt that on the highest level of Cuban political leadership and economic management, as well as on other levels, including the lower ones of educational, scientific, medical, and artistic activities, true inner dedication to the interests of the community does, in fact, prevail. In most instances, moreover, it is combined with a deeply ingrained "instinct of workmanship." The Cuban programs of health, education, and social welfare seem major accomplishments, especially in view of the limited resources available for investment in them.

However, at every other level of productive activity, on which the overall performance of any modern economy so critically depends, the abolition of the old profit system has not eliminated the driving forces of individualistic interest. The new institutional apparatus of education, propaganda, public honors, and popular disgrace has only directed these forces in different, often invisible, channels. The effect of such displacement is a marked lowering of the total productivity of labor.

All this, combined with poor over-all planning, leads to the rapid deterioration of the economic performance so dramatically described by Fidel himself. Other socialist countries, while maintaining centralized planning and continuing to stress social and moral aims, have at the same time developed elaborate systems of economic incentives. Although much less effective than ours, particularly on the lower and middle management levels, they nevertheless work reasonably well. It clearly helps to maintain labor discipline and production on a higher level than the one to which they would have sunk under the system of moral incentives practiced in Cuba now and in Russia immediately after the revolution.

Does all this mean that the attempt to build a new society in which equality will be given precedence over prosperity and public over private interest must fail? Not at all. Socialist and particularly Marxist thought was traditionally based on the assumption that moral incentives—as compared to material incentives—can better serve not only the higher aspirations but also the material, economic needs of the society. All available evidence—and Cuba is the most recent of many tests—demonstrates that this is not the case. In prompting an average laborer, sales clerk, manager, or technician to exert himself day in and day out in steady purposeful, i.e., productive, work nothing seems as effective as a steady flow of material benefits closely commensurate with the results of his individual efforts.

This is not to imply however that human nature cannot change in the long run, especially if the economy reaches a point where it can comfortably supply material needs and work itself becomes less arduous. But in the short run Cuba is facing a dilemma, and in questions related to human nature the short run means not one, or two, but several generations. (The socialist regime in Russia celebrated its 50th anniversary two years ago.). . . .

Castro is facing a difficult choice, one somewhat analogous to the one Lenin was confronting on the eve of the inauguration of the so-called New Economic Policies. To continue on the present course means risking further economic deterioration, or at least stagnation, and with it rising discontent, which is bound to change the mood of the revolution. Reintroduction of material incentives would also change that mood and it would require a great deal of public explanation. One hopes that whatever road is chosen will bring the country out of its present impasse. A collapse of the aspirations of the revolution would be a great calamity, not only for the Cuban people, but also for the rest of the world.

13. Development Strategies and Basic Human Needs*

BY CLAES BRUNDENIUS

It is today widely recognized that revolutionary Cuba has done comparatively well in solving the most urgent problems of poverty inherited from the past. It has also been assumed that the Cuban performance has been associated with a radical redistribution of income although quantitative evidence has been lacking.[1] What is perhaps not so universally known is the boom of the Cuban economy during the first half of the 1970s with growth rates paralleling those of the Brazilian "miracle" which took place about the same time. Economic growth in the postrevolutionary period (1959–1979) compares very favorably with the prerevolutionary era as will be shown in this paper. What is true is that economic growth was very sluggish in the 1960s and was even negative during some bad years in the middle of the decade, but it is argued that this failure to meet growth targets was less a result of incompatibility between growth and equity goals than of gross inefficiencies of an overcentralized and bureaucratic planning system.

1. PHASES OF A REVOLUTION

Paradoxically, there was no deliberate strategy behind the redistributive reforms enacted during the first years of the revolution. It is true that the

*From Claes Brundenius, "Growth with Equity: The Cuban Experience (1959–1980)," *World Development* Vol. 9, No. 11/12 (1981) pp. 1083–96.

redistributive measures coincided with a forced drive towards collectivization of the means of production, but this was a growing necessity rather than a premeditated strategy, in view of the mounting attacks on the reforms by the enemies of the revolution, outside as well as inside Cuba. However, even if there was no explicit development strategy, Fidel Castro made it no secret that his revolution would be adamant and implacable in carrying though reforms that would substantially improve the living conditions of the large majority of Cubans, especially those in the rural areas. Thus Castro pushed through reform after reform yielding nothing to his opponents.

The reforms that most aroused the wrath of the bourgeois opposition were the Agrarian Law and the Rent Reform, both enacted within the first five months of the revolutionary rule. Although neither of the reforms could be considered revolutionary in the strict meaning of the word, they were profound enough to constitute uncomfortable blows to vested capitalist interests in the urban as well as in the rural areas. During the first two turbulent years (1959 and 1960) the revolutionary government was more preoccupied with con-solidating power through mass mobilizations in support of the revolution than with the formulation of development strategies. Nevertheless, development goals such as eradication of unemployment, redistribution of income and opportunity, and raising the educational and health levels of the population had all been self-evident goals in the minds of the *barbudos* in the Sierra Maestra.

The success in terms of both redistribution and growth during the first two years no doubt explains the overoptimistic and somewhat romantic develop-ment strategy formulated in 1960–1961 and intended to be implemented dur-ing the following four years. This strategy focused on the importance of breaking Cuba's traditional dependence on sugar.[2] The first so-called Perspec-tive Plan for 1962–1965, or the early Cuban model as it is sometimes referred to, foresaw rapid economic growth coupled with a radical structural transfor-mation of the economy through diversification of agriculture with self-suffi-ciency in food production to be achieved within the plan period.[3] At the same time a wide range of new import-substituting industries, including metallurgy and heavy engineering were to be installed. This industrialization program was to be implemented simultaneously with accelerating housing construction and the continued expansion of education and health services. In 1961 and 1962 serious difficulties ominously turned up, not so much because of inherent error in the model as because of the impossibility of carrying through such an optimistic plan considering the mounting pressures against resources, the embargo policies of the United States, the loss of highly qualified manpower through emigration and the inevitable weaknesses in a new economic organiza-tion that was replacing an old one.

The difficulties made the planners revise the plan targets before the plan even entered into operation and the unlikelihood of Cuba becoming self-sufficient in food within the plan period was evident when in March 1962 the government had to introduce a rationing system on most foodstuffs—a system largely still in effect at the end of the 1970s. The unexpected reversal of events, which mercilessly revealed the weakness and the obvious inefficiency of the planning system, led to the so-called great debate (1962–1965) where the discussions centered on the applicability of the law of value in a transitional society (towards communism), on moral vs material incentives in production, on centralization vs decentralization, and in decision making on whether to apply a budgetary system of finance or the economic accounting (self-finance) system gradually being applied in the Soviet Union and Eastern Europe at that time. . . .[4]

The new development strategy that emerged from these debates was sugar-centered and export-oriented. It was no longer assumed that sugar exports would increase by themselves without any effort to increase yields. Reckoning with favorable sugar prices on the world market, and with a target of 10 million tons of sugar for the 1969/1970 *zafra* (the period from November to April), the foundation was to be laid, it was hoped, for the rapid industrialization of the country in the following decade.[5] This sugar-oriented strategy was to be coupled with a decentralized version of the budgetary system of finance, or "a fidelista variant of the guevarista model."[6] Further, the principle of moral incentives should predominate over material incentives following closely the views of Che Guevara that "man is a conscious actor in history. Without his *consciousness* which embraces his awareness as a social being, there can be no communism."[7]

Although economic growth became the overriding priority when production problems intensified in the 1960s, it should be emphasized that while aggregate consumption levels were sacrificed in order to increase investment, income distribution was never sacrificed for growth. This policy was not without problems, however. Lowering the levels of consumption, especially of durable consumer goods which had been in abundance before the revolution, and rationing basic goods created a growing gap between the total wages paid in the economy and the availability of goods for sale. People who earned more simply could not do anything with the excess money but hoard it. This naturally constituted a tremendous problem. How could a worker be morally stimulated to work and produce more, if he could not even buy products for the money that he had supposedly been *materially* stimulated to earn? This was one of the many issues discussed by Fidel Castro in his famous address to the Thirteenth Workers' Congress in 1973.[8] With the resolutions from the congress the work quota system from 1966 was changed. Unlike the previous period, when a less productive worker had been remunerated as much as a more productive worker for the same type of work, the new work quotas were linked to productivity.

The shift in strategy in the 1970s, following the failure of the 10-million-ton *zafra,* could be summarized as follows: No more quick roads to communism, a balance between moral and material incentives; no quixotic planning, the working population had to be organized and the trade unions revitalized. In order to satisfy the demand for consumer goods and to siphon off the amount of money in circulation, the abolition of house rents was postponed, electricity and water rates were increased, free public telephones were suppressed, and the prices of stimulants such as cigarettes and rum were substantially raised. These measures, sometimes labelled "socialist inflation," were designed to deal specifically with the dislocations of previous planning decisions since the pricing of individual commodities had not been determined by the market.[9] The policies of the revolutionary government had always, implicitly or explicitly, given priority to the basic needs of the people, and the state's provision of basic goods and services at low cost had had the effect of raising the real wages for most people, creating an excess of money in circulation. As a consequence luxury goods and durable consumer goods had to be deliberately overpriced.[10]

2. THE ERADICATION OF OPEN UNEMPLOYMENT

The perhaps most serious problem, haunting many underdeveloped countries, not least in Latin America, is that of high rates of open unemployment coupled with perhaps half of the population of working age being underemployed in subsistence agriculture and in the service sector in exploding cities. The eradication of mass unemployment had been one of the priorities outlined in the program manifesto of the 26th of July Movement where it was stated "that there cannot be democracy or social justice if man does not have the means to satisfy in an honorable way his material needs . . . [and] that the state is obliged to provide those means, principally in the form of adequate production instruments and well-paid opportunities to work."[11] On the eve of the revolution over half of the rural labor force of 900,000 workers was employed in the cane fields and during the "dead season" it has been estimated that more than 400,000 workers were unemployed, the majority of them being sugar workers.[12] These numbers represented about 20 percent of the total labor force but even during the *zafra* (November–April) open unemployment was as high as 9–11 percent.[13]

Despite determined efforts by the government to tackle the problems of those deprived of adequate work, open unemployment was as high as 9 percent as late as 1962. But then, during the following six years, the unemployment rate went down to 4.3 percent thanks to mass mobilization, the expansion of the educational system, making young people stay longer at school, and not least, the effects of massive emigration during especially the first five years of the revolution. By 1970—the year of the 10 million *zafra*—the unemployment rate was as low as 1.3 percent. Probably, at least some of these people belong to what is sometimes referred to as *frictional* unemployment in the industrial countries in the capitalist world. At any rate, the problem by the end of the 1960s was no longer to eradicate open unemployment so much as to get enough skilled people to do a particular job at a particular time.

Women have always constituted a large labor reserve in Cuba, as in most other parts of Latin America, but they have seldom been motivated to join the labor force. This is partly due to attitudes, partly it is a reflection of already high unemployment and underemployment rates. After the revolution considerable efforts have gone into changing these attitudes and with the expansion of the educational system it has been natural for girls to look for jobs after leaving school. When this new generation of girls, with at least six years of primary education, started leaving school at the beginning of the 1970s, female participation rates also started increasing dramatically. These new entries into the labor force came at a time when the Cuban economy was experiencing an unprecedented boom period, at the peak of which (1972–1976) the female labor force increased by some 226,000, or by almost 50 percent, explaining over 75 percent of the new entries into the work force during that period.

The employment policy has, however, also led to new problems. While the drive towards full employment was apparently successfully accomplished in the 1960s, there were also inherent contradictions in this process. Thus, quite a lot of people were employed in low productivity work places. At the same time, as the labor force became rigid and immobile, investments went more and more into capital-intensive projects.[14] These contradictions came to light in the 1970s when the earlier labor deficit was replaced by a labor surplus by the end of the decade. Much less labor is now needed for the sugar harvest, to a large degree mechanized today, and this together with the new priority given to raising productivity as opposed to employment creation, has led to an increasing army of "abundant" workers or *disponibles,* who receive 70 percent of their wage while waiting for job reassignment. The leadership of the revolution seems to have been well aware of the danger of the reappearance of the specter of unemployment and already in 1973 Fidel Castro warned that "the time may come when we will have a headache finding jobs for all those who want to work."[15]

To a certain extent the supply of labor has been offset by a very progressive retirement law, applicable to women from the age of 55 and for men over 60 years of age. It is no exaggeration to claim that Cuba has the most advanced social security system in Latin America, covering practically 100 percent of the population. The corresponding coverage is in Brazil 32 percent, in Chile 69.5 percent (before Pinochet), in Mexico 25 percent, and in Peru 36 percent.[16] On the other hand, such an advanced social security system is becoming increasingly costly and makes the pressure against resources and low productivity even more obvious.

3. SATISFACTION OF BASIC NEEDS

When the Program of Action, adopted by the World Employment Conference in 1976, declared that "strategies and national development plans should include explicitly as a priority objective the promotion of employment and the satisfaction of the basic needs of each country's population,"[17] the Cuban delegation probably could not agree more. Even if these priorities have not always been explicitly spelled out, they had no doubt been self-evident goals in all Cuban development plans since 1959. But how successful have these basic needs oriented strategies of Cuba been? In order to get at least some quantitative indicator of Cuban performance in satisfying the basic needs of its population, I have tried to construct indices of the availability of basic goods and services per capita in Cuba after the revolution. The index is based on quantity data for the following broad basic needs categories: food and beverages, clothing, housing, education and health. The quantity data have then been weighted with constant shadow prices.[18]

Table 1: *Availability of Basic Goods and Services per Capita—Cuba 1958–1978 (1958 = 100)**

	Food and beverages	Clothing	Housing	Education	Health
1958	100	100	100	100	100
1962	99	52	107	173	105
1968	102	86	104	201	122
1972	110	90	103	224	120
1974	120	95	103	275	151
1976	123	100	103	363	175
1978	125	100	104	446	202

*Source: Claes Brundenius, "An Assessment of Basic Needs Satisfaction in Cuba 1958–78" (mimeo) (Lund, Sweden: Research Policy Institute, 1980), Tables 17 and 18.

The indices in Table 1 show that Cuba has done fairly well with respect to food and beverages, very well in health, extremely well in education (that was expected) but has a rather poor record with regard to clothing and housing. The food situation remained critical during the first decade, above all due to inefficient planning, and the textile industry suffered heavily from the embargo policies adopted by the countries that were "enemies of the revolution," notably the United States.[19] Quite a lot of raw material for the textile industry, which had formerly been imported, had to be produced with local inputs, a structural transformation that has been a long and difficult process.

Housing construction boomed during the first years of the revolution when on the average some 17,000 dwelling units were built annually.[20] Then during the hard years after 1963 and through to 1970, annual housing construction dwindled drastically when priority for the construction industry was given to building infrastructure, schools and industrial plants. By the end of the 1970s housing construction again reached an annual level of 17,000 to 20,000 units but far from the goal of 70,000 to 80,000 new homes to be built annually beginning in 1975, and only just about enough to make up for the population growth and the annual demolition of old houses.[21]

The Cuban health record is impressive, not least considering that about one third of all doctors left the country during the first three years after the revolution. Medical services also suffered during the first decade when the Ministry of Education and the universities, in order to compensate this brain drain, reduced the requirements for medical professions.[22]

The health situation also deteriorated in these years. Thus, the infant mortality rate went up from 34.9 to 46.7 per thousand in 1969 but has then gradually fallen and was in 1978 as low as 22.3, one of the lowest rates recorded in the Third World.[23] During the second decade many diseases have been completely eradicated in Cuba (malaria and poliomyelitis), and mortality rates sharply reduced as in the cases of tuberculosis, diphtheria and intestinal parasitism.[24] This is no doubt the result of the rapid expansion of medical facilities in the 1970s, especially as regards number of physicians, dentists and nurses. The success is particularly due to the extension of medical services to the *rural areas.* Medical treatment is totally free and newly graduated doctors have to do obligatory service for at least two years in the countryside. At the same time that the administration of health has been centralized, its execution has been very much decentralized. Medical care has been provided free side by side with the active mobilization of the population to attain massive immunization, blood donations, the clearing of garbage dumps and similar activities, in most cases organized by the numerous Committees for the Defense of the Revolution.[25]

The educational expansion is perhaps the most spectacular accomplishment of the Cuban Revolution. In the 1960s the stress was laid on raising the minimum levels of education of the population and one of the first achievements was the historic literacy campaign in 1961 when some 200,000 Cubans were mobilized under the slogan "Let those who know more teach those who know less."[26] In this way, in less than one year the illiteracy rate went down from 23.6 percent for Cubans aged over ten (and in the countryside the figure was double that rate) to 3.9 percent, an accomplishment later corroborated by UNESCO and described as probably unequalled in the history of education.[27] An important aspect of this campaign was the fact that making people literate was not seen as an end in itself but rather a means for the integration of these earlier marginalized sectors of the population into the new society.[28] When the literacy campaign ended, an ambitious program to elevate the educational levels of people at large was launched, and primary and secondary schooling was offered in farms, factories, offices and night schools.[29] Courses leading to third-grade education were made available to more than 500,000 adults, culminating with 848,000 adults enrolled in 1964. The next phase was the "battle for the sixth grade," the target being that all workers and farmers should attain an educational level corresponding to the sixth grade of primary school. This target was reportedly reached by the end of the 1970s.[30]

The most spectacular expansion of education did not, however, take place in the 1960s but in the 1970s, the reason being the explosion, to say the least, of secondary education—enrollments by the end of the 1970s were more than ten times higher than before the revolution. In 1979 compulsory schooling embraced no less than 92 percent of all children between 6–16 years old, and more than one third of the total population was attending some type of school.[31]

Here again the upsurge in the rural areas has been remarkable. Before the revolution there were no secondary schools at all in the countryside and as late as in 1971 secondary rural enrollment only amounted to some 3,000 children.[32] During the 1970s, however, a continuous effort has gone into the construction of full boarding schools in the countryside based on the principle of half-time work and half-time study, in order to eliminate traditional attitudes looking down on manual work. By 1978 there were 368 such *escuelas en el campo* with some 200,000 students, accounting for 25 percent of total secondary enrollments.[33]

4. REDISTRIBUTION OF INCOMES AND ASSETS

Although little quantitative information has been supplied by the Cuban government to support the claim that a radical redistribution of incomes and assets has taken place in the country after the revolution, few observers of the Cuban Revolution seem to doubt it. As a matter of fact, Dudley Seers considers that "the degree of equality in Cuba is now probably unique,"[34] and Robert Bernado even argues that Cuba "is the first [country] to institutionalize the communist or egalitarian rule of production and distribution."[35] Although those claims may be somewhat exaggerated they nevertheless reflect the large number of redistributive reforms and laws enacted after the revolution, especially during the first ten years.

The most important reform was the Agrarian Reform Law of May 1959. Its provisions can be summarized as follows:

1. a maximum limit of 400 hectares [1000 acres] on land ownership,
2. the transfer of land to those who farm it but do not own it,
3. the establishment of people's farms and sugar cooperatives in place of the large expropriated sugar estates,
4. the nationalization of 40 percent of all rural property,
5. compensation to owners of expropriated land in the form of Agrarian Bonds, redeemable within a period of 20 years and with a 4 1/2 percent interest rate.[36]

The Agrarian Reform had, of course, a tremendous effect on income distribution in the rural areas, not only because the large *latifundistas* were deprived of much of their land but also because the small farmer could get land very cheap. The first 27 hectares of land were given to the small farmer *(campesino)* free, with the right to purchase a further 40 hectares. It has been estimated that some 100,000 *campesinos* benefited from this reform.[37] In October 1963, a second and final Agrarian Reform Law was passed, limiting the area of land which could be owned privately to 66 hectares.[38]

In the urban sector the most effective redistributive reform was the Rent Law of March 1959, implying reductions of 50 percent in the rents of all who paid less than 100 pesos per month and of 30 or 40 percent for tenants in the higher brackets. The wealthy were shocked by this drastic measure denounced as virtual confiscation of their private property, and considered to be Castro's first "betrayal" to the bourgeois supporters of the revolution.[39] But there were many other reforms or laws that meant de facto redistribution of income and wealth. Thus, for instance, the minimum salary was raised, prices of medicine, electricity and gas were lowered, gambling and prostitution were suppressed, back payments of salaries and retirement pensions of people fired during the Batista regime were honored, and the establishment of "people's stores" (especially in the rural areas) guaranteed the supply of basic goods at low prices.[40]

Table 2: *Estimated Income Distribution in Cuba 1953, 1962 and 1973**
(IS, Income Shares; CS, Cumulative Shares)

	1953		1962		1973	
Deciles	IS	CS	IS	CS	IS	CS
0–10	0.6	0.6	2.5	2.5	2.9	2.9
10–20	1.5	2.1	3.7	6.2	4.9	7.8
20–30	1.9	4.0	4.8	11.0	5.4	13.2
30–40	2.2	6.2	6.2	17.2	7.1	20.3
40–50	4.6	10.8	6.8	24.0	8.7	29.0
50–60	6.4	17.2	9.5	33.5	10.5	39.5
60–70	10.8	28.0	12.0	45.5	12.5	51.5
70–80	12.0	40.0	13.1	58.6	13.5	65.0
80–90	21.5	61.5	18.4	77.0	15.1	80.1
90–100	38.5	100.0	23.0	100.0	19.9	100.0
(Top 5%)	(28.0)		(12.7)		(9.5)	
Total	100.0		100.0		100.0	
Gini coefficients		0.56		0.35		0.28

*Source: Claes Brundenius, "Measuring Income Distribution in Pre- and Post-Revolutionary Cuba," *Cuban Studies,* Vol. 2 (1979). Figures for 1962 are revised. The above figures include estimates for the private sector.

The redistribution of income that took place during the first two years was indeed impressive. Exactly how much was redistributed is not known, but it has been calculated that more than 500 million pesos annually, or 20 percent of the average national income in the period 1959–1960, was redistributed in those years.[41] According to one official source, the proportion of the labor force earning more than 75 pesos a month rose from 51.5 to 60.8 percent, and in the rural areas from 27.2 to 34.2 percent between January 1958 and January 1961.[42] It has been estimated that in the same period, as a result of the renegotiation of new labor contracts, wages and salaries increased between 15 and 30 percent.[43]

Although no official statistics exist on distribution of income in Cuba, neither before the revolution nor after, I have myself ventured to make some estimates for the years 1953, 1962 and 1973; of which the summary findings are presented in Table 2. The methodology behind these calculations has been explained in another context,[44] and will not be repeated here, although it should be pointed out that the 1962 figures are slightly revised, since they did not, in the earlier version, include estimates for the private sector (which was still important, in the agricultural sector above all, at the time).

The figures in Table 2 suggest that an important redistribution of income took place just after the revolution, benefiting principally the poorest 40 percent of the population, although the middle deciles also appear to have gained in the process. Between 1962 and 1973 a further redistribution of income took place but at a much slower pace than before. This is somewhat surprising, considering that the new, more profound, Agrarian Reform was decreed in October 1963, and moral incentives were to take priority over material incentives in accordance with resolutions adopted at the Twelfth Workers' Congress in 1966.[45] Of these events, however, perhaps only the second Agrarian Reform had any deeper effect on income distribution. In retrospect, it seems that moral incentives produced increased inequalities rather than the reverse. The reason is, it is argued, that income increases went to the wrong people. Those who wanted to work more did not get any more money out of it, while those who did not want to work more for the same rate still could earn money doing an extra job.[46]

At any rate, it is clear that the redistribution which did take place in the period 1962–1973 was largely the result of the continuing rise of the average wage in the agricultural sector. Thus, in 1962 the annual average wage in agriculture was only 954 pesos, or 62 percent of the average wage in the state sector as a whole, and only 49 percent of the average industrial wage.[47] In 1973 the income differentials had narrowed considerably, the average agricultural wage being 1,416 pesos per year, or 93.5 percent of the national average, and 88 percent of the industrial average.[48] By 1978, however, it seems that the income gap between the sectors had again increased with the average wage in agriculture amounting to 81 and 73 percent of the national and industrial averages, respectively.[49] This indicates that the drive toward income equality might have reached its climax around 1973, at least temporarily, although it is not so certain what impact the new wage reform announced in June 1980 might have.[50] Even if strong material incentives are reinforced, many of the lower salary steps are eliminated at the same time, and the latter effect might make up for the effects of the former on income distribution at the aggregate level.

Although not unique in the world, the income redistribution for the benefit of the poor that has taken place in Cuba after 1959 is by all means unique in Latin America. In most of the Latin American countries the income share of the poorest 40 percent of the population seldom reaches 10 percent,[51] and in many countries the share has even been decreasing during the last two decades. In the case of Brazil, the poorest 40 percent received only 7.9 percent of the income in 1976, which should be compared with 10.1 percent in 1970, and 11.5 percent in 1960.[52] In Peru the trend has been the same. While the two first quintiles in 1961 got 10 percent of the income, this share had by 1972 decreased to 8 percent, and for the lowest quintile the situation has aggravated even more drastically, from 3.0 percent to 1.4 percent.[53]

Brazil and Peru are interesting cases to compare since both countries have, rightly or wrongly, been associated with alternative development strategies. Brazil has been the most pronounced advocate of the theory that a growth-oriented strategy will in the long run also benefit the poor, and that "the cake has to grow before it can be eaten."[54] Peru is interesting because the military government, which came into power in 1968, promised to redistribute both assets and income through radical measures such as land reform, nationalizations of basic industries, and workers' participation in profits and management,[55] but all measures were to be carried out in accordance with a genuine Peruvian model that would be "neither reformed capitalism nor authoritarian communism."[56] . . .

5. GROWTH VERSUS BASIC NEEDS AND REDISTRIBUTION

It has sometimes been argued by critics of basic needs oriented strategies that such an approach is bound to inhibit growth since it is basically consumption oriented. Cuba has been used as a case in point in view of the sluggish growth rates recorded in the 1960s. Dudley Seers, however, finds the issue to be misleading and says that "the important question to pose about a country's performance is not, how much did the nation's income grow? But rather, whose income grew? And what sort of production increased?"[57] Furthermore, Norman Hicks has tried to estimate through regression analysis the relationship between growth performance and basic needs oriented strategies among the developing countries in the 1960–73 period, and has found that:

> first, it would appear that countries making substantial progress in meeting basic
> needs do *not* have substantially lower GNP growth rates; and

second, the attainment of higher level of basic-needs satisfaction appears to lead to higher growth rates in the future.[58]

Few countries could illustrate this finding better than Cuba. First of all, the relatively slow growth rates of the sixties were not slow compared to the prerevolutionary rates.

. . . Secondly, the relatively slow growth certainly is not the result of lower investment levels. On the contrary, what happened was that while before the revolution the economy had been highly consumption-oriented (for the upper-middle classes), with lots of the consumer items imported from abroad, the economy rapidly ran into difficulties when, after the revolution, the income redistribution to the benefit of the bottom half of the population led to a drastic increase in the demand for basic goods. Since there was not enough installed capacity to satisfy demand, and there was little chance of getting these goods on the world market due to the embargo by the United States and its allies, a good deal of resources had to be devoted to investment in new plants and equipment, most of which had to be imported from the socialist countries. Thus, state investments as a percentage of the gross material product increased from 16.4 percent in 1962 to 22.8 percent in 1966, to 27.4 percent in 1967 and, reportedly, to no less than 31 percent in 1968.[59] The high rates of investment are also corroborated by the high rates of growth of the construction industry in the same period.

The priority given to investment in industry and the expansion of the educational and health services in the 1960s explain most of the story behind the economic boom during the first half of the following decade. Since most of the investment goods had to be imported, the main concern was over the rising balance-of-payments deficit.[60] It was this concern, coupled with low productivity and overcentralized and bureaucratic planning, that became the headache of the government, and not that basic needs satisfaction and redistribution in any way would inhibit growth. In retrospect it is clear instead that the equity strategy of the 1960s has induced growth in the 1970s.

Table 3: *Annual Growth Rates during the First Five-Year Plan* (1976–1980)*
(Constant Prices)

	Agriculture, forestry and fishing	Mining, manufacturing and electricity	Construction	Total material production
1976	3.6	3.1	5.6	3.6
1977	4.2	1.1	9.9	3.1
1978	6.2	9.0	7.4	8.2
1979	2.7	1.9	0.8	1.9
1980	4.5	2.5	0.4	2.4
Average 1976–1980	4.2	3.7	4.9	4.0

*Sources: CEE (Committee for National Statistics), *Anuario Estadístico de Cuba* 1979 (Havana: 1980); *Boletín Estadístico Mensual de Cuba, Marzo de 1981* (Havana: 1981).

6. PROSPECTS FOR THE 1980s

What is perhaps the most impressive feat of the Cuban development strategy is that it has been committed to satisfy the basic needs of the population as a first priority in spite of mounting economic problems during the latter part of the 1970s. From 1976 the growth rates of the economy started slackening considerably and were below 4 percent during each of the years 1976 through 1980 except for 1978 (see Table 3). What was worse, this period coincided with the launching of the First Five-Year Plan. In other words, the plan could not have had a worse start. No doubt one of the major reasons for the disappointing performance of the economy during the first plan (total material production increased at a rate of 4 percent compared with a planned rate of 6 percent) was the sudden reverse in the behavior of the world sugar market. Sugar prices had soared in 1974, and were for a brief period as high as 70 cents per pound, an unprecedented figure, and although prices quickly went down to more normal levels, the Cubans still were optimistic that they would stabilize around 20 cents. But the prices went down the drain and, during most of the plan period, were below 10 cents, at times below costs of production. This was very serious indeed because the boom years had generated 3.7 billion dollars of credits from the Western world.[61] Now, as a result of disappointing price movements, many industrial projects envisaged by the plan had to be discontinued. As so many times before, the Soviet Union had to come to the rescue of the Cubans and thanks to improving terms of trade with the Russians the trade balance with them was favorable for the first time since the early 1960s and the overall trade deficit was kept at a lower level than during the preceding quinquennium.[62]

However, it is not only the fall in terms of trade with the West (30 percent lower during 1976–1979 than during 1971–1975)[63] which explains the sluggish growth rates during the last years of the plan. There were also important difficulties in agricultural and livestock production at the end of the period due to plagues and pests, such as sugar rust, tobacco blue mold and African swine fever. . . .

Cuba has just launched its Second Five-Year Plan (1981–1985) and the tone of the declared goals of the plan is what one might call cautiously optimistic. The plan envisages an annual rate of growth of the economy of 5 percent and personal consumption is expected to increase by 4 percent a year.[64] At the same time important resources are going to be diverted to the heavy industry in order to diminish the foreign dependency in the long run. One of the most determined efforts of the plan will go into the construction of some 200,000 housing units, more than twice the number achieved during the first plan. As before, the key element for the success of these targets is the performance of the sugar sector. The plan is made on the prediction of an increase of sugar production of between 20 and 25 percent over the former plan period, which would mean an average of about 8.5 million tons. But even if this target is reached, the big question mark still remains. How will the sugar prices on the international market behave? If their movement will turn out to be as disappointing as during the first plan, the fulfillment of the plan can only be achieved at the price of still heavier dependence on the Soviet Union.

NOTES

1. See, for instance, Dudley Seers, "The Cuban Experience," in H. Chenery, *et al., Redistribution with Growth* (Oxford: Oxford University Press, 1974), p. 262.

2. Archibald R. M. Ritter, *The Economic Development of Revolutionary Cuba* (New York: Praeger, 1974), p. 134.

3. Ibid.

4. For a definition and discussion of these systems, see Alex Dupuy and John Yrchik, "Socialist Planning and Social Transformation in Cuba: A Contribution to the Debate," *The Review of Radical Political Economy,* Vol. 10, No. 4. (1978), pp. 51–52.

5. A. Ritter, *The Economic Development . . . ,* p. 167.

6. Nelson Valdés, "The Cuban Revolution: Economic Organization and Bureaucracy," *Latin American Perspectives,* No. 1 (Winter 1979), p. 17.

7. Ernesto "Che" Guevara, "Man and Socialism in Cuba" in Bertram Silverman, ed., *Man and Socialism in Cuba: The Great Debate* (New York: Atheneum, 1973), pp. 337–54.

8. Fidel Castro, "Discurso en al Acto de Clausura del XIII Congreso CTC," (November 11–15, 1973), *Granma* (November 25, 1973).

9. A. Dupuy and J. Yrchik, "Socialist Planning . . . ," p. 55.

10. Ibid.

11. "Program Manifesto of the 26th July Movement," in Rolando Bonachea and Nelson Valdés, eds., *Cuba in Revolution* (New York: Anchor Book, 1972), p. 131.

12. James O'Connor, *The Origins of Socialism in Cuba* (Ithaca, N.Y.: Cornell University Press, 1970), p. 182.

13. Dudley Seers (ed.) *Cuba: The Economic and Social Revolution* (Chapel Hill, N.C.: University of North Carolina Press, 1964), p. 84.

14. Carmelo Mesa-Lago, *The Economy of Socialist Cuba: A Two-Decade Appraisal* (Albuquerque, N.M.: University of New Mexico Press, 1981), Ch. 6.

15. F. Castro, "Discurso en al Acto de Clausura . . ."

16. Carmelo Mesa-Lago, "A Model to Compare Alternative Strategies of Socioeconomic Development in Latin America" (mimeo) (Pittsburgh: University of Pittsburgh, 1978), Table 3.

17. ILO (International Labor Office), *Employment, Growth and Basic Needs: A One-World Problem* (New York: ILO 1977), p. 191.

18. For a definition of methodology and more details, see Claes Brundenius, "An Assessment of Basic Needs Satisfaction in Cuba 1958–78" (mimeo) (Lund, Sweden: Research Policy Institute, Univ. of Lund, 1980).

19. For an interesting discussion on the effects of the U.S. embargo policy against Cuba, see Gunnar Adler-Karlsson, *Western Economic Warfare 1947–1967* (Stockholm, Sweden: Almqvist and Wiksell, 1968), Ch. 17.

20. MINREX (Ministerio de Relaciones Exteriores), *Profile of Cuba* (Havana: MINREX, 1966), p. 205.

21. Carmelo Mesa-Lago, *Cuba in the 1970s* (Albuquerque, N.M.: Univ. of New Mexico Press, 1974), p. 46.

22. —————, "Economic Policies and Growth," in Carmelo Mesa-Lago, ed., *Revolutionary Change in Cuba* (Pittsburgh: Univ. of Pittsburgh Press, 1971), p. 292.

23. CEE (Comite Estatal de Estadistica), *Anuario Estadistico de Cuba 1979* (Havana: JUCE-PLAN, 1980), Table 21, and World Bank, *World Development Report 1980* (Washington, DC: World Bank, 1980), Table 21.

24. Ministerio de Salud, *Informe Anual 1979* (Havana: MINSAP, 1980).

25. Ricardo Leyva, "Health and Revolution in Cuba," in R. Bonachea and N. Valdés, *Cuba in Revolution,* p. 495.

26. Lee Chadwick, *Cuba Today* (Westport, Conn.: Lawrence Hill and Co., 1975), p. 91.

27. Ibid.

28. Peter Griffiths, "Fidel Castro's Report on Education, 1976," in John Griffiths and Peter Griffiths, *Cuba, The Second Decade* (London: Writers and Readers Books, 1979), p. 173.

29. Nelson Valdés, "The Radical Transformation of Cuban Education," in R. Bonachea and N. Valdés, eds., *Cuba in Revolution,* p. 429.

30. *Granma* (October 31, 1980).

31. Ministerio de Educación, *Algunos Datos de la Educación Cubana* (Havana: MINED, 1980), p. 56.

32. C. Brundenius, "An Assessment . . . Cuba 1958–78," Table 13.

33. CEE, *Anuario Estadistico. . . .*

34. D. Seers, "The Cuban Experience," p. 262.

35. Robert Bernard, *The Theory of Moral Incentives in Cuba* (Tuscaloosa, AL: Univ. of Alabama Press, 1971), p. ix.

36. MINREX, *Profile . . . ,* p. 120.

37. Ibid.

38. Ibid, p. 121.

39. J. P. Morray, *The Second Revolution in Cuba* (New York: Monthly Review, 1962), p. 24.

40. A. Ritter, *The Economic Development . . . ,* p. 107.

41. Jose-Luis Rodríguez García, "Politica economica de la revolución Cubana 1959–60," *Economia y Desarrollo,* No. 54 (1979), p. 148.

42. Employment Survey cited in O'Connor, *The Origins of Socialism . . . ,* p. 245.

43. A. Ritter, *The Economic Development . . . ,* p. 107.

44. Claes Brundenius, "Measuring Income Distribution in Pre- and Post-Revolutionary Cuba," *Cuban Studies,* Vol. 2 (1979).

45. Roberto E. Hernández and Carmelo Mesa-Lago, "Labor Organization and Wages," in Mesa-Lago (ed.) *Revolutionary Change in Cuba* (Pittsburgh: University of Pittsburgh Press, 1971), p. 211.

46. Opinion expressed to the author by Dr. Carlos Rafael Rodríguez, Vice-President of the Council of State and the Council of Ministers, in Havana, November 4, 1980.

47. C. Brundenius, "Measuring Income Distribution . . . ,"

48. Ibid.

49. CEE, *Anuario Estadistico* . . . , p. 57.

50. *Granma* (April 6, 1980).

51. World Bank, *World Development Report 1980,* op. cit.

52. Carlos Langoni, *Distribuiçao de Renda e Desenvolvimento Economico no Brasil* (Rio de Janeiro: Editora Expressão e Cultura 1973), and PNAD (Pesquisa Nacional por Amostra de Domicilos 1976), (Rio de Janeiro: 1978).

53. Carlos Amat y León and Hector León, *Estructura y Niveles de Ingreso Familiar en Perú* (Lima: Universidad del Pacífico, Centro de Investigación, 1979), p. 105.

54. Governo Federal, *II National Development Plan, 1975–79 (Brazil)* (Rio de Janeiro: Instituto Brasiliero de Geografia e Estadistica 1974), p. 69.

55. Claes Brundenius, *Structural Changes in the Peruvian Economy 1968–75* (Lund, Sweden: Research Policy Institute, 1976).

56. Juan Velasco Alvarado, *Velasco: La Voz de la Revolución* (Lima: Oficina Nacional de Difusión del SINAMOS, 1972), p. 10.

57. Seers, "The Cuban Experience," p. 262.

58. Norman Hicks, "Growth vs. Basic Needs: Is There a Trade-Off?" *World Development,* Vol. 7 (1979), p. 992.

59. JUCEPLAN (Junta Central de Planificacion), *Boletín Estadístico de Cuba 1970* (Havana: JUCEPLAN, 1972), and Fidel Castro, "Speech on March 13, 1968," *Granma* (March 15, 1968).

60. See, for instance, Ritter, *The Economic Development* . . . , Ch. 5.

61. Carmelo Mesa-Lago, "The Economics of U.S.-Cuban Rapprochement," in Cole Blasier and Carmelo Mesa-Lago, *Cuba in the World* (Pittsburgh: Univ. of Pittsburgh Press, 1979), p. 209.

62. Olga Ester Torres, "El desarrollo de la economia cubana a partir de 1959," *Comercio Exterior,* Vol. 31, No. 3 (March 1981), Table 1.

63. Ibid., Table 3.

64. Fidel Castro, *Informe Central al II Congreso del Partido Comunista de Cuba* (Havana: Editora Politica, 1980), p. 7.

CHAPTER 6

The Contemporary Cuban Economy

14. Main Report to the Third Party Congress: The Economy*

BY FIDEL CASTRO

Excerpted from Fidel Castro's report on behalf of the Central Committee to the Third Congress of the Communist Party of Cuba, 1986.

The five years that have elapsed since the Second Congress have been, without a doubt, rich in the creative work of our people and the advances of the revolution; perhaps one of our most prolific and successful periods.

The Gross Social Product grew at an average rate of 7.3 percent—far above the 5 percent forecast for the period—while industrial production increased by 8.8 percent.

Investments in the State civilian sector during the five-year period amounted to 17.88 billion Cuban pesos at current prices: 34.2 percent higher than during the 1976–80 period. Of this, 36.2 percent was invested in industry; 23.3 percent in agriculture; 11.8 percent in transportation. These three sectors accounted for 71.3 percent of total investments.

Labor productivity increased during the five-year period at an annual rate of 5.2 percent. This factor accounted for 74 percent of the increase in production. . . .

Personal consumption grew at an annual rate of 2.8 percent while the

*From Fidel Castro, "Main Report to the Third Party Congress of the Communist Party of Cuba, February 4, 1986," *Granma Weekly Review* (February 10, 1986), pp. 2–21.

corresponding rate for social consumption grew by 7.1 percent. Average monthly salaries increased by 26.4 percent during the period.

Daily per capita calorie intake rose to 2,900 and protein intake to 78 grams.

By 1985 there were 50 refrigerators, 91 television sets, 152 radios, 59 washing machines and 69 fans per 100 homes with electricity. . . .

ADVERSE CONDITIONS

Thus far, comrade delegates, I have reviewed our major economic and social development achievements of the past five-year period, and they are considerable. It must be borne in mind that, in this period, our country has suffered a prolonged drought, which became more intense as of May 1983, and further worsened in 1985, when the country registered its driest rainy season since the triumph of the Revolution. During three of the five years of this period, rainfall was less than 80 percent of the historical rainy season average. These climatic irregularities were compounded by five tropical storms in the five-year period and by unseasonable torrential downpours that hit the sugar harvest and other crops in the first quarter of 1983.

In evaluating our economic and social performance, the profound economic crisis that has been scourging the developed capitalist world and, particularly, the Third World countries must also be kept in mind. The past five-year period has been one of the most disastrous for the domestic economies of Latin America: all economic indicators dropped; many of them registered negative growth and some fell back to the rates of 20 years ago. Moreover, sugar prices on the so-called world market reached their lowest buying power this century, and there is still an imperialist blockade against our country. The fact that Cuba has achieved what it has in this period attests to our excellent and fair economic relations with the socialist community.

DEFICIENCIES AND SHORTCOMINGS

Nevertheless, we could have made better use of our resources and our efforts. Our work has been far from its best. Deficiencies and shortcomings still persist, and we must call them by their names and fight against them with all our might. Only thus will we be worthy of the name communist! Only thus will we be able to advance with ever faster and firmer steps!

The country's main economic problem during 1981–85 was that although overall growth rates were satisfactory, they proved sluggish where we most needed them: exports of goods and services and import substitution.

Traditional exports to capitalist markets were effected, and, despite the increase in new export items, they are still not sufficient to counter the deficits in our balance of payments in convertible currency. Tourism, notwithstanding its sustained growth, has not yet fulfilled our expectations. It will have to overcome subjective difficulties that would jeopardize our excellent prospects were they to persist.

Some delivery commitments to the socialist countries were not met. It should also be pointed out that very few new export items have been added to our trade with the socialist countries in these five years. We must take more vigorous steps in this field, given the huge market and favorable terms the CMEA member countries offer us for further economic integration.

Imports were reduced in this quinquennium, but still not as far as is necessary and feasible. . . .

There are still some subjective conditions in the national economy that conspire against reducing production costs, increasing profitability and saving material, labor and financial resources.

We have not made the best use of industrial capacities. Lack of skills and labor force instability are basic factors in the slow assimilation of new facilities. We are still facing technical and organizational deficiencies in production, failure to make the best use of foreign technical assistance, lack of technical discipline and precision in industrial repair and maintenance. Inter-industry production cooperation has not been developed, nor has secondary production for consumer goods. . . .

Cost effectiveness is still hampered by idle raw materials, spare parts and other goods and resources frozen because of problems in planning and administering supplies.

The still inadequate application of the principle of payment for completed work is reflected in the quantity of elementary, nontechnical standards in effect, and the inadequate implementation of payment according to the quantity and quality of finished goods; and the system of premiums and bonuses in many enterprises is not always in line with production results. Management has been weak in this area.

One of our most serious problems has been the absence of comprehensive national planning for economic development, particularly where individual sectors have planned and executed investments on their own initiative without adequate centralized control. Examples abound: new industries and agricultural projects in sparsely populated areas lacking housing facilities for the labor force; extremely important agricultural plans, such as the citrus fruit plan, where we still have areas planted without irrigation; irrigation systems where there are no pumping stations or electric power to run them; workshops and facilities without the corresponding power supply; housing developments completed without the necessary urban infrastructure, etc.

We have not lacked external financing for different initiatives, but they have not always been undertaken with the rational and disciplined approach needed to ensure the prompt use of the resources invested. . . .

There has been an inadequate and unstable supply of consumer goods, particularly clothing, footwear, home furniture and linens, as well as a lack of variety, inappropriate sizes, poor finishing and outdated and repetitive designs, aggravated by irrational distribution.

In the service sector there are incidences of insensitivity to the population's problems, treatment that is incompatible with the revolution's principles, administrative attitudes that allow for irregularities which discredit the State's role and some schedules that do not meet customers' needs, all of which exacerbate the problems of a still insufficient network of services.

There are serious service problems in Havana, particularly in housing maintenance, public facilities and public transportation. The water supply is inadequate, aggravated by leaks resulting from the poor condition of the conduits. There are serious problems with the telephone service. The number of hospital beds in the capital, where some services are made available on a national level, has not increased at an adequate rate.

Procedures for solving simple legal problems remain excessive and bureaucratic.

Despite undeniable progress in public health, insistence on quality services is still inadequate. . . . The quality of medical care in some emergency rooms is affected by the large number of patients requiring attention. . . . Hygienic conditions in some facilities are substandard. There have been delays in putting expensive equipment to use, and maintenance is still inadequate. The production of a number of medications has been unstable and their distribution has been inconsistent.

Although there has been a growing awareness of the need to protect the environment, little progress has been made in the struggle against pollution, and industrial waste recycling is being done at only a small number of plants. . . .

The quality of our education still leaves much to be desired. Some classes are still mediocre or poor; notes, rather than textbooks, are often relied upon; some students are promoted without having gained the required knowledge, due to certain mechanisms operating in the school system. . . .

As regards employment, one of the fundamental rights of the people, many parts of the country have a labor shortage while others have a surplus; these must be given special consideration in our development plans. . . .

Following the initial thrust in implementing the Economic Planning and Management System there has been no consistent follow-through to improve it. The initiative was lost and the creativity needed to adapt this system to our own conditions—a system largely taken from the experience of other countries—never materialized.

The result was a proliferation of isolated enterprises and it was only due to the pressures exerted by a few ministries that the first joint enterprises began to be organized. Some of these mergers are too narrowly focused, or were put together piecemeal, and should be reviewed. Supply administration—which was overly centralized—remained practically stagnant and little was done to streamline that of foreign trade. Discipline was lax in agreeing on contracts and fulfilling contract obligations. Progress was made in incentives, but in a scattered, unsystematic way; they were not always effective as an economic stimulus. Statistics continued to be a mountain of data of debatable usefulness. The accounting system shows serious shortcomings, from the primary entry on; and until very recently no progress was made to facilitate practical participation by all administrative levels and workers' collectives in designing the plan—whose implementation remained rigid—or to establish a coherent system of controls. . . .

The Economic Planning and Management System could become a complete farce, as regards enterprise efficiency, if we attempt to achieve enterprise profitability by raising the prices of products, construction and productive services.

Prices in maintenance, construction and transportation, to mention just a few sectors, are scandalously high, covering up for inefficiency, over-staffing and over-spending. I believe we still have a lot to learn in the field of efficiency, and becoming the sorcerer's apprentice, i.e., apprentice capitalists, is not the solution. If these defects are not overcome, the Economic Planning and Management System will cease to be the driving force of our development.

. . . [On] December 28, 1984, speaking before the National Assembly we explained that a Central Group—including the vice-presidents of the Council of Ministers and the ministers, with the participation of secretaries and heads of the Central Committee departments and the presidents of provincial People's Power bodies—had been organized, and that, based on these principles, and working tirelessly, it had restructured the 1985 Plan. Furthermore, we said that the same thing would be done with the 1986 Plan, the Five-Year Plan and the Long-Term Plan for the year 2000.

We had thus embarked upon a new, qualitatively superior stage of the revolution. The methods for drawing up, supervising and executing the plans with the participation of all agencies and sectors, from the very beginning of the process, have been a considerable step forward.

Undoubtedly, 1985 was the year that afforded the greatest savings and efficiency, the year in which the revolution obtained the best economic results. However, this is just a beginning. . . .

The Central Group will continue its work. Improvements in the structure of State agencies and replacement of unsatisfactory officials will continue.

We have become increasingly aware of the difficulties, obstacles and deficiencies that can and must be overcome, and especially of the need to do more efficient, energetic and sustained work. There will be no tolerance whatsoever for laziness, negligence, incompetence or irresponsibility. The apprentice stage must be left behind once and for all. The time has come to fully apply the enormous experience and know-how accumulated over the years of the revolution. This implies absolute dedication and selflessness!

THE 1986–1990 PERIOD

During the 1986–90 period, we project a 5-percent annual growth rate, a target which—despite the unfavorable world economic situation—is feasible thanks to our economic relations with the socialist countries.

Exports will grow at an annual average rate of 5 percent, while the growth rate for imports will be only 1.5 percent.

The policy of reducing energy consumption will be maintained. A national plan has been drawn up for saving and making rational use of energy. The plan comprises 10 large spheres of action and 34 main themes. This will reduce the consumption of petroleum-based fuels in 1990 by 10 percent relative to 1985.

Cost-effectiveness will be increased primarily through higher labor productivity, which will grow at an average annual rate of 3.5 percent, and which, in turn, will depend on a better organization of work based on a broader use of permanent and comprehensive brigades and cost-profit accounting at the brigade level.

During this quinquennium, which is the one that has shown the greatest growth of labor resources, a high level of employment will be maintained.
. . .

In order to revitalize the work to be done in the Economic Management System a national commission will be set up, attached to the Executive Committee of the Council of Ministers, to monitor implementation and improvement of the System. The commission will operate as an autonomous agency and its chairman will have the rank of Minister; it will oversee, coordinate, promote and monitor all the work to be done on management methods and operations.

The commission will be made up of representatives of the different State agencies, who will discuss and analyze the System's problems, and come to collective and comprehensive conclusions to improve coordination among all the agencies and institutions that have to do with economic management. It will have the services of a highly qualified and experienced group of consultants. . . .

DEVELOPMENT STRATEGY UP TO THE YEAR 2000

The strategy's main economic objective is to speed up the country's industrialization process.

The determining factors of future economic development and the industrialization process demand increasing and diversifying exports; substituting imports (particularly from the capitalist area); further integrating the national economy; using natural resources rationally; increasing efficiency in social production while economizing on resources (especially imports); recovering and recycling raw materials along with protecting the environment; moving idle stock; planning investments comprehensively and assigning investment priorities according to their impact on the balance of payments; concentrating on works in progress to reduce ongoing investments and make them operational more quickly; and keying improvements in the standard of living strictly to real development and our own resources.

Our socialist economic integration within the framework of the CMEA will be increased. Priority will be given to developing the machine and electronics industry, light industry, pharmaceuticals, biotechnology, and sugarcane by-products as important areas that will generate new exports. International tourism will be promoted as an important source of convertible currency. Agricultural development will be stepped up with intensive soil exploitation and increased yields contributing to more exports of traditional agricultural products and increasing satisfaction of the population's nutritional needs. . . .

All efforts should be aimed at sustained labor productivity increases, full use of labor power, cost reduction, increased profitability of enterprises, in short: efficiency.

The economic development strategy encompasses the experience of the revolution over more than 25 years, the ideas and concepts adopted by the Party and government in December 1984, and the Draft Party Program and economic guidelines that will be analyzed by this Congress. . . .

15. Patterns of Cuban Development: The First Twenty-five Years*

BY ANDREW ZIMBALIST AND SUSAN ECKSTEIN

The second half of the 1970s witnessed Cuba's first Five-Year Plan as well as the gradual introduction of an economic reform known as the "New System of Economic Management and Planning" (SDPE). Each represents the evolving maturity and institutionalization of Cuba's economic organizations.

The SDPE in many respects is modeled after the 1965 Soviet reforms. It attempts (1) to put enterprises on a self-financing basis, (2) to introduce a profitability criterion with its attendent incentives, and (3) generally to promote decentralization, organizational coherence, and efficiency. As with the Soviet reform it has met with the obstacles of, *inter alia,* bureaucratic resist-

*From Andrew Zimbalist and Susan Eckstein, "Patterns of Cuban Development: The First Twenty-Five Years," *World Development* Vol. 15, No. 1 (1987), pp. 5–22. Edited for this volume.

ance, an irrational price structure, and the weakness of financially based incentives in a shortage-type economy.[1] Both official studies and privately conducted interviews with enterprise administrators as well as other economic planning personnel who have emigrated to the United States suggest that there are still many snags to be worked out before the SDPE is fully and effectively implemented.[2] To be sure, Cuban officials have repeatedly expressed frustration with the bureaucratic encumbrances of planning as well as with the delays in implementing various parts of the new system. The speeches by former JUCEPLAN President, Humberto Pérez, at the Fourth Plenary evaluation of the SDPE in May 1985 and by Fidel Castro at the recent Party Congress in February 1986 are rather outspoken regarding these ongoing problems.[3]

Since the Cubans began introducing the SDPE they have found this Soviet-styled apparatus too inflexible and too centralized for the Cuban political culture. Each year between 1976 and 1980 innovations, intended to allow for decentralization and greater local initiative, were introduced. By 1980, however, it was decided that the system was being modified too rapidly and this engendered uncertainty about the rules of the game and, in turn, counterproductive instability. A general moratorium on decentralizing reforms ensued and was to last until the Third Party Congress, scheduled for December 1985. Following intensive study, it was projected that major reforms would be carried out to correspond with the Third Five-Year Plan, 1986–90.[4]

Major reports on the deficiencies of the SDPE were presented to the Third Party Congress, but the actual reform proposals were delayed until at least December 1986 when the Congress will be called back into session. In the meantime, the *Grupo Central* and a special planning commission are considering substantial decentralization efforts. As a prelude to such changes, several top planning figures, such as Humberto Pérez and Miguel Figueras, have been replaced. While these personnel changes have been interpreted by some Western scholars as indications that the SDPE has failed, it appears that they are better understood as an attempt to invigorate the planning apparatus with new ideas and fresh relationships unencumbered by previous methods and patterns.

The open, public criticism of the continuing weaknesses of the SDPE is consistent with the long-standing style of self-criticism and high expectations on the part of the revolution's leadership. It is important to stress, however, that at the same time that the Cubans have expressed dissatisfaction with the slow progress and imperfections of the SDPE they have also repeatedly credited the SDPE with rationalizing and improving the functioning of the Cuban economy. That is, on balance the SDPE has had a positive impact on the Cuban economy. To understand this salutary effect it is necessary to consider several of the concrete, decentralizing measures that have been introduced.

One of the first measures was the 1976 legalization of certain private sector activity. Since then individuals can offer such services as appliance and auto repair work, carpentry, licensed and done on a self-employed basis. The licensing requirement, in principle, enables the government to permit only activities which do not conflict with planned state activity. This economic "opening" does not necessarily represent "capitalist backsliding" but rather represents an effort to correct for the inefficiencies and inadequacies of the bureaucratized state sector and to allow fuller use of labor. License fees also enable the government to profit directly from private activity. In the first month of operation 2,000 people took out licenses to be street peddlers in Havana alone, and in 1981 private contracting cooperatives were responsible for 38 percent of new housing units.[5] Yet the contained reprivatization of the economy may have the unintended effect of reducing state enterprise productivity if, for example, workers pilfer state enterprises for private supplies, if they absent themselves from work to pursue private jobs, and if they become less committed to their official job because of their preference for the private work. Small-scale private activity is difficult to regulate.

Beginning in the mid-1970s the government also shifted its rural strategy. In raising prices paid by the state procurement agency and by permitting farmers and wage workers to market privately output exceeding their official quotas, material incentives stimulated farm production. The government also pressured farmers less to work on state farms and to cooperate with official agricultural plans. As a result, the number of private farmers who affiliated with state plans dropped—by half, for example, between 1973 and 1977.[6] Instead, the government encouraged farmers to form production cooperatives in which they retained private property rights while benefiting—at least in theory—from economies of scale and a less individualized (and therefore "higher") stage of organization. The number of cooperatives jumped from 44 in 1977 to almost 1,400 in 1985, and cooperatives came to involve over 60 percent of the land that remained in private hands.[7] Production brigades, along with team and modified household contracting, have also been introduced on state farms in recent years. The agrarian restructuring has had such a positive effect on production that the government has greatly expanded "parallel markets" and begun to tax the income from private sales. (In May 1986, in response to the emergence of a wealthy group of marketing middlemen who transported goods to the peasant markets and as an outgrowth of the expansion of rural production cooperatives and state-run parallel markets, the government announced the demise of the experiment with free farmers' markets. Since the government has raised procurement prices for production in excess of the quota to "free market" levels, peasant income and production incentives should not be significantly affected by this measure.) . . .

The government also modified its wage and consumer policies. Not only have wages—as previously noted—been increasingly linked to productivity (with slightly less than 50 percent of all jobs normed by 1979) and enterprise performance, they also have been raised and more closely tied to skill level.[8]

The new wage and labor policies appear to have had a positive economic impact because the government concomitantly modified its consumer policies. There has been a rapid expansion in the number and variety of consumer goods available to the public. Many goods are now available off the ration system. Indeed, while in 1970 95 percent of consumer spending was on rationed goods, in 1980 this proportion had diminished to approximately 30 percent.[9] New state housing policies allow dwellers to exchange housing units, tenants to purchase their homes and owners to rent out rooms.

Government concern with consumer preferences is reflected also in the activities of the Institute of Internal Demand. It surveys regularly consumer preferences and makes inventories of available supplies. The Institute relies on a network of thousands of volunteers to provide information on consumer preferences biweekly. The Institute, in addition, publishes a monthly magazine *(Opina)* with consumer information, which since 1976 has included ads for a panoply of private services available on a fee basis, as discussed below. While consumer allocations entail an immediate investment trade-off, they are central to the government's emphasis, since 1970, on a domestically based accumulation strategy. The increased availability of consumer goods and services should stimulate greater worker motivation and, in turn, productivity.

Although clear progress has been made in using domestic resources more fully and efficiently, the process of decentralization has been slowed by ongoing resource constraints and the related inability of Cuba's planning mechanism to develop slack. Thus, for example, as part of the material incentive scheme of the SDPE, enterprises were to be allowed to retain a certain share of their profits (or reduction in losses) through the so-called "stimulation fund." Largely due to the inability of the Cuban economy to develop slack, however, the "stimulation fund" has been slow to take effect. As long as there are insufficient goods available for enterprises to purchase outside the plan, the ability to retain earnings generally provides only a weak incentive at best. By 1979, only 2.8 percent of enterprises earned stimulation funds.[10] Moreover, it was originally contemplated by the SDPE that stimulation funds would be used for three purposes: worker bonuses, enterprise; sociocultural expenditures; and, small investments on new machinery and equipment. Yet, again due to the absence of slack and problems with surplus accumulation, the last use of the stimulation fund has been indefinitely suspended. . . .

While the government reemphasized a domestically rooted development strategy in the 1970s, it never abandoned its externally rooted strategy. CMEA and Western trade and financing came to be central to the regime's recovery from the political and economic crisis caused by the policies of the late 1960s. As the Western trade gave rise to new problems that have yet to be resolved, relations with the Soviet Union have resurged in economic importance.

Sugar continued to play a key role in the economy. After the crisis caused by the 1970 10-million-ton sugar target, the government lowered the output goal, but successful mechanization of production kept sugar yields high (though below the 1970 record yield) with much less use of labor. Indeed, the government's more permissive stance toward private economic activity, in both the cities and the countryside, undoubtedly partly results from the decline in the need for labor in the sugar sector. Whereas in 1975, 25 percent of cane cutting and 95 percent of lifting were mechanized, in 1981 46 percent of cutting and 97.5 percent of lifting were mechanized, and in 1985 these shares were 62 percent and 100 percent, respectively.[11]

The early 1970s success of the sugar strategy, however, is explained less by the reorganization of production or output than by world sugar prices. The world market price of raw sugar reached an all-time high in 1974, and the Soviet Union responded by raising the price it paid for Cuban sugar and by allowing the island to sell on the world market some of the sugar it had contracted to CMEA countries. Island export earnings accordingly reached an unprecedented high. . . . High export earnings provide revenue for the importation of inputs that are essential for domestic production and the slack that makes for effective decentralization.

The 1970s export based growth was distinctive in that it was heavily centered around Western trade. Indicative of the trade shift, in 1974 the hard currency earnings enabled the Castro government to import goods and technology from the West for the first time on a significant scale.

The country's capacity to stimulate domestic economic growth through Western trade proved, however, to be contingent on a short-lived favorable conjuncture in the international economy. World market sugar prices dropped from a record high of 68 cents a pound in November 1974 to around seven cents within three years. Since output did not expand at a rate sufficient to offset losses in unit sales, the island's capacity to stimulate capital accumulation through the purchase of imported raw materials, machinery and technology diminished. Moreover, the government was left with outstanding loans contracted when world market sugar prices were high.

Cuba arranged for Western loans to acquire goods and technology unavailable from CMEA. A good portion of the economic improvement of the early 1970s therefore is attributable to the growth in export earnings and the financing to which it gave rise; the previously delineated organizational changes may have been necessary but they in themselves do not fully explain the period's rapid economic growth.

Western banks, in turn, extended the financing to Cuba because their liquidity expanded dramatically following the post-1973 OPEC oil price hikes, and Western governments and banks alike viewed Cuba as a good credit risk given the high world sugar prices at the time and the then excellent credit ratings of the CMEA bloc. Yet, the collapse in the sugar market and then a rise in interest rates caused Cuba's Western debt to climb dramatically, from $660 million in 1974 to $2.86 billion by the end of 1983.[12] Cuba's debt service (amortization plus interest) to hard currency exports ratio reached 48% in 1980 (or 18.7 percent in relation to total export earnings).[13] Like other Latin American countries, Cuba has sought and achieved a renegotiation of its debt servicing in recent years; however, because of political discrimination, the terms of the renegotiation have been less favorable than in neighboring countries with more serious debts.

Despite the ongoing burden of its hard currency debt and the continuing drop in world sugar prices, Cuba's debt has not caused a severe dislocation to overall economic activity. . . . Cuban real Gross Social Product grew at about 7 percent per annum according to official figures during 1981–85 (attributable in large part to improvements in organizational efficiency and the high investment ratios during 1976–80), while the rest of Latin America on average has experienced real national income decreases. . . . Unemployment in Cuba continues to be negligible at a time when it has reached mammoth proportions in most of Latin America. Moreover, to the extent that labor is unemployed it does not have the same adverse social and economic consequences as in the rest of the region; in Cuba, for example, most unemployed workers are guaranteed a minimum wage as well as free health care and heavily subsidized basic services.

Nonetheless, the burden of debt service has impelled Cuba to concentrate on export production and import reduction. As a result, Cuba has had to curb investment spending. The projected investment ratio (gross investment as a share of Gross Material Product) for 1984 is a relatively low 18 percent. In contrast, the average investment ratio during 1976–80 was 29.3 percent.[14] The lower investment ratio, *inter alia,* is likely to slow down the growth rate for the remainder of the decade.

On the brighter side, Cuba has begun to make significant strides in the areas of import substitution and export diversification. Capital goods, consumer durables, chemicals, medicines (Cuba produces 83 percent of its needs), electronics, computers and steel are all sectors with negligible or zero output in 1958 that are now substantial and growing rapidly. For instance, whereas engineering and capital goods industries (ISIC 37 and 38) accounted for approximately 1.4 percent of total industrial production in 1959, due to an annual growth rate of 16.6 percent since 1970, this sector accounted for 13.2 percent of industrial gross value of output in 1983.[15]

Other products, such as citrus, fish, eggs, nickel, cement and electricity, have expanded several times over since 1958. Cuba currently produces a large share of its new cane harvesters, buses, refrigerators and other durables.[16]

Regarding export diversification, the share of sugar in total exports fell from an average of 86.8 percent during 1975–79 to 79.9 percent during 1980–82.[17] This decreased dependence on sugar exports cannot be attributed to lower world sugar prices in the latter period.[18] On the contrary, world sugar prices averaged 11.49 cents per pound during 1975–79 and 18.16 cents per pound during 1980–83. That is, world sugar prices were 58.1 percent higher on average during the second period, yet the sugar export share was 9.1 percent lower. Adjusting for sugar prices, then, would indicate even lesser rather than greater dependence on sugar exports. The sugar share in total exports fell further to an average of 75.7 percent during 1983–84.

From 1976 to 1980 Cuba introduced 115 new export products and in 1981 it introduced 17 more.[19] Whereas nonsugar exports equalled 230.5 million pesos in 1978, in 1982 they equalled 640.9 million pesos.[20] Nonsugar exports grew by an additional 27.5 million pesos in 1983.[21] After falling in 1984, nonsugar exports rose to record levels in 1985.[22] In addition, Cuba earned over 15 million pesos in 1983 from reexported petroleum; the Soviet Union now allows the island to sell a portion of its oil allotment for hard currency. (These exports, aided by a tripling of domestic crude oil extraction between 1981 and 1984 and a highly successful domestic energy conservation program, accounted for 39.5 percent of Cuba's hard currency earnings during 1983–85.[23] Indeed, the precipitous drop in oil prices in 1986 is projected to reduce Cuba's 1986 hard currency earnings by over $200 million.)

Yet hard currency commodity export earnings have been insufficient to address Cuba's debt repayment and import needs. Consequently, the leadership has tried still another externally linked surplus accumulation strategy since the late 1970s: direct foreign investment and use of foreign management expertise and technology. In 1977, for example, the Cuban leadership began to encourage contract manufacturing and joint ventures. Contract manufacturing is seen as a strategy whereby Cuba can expand its plant capacity with foreign capital and management skills. Under contract manufacturing arrangements, the government need not draw upon its own capital resources for initial plant investment outlays; rather, the plant is to pay for itself over time through the sales it generates.[24] Joint ventures require the government to furnish some but not all of the capital requirements. The government has implemented joint ventures with Japan in shipping, with Mexico in agricultural machinery-building marketing, with Panama in finance and sugar refining, and it has encouraged a variety of other projects. In 1982, Cuba issued a new foreign investment code, formalizing its efforts to attract foreign investment. The code permits foreigners to own up to 49 percent of local enterprises, to repatriate profits, and to control labor, pricing and production policies. The code is designed to attract a form of capital that compels foreign investors to absorb more of the risks than is true in the case of finance capital. Negotiations were initiated with a number of Canadian and West European firms but pressure from the Reagan Administration has indefinitely delayed potential investment projects.

Nonetheless, in part because of effective import substitution and export diversification as well as petroleum re-exports, Cuba achieved hard currency trade surpluses in 1982 and 1983 of 749.9 and 450.7 million pesos, respectively.[25] In this and other indicators Cuba has surpassed the performance targets stipulated in the 1982 Club of Paris debt renegotiations. These gains, it must be stressed, have been made despite the tightening blockade imposed by the Reagan Administration (through effectively pressuring third parties not to trade with Cuba and prohibiting US tourism to Cuba) and the precipitous fall in sugar prices since 1981.

It is also true, of course, that Cuba continues to be cushioned from changes in world market conditions by its privileged position within CMEA. Through significant sugar and nickel price subsidies as well as generous technological transfers and development and payments aid, the Soviet Union has buffered the Cuban economy over the years. This aid, however, has not been nearly as large as claimed by official US sources.[26] Official Western calculations overestimate the sugar subsidy (by comparing Soviet prices with world market prices, rather than with the subsidized prices at which most Western sugar is traded and by using official peso/dollar exchange rates) and they underestimate the costs of the "tied" nature of Soviet aid (i.e., the high cost and poor quality of Soviet imports that must be purchased with the rubles received for Cuban exports). A full assessment of Soviet aid must also take into account the opportunities thereby forgone, namely the consequent loss of aid from and trade with the United States.

Some have suggested that Soviet generosity toward Cuba has diminished in recent years. We, however, have not seen convincing evidence that the 1976 agreement to maintain bilateral terms of trade at unity has been violated. Moreover, it appears that the Cuban debt postponed from 1972 to 1986 has once again been put on hold. Nonetheless, Cuba's slow diversification out of sugar and the continuance of world sugar prices below six cents per pound, along with the ongoing hard currency debt amortization and interest payments, assure that Cuba's foreign sector will be a surplus detractor, imposing constraints on development possibilities through the remainder of this decade. . . .

As Cuba has institutionalized its system of central planning over the last 15 years, it has become apparent to Cuban planners that greater decentralization is needed to mitigate bottlenecks, delays and general inefficiencies as well as to promote the flow of information within the planning apparatus and improve worker/manager motivation. . . .

The process of successful planning reform and decentralization, however, has been constrained by resource shortages imposed by the external sector since the 1974–75 period of high sugar prices. Since then low sugar prices and costly debt repayment obligations have constricted external accumulation efforts. With the foreign sector a surplus consumer (rather than producer), the necessary resources for meaningful decentralization have been lacking. This circumstance, in turn, threatens to further entangle the planning bureaucracy and to engender frustration in the micro-units of the economy, thereby hindering the operation of the domestic surplus generation process as well. To be sure, this sequence of reactions represents only a potential force that may make itself felt in varying intensity and may be counteracted by other forces. Not-withstanding the pains of growth and the vagaries of world market pressures, the Cuban economy has emerged with a strong record for the first 25 years of the revolution. Although short and medium-run hurdles and tests remain, the overall outlook is positive—especially in comparison with Cuba's Latin neighbors.

NOTES

1. JUCEPLAN, *Segunda Plenaria Nacional de Chequeo de la Implantación del SDPE* (Havana: Ediciones JUCEPLAN, 1981); and Andrew Zimbalist, "Cuban Economic Planning: Organization and Performance," in S. Halebsky and J. Kirk, eds., *Twenty-Five Years of Revolution* (New York: Praeger, 1985).

2. JUCEPLAN, *Segunda Plenaria* . . . (1981); and JUCEPLAN, *Dictámenes Aprobados en la IV Plenaria Nacional de Chequeo del SDPE* (Havana: Ediciones JUCEPLAN, 1985). Each of these official studies is quite candid and blunt about the ongoing problems of inefficiency, bureau-cratic delays, etc. They also are clear that the SDPE is yielding increasingly positive returns.

3. Humberto Pérez, Speech given at the closing of IV Plenaria Nacional del Chequeo de la Implantación del Sistema de Dirección y Planificación de la Economia, to the SDPE, May 25, 1985, in JUCEPLAN, *Dictámenes Aprobados* . . . (1985); and Fidel Castro, "Main Report to the Third Congress," *Granma Weekly Review* (February 16, 1986).

4. The shortage of trained managerial and technical personnel has been an important constraint on the speed of the decentralization process. This account is based on conversations held in October 1985 and March 1986 with Miguel Figueras, Vice-President of JUCEPLAN until April 1986.

5. Fred Ward, *Inside Cuba Today* (New York: Crown Publishers, 1978), p. 31; also see Andrew Zimbalist and H. Sherman, *Comparing Economic Systems: A Political-Economic Approach* (New York: Academic Press, 1984), p. 381.

6. Jorge I. Domínguez, *Cuba: Order and Revolution* (Cambridge, MA: Harvard University Press, 1978), p. 459. For an interesting treatment of recent agricultural policies, see Medea Benjamin, *et al., No Free Lunch: Food and Revolution in Cuba Today*, (San Francisco: Institute for Food and Development Policy, 1985), Chs. 9 and 12.

7. *Granma Weekly Review* (May 27, 1984), p. 2; also, see CEPAL, *Estudio Económico de América Latina y el Caribe: Cuba 1984,* (August 1985), p. 9.

8. A. Zimbalist, "Cuban Economic Planning . . . ," p. 219.

9. A. Zimbalist and H. Sherman, *Comparing Economic Systems* . . . , p. 383.

10. JUCEPLAN, *Dictámenes Aprobados* . . . p. 385.

11. Humberto Pérez, "La Plataforma Programática y el desarrollo económico de Cuba," *Cuba Socialista,* Vol. 3 (June 1982), p. 10.

12. Banco Nacional de Cuba (BNC), *Informe Economico* (La Habana: BNC, 1984), p. 18.

13. Susan Eckstein, "Revolution and the Restructuring of National Economies: The Latin American Experience," *Comparative Politics,* Vol. 17, No. 4 (July 1985), pp. 474–94. Table 4.

14. CEE (Comite Estatal de Estadistica), *Anuario Estadístico de Cuba* (Havana: JUCEPLAN, various years); also see, Claes Brundenius, *Revolutionary Cuba: The Challenge of Economic Growth with Equity* (Boulder, CO: Westview Press, 1984), pp. 32–33.

15. Calculated from data presented in Claes Brundenius, "The Role of Capital Goods Produc-tion in the Economic Development of Cuba," Paper presented to workshop on "Technology

Policies for Development" (Lund, Sweden: Research Policy Institute, Univ. of Lund, May 29–31, 1985), pp. 11, 20 and 21.

16. On the development of an indigenous technological base in Cuba, see Charles Edquist, *Capitalism, Socialism, and Technology: A Comparative Study of Cuba and Jamaica* (London: Zed Books, 1985), Chs. 4, 6 and 7.

17. BNC, *Informe Economico,* (1982), pp. 21, 49.

18. C. Mesa-Lago has claimed that assertions of decreased dependence on sugar are misleading because they overlook the trend of sugar prices. As the numbers in the text demonstrate, Mesa-Lago's observation does not apply to the period since 1975. See Carmelo Mesa-Lago, "Cuba's Centrally Planned Economy: An Equity Trade-off for Growth," Paper presented at the Conference on Latin America (Nashville, TN: Vanderbilt University, November 3–5, 1983), p. 34; and William M. LeoGrande, "Cuban Dependency: A Comparison of Prerevolutionary and Postrevolutionary International Relations," *Cuban Studies,* Vol. 32 (July 1979), pp. 1–28.

19. H. Perez, "La Plataforma Programática . . . ," p. 39.

20. BNC, *Informe Economico* (1982), p. 49.

21. BNC, *Informe Economico* (1984), p. 20.

22. BNC, *Cuba: Quarterly Economic Report* (September 1985), p. 6; and BNC, *Cuba: Quarterly Economic Report* (February 1985), pp. 32–35.

23. The results of this conservation effort are most dramatically seen in the sugar sector. In 1976 Cuba's sugar mills consumed 2.11 gallons of oil per metric ton of processed cane; in 1983 the rate had dropped to 0.11 gallon. See Research Team on the Cuban Economy, *The Most Outstanding Aspects of the Cuban Economy, 1959–83* (Havana: University of Havana, Economic Sciences Area, 1984), p. 39.

Oil reexports grew from 96 million pesos in 1980 to 262 million pesos in 1982 and 486 million pesos (8.9 percent of total exports) in 1984. See CEPAL, *Estudio Económico . . .* (August 1985), p. 17; and BNC, *Informe Económico* (1984), p. 31.

24. *New York Times* (April 25, 1977), p. 4.

25. BNC, *Informe Económico* (1984), p. 12. A variety of production and price problems, however, turned this balance slightly negative in 1984 and the first three quarters of 1985.

26. CIA (Central Intelligence Agency), *The Cuban Economy: A Statistical Review* (Washington, D.C.: U.S. Government Printing Office, 1981); Lawrence H. Theriot, *Cuba Faces the Economic Realities of the 1980s,* Prepared for the Bureau of East-West Trade (Washington, D.C.: U.S. Department of Commerce, 1982); and Andrew Zimbalist, "Soviet Aid, U.S. Blockade and the Cuban Economy," *Comparative Economic Studies,* Vol. 24, No. 4 (Winter 1982).

16. Castro Takes the Economy in Hand*

BY MARIFELI PEREZ-STABLE

In August 1984 Silvia Marjorie Spence, a 42-year-old Jamaican-born woman who has lived in Santiago de Cuba since 1955, was fired from her job as chief accountant of a Santiago cement plant. Management charged that she

*From Marifeli Perez-Stable, "Castro Takes the Economy in Hand," *The Nation,* September 26, 1987, pp. 298–300.

had "acted on her own, mistrusted her superiors and voiced unsubstantiated gossip."

For two years, Spence had persistently questioned bookkeeping and payroll irregularities. Workers were being paid three times the national average wage; bonuses were being awarded without corresponding increases in productivity; and cement was being illegally bartered to a nearby agricultural enterprise for meat and vegetables.

Spence appealed her dismissal both to the Ministry of Construction and the Cuban Communist Party. The ministry's response was slow and unsympathetic, and in the end the minister himself confirmed the firing. Local party officials were more receptive, but her case hit a dead end when it reached the provincial party committee, whose secretary in charge of construction-industry issues was a personal friend of the cement plant's director. Undaunted, Spence appealed to the party's national review board. In February 1985 it concluded that her dismissal was unwarranted and ordered her reinstatement and an audit of the plant. But twenty-one months passed before the board's directives were implemented. In November 1986 Spence was reinstated in her old job and awarded more than 7,000 pesos in back pay. That December 25 and 26, the official party newspaper, *Granma,* published a two-part exposé of Silvia Marjorie Spence's ordeal.

That outcome was in no small way attributable to a speech that Fidel Castro had delivered on April 19, 1986—the twenty-fifth anniversary of the Bay of Pigs—in which he lambasted corruption, negligence and profiteering. New mercenaries, Castro charged, were now threatening the revolution from within. Managers were looking out for the well-being of their own industries without considering the national interest; artists were selling their works to the state at exorbitant prices; and peasants were making hefty profits on the parallel market. A 1985 housing law allowing direct transactions between buyer and seller was abetting runaway speculation. The informal economy was buzzing with street vendors and jacks-of-all-trades. The revolution, Castro reminded his audience, was not about making a quick peso. "We do not want to launch a cultural revolution," he declared. "We do not want to solve our problems by extremist methods and hurl the masses against those responsible for these irritating deeds."

The modest private sector that had flourished since the 1970s had become intolerable. Some Cubans were pursuing their individual enrichment and the private economy was draining the state sector of increasingly scarce resources. Meanwhile, Cuba's open economy remained as vulnerable as ever. Its annual export earnings had in the recent past provided sufficient hard currency for imports of between $1.2 billion and $1.5 billion, but in 1986 those had been reduced to some $600 million. Today, real sugar prices on the world market have fallen to 1930s levels, and the value of petroleum exports (domestic savings from the crude oil that the Soviet Union supplies to Cuba) has declined by half. While the Cuban-Soviet relationship is stable, Soviet sugar price subsidies and oil supplies beyond the island's domestic needs are reportedly being reduced.

The U.S. embargo, tightened by the Reagan Administration, continues to impose a heavy burden on the Cuban economy. Since, for example, the U.S. market remains out of bounds for Cuba, the devaluation of the dollar has increased import costs from other Western suppliers. Were there no embargo, Cuba could purchase cheaper U.S. goods. Western banks are much less willing to make loans, and Cuba still has to reschedule payments on a substantial part of its $4 billion foreign debt. The United States, moreover, has pressured the island's Western creditors to exact considerably harsher repayment terms than those imposed on other Third World countries. Natural disasters—a hurricane in late 1985 and a severe drought throughout 1986—have taken their toll on agricultural output. All told, both ideological considerations and harsh economic realities are spurring a reexamination of the modest economic reforms of the past ten years.

During the 1960s the revolution sought to make its special mark on history by attempting the parallel construction of socialism and communism. If Cuba was to promote social justice, then the logic of the market had to be challenged. If Cuba was to harness mass enthusiasm and channel it into economic development, then a more responsive political system was needed. Or so the Cuban leadership reasoned as it contemplated the face of socialism in the Soviet Union and Eastern Europe.

By 1970 Cuba had eliminated nearly all private-sector activity. Accounting and planning controls over economic activity had been virtually discarded. High investment rates and poor economic performance had drastically curtailed consumption. And worker absenteeism soared as bare store shelves rendered money worthless. Moreover, a political system that depended on Castro's stature and prestige, and on popular élan and commitment, wore thin amid mounting austerity. The combination of highly centralized economic planning, moral incentives and charismatic leadership ground to a halt with the failure to achieve the goal of a ten-million-ton sugar harvest in 1970.

In the 1970s Cuba embarked on the institutionalization of its revolution. In 1976 the economy acquired a blueprint for the first time, with the introduction of a management and planning system of relative decentralization and material incentives. At the same time, the Communist party expanded its membership, mass organizations were strengthened, a socialist constitution was promulgated and the institutions known as Popular Power were set in place, allowing a semblance of supervision over government facilities such as schools, supermarkets, cultural and sports centers, especially at the local level. Trade unions and the Federation of Cuban Women became active, albeit within the confines of vanguard party leadership. At least in principle, most Cubans had a set of rules to govern their daily lives at work and in their neighborhoods.

The management and planning system did not work miracles, but it did introduce a modicum of rationality into the economy, which began to register modest, if irregular, growth rates. The standard of living improved noticeably and daily life for the average Cuban became easier. Wages were linked to performance and the "parallel market" offered a greater variety of goods at higher prices than state stores did, as an incentive to productivity. The free market spurred peasants to increase their output and offered consumers fruit and vegetables, which had disappeared from the state market long ago. The government enacted wage and price reforms and allowed free contracting to encourage a more rational use of labor. Voluntary work was reduced. The 1960s were indeed receding.

Yet, Cuba's efforts to decentralize and streamline its economy did not proceed smoothly. A trade-dependent economy facing a U.S. embargo could not guarantee the flow of much-needed hard currency. Decentralization was in part hindered by the irregular supply of raw materials needed to give enterprises greater autonomy over planning and production. Faced with the need to show a profit, many of them resorted to inflating prices. Even so, state subsidies rose substantially in 1985. Scarcity of resources and supply bottlenecks encouraged an ad hoc barter system among firms.

At the same time, there is no doubt that the central bureaucracy resisted the effort to loosen planning controls. The government never created a local development fund that could reinvest industry profits, for example, and the allocation of investment capital remained haphazard. Most important of all, perhaps, the top party leadership—particularly Castro—was ambivalent about the new planning system, which was introduced only in the aftermath of the 1970 sugar harvest fiasco. For Castro, socialism was not reducible to the smooth functioning of economic control mechanisms. Mass enthusiasm and *conciencia* ("social consciousness"), rather, were the forces behind Cuba's struggle for national independence and social justice, and Castro was their anchor. Though Castro nominally endorsed the reforms at the first two Communist party congresses, in 1975 and 1980, he stopped short of giving them his personal political imprimatur. By the time the 1986 congress came around, Castro had taken the reins of the economy firmly back into his own hands.

In late 1984 the state Central Planning Board, JUCEPLAN, was partially divested of its powers in favor of a more broadly based Central Group, which includes government ministers and vice-ministers, central committee department heads, leaders of the mass organizations and Popular Power representatives. The new body aims to institute truly global economic planning and is more directly under Castro's personal direction than was its predecessor. In December 1986, at its closing session, the party congress ratified a "strategic counteroffensive to rectify mistakes and negative tendencies," something Castro had repeatedly called for during the course of the year.

Underlying the counteroffensive is the old 1960s Cuban vision that socialism without *conciencia* is no better than capitalism. The party abolished or restricted all the extraordinary sources of income that had been tolerated since the 1970s—peasant markets, freelance work, market regulation of housing costs—in the belief that the self-interested quest for material rewards was undermining the resolve that had sustained the revolution and was allowing the successful few to breach its commitment to equality. "A Communist spirit and *conciencia,* a revolutionary will and vocation were, are and always will be a thousand times more powerful than money!" Castro recently proclaimed.

To meet its current economic predicament, Cuba adopted a domestic austerity program last December that includes increases in public transportation fares, consumer utility costs and select parallel market prices, as well as cutbacks in the number of state-assigned automobiles, per diem payments to government officials, and foreign travel budgets. Together with the retrenchment of the private sector, these measures may save the state up to 500 million pesos a year.

The "strategic counteroffensive" is an attempt to infuse this belt-tightening with cherished revolutionary values of national purpose and self-sacrifice. The Cuban leadership has shown itself unwilling to risk a full-fledged market socialism like Hungary's, refusing to accept the proposition that the inner logic of socialism lies in a new "invisible hand" or to resign itself to widening social inequality. It has reaffirmed its view that the island's economy, historically deformed and currently embargoed, cannot implement a socialist version of the law of supply and demand without intolerable social costs. It has once again staked a claim to its own road to socialism. Since 1959, the Cuban leadership has preferred to believe that politics—not economic mechanisms— lie at the heart of socialism, and the current counteroffensive, with its reliance on charismatic authority, is a reassertion of that belief.

The 1980s, however, are not the 1960s. Although under evaluation, the planning and management system remains in place and Castro has warned that the "idealistic mistakes" of the past must not be repeated. However weak and constrained, there is an institutional order in Cuba today, and strengthening party authority over the state, especially at the local level, is a key element of the effort to "rectify mistakes and negative tendencies." The institutional order introduced in the 1970s has not so far been challenged. The government is encouraging a more critical, less controlled press and urging Cubans—like Silvia Marjorie Spence—to voice their concerns and keep management under close scrutiny. The 1986 party congress underscored the need for women, blacks and young people to be promoted to leadership positions in Cuban society. Present policies are indeed contradictory, as old visions are resurrected under new conditions.

Cuba's challenge, however, lies beyond the strategic counteroffensive. However evocative the 1960s may be of revolutionary sacrifice and moral exaltation, the generation of the 1980s may prove resistant to that appeal. About one of every two Cubans on the island was born after 1959; more than 1 million

Cubans live in the United States. No other socialist country has a history and a culture so intimately marked by the United States, and despite the present freeze of relations, a rapprochement cannot be ruled out forever. The revolution is nearing its 30th anniversary, and Castro is 61 years old. The present counteroffensive would be inconceivable without him, but by and large it is not providing any clues about how Cuba should be governed after he is gone from the scene.

Cubans may well respond to the moral exhortations of the present moment—for a time. But the exigencies of everyday life may in the end prove too compelling. Winds of change are blowing everywhere in the socialist world, and Mikhail Gorbachev's view that the United States is "worried about one thing: If democracy develops here . . . we will win" strikes a long-neglected chord in socialism. Younger generations of Cubans may conclude that Cuban socialism, without reneging on its own special legacy, should heed the calls for change that are now stirring the entire socialist world.

PART III

Politics in Cuba

Introduction

Cuba's revolution was unusual from the beginning. In its moment of triumph, it was an extraordinarily broad-based movement against the hated military dictatorship of Fulgencio Batista. The revolutionary government came to power with enormous legitimacy and support. Polls taken shortly after Batista's fall showed that over 90 percent of the people supported the new government.

The Cuban Revolution was always a social revolution, in the sense that many of the people who fought against Batista were motivated as much by social and economic grievances as by political ones. But it was not initially a socialist revolution. The ideologically heterogeneous July 26th Movement that led the struggle against Batista demanded sweeping social change, but it did not have a clear vision of how such change was to be achieved.

It was only after the triumph of the revolution, when the broad anti-Batista coalition began to break down over the issue of what Cuba's future should look like, that the revolution embarked on a socialist path of development—the first socialist revolution in the Western Hemisphere. The choice of socialism by the revolutionary leadership split Cuba politically along class lines, but much of the support and legitimacy gained from the struggle against Batista held over into the socialist stage of the revolution's development. Thus the transition was relatively peaceful. There was a counterrevolution, to be sure, but there was no civil war as in Russia or China.

Cuba's socialist revolution was the first to succeed without a Communist party in the vanguard of the struggle, a development that challenged Leninist orthodoxy. At the center of this process—both the initial seizure of power and the subsequent transition to socialism—was Fidel Castro.

A social revolution is never the work of a single person, and no individual can exercise personal control over the complexities of a modern society. But the Cuban Revolution, more than any other revolution in the 20th century, is identified with the name of Fidel Castro.

During the six-year struggle against Batista, Castro emerged as more than just the leader of the revolution; he came to embody it. He led the attack on Moncada Barracks that launched the revolution in 1953. With Frank Pais, he founded the 26th of July Movement, the principal opposition to the dictatorship. He commanded the Granma expedition from Mexico, and the rebel army that grew from it and fought the guerrilla war.

Castro inspired Cubans with his audacity, and they had faith in the revolution because they had faith in Fidel. On the eve of the Bay of Pigs invasion, Castro announced that the revolution was a socialist revolution. For months thereafter, Cuban crowds voiced their support by chanting, "If Fidel is Communist, so are we!"

Castro not only stood head and shoulders above the other important leaders of the revolution—Ernesto "Che" Guevara, Camilo Cienfuegos, and Raúl Castro, to name a few—he also stood above the revolutionary political system itself. Just as the triumph of the revolution had not followed orthodox patterns, the process of building socialism in Cuba did not either—not in the political realm any more than in the economic.

Throughout the 1960s, Cuban politics remained amazingly fluid. Few permanent, stable institutions were built. Instead, organizations were created and dissolved at a dizzying pace, usually at Castro's direction, depending upon the needs of the moment. Even such basic institutions as the vanguard party were not fully formed. The result was that the legitimacy of the revolution continued to be vested in Fidel, rather than in enduring institutions of party or state. And perhaps inevitably, the institutions that were created did not perform well. The party was incapable of assuming the leading role in politics that is the norm for Communist parties in power, and the government bureaucracy was so overblown and inefficient that the revolutionary leadership launched two major "struggles against bureaucratism" in the second half of the decade alone.

One consequence of these institutional weaknesses was a severe limitation of the ability of ordinary Cubans to hold political leaders accountable. The Cuban political system was intensely participatory during the 1960s, but participation was largely limited to mobilizing supporters of the revolution to carry out tasks such as the literacy campaign, public health campaigns, and voluntary labor. There were few opportunities for Cubans to make political demands, or to have input into policy decisions.

It was not until after the failure to produce ten million tons of sugar in 1970 that a serious reassessment of the structure of the political system was undertaken. The result of this reassessment was the campaign to "institutionalize" and "democratize" the revolution. Institutionalization meant the strengthening of the party and state to make them less dependent on Fidel. Democratization meant the creation of channels for ordinary citizens to have a greater say in politics. The mass organizations, especially the trade unions, were democratized by the holding of free elections at the base. But the most important aspect of democratization was the creation of the Organs of People's Power—elected legislative assemblies operating at all levels of government—that were specially designed to provide greater opportunities for local communities to make demands on the political system. Their success was partial at best.

Of course, democracy in Cuba must always be understood within the Marxist-Leninist framework of the Cuban political system. In the 1960s, Castro defined the limits of dissent when he said, "Within the revolution, everything; outside the revolution, nothing." It is a criterion that still frames the limits of political liberty in Cuba.

The intensity of the political restructuring that characterized the 1970s gave way to greater stability in the 1980s. But by mid-decade, persistent shortcomings in governance led Castro and the Communist party to launch a "rectification" campaign aimed at revitalizing the revolutionary leadership. Many veteran leaders whose job performance was judged below par were replaced. Many new leaders were moved quickly up the hierarchies of party and state in a process of renovation that clearly marked the beginning of a transition from the generation that made the revolution to the first generation to come of age since the triumph.

New York Times correspondent Herbert L. Matthews was one of the earliest writers on the Cuban Revolution. His exclusive interviews with Fidel Castro in the Sierra Maestra gave him unparalleled access to Castro after the revolution's triumph. Reading 17 is an excerpt from Matthews' last book, in which he provides a short biography of Castro and a discussion of his centrality to Cuban politics.

William M. LeoGrande's article on the development of the Communist Party of Cuba (Reading 18) details the efforts to build a new Communist Party in the 1960s and 1970s. The severe internal strife that divided the leadership of the revolution crippled the party-building process and left the party a weak and dependent organization. Not until the 1970s did the revolution's leaders make a concerted effort to build a permanent institutional framework for the political system with the Communist Party of Cuba in the central role.

In Reading 19, Nelson Valdés reviews the far-reaching changes in the composition of the party leadership that came out of the Third Congress of the

Communist Party of Cuba, held in 1986. The rate of turnover in the Central Committee was unprecedented, and the new leaders were selected with the aim of giving greater representation to women, blacks, and youth—three sectors that had traditionally been underrepresented in the revolution's highest councils. Jorge Domínguez explains the revamping of the party leadership in terms of Castro's effort to address problems in the economy and in the management of Cuba's government (Reading 20).

As the Communist party has been institutionalized since 1959, so too the way people participate in politics and the basic institutions of the state have been institutionalized. William M. LeoGrande shows the varied channels through which Cubans are involved in politics and the varied types of participatory activity available to them—from electoral activity to community affairs to direct contact with political leaders (Reading 22).

Debra Evenson's description of how the legal system has evolved since 1959 (Reading 23) indicates the fluid character of legal norms during the 1960s, and the extent to which the revolutionary leadership built legal institutions in the 1970s. By the end of the decade their commitment to "socialist legality" had produced a full-scale reform of the legal system.

We conclude Part III on Cuban politics with a chapter about human rights and freedoms. Margaret Crahan reviews the activity of various religious denominations since 1959 and the recent improvement in relations between the government and Catholic Church after nearly a quarter century of antagonism (Reading 24). It took almost a decade for the Church to accept the permanence of the revolution and to begin to seek a rapprochement. It took the state more than another decade to be willing to enter into a dialogue with the Church.

John S. Nichols describes the role of the press in Reading 25. Its purpose is to convey the message of the revolution consistently and effectively, but Nichols notes that within the limits of state control, the Cuban press is quite varied in both the subjects and viewpoints expressed.

International human rights groups have not been permitted to do studies in Cuba, but several reports have been issued about general conditions and about prison conditions. In Reading 26, an excerpt from the most recent report from the Inter-American Human Rights Commission of the Organization of American States, Cuba is given a mixed evaluation with respect to human rights. Both a 1986 report on prisons by Amnesty International (Reading 27 I) and one by human rights observers in 1988 (Reading 27 II) note that charges of abuse occurred in the early years of the revolution and that many political prisoners have since been released. Both reports indicate that prison conditions have improved in recent years.

Finally, Patricia Weiss Fagen's review of the laws and policies in Cuba that permit the rights of free movement internally and of international migration dispels commonplace myths about the total limitation on such freedoms (Reading 28).

CHAPTER 7

The Cuban Communist Party

17. Fidel Castro*

BY HERBERT L. MATTHEWS

> *Herbert L. Matthews covered the Cuban Revolution for the* New York Times *and obtained the first interview with Fidel Castro in his guerrilla camp in the Sierra Maestra mountains in 1957.*

With Fidel Castro, as with virtually all important historic figures, the years before his prominence are a reconstruction, true and false, imaginative, distorted, colored by favorable or unfavorable bias, and full of gaps. Fidel is a reserved, self-centered, and extremely complex character. He is only superficially an extrovert. He seems to live in a goldfish bowl; in reality, he has an inner self and an inner life that nobody I have met or know of has ever reached or, I think, ever will reach, unless the equally enigmatic Celia Sánchez, his faithful companion, has done so. If she has, she will keep it to herself. Fidel does not give of himself in any intimate way, and he has taken affection only from a few persons in his life. He is a lonely man.

One could draw up a long list of figures famous to history who lived in a constant blaze of publicity, surrounded by apparent intimates, but whose private lives and characters as human beings remained mysteries. They are the enigmas of history, the unsolved puzzles of the chroniclers. Fidel Castro belongs in this class, as did—to pick a perhaps appropriate modern example—Vladimir Ilyich Lenin.

Fidel does not have an affectionate nature; he does not, as I said before, wear his heart on his sleeve; he is one of those people who feel deeply without being

*From Herbert L. Matthews, *Revolution in Cuba: An Essay in Understanding* (New York: Charles Scribner's Sons, 1975), pp. 40–48.

able to express their emotions. The July 26, 1970, address was one of the very rare speeches in which he publicly showed a deep, personal emotion. Another was in his elegiac tribute to Che Guevara. There are men who steel themselves against a display of emotion—the stiff upper lip of the English, for instance—but there is also the inherited stoicism of the Spanish.

Yet Fidel has had the rare gift of inspiring the men and women around him with a feeling that can only be called worship. This is why the comrades of the "Generation of '53" have remained a cohesive, blindly loyal group.

He could not have been a sociable young man while he was at Havana University from 1945 to 1950. He shunned dancing and parties—in fact, I am sure that he does not know how to dance. Even now, he dresses formally only when it is absolutely necessary. He hates formality. His brother Raúl once said to me: "Diplomatic protocol and behavior bore and irritate him. Fidel just cannot be bothered." Banquets with toasts are anathema. He is best at public appearances with visiting celebrities, especially when he can make a speech. Gina Lollabrigida found him "unsure of himself; he was afraid of me," although he seemed far from inhibited during her visit in September 1974.

I have had to change my mind about Fidel Castro in some respects as the years passed and as I saw more of him. I have watched him mature from youth into middle age. (He was 31 when I first met him and was 46 in September 1972 when I last saw him.) In my opinion, he has grown in humanity and in his feeling for the people. The idealism, patriotism (or nationalism), the dedication and courage that were always there, but that had a romantic, fanatical, almost frantic quality, are under better control now and more calmly and practically directed. He responds more often and more readily to his innate pragmatism. I think that posterity, including future generations of Cubans, will grant him more respect as a moral being, as well as a revolutionary, than he has been accorded during these hectic years.

Fidel was born on August 13, 1926 (not in 1927 as was sometimes said, even in official publications), on his father's *finca,* Manacas, outside the village of Birán. The nearest town was Mayarí, about twenty miles inland from Nipe Bay on the northern coast of Oriente Province. It was a region partly owned and dominated by the United Fruit Company, which had great properties, mostly in sugar, acquired after the 1898 war. His father, Angel, worked for a time for United Fruit.

Angel, the former Spanish soldier and manual worker from Galicia, was by 1926 a landowner with thousands of acres of mostly sugarcane land. He was rough, tough, bold, unscrupulous, uneducated. Legality and morality—church or otherwise—bothered him little. One sensed that he was irascible. If he had any political coloring it was rightist, but also anti-Yankee.

Respectability was thrust upon him. His first wife was a schoolteacher. There were two children by the marriage, Pedro Emilio and Lidia. A young woman named Lina Ruz, who was born in Cuba, entered the house as a cook. Angel and Lina would be the parents of five more children—Ramón, Fidel, Juana, Emma, and Raúl—all illegitimate. Lina's family had also come from Galicia in Spain. This made Fidel, like Generalissimo Francisco Franco, a pure *Gallego* by blood. However, nothing should be made of the fact that Fidel was an illegitimate child during the earliest years of his life. In Cuba illegitimate children are never deprived of a normal family life and they have the legal status of legitimate offspring.

When the parents wanted to send several of the boys to the Colegio La Salle, a primary school in Santiago de Cuba run by a religious order, the headmaster insisted on all his pupils being baptized, confirmed, and legitimate. So Angel, his wife having died, married Lina Ruz with the help of the then bishop of Camagüey, Enrique Pérez Serantes, who likewise had been born in Galicia. He was a friend of the family and was later, as bishop of Santiago de Cuba, to play a prominent role in the Moncada Barracks affair.

Fidel's mother, like her husband, had a peasant hardness and that special, covetous attachment to the land that one finds in the farmers of Spain and France. She was angry and dismayed when the 26th of July Movement set about burning sugarcane, including hers, and later, early in the revolution, expropriating the family property along with all other large holdings. Like nearly all Latin women, she was devoutly religious.

The children were rebellious and must have been hard to handle. Unlike the oldest son, Pedro Emilio, Fidel did not break with his father, although he quarreled with him often and in 1940, when he was thirteen, according to Hugh Thomas, tried to organize a strike of sugar workers against his father. In later life he spoke critically of Angel. At the same time, he let his father support him generously through schools and the university, but I cannot imagine what he did with the money he may have inherited from Angel, who died in 1956 while Fidel was in Mexico. By the time his mother died, in 1963, money meant nothing to Fidel.

After the Colegio La Salle, in Santiago, Fidel went to the Colegio Dolores, a Jesuit primary school in the same city—like his previous school, for children of the well-to-do. In 1941 he started his *bachillerato* in the fashionable Belén preparatory school in Havana, one of the best secondary schools in Cuba. There he excelled in athletics and did well as a student. The note under his photograph in the June 1945 graduating class annual, *Ecos de Belén,* stated: "We do not doubt that he will fill the book of his life with brilliant pages." He was evidently popular, as the reference also said that he won "the admiration and affection of all."

. . . In 1945, at the age of eighteen, Fidel entered Havana University and elected to study for the bar. While there he fell in love with a student in the faculty of philosophy, Mirta Díaz Balart, whose brother, Rafael, was a fellow student at the university and whose father was an official in the Batista government. Rafael also was to take a post with the Batista government. The family did not approve of the marriage, while Fidel, for his part, was to find the connection a great embarrassment.

He and Mirta were married on October 12, 1948, in the Roman Catholic church at Banes, Oriente Province, where Mirta was born. Their only child, Fidelito, was born on September 1, 1949. The marriage was clearly unhappy. Fidel must have been a hopeless husband. While he was in the Isle of Pines prison after Moncada, Mirta accepted a salary through her brother from Batista's Ministry of the Interior, causing a scandal. Fidel was bitter. Mirta divorced him while he was still in jail, remarried, divorced again, and, I was told in 1972, had a third husband. Except for a few years at school on Long Island, New York, when Fidel was in the Sierra Maestra, Fidelito had always been in Cuba under his father's care until he went to Moscow in 1974 to take graduate courses in physics.

Fidel's career as a student is tangled in myths, truths, and mysteries. He was exceptionally intelligent, so that when he applied himself he was a brilliant pupil. The system at the university made it possible for students to neglect classes and cram at the very end of the term in order to pass the all-important examinations. This method was ideal for Fidel, who called on his retentive memory.

As an athlete he was always outstanding. His reading was eclectic. He could boast, and be accused of, reading Lenin, but then he also read Hitler's *Mein Kampf.* All that one can glean from Fidel's voracious reading as a youth is that he was not interested in one field of thought, such as Marxism-Leninism, any more than another, despite his opportunistic and demagogic boasts in later years. Because of his excellent memory, surprising literary, philosophical, or historical allusions crop up in his speeches. Raúl Castro once showed me Fidel's university reports for his graduating year, which he had saved. Eight or nine of the professors had written *sobresaliente* (excellent), three gave him *notable,* and only two graded him *aprovechado* (passing).

Fidel is not the most reliable biographer of his own life. Early in the revolution he was persuaded by the Italian publisher Feltrinelli to attempt an autobiography. Carlos Franqui, a former editor of the newspaper *Revolución,* was entrusted with the task of writing it for him and given the material. He told me in 1963 that he had accumulated the equivalent of eleven volumes.

I asked Castro about it in 1967. He laughed. "I want to *make* history, not write it," he said. This was, perhaps, an unconscious variation on Karl Marx on the role of philosophers: they "have only *interpreted* the world in various ways; the point, however, is to *change* it." In 1972 Fidel again brushed aside the idea in the conversation we had. "I'm too busy living to waste time writing," he said.

But he has never been too busy to talk, starting with his student life. Fidel

Castro is a great orator, one of the greatest of our times and, I would think, without a peer in Latin American history. A conversation with him is usually very one-sided because Fidel's flow of ideas and language is close to inexhaustible. He has a remarkable memory, as I said, but perhaps one should add: for what he wants to remember. His hearer is overwhelmed by the talker's enthusiasm, passion, conviction, and complete assurance. One goes away convinced, and then sometimes gets doubts—too late.

His speeches, as I remarked before, are to be listened to, not read. They have no polish, not much form, much repetitiveness, and plenty of declamation. They will never be studied for their literary quality, as Englishmen will always read Churchill or Frenchmen De Gaulle. Fidel uses his speeches as a form of popular education, often going into great detail, with endless data. There is no telling how much is understood, but his efforts seem to be appreciated. The speeches show a respect for the people and for their intelligence and seriousness.

He began to teach himself to be a public orator at Havana University. A feature of Cuban university life all through republican history, and especially from the Machado era onward, was its preoccupation with politics. The romantic, revolutionary fervor of the *Machadato*—what Fidel called "the legend of a heroic epoch"—still permeated the university. It expressed itself in factional quarrels and opposition to the government. The violence had a gangster-like character.

There were two chief "action groups" while Fidel was there, the MSR (Movimiento Socialista Revolucionaria), whose leader was Mario Salabarría, and the UIR (Unión Insurreccional Revolucionaria). The "revolutionary" names were typical. Fidel joined the UIR after Salabarría's gang almost murdered him in an ambush, writes K. S. Karol in *Guerrillas in Power.* One of the leaders of the MSR was Rolando Masferrer, then Communist, later a strong man for Batista with his own private army of terrorists during the dictatorship; now he is an exile in Florida.

Karol, whose book is venomously anti-Castro, nevertheless asserts that there is no evidence that Fidel indulged in the university gangsterism. This is also my information from some of his fellow students. There is a "black legend" about Castro's supposed hoodlumism and even murders at the university, but no proofs or police convictions. Fidel was never interested in violence for the sake of violence. In fact, in the newspaper articles he was writing for *Alerta* at the time and in his first appearances at the bar he vehemently denounced the prevailing violence.

He and a student named Justo Fuentes had a daily program on the radio station COCO, which apparently led to an MSR ambush in 1949 in which Fuentes was killed. The head of COCO, Guido García Inclán, is still (1975) running the station and ranks as one of Fidel's oldest and most loyal supporters.

The two most sensational episodes in Castro's university career were the abortive Cayo Confites expedition to invade the Dominican Republic in 1947 and the extraordinary outburst of popular fury in Bogotá, Colombia, in 1948, in which Fidel was involved.

The first was a plot to land about a thousand men in the Dominican Republic, then headed by the monstrous General Rafael Leónidas Trujillo. The MSR and UIR went along to help Dominican rebels, one of whose leaders was Juan Bosch. Castro, as a member of the UIR and perhaps looking for adventure, joined the rebels who gathered at Cayo Confites, a little island off the coast of Camagüey. Trujillo, learning of the plot, brought enough pressure on the United States and the Grau administration to get the expedition broken up. Reliable witnesses say that Fidel swam ashore with his submachine gun lashed to his back.

The *Bogotazo,* as it came to be called, took place during a Pan-American Conference of American States in the Colombian capital. At the same time, a "Conference of Latin-American University Associations" was planned, with General Juan Perón of Argentina providing most of the money on behalf of the Perón Youth League. Perón's interest was to protest against the British possession of the Falkland Islands in the Atlantic, which were claimed by Argentina. There were four in the Cuban delegation. Fidel went to Bogotá with a UIR friend named Rafael del Pino, who was later to betray the *Fidelistas* in Mexico. Early in the Cuban Revolution he joined a sabotaging landing party from Florida and was caught. He is now in a Cuban prison.

On April 9, 1948, the popular Colombian Liberal party leader, Jorge Eliécer Gaitán, was murdered by a madman in the streets of the capital during a demonstration. The killer was lynched on the spot, and an extraordinary explosion of looting, burning, and murder (perhaps three thousand were killed) went on for three days. The Communists tried to take advantage of the situation but failed. This did not inhibit Secretary of State George G. Marshall and the American delegation from labeling the uprising as Communist.

Fidel and del Pino were involved in the rioting and seem to have been asked by the police to get out. The Cuban ambassador, Guillermo Belt, a lawyer for American firms in Cuba, took them into the Embassy and arranged for them to be flown back to Havana. He told me in 1960 that he wished to God he hadn't. . . .

Fidel once spoke of his "vocation for revolution." If there is such a person as a born revolutionary, he is one. Some of Castro's fellow students and his critics and enemies believe that he saw revolution as his road to power and would have made any kind of revolution, right-wing or left-wing, as opportunity presented itself. This makes no sense, if only because a Cuban revolution in the 1950s made by a man born in 1926 could only be anticapitalist and anti-American. Castro was a rebel against the society of his times, which was rightist and conservative. Moreover, he was later to show a genuine feeling for the poor and an absorbing desire to do something to help the mass of the people, and this could be done only with a radical, leftist revolution.

However, the more one studies his actions and opinions in the prerevolutionary period, the more obvious it is that he had no systematic ideas, no ideology, no political connections. This is one reason why in the Sierra Maestra he was able to make all sorts of democratic, as well as radical, promises with authentic acquiescence and a certain degree of innocence. He was politically immature. In economics, he was a child. If, as he later asserted, he was a Marxist-Leninist in embryo at Havana University, there is no evidence that he, or any reliable witness, can submit to substantiate the claim.

"Fidel never wanted to join any party," his brother Raúl said to me in 1967, "because he didn't want to be restricted or be under any orders or discipline. He never could stand for any kind of formalism. This is a trait of his that he has never abandoned."

Early in the revolution I suggested that Castro picked up movements and ideas as one would garments, putting them on, taking them off, throwing them away, placing them in the wardrobe—but that in all cases the wearer was the same Fidel Castro. He is not, and cannot be, emotionally dogmatic or orthodox; it is against his nature. It is a vital feature of his character that he must be his own master.

This does not mean that he will not, as he says, be a Marxist-Leninist until the day he dies. It means that Cuban Marxism-Leninism will be what Fidel Castro makes it, not what Marxist ideologues in Moscow or academic scholars consider it should be. Of course, communism is a determined political and economic system, but so is liberal democracy. Within its limits, Fidel has at all times consciously or unconsciously avoided being caught in a "shirt of Nessus." In a speech in 1968 he said: "Nothing is more anti-Marxist than dogma and thought which are petrified."

His politics had to fit his character, which is that of the "lone wolf," and above all, the leader. The Latin American scene has had a long history of *personalismo*. It is not necessary to be an embodiment of ideal qualities like George Washington or Abraham Lincoln. José Martí was an exceptional figure in Cuban history who died before his image could be tarnished. Latins want their *caudillo* or *jefe* to be different, commanding, strong. His right to rule is his charismatic stature as a hero, and he can achieve that image as much by defying the laws of his country as by climbing a political ladder. A leader whose supreme virtue is to be like everybody else, only more so (an Eisenhower, for example), would have little attraction in a country like Cuba. Anglo-Saxon historians are wasting their time when they judge Fidel Castro by their own standards of morality and virtue.

Revolution was taking form in Fidel's mind in 1952 when General Batista made his garrison coup. The time had come to do something—but what he did brought on the first of his three shattering defeats. However, as Raúl Castro said to me: "The most important feature of Fidel's character is that he will not accept defeat."

18. Party Development in Revolutionary Cuba*

BY WILLIAM M. LEOGRANDE

During the Cuban Revolution's first decade, Fidel Castro's charismatic authority and predominant position eclipsed the significance of the new institutions created to replace the prerevolutionary political order. The "institutionalization" under way in Cuba since 1970, however, has strengthened and formalized the political structure to the extent that the island's institutions can no longer be regarded as peripheral to the dynamics of Cuban politics. This is particularly true of the Communist party of Cuba, which has emerged from the 1970s as the central political institution. The way in which the party has developed not only highlights some of the problems inherent in the process of creating a new political order, but is also essential for understanding contemporary Cuban politics.

BUILDING A NEW PARTY APPARATUS

The ORI: The Abortive Attempt to Build a Party

Most Socialist revolutions undertake the process of forming new political institutions with the Communist party at center stage. Forged during the struggle for state power, the party constitutes the organizational core around which the new political system is erected; other institutions are constructed under its guidance and at its direction. The Cuban Revolution, however, was the first socialist revolution to succeed without a Leninist party in the vanguard of the revolutionary struggle. The victory over Batista's dictatorship was won instead by a loose coalition of political groups, foremost among them Fidel Castro's 26th of July Movement, (M-26-7). Shortly after victory, the anti-Batista coalition began to disintegrate over the issue of what the future course of the revolution should be, and even the M-26-7 divided into warring factions. Always more a movement than an organization, the M-26-7 was by

*From William M. LeoGrande, "Party Development in Revolutionary Cuba," *Journal of Inter-American Studies and World Affairs,* Vol. 21, No. 4 (November 1979), pp. 457–80. Edited for this volume.

1961 so atrophied from disuse and so riddled by defections that the meager infrastructure it had possessed initially no longer existed. Thus, as the revolutionaries turned to the task of creating a new Cuba, there was no party apparatus through which to govern.

In order to provide such a political apparatus and perhaps to convince the Soviet Union that Cuba's revolution was authentically socialist, the creation of a new vanguard party was begun in early 1961 with the merger of the only three groups remaining in the political arena: the M-26-7, minus its right wing; the Revolutionary Directorate (Directorio Revolucionario—DR), essentially a student group; and the Popular Socialist party (Partido Socialista Popular—PSP), the old Communist party. In July 1961, Castro formally announced the merger of these three organizations into the Integrated Revolutionary Organizations (Organizaciones Integradas Revolucionarias—ORI.)[1]

Since only the PSP had cadres with both the requisite organizational experience and a long history of commitment to the revolution's newly adopted socialist goals, construction of the ORI was entrusted to veteran leaders of the PSP. Under the direction of Aníbal Escalante, former PSP Executive Secretary, the development of the ORI proceeded rapidly. Within a few months, hundreds of ORI members had been selected and appointed to key governmental posts, giving the ORI tremendous influence over the most fundamental policies and programs of the revolution.

The process of building the ORI did not proceed without friction, however. On July 26, 1961, Castro had implied that the ORI would be a transitional institution through which the M-26-7, DR, and PSP would cooperate in the creation of a unified party—the United Party of the Socialist Revolution (Partido Unido de la Revolución Socialista—PURS). He reaffirmed this view explicitly on December 2, 1961, when he declared himself a Marxist-Leninist. Aníbal Escalante's view, however, was that the ORI would *be* the new party. In September 1961, he called the ORI "the backbone of the revolutionary state" and implied that a simple change in name would constitute the change from the ORI to the PURS.[2]

Behind these disparate conceptions of the ORI was a growing controversy over how its construction was being handled. Lauded as the organization which would structurally integrate the three major revolutionary groups, the ORI was, in fact, nothing but the apparatus of the PSP under a new name. Escalante used his dominant position to pack the new party with his old comrades from the PSP, to the virtual exclusion of veterans from the M-26-7 and DR. In fact, as ORI members were appointed to posts in the government and mass organizations, hundreds of M-26-7 and DR veterans lost their positions in those institutions because of their "low political level."[3]

Given the relatively marginal role played by the PSP in the struggle against Batista, such practices engendered much bitterness. Equal in seriousness to the aggravation of divisions within the revolutionary leadership caused by the

PSP's capture of the ORI was the manner in which the party undertook its role of directing the revolutionary process. In order to attain hegemony over the other institutions of the political system, the vast majority of newly selected ORI members were appointed to administrative posts in these other institutions, leaving virtually no membership among rank and file workers. As a result, the ORI was neither capable of perceiving the degree of support or opposition among the people for various policies nor of mobilizing the people in support of policy. When resistance was displayed toward ill-conceived policy, the ORI responded with coercion. The popular reaction to this arbitrary and sometimes illegal repression was disillusionment, intensified by the appearance of special privileges for those in the ORI hierarchy.

The ORI's response to the 1961 agrarian problem offers, in microcosm, an excellent picture of the dimensions of the political crisis then brewing. The 1959 agrarian reform expropriated only the largest of the private estates, leaving some 57 percent of the cultivable land outside the public sector in the form of small and medium-sized farms. In the fall of 1961, resistance developed among the remaining private farmers to the regulations compelling them to sell their produce solely to the government at fixed rates. The ORI's response was to crack down on the private farmers indiscriminantly; produce was seized, people arrested, and some lands were even confiscated, although the Council of Ministers had passed no law authorizing the expropriation of medium-sized farms. The farmers defended their interests in classic fashion—they planted only enough for their own consumption, so that by 1962 the regime was faced with a critical shortage of food, resulting in considerable popular discontent and several overtly antigovernment demonstrations. In the first major test of its ability to guide the revolution forward, the ORI proved to be a miserable failure—alienating en masse the private farmers, and provoking such privation that general support for the revolution was jeopardized. For Castro, who had resolved in December to institutionalize his "one-man rule" in the collective wisdom of the party, the result could not have been more disturbing. Perhaps it is not coincidental that Castro's first public intimation that significant changes in the ORI were required came on March 12, 1962, when he announced the need to ration food.[4]

The following day, at a ceremony commemorating the DR's assault on the presidential palace and the death of the DR's founder José Antonio Echevarría, a student leader reading Echevarría's political testament omitted a passage referring to God. Outraged at the alteration of the text, Castro denounced such rewriting of history as foreign to Marxism.[5] Such attitudes were turning the revolution into a tyranny, he said; a struggle had to be waged against them and also against vagrants and privileged persons who had ensconced themselves in the ORI. Speaking five days later at the Conrado Benítez School of Revolutionary Instruction, Castro escalated his attack on the ORI; it had lost touch with the masses, he charged, and had imposed on the nation a despotism "almost indistinguishable from Batista and his henchmen." It was necessary, he continued, to wholly reorganize the party, doing away with sectarianism and privilege once and for all.[6]

On March 22, the National Directorate of the ORI met and created the apparatus for conducting this reorganization—the National Secretariat of the ORI.[7] Only one of the Secretariat's six members, Blas Roca, was a PSP veteran, and his assignment to edit the newspaper *Hoy* effectively removed him from the reorganization of the ORI. To undertake the reorganization, the Secretariat created an Organizational Commission composed of M-26-7 veterans Osvaldo Dorticós and Emilio Aragones, formerly the M-26-7's National Coordinator. Aníbal Escalante was removed from the National Directorate and went into exile in Czechoslovakia shortly thereafter.

Finally, in a televised address to the nation on March 26, Castro presented a detailed criticism of Escalante and the ORI. The party had, he said, degenerated into a pervasive sectarianism—"the sectarianism of believing that the only revolutionaries . . . who could hold positions of trust . . . had to be old Marxist militants." This attitude had created not a political apparatus, but "a nest of privilege, toleration, favoritism, a system of immunities and favors," the authority of which "came from the fact that from it one might expect a favor, some dispensation, or some harm or good." Through its appointees, the ORI had reduced the government to an appendage by directing even the day-to-day operations of state agencies. The result of these deficiencies was "the destruction of the prestige of the Revolution."[8]

Castro's criticism alone destroyed the political influence of the ORI. It halted all operations after March 26 and was completely dismantled within months; but the political aftershocks of the sectarianism of the ORI reverberated through the Cuban political system long after the party's dissolution. The most significant long-term effect was to retard severely the institutional development of a political apparatus capable of assuming the central role of directing the political system. The building of the ORI was the first major attempt at institutionalization undertaken by the revolution, and its disastrous effects upon both the fragile unity of the revolutionary leadership and upon the regime's mass support resulted in a marked reluctance to resume the institutionalization process even after the reorganization of the ORI. . . .

Castro's criticism of the ORI represented a clear reassertion of the charismatic authority against that of the developing party apparatus. In effect, he stepped outside the new institutional framework to condemn the manner and direction in which it was evolving. That his charismatic authority remained intact was demonstrated by the ease with which Escalante was deposed and the ORI discredited. The catastrophic results of the attempt to institutionalize that authority in the ORI discredited the process of institutionalization in Cuba before it had hardly begun. The ORI had been a "straitjacket, a yoke" binding the revolution rather than advancing it, and the fear of freezing the political system prematurely in an inadequate set of political institutions continued to weigh upon the development of the party throughout the decade.

The PURS and the Trial of Marcos Rodríguez

In the wake of Castro's denunciation, the party apparatus which had been built up over the preceding months was completely dismantled, and the ORI's control over the other institutions of the political system was liquidated with the wholesale dismissal of Escalante's appointees. In many localities, popular feeling ran so high against the ORI that meetings convened spontaneously to purge the nuclei from the bottom up.[9] This practice was discouraged, however, in favor of a systematic process of "reorganization and purification" supervised by the National Directorate and implemented by President Dorticós's Organizational Commission. Whereas previously, ORI officials had merely appointed, sometimes secretly, whomever they pleased to form a party nucleus, members of the PURS were chosen by the "mass method" designed by Castro.[10] The "mass method" gave the workers themselves the power to nominate and ratify the people in their work places who would become party members. This procedure began with the ORI commission calling an assembly (asamblea de selección) in the workplace and soliciting nominations for prospective party members. If, after discussing the merits of a nominee, the assembly voted its approval of the nomination, the individual became an "exemplary worker." The commission would then conduct an investigation of the candidate and decide whether to admit him/her to the new United Party of the Socialist Revolution. This mass method of party recruitment continues to be employed today.

The "reorganization and purification" of the ORI was a long and difficult process, both because the mass method was extremely time-consuming and because of the mutual distrust sown within the revolutionary leadership by the sectarianism of the ORI. It took over a year just to reorganize the nuclei originally created by the ORI. Even then, the PURS stood in marked contrast to the ORI in terms of political influence. Whereas the ORI under Escalante had firmly asserted its primacy over the other political institutions, the PURS had no discernible influence at all with regard to policy. It was not until mid-1963 that newly constituted PURS nuclei began to undertake any political work. The party then concentrated on stimulating productivity, aiding socialist emulation, and mobilizing voluntary work brigades at the workplace level; it had no responsibilities beyond those until 1965. Its apparatus remained too limited in terms of the number of work places covered and too weak in terms of the capabilities of intermediate bureaus to act effectively in any other capacity. Thus, the new Communist Party of Cuba was an institution still in gestation when, in March 1964, it was rocked by a political crisis nearly as severe as that which destroyed its predecessor.

In the aftermath of the Revolutionary Directorate's 1957 assault on the presidential palace, four of the DR's surviving leaders took refuge in an apartment at 7 Humboldt Street. Betrayed by an informer, they were murdered by Batista's police. The DR long suspected one Marcos Rodríguez of being responsible for the massacre and had him arrested in 1959. However, the PSP, of which Rodríguez had become a member, protested his innocence, and since the DR could furnish no evidence against him, Rodríguez was freed. When Rodríguez was arrested again in 1961 on an unrelated charge, the earlier investigation was reopened, and he continued to receive the support of Joaquin Ordoqui, a founding member of the PSP, member of the National Directorate of PURS, and Vice-Minister of the Armed Forces. In 1963, Rodríguez finally confessed his guilt and, more importantly, claimed he had confided his treachery to Ordoqui as early as 1958, thus implicating Ordoqui in a cover-up of the crime.

In March 1964 Rodríguez was tried, convicted, and condemned to death. The veterans of the DR, however, used the trial to attack all the old Communists. Faure Chomón, former President of the DR, charged the PSP as an organization with responsibility for Rodríguez's action. . . . Faced with mounting attacks on their revolutionary credentials, the former members of the PSP in the revolutionary leadership began mobilizing their defense, demanding a full hearing and an opportunity to refute the charges against them. The National Directorate took up the matter and ordered an appeals trial for Rodríguez before the Supreme Court. Rodríguez, of course, was not the real subject of the new trial; his guilt had been sealed by his own confession. Broadcast live on radio and fully covered by the press, the trial was a public airing of the charges made by Chomón against the PSP. Chomón repeated his accusations, albeit in less virulent prose, and the former members of the PSP, one by one, took the stand to defend their pasts.

On the fourth day of the trial, Castro himself spoke for nearly five hours, rendering, in effect, the political verdict. He called for unity among the already formally unified revolutionary groups, observing that the Rodríguez trial had been "unexpectedly converted into a trial of political character." He criticized Chomón for exacerbating divisions within the revolutionary leadership, thereby "giving arms to the enemy."[11] . . . The PSP as an organization was thus vindicated, although Ordoqui's behavior was described as negligent, and he was stripped of his leadership positions.

The Marcos Rodríguez affair demonstrated that the fragility of the formal unity between the M-26-7, DR, and PSP had improved little since 1961. Their merger had not wiped out memories of old antagonisms, and the ease with which these erupted in bloody infighting, threatening to rend the party before it was even fully constructed, did not bode well for the process of institution building in the new Cuban political system. As had happened so many times previously, Fidel Castro was obliged to step in and, asserting his overwhelming personal authority, rescue the revolution from a debilitating political crisis. . . .

In October 1965 the National Directorate and National Secretariat of PURS were replaced by a Political Bureau, Central Committee, and Secretariat, and the name of the party was changed to the Communist Party of Cuba (Partido Comunista de Cuba—PCC).

The PCC's initial recruitment drive, begun in 1962, had been completed and its chain of command had been strengthened in anticipation of the party taking on major responsibilities in the supervision of production and in the struggle against bureaucracy. As the party undertook its new duties, however, it rapidly became apparent that the problem of forging a political apparatus capable of playing the central role in the political system had not yet been solved.

Foremost among the difficulties which plagued the party from the time it began nationwide tasks in 1965 through the end of the decade was the fact that it remained a severely underdeveloped quasi-institution. Twice during the decade, first in 1967 and then again in 1969, the founding Congress of the PCC, which would have given the party a set of statutes and a program, was scheduled and then postponed.

Table 1: *Party Membership in Cuba, 1962–1975*

Year	Members and Candidates	Members and Candidates as % of Population
1962	2,109	.03
1965	50,000	.5
1970	100,000	1.2
1975	202,807	2.2

SOURCE: William M. LeoGrande, *The Development of the Party System in Revolutionary Cuba* (Erie, PA: Northwestern Pennsylvania Institute for Latin American Studies, 1978).

The most compelling indication of the party's underdeveloped character was its size, with the resultant shortage of competent cadres and disorganization of operations (Table 1). If we take the prevailing size of other Communist parties as a measure, the PCC was tremendously undersized throughout the 1960s. Not only was it by far the smallest ruling Communist party (only one fifth the per capita size of the next smallest party, the Albanian Labor party), but it was also smaller than nonruling parties in Italy, Finland, and Indonesia. The underdevelopment of the PCC was also apparent from the party's incomplete coverage of Cuban society. In the late 1960s no more than 16 percent of Cuba's work centers had PCC organizations. Though the party was organized primarily in the island's larger work places, data from the 1966 Industrial Efficiency Plan suggests that less than half the Cuban working class were employed in places that had a party nucleus.[12]

Another symptom of the party's low level of institutional development was the emergence of serious organizational difficulties when the party began work on its newly assigned tasks in 1965. Part of the reason for this was the persistent shortage and poor quality of party cadres. The general shortage of qualified personnel generated an intense competition among various bureaucratic structures for the talents of the few skilled people who were available. Paralyzed for over a year by the purge of the ORI, the party became a hunting ground for the state administration in its search for good leaders. Government agencies had considerable success hiring away the party's best activists; the problem became so severe that Castro (1963) was finally moved to condemn the practice publicly, warning that such "piracy" would lead to the "progressive anemia" of the party. Protecting the party apparatus from the state bureaucracy's recruiters could not, however, solve the more serious problem of the general shortage of qualified personnel.

After over a year of working at various national projects, the weaknesses in the party organization had become all too clear. At a PCC meeting in Oriente, Organizational Secretary Armando Hart surveyed them candidly: "Our party organization," he began, "is extraordinarily weak." He described virtually every area of party activity as deficient, blaming poor organization and a shortage of skilled cadres. Party organs were characterized by "the absence of aggressiveness" and a "contemplative attitude in the face of problems."

. . . Most of the problems outlined by Hart in 1966 persisted through the end of the decade. The educational level of party members improved hardly at all. In 1969, 79 percent of the party's membership still did not have even a sixth-grade education, and only 29 percent were studying.[13] Disorganization within the party apparatus also remained pronounced. José Machado, Political Bureau delegate to Matanzas Province, acknowledged that a shortage of party members and poor organizational work had left many key work centers without any party nucleus. In some factories, Machado said, party members were not even functioning together as a nucleus because things were so disorganized.[14]

The 1960s produced in Cuba a nominally Marxist-Leninist political system in which the Communist party, beset by organizational weakness and intraelite conflict, was incapable of truly directing the other institutions of the polity. It remained one of Cuba's "provisional institutions," more an extension of Castro's charisma than an independent base of political authority. When the party finally began to function in 1965, its attempts to exert control over other institutional centers of political power were met with resistance.

PARTY-STATE RELATIONS, 1965–1970

The first year in which the party was assigned nationwide duties was 1965; it was mandated to launch a fight against bureaucracy, and it was given responsibility for aiding economic development by overseeing the administration of key economic sectors and by mobilizing the work force to increase productivity.

. . . The struggle against bureaucracy graphically demonstrated the basic weakness of the party apparatus. Bureaucratic inefficiency was by no means a new problem to Cuba, but the advent of socialism had done little to ameliorate the problem. The chaotic fashion in which the state apparatus developed after 1959 and the shortage of trained personnel had, in some instances, made matters worse. As early as 1963 Che Guevara had warned of the spread of "bureaucratism," and called for the party to lead a "war" against this malady.[15] Between 1963 and 1965, Castro devoted several speeches to the pernicious effects of bureaucracy, but it was not until the party had installed its strengthened chain of command that a program for eradicating bureaucratism was presented.

On January 2, 1965, Castro devoted a major portion of his annual report on the state of the revolution to the problem of bureaucratism and how to combat it. The solution Castro proposed was to freeze the number of office jobs and to introduce a system of "labor control boards" in every locality to enforce the freeze and to begin reducing the number of administrative employees. The formation of these boards, later christened the "Commissions for the Fight Against Bureaucracy," was delegated to the party. This battle, Castro emphasized, required concerted and organized effort, perhaps explaining why it had not been launched before the party apparatus was in a position to undertake it.[16]

In its first two years the campaign against bureaucracy was not very successful because the PCC proved unequal to the task of overseeing the government administration. Still extremely small, the party apparatus was simply unable to keep track of what the state apparatus was doing; government bureaucrats showed little hesitance to ignore both the hiring freeze and the commissions designed to enforce it. A 1967 survey by a special PCC committee created to evaluate the campaign discovered that 75 percent of the administrative units surveyed were in violation of the directives on personnel reduction.[17] During 1965 and 1966, the Commissions for the Fight Against Bureaucracy eliminated 21,066 administrative posts, either reassigning the personnel to other jobs or sending them to school. By the end of 1966, however, nearly half these people were back in jobs "similar to their old ones." Bureaucracy had gone "back on the offensive," and Castro declared that the Commissions for the Fight Against Bureaucracy had themselves become bureaucratized.[18]

A renewed and intensified campaign against bureaucracy ensued. New regulations on the hiring and transfer of personnel were promulgated, and bureaucrats were warned that violators would be punished this time.

In its new phase, however, the campaign against bureaucracy focused upon the central agencies of the state. Since the party had not yet been organized in the central agencies, the campaign had to be handled directly by the national leadership of the party through directives restructuring administrative operations. This, of course, required little reliance upon the party apparatus. In fact, the party organization found itself among the targets of the new antibureaucracy drive; over 1,000 PCC officials from Havana alone were dispatched to the countryside for three years to do agricultural work.[19]

In addition to the struggle against bureaucracy, the PCC's other principal mission after 1965 was to advance the economic development of the nation. Prior to 1965, the activities of the PURS were almost exclusively in the economic sphere—i.e., stimulating production by political agitation and mobilizing voluntary labor campaigns. When the party expanded operations nationally in 1965, the PCC's responsibilities in the economic field increased dramatically.[20] The PCC was assigned to supervise the administration of production in key work centers and in the economically strategic sugar industry. In 1966, the first Plan for Industrial Efficiency was introduced, systematizing both the PCC's mobilization and supervisory duties in the economy. The plan left no doubt as to the preeminence accorded to this area of party work by asserting that the only yardstick for measuring overall party performance was the level of production.[21]

The PCC's two major projects during the 1960s—the struggle against bureaucracy and assistance to the economy—led to political conflict which, in the long run, proved to be critically important in molding the development of the PCC's role in the Cuban political system. Fighting bureaucracy and supervising production were both tasks which posed the party as an institutional rival and threat to the government bureaucracy. Conflict was engendered because, in both projects, the party was mandated to seek out and expose government inefficiency, corruption, and noncompliance with policy directives. Moreover, this supervision was imposed suddenly; until 1965 the government had not been faced with any systematic external review of its operations.

The political conflict stemming from the initiation of party supervision of the state was severe and persistent, lasting until the end of the decade. The government bureaucracy resisted party supervision by meeting disagreeable directives with passive noncompliance, and the party routinely ignored the prohibition against issuing directives to administrators. Relations between the two institutions progressively deteriorated.[22]

Something of a stalemate existed until 1967; the state apparatus was unable to challenge openly the supervisory role of the party since that role had been assigned to the party by the Political Bureau and by Castro himself. On the other hand, the weakness of the party apparatus prevented it from adequately overseeing the bureaucracy's operations or putting a halt to noncompliance. We have already reviewed the government's disregard of the directives on personnel reduction during the first phase of the antibureaucracy campaign. In January 1967, President Dorticós revealed that similar resistance had been encountered with regard to the voluntary labor campaigns.[23] There was opposition within the state apparatus because, so it was argued, the campaigns disrupted administrative operations. Perhaps so, Dorticós conceded, but that could not justify the erection of procedural roadblocks to thwart the mobilizations. Some officials, he warned, were verging on a "criminal stance." The renewal of the antibureaucracy campaign in early 1967 marked the end of this stalemate between the party and state organizations, not by increasing the strength of the party, but by overcoming the centers of resistance in the state bureaucracy. . . .

Conflict within the revolutionary leadership concerned not only party-state relations, but also the general development policies advanced in the late 1960s. This conflict was highlighted by the 1968 trial of the "microfaction"—a group of 43 state and party officials charged with treason for their organized, clandestine opposition to the leadership's economic policy. The microfaction's admitted intent was to convince the USSR and other socialist countries to exert economic pressure on Cuba, forcing a change in policy and even a change in leadership. To this end, they were in contact with foreign diplomats.[24]

Led by none other than Aníbal Escalante, who had returned from exile in 1966 to manage a state poultry farm, the microfaction was composed primarily of PSP veterans. They were, however, second- and third-echelon officials; only two junior members of the Central Committee were among the 43, and their involvement was peripheral. Thus the microfaction itself posed no serious threat to the leadership of the revolution.

Its members were so obscure and so few as to be inconsequential, not even really constituting a faction—only a microfaction. Yet the incident was regarded seriously because its political significance transcended the individuals involved. The trial served as a warning to potential dissidents that opposition to prevailing policies was, in itself, counterrevolutionary. Thus it had a chilling effect on PCC and state officials critical of the deteriorating economic situation at a time when the ranks of those critics were expanding.[25]

THE COMMUNIST PARTY OF CUBA IN THE 1970s

Cuba's failure to produce ten million tons of sugar in 1970—a goal upon which Castro had staked both his personal prestige and the prestige of the revolution—catalyzed a thorough reassessment of the political system created over the previous decade. As a result of this reassessment, the Cuban Revolution entered a "new phase" in which "institutionalization" and "democratization" became the watchwords of a far-reaching reorganization of the entire political process.

The institutionalization of Cuban politics since 1970 has had a profound effect on the Cuban Communist party: The size of the party has been greatly expanded, internal coordination and control have been systematized, institutional functions have been specified, and individual roles have been codified. Moreover, the functional boundaries *between* the party and other institutions are, for the first time, clearly delineated and enforced, and the subordination of the PCC to Fidel Castro's personal authority has been reduced.

By 1969, even before the beginning of the new phase, it had become clear that the PCC was too small to fulfill even the purely administrative duties to which it had been assigned during the 1960s. Consequently, in the middle of 1969, a campaign of "construction and growth" was begun in order to expand overall party membership and to increase the number of nuclei.[26] After 1970, the policy of increasing party membership continued to be an important aspect of the overall campaign to strengthen the PCC. By September 1975 membership had reached 200,000—nearly four times the 1969 membership. The average size of the nuclei also increased by nearly fifty percent—from 7.4 members per nuclei in 1964 to 10.6 in 1974—and by 1974 nearly half the nation's work centers—that is, almost all the medium-sized and large work centers—had party organizations. Another aspect of the drive to strengthen the PCC was the policy of increasing the percentage of rank and file workers in the party.[27]

Improving internal coordination and information flow became a concern after 1970. The first stage of this process was the convening of evaluation meetings at various levels of the party apparatus in order to evaluate past work, adopt plans for future work, and elect delegates to higher-level meetings.

Once the system of evaluation meetings had been established and the information on party operations which they provided had been analyzed, the next step in strengthening the PCC was the full-scale reorganization of its apparatus in 1972. The most important results included the establishment of a routine reporting system from lower to higher party bodies, something which had not existed previously; a specific delineation of the PCC's relationship to the government administration and the mass organizations; the beginning of regularly scheduled meetings of PCC organs which heretofore had met only sporadically; and the expansion of the national Secretariat from 7 to 11 members to facilitate a wider division of responsibilities. Toward the end of 1973 and in the early months of 1974, the annual evaluation meetings were accompanied by the election of PCC officers from the nuclei up through the provincial level.

In December 1975, fully ten years after the party's founding and 17 years after the victory over Batista, the Communist Party of Cuba held its First Congress. Lauded as the most important event in the history of the revolution since the party's founding in 1965, the First Congress marked the culmination of the "institutionalization" of the PCC. Formal statutes and a preliminary party program were adopted, thus giving the party, for the first time, coherent operational and policy guidelines.[28] In the years since the First Congress, the PCC has further codified its procedures with a series of regulations on the operation of various party organs, and in 1978 its organizational structure was finally completed with the creation of the National Commission for Control and Revision to oversee adherence to party regulations.[29]

The strengthening of the PCC in the years since 1970 was also reflected in the composition of the Central Committee elected at the First Congress. In 1965, only 12 percent of the committee's members held positions in the party apparatus; in the 1975 Central Committee, this figure rose to 29 percent, indicating the growing influence of the PCC in the political system as a whole.[30]

The composition of the new political elite also suggests that the intraelite conflict between PSP veterans and other revolutionary leaders, which plagued the party during the 1960s, has diminished considerably. The Political Bureau of the 1965 Central Committee did not contain any veterans of the old Communist party, whereas the new Political Bureau contains three out of a total membership of 13. This increasing integration of the elite is mainly attributable to the fact that policy differences between the old communists and the veterans of the M-26-7 have been considerably reduced since 1970. Also, the mere passage of time may be partially responsible for the reduction of hostilities. Along with the strengthening of the PCC, there has been a subtle but discernible shift in its relationship to its First Secretary. During the 1960s the party was an extremely weak institution, dependent upon Fidel Castro personally for its cohesion, its legitimacy, and its direction. Meetings of its national bodies were rare and directives from them were rarer still. Important policy decisions were made by Castro and his inner circle of trusted advisers, and if Castro's opinion contradicted a decision of the Central Committee, then the Central Committee was overruled.

Now, however, the party is becoming a cohesive and legitimate institution in its own right, capable not only of directing its own organs but also of giving direction to the other institutions of the political system. It is no longer true that without Castro the whole edifice would fall apart, as one Cuban official indicated it would in 1965.[31] Castro has also begun to treat the party as if he were responsible to it, rather than vice versa. This shifting relationship between Castro and the PCC is but one aspect of the ongoing process of institutionalizing his charismatic authority. As Castro himself observed, "Men die, but the Party is immortal."[32]

One of the major criticisms leveled against the PCC's performance during the late 1960s was its usurpation of the administration of the economy and the consequent fusion of state and party functions. In the early 1970s the distinction between state and party was redrawn and reinforced.[33] The first step taken to reverse the fusion of these two institutions was the stricture that the roles of plant manager and Party Secretary in a plant could no longer be held by the same person, a practice which had become almost universal in the late 1960s. Such a division of functions was seen as necessary if the party was to supervise adequately the work of the administration and report on its deficiencies.[34]

In the long run, of course, personnel changes could not by themselves resolve the problem of state-party relations; that required a clear delineation of the respective duties of the two institutions and their relationship to one another. After more than a year of study, the necessary guidelines were spelled out in a document entitled "The Structure, Mechanisms, and Means of the

Party to Direct and Control the State and Society as a Whole," adopted by the Political Bureau of the party in January 1973.[35]

The restructuring of the Cuban political system since 1970 has also involved the creation of an entirely new set of institutions—the Organs of People's Power. These elected assemblies, which now exist at all administrative levels, are analogous to soviets in the USSR. The relationship between the PCC and the People's Power assemblies typifies the new relationship between the party and government in Cuba. The PCC leads the state through its right to nominate the executive committees of the People's Power assemblies, its right to introduce proposals, and through party members who sit on the assemblies. The party is proscribed, however, from issuing directives to People's Power or intervening in routine administrative matters.[36]

In the event of disagreement between a party organization and an organ of People's Power that mutual consultations cannot resolve, the party must refer the matter to the next higher party organization which will then take up the matter in consultation with the next higher Organ of People's Power. If a solution still cannot be reached, the matter continues to be referred upward, to the national level if necessary. Though this is similar to the consultation process outlined in 1965–1966, both the party and the state are more clearly defined now than they were a decade ago and the prohibition on party interference in administrative affairs has been advanced much more adamantly. Thus the prospects for this consultation process succeeding are better now, but whether it will actually operate as designed is something that is still too early to evaluate.

CONCLUSION

The absence of a Leninist party in the leadership of the struggle against Batista meant that when the dictatorship was overthrown and the old political system was swept away, there was no party organization around which to build a new set of political institutions. The dynamics of Cuban politics in those early years of the revolution revolved around the military as the only institution with any significant degree of cohesion and capacity and, moreover, around the charismatic leadership of Fidel Castro.

Early attempts to institutionalize Castro's authority were largely unsuccessful. Despite its purported "leading role," the Cuban Communist party did not develop the organizational capacity to direct the political process during the 1960s. This was due, in part, to the intense distrust and hostility among veterans of the M-26-7, DR, and PSP, feelings that repeatedly threatened to fragment the revolutionary leadership. The experiences of the ORI and the Marcos Rodríguez affair demonstrated that elite cohesion could not be maintained in Cuba by institutional means. Only Castro's preeminent authority was able to hold this fragile coalition together.

The experience of the ORI also revealed how easily new and untried institutions might dissipate the regime's popular support and legitimacy rather than institutionalizing it. The ORI brought to reality all the hypothetical dangers inherent in the process of transferring authority from a charismatic to an institutional foundation. The failure of the ORI instilled in the leaders of the revolution a distrust of institutions, with the result that Cuba's political structures remained "provisional" until 1970. The ORI's successor, the Communist party of Cuba, did not even begin operating nationally until 1965, and by 1970 it was still small, disorganized, and incapable of directing the political process. Its relations with the government bureaucracy were more conflictual than cooperative, partly because neither structure had a clearly defined functional domain.

After the failure to produce ten million tons of sugar in 1970, the basic institutional relationships in the Cuban political system began to shift considerably with the campaign to "institutionalize" the revolution. For the first time, internal coordination and control were systematized, institutional functions were specified, and the boundaries between institutions were clearly demarcated. The military, which had been a dominant force in politics during the 1960s and had literally taken over the administration of the economy in 1969–1970, was in the 1970s separated from political and administrative tasks unrelated to national security policy.

The focal point of the "institutionalization" process has been the strengthening of the Communist party. Its expanded size, its improved cohesion and coordination, and its increasingly important role in the routinization of Castro's charismatic authority have all combined to make the PCC the dominant institution in post-1970 Cuba. It is no longer possible to view the PCC simply as an organizational extension of its First Secretary's authority, and therefore it is no longer possible to understand Cuban politics without analyzing the central, leading role played by the Communist Party of Cuba.

NOTES

1. Fidel Castro, "La revolucion no será tolerante con los traidores," *Revolución* (July 27, 1961), pp. 3–5, 7, 13–14.

2. Aníbal Escalante, "Las ORI son la vanguardia," *Bohemia* (October 8, 1961), pp. 72–73.

3. Fidel Castro, *Fidel Castro Denounces Sectarianism,* (Havana: Ministry of Foreign Relations, 1962).

4. Fidel Castro, "Reparto equitativo de alimentos sin privilegios," *Obra Revolucionaria,* Vol. 7 (1962), pp. 7–21.

5. Fidel Castro, "Hay que crear en la juventud un mayor espiritu comunista," *Revolución* (March 14, 1962), pp. 1, 6, 9–10.

6. Fidel Castro, "Ahora damos a los trabajadores las cosas que antes tenian los burgueses," *Bohemia* (March 23, 1962), pp. 36–39, 89–90.

7. "Integración del secretario y de comisiones de la dirección nacional de las ORI," *Cuba Socialista,* Vol. 8 (April 1962), pp. 136–37.

8. F. Castro, *Fidel Castro Denounces . . .* (1962).

9. A. Suarez, *Cuba: Castroism and Communism, 1959–1966* (Cambridge, MA: MIT Press, 1967).

10. "La selección del trabajador ejemplar," *Cuba Socialista,* Vol. 9 (May 1963), pp. 129–32.

11. Fidel Castro, "Declaración del Primer Ministro . . . en el juicio contra el delator de los mártires de Humboldt 7," *Obra Revolucionaria* (March 27, 1964), pp. 5–47.

12. J. Domenech, "Activity of the Party Nuclei in the Plan for Industrial Efficiency," *Granma Weekly Review* (October 16, 1966), p. 2.

13. Armando Hart, "Production's First Need Is Technical and Cultural Improvement . . . of Party Cadres and Members," *Granma Weekly Review* (July 20, 1969), pp. 10–11.

14. José Machado, "In the Face of All Difficulties We Will Not Forget the Fundamental Factor," *Granma Weekly Review* (June 29, 1969), p. 5.

15. Ernesto "Che" Guevara, *Venceremos: The Speeches and Writings of Che Guevara* (New York: Simon & Schuster, 1968), pp. 220–25.

16. Fidel Castro, "Discurso . . . en la concentración commemorativa del VI aniversario de la revolución," *Obra Revolucionaria,* Vol. 1 (1965), pp. 5–34.

17. "General Offensive Against Bureaucracy Is Stepped Up," *Granma Weekly Review* (March 2, 1967), p. 4.

18. Fidel Castro, "Speech to the 5th National Plenary of the FMC," *Granma Weekly Review* (December 18, 1966), supplement.

19. "One Thousand Party Militants," *Granma Weekly Review* (April 23, 1967), p. 8.

20. Armando Hart, "How Should the Party Units Perform Their Role in the Revolution's Tasks of Production?" *Granma Weekly Review* (March 6, 1966), p. 2.

21. PCC (Partido Comunista de Cuba), "Acerca de las tareas y los métodos de dirección del partido," *Granma Weekly Review* (October 26, 1967), p. 2.

22. Armando Hart, "Debemos elevar la organización del partido a la altura de nuestra revolución," *Granma Weekly Review* (September 19, 1966), pp. 2–3.

23. Osvaldo Dorticós, "We Base the Future of Our Homeland on Revolutionary Honor, Dignity and Enthusiasm," *Granma Weekly Review,* (January 29, 1967), p. 5.

24. Raúl Castro, "Report to the Central Committee on the Activities of the Microfaction," *Granma Weekly Review* (February 11, 1968), pp. 7–11.

25. Fidel Castro, "Speech on the 11th Anniversary of the Attack on the Presidential Palace," *Granma Weekly Review* (March 24, 1968), pp. 2–8.

26. Armando Hart, "The Process of Building and Developing the Party Has Tremendous Importance," *Granma Weekly Review* (May 5, 1969), pp. 3–4.

27. Carmelo Mesa-Lago, *Cuba in the 1970s* (Albuquerque, N.M.: Univ. of New Mexico Press, 1978), p. 71; and PCC, "Sobre la vida interna del partido: tesis y resolución," in *Tesis y Resoluciones: Primer Congreso del Partido Comunista de Cuba* (La Habana: Departamento de Orientación Revolucionaria, 1976), pp. 13–54.

28. PCC, *Estatutos del Partido Comunista de Cuba* (La Habana: Departmento de Orientación Revolucionaria, 1976); *Plataforma Programática del Partido Comunista de Cuba* (La Habana: Departamento de Orientacion Revolucionaria, 1976); and Fidel Castro, "Report of the Central Committee to the First Congress," in *First Congress of the Communist Party of Cuba: Collection of Documents* (Moscow: Progress Publishers, 1976), pp. 16–279.

29. José Machado, "The Party Leadership Has Confidence in the Work You Will Be Doing," *Granma Weekly Review* (October 8, 1978), p. 4; "Central Committee of Cuba Holds 5th Plenary

Meeting," *Granma Weekly Review* (December 25, 1977), p. 1; and "Communist Party of Cuba Holds 6th Plenary Meeting" (June 11, 1978), p. 1.

30. William M. LeoGrande, "Continuity and Change in the Cuban Political Elite," *Cuban Studies,* Vol. 8, No. 2 (July 1978), pp. 1–31.

31. L. Lockwood, *Castro's Cuba, Cuba's Fidel* (New York: Vintage, 1969), p. 329.

32. Fidel Castro, "Speech on the 20th Anniversary of the Attack on Moncada," *Granma Weekly Review* (August 5, 1973), pp. 2–5.

33. "The Party, the State, and the Mass Organizations in the Dictatorship of the Proletariat," *Granma Weekly Review* (January 27, 1974), p. 10.

34. Fidel Castro, "Speech on the 17th Anniversary of the Attack on Moncada," *Granma Weekly Review* (August 2, 1970), pp. 2–6.

35. Raúl Castro, "Speech to the Delegates to People's Power," *Granma Weekly Review* (September 8, 1974), pp. 2–5.

36. Ibid.; and PCC, *Constitution of the Organs of People's Power* (New York: Center for Cuban Studies, 1975).

19. The Changing Face of Cuba's Communist Party*

By Nelson Valdés

The Third Cuban Communist Party Congress was held in Havana from February 4–7, 1986. On the first day the Congress discussed the work carried out in the last five years. On the second day the Congress discussed a projected draft program (the actual program had not been finished), the social and economic guidelines for the 1986–90 period, changes in the party statutes and two draft resolutions on the management and planning of the economy and the country's politico-administrative division. After the reading of the *Main Report* by Fidel Castro, on the second day, separate commissions discussed the party's statutes. There were some resolutions referring to the political and administrative division of the country, the economic and social guidelines for the 1986–90 five-year plan, and the management of the economy. The new procedure by which the draft program will be discussed by everyone in Cuba is a new concept in the Cuban Communist Party (PCC). The program, said a resolution, will determine the immediate and final goals of the revolutionary process and the specific activities in each sphere.

Cuba watchers eagerly awaited the results of the Congress amidst rumors that great changes could be expected. Indeed, some significant changes occurred at this unusual Congress. The Congress, which was postponed from

*From Nelson Valdés, "The Changing Face of Cuba's Communist Party," *Cuba Update* Vol. 7, Nos. 1–2 (Winter–Spring 1986), pp. 1, 4, 16.

December 1985 to February of 1986, did not end with the closing speech given by Fidel Castro on February 7th since the Central Committee will have to convene again in late December to discuss the social and economic projections of the party for the next 15 years. Thus, in this brief report, only matters related to the Communist party proper will be reviewed.

PARTY GROWTH

The Communist party has continued to grow since 1965. From just 50,000 members in 1965 it now has 523,639 members. Perhaps more revealing is the number of members per 1,000 inhabitants. In 1965 there were just 6.5 party members for every 1,000 Cubans. In February the figure was 51 per 1,000. The annual growth rate of party membership has shown some fluctuations, going from an average growth rate of 32 percent per year (1965–75), to 21 percent (1975–1980) and down to 4.1 percent (1980–1986). The dramatic drops in the rate of growth seem to be connected to the prerequisites for joining the party. In 1975 only 19.6 percent of the members had a 9th grade education or more; by 1986 the figure was 72.4 percent, an extraordinary improvement in just 11 years.

PARTY ORGANIZATION

Perhaps more significant than the actual growth in membership have been the changes in the internal organization and makeup of the party. From its inception in 1965 the critical structures within the PCC have been the Central Committee, the Political Bureau, and the Secretariat. A review of each of these follows:

The Central Committee

The Central Committee membership can be divided into full members (who actually participate in decision making) and alternates (who may take the place of full members due to death, promotion, etc.). In 1965 the CC had 100 full members with no alternates. But as the PCC grew in members it was necessary to incorporate more people into positions of leadership. The PCC avoided the process of demoting some of the CC full members by inventing the concept of alternates. Thus, in the 1976 Party Congress, 12 new alternates were incorporated, so the Central Committee had 100 full members and 12 alternates. In 1980, the practice continued. Rather than demoting the old full members, the PCC opted for the increment in CC membership. Thus, in 1980, the number of full members jumped to 148, while the alternates increased to 77 members. This meant a combined CC membership of 225 members, or 113 more members than five years earlier.

At the Third Congress the party decided that a policy of promotion without demotions could not continue. The combined CC membership remained at 225 members while the actual full members were reduced from 148 to 146 and the alternates were increased by 2 (from 77 to 79). Of the total, 20 are 28–35 years old (8.9 percent), 91 are 36–45 (40.5 percent), 86 are 46–55 (38.2 percent) and 28 are over 55 (12.4 percent). Almost half of the PCC Central Committee members were under 18 at the triumph of the revolution in 1959. The average age of the 225 CC members is now 47 as a result of the inclusion of many young people. This shift in policy is the very bread and butter of so-called "Cubanologos" (that is, those who spend numerous hours trying to figure out what group, faction or elite is gaining or losing influence). Sam Dillon of the *Miami Herald* (February 14, 1986) reported that the magnitude of the changes "has left European and western diplomats shaking their heads in amazement." More than 50 percent of the CC full membership was replaced. Of the newly elected alternates (79) only eight were reelected (from 1980). There were also major changes in the Political Bureau.

The Political Bureau

In 1965 the PB had eight members. At the First Party Congress (1975) it was increased to 13 and at the Second it went to 16. Again, the policy of growth without demotion was at work. But not so at the Third Congress. In fact the number of full members was reduced to 14. (In 1965 there were no alternate members in the PB, nor in 1975. In 1980 the position was created and 11 people elected to it. In 1986 the number of alternates was reduced to ten.) Thus, at present the combined membership of full and alternate PB members has declined from 27 (in 1980) to 24.

Of the original 14 full members of the PB in 1975 six have been replaced, and eight have been reelected. The two persons that were added in 1980 to the PB were reelected again, and four new persons have been added. The changes were much more profound among the alternate PB membership. Of the 11 elected in 1980 only two were reelected. That is, 72 percent were replaced by totally new people.

Secretariat

In 1975 the Secretariat had nine full members. At the Second and Third Party Congresses the number of full members remained constant. But the personnel changed in a major way as well. One third of the 1980 members were not reelected, 66 percent were reelected (five members), and three new members joined the Secretariat.

Fidel Castro was reelected first secretary of the party, just as Raúl Castro was reelected second party secretary. Don Shannon of the *Los Angeles Times* wrote that "Fidel formally" designated Raúl Castro "as his heir." (LAT, February 14, 1986). This is inaccurate since it was the PCC that did so; moreover, this practice had been going on at least since 1965, if not earlier (i.e., March 1962). Interestingly enough, the U.S. media reported these dramatic changes as evidence of Fidel Castro's charismatic influence and rule (so did the "Cubanologos"). This is a rather peculiar interpretation. After all, three so-called "Fidelistas" were removed from the PB (Ramiro Valdés, Guillermo García, Sergio del Valle and just one "old PSP," Blas Roca). Thus, Fidel was getting rid of the Fidelistas! The same logic would be applicable with the Secretariat and the CC.

It is obvious that the Cuban PCC has learned from the Soviet and Eastern European experience. The recent history of the Soviet CP, with its litany of deaths, suggests that a gerontocracy is hardly the best way of running a political party. Thus, it is not surprising when Fidel declares, "we had to renew or die." He went on, "we must trust our youth." This sensitivity to youth is also the by-product of Cuban political culture as well as the very demography of the country.

AFFIRMATIVE ACTION

In previous Congresses the PCC has stressed the need to incorporate a larger number of workers, or to improve the overall educational/cultural level of the membership. At the second Congress, for example, particular attention was given to the incorporation of women. The same theme was repeated at the Third Congress, but the PCC went further this time, enunciating a policy of affirmative action for women, blacks and the young. The *Main Report* read by Fidel Castro stated,

> The mechanisms that ensure the correct selection, permanence and promotion of cadre must be improved constantly on the basis of thorough, critical, objective and systematic evaluations and with appropriate attention to development and training.
>
> Women's representation, in keeping with their participation and their important contribution to the building of socialism in our country, must be ensured, along with the existence of a growing reserve of promising young people born and tempered in the forge of the revolution.

In 1975 women accounted for 13.2 percent of the total PCC membership, five years later it was 18.8 percent and in 1986 reached 21.5 percent. Although below the distribution of the entire female population the figure indicates that efforts continue to be made in this area. The number of women in the Central Committee has increased to 41 (or 18.8 percent of the combined CC membership), one is a full member of the Political Bureau, Vilma Espín, and two alternates, Yolanda Ferrer (from the FMC) and Rosa Elena Simeon (head of the Academy of Sciences).

A new development seems to be taking place as far as ethnicity and race is concerned within the PCC. The *Main Report* states,

> In order for the Party's leadership to duly reflect the ethnic composition of our people, it must include those compatriots of proven revolutionary merit and talents who in the past had been discriminated against because of their skin color.

Fidel elaborated on this theme at the closing of the Congress. He noted that the "rectification of historical injustices" such as racial discrimination "cannot be left to spontaneity." He noted that it is not enough that the laws recognize equality. He added that "in the mass organizations, in the youth, and in the party it is necessary to promote." And the revolution has to promote women, the young and blacks. "It has to be party work . . . because we have to straighten out what history distorted." At present 28.4 percent of the CC membership is black or mulatto (self-defined). It remains to be seen how this new "política" is translated into a comprehensive program of affirmative action throughout the society.

SOCIAL COMPOSITION

The social composition of the CC reveals some interesting trends. People who work professionally in party activities have become the dominant sector within the CC. In 1965 they represented just 10 percent of the total membership, but by 1986, 32.4 percent. A reverse trend has taken place as far as the military presence in the CC. In 1965 the military represented 58 percent, but in 1986 only 19.1 percent of the combined membership. Mass organizations, on the other hand, began with seven percent in 1965, climbed to 15.6 percent of the combined membership in 1980, but dropped six years later to 8.9 percent. Also, the overall trend seems to indicate a growing presence of workers not related to state, party or mass organization work. The increased presence of party workers as well as state bureaucrats reflects the increasing importance of these two sectors in the society. The decline in the influence of the military, although not new, has reached a new low in the history of the revolution.

In the future it may be pertinent to discuss the actual meaning of all these changes, and what they may portend for the future of the revolution. Moreover, these changes should be placed in the context of the separation of party functions from state functions.

20. Cuban Leadership in the 1980s*

BY JORGE I. DOMÍNGUEZ

Cuba is at a turning point. President Fidel Castro has been using his power boldly during the past two years to reshape internal affairs along lines not seen since the late 1960s. Instead of delegating authority to powerful subordinates,

*From Jorge I. Domínguez, "Cuba in the 1980s," *Foreign Affairs,* Vol. 65, No. 1 (Fall 1986), 118–135. Edited for this volume.

as he had done since the early 1970s, he has recentralized it. Instead of liberalizing the economy, he has reversed several market-reliant policies of the past decade. And instead of stressing pragmatic policy goals, he has again been emphasizing the need to follow the "correct" ideological route in building socialism. . . .

In late 1984, President Castro looked around and did not like what he saw at home. He began a reorganization of internal affairs, dismissing many top government and party leaders from various organizations and factions. The three key changes have been the 1985 dismissals of the interior minister, Ramiro Valdés; the president of the Central Planning Board, Humberto Pérez; and the party secretary for ideology, Antonio Pérez Herrero. One common theme of these dismissals is that the officials' work, though on some counts successful, displeased President Castro, as did their conspicuous display of decision-making autonomy.

Before his ouster, Ramiro Valdés was considered the third-ranking official, after Castro's brother Raúl. (Raúl, who heads the armed forces, is Fidel's designated successor.) Valdés, a commander of the revolution since the war against the government of Fulgencio Batista in the 1950s, worked to consolidate the new government's power after victory in 1959 and during the critical decade of the 1960s. He used all means, including repression of any opposition, widespread imprisonment of dissidents and ample use of the death penalty. When he stepped down at the decade's end, the counterrevolution had been crushed. He returned as interior minister in late 1979 to stifle the discontent that became evident to the world in 1980 when more than 125,000 Cubans left from Mariel harbor for the United States. Again he succeeded. Valdés' dismissal in December 1985, which was announced in curt, cold tones, may have stemmed from allegations of corruption and abuse of power against him. Valdés was also blamed for failing to stop a wave of common crime, and he may have opposed some of the liberalizing trends that have not been reversed, such as more permissive social and religious attitudes and an openness to non-Communist influences. At the Cuban Communist Party's Third Party Congress in February 1986, Valdés was dropped from the Politburo, which completed his fall from power.

Humberto Pérez was the architect of Cuba's economic recovery during the past decade. To understand his achievement, recall Cuba's circumstances in the 1960s. This allegedly centrally planned economy did not have a five-year plan until 1976. In the late 1960s, it had no plan of any kind, no budget, no auditing, and not even financial statistics to determine costs. Labor unions were moribund, and workers were expected to work overtime without pay. Wages were paid with little regard to effort, quality or hardship.

Pérez was able to make some headway; the economy did recover from its collapse of the 1960s. It withstood even the much lower prices for sugar (the commodity which still accounts for at least three quarters of Cuban export earnings) that have been typical since 1975. It even grew somewhat in the early 1980s, weathering the economic storm that has devastated most of Latin America. Living standards rose. Cuba may be one of the few countries where the application of Soviet economic procedures, including some modified market mechanisms, increased production and even efficiency.

But Pérez did not perform the miracles expected of him; the Cuban economy remains troubled and dependent on external aid. He was dismissed in July 1985 because the results were not good enough. There was insufficient plan discipline and too much reliance on the market, and his policies by late 1984 seemed to have led to serious balance-of-payments problems. The new top official for the economy, Osmani Cienfuegos, scored high on loyalty to the Castro brothers and on organizational skills, but his main prior experience was training insurgents for overseas revolutions in the late 1960s.

Antonio Pérez Herrero tried to create a real Communist party. To understand the magnitude of his task also requires looking back to the 1960s, when the allegedly Marxist-Leninist state barely had a functioning Communist party. No party congress was held until 1975; the Central Committee had met rarely. That presumably democratic regime had a makeshift constitution, no nationwide elections and no legislative assemblies. Pérez Herrero was no democrat, but he sought to apply Marxism-Leninism systematically to run Cuba. His dismissal in 1985 was the first since 1968 which publicly linked a party official's departure to a policy dispute—in his case, the new, short-lived opening toward the United States, and the new opening toward the Roman Catholic Church, which is still under way. He was opposed to both overtures.

As a means to infuse new leadership at the top, at the Third Party Congress in February 1986 nearly half of the alternate Central Committee members were dropped, as were 37 percent of its full members. For the first time since the Politburo's creation in 1965, there was a major change in its membership, including the departure of two commanders of the revolution. The following were also "firsts": the new interior minister (Division General José Abrantes) is not a Politburo member; no naval officer is a full member of the Central Committee; and a black man who was not a part of the original revolutionary coalition, Esteban Lazo, entered the Politburo. Also, both the proportion and the absolute number of military members of the Central Committee fell to the lowest levels ever, in order to assert the power of civilian party elites more clearly.

This was not, however, a bloody or vicious purge. No one dropped as a member or alternate of the Politburo was also asked to leave the Central Committee. No faction was crushed, no overarching policy dispute surfaced. Recruitment was also rational. Promotion to the top organs rewarded good performers and followed appropriate hierarchical channels. No one was promoted to the Politburo who had not been at least a Central Committee alternate. Many appointments to replace ministers or party officials who had been dismissed were promotions of those with experience. In short, the shake-up has been radical, but not reckless.

What had gone so wrong that required so much change? Castro's criticism stresses lack of economic efficiency (despite the growth) and discipline, and too much reliance on market methods. He blamed these substantive and ideological failings on top officials. Castro seems motivated by ideological, political and economic factors. His solutions apparently are to recentralize economic decision-making authority as a means to achieve efficiency, and to reemphasize socialist, revolutionary values as a means to motivate people. Both solutions were tried and failed in Cuba in the 1960s, but Castro seems determined nevertheless to try them again. He believes that the regime is today more ideologically mature and better organized, and thus is able to achieve these goals without the costs incurred in the 1960s. I think he is wrong.

As a result of Castro's critique, personnel changes were most drastic in the malperforming sectors. The military personnel who lost seats on the Central Committee were mostly from the Interior Ministry and the navy; the first was blamed for abuses, corruption and its inability to stop a crime wave in 1985, and the second for its serious disarray. Similarly, the Interior Ministry general in charge of intelligence from Grenada was dropped from the Central Committee; Cuba had been in the dark about many changes that led the Grenadian government to commit suicide in 1983, setting the stage for the U.S. and English-speaking Caribbean intervention.

Fidel Castro criticized (generally accurately) his government's performance in his report to the Third Party Congress, thereby explaining the dismissal of many on his economic team. He noted "the absence of comprehensive national planning for economic development." The budget, he said, "continued to be ineffective. Rather than regulating spending, it, in effect, promoted it along with improper social consumption." He questioned the reliability of government statistics. He criticized the poor use of external financing for projects that "have not always been undertaken with the rational and disciplined approach" needed. He indicted industry: "We are still facing technical and organizational deficiencies in production, failure to make the best use of foreign technical assistance, lack of technical discipline and precision in industrial repair and maintenance." He regretted that there "are serious service problems in Havana, particularly in housing maintenance, public facilities and public transportation" (there is little private car ownership). Havana suffered, too, he said, from "inadequate" water supply and from "serious problems with the telephone service." He criticized education, the revolution's pride: "Some classes are still mediocre or poor . . . [and] some students are promoted without having gained the required knowledge."

Indeed, he complained about everything except his own performance. Born in 1926, Castro seems healthy, able and ready to rule Cuba until the next

century. Supremely confident as ever, conscious that he still has the support
and affection of many Cubans, shrewd and politically effective, he still towers
over Cuba's national life. One of the world's most experienced leaders, with
a prodigious memory, he is a powerful and tireless orator as well as seductively
persuasive in conversation. He still pays detailed attention to animal genetics,
elementary school texts and the quality of baseball teams. Castro can be
charming, or ruthless if he must be, but his style of rule has come to rely more
on listening, choosing and mediating than on shouting, initiating or imposing.
And yet he, above all, is responsible for his government's problems.

Although Castro rightly criticized his deputies' performance, he is to blame
to the extent that the flaws have been in design and not implementation. He
has promoted military and social expenditures that have broken the budget.
He has demanded infeasible goals in national plans. He has promoted the
interests of the countryside at Havana's expense. And he is personally disorganized in his management of the government. Furthermore, Castro is certainly responsible for the risky direction in which he has been taking the
country in the past two years.

There is a specter haunting Cuba. It is the specter of capitalism. It impedes
Fidel Castro's political control of the economy. It threatens his core, radical
ideological beliefs. To protect them, he has launched new policies to rediscover
the regime's "revolutionary roots." At the Third Party Congress, he vented
his anger. The management system (borrowed from the Soviet Union) "could
become a complete farce, as regards enterprise efficiency, if we attempt to
achieve enterprise profitability by raising the price of products, construction,
and productive services." Indeed, he said, "prices in maintenance, construction and transportation . . . are scandalously high." He concluded: "I believe
we still have a lot to learn in the field of efficiency, and becoming the sorcerer's
apprentice, i.e., apprentice capitalists, is not the solution." Unlike the Soviet
Union, most of Eastern Europe, and certainly China, Cuba may be the first
Communist regime in the late 1980s to back off from market mechanisms in
order to improve production and efficiency.

In the 1970s, the government authorized private contracting for services,
such as plumbing repairs. That change was popular and successful. Provided
workers met their obligations to their state enterprise employers, they could
contract privately for work on evenings or weekends. State firms had been
incompetent and slow to meet customer needs. In 1986, however, Castro
warned that "some people have confused freelancing with capitalism." Moreover, in the plastic arts, where high rates stimulated artistic production and
rewarded quality, Castro said that "there are those who paint and sell paintings
or do decorating work, mostly for state agencies, who have even earned over
200,000 pesos a year." To him, this "showed some state officials are irresponsible." A new commission has been appointed to change this and perhaps other
cultural policies.

In an April 1986 speech, Castro charged that "some of our enterprise heads have also become capitalistlike entrepreneurs." (The official newspaper ambiguously reported that there was applause.) Castro continued: "The first thing a socialist, a revolutionary, a Communist cadre must ask himself is not if his firm is making more money but how the country makes more." He criticized managers "who want their enterprises to be profitable by increasing prices and distributing bonuses by charging the earth for anything." He cited the example of elevators reinforced with stainless steel sheets installed in the Hermanos Ameijeras hospital. At first, he said, he admired the high quality of the work, but he recoiled when he learned of the high prices one state agency had charged another for the work.

Castro could have admired the work and recognized that it was done well because the management system was working as designed. Firms had been urged to show their efficiency by becoming profitable; they could retain part of their profit and declare a bonus for workers and managers. In return, it was hoped that the quality of work would be better. The hospital example showed how performance and profitability did improve. Castro was questioning the success of his government's policies.

Some of Castro's reform policies are akin to Mikhail Gorbachev's in the Soviet Union. In 1985 the Cuban government launched a campaign against corrupt and incompetent officials. The government has also taken steps against anyone who is "diverting resources" for private use "thanks to his friends and connections." Another Gorbachev-style policy ordered bars not to serve beer before 3 P.M. so as not to disrupt work or the neighbors during the day. But Castro's new policies go beyond this to question the very mechanisms of material incentives. "Although we recognize that there is room for bonuses under socialism," he warned, "if there is too much talk of bonuses, we will be corrupting workers." Instead of money, "is there no appeal to the obligation of the workers? Is there no appeal to the duty of young people, telling them that this is an underdeveloped country that needs to develop, that it cannot be on the basis of offering pie in the sky?"

To stamp out the curse of the market, in May 1986 the government banned the free peasant markets. They had been legalized in early 1980, following the example of other Communist countries. All those who raised crops could sell freely in these markets, without price controls, any surpluses remaining after national plan target commitments to state agencies had been met. This measure rewarded peasants, increased output of food crops and improved supplies in the cities. But Castro became incensed by the emergence of middlemen and the new wealth that these policies made possible. In mid-1986 the government also amended its 1985 housing law to forbid private sales of homes. The law had promoted home ownership, but some thought it meant that they could sell their homes or those they built as they wished.

Such market means, Castro told the Interior Ministry on its 25th anniversary, reflected unacceptable "liberal bourgeois" tendencies. Instead, "socialism must be built through political work." These market "mechanisms only build capitalism." The glories of the revolution, he said, were "not based on money" but "on concepts, on ideas, on principles, and based on certain moral values that people treasure."

Appeals to patriotism, to socialist values or to the commitment to build a revolutionary society are a depletable resource. People may tire as time passes or may become skeptical of being called upon to perform miracles again. In the late 1960s, Cuba sought to build a better society based on higher values and to create a "new man," motivated by political consciousness, not by "evil money." In those years, the government closed down the bars, determined the right length of women's skirts, sent homosexuals for "rehabilitation" to forced labor camps, called on workers to work overtime without pay, and disdained the use of financial incentives. These efforts failed. With understatement, Cubans refer to those times as the "tough years." Will Cubans in the late 1980s work for values greater than self-interest? Castro has said that he is not launching a cultural revolution, and yet that is what people fear. He and his government seem to be moving backward.

In discussions I held in Cuba in June 1986, many people deeply committed to the revolution said that the closing down of the free peasant markets was a mistake. The government, they said, could have adopted intermediate steps, such as a better tax and auditing policy, or the normal use of police powers against crime. Instead, the policy swung from unregulated markets to no markets. Beneath this, they had a more serious worry. The trend toward the use of some market means (promoted by Humberto Pérez) had been part of policies since the early 1970s. Castro's explanation of recent changes seemed to herald a renewed ideological zealotry to alter what had seemed like the "rules of the game" for over a decade. This larger fear created even greater anxiety.

There were reports about overzealous officials who ordered that houses built without state authorization be torn down, leaving people homeless. In northern Holguín province, 17 peasant families were evicted and their homes destroyed. They appealed to the local Roman Catholic bishop, who protected them from further harm. Town citizens gathered in front of party offices to protest. Mothers threw down their children's emblems from the Young Pioneers' Union and stepped on them. Some asked how the Batista regime's evictions differed from these. Other officials eventually intervened and promised to build new housing, giving temporary shelter to those who had lost their homes.

The new anticapitalist values have a counterpart in economic organization. Beginning also in late 1984, when Humberto Pérez' power declined sharply, economic decision making has been increasingly centralized. Cubans report that top leaders at times decide simple details that had been delegated in years past to state enterprises. These leaders' preferred alternative to Cuba's mild and successful use of market means is ideology and centralization or, as they might put it, the call to better discipline, sacrifice and organization to build a new society with new and better citizens who respond to the revolution's vision. In the past, this "vision" led to economic collapse.

These criticisms that I heard in Cuba (with which I agree) could not have been recorded had people not been willing to discuss them. I detected no fear. Many stressed their loyalty to the revolution and told me that they criticized it as a sign of their faith in its capacity to overcome error. They stressed, too, that there were party policies to tolerate and promote such criticism as means of rectifying errors. Nor would a Roman Catholic bishop have dared to intervene against the authorities had there not been a change in church-state relations. But would the new path to virtue continue to tolerate disagreements? The government's history provides little reassurance: its past pursuit of a socialist utopia unleashed arbitrary, ruthless repression. . . .

CHAPTER 8

The State and Political Participation

21. The Politico-Administrative System of Cuba at the End of the 1970s (opposite)

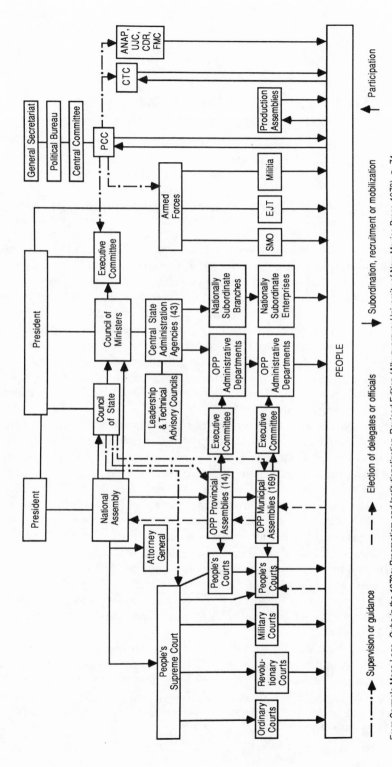

General Secretariat
Political Bureau
Central Committee

ANAP, UJC, CDR, FMC

CTC

PCC

Production Assemblies

President

Executive Committee

Armed Forces

Militia

EJT

SMO

President

Council of Ministers

Council of State

National Assembly

Attorney General

People's Supreme Court

Central State Administration Agencies (43)

Leadership & Technical Advisory Councils

Nationally Subordinate Branches

Nationally Subordinate Enterprises

OPP Administrative Departments

OPP Administrative Departments

Executive Committee

Executive Committee

OPP Provincial Assemblies (14)

OPP Municipal Assemblies (169)

People's Courts

People's Courts

Military Courts

Revolu-tionary Courts

Ordinary Courts

PEOPLE

Participation

Supervision or guidance

Election of delegates or officials

Subordination, recruitment or mobilization

From Carmelo Mesa-Lago, *Cuba in the 1970s: Pragmatism and Institutionalization*, Revised Edition (Albuquerque: University of New Mexico Press, 1978), p. 74.

22. Mass Political Participation in Socialist Cuba*

BY WILLIAM M. LEOGRANDE

THE ROLE OF PARTICIPATION IN A REVOLUTIONARY IDEOLOGY

Promoting mass political participation has always been a key aspect of the revolutionary leadership's plans for building socialism and communism in Cuba. Participation is regarded as indispensable to achieving both the objective conditions (economic development) and the subjective conditions (new socialist man) for a revolutionary transformation of Cuban society. As Fagen (1969, p. 7) writes, "A primary aim of political socialization in Cuba is to produce a participating citizen, not just one who can recite the revolutionary catechism perfectly. The test of the new Cuban man is how he behaves." Nevertheless, the particulars of precisely *how* Cuban citizens ought to participate in the revolutionary process and the actual opportunities available for participation have changed considerably over time.

The earliest concern of the revolutionary government was to organize and mobilize the population to support the new regime and to protect it from both internal and external threats. While the revolutionary government enjoyed widespread popular support after the collapse of the old regime (Free 1960; Zeitlin 1970), few people had actively participated in the struggle against Batista (Bonachea and San Martín 1974). Moreover, there was no organizational vehicle to convert attitudinal support into behavioral support. Initially, then, the principal form of mass participation was the mass rally. Dozens of such rallies, with tens of thousands in attendance, were held in the first few years of the revolution, and they were an important factor in the struggle between left and right wings of the anti-Batista coalition. The inability of the Right to mobilize mass support as could the Left contributed significantly to the Right's feelings of political isolation and impotence (Thomas 1971, pp. 1232–33, 1246–47).

The first formally organized vehicle for mass participation in revolutionary Cuba was the Militia, created in late 1959. At its peak in the mid-sixties, the Militia included half-a-million armed civilians, drawn largely from the work-

*From William M. LeoGrande, "Mass Political Participation in Socialist Cuba," in John A. Booth and Mitchell A. Seligson, eds., *Political Participation in Latin America: Citizen and State* (New York: Holmes and Meier, 1981), pp. 114–128. Edited for this volume.

ing class (Blutstein, et al. 1971, p. 454). It constituted an important supplement to the military might of the Revolutionary Armed Forces (as demonstrated at the Bay of Pigs), and also acted as a politico-military counterweight to the armed forces. Since the mid-sixties, however, the status of the Militia has been reduced to that of a civil defense force and military reserve; it is no longer a significant vehicle of mass participation in politics.

The conception of how Cuban citizens ought to participate in politics and the range of participatory opportunities available have been inextricably linked to the revolutionary leadership's conception of socialist democracy. Throughout the 1960s, the concept of "direct democracy" predominated. This conception rested upon several distinct premises: (1) that the essence of democracy is the pursuit of policies which serve the interests of the people; (2) that democracy requires the active support of the people through their direct participation in the implementation of public policy; and (3) that a direct, informal, and noninstitutional relationship between the people and their leaders is sufficient to ensure governmental responsiveness to popular needs and demands.

In practice, direct democracy meant that virtually all organized political participation was supportive activity. Fagen (1969, p. 9) refers to this activity as mobilization participation and describes it aptly as "a matter of enlisting supportive hands in the service of national goals. . . . Mobilization as used here means 'getting the troops out' to do whatever the leadership feels needs to be done." With the exception of the brief interlude of Local Power (1966–68), which has been described elsewhere (LeoGrande 1976), there were no formal channels through which Cuban citizens could participate in policy formation or elite selection during the 1960s.

There was one informal way, however. Fidel Castro's numerous inspection tours throughout the countryside constituted the principal opportunity for the Cuban people to communicate with their leaders and thereby to exert some influence over policy. Frequent, usually unannounced, and always informal, these visits were an integral part of direct democracy. "No one could accuse him," wrote Hugh Thomas (1971, p. 1345), "as Fanon in *The Wretched of the Earth* did of so many leaders of new states, of retiring to the palace and never visiting the country. On the contrary, Castro never seemed to be in the capital, always travelling by helicopter, or jeep, or Oldsmobile, always looking at some new project, always speaking, encouraging, threatening, denouncing, never indifferent."

In his travels, Castro gave the ordinary Cuban direct access to the center of governmental power—himself. He would often spend hours with small groups of people discussing local problems, ordering action to solve the problems, or explaining why the problems were unsolvable. Not infrequently, he would take the side of the citizenry against abuses or inefficiency by local officials. Castro personally came to be regarded as a more reliable bulwark against governmental irregularity than any set of structural safeguards. González (1974, p. 184) writes:

> As the personal link between the rulers and the ruled . . . Castro also supplied an element of regime responsiveness to popular pressures. Constantly making personal inspection tours throughout the length and breadth of the island, he functioned, in effect, as an ombudsman for the populace. Only he possessed the singular ability to redress local grievances in a political system that had yet to develop truly responsive (as opposed to command) institutions. By the same token, he served as the regime's intuitive barometer of popular sentiment, sounding out public opinion and eliciting criticisms from among the rank and file regarding the performance of local party and government officials in the management of state enterprises.

Since direct democracy placed such emphasis on direct personal mass-elite relationships, institutional mechanisms for mass participation in policy making or to ensure elite accountability were virtually nonexistent.

The Cuban conception of democracy underwent substantial revision in the reorganization of the political system which began in 1970. The failure of the economic policies of the late 1960s, culminating in the failure to produce ten million tons of sugar in 1970, was a severe blow to the prestige of the revolution. These failures prompted a reassessment not only of economic policy, but also of the political system which had allowed such mistakes to be made. The problems in the economy were blamed, in part, on the weakness of Cuban political institutions and on the lack of popular participation in the formation of public policy (Castro 1970a). To remedy these failings, a total reorganization of the political system was initiated, a reorganization aimed at "institutionalization" (i.e., strengthening the institutional structure of the political process) and "democratization" (i.e., increasing mass participation in policy decision making). This new phase of the Cuban revolution marked a shift away from the precepts of direct democracy, and the recognition that more than supportive participation was required for building socialism:

> The people must be given the opportunity to decide the persons to whom they delegate their power and, moreover, the channels should be established through which every member of society may, to the greatest extent possible, participate directly in the governing of that society, in the administration of that society (*Granma Weekly Review* 1974a, p. 10).

In practice, this has meant an expansion of political participation and participatory opportunities beyond the narrow bounds of supportive activity which, during the 1960s, constituted by far the greatest part of political participation in Cuba.

One aspect of political participation in Cuba which has remained relatively constant over time is the boundary delineating the limits of legitimate participation. Since 1961 when Castro declared himself a Marxist-Leninist, the

Cuban political system has been officially characterized as a proletarian dictatorship. As such, it is thoroughly antipluralistic; many political activities
regarded as essential to pluralist democracy are beyond the bounds of legitimacy in Cuba's socialist democracy. Specifically, mass participation aimed at
altering the form of rule (i.e., the basic ideological and institutional framework
of the political process), replacing the existing political elite with a counter-
elite, or blocking the implementation of policy are all regarded as strictly
illegitimate. The formation of political organizations that might pursue such
goals—e.g., opposition political parties, autonomous voluntary associations, or
even organized factions within existing political structures—is likewise prohibited.

POLITICAL PARTICIPATION IN CUBA IN THE EARLY 1970s

Legitimate forms of political participation in Cuba are concerned primarily
with influencing the allocation of public goods within the context of the
existing political system. Such participatory activity is channeled through and
structured by a variety of political institutions, three of which are especially
important: the mass organizations, the Communist party, and the elected
government assemblies.

The mass organizations. Like all socialist countries, Cuba has a variety of mass
organizations which organize people on the basis of common characteristics
such as age, occupation, and gender. Four of these stand out as being, by far,
the most important: the Committees for the Defense of the Revolution (Co-
mités de Defensa de la Revolución—CDR); the Confederation of Cuban
Workers (Confederación de Trabajadores de Cuba—CTC); the Federation of
Cuban Women (Federación de Mujeres Cubanas—FMC); and the National
Association of Small Farmers (Asociación Nacional de Agricultores Peque-
ños—ANAP). Together, these four organizations constitute the most important mechanism through which Cuban citizens participate in politics. The
activities comprising three of the five modes of participation under consideration (supportive activity, communal activity, and self-management activity)
occur largely under the rubric of these mass organizations.

During the 1960s, the mass organizations constituted virtually the *only*
channel through which Cubans could participate, and the activity of these
organizations was then concentrated primarily on mobilizing people for supportive activities. This emphasis characterized all the mass organizations from
their inception: the CDR was created to mobilize supporters to defend the
regime against internal opponents; the CTC was reoriented in 1961 to mobilize
workers to raise productivity and thereby to accelerate economic development;
the FMC was created to mobilize women to participate in all the various

activities of the revolution; and the ANAP was organized to mobilize support among small private farmers. Indeed, the Cubans themselves portrayed the mass organizations as instruments of mass mobilization. "In order to organize and mobilize the masses," said party official Jorge Risquet in 1963, ". . . the Party depends upon the mass organizations, which are like its arms and legs" (Risquet 1963). Not until the political reorganization of the 1970s was the role of the mass organizations expanded to allow for any significant input to the policy-making process.

Today, the mass organizations are still the main vehicle for political participation. Mass organization membership is so extensive that virtually everyone belongs to at least one mass organization, and a majority of Cubans belong to at least two. Since their reorganization in 1961, the trade unions have had a membership of over two million, or more than 80 percent of the state sector work force (Castro 1976, p. 188). Similarly, the Farmers' Association has included nearly all small private farm owners since its inception in 1961; present membership stands at 232,000, or about 85 percent of private farmers and the members of their families (Castro 1976, p. 193; Mesa-Lago 1976, p. 283). The memberships of the CDR and FMC have grown more slowly. After burgeoning rapidly in the first two years of their existence (1960–1962), they settled into a fairly steady rate of expansion of about 15 percent per year. This continued into the early 1970s when membership in both organizations peaked at what appears to be a saturation point of 80 percent of the eligible populations. At present, the CDR has nearly five million members, and the FMC has over two million (Castro 1976, pp. 197, 201). Unlike the other mass organizations, the CDR is open not just to one social sector, but to anyone who supports the revolution. The CDR's goal is to incorporate the entire adult population into its ranks.

There is considerable social pressure to join a mass organization, thereby demonstrating that one is "integrated" into the revolution—i.e., that one is a supporter and a participant. Consequently, membership figures probably overstate the number of citizens who are actually participants in any mass organization activities. Intense organizational efforts to mobilize the entire membership of a mass organization (e.g., to elect delegates to a national Congress, or to discuss drafts of important legislation) typically result in a participation rate of about 85 percent (e.g., Granma Weekly Review 1968b, p. 8; 1974b, p. 3; Castro 1976, p. 192). At the other extreme are those members who participate a great deal. Such members are referred to as "activists" and comprise 19 percent of the CDR's membership, and 16 percent of the FMC's (Granma Weekly Review 1970, p. 3; 1975, p. 6).

The specific tasks undertaken by the mass organizations have been as diverse as they have been numerous, changing considerably over time as the national goals and policies of the regime have evolved. As memberships have expanded, the mass organizations have taken on a larger number and a wider variety of tasks.

Participatory opportunities available through the mass organizations fall primarily into the modes of supportive and communal activity. Both modes are extremely variegated and the constraint of space prohibits a full listing of all the participatory acts that comprise them. The three most important types of supportive activity, though, are voluntary labor campaigns (usually in agriculture at harvest time), work on community improvement projects (such as adult education, public health classes, vaccination campaigns, blood donation drives, school improvements, etc.), and socialist emulation (contests between individuals or groups to see who can fulfill or overfulfill their work plans most quickly). Since different individuals devote their time to different projects, it is extremely difficult to estimate how many people participate in these supportive activities taken together, although it appears to be a majority of the membership.

Communal activity is defined as nonelectoral behavior aimed at influencing policy, especially within the community. Much of the communal activity engaged in by Cubans involves internal decisions about how the mass organizations will conduct their various work programs. At the base level, branches of the mass organizations have considerable autonomy to organize their own programs of work and to elect their officers (Fagen 1972). Candidates for leadership positions in the mass organizations at the local level are nominated by the membership itself, with the requirement that there must always be at least two candidates for every position. The Communist party is prohibited from either nominating or endorsing any candidate. After a discussion of the merits of the candidates, the membership votes (in the trade unions, at least, this vote is by secret ballot). One indicator of the effectiveness of this process is the very high turnover in mass organization leaders at the local level. For example, in the trade union elections of both 1966 and 1970, three quarters of the candidates elected had not previously held leadership posts (*Granma Weekly Review* 1966, p. 3; Mesa-Lago 1974, p. 77). Participation in this electoral process varies somewhat from one mass organization to another. About 84 percent of the trade unions' membership participated in the 1966 elections, while only about 60 percent participated in the elections of 1970 (*Granma Weekly Review* 1966, p. 3; Mesa-Lago 1974, p. 77).

Mass organization members also have some opportunity to influence the work of their organizations at the national level. National plans of work are adopted at a mass organization's national congress. "Draft theses," i.e., a proposed work plan, circulates throughout the organization before the congress convenes so that the membership can discuss it and suggest changes. In addition, most national congress delegates are drawn from the base of the organization; local units elect delegates to congresses in the way that they elect local leaders.

The degree of influence these procedures actually give the membership over national work plans is debatable; no doubt the Communist party and the national leadership of the mass organizations retain the ability to control this process. That, however, does not make participation by the general membership "inauthentic." The whole process is not merely a charade; rather, it is a way for the national leadership to assess the reactions of the membership to a program which depends for its success upon mass participation in its execution.

Mass organization members also have opportunities to influence policies outside the organizations themselves. The main mechanism for doing this is the mass discussion of drafts of laws. The process here is similar to the mass distribution of draft theses before a national congress, except that all the mass organizations are involved. Drafts of important legislation are discussed by mass organization members at the local level, suggested changes are solicited, and these changes are then communicated to the Council of Ministers for use in drawing up the final text of the law. In at least some cases, the suggestions that emerge from the discussion process have led to substantial revisions in the draft law. The mass discussions of draft legislation are typically attended by about 60–80 percent of the mass organizations' membership (Castro 1976, p. 192; *Granma Weekly Review,* 1968a, p. 1).

Individual mass organizations also serve a "watchdog" function in various settings. The trade unions are responsible for overseeing the behavior of plant managers, the CDR is responsible for maintaining a "patient advocate" service to assure proper treatment of people receiving medical services, and the FMC and CTC have created the "Women's Work Front" which is essentially a women's caucus within the trade unions. The Women's Work Front is responsible for seeing that the trade unions give proper attention to the concerns of working women.

Self-management activity in Cuba takes place almost entirely in the work place through the trade unions. While there were several experiments in worker self-management during the 1960s, they were largely ineffective. The trade unions, like the rest of the mass organizations, devoted most of their energy to mobilizing supportive activity. In the late 1960s, the trade unions were replaced by the Advance Workers Movement—a cadre organization of the most productive workers in a plant. The function of the Advance Workers Movement was to spur production. At its peak, the Movement included only 450,000 workers, about 17 percent of the labor force (Mesa-Lago 1974, p. 237). Thus the vast majority of workers had no mass organization of their own to represent their interests or through which they could participate in politics.

One conclusion of the post-1970 reassessment of the political system was that the replacement of the unions by the Advance Workers Movement had been a mistake (Castro 1970b). Beginning in 1970 and culminating in 1973 with the Thirteenth Congress of the CTC, the trade unions were rebuilt. The self-management activities now available stem largely from resolutions passed at the Thirteenth Workers' Congress (CTC 1973). Workers' participation in decision making within the workplace is exercised through three channels: production assemblies, management councils, and work councils. Through the production assemblies, which are meetings of a plant's entire work force, workers have the right to participate in decisions concerning production quotas, individual work norms, overtime, working hours, socialist emulation plans, voluntary labor mobilizations, etc.

Proposals passed at production meetings are not binding on the plant manager, but rejections of such proposals must be justified at the next production assembly. The assemblies are held at least every two months, though many work centers hold them more frequently. Zimbalist (1975, p. 20) reports that worker attendance at production meetings is between 80 and 100 percent and that worker participation is "extensive and vocal." In interviews with Cuban workers, Perez-Stable (1976, p. 40) found that 85.9 percent of her respondents said the workers must be consulted in enterprise management, 57.8 percent felt that workers' input through the production assemblies was influential, and 52.6 percent believed that the management had to respond to workers' proposals.

Management Councils offer an additional avenue for worker participation in plant administration. The councils are composed of the plant administrator, his/her top assistants, elected trade union representatives, a representative of the Women's Work Front, and representatives of the Communist party. The Management Councils do not have the power to overrule the plant manager, but all administrative matters must be brought before it for discussion. "From my interviews with administrators, Party representatives, union representatives, and workers," writes Zimbalist (1975, p. 19), "it seems that the workers' input at these meetings is quite significant."

The Work Councils, on the other hand, are comprised entirely of workers elected by their coworkers. These councils handle all labor grievances, and their decisions are not subject to review by the plant management.

The Communist Party of Cuba. During the 1960s, the only avenue for political participation besides the mass organizations was the Communist Party of Cuba (Partido Comunista de Cuba—PCC). As a Leninist party, the PCC is a cadre party; membership is highly selective and limited to a very small portion of the population. . . . However, the PCC's unique method of selecting party members does provide the mass populace with at least some opportunity to participate in party affairs. Since 1962, PCC members have been chosen by the "mass method." Periodically, the workers in each plant meet to decide who among them deserves to be a party member. Nominations are made, discussed, and voted upon. Those who are approved are then recommended to the party for membership. If the party decides to accept these nominees, it must still return to the workers' assembly for ratification of the individuals' membership (*Cuba Socialista* 1962, pp. 129–32).

THE ORGANS OF PEOPLE'S POWER: 1976 AND BEYOND

During the 1960s, all government officials in Cuba were appointed from above. There were no elections and there were no representative assemblies analogous to soviets in the USSR. This was consistent with the general absence of mechanisms for assuring elite accountability to the populace and it was consistent with the precepts of direct democracy. It meant, however, that the government institution provided no opportunities for mass political participation.

The shift away from direct democracy in the 1970s brought with it a thorough reorganization of the government and the initiation of "People's Power." Composed of elected delegates, these legislative assemblies constitute the primary organs of government at all levels of administration (municipal, provincial, and national), and all administrative agencies are, in theory, subordinate to them. After a two-year pilot project in Matanzas Province, Organs of People's Power were instituted nationwide in 1976.

The stated purpose for creating People's Power was to provide the citizenry with more opportunities to participate in policy formation and elite selection, especially at the local level (R. Castro 1974). The delegates to the municipal assemblies are directly elected by the general populace. These delegates, in turn, elect the members of the provincial and national assemblies. The legal powers of these assemblies are formidable (Constitution of the Organs of People's Power 1975). The Organs of People's Power has the authority to set governmental policy, to oversee administration of that policy, and to appoint or dismiss administrative officials. The Communist party explicitly retains the "leading role" in the political process, however, and it is still too early to assess the degree of actual control over decision making that the People's Power Assemblies will be able to exercise.

The electoral process for municipal delegates is complex, but is worth discussing at length. Municipalities are divided into electoral districts called "circumscriptions." Each circumscription sends one delegate to the municipal assembly. Circumscriptions are divided into neighborhoods, each of which runs one candidate for the delegate seat of the circumscription in which the neighborhood is located. A mass meeting of all eligible voters is held in each neighborhood for the purpose of nominating that neighborhood's candidate. The meetings are chaired by a local resident who was himself elected to chair the nominating meeting at a prior meeting of the neighborhood's residents. Nominations are made from the floor; any number of people may be nominated, so long as there are at least two nominees. The Communist party is explicitly prohibited from making nominations or endorsing nominees, although individual party members may make nominations. The nominees are then discussed and voted upon by a show of hands. The nominee receiving a simple majority becomes the neighborhood's candidate for the delegate election. During the nominating process for the 1976 elections, 76.6 percent of the eligible voters attended these nominating meetings (*Granma Weekly Review* 1976a, p. 2).

Since each circumscription encompasses several neighborhoods, each delegate seat is contested by several candidates. Once candidates have been nominated by the neighborhoods, an election commission compiles their biographies and distributes them to all eligible voters in the circumscription. No other form of campaigning is permitted.

The first nationwide election of delegates to the municipal assemblies was conducted in 1976 with some 30,000 candidates contesting 10,725 seats. Voting was by direct secret ballot in closed voting booths. Although voting is voluntary (it was compulsory before 1959), voter turnout was 95.2 percent, the highest in Cuban history. Given the multiplicity of candidates, in many circumscriptions no one received a majority of ballots cast. Runoff elections had to be held to fill about a quarter of the delegate posts; turnout in the runoff election was 94.9 percent (*Granma Weekly Review* 1976b, p. 1; 1976c, p. 6).

The delegates' mission is to act as a "true vehicle of communication between the electorate and the municipal assemblies" (Constitution of the Organs of People's Power 1975, p. 22). Consequently, the Cubans have introduced a formal set of procedures to assure ongoing contact between delegates and the populace. Delegates are mandated to meet regularly with their constituents, both to report on governmental operations and to listen to people's complaints and suggestions. The principal forum for such contacts are the "Assemblies for Rendering Accounts." These are mass meetings of the delegate's entire constituency which are held every three months. Delegates are required to report on the actions of the municipal assembly, report on their own performance in the assembly, and to solicit the people's grievances and proposals. All proposals are submitted to a vote, and if they are passed, the delegate is required to introduce them to the next meeting of the municipal assembly. Finally, the delegate must report back at the next Rendering of Accounts what the disposition of the proposal was. Delegates are also required to meet every three months with all the CDR committees in their circumscription to receive input from those organizations. Finally, delegates are required to set aside several hours every week as "Consulting Hours," during which time members of the community can meet with them on an individual basis.

Since People's Power has only been recently created, it is still too early to evaluate the effectiveness of its mechanisms for increasing elite accountability and popular input to local policy making. Results of the two-year pilot project in Matanzas, however, offer preliminary indications that these procedures are functioning fairly well. The meetings for "Rendering Accounts" were held regularly and attended by between 50 and 70 percent of the electorate. People also took advantage of the consulting hours by visiting their local representative, though estimates as to the extent of such contacting are unavailable (Bengelsdorpf 1976; Casals 1975).

The creation of People's Power has significantly expanded the participatory opportunities of the Cuban population, and large numbers of people seem to be taking advantage of those opportunities. People's Power provides the first opportunity since 1959 for the Cuban people to vote for government officials; it provides several important new opportunities for communal activity (the nomination of candidates, the Rendering of Accounts assemblies, and the delegate meetings with CDR); and it provides a formal procedure to facilitate individual contacting of delegates (Consulting Hours).

CONCLUSION: PARTICIPATION AND THE ALLOCATION OF PUBLIC GOODS

The available data clearly indicate that participatory opportunities in Cuba have expanded greatly since 1970, and that the vast majority of Cubans participate in politics in a variety of ways. The effects of this participation on the allocation of public goods is more difficult to assess, but several preliminary conclusions seem warranted.

Supportive activity has been and continues to be an important political resource for the successful realization of the regime's policy goals. Numerous accomplishments in such fields as housing, education, and public health would have been unattainable without active participation by thousands of citizens.

Electoral, communal, and self-management activity differ from supportive activity in that they are aimed directly at influencing policy—i.e., influencing the distribution of public goods by the state. Such participation in Cuba is not merely symbolic or manipulated, though the scope of its effectiveness is clearly limited by the ideological and institutional context in which it occurs. Fundamental challenges to the regime, its leadership, or its basic policy orientations are proscribed, as are political structures through which people might organize to pose such challenges. Virtually all opportunities for legitimate participation are provided by regime-sanctioned institutions. This does not mean that participation is therefore devoid of influence, but it does mean that popular influence is restricted to policy decisions about the allocation of particular public goods rather than the structure of the allocation process itself.

Since the institutions which structure participation in Cuba are organized on the Leninist principle of democratic centralism, there is also a significant difference between the effectiveness of popular influence at the local and national levels. Mass participation affords citizens considerable opportunity to affect local policy, local implementation of national policy, and even the composition of local elites. Above the local level, however, the role of the Communist party becomes increasingly important, and policy at the national level is undoubtedly the least responsive to popular influence.

Even national policy is not wholly impervious to popular demands, however. The expansion of participatory opportunities since 1970 reflects the national leadership's desire to provide policymakers with information concerning popular opinions and demands—information which is essential to the formulation of realistic policy at the national level.

The evolution of political participation in revolutionary Cuba has been toward increasing levels of participation, and toward greater participation by the populace in influencing the formulation of public policy. For Cubans in accord with the socialist character of the revolution, the expansion of political participation has provided extensive and meaningful opportunities to influence the allocation of public goods.

REFERENCES

BAYLIS, THOMAS A.
1978 "The Faces of Participation: A Comparative Perspective," in *Political Participation in Latin America,* volume 1: *Citizen and State,* edited by John A. Booth and Mitchell A. Seligson. New York: Holmes and Meier Publishers.

BENGELSDORPF, CAROLEE
1976 "A Large School of Government." *Cuba Review* 6 (September): 3–18.

BLUTSTEIN, HOWARD I., ET AL.
1971 *Area Handbook for Cuba.* Washington, D.C.: Government Printing Office.

BONACHEA, RAMON L., AND MARTA SAN MARTÍN
1974 *The Cuban Insurrection,* 1952–1959. New Brunswick: Transaction.

BOOTH, JOHN A.
1976 "A Replication: Modes of Political Participation in Costa Rica." *Western Political Quarterly* 29 (December): 627–33.

BOOTH, JOHN A., AND MITCHELL A. SELIGSON
1976 "Peasant Political Participation: An Analysis Using Two Costa Rican Samples." Paper presented to the Seminar on the Faces of Participation in Latin America: A New Look at Citizen Action in Society, San Antonio, Texas (November 12–13).

CASALS, LOURDES
1975 "On Popular Power: The Organization of the Cuban State during the Period of Transition." *Latin American Perspectives* 2 (no. 4): 78–88.

CASTRO, FIDEL
1970a "Speech on the 10th Anniversary of the FMC." *Granma Weekly Review* (August 30): 1–6.
1970b "Speech on the 10th Anniversary of the CDR." *Granma Weekly Review* (October 4): 2–4.
1976 "Report of the Central Committee of the Communist Party of Cuba to the First Congress." In *First Congress of the Communist Party of Cuba.* Moscow: Progress Publishers.

CASTRO, RAÚL
1974 "Speech on the 15th Anniversary of the Triumph of the Revolution." *Granma Weekly Review* (January 13): 2–3.

CHAFFEE, WILBER A., JR.
1976 "Entrepreneurs and Economic Behavior: A New Approach to the Study of Latin American Politics." *Latin American Research Review* 11 (no. 3): 55–68.

Forthcoming   "Let Jorge Do It: A Rational Choice Model of Political Participation." Mitchell A. Seligson and John A. Booth, eds., *Political Participation in Latin America,* volume 2: *Politics and the Poor.* New York: Holmes and Meier Publishers.

CONSTITUTION OF THE ORGANS OF PEOPLE'S POWER
1975   *Constitution of the Organs of People's Power.* New York: Center for Cuban Studies.

CUBA SOCIALISTA
1962   *Cuba Socialista* 9 (May): 129–32.

FAGEN, RICHARD R.
1969   *The Transformation of Political Culture in Cuba.* Stanford: Stanford University Press.
1972   "Continuities in Cuban Revolutionary Politics." *Monthly Review* 23 (April): 24–48.

FREE, LLOYD
1960   *Attitudes of the Cuban People Toward the Castro Regime.* Institute for International Social Research.

GONZÁLEZ, EDWARD
1974   *Cuba under Castro: The Limits of Charisma.* Boston: Houghton Mifflin.

GRANMA WEEKLY REVIEW
1966   *Granma Weekly Review.* (August 28).
1968a   *Granma Weekly Review.* (September 22).
1968b   *Granma Weekly Review.* (October 6).
1970   *Granma Weekly Review.* (October 4).
1974a   *Granma Weekly Review.* (October 20).
1974b   *Granma Weekly Review.* (December 1).
1975   *Granma Weekly Review.* (August 31).
1976a   *Granma Weekly Review.* (October 10).
1976b   *Granma Weekly Review.* (October 17).
1976c   *Granma Weekly Review.* (October 31).

GREEN, GIL
1970   *Revolution Cuban Style: Impressions of a Recent Visit.* New York: International Publishers.

HOUGH, JERRY F.
1975   "The Soviet Experience and the Measurement of Power." *Journal of Politics* 37 (August): 685–710.
1976   "Political Participation in the Soviet Union." *Soviet Studies* 28 (January): 3–20.

LEOGRANDE, WILLIAM M.
1976   "Cuban Democracy in Theory and Practice since 1959: Mechanisms of Elite Accountability." Paper presented at the annual meeting of the New York State Political Science Association, Albany, New York.

LITTLE, D. RICHARD
1976   "Mass Political Participation in the U.S. and U.S.S.R.: A Conceptual Analysis." *Comparative Political Studies* 8 (January): 437–60.

MESA-LAGO, CARMELO
1974   *Cuba in the 1970's: Pragmatism and Institutionalization.* Albuquerque: University of New Mexico Press.
1976   "Farm Payment Systems in Socialist Cuba." *Studies in Comparative Communism* 9 (autumn): 275–84.

PEREZ-STABLE, MARIFELI
1976   "Institutionalization and Workers' Responses." *Cuban Studies/Estudios Cubanos* 6 (May): 323–41.

RISQUET, JORGE
　1963　"El PURS en las montañas de Oriente." *Cuba Socialista* 24 (August): 115–19.

SALISBURY, ROBERT H.
　1975　"Research on Political Participation." *American Journal of Political Science* 19 (May): 323–41.

SELIGSON, MITCHELL A., AND JOHN A. BOOTH
　1976　"Political Participation in Latin America: An Agenda for Research." *Latin American Research Review* 11 (fall): 95–119.
　Forthcoming　"Structure and Levels of Political Participation in Costa Rica: Comparing Peasants to City Dwellers." In Mitchell A. Seligson and John A. Booth, eds., *Political Participation in Latin America,* volume 2: *Politics and the Poor.* New York: Holmes and Meier Publishers.

THOMAS, HUGH
　1971　*Cuba: The Pursuit of Freedom.* New York: Harper & Row.

VERBA, SIDNEY, AND NORMAN H. NIE
　1972　*Participation in America; Political Democracy and Social Equality.* New York: Harper & Row.

VERBA, SIDNEY, NORMAN H. NIE, ANA BARBIC, GALEN IRWIN, HENK MOLLEMAN AND GOLDIE SHABAD
　1973　"The Modes of Participation: Continuities in Research." *Comparative Political Studies* 6 (July): 235–50.

VERBA, SIDNEY, NORMAN H. NIE AND JAE-ON KIM
　1971　*The Modes of Democratic Participation: A Cross-National Comparison.* Beverly Hills: Sage Publications.

ZEITLIN, MAURICE
　1970　*Revolutionary Politics and the Cuban Working Class.* New York: Harper & Row.

ZIMBALIST, ANDREW
　1975　"The Development of Workers' Participation in Socialist Cuba." Paper prepared for presentation at the 2nd annual Conference on Workers' Self-Management Ithaca: Cornell University.

23. *Law and Revolution in Cuba**

BY DEBRA EVENSON

Since the Cuban Revolution did not merely change the leadership of the country but transformed its social, economic and political order, it was inevitable that the preexisting legal system would be modified as well. The development of Cuban law since the revolution has reflected events in the history of the revolution and of the directions taken within Cuban society and politics. Much like the social, economic, and political changes, Cuban law and legal institutions have evolved considerably since 1959.

*This essay was written for this volume. Copyright 1988 by Debra Evenson.

Many commentators have noted three distinct periods within the revolution that correspond roughly to the decades of the 1960s, 1970s, and the 1980s. Significant changes in the development of law match these periods as well. With respect to the development of the legal system, these periods can be characterized respectively as periods of upheaval, institutionalization, and reform. The following discussion will focus primarily on the evolution of the criminal justice system in Cuba, but since law relates to all the complexities of social, economic and political organization, parallel developments can be seen in other areas of the law.

UPHEAVAL

The evolution of the criminal justice system in Cuba cannot be viewed in isolation from surrounding events. Within a few years following the overthrow of the Batista regime in 1959, the revolutionary government overturned the economic order and replaced former political elites with leadership dedicated to radical social and economic change.[1] It was a decade marked by wrenching upheaval and violence which profoundly affected Cuban society. Within a short period of time, much of the economy was socialized, and much of the capitalist and professional class had fled the country (including many lawyers and judges). The new leadership had little expertise in running the national economy or its institutions, a factor immensely complicated by the total economic embargo imposed in 1961 by the United States which had previously supplied Cuba with over 70 percent of its food and other products.[2] In addition to the socialization of the economy, the leadership embarked on ambitious social programs, such as the national literacy and mass health and inoculation campaigns. At the same time, the country was facing armed insurgency by counterrevolutionaries supported from abroad (primarily from the United States). Sabotage and bombings of buildings and plants were commonplace.

Criminal prosecution in the 1960s targeted three major groups: the Batista forces accused of abuses, torture, and assassination prior to 1959; those trying to sabotage and undermine the revolution; and those committing common crimes, particularly the entrenched criminal element engaged in drug trafficking, gambling, and prostitution.

One of the first changes the new government made in the judicial process was to formally establish special Revolutionary Tribunals to prosecute the members of the Batista regime, including the hated secret police. These tribunals were placed under the control of the military. Similar courts had been created in the Sierras to prosecute "war criminals" during the armed rebellion. The existing criminal courts were not controlled or trusted by the new government, and many of the judges of these courts were unsympathetic to the revolution. By the end of 1959, the Revolutionary Tribunals also tried the cases of those accused of participating in counterrevolutionary activity.

Because the Revolutionary Tribunals kept citizens from indiscriminately executing former members of Batista's secret police force and army, Cuba did not experience a "bloodbath" in the aftermath of the revolution.[3] Although hundreds of people were sentenced to death by the Tribunals during this period,[4] the Revolutionary Tribunals did not serve merely to impose death sentences. Many thousands were tried and sentenced to prison terms, the maximum term being 30 years. By 1967, the armed insurgency was quelled and relatively few cases were brought to the Revolutionary Tribunals after this period.

During the mid-1960s the Cuban government also established the infamous UMAP work camps (Unidades Militares de Ayuda a la Producción), where thousands of persons accused of counterrevolutionary activity were sent. Many homosexuals, targets of homophobia and irrationally suspected of conspiring against the government, were arrested and sent to these camps. In 1967, the same year as the armed counterinsurgency ended, these camps were closed.

Several factors weighed against the immediate establishment of meaningful due process protections for persons accused of crime. First, Cuba did not have a solid tradition in criminal justice. Second, many of the judges of the Revolutionary Tribunals were appointed because of their commitment to the revolution and were untrained or inexperienced in law. Revolutionary fervor and disdain for those opposing the revolution played heavily in shaping the judicial attitudes of the newly appointed judges who were more concerned with "moral justice" than with process. Moreover, Cuba was in a state of siege, internal power struggles were a concern, and leadership was struggling to provide basic necessities cut off by the blockade to its population.[5]

In the context of disorder and revolutionary fervor, it would be remarkable if the leadership had replaced a corrupt legal system with a smoothly functioning system with enhanced procedural protections. Yet, even during this tumultuous period, Cubans never experienced the state terrorism prevalent in other Latin American countries that practiced systematic torture, disappearances, and assassinations against opposition groups.

Some steps were taken to improve justice. In 1962 the government established new courts, Popular Tribunals, to handle private disputes and petty crimes in rural areas which previously had little access to the judicial system.[6] The Popular Tribunals were presided over by lay judges elected from the community. The practice was the first introduction of a quasi-jury system in Cuba. By the end of the decade similar tribunals functioned in the cities as well. Thus, three different court systems functioned during the 1960s: the Revolutionary Tribunals, the Popular Tribunals, and the previously existing court system.

PROFESSIONALISM AND INSTITUTIONALIZATION

By the 1970s Cuba had clearly established itself as a one-party, socialist state. Its program of a socialized economy, its commitment to social programs, such as a national health and education system, and its policy of achieving full integration of women and racial groups into the social, political, and economic life of the country were firmly in place.[7] Although the political structure would not be formalized until after the First Congress of the Cuban Communist Party in 1975 and the adoption of the new constitution in 1976, many important institutional changes in the legal system were already taking place.

In the late 1960s a number of jurists recognized the need to rationalize the system, to create greater predictability and fairness in the resolution of disputes and to educate the population to the socialist legal order. As a result, in 1973 the Revolutionary Courts and the People's Tribunal were abolished and replaced by a national unified court system under civilian control.[8] Under the 1976 Constitution, the new courts are accountable to the National Assembly.[9]

The present court system consists of municipal and provincial courts and a national supreme court. Each has its own sphere of original jurisdiction and appellate review of decisions of the next lower court. The new system incorporated some aspects of the institutions it replaced. For example, lay judges serve in each of the courts along with professional judges. At the provincial and supreme courts each case is decided by a panel of three lay judges and two professional judges; at the municipal courts the panels consist of three judges, two lay and one professional. The inclusion of lay judges preserves the popular participation in the judicial process begun with the People's Tribunals. Persons committing counterrevolutionary crimes are no longer tried by military courts, but are tried instead by specified provincial courts and the supreme court.

The process of modifying and refining the legal system was strengthened by developments in the legal profession. By the 1970s, Cuba had the beginnings of a trained bar educated in the principles of the revolution.[10] The National Union of Cuban Jurists, founded in 1977, plays an important role in improving professional skills and expressing the concerns of lawyers on legal issues.[11]

Many of the most significant codes that embody the social and economic principles of the revolution were enacted in this period. In 1973, a new Code of Criminal Procedure was adopted. By the end of the decade, Cuba had a new constitution,[12] a new Family Code, and a new Criminal Code. The developments in family, constitutional and criminal law demonstrate how the revolution has utilized law both to establish revolutionary principles as societal norms and to serve as a mechanism to further the achievement of those principles.[13]

Prior to enacting the Criminal Code of 1979, Cuba enforced, with some modifications, the Social Defense Code originally enacted in 1896. The 1979 code, like its predecessor, treated criminal conduct severely, but it also contained major differences from the previous law. For example, the new code gave judges more flexibility in applying sanctions by allowing for alternatives to imprisonment for minor offenses. Further, the age of criminal responsibility was fixed at 16 under the new code;[14] the prior law merely provided that no criminal responsibility could attach to the acts of children under the age of 12. New crimes were defined in the 1979 Code such as crimes against social property and some forms of misfeasance.

In addition to provisions dealing with theft, assault and other common crimes, the 1979 code contains a section dealing with Crimes Against State Security. Included in this category are actions that threaten state security, such as espionage, sabotage, treason, and armed rebellion. Sanctions for such crimes can be imprisonment for periods of 4 to 20 years or death in cases where violence is used or the threat to security particularly serious.[15] Also included is the crime of "Enemy Propaganda," which criminalizes conduct that incites opposition to the social order, international solidarity and the socialist state. Sentences for violation of this section are lighter, ranging from one to eight years.[16]

REFORM

While providing substantial improvement, the 1979 Criminal Code left much to be desired. It maintained a regime of severe sentencing, which gave judges little flexibility to treat individually defendants who committed minor offenses.[17] Further, while it eliminated criminalization of homosexuality, it contained a catchall provision sanctioning conduct that was "socially dangerous," which in its vagueness left too much room for biased interpretation.

The imperfections in the code were recognized even as it was enacted, but according to one jurist, it was enacted anyway because Cuba needed a new code that gave definition to its criminal law and the 1979 code was far better than the previous law. The new code was not in effect long before Cuban jurists embarked on an extensive analysis of its effectiveness and consistency with the principles of justice. By 1983, new leadership was in place at the Ministry of Justice, soon to be followed by changes at the top of the Ministry of Interior (responsible for running the prison system) and the office of Attorney General. This new leadership formed a commission to analyze the 1979 code and its effect and to propose reforms. Deficiencies in the Code of Criminal Procedure in 1973 were also placed under study for revision.

To accomplish its goal of improving Cuba's criminal justice system, the commission studied the contemporary criminal codes of many countries, including some from the United States. Moreover, several international conferences were held in Cuba to discuss approaches to criminal justice. As a result of the commission's work, a proposal for major reform was presented to the

National Assembly for adoption in December 1987 and a new, revised Criminal Code was adopted.

Some insight into the evolution of thinking with respect to criminal justice in Cuba is found in a statement by Vice-Minister of Justice Carlos Amat in June, 1987:

> In the first period, we operated under the idealistic criteria which governed law making in the country. One of the basic principles governing our philosophy was that if delinquency and criminal behavior is a product of the social system of exploitation and oppression, then if we change that situation and do away with exploitation and oppression, then crime and criminals would be eliminated. That was the "bobo" (stupidity) at the beginning. So we began to deal with crime very severely, imposing very heavy penalties to suppress crime, because we thought that any manifestations of crime had to be carryovers of the prior system. And this same approach was adopted in the Criminal Code of 1979, which was very severe.
>
> But experience has shown us that severe treatment has neither prevented crime nor eliminated criminals. New forms of crime developed, and harsh sanctions did not serve as the slightest deterrent to crime.[18]

As a result, among the many modifications adopted are reduced sentences and greater flexibility in sentencing for first-time offenders. Even before the National Assembly considered the proposed reforms, however, review of sentencing of individual cases was begun. A decree-law passed in 1985[19] established a new procedure of sentence review called "revision" that gives the Supreme Court authority to review cases to determine whether sentences imposed were too severe. Review can be requested by anyone. A commission comprised of persons from the Ministry of Justice, the President of the Supreme Court, and members of the Provincial Tribunals studied more than 4,000 cases in 1986 and 1987. As of June 1987, 1,000 cases had been submitted to the Supreme Court for revision, and many of the prisoners were released or received reduction of their sentences.[20] For example, under the 1979 code, robbery of state property (such as goods from a factory) carried a sentence of four to ten years. After revision, the sentence could be reduced to three years or less in cases where no force or violence was used unless it involved a repeat offense. Under the revised Code, the sanction has been reduced to two to five years and even less where the item stolen is of small value.

Further, under the new modifications a number of minor offenses, such as traffic violations and some misdemeanors that were included as crimes in the 1979 code, were removed and will be dealt with administratively. Most significantly, the catchall provision for unspecified conduct that is "socially dangerous" has been substantially limited to encompass violent behavior and drug use. Thus, with the limitation of this vague section, no provision remains that could be used to punish consensual, private homosexual conduct.[21]

Cuban law does permit imposition of the death penalty. Since 1979, however, the death penalty is not applicable to youths who committed a crime while under the age of 20. According to Cuban officials, it is used very infrequently and only in the most heinous cases involving infliction of severe injury or death. A mandatory, extensive review process prevents the death penalty from being applied arbitrarily. There is an automatic appeal to the Supreme Court in every instance in which the trial court imposes the death penalty. The appeal involves complete review of the evidence tantamount to a new trial. If the Supreme Court ratifies the death sentence, it must be reviewed again by the Council of State (the highest executive body of the state) before it can be carried out. Execution is by firing squad. According to the president of the Supreme Court, there were no executions in 1985 or 1986; three executions took place in 1987.[22] Although the death penalty is reportedly rarely applied, there is no proposal to eliminate it.

Criminal Procedure

Although the procedures by which an accused person is prosecuted in Cuba are very different from the adversarial process in the United States, Cuba subscribes to many of the procedural protections familiar in the United States, such as the principle that the accused is innocent until proven guilty. Cubans also enjoy protections against unauthorized searches and seizures and against self-incrimination.

Criminal procedure in Cuba is based on the investigatorial system that is commonly followed throughout Europe. After making an arrest, the police must turn the accused over to an investigator within 24 hours, or he/she must be released. Family members are notified promptly. The investigator has 72 hours to determine whether there is sufficient evidence to bring charges against the accused and to present the case to a prosecutor. The prosecutor then has 72 hours to make a preliminary determination of sufficiency of the evidence to make a recommendation concerning provisional detention. The prosecutor then makes his/her recommendations to the court, which has 72 hours to accept or reject the preliminary recommendations of the prosecutor. During this investigatorial phase, the accused may be held without the service of an attorney. The accused may hire a defense attorney at the end of this phase, and if he/she does not do so, the court will appoint one at state expense. An important reform that is under review for inclusion in the Code of Criminal Procedure is the guarantee to all accused the right to defense counsel from the time of arrest.

Once formal charges have been made in court, the prosecutor and the defense attorney have up to six months to prepare their cases. By law, a trial is to be completed within six months of arrest or the accused must be released if held in detention.

Prisons

Consistent with the current approach to criminal justice, considerable attention is being paid to the rehabilitative function of incarceration. Sentences for most crimes, particularly those committed by first time offenders, have been substantially reduced, because it has been recognized that long sentences do not serve the goal of rehabilitation. In addition, innovative programs for counseling, education and training are being developed.

Among the more remarkable features of the Cuban prison system is its individualized approach to rehabilitation. After the initial orientation program, the prisoner is assigned to a group—called a detachment—of approximately 80 inmates supervised by a rehabilitation counselor. Civilians and prison officials also work directly with the prisoners. Each detachment elects a council that expresses the concerns of the detachment to the prison management.

The prisoner is provided educational programs in basic learning skills, if needed, and courses in history and the sciences. Prisoners who have the requisite education may work as teachers within the prison. There are also a variety of cultural activities.

With the exception of prisoners considered violent or dangerous, each prisoner is expected to work, although it is not obligatory, and everyone is expected to learn a trade if he or she does not already have one. At Aguica, a maximum security prison for men in Matanzas Province, the major enterprise is the construction of prefabricated parts for housing. There is also work in carpentry and crafts. Combinado del Este, a maximum security prison for men outside Havana, also has several light industries including furniture building and leathercraft. About 10 percent of the inmates work outside the prison in areas such as maintenance, carpentry, or electrical work. However, unlike their U.S. counterparts, Cuban inmates not only engage in productive work but they are also paid the same wage as workers on the outside doing comparable work whether it be construction, mechanical, or handcrafts. The prisoners pay one third of their salary for their maintenance; therefore, the major portion of their income is available for their own use: to save money for themselves for use later on or to support their families.

Moreover, the system encourages family contact. When a prisoner first enters the prison, his or her family is interviewed, along with the prisoner, by the head of the prison. The prisoner's counselor also convenes regular meetings with the family and inmate to discuss the inmate's progress. Visits are encouraged and are normally scheduled monthly. Families and friends can be seen visiting every day of the week. At Aguica, they meet inmates in a large open pavilion with long tables. Combinado del Este and the Women's Prison have similar arrangements. There is no barrier between the prisoner and visitor. Guards are present, but do not stand close by.

Another striking feature, which is strikingly absent in most U.S. prisons, is the general right to conjugal visits. Prisoners (both men and women) are generally permitted three-hour conjugal visits every three to four months and some more frequently. Special quarters—pavillons—are provided for these visits. The rooms are separate and private, and look much like normal bedrooms. Each brightly decorated with a double bed, private bathroom, and a small kitchen.

Physical conditions have improved markedly in Cuba's prisons since the 1960s. At present, Cuba's prisons are operated well below capacity and some are being phased out. For example, Aguica, built in the mid-1960s to accommodate 1,000 inmates, presently houses approximately 700 to 800 male prisoners. Combinado del Este is three times the size of Aguica and is also presently operated below capacity with a population of approximately 2,500. Officials report that the prison population in Cuba in the first half of 1987 numbered approximately 25,000 to 30,000.[23] The current policy of reducing sentences and releasing prisoners under the process of sentence review, should result in a substantial reduction of the prison population.

There have been no major complaints from common prisoners about their treatment in the prisons. Some prisons are known to be rougher because of the prison population: for example Kilo 7 in Camaguay Province. Others are extremely supportive such as Melena del Sur in Havana Province where a local chapter of the Union of Writers and Artists takes an interest in prisoners interested in the arts. In Combinado del Este, prisoners have related that the relationship between inmates and guards is not tense, although there are occasional blows from guards but not beatings. They also report occasional fights between inmates over personal differences.

Reports of mistreatment come from prisoners who were convicted for crimes against the security of the state and who have refused to work or accept other prison programs. The major group are the *plantados* (the planted ones) who were convicted in the 1960s. For over 20 years they have continued to reject socialism and the authority of the Cuban government. The resistant *plantados* have called hunger strikes and have refused to wear normal prison garments. Even among these prisoners, however, the complaints date primarily to the 1960s and early 1970s. Until recently, many *plantados* were kept at the century-old Boniato prison on the east coast of the country. As another indication of change, they are no longer held in separate facilities and all have been moved to the more modern facility at Combinado del Este.

Cuban officials state that there has been no torture or mistreatment of any prisoners, and that the statements of the *plantados* are made for political purposes to denigrate Cuba in the international community. And indeed, most of those making such statements are supported by influential anti-Castro exile groups. Amnesty International, which has never received permission from Cuba to visit its prisons, reports on information received from *plantados*.

Although Amnesty reports incidents of ill-treatment, it has not reported receiving evidence of torture.[24] Cuba recently granted permission to the Human Rights Project, members of Americas Watch and the National Lawyers Guild to inspect prisons. These groups report no evidence of torture.

Cuba has also been releasing these prisoners, including the *plantados,* at a steady pace. Officials reported that there was a total of approximately 1,000 such prisoners in June, 1987,[25] and some officials privately state that all will be released by the end of 1988. Release of these prisoners may signal a new policy with respect to the penalization of activity considered to be against state security. A more lenient attitude is already visible with respect to a self-proclaimed human rights group, *Comité Cubano pro Derechos Humanos,* which is critical of the Cuban government and which has ties to exile groups. Members of its executive committee were released last year after serving several months in prison and it now functions openly in Cuba.

CONCLUSION

With respect to criminal justice, Cuba has come a long way since 1959 and the turbulent 1960s and is presently receiving the benefits of maturity. Now in its third decade, the Cuban Revolution has a body of experience from which it can learn and that it can apply to the process of reform. A new generation of trained jurists who bring professionalism to the task of reform are taking positions of leadership. Moreover, although it still faces hostility and attempts at destabilization from abroad, Cuba has achieved a state of normalcy and security that provides a positive environment for reflection and reform.

The stabilization and institutionalization of the revolution has also permitted the government to apply more resources, both material and personnel, to the improvement of criminal justice. It is an often ignored fact that justice requires considerable resources to function efficiently as well as fairly. Lawyers, prosecutors and judges must be sufficient in number and well trained. Simple record keeping requires typewriters, if not computers, duplicating machines, paper, etc. Cuba has dedicated substantial national resources to the improvement of criminal justice and its prison system. Its ability to continue to improve will be dependent both on continuing commitment and on the health of the nation's economy.

NOTES

1. New laws were quickly drafted and enacted to bring about economic reform. For example, the Urban Reform Law of 1960 prohibited the private rental of housing, nationalized rental property, and set a maximum for rentals at 10% of family income. The Agrarian Reform Law enacted in 1961 broke up the large landholdings of U.S. corporations and large landowners and distributed land to individual peasants and newly created agricultural cooperatives. Other laws were passed, affecting the equal participation of women in the economic and social life of the country. For example, Cuba adopted a very progressive law that provided extraordinary maternity benefits to working women.

2. Medea Benjamin, *et al., No Free Lunch: Food and Revolution in Cuba Today* (San Francisco: Institute for Food and Development Studies, 1984), p. 20.

3. Tad Szulc, *Fidel* (New York: William Morrow and Company, 1986), pp. 482–85. Szulc quotes several people connected with the tribunals who have since left Cuba, but who felt the tribunals were justified, since they prevented mobs from taking justice into their own hands.

4. Ibid., p. 483. According to T. Szulc, Fidel Castro has acknowledged approximately 550 such executions.

5. Armando Valladares, *Against All Hope* (New York: Alfred Knopf, 1986). In this polemical account of his experience in jail, Valladares protests the poor quality and small quantities of food fed prisoners in this period. In fact, the crisis in food supply was experienced by everyone; prisoners were not starved, neither were they given special treatment.

6. For a discussion of the development of the Popular Tribunals, see Luis Salas, "Emergence and Decline of Cuban Popular Tribunals," *Law & Society Review,* Vol. 17, No. 4. (1983), pp. 588–612.

7. For a discussion of the development of women's equality in Cuba, see Debra Evenson, "Women's Equality in Cuba: What Difference Does a Revolution Make?" *Law & Inequality Journal,* Vol. 4, No. 2 (1986), pp. 295–326.

8. Law No. 1250 (June 23, 1973).

9. Constitution, Article 122; and Salas, "Emergence and Decline . . . ," p. 594. The constitution speaks of the judiciary as "independent," but it is not an autonomous, equal branch of government. Abolition of judicial autonomy and the notion of separation of powers did not come without controversy. Cubans explain that since there is only one source of authority—the people—all authority is unitary and cannot be divided.

10. Salas, "Emergence and Decline . . . ," p. 598. The legal profession was all but decimated during the 1960s. Not only had many lawyers and judges emigrated, but the entire profession was stigmatized, and enrollment at the nation's law schools dropped precipitously from 2,853 in 1958–59 to 159 in 1971–72.

11. The National Union of Cuban Jurists (UNJC) publishes a scholarly law review and organizes conferences and seminars on various legal subjects as a means of stimulating discussion of important legal issues and also to improve professional skills. Also concerned with maintaining professional discipline, the UNJC adopted a code of ethics for the legal profession in Cuba in 1987.

12. The constitution affirmatively declared Cuba a socialist state. It also created a new governing structure. Popular Assemblies were established at the municipal, provincial, and national levels to govern the country along with the executive branch (the Council of State and the Council of Ministers). The constitution also declared the rights and duties of Cuban citizens based on principles of racial and gender equality.

13. For example, the Family Code reflects the revolution's concept of the family: ". . . [T]he elementary cell of society" that plays a central role in the development of the new generations and is the "center for relations of common existence between men and women and between them and their children and between all of them with their relatives." The Family Code attempts to maintain the perceived social and psychological benefits of the nuclear family while eliminating objective features of the traditional family that kept women in a perpetual condition of subordination and inequality to men. While the 1950 amendments to the Civil Code gave women and men the same rights in marriage, the Family Code of 1975 affirmatively expresses and establishes equality between the marriage partners. Thus, it declares that husband and wife are equal partners in marriage and share equally in duties and obligations, including childcare and maintenance of the home.

Naturally the code was not able to legislate a new relationship between men and women that would eradicate centuries of patriarchy. However, it did establish a new norm that is slowly having effect, and it gave women leverage to achieve equality in marriage, including its dissolution through simple divorce procedures.

14. This change had been made in 1973 by an amendment to the Code of Social Defense. In 1983, legislation created a separate process for dealing with juveniles that does not involve the court system.

15. Cuban Criminal Code, Articles 95–136. Included in this section also are crimes that violate international law, such as the crime of genocide (Art. 124) and of racial violence and persecution (Art. 128).

16. Cuban Criminal Code, Article 108. The sentence for the distribution of false malicious information for the purpose of stirring public alarm or discontent under this section is one to four years unless the convicted person has used mass media to distribute the information, in which case the sentence is seven to 15 years.

17. For example, theft without the use of force carried a sentence of from three to eight years. Theft with the use of any kind of force, such as breaking a car window to steal something inside, carried mandatory sentencing of 10 to 20 years. Theft of state property regardless of value also carried a sentence of 10 to 20 years.

18. Interview with Carlos Amat Fores, Vice-Minister of Justice, June 12, 1987, Havana, Cuba.

19. Decree-Law 87, July 22, 1985 (Council of State). A decree-law is a law adopted by the Council of State or the Council of Ministers while the National Assembly is in recess. The statute is then presented to the Assembly at its next session for rejection or approval. It takes effect, however, upon adoption by the Council.

20. Ibid.

21. There is substantial evidence that the situation of homosexuals in Cuba has vastly improved in the 1980s. Official discrimination no longer exists, and acceptance is slowly being gained in a once fiercely homophobic society. One can find homosexuals in a wide variety of professions and even among party members.

22. Interview with Raul Amaro Salup, President of the Cuban Supreme Court, Havana, Cuba, June 14, 1987.

23. This number is substantially lower than the exaggerated claims of anti-Castro exile groups whose estimates vary from somewhat less than 100,000 to 200,000.

24. Amnesty International Report 1987, pp. 150–154. Treatment of prisoners in Cuba has become a major focus of anti-Cuban political movements. In February 1987, the U.S. used the issue to attempt to obtain censure of Cuba by the United Nations Human Rights Commission for outrageous violations. At the same time, the U.S. delegation fought to keep the commission from considering the case of Chile. This clear attempt to politicize the issue of human rights was rejected by a narrow vote of the commission.

The politicization of the issue on the world scene has not necessarily enhanced the reliability of information. On the one hand, it has encouraged activities by the *plantados* and dissidents to embarrass the Cuban government. For example, in a recent interview with me in Havana, Elizardo Sanchez, an official of the dissident *Comité Cubano pro Derechos Humanos,* wildly exaggerated the numbers of executions taking place in Cuba. A list of persons allegedly executed contained the names of persons who had previously been released from prison. On the other, world focus has led to Cuba's recent opening up of its prisons for inspection by outside visitors.

25. As of June 1987, there were approximately 50 to 60 *plantados* remaining in prison.

CHAPTER 9

Human Rights and Freedom

24. *Freedom of Worship in Revolutionary Cuba**

BY MARGARET E. CRAHAN

In January 1985 a delegation of three U.S. Catholic bishops visited Cuba at the invitation of the Cuban hierarchy. While there they met with President Fidel Castro, at his invitation, to discuss the need for dialogue between the Cuban bishops and high government officials. They also expressed concern about reports of discrimination against practicing Catholics. Castro expressed interest in pursuing these issues in conversations with the Cuban bishops, as well as with Pope John Paul II, and stated that "pressure against Catholics was not a part of Cuban government policy."[1] He did, however, admit that historical circumstances could result in discrimination.

The U.S. prelates led by James W. Malone, head of the United States Catholic Conference, also indicated their willingness to provide humanitarian aid to the Catholic church in Cuba. A spokesperson for the bishops, Reverend David Gallivan, stated that "We are anxious to give, and they are anxious to receive. . . . But there are problems on the level of national relationships, and a lot depends on the normalization of that relationship."[2] In addition to limited financial resources, the bishops noted a scarcity of priests and religious and a substantial decline in church membership. Nevertheless, their overall conclusion was that improved communication between the Catholic church and the Castro government was a "real cause of hope."[3]

Some six months earlier the visit of the Reverend Jesse Jackson to Cuba

*This essay was written for this volume. Copyright 1988 by Margaret E. Crahan.

and his conversations with high government officials had served to improve relations between the Protestant churches and the government. During that visit Castro had appeared on Cuban television, speaking from the pulpit of a Methodist church in Havana, surrounded by leaders of virtually all the religious denominations in Cuba. This event had substantial impact on public opinion in Cuba, lessening the impression that church people were inclined to be counterrevolutionaries. In addition, in the aftermath of the Jackson visit, Protestant leaders had greater access to high government officials, who helped cut red tape in order to facilitate foreign imports for the churches. The government has traditionally assisted the Jewish community in obtaining abroad those goods needed, particularly for the high holy days. As one Protestant leader phrased it, "relations with the government have never been better."[4]

This situation reflects a remarkable evolution from the tension and conflict of the early 1960s on the part of both government officials and Catholic, Protestant, and Jewish leaders. At the outset of the Cuban Revolution most church people expected the government to implement substantial, but not radical change. While there had been fairly widespread support on the part of the churches for the overthrow of the Batista dictatorship, there was little expectation of substantial land reform, nationalization of foreign holdings, or the emergence of a single-party Communist state. The Catholic and Protestant churches, together with the Jewish community, were largely unprepared to respond positively to such changes as they lacked organizational flexibility, ideological and political openness, and commitment to substantial socioeconomic change. All were closely linked to foreign institutions as sources of funding and personnel. Approximately 2,500 out of the 3,000 Catholic priests and religious in Cuba in 1959 were from Spain, while the principal Protestant denominations were U.S.-based missionary operations. The Jewish community also had close relations with the United States. Such ties encouraged Cuban church people to leave, and by 1965, 20 percent of Catholic priests and 90 percent of religious Catholics had done so, while over 50 percent of Protestant clerical and lay leaders departed. The Jewish community, which was concentrated in Havana, was reduced from approximately 12,000 in 1959 to 1,200 in 1965. Most left voluntarily, with 8 percent of Catholic clerics being expelled.[5] This exodus sorely depleted the churches of clerical and lay leadership and left them with few resources to participate actively in Cuban society. Hence, the churches and Jewish community became marginalized, often serving as refuges for those Cubans opposed to the construction of a socialist society in Cuba.

Throughout the period 1959 to 1962 the Vatican counseled, with limited success, the Cuban bishops to avoid exacerbating tensions with the Cuban government. Castro maintained normal diplomatic relations with the Vatican, and in 1963 the government published and circulated Pope John XXIII's encyclical *Pacem in Terris*. Some of the priests who left Cuba began to return, joined by missionaries, particularly from France and Belgium.[6] The papal nuncio, Cesare Zacchi, undertook the arduous task of rebuilding Church-State relations, achieving considerable success by the early 1970s.

Progress in rapprochement between the Catholic church and the government was signaled by two pastoral letters issued by the bishops in April and September of 1969. In an attempt to diminish the counterrevolutionary image of the Catholic church, the first condemned the U.S. economic blockade of Cuba. It also urged Catholics to support those government programs which were conducive to the common good. The second reassured Catholics that cooperation with Marxists for the betterment of humanity was moral. Both letters reflected the conclusions of the Second Vatican Council (1962–65) and the Latin American Bishops' Conference in Medellín, Colombia (1968). A prime emphasis at each of these meetings had been cooperation with all those of good will who were struggling for peace and social justice. For the first time, dialogue with Marxists was accepted and some theologians began making use of certain elements of Marxist analysis.

The pastoral letters were not, however, enthusiastically received by all Cuban Catholics. Some felt they were a sell-out, while others criticized them for not supporting the revolution more strongly. A number of Catholic Action leaders felt that support for the accomplishments of the revolution should only have been offered by the bishops in exchange for government recognition of the church as a legitimate critic of the revolutionary process. These differences were not easily resolved, in spite of the attempted mediation of a papal representative sent from Rome in October 1969, as indicated by the fact that some Catholic activists left the church.[7]

Mainline Protestant denominations, especially the Methodists, Presbyterians, and Baptists, were also seeking to adapt to Cuban realities by the late 1960s. The Cuban Council of Evangelical Churches not only encouraged Marxist-Christian dialogue, but also exchanges within and among churches. Such work was encouraged by the World Council of Churches in Geneva which, with the cooperation of the U.S. and Cuban governments, transferred funds from the U.S. to the Cuban churches. Foreign donations to the Catholic Church were also permitted by the Cuban government.[8] These funds helped the churches survive, but were sometimes criticized by church people for maintaining dependence on foreign institutions.

Church people from abroad visiting Cuba in the late 1960s and early 1970s regarded the churches as being in a transition period in which there were some tentative attempts to reconcile religious beliefs with an increasingly institutionalized revolution. One U.S. Protestant felt that the government's attitude toward the churches was positive and that active Christians did not run afoul the government unless they were counterrevolutionaries.[9] Rabbi Everett Gendler, who visited Cuba in 1969, felt that those Christians and Jews who were recognized as making positive contributions to Cuban society did not suffer discrimination except by "sectarian" Communists, whom he felt were outnumbered by "liberal" Communists. He also concluded that there was little obvious antireligious indoctrination and complimented the government for allowing Jews time off from work on the Sabbath and permitting soldiers to attend services on the high holy days.[10]

Cuban Catholics, Protestants, and Jews began the 1970s with an increasing desire to adapt to their existential situation. Church leaders and young people went farther and lobbied for integration into revolutionary society. Hence, the early 1970s witnessed more theological reflection and pastoral efforts to deal with the reality of a socialist society. Such efforts by Christians and Jews challenged Marxists within and without the government to reevaluate their own attitudes towards religion and church people. The result was increasing contact and dialogue during the course of the 1970s, at least at the level of the leadership.

Ecumenical conferences, such as the Jornadas Camilo Torres, aimed at exploring the role of Christians in revolutionary society, while study groups and new seminary curriculums served to disseminate progressive views within the churches. These were reinforced by the emergence of liberation theology throughout Latin America, as well as such groups as Christians for Socialism in Chile and the Third World Priests in Argentina. Such developments caused occasional discord within the churches and criticism was frequently focused on the Cuban Council of Evangelical Churches which increasingly identified itself with the revolution.[11] By the end of the 1970s, however, progressives and liberals had consolidated themselves in leadership positions in most Catholic and Protestant churches, even if the laity was sometimes left far behind.

Changes within the churches, beginning in the late 1960s, prompted the Castro government to reevaluate its own positions. The first major reassessment occurred at the 1971 Cuban Educational and Cultural Congress, which publicly noted the growing progressivism of the Catholic church and mainline Protestant denominations worldwide and the inclination of church people towards greater ideological openness. The Congress was strongly influenced by the view that religion was a private matter and that the state should have nothing to do with religion, either in support or in opposition. Every person was free to adopt any religious belief as an individual right and not suffer discrimination as a consequence. However, the Communist party was not to be indifferent to religious obscurantism, which had to be combatted through the media and education in scientific materialism. The Congress concluded that overall there was a need for more sophisticated attitudes on the part of Marxists toward religion.[12]

While the Catholic and mainline Protestant denominations benefitted from the Congress' conclusions, the Jehovah's Witnesses, Evangelical Gideon's Band, and Seventh Day Adventists did not, for they were deemed obscurantist and counterrevolutionary. This stemmed, in the case of the Jehovah's Witnesses, largely from their continued links to the United States, insistence on proselytizing in the streets, and opposition to universal military service and public education. The Evangelical Gideon's Band was regarded as strongly counterrevolutionary, while the Seventh Day Adventists were criticized for refusing to work or send their children to school on Saturdays. Young male members of these groups were jailed for refusing military service. All three denominations became the objects of a nationwide campaign categorizing them as counterrevolutionary, antisocial, and unpatriotic.[13]

Church-State relations were further clarified by the promulgation of the 1976 Cuban Constitution, Article 54 of which held:

> The socialist state, which bases its activity and educates the people in the scientific materialist concept of the universe, recognizes and guarantees freedom of conscience and the right of everyone to profess any religious belief and to practice, within the framework of respect for the law, the belief of his preference.
>
> The law regulates the activities of religious institutions.
>
> It is illegal and punishable by law to oppose one's faith or religious belief to the Revolution, education or the fulfillment of the duty to work, defend the homeland with arms, show reverence for its symbols and other duties established by the Constitution.[14]

As in the prerevolutionary Cuban constitutions of 1903 and 1940, religious freedom was guaranteed with restrictions. The 1940 Constitution, for example, provided for freedom of worship within the limits of social mores and the requirements of public order.[15]

The response of Cuban church leaders to the 1976 constitution was generally positive. An official of the Cuban Conference of Bishops stated that the Catholic church was gratified that the status of the faithful and the churches as institutions was defined. There was, however, some regret expressed about the emphasis on atheistic materialism.[16] Several students at the Catholic seminary of San Carlos felt that the constitution opened the way for improvements in Church-State relations. Father José Manuel Mijares, rector of the seminary, stated that "it is extremely . . . consoling to see that . . . all types of coercion and discrimination against believers are clearly proscribed."[17]

The 1978 Communist Party Platform and the Second Congress of the Cuban Communist Party in December 1980 both emphasized that the creation of a new society required the efforts of all Cubans, and hence, believers should be encouraged and welcomed to participate. In addition, the 1978 Party Platform supported liberty of conscience and freedom to worship within the law. Believers and nonbelievers were to have the same rights and social responsibilities.[18] The Second Party Congress noted that the increasing support of Christians for more just societies via structural changes throughout Latin America provided a basis for strategic alliances between Christians and Marxists.[19]

Such a position had been initially suggested by Fidel Castro in an October

11, 1977, speech to the Jamaican Council of Churches in which he asserted
that there were "no contradictions between the aims of religion and the aims
of socialism." When he was asked how he could justify such a strong emphasis
on Marxism–Leninism in Cuban education, and not Christianity, Castro responded that he felt it was proper for public education to have "an orientation
that opposes the religious view in the fields of philosophy or history."[20] Castro
also claimed that no revolution as extensive as Cuba's had fewer problems with
the churches. This he attributed to the wisdom of church leaders, the growing
progressivism of Christians, as well as the intention of the government not to
portray itself as an enemy of religion and thereby open it up to criticism by
opponents of the revolution.[21]

Many religious leaders in Cuba today accept the validity of a strategic
alliance with the revolution to promote the common good, although they do
not accept Marxism. As a professor at the Seminary of San Carlos explained:

> Socialism is the only economic solution available to us. As our witness to God,
> we must work inside the process for mutual social goals. We are "Christian
> revolutionaries." That is possible. What is not possible is to be "Christian Marx-
> ists." That would be like putting a circle in a square. In Cuba, the word "Marx"
> means atheism, the word "revolutionary" does not. We teach our students how
> it is possible to separate economic reality from atheism.[22]

Such a position was affirmed in a report presented by Cuban Catholics to
the 1979 Conference of Latin American Bishops in Puebla, Mexico. They
affirmed that differences between religious and Marxist views should not impede the construction of a new, and better, society.[23] Hence, while there was
acceptance on the part of some Cuban church people of a strategic alliance
with Marxists to achieve common goals, there was also recognition of somewhat different world views and values.

What, as a consequence, is the present status of freedom of worship in Cuba?
According to the former Archbishop of Havana, Francisco Oves Fernández,
"the churches [and] the various ministries enjoy complete freedom. Freedom
of conscience is guaranteed. . . ."[24] His successor, Archbishop Jaime Ortega
Alamino, agrees while noting that antireligious statements and occasional
discrimination have not been eliminated, although they are contrary to official
government policy.[25]

This opinion is shared by officials of the Cuban Ecumenical Council, as well
as the leaders of individual Protestant denominations. In 1979 the president
of the World Council of Churches visited Cuba and concluded that Church-
State relations were cordial and believers free to proclaim their faith.[26]

The most serious problem, according to Catholic, Protestant, and Jewish
leaders, is the exclusion of active Christians and Jews from the Communist
party and the Union of Communist Youth. This prevents them from gaining
positions of influence in the government and armed forces and, thus, limits

their capacity to criticize the direction of the revolution. Hence, the degree to which believers can participate in the major institutions of Cuban society is restricted, although they are free to contribute to grass-roots mass organizations.

Other complaints include not being able to mount massive evangelization campaigns, lack of access to the media, inability to hold meetings or services in public places or proselytize in the streets. In addition, the emphasis on materialist atheism in public education and the restriction of religious education to church buildings is frequently criticized. One Catholic church official held that the main problem boiled down to the fact that "in this country . . . materialism is proclaimed officially. In other countries, the priest faces a practical materialism."[27]

In general, most religious leaders today have a positive outlook, arguing that their believers have a more profound faith than those of the prerevolutionary era and that the loss of members has been partially offset by improvements in the quality of the faithful. In addition, in recent years there has been increasing opportunity to revitalize their institutions to make them more attractive to Cubans. Some hold that religion is at its best when slightly out of step and, hence, forced to plumb more deeply into its spiritual resources.[28]

This attitude has been influenced by the new-found vitality of religious institutions that have assumed prophetic roles in other Latin American countries, particularly as champions of human rights and social justice. To date the Cuban churches have not demonstrated that they have the theological, pastoral, and spiritual resources to achieve a commensurate rebirth. Hence, while an annual Protestant survey of religious freedom worldwide holds that "Marxists come through as great oppressors of religion everywhere but in Cuba and Nicaragua . . . ,"[29] Catholics, Protestants, and Jews in Cuba continue to play a limited role in their society.

NOTES

1. United States Catholic Conference (USCC), National Catholic Office for Information, "Bishops See Hope for Improvement in Church-Government Relations in Cuba," (January 28, 1985), p. 1.

2. "Castro Tells U.S. Bishops He'd Like to Meet Pope," *The New York Times* (January 29, 1985), p. 3.

3. USCC, p.5.

4. Interview IH 480121. In order to maintain the confidentiality of sources, interviews will be identified by letter and number.

5. Nominal Catholics were estimated at 70–75% of the total population of Cuba (approximately 7,500,000) in 1960, Protestants at 3 to 6%. In 1985 the Catholic church claimed there were 3,973,000 Catholics in Cuba or 38% of the total population (10,484,000). Protestant estimates ranged from 25,000 to 80,000. The Jewish community is slightly under 1,000. Practicing Catholics are estimated to number between 150,000 and 200,000, while Protestants are more active with about 45% regularly attending services. See *Anuario Pontificio, 1985;* René F. de la Huerta

Aguiar, "Espiritismo y otras Supersticiones en la Población Cubana, *Revista del Hospital Psiquiá-trico de la Habana,* Vol. 2, No. 1 (enero, febrero, marzo, 1960), pp.46–47; D. P. Noonan, "Religion in Cuba: Christianity in the Catacombs," Xerox, United States Catholic Conference Files (1982), p. 7; Alice L. Hageman and Philip E. Wheaton, eds., *Religion in Cuba Today: A New Church in a New Society* (New York: Association Press, 1971), pp. 30–31; Joseph Beckman, "The Future of Religion in Cuba," *LADOC,* Vol. 9, No. 5 (May/June 1979), p. 27; Jacinto Ordóñez, "Informe Sobre Una Visita a Cuba, 20 a 28 de junio 1974," Xerox (15 de agosto de 1974), p. 4; Jim Wallace, "Christians in Cuba," *Cuba Resource Center Newsletter,* Vol. 3, No. 1 (April, 1973), p. 6; James W. Wall, "A New Use for the Miramar," *Christian Century,* Vol. 97 (November 12, 1980), pp. 1083–84; United Methodist Board of Missions, p. 3; Theo Tschuy, "Responses to Questions in Mr. Davis' letter of February 11, 1971, Tannay, Switzerland," 1971; Germinal Rivas, Minutes of the Cuba Sub-Group, Latin American Methodist Task Force, March 1, 1971, p. 7, Interviews IH 97326 and IH 67328.

6. Francois Houtart and André Rousseau, *The Church and Revolution* (Maryknoll, N.Y.: Orbis Books, 1971), pp. 124–25.

7. Antonio Benitez Rojo, "Fresh Air Blows Through the Seminary," Cuban Christians for Socialism, "How Christians in Cuba See Their Future," and Episcopal Conference of Cuba, "Pastoral Letter, April 10, 1969," *LADOC* "Keyhole" Series 7 (Washington, D.C.: United States Catholic Conference, nd), pp. 4; 46–49; 76–77; F. Houtart and A. Rousseau, p. 125; Interview IM 5771112.

8. Iglesia Metodista de Cuba, *El Evangelista Cubana,* Vol. 57, No. 2 (enero de 1965), p. 7; United Methodist Board of Missions, Minutes of May 14, 1971, Meeting, Cuba Sub-Group, Latin American Task Force, p. 5; Theo Tschuy, "Cuban Protestantism: A Historical Sketch, Memo to Faith and Order Team to Cuba, Geneva" (February 3, 1971), p. 8; Tschuy, April 25, 1971, p. 2; Wallace, p. 8; World Council of Churches Archives (WCCA) 280. 57291 (Box 1), Cuban Council of Evangelical Churches, "Informe del Secretario Ejecutivo, Adolf Ham, 1967," p. 2; WCCA, 425. Division of Interchurch Aid, DICARWS Divisional Committee, Projects Subcommittee, Tutzing, July 22–26, 1964, pp. 2–3.

9. J. Wallace, "Christians in Cuba," pp. 3–4.

10. Everett E. Gendler, "Cuba and Religion: Challenge and Response," *Christian Century,* Vol. 86 (July 30, 1969), pp. 1013–14.

11. J. Wallace, "Christians in Cuba," p.8.

12. National Congress on Education and Culture, "Declaration, April 30, 1971," *LADOC,* "Keyhole" Series 7 (Washington, D.C.: United States Catholic Conference, nd), p. 51.

13. Ibid., pp. 50–51; IH 67038; IH 47412–2; IM 5771112.

14. *Constitution of the Republic of Cuba* (Havana: Instituto Cubano del Libro, 1975), p. 30.

15. Leonel-Antonio de la Cuesta, "The Cuban Socialist Constitution: Its Originality and Role in Institutionalization," *Cuban Studies,* Vol. 6 (July, 1976), pp. 18–20.

16. IH 67328.

17. Elmer Rodríguez, "Cuba: Who Said There Is No Religious Freedom in Cuba?" Prensa Latina Feature Service, Vol. 168 (May 1, 1977), pp. 2–3.

18. Partido Comunista de Cuba, *Plataforma Programática: Tesis y Resolución* (Havana: Editorial Ciencias Sociales, 1978), pp. 100–102.

19. Partido Comunista de Cuba, Segundo Congreso, "La construcción del socialismo y la libertad de conciencia," (1980), photocopy, np.

20. Fidel Castro, "There Are No Contradictions Between the Aims of Religion and the Aims of Socialism," *Granma,* (November 20, 1977), p. 5.

21. Ibid., pp. 3–9.

22. Dow Kirkpatrick, "U.S. Christians and Cuba," *Christian Century,* Vol. 94 (August 3–10, 1977), p. 687.

23. Maria Teresa Bolívar Arostegui, *et al.,* "Cuban Christians and Puebla," *LADOC* "Keyhole" Series 17 (Washington, D.C.: United States Catholic Conference, 1980), p. 46.

24. Luis Suárez, "Is There Religion in the New Cuba: Interview with Archbishop Francisco Oves Fernandes," *LADOC,* Vol. 9, No. 3 (January/February 1979), p. 29.

25. Ibid.; D.P. Noonan, Interview with Jaime Ortega Alamino, Archbishop of Havana, July, 1982, photocopy, np.

26. Juana Berges, "President of the World Council of Churches Visits Cuba," *Granma* (February 11, 1979), np.

27. James M. Wall, "Worshipping God in a Communist State," *Christian Century,* Vol. 98 (April 29, 1981), p. 467.

28. Walter Owens Owensby, "Cuba: A Report," *Church & Society* (July-October 1979), p. 80.

29. James A. Gittings, "In Many Places It's Still Dangerous to Believe," A.D., X, 4 (April 1981), p. 27. See also James A. Gittings, "It's Still Dangerous to Believe," A.D., XI, 4 (April 1982), pp. 14–16 and "Another Precarious Year for Religious Freedom," A.D., 4 (April 1983), pp. 15–16.

25. *The Press in Cuba**

BY JOHN SPICER NICHOLS

When Fidel Castro and his guerrilla army came down from their mountain stronghold to take control of the Cuban government in 1959, one of their earliest and most widely criticized acts was the swift takeover of the country's mass communication system. In the 18 months following Castro's victory, all mass media opposing the revolutionary government were closed down or starved out of business, and by 1961 all Cuban media, regardless of political stance, were owned or controlled by Castro forces.

Castro had learned, through his effective use of a clandestine press and radio station during the guerrilla campaign, that the mass media are precious resources for fostering revolution. When he came to power in 1959, Cuba's broadcast media were among the few useful assets in that extremely poor country. Most homes outside of Havana lacked running water but not a radio receiver. Cuba also had more television sets per capita than any other Latin American country. Castro believed that those resources could not be left to the helter-skelter management of private owners under a libertarian media system. Rather, they had to be used as a government tool for national development.

*From John S. Nichols, "Republic of Cuba," in George Thomas Kurian, ed., *World Press Encyclopedia* (New York: Facts on File, 1982), pp. 257–271. Edited for this volume.

"What is freedom to write and to speak for a man who doesn't know how to write, who doesn't know how to read?" Castro would ask those who questioned his decision.

Castro frequently is charged with the destruction of a free press in Cuba; in reality, however, he merely substituted one form of strict government control for another. The prerevolutionary media were seedy, censored, venal puppets of government and industry. Every Cuban president from the time of independence to the revolution either had overtly censored or more subtly bribed editors and reporters into submission. In the period immediately before the overthrow of dictator Fulgencio Batista in 1959, press censorship and corruption reached their worst. The government was paying the press approximately $450,000 a month in bribes, allowing some prominent journalists to pocket tens of thousands of dollars per month. Only six of the 58 newspapers publishing in Cuba in 1958 were surviving without government advertising and subsidies, and many of the papers that did not cooperate with the government were forced out of business through trumped-up taxes or restrictions on vital imports such as newsprint and equipment. Still other newspapers were owned outright by Batista and his collaborators.

In the long run, though, government censorship worked in favor of Castro's revolutionary movement. Cuban audiences eager to hear news not censored by the Batista government consequently tuned in to Radio Rebelde, the guerrillas' clandestine radio station. Radio Rebelde, which was inaugurated in February 1958 by Ernesto "Che" Guevara, eventually became one of the most listened-to voices in Cuba and much of the Caribbean. Each night, a growing number of Cubans would tune in to the station and hear a barrage of reports of guerrilla victories, manifestos, patriotic poems and music. Castro frequently polished his oratorical skills over the air, and by the time the revolutionaries took control of the government he had refined his ability to the point that many analysts considered him the world's greatest political speaker of the era.

In 1959, the new revolutionary government immediately ended bribes and subsidies to the press (except to the official newspaper, *Revolución*), and as a result, most newspapers shortly went out of business. Even those newspapers not dependent on government subsidies for their survival also had financial difficulties. As the government rapidly nationalized private industry and business, the remaining media found it increasingly difficult to find advertising revenues to support themselves.

Despite the economic problems, the few privately owned media were not censored by the government for a year or so, and had considerable latitude to criticize Castro and his government. But as the revolution gathered steam, the adversary press became progressively more cautious, and in late 1960, by intimidation, expropriation and increased economic pressure, the revolutionary government had closed almost all of the privately owned print media and gained complete ownership of the broadcast media.

. . . Despite government intervention, the controls were not monolithic, and a considerable amount of debate still could be found in the Cuban media, particularly the print media. Two groups, one headed by the revolutionary Che Guevara and the other by old-line, Soviet-style Communists, argued over the future path of the revolution. Some of the ideological debate spilled onto the pages of Havana's two major newspapers, each controlled by a contending group.

By 1966 Cuba had entered a phase of mobilization and radicalization of the media under the newly adopted policies of Guevara, the victor in the debate. The revolutionary elite moved to consolidate their direct control over the media, starting by merging the warring newspapers of the preceding years into *Granma,* the single and official voice of the Cuban Communist party.

For the most part, Cuban newspapers are organs of various divisions of the Cuban Communist party and have similar staff organization, format and content. *Granma,* the highest-circulation daily, is the official voice of the party and is organized as a political division of the party's Central Committee. . . . The newspaper (named for the vessel that transported Castro's guerrilla force from Mexico to Cuba to begin jungle warfare against Batista) has an estimated daily circulation of more than 560,000.

Granma was founded in October 1965 when Castro merged *Revolución* and *Hoy,* the newspapers representing the debating factions of the revolution. The editor of *Granma* since 1967 has been Jorge Enrique Mendoza, a member of the Central Committee, former propagandist for Castro's prerevolutionary guerrilla forces. . . .

The other national daily, *Juventud Rebelde,* is published by the Union of Young Communists. . . . The newspaper circulates about 230,000 copies Monday through Friday and 325,000 copies on Sunday. Both *Granma* and *Juventud Rebelde* are distributed throughout the nation.

. . . Each is widely read by party workers and government bureaucrats—and also frequently read aloud, along with other revolutionary literature, over the public address systems in many Cuban factories.

In addition, the party committees of 10 provinces publish daily newspapers that are closely modeled after *Granma.* Although the circulation and influence of these regional papers are limited, they appear to have greater leeway to comment on local affairs than the national dailies have to comment on national issues. The total press run for these provincial dailies is about 122,000.

Cuban media content is extremely dull. According to surveys conducted by Cuban researchers, the vast majority of the Cuban population disapprove of media content, and top government officials and media policymakers have called for improvements. In a speech to the Fourth Congress of the Union of Cuban Journalists in 1980, Raúl Castro (Fidel's brother), commander of the military and second in command of the Cuban government, chided the group for the low quality of Cuban journalism. He criticized the journalists for being "boring" in their style, failing to "delve deeper into basic problems" and practicing self-censorship. He called on the journalists to criticize malfunctions of government operations, although *not* the revolution itself. "Criticism within our ranks is a political duty and social responsibility," he said. And after he finished his address and was walking off stage, he shouted, "Criticize all you want! The party is behind you!"

More than 100 magazines, journals and specialized newspapers are published in Cuba, and each is governed by a specific sector of the Cuban government or one of the mass organizations. Examples are *Mujeres,* Cuban Federation of Women; *Política Internacional,* Ministry of Foreign Relations; *Cuba Azúcar,* Ministry of the Sugar Industry; and *El Deporte,* National Institute of Sports. The sponsoring group has the sole responsibility for the organization, editorial policy and operation of its publication, although party ideological planners and central government officials have coordinating powers and considerable influence on matters of policy. Because of the diversification of control of the periodical press and its insulation from direct supervision, most magazines and journals enjoy increasing latitude to comment on issues, although mostly from the perspective of their sponsoring organizations or their constituencies. Not surprisingly, the most influential magazine, *Verde Olivo,* is published by the Revolutionary Armed Forces, probably the most powerful sector in Cuban government.

A new periodical, *Opina,* is Cuba's largest-selling magazine. *Opina,* which is published by the Cuba Institute for Consumer Research and Planning and is filled with relatively lively articles about consumer products and affairs, current events and cultural activities, usually sells its entire press run of 500,000 copies within hours after it reaches the newsstands. Other Cuban magazines of hemispheric influence are *Bohemia, Casa de las Américas* and *Tricontinental.*

ELECTRONIC NEWS MEDIA

Radio and television are the most important media in Cuba. Owing largely to Castro's early success with his guerrilla radio station, the government relies heavily on its broadcasting system as a means of information transmission and national integration. In the early years of the revolution, Castro would appear on national radio and television, often daily, to explain revolutionary goals and encourage popular cooperation. The media became so crucial to the revolutionary process that Herbert Matthews of *The New York Times* coined the phrase "government by television." Although Castro speaks less frequently on Cuban radio and television today, the broadcasting system continues to shoulder a large portion of the educational and political responsibilities for the nation.

All facets of the broadcast media are centrally administered by the Cuban

Institute of Radio and Television, and although directors of individual stations claim considerable programming autonomy, in-country research indicates that radio and television are the most tightly controlled of all Cuban media. Nonetheless, University of Texas researchers Elizabeth Mahan and Jorge Reina Schement noted several important similarities to the U.S. broadcasting system, and argued that much of the greater diversity in U.S. broadcast content was merely the product of the larger scale of that system.

PRESS LAWS AND CENSORSHIP

Cuban press law is predicated on the socialist principle that the rights of the collective take precedence over the rights of the individual. . . .

In the view of the Cuban leadership, social and economic equality is a precondition to civil and political rights, such as the Western concept of freedom of the press; therefore, society has the right to use the mass media as tools to achieving collective goals. The new Cuban constitution, ratified by popular referendum in 1976, legitimizes the concept that a citizen's right to speak freely is subordinate to the good of the state. Article 52 states:

Citizens have freedom of speech and of the press in keeping with the objectives of socialist society. Material conditions for the exercise of that right are provided by the fact that the press, radio, television, movies, and other organs of the mass media are state or social property and can never be private property. This assures their use for the exclusive service of the working people and in the interest of society.

Those rights are further limited by Article 61:

None of the freedoms which are recognized for the citizens can be exercised contrary to what is established in the Constitution and the law, or contrary to the existence and objectives of the socialist state, or contrary to the decision of the Cuban people to build socialism and communism. Violations of this principle can be punished by law.

Although the punishment of Cuban journalists guilty of counterrevolutionary behavior is legitimized by the new constitution, the legal provisions are, as in most Latin American countries, largely a matter of form, and other means of media control are more significant. Subtle controls over the operation of the mass media are so effective that jailings, censorship and other forms of overt repression are comparatively rare.

Nevertheless, the Inter-American Press Association has listed about a dozen journalists as among the 2,000 to 5,000 political prisoners held in Cuban jails in the late 1970s. Despite several recent releases of political prisoners, including some media people, several Cuban journalists still are imprisoned, a few since the early 1960s. (While the Cuban government concedes that former journalists are in Cuban jails, it also says that they were imprisoned for ordinary criminal behavior rather than for what they wrote.)

Formal government censorship has been practiced in Cuba and, to a limited extent, continues today, but its use as a media control is grossly overestimated by observers outside of Cuba. The reason that censorship and other overt controls generally are not required is that Cuban journalists, with rare exceptions, are ideologically aligned with the goals of the revolution and, in numerous instances, also hold top leadership positions in the government and party. For example, Jorge Enrique Mendoza, the editor of *Granma,* also is a member of the Central Committee and a deputy in the national assembly, formerly held several top ministerial posts in the government, and was one of Castro's top propagandists in the pre-1959 guerrilla warfare. And Mendoza is not an exception. A study by this author published in *Journalism Monographs* documents that at least 71 percent of Cuban editors and other top media policymakers also hold leadership positions in the party and the government and/or were prerevolutionary allies of Castro.

The control of rank-and-file journalists is almost as complete as for their editors. More than 40 percent of all Cuban journalists are members of the Cuban Communist party or the Communist Youth Union. Only a few sectors of Cuban society, such as the police force and military officers, have a higher percentage of membership. In addition, all journalists must be members of the Union of Cuban Journalists, which establishes and strictly enforces standards that govern the media and, to some extent, the private behavior of all its members. Those who violate union policy can lose their accreditation, and thus, their right to publish.

Despite the effectiveness of these controls, the Cuban government on occasion has been forced to resort to more overt methods. The most sensational case was that of Cuban writer Heberto Padilla. Padilla was a correspondent for the Cuban news agency Prensa Latina and for *Granma* in both Prague and Moscow, but lost his job following a run-in with the government in 1968. The disgruntled Padilla continued, as a poet and novelist, to write what some considered veiled criticism of the government.

In March 1971 Padilla was jailed without charges. The word of his arrest filtered abroad, and in April a large group of European and Latin American leftist writers and intellectuals (among them Jean-Paul Sartre, Gabriel García Márquez, Carlos Fuentes, Octavio Paz and Mario Vargas Llosa) published an open letter to Castro expressing concern over the imprisonment and "the use of repressive methods against intellectuals and writers who exercise the right of criticism." After being held incommunicado for more than a month—and after writing a long, abject confession of his "errors against the Revolution"—Padilla was released from jail. Two days later, he appeared before the Cuban Congress on Education and Culture and read his letter of self-criticism. The congress responded with a hard-line declaration on the mass media and cultural affairs. Among other things, the assembled writers and artists said that the mass media "are powerful instruments of ideological education whose utilization and development should not be left to spontaneity and improvisation."

A month later, the international group of writers wrote Castro and his congress a second letter charging that Padilla's confession had been obtained through torture, and likened the episode to "the most sordid moments of Stalinism." Both Castro and Padilla denied the charge, but worldwide criticism of the affair continued.

Afterwards Padilla worked in obscurity as a translator in Havana, but was not allowed to publish his own works. In 1980, after a year of petitioning the government and with the sponsorship of U.S. Senator Edward M. Kennedy, Padilla was allowed to emigrate to the United States. . . .

STATE-PRESS RELATIONS

The Cuban government has no information ministry that administers all, most, or even a large share of the country's mass media. At least a dozen government divisions have some administrative control over the media.

Despite this hodgepodge of organizational controls, some centralized supervision does exist. The Department of Revolutionary Orientation, a division of the Central Committee of the party, seems to have some authority to coordinate Cuba's propaganda activities and to set general media policy. According to the limited evidence available, the department's authority has fluctuated greatly in past years and has frequently been contested by other agencies. In the 1960s the department had great power in matters of ideology and was often referred to as the "censorship board," but in the 1980s its power seems to have deteriorated and its responsibilities today are less policy setting and more operational—implementing policy determined elsewhere in the Cuban hierarchy.

Of course, the relationship of the government and the press is reciprocal—even in a Communist system such as Cuba's. Not only does the Cuban government affect the media, but the media also affect the Cuban government. The best example is the increasing ability of the Cuban press to criticize the government and force changes in its tactical operations. . . . In 1975, *Granma* launched a "consumer action" column, to force bureaucrats to account for their mistakes and inefficiency and to relay reader concerns to the government. Editors of the column, titled "By Return Mail," invite readers to blow the whistle on unresponsive administrators, long waits in the local hospital, lack of garbage collection, or any other cases of negligence and waste. A team of reporters is then assigned to investigate the charges and report on their findings. As the column continues to build a reputation and wide readership, it increasingly has been demanding "accountability," in essence fixing blame for the abuses that are uncovered. For example, an investigation initiated by the column staffers led to the firing of three top officials in Havana's sanitation department after a reader reported that two department vehicles were abandoned for months on a city street.

The column was so successful and popular with the readers that Havana's other daily, *Juventud Rebelde,* started one of its own, and the idea is now spreading to newspapers in the provinces. *Juventud Rebelde* receives between 800 and 900 letters a week. . . .

SUMMARY

Cuban mass media policy is a highly flexible adaptation of the Marxist philosophy of the press. While all media are owned, operated and at the service of the state, in accordance with Marxist principles, they also have many characteristics that set them apart from other Soviet-bloc nations. Their individuality results from the country's early revolutionary experience, frequent modifications to adjust to the changing winds of international affairs and domestic problems during the past two decades, and the flamboyant yet pragmatic nature of Cuban President Fidel Castro.

The Cuban media are viewed by the government and party as essential tools for solving the basic problems of society, but their centralized use in education, development programs, and political formation has been a mixed blessing for Cuba. On one hand, the Cuban government replaced the prerevolutionary media system, which by all accounts was seedy, corrupt and U.S.-dominated, with one of the most developed media systems among countries at the same level of economic development. . . .

On the other hand, the Cuban approach means the automatic end of libertarian media practices. Individuals and dissident sectors of Cuban society have only limited opportunities to discuss the tactical operation of the government and no opportunities to criticize the revolution itself in the mass media. And, although in contradiction to official policy, the Cuban leadership, especially the second-echelon bureaucrats, tend to conceal and distort facts that they feel might tarnish their image with the public. The result is rigid government control of media content. The top leadership is concerned about these maladies and has issued directives intended to cure them, but the prognosis is guarded.

It is often said that the one thing to expect in Castro's Cuba is the unexpected. That is probably true for the Cuban press. Nevertheless, whatever media structures or policies evolve in the future will certainly be constrained by the country's revolutionary ideology and harsh economic realities. Within those limits, a continuation of the post-1975 trend toward greater press criticism of lower-level government operations would be expected. However, no attacks on the basic principles of the revolution and its top leaders will be tolerated, and some consolidation within the media would be expected to occur during times of turmoil, such as during the exodus of 1980.

. . . In sum, Castro will use the press to balance both domestic and external forces so that he has greater power to conduct the Cuban revolution as he deems best for the Cuban people.

26. *Human Rights in Cuba**

By Organization of American States Inter-American Commission on Human Rights

> *The Inter-American Commission on Human Rights is an official body of the Organization of American States. The Cuban government has refused to allow the Commission into Cuba to conduct its inquiries on the grounds that it has no jurisdiction because the OAS suspended Cuba's membership in 1962.*

Introduction

For over twenty years, the Inter-American Commission on Human Rights (IACHR) has given special attention to the situation of human rights in Cuba. The result of this has been preparation of the six reports that precede this one.[1] Several special situations characterize relations between the IACHR and the government of Cuba; the changes that have taken place in that country since January 1, 1959, have been numerous and far-reaching. The commission therefore considered it an opportune time to evaluate the concrete results of the policies carried out by the government of Cuba insofar as they affect the situation of human rights in that country.

This report includes a treatment of civil and political rights, which, in general, have been the primary focus of attention in the reports of the commission. Thus, the structure of the Cuban state is examined on the basis of recently promulgated laws, especially the Constitution of 1976. The examination of civil and political rights is approached on two levels; on the normative level, in order to establish the correspondence between current Cuban legislation and the revelant international instruments, and on the practical level, in order to specify the forms assumed by the concrete exercise of those rights and the behavior of the Cuban government with respect to them. Po-

*From Inter-American Commission on Human Rights, Organization of American States, *The Situation of Human Rights in Cuba: Seventh Report* (Washington, DC: OAS, 1983), pp. 1–2, 177–83.

litical rights are examined in the corresponding chapters; the right to a fair trial, to personal liberty and to due process of law; the right to physical integrity; the right to freedom of investigation, opinion, expression and dissemination; the right to life; the right to religious freedom; and the right to residence and movement.

The Inter-American Commission on Human Rights has drawn attention to the growing importance of economic, social and cultural rights, both in themselves and in their relation to civil and political rights. In this respect, it has pointed out that:

> the essence of the legal obligation incurred by any government in this area (economic, social and cultural rights) is to strive to attain the economic and social aspirations of its people, by following an order that assigns priority to the basic needs of health, nutrition and education. The priority of the "rights of survival" and "basic needs" is a natural consequence of the right to personal security.[2]

For the purposes of the analysis presented in this report, the following rights have been selected: the right to property, to work, to social security, to adequate nutrition, to health and sanitary living conditions, and to education. The concrete attainment of these rights imposes on the state a duty to assume an active position; in effect, the content of economic, social and cultural rights is made up of a number of basic needs that must be satisfied directly or through the creation of conditions that are effective in meeting them. Thus, the observance in practice of these rights implies the formulation of appropriate policies, the execution of which entails the allocation of resources—in some cases substantial—both in goods and in services. The concrete results obtained by such state action will make it possible to determine the degree to which a state meets its obligation to observe the above-mentioned rights in practice.

These concrete results can be evaluated with the aid of a number of indicators which can be quantified with relative precision. In this report, the fundamental criterion used to evaluate these results has been the access of the population to the goods and services provided to meet the basic need in question. This criterion has been adopted bearing in mind the difficulties associated with quantification of the quality of the goods and services in question; nevertheless, the use of some indicators has made it possible, in certain cases, to obtain a satisfactorily correct assessment of these qualitative aspects.

It should be pointed out that the Cuban Revolution has consistently identified human rights with basic needs, and even calls them "the true human rights." These rights are: nutrition, health, education, social justice, and work, as well as the prohibition and elimination of gambling, prostitution, begging, and discrimination. Official Cuban statements never make reference to civil and political rights. . . .

CONCLUSIONS

In accordance with what has been set forth in the body of this report, the commission has reached the conclusions presented below:

1. With respect to the structure of the State and political rights, the commission considers that the Communist party plays an excessively preponderant role in the Cuban political system. This party, in reality, is a force above the State itself which impedes the emergence of healthy ideological and party pluralism that is one of the bases of the democratic system of government. The most important state organs are controlled by members of the Communist party who wield decisive influence in the selection of candidates to hold elective office. All of this combines to impose an adherence to ideology that may be described as uncritical and dogmatic.

2. The above is reinforced by the Cuban constitution's use of terms and concepts taken from political-philosophical doctrines, which serve little to promote the observance of the rule of law, the guarantee that protects the rights of citizens against impairment by the State. A source of particular concern to the IACHR is the Cuban legislation which establishes limits on the exercise of the recognized rights and freedoms of its citizens. According to this formulation of the laws, it is the citizen who must adapt to the purposes set by the State; whereas the concept of democracy envisions exactly the opposite: it is the State that must limit its action in the face of the inherent rights of man and may interfere only to bring about the full observance of civil, political, social, economic, and cultural rights of those governed. The subordination of the individual to the State is further entrenched in Cuba by the nonexistence of a separation of governmental powers, which results in the dependence of the system for the administration of justice on the executive.

3. Thus, with respect to the right to a fair trial and to due process, the commission considers that the subordination, in fact and in law, of the system for the administration of justice to the executive, affects one of the conditions it considers fundamental for the observance of that right. It creates an environment of uncertainty and fear among the populace, which has further deteriorated by the weakening of procedural guarantees. This is seen especially in those judicial decisions which refer to cases which may, directly or indirectly, affect the power structure that exists today in Cuba.

4. In the opinion of the commission, the existence of political organs of a collective nature in Cuba is a positive feature, since they employ negotiating procedures designed to obtain a consensus for political action; in principle, the collective organs constitute a sound basis to facilitate broad citizen participation in the formulation of national policy. In practice, however, the principal organs of the State and the Communist party have been dominated by a small

group since the very beginning of the current Cuban political process. This situation was created and is sustained by a marked intolerance toward any form of political opposition, which consequently, has been virtually eliminated. The commission considers the high level of participation of the people in matters of a sectoral and local nature, and the progressive conversion of municipal administrative positions to elective offices, as positive developments of the Cuban political system.

5. With respect to freedom of expression, the IACHR considers noteworthy the campaign undertaken by the government of Cuba to create the social conditions to allow for the effective exercise of the right to freedom of expression, in particular, the literacy campaign. It is senseless to postulate the observance of this right in a social context characterized by illiteracy. The strict control and subjugation of any political and ideological divergence from the dominant ideology of the government and the party however, has led to a situation where only those groups identified therewith may express themselves through the means of communication. Hence, the commission considers that there is no freedom of the press in Cuba such as would allow political dissent which is fundamental in a democratic system of government. On the contrary, the oral, written, and televised press is an instrument of the ideological struggle, and notwithstanding the self-criticism that is transmitted by these channels, even that follows the dictates of the group in power and serves to transmit the messages of that group to the lower levels.

6. Furthermore, the commission regards as reprehensible the limitations on the freedom of artistic expression imposed by the government of Cuba, and the pressures and punishment applied to artists who do not share the official ideology or who dissent from the political practice of the authorities. At the same time, the commission recognizes the efforts made by the Cuban government to create the conditions that would allow the bulk of the population to express itself artistically; it emphasizes in this respect that although extending the benefits of culture to the entire population is an inherent element of democracy, also, the open exercise of the freedom of expression is another of its fundamental elements.

7. With respect to the right to life, the commission considers that the range of crimes punishable by the death penalty is excessively broad. Although the appeals process, in terms of procedure, aims at guaranteeing a careful application of the death penalty, it is also true that the absence of an independent system for the administration of justice suggests that this remedy does not function as a true guarantee in the case of crimes committed against the security of the Cuban State. This means that the death penalty for political crimes is a latent threat. It should also be recognized however, that under the current legal system, the death penalty is always handed down with the alternative of incarceration, which represents an improvement over other Cuban laws in which death was the only penalty provided for certain kinds of crimes.

8. Also in relation to the right to life, the commission is concerned that Cuba appears to have markedly regressed in so far as courts continue to impose the death penalty for political crimes, and it notes the numerous executions which may have occurred during 1981 and 1982. Furthermore, the IACHR considers that prison conditions with respect to political prisoners have improved in recent years, which would seem to explain why no recent cases of prison deaths have been reported.

9. With respect to the right to liberty and personal security, there is an absence of adequate guarantees against arbitrary detention, although denunciations of this kind have fallen. With respect to the conditions under which political prisoners serve their sentences, although a relative improvement in comparison with the initial period of the revolution can be noted, there continue to be serious violations of human rights, which have given rise to physical confrontations and hunger strikes. The deliberately severe and degrading conditions imposed on many political prisoners are exacerbated in the case of the "resentenced" prisoners, whose deprivation of freedom is prolonged arbitrarily. This practice warrants the strongest condemnation by the IACHR.

10. With respect to the release of political prisoners begun in 1979, the commission recognizes and values the efforts made and those being made, to continue this process, and urges that it be completed. The IACHR is also deeply concerned about the obstacles posed by the Cuban authorities to the emigration of several former political prisoners. Likewise, the commission requests the governments of the countries affected to facilitate immigration of released Cuban prisoners and their families.

11. The IACHR is aware of the fact that former political prisoners are the victims of various kinds of discrimination. The commission considers that the treatment given by the Cuban authorities to former political prisoners is in violation of their rights; in addition, it considers that this discriminatory treatment prolongs in time, under other forms, the punishment they suffered while deprived of their liberty. For that reason, the Commission urges the government of Cuba to provide released prisoners with access to the same living conditions as is granted to other individuals with equivalent professional qualifications, without subjecting them to any kind of discrimination by virtue of having served a prison sentence for political reasons.

12. The commission considers that freedom of religion and worship in Cuba is limited in two fundamental ways: in the use of the mass media and in education. The IACHR considers that both restrictions should be eliminated, since they undermine the exercise of the right to religious freedom and worship. The early antagonism between the Cuban government and the churches has given way to ideological competition, in which the government has—and uses—the vast resources at its command to actively promote the official Marxist-Leninist philosophy. In this respect, the Commission considers that it is the right of religious institutions to promote the application of social principles

based on their ethical concepts when this leads to a greater observance of inalienable human rights. Likewise, the IACHR finds that there has been an evolution in the positions of the churches and the government, which has resulted in an environment of mutual tolerance. However, there continue to exist indirect restrictions which give rise to promote discrimination against religious groups affecting central aspects of life and politics in Cuban society. There is no religious persecution per se; the restrictions to which certain religious groups have been subjected—including imprisonment of some of their members—can be traced to the political impact of their action and not to the fact of professing a religious faith.

13. With respect to the right to residence and movement, the commission considers that its exercise is extremely restricted in fact and in law. The restrictions are particularly severe in the case of those who wish to leave Cuba permanently, and especially in the case of political dissidents. At this time, some intellectuals are barred from leaving the country although they have been granted visas by countries willing to receive them. The commission has learned that the mere fact of having emigrated has been grounds for the loss of Cuban nationality, a practice that the commission considers unjust and incompatible with the observance of human rights. In order to regularize such situations, the Commission urges the government of Cuba to adopt the pertinent measures in order to allow an unimpaired movement of people.

14. With respect to the right to property, it may be affirmed that the means of production are owned entirely by the State with the exception of one fourth of the quasi-private agricultural sector, in which the farmers do not enjoy the right of alienation and are subject to serious limitations with respect to their rights of use and usufruct. This nonstate sector has been gradually reduced in the last 25 years and its disappearance is foreseen through its integration into cooperatives and state farms. Personal ownership of housing also exists (although limited in terms of the rights of alienation, use and usufruct) as does ownership of the instruments of personal and family labor.

15. Analysis of the right to work in the Republic of Cuba makes it possible to state that significant progress has been made with respect to employment, both in absolute and comparative terms, through the organization of an economic system which strives for full employment; this is a worthy achievement and deserves to be highlighted. However, it should also be pointed out that unemployment still continues in limited sectors of the Cuban economy, and that, in certain cases, this is the result of political discrimination against those opposed to the regime. Likewise, it should be noted that there is hidden unemployment—how much is difficult to determine—which entails a high economic cost; an economic strategy that promotes activities capable of productively absorbing underemployed sectors is not compatible with the rigid and dogmatic practice of the Cuban government.

16. Labor mobility that allows individuals to follow their vocations is limited by an economy that still suffers from serious structural defects (preponder-

ance of single-crop farming, meager industrial development, low productivity, etc.). Labor options are also restricted by the various forms of governmental and social controls with the consequent chain of bureaucratic processes necessary to obtain the authorizations to change employment and the operations characteristic of a highly centralized economic system that has consistently discouraged private initiative.

17. With respect to working conditions, the positive results brought about by efforts to achieve a more equitable distribution of income should be noted. This has been possible as a result of wage policy and the adoption of other measures, such as the massive extension of social services. There are indications however, that practices that violate traditional labor gains such as the eight-hour workday and leisure time, have become widespread, through the extension of the workday by "voluntary" work, obtained to a large extent as a result of various forms of pressure brought to bear on the workers.

18. It is in the field of collective labor rights that the commission finds the greatest contradiction between the ideological principles of the system and its operation in practice. The right to associate, in labor unions, is not recognized and is not observed in practice; rather, only the official unions are authorized. The very nature of unions has been distorted, their function having shifted from the protection of the workers' interests to that of serving as conduits for government directives; the unions have become one more instrument of State control. In this context, a strike has become a punishable act, and collective bargaining is unknown. As concerns enterprises, a vertical structure has been set up in which there are no institutional channels to allow for worker participation, even though, in theory, the workers are the owners of the means of production.

19. The IACHR notes that both in law and in practice, social security and welfare are rights available to the Cuban people. In the case of unemployment, disability, sickness, widowhood, advanced age, or for other reasons, Cubans receive assistance from the State. This is unquestionably progress. Those who receive social security and welfare benefits do not have to contribute directly to a national fund to be entitled to such assistance, because the system is financed by the State budget. The system is unified and is applied equally throughout the country. There is no evident discrimination on the basis of sex, race, place of residence, or any reason.

20. With respect to the right to food, the IACHR notes that although there is no legislation in Cuba that obliges the State to provide the population with a certain nutritional level, the widespread changes that have taken place have contributed to a very marked improvement in the nutritional levels of the Cuban people.

21. With respect to the right to health in Cuba, the commission notes that health services—in the form of medical and dental care—are provided free of charge and under the responsibility of the State. Numerous positive measures have been undertaken to extend this right to all sectors of society, regardless

of sex, age, color, belief, income, or place of residence. In addition, the IACHR finds that considerable progress has been made in reducing the rate of still-births, infant mortality and in improving the healthy development of children. Prevention, treatment, and control of epidemic diseases has progressed since the revolution, in particular in terms of mortality, although morbidity rates have risen for some diseases. Nevertheless, the increase in the suicide rate is a source of concern, and the commission considers it important to investigate the reasons that may have led to this phenomenon.

22. With respect to the right to education, the IACHR considers that highly significant progress has been made in Cuba. Primary and secondary education is accessible to all, is free of charge at all levels, and is compulsory up to the ninth grade. Technical, vocational, and university education is available to a larger segment of the population than previously. Adult education has been promoted and intensified and the positive results of that effort have been numerous. Furthermore, scholarships have opened up more opportunities and the material infrastructure for teaching has been improved. Neither social class, nor race, nor sex appear to influence access to education. The rural population is still at a disadvantage, but the trend is toward greater equality between urban and rural areas. However, discrimination in education for political and even religious reasons is a fact that persists and that needs to be emphatically condemned. A further negative aspect of the Cuban educational system is the dogmatic rigidity of the content of the educational material, which converts the system into an additional channel for political indoctrination. In this context, parents have been unjustly denied of their right to choose the type of education they consider most appropriate for their children.

23. In light of the above, the commission considers that there are two characteristics of the Cuban political, economic, social, and cultural system that permit one to interpret how it operates and to evaluate how it promotes and limits the observance of human rights. The first is the subordination of Cuban society to the political group in power; the second is its organization designed to satisfy the basic needs of the population. The first is manifested through the political practice of the regime and the legal and institutional order upon which that practice is based; features of the system are its exclusion of any dissident political views, the use of coercion—direct or indirect—to bring about adherence, and the absence of any effective guarantees which could render the State accountable to the people and protect them in the exercise of their rights. As a consequence, it is a totalitarian political system. That system, however, has shown itself to be notably efficient in meeting the basic needs of the population, especially of those sectors that were the most disadvantaged prior to the revolution.

24. The commission considers that there are elements of the Cuban political system which, if developed, would allow for the progressive evolution of a democratic order—today absent—and which is the only way of consolidating

the advances made in the social area and of overcoming the deeply rooted distortions that affect its economy. The commission hopes that the internal and international conditions will be created that will make it possible to bring about the effective and authentic participation of the citizens of Cuba in the political decisions that affect them, in a context of liberty and pluralism which is necessary to bring about the observance of all human rights.

NOTES

1. a. Report on the Situation of Human Rights in Cuba (OEA/Ser.L/V/II.4, Doc. 30, May 1, 1962).

b. Report on the Situation of Political Prisoners and their Families in Cuba (OEA/Ser.L/V/VI.7. Doc. 4, May 17, 1963).

c. Report on the Situation of Human Rights in Cuba (OEA/Ser.L/V/II.17, Doc. 4, Rev. 1, April 27, 1967).

d. Second Report on the Situation of Political Prisoners and their Family Members in Cuba (OEA/Ser.L/V.II.23, Doc. 6, Rev. 1, May 7, 1970).

e. Fifth Report of the IACHR on the Situation of Human Rights in Cuba (OEA/Ser.6 CP/INF.872/76, June 1, 1976).

f. Sixth Report of the IACHR on the Situation of Political Prisoners in Cuba (OEA/Ser.L/V/II.48, Doc. 7, December 14, 1979).

2. IACHR, *Annual Report 1979–1980,* p. 152.

27. *Political Imprisonment in Cuba: Two Readings*

I. By Amnesty International*

> *Amnesty International is an independent human rights monitoring organization and recipient of the Nobel Prize for Peace for its work on behalf of political prisoners. The Cuban government has not allowed Amnesty to send formal missions into the country.*

Introduction

During the early years of the revolution which brought Fidel Castro to power in January 1959, thousands of political opponents were tried by Revolutionary Tribunals and convicted of crimes against the security of the State on accusations of "counterrevolutionary activities" (a charge covering a variety of political activities including armed political opposition) and related crimes against

*From Amnesty International, *Political Imprisonment in Cuba* (London: Amnesty International, 1986), pages excerpted throughout.

the security of the State. Evidence in Amnesty International's possession suggests that the summary procedures followed in these trials did not always conform to internationally recognized standards for a fair trial; for example, the right of defense appears to have been severely limited. Sentences imposed by the Revolutionary Tribunals (abolished in 1973) were harsh, often as much as 60 or 90 years. The death penalty was also widely applied during the period immediately after the revolution: hundreds of political prisoners were sentenced to death by Revolutionary Tribunals and executed by firing squads. In the 1970s the judiciary underwent a number of changes. For instance, the new Penal Code introduced in 1979 fixed a maximum sentence of 20 years for crimes not punishable by the death penalty and 30 years as a possible alternative to the death penalty. It is believed that, in accordance with Article 3.2 of the new code, which reads ". . . la nueva ley es aplicable al delito cometido con anterioridad a su vigencia si es más favorable al encausado," (The new law is applicable to crimes committed prior to its coming into force if it is favorable to the accused) those still serving their prison terms at that time had their sentences reduced accordingly.

In September 1978, a release program was announced by the government bringing about the release of almost 4,000 political prisoners between December 1978 and the end of 1979. Those released included hundreds of *plantados*—a category of prisoner known for their refusal on political grounds to take part in the government's "rehabilitation" programs (these originally involved prisoners' participation in political reeducation and paid manual work, though later "rehabilitation" is said to have focused on the work schemes only), and to wear the prison uniform worn by ordinary (as opposed to political) prisoners. Some 250 *plantados* were not included in the 1979 releases and remained imprisoned in several prisons, principally Combinado del Este in Havana, Boniato in Oriente Province and Kilo 7 near Camagüey.

. . . Since then, a number have been released upon expiry of their sentences while many others were reportedly held for variable periods of time after their original sentence had expired. As many as 50 prisoners are known to have been kept beyond their original sentence between 1977 and 1983. All, however, were subsequently released. Amnesty International appealed to the Cuban government on behalf of the resentenced prisoners on the grounds that the prisoners were kept in detention following summary proceedings which did not conform to internationally recognized standards.

The practice of not releasing political prisoners after the expiry of their original sentence seems to have first appeared in the mid-1970s when, according to official statistics, many prisoners serving terms of 10 or 12 years were released only after having served between one and four additional years in prison. With few exceptions, it appeared that formal judicial procedures were not used to resentence prisoners. In some instances, prisoners were reportedly subjected to summary trials on charges such as having "a rebellious attitude," often because they had participated in hunger strikes or refused to work and/or wear prison uniform. (The *plantados* reportedly claimed that such regulations and tasks constituted a denial of their political prisoner status.) Most, however, were simply informed orally by prison guards that they had been resentenced to a further period of imprisonment, usually one or two years, although some were given what appeared to be official court documents stating that a further sentence had been passed.

Following a hunger strike staged by 11 *plantados* in Boniato Prison in October/November 1982 in protest against their continued detention after completing long sentences, many were transferred to a maximum security building in the prison and reportedly told by the authorities that their release was imminent. From the last months of 1982 until August 1983 approximately 35 *plantados* were released from both Boniato and Combinado del Este prisons. Many had served two years in excess of their original sentences . . .

Amnesty International has not been able to establish whether any prisoners have been resentenced in this way in the past two or three years, although it is thought that some prisoners may have been tried for a second time while still serving their sentence after having tried to escape or for having breached prison discipline. . . .

At the time of writing, Amnesty International has received the names of some 90 political prisoners who have been released in the course of 1986, some upon expiry of their sentence and others as the result of interventions by foreign delegations. They include many of the long-term *plantado* prisoners. In September 1986, a group of 68 former political prisoners and members of their families arrived in Miami. While some had been released only days earlier, many had been released earlier in the year or during 1985.

PRISON CONDITIONS

According to a publication of the Ministry of Justice dating from 1985 called *El Sistema Jurídico Penal en Cuba* (The Penal Legal System in Cuba), "the main function of the penitentiary institutions in Cuba is to correct and reeducate the convicts in work habits, the strict observance of law and respect for social living conventions, to prevent them from perpetrating new crimes." Amongst the "fundamental means of correction and reeducation of convicts" are the following:

—the progressive penitentiary regime, through which the convict's situation may be improved according to his attitude towards work and other indicators, and pass from a more severe phase to another less rigorous.
—socially useful work, as a means of education, which is done according to a work regime similar to that applicable to all workers in the country. . . .

In addition to these, the prisoners are said to be provided with "indispensable living conditions according to acceptable dietary, sanitary and hygienic norms," free hospitalization and medical care, socioeducational activities, general and technical professional education, and sport and recreational activities. They are also said to have the possibility of using the *pabellones conyugales* (conjugal pavilions) so that married prisoners may maintain their relationship with their partner, and to be permitted "to exchange mail with residents outside the penitentiary, as well as to receive visitors and consumer goods." All of these, according to the brochure, "indicate the respect shown to the dignity and human rights of the convicts."

As already mentioned above, over the years large numbers of political prisoners have, as a political act, consistently rejected participating in the rehabilitation program, known as the *Plan Progresivo* (Progressive Plan) and have refused to wear prison uniform and to adhere to other aspects of prison discipline. They have become known as *plantados,* literally "those who stand firm." At the time of writing, some 80 long-term *plantados* are believed to be held in Combinado del Este, Boniato, and Kilo Siete prisons. However, Amnesty International has recently received reports that there is a group of prisoners mostly convicted in the 1980s known as the "new *plantados*" in Combinado del Este Prison, 19 of whom went on hunger strike in January 1986, apparently in protest at the suspension of family visits. In a letter smuggled out of the prison, they also claimed to have been deprived of sunlight for two years and that they were not receiving adequate medical attention. Amnesty International has so far received no further information concerning the outcome of the hunger strike.

Because of their refusal to engage in any activities which they believe to be incompatible with their beliefs, the long-term *plantados* have claimed that they have frequently been denied certain of the "privileges" that, according to the publication cited above, are guaranteed to prisoners. Amnesty International has often received reports that they have been denied visits, access to correspondence (both sending and receiving), adequate medical care, fresh air, etc., although, in some cases, it is believed that the prisoners themselves have refused to see their relatives in protest at the conditions imposed by the authorities for such visits, i.e., that the prisoners have to be strip-searched and to wear the prison uniform. They have also participated in a number of hunger strikes in order to put pressure on the Cuban authorities to accede to their demands. Several reports have also been received by Amnesty International of *plantados* having been badly beaten by guards or placed in cells whose grilled doors have been totally covered with steel plates, known as *celdas tapiadas,* for prolonged periods after refusing to obey an order or refusing to conform to prison discipline, or of being held in other kinds of punishment cells for several weeks at a time. Many of the long-term *plantados,* most of whom have spent a least 15 or 20 years in prison, are reported to be suffering from serious illnesses. Their condition may have been compounded by ill-treatment and the effects of the hunger strikes, prolonged detention and a reportedly inadequate diet. As already stated above, medical treatment is in principle freely available to all prisoners and every major prison has a prison hospital. However, Amnesty International has received reports that, on occasion, medical care has been withheld or only very basic assistance provided as a form of punishment. Serious illnesses, however, do appear to receive attention, and several prisoners have reportedly been released on health grounds, although a number of others have died in prison in recent years, apparently as the result of illness or old age. . . .

PRISONERS OF CONSCIENCE

At a press conference on socialist legality in Cuba, reported in the international edition of *Granma* (April 14, 1985) the Deputy Minister of Justice, Ramón de la Cruz, stated that "Any unbiased observer can come to the conclusion that in our country there's absolute respect for human rights. For example, those involved in crimes against state security and confined to prison have all had maximum guarantees. All were tried by the corresponding court and had the opportunity to have counsel, either selected by them or appointed by the court. None of them are prisoners of conscience. All engaged in concrete activities. Thousands of counterrevolutionaries who had been serving time have left Cuba, and not a single one showed signs of ill-treatment."

Despite these assurances, Amnesty International has come to the conclusion that a number of political prisoners in Cuba are prisoners of conscience under the terms of the organization's mandate and may have been subjected to certain kinds of ill-treatment.

1. People imprisoned on charges of "enemy propaganda"

One charge that is sometimes applied to those who disagree with the Cuban system of government or are critical of some of its methods is that of *propaganda enemiga* (enemy propaganda). According to Article 108 of the Cuban Penal Code . . . , anyone who "incites against social order, international solidarity or the Socialist State, by means of oral, written or any other kind of propaganda" or "prepares, distributes or possesses" such propaganda, faces imprisonment for between one and eight years. If such activities are carried out via the mass media, the penalty is between seven and 15 years' imprisonment. . . .

2. People imprisoned for trying to leave Cuba illegally

According to Article 247 of the Cuban Penal Code . . . , those who leave or try to leave Cuba without fulfilling the legal formalities face from six months to three years' imprisonment. The sentence for those who use violence or intimidation in order to leave or try to leave is from three to eight years. Those who by deceit, coercion, force, violence or intimidation try to enter an embassy (to seek asylum) risk between one and eight years' imprisonment. According to Article 12 of the International Covenant on Civil and Political Rights, everyone shall be free to leave any country, including their own. Amnesty International therefore believes that anyone held under Article 247 who has neither used nor advocated violence can be considered to be a Prisoner of Conscience under the terms of its mandate.

Since 1979, tens of thousands of Cubans have been allowed to emigrate, mainly to the United States. However, Amnesty International has continued to receive reports that administrative procedures for leaving the country are extremely slow and bureaucratic, and that some individuals, whose skills are particularly valued, such as medical doctors, or who are considered to constitute a risk to the Cuban authorities, from a political point of view, have faced harassment and, in some instances, imprisonment as a result of having expressed their wish to leave or having initiated enquiries with the authorities with a view to seeking emigration. Amnesty International has received reports that some people who have applied to leave the country, while not being imprisoned, have been unable to continue with their normal occupation and in some cases forced by police order to do manual work on construction sites or other kinds of unskilled labor. . . .

3. Other political prisoners
    . . . There are believed to be at least several hundred other political prisoners currently in detention in Cuba for politically related offenses. In many cases, the charges are criminal ones; however, Amnesty International has concluded that in several cases there is reason to believe that the person may have been convicted solely on account of his/her known opposition to the Cuban Government. In Cuba all press and media are government controlled and independent human rights groups are unable to operate officially. It is, therefore, extremely difficult to obtain precise information concerning political prisoners. A great deal of the information at Amnesty International's disposal has come from relatives or friends of the prisoners living abroad, who have either left since the prisoner was detained or who have managed to correspond with them, often clandestinely, since then. Amnesty International has also received copies of some trial documents that indicate that political detainees may sometimes be convicted despite serious lack of evidence. . . .

Political Imprisonment—An Update (January 1988)

Long-term prisoners have continued to be released over the past few months, and it is hoped that all of the remaining *"plantados históricos,"* "historical *plantados,"* will benefit from the recent immigration agreement between the U.S. and Cuba by which the U.S. agreed to accept a certain number of Cuban political prisoners and their families each year. . . . In January 1988, the first of the 348 current and former political prisoners on a list presented to the Cuban authorities by the U.S. Catholic Conference started arriving in the

United States. All of the *"plantados históricos"* formerly held at Boniato and Kilo 7 prisons were transferred to Combinado del Este Prison in May 1987 where conditions for them have reportedly improved to a certain extent. For example, they are now said to be permitted monthly family visits and daily exercise in the prison yard. About 65 *"plantados históricos"* are believed to be still in detention at the time of writing. It is difficult to know how many prisoners are in the group of *"nuevos plantados,"* new *plantados,* held in Combinado del Este—estimates range from 23 to some 50 or 60. However, conditions for them appear to have changed little in recent months with reports still being received that medical attention is inadequate, and that fresh air, exercise, family visits and correspondence are seriously restricted, because of their refusal to participate in the "reeducation" program. [*The above information reflects Amnesty International's concerns in Cuba as of January 1988. The secretary general of Amnesty International, accompanied by two staff members, visited Cuba in March 1988 at the invitation of Vice-President Carlos Rafael Rodríguez. An updated version of the organization's concerns about Cuba, based on information obtained during the visit, was published as this book went to press. Readers should contact Amnesty International directly to obtain a copy.—eds.*]

II. By Institute for Policy Studies*

The Institute for Policy Studies is a nonprofit research organization founded in 1963. In 1987 it began a program, the U.S.-Cuba Dialogue Project, to organize meetings in the United States and Cuba between leaders from both countries to address key issues that stand in the way of normalizing relations.

Introduction

From February 26 to March 5, board members from the Institute for Policy Studies (IPS) led a delegation to Cuba to conduct an inquiry into present prison conditions and the treatment of prisoners in Cuba. (The delegation members were: Diana de Vegh, Vice-chair of IPS board of directors; Adrian DeWind, Chairman of Americas Watch and former president of the Bar Association of New York; Peter Bell, President of the Edna McConnell Clark Foundation; Howard Hiatt, former dean of Harvard University School of

*From Institute for Policy Studies, *Preliminary Report: Cuban Prisons* (Institute for Policy Studies, 1988).

Public Health; Aryeh Neier, Vice-chair of Americas Watch; and Herman Schwartz, professor of law at American University. Julia Sweig was the coordinator of the IPS U.S.-Cuba Dialogue Project.) This investigation was made possible by an agreement signed in February between IPS and the National Union of Cuban Jurists (NUCJ). The agreement called for NUCJ to obtain open access to all facilities in six Cuban prisons chosen by the U.S. delegation to facilitate confidential interviews with present and released prisoners selected by the delegation. In exchange IPS agreed to seek similar access to United States prisons for a Cuban delegation from NUCJ. A condition in the agreement that U.S. visas for the Cubans be obtained prior to the visit to Cuba was waived by NUCJ in reliance upon good faith efforts to accomplish the reciprocity.

This visiting program is an early part of an IPS project to explore possibilities for bettering relations between Cuba and the United States. Since the treatment of prisoners and prison conditions, both in the U.S. and Cuba, has been a festering issue between the two governments for years, the proposal for open reciprocal exchange offered some promise for an initial test of possibilities, through a specific, tangible approach to one divisive issue that has stood in the way of better relations. The reciprocity feature is essential to the success of the effort. The IPS delegation hopes that the United States administration will recognize this and support a program that will help to advance human rights and open doors to future progress.

TASK OF DELEGATION

We visited the six prisons that we had asked to see located in four provinces of Cuba and conducted confidential interviews with more than 120 prisoners. (We also conducted brief visits to one other prison and one police detention facility, but we omit these from our report because our research was not sufficiently thorough.) More than 40 of the interviews were conducted with prisoners we had asked to see in advance; the remainder of the prisoners were selected by us at random. At least 50 of the interviews took place with prisoners incarcerated for politically motivated offenses. Most of these interviews were with prisoners we had selected in advance. More than half of our interviews were conducted out-of-doors at places we chose at random. The interviews that took place indoors were also conducted at places we chose at random. At no time were Cuban authorities present during these interviews.

The Cubans with whom we were in contact—NUCJ officials, officials of the Ministry of Foreign Relations and the Ministry of the Interior, which operates the prisons—facilitated our visit throughout, providing access, transportation and lodging, including a plane to make possible our visits to prisons in the provinces. IPS will provide accommodations and transportation for the Cubans who travel to the U.S. to see prisons here.

The Cuban authorities gave us access to all areas of each prison that we chose to see, including dormitories, workplaces, conjugal pavilions, visiting areas, infirmaries, punishment cells and segregation cells for prisoners designated as high risk or troublesome inmates, kitchens, laundries, dining areas, classrooms and libraries. Of those prisoners we asked to see in advance, we saw all but a handful. Some few, we were told, had already been released. (We will try to verify this.)

In addition to visiting the prisons, we met with Cuban officials in each of the four provinces and nationally to discuss the prisons. We also arranged meetings with the leaders of two unofficial human rights group in Cuba to obtain through them the testimony of recently released prisoners about prison conditions. We did not visit pre-trial detention facilities, military prisons, or reform schools. At one of the prisons that we visited, Nieves Morejon in Sancti Spiritus province, which also has facilities where juveniles of 16 years and older are confined, we devoted some of our inspections and interviews to juveniles.

Our principal focus was on current conditions. Our interviews with prisoners dealt primarily with the present and recent conditions and changes in conditions since the beginning of 1987.

Also, we did not examine the reasons for confinement or the procedures leading to confinement. That was not part of our mandate. Our examination was limited to the conditions within the prisons.

Reeducation for the purpose of reintegration into civilian life is the central principle of the Cuban penal system. In carrying out reeducation, the system relies principally on:

1. employing as many prisoners as possible in productive remunerated labor;
2. technical education to provide prisoners with skills that they will continue to use after release from prison;
3. political education;
4. discipline.

We encountered a very strong sense of mission in most of the prison officials we met. They expressed great faith in their system, and though they concede faults in practice, they seem determined to work increasingly on their plan for reeducation and for incorporation of the penal population into work and later society. At present, officials say that 85 percent of the Cuban penal population works. Their goal for 1990 is to incorporate 95 percent of the penal population into work. They claim that at present 80 percent of all operations costs to run Cuban prisons are covered by production that takes place within the prisons.

The humane and constructive features of the system, particularly the paid work opportunities and the training in basic skills, as well as the harsh and cruel features, appear to us to be directly attributable to the determination to reeducate prisoners.

The constructive aspect of the system is reflected in the following facts:

1. The great majority of prisoners work a regular work week at productive jobs under conditions similar to those of workers not serving sentences.

2. Almost all the prisoners who work are paid. The remuneration is the same as for civilians before certain discounts for cost of living. We were told that the amount remaining to them after these discounts is sufficient to help to provide support for families or to accumulate substantial savings for prisoners without family-support responsibilities, which can aid their reentry into normal life.

3. The regular prison facilities we saw were all clean and hygienic, and we heard no great complaints in this regard.

4. We heard no complaints of the use of instruments of torture to inflict pain; we did not find any policy of extrajudicial executions or disappearances.

5. A system of conjugal visiting is well established at all the prisons we saw. Visits at conjugal pavilions range from three to eight hours every one to six months, depending upon inmates' compliance with prison rules.

6. Many prisoners do acquire practical skills during confinement.

7. Prisoners are provided with education to bring them up to the ninth grade level. A program is underway for prisoners who have already completed the ninth grade to secure further education.

8. We heard no complaints that prisoner-against-prisoner violence is commonplace (as it is in some other prison systems).

9. The outpatient, hospital, physical therapy, laboratory, and pharmacy facilities we saw were good. Doctors and nurses, as well as laboratory and other personnel, were present in sufficient numbers required for the prison population. Prisoners expressed satisfaction with the care available for major medical problems, but we heard some complaints, mostly from prisoners held on politically related charges, about failure or delays in access.

The harsh and cruel part of the system is reflected in these following facts:

1. Those who resist reeducation or violate prison discipline, including passive violation such as hunger strikes, are confined for extended periods sometimes in extremely harsh punishment cells—bare, tiny, dark, cold (or hot, depending on the season)—sometimes with not enough food. We heard of a few cases of prisoners in these cells without clothes and some cases of prisoners dressed in undershorts and shoes.

2. Other prisoners, who are considered to be problems and who do not work, have only slightly better facilities than the punishment cells and go out into the sun only once a week for an hour or two. In some prisons they are then placed in large iron cages too small for walking.

3. Visits have been infrequent in the past, though new rules now make them somewhat more frequent. Up to now, many prisoners could only get visits once every six months; the new rules reduce this to once every 60 days. In the best of circumstances—that is, for the prisoners considered to be doing best in the prisons and under the new rules just put into effect that liberalize visiting

considerably—visits may take place only every 21 days (family visits for juveniles are more frequent); incentives, *estimulos,* for good conduct include additional visiting privileges.

4. In general, letters may be sent with almost the same infrequency as visits, though regulations for some prisoners in some prisons allowed for letters to be sent and received every two weeks or more often in some cases.

5. In two prisons, Boniato and Combinado del Este, we encountered frequent complaints that prisoners who did not conform to the prison regime had been beaten with rubber hoses, *mangueras,* or with fists or sticks. We spoke to prisoners in Combinado del Este who had witnessed such beatings. We heard of one case in which a prisoner in 1987 was allegedly kicked to death by guards, but could not verify this. We heard that the two offending guards faced disciplinary procedures, but we were unable to verify this. We did not hear such complaints of beatings in the other four prisons we visited.

As to some other matters, some prisoners told us the food was good, and others said it was adequate but tasteless. Except in the case of prisoners in some the punishment cells, no one told us it was insufficient. In those punishment cases, prisoners received a small breakfast and a larger supper, but no lunch, a very deprived diet.

Except in the case of the punishment cells and harsh protection cells, toilet facilities were minimally adequate. In the punishment cells, toilets are holes in the grounds. Most punishment cells in most prisons contained facilities for running cold water. In one building in one prison the facilities were less good, accompanied by stench and inadequate water and ventilation.

Bathing facilities in dormitories in all prisons were primitive but adequate relative to the number of prisoners in each detachment.

In the dormitories in men's prisons, there was little place for prisoners to keep private possessions. In one prison, inmates could only keep their possessions in a numbered bag hung in a room that is normally locked; access over the course of the day is permitted according to schedule. Elsewhere—particularly in the women's prisons—there was adequate space for the storage of private possessions.

For most prisoners overcrowding is not a problem. Some prisons we saw have empty dormitories. Typical dormitories had double and triple bunks, though we saw only partial evidence of use of the top bunk in the triple bunk facilities. We calculated an average of about 30 square feet of floor space per prisoner. For those prisoners, the fact that they work elsewhere, study elsewhere, take part in sports elsewhere, and eat elsewhere prevents the lack of space from being particularly oppressive.

On the other hand, we saw extremely crowded conditions in punishment cells. At their worst, we saw a few cells with three prisoners in which they were confined for 24 hours a day and that measured five feet by seven feet—35 total square feet or 12 square feet per prisoner. Most punishment cells in most prisons we saw contained one or two prisoners. Some punishment cells were slightly larger, measuring 6 feet by 12 feet. In the punishment cells in three of the prisons we saw, prisoners slept on bare cement slabs without bedding on which regular prisoners may sleep. In others, adequate bedding with mattresses is provided. The toilet (a hole in the floor) is in the cell, as is a spigot for water. Light is minimal. All but one of the prisoners we saw in punishment cells were common criminals, not those confined for politically motivated offenses.

Complaints by prisoners are supposed to be investigated by the office of the Fiscal General. The office of the Fiscal General performs an inspection function—carrying out unannounced on-site visits to prisons to review compliance with requirements for conditions, prisoners' rights, and completion of sentence, parole, and release. We obtained evidence that this system works at least some of the time, though how often we could not determine. Some prisoners expressed skepticism about seeking assistance from the Fiscal General and believed their communications would never reach his office. They told us that letters of complaint must be entrusted to their reeducators. Cuban judicial theory does not provide for independent advocates for prisoners. It is considered not an appropriate function of lawyers to represent prisoners in matters dealing with prison conditions. Pastoral visits by clergy are unknown and are apparently prohibited in Cuban prisons.

Two private, unofficial human rights groups have recently begun to operate, most of their members fresh from prison themselves. The government is hostile to such groups, and they have no rights of access to prisoners, though both have sources of information. In recent years foreign delegations have visited the prisons. The International Committee of the Red Cross, however, has not yet been permitted to establish a presence in Cuba, though there have been recent official contacts with the ICRC, and indications are that it may gain entry. At present, officials from the prison system itself or from the office of the Fiscal General are the only ones who can be counted upon to protect the rights of prisoners.

There was one exceptional prison we visited: the Women's Prison of the Western Provinces in Havana. It is a model prison in terms of all physical facilities. The working conditions, the cells (including punishment cells), and the facilities for activities were very good. Relations between officials and prisoners seemed generally courteous and respectful. The prison reflects the positive influence of a dedicated warden. While this is a showplace and intended and paraded as such, the fact remains that some 600 women are imprisoned under humane conditions.

The Cuban prison system is made very hard by the prolonged prison sentences that have prevailed. Although the officials with whom we spoke are quick to say that Cuba has a low crime rate (no statistics are published), and though this claim seems valid, the ratio of prisoners to population is high.

Assuming that the Cuban government's figures are correct, there are 32,000 inmates currently in prisons and detention centers. We got no figures on reform schools or military prisons. Given a population of about ten million, and using just the figure given to us, the rate of imprisonment is 3.2 per thousand. In the United States, including military prisons, we have 820,000 prisoners in prisons and jails. Given a population of about 240 million, the rate is approximately 3.4 per thousand. If we add the military prisons, which include draft resisters and draft evaders in Cuba, the rate must be as high or higher than in the United States. The United States has a very high crime rate and among the world's longest prison sentences. In Cuba, with a low crime rate, the comparable rate of imprisonment indicates long sentences. In the case of those prisoners who experience the worst of the Cuban prison system, this can mean several years in cramped, poorly lighted, locked cells with an hour a week in the sun and infrequent visits. Such prisoners may see relatives only through iron grills, though most prisoners are entitled to contact visits.

Cuba has recognized that its sentences are greatly prolonged, and some changes are underway. In 1987, 14,000 prisoners were reportedly released on parole. Some crimes have been eliminated in the new penal code effective April 1, 1988; some sentences are being reduced; parole is abbreviating some sentences; the same is the case with reductions of sentences for good behavior.

We applaud the fact that the Cuban government permitted the IPS delegation access to its prisons. While our visit was constructive, it is only a single visit, and we would hope that present discussions with the International Committee of the Red Cross about a permanent presence in Cuba will come to a successful conclusion.

28. Cuba's Policies on Immigration and Emigration*

BY PATRICIA WEISS FAGEN

THE MIGRATION LAW AND THE FOREIGNERS LAW

Travel Outside of Cuba

Cuba's migration laws cover citizens, resident foreigners, temporary residents, transients, invited visitors and tourists. There are measures governing Cubans

*From Patricia Weiss Fagen, "Immigration, Emigration and Asylum Policies in Cuba," *Migration News,* No. 2 (April–June 1984), pp. 19–27.

who travel for diplomatic or official purposes, for personal business or for family visits, and non-Cubans who enter the national territory for the same purposes. The Foreigners Law defines who are considered foreigners, and what their rights and obligations are in Cuba.

Cubans leaving the national territory, either temporarily or permanently, require passports. These are available, upon request, to anyone 18 years or over. Notarized requests are filed with the Dirección de Inmigración y Extranjeria, and must be accompanied by proof of identity and a payment. Cuban nationals living outside of Cuba may request passports in designated Cuban diplomatic and consular offices. Passports are valid for two years and may be renewed. Cubans with ordinary passports *(pasaportes corrientes)*, as well as any foreigners or persons without citizenship who reside in Cuba for more than 90 days and are not serving in official capacities, must obtain exit visas in addition to their passports. Applicants for exit visas must present statements of character from their places of work or study, any criminal records and, if travel is for the purpose of visits to family or friends, the applicant must have information on and invitations from those who will be visited. In the case of visits or travel for personal reasons, it is also necessary for those of military age to present documents verifying military service, and for prospective travelers to non-socialist countries to deposit or otherwise assure funding corresponding to the cost of the trip. Temporary exit visas are valid for specific periods of time, but may be renewed. When permanent exit visas are issued, prospective emigrants must undergo an inventory of their goods which is described below.

Travel overseas by Cubans and resident non-Cubans is entirely regulated by government agencies, by means of exit visas. If, for example, a Cuban writer or singer receives an invitation to participate in a conference or to perform in another country, the invitation is presented to the appropriate ministry where the decision will be made, the Ministry of Culture in these examples. If there are no problems, that ministry sends a memo to the Ministries of Foreign Relations and Interior, and the exit visa is issued. If there are objections of some kind, the issuance of the exit visa may be delayed or the visa may be denied.

The neighborhood Committees for the Defense of the Revolution (CDR's) may be consulted to verify addresses and other information submitted for purposes of travel and family visits. These organizations implement a number of public services (vaccination programs, for example), but also function as committees of political vigilance. Citizens who are not well-regarded by the CDR's may on occasion find it difficult to obtain permission to travel. However, exit visas for the kinds of activities described above normally are obtainable, providing the travel does not imply costs in terms of foreign currency.

Tourist visas for family visits overseas are issued relatively automatically for

Cubans over 60 years of age. In emergency family situations involving sickness or death, they are usually issued quickly for anybody. In general, when Cubans apply for an exit visa in order to visit family abroad, the visa takes about a month to be processed. Although most professionals do eventually obtain temporary visas for travel when invited by organizations overseas, it is sometimes difficult for professionals in certain categories to obtain permission to travel. Young men usually have to complete military service before they are given exit visas.

Over the years, the procedures for obtaining emigrant visas have become more regularized and less punitive. It is still the case that Cubans must leave behind all but their personal possessions. Once a permanent exit visa has been issued, officials take an inventory of household goods, and these must be present at the time of the individual's departure. If, however, only one member of a family unit leaves permanently, the household remains basically intact. Several years ago, when Cubans declared their intention to leave, they often lost their jobs—if they had desirable jobs—and were obliged to work at manual labor or to remain without work until they actually left. This has rarely occurred in recent years. However, once a person does declare that he or she intends to leave permanently by requesting an exit visa for this purpose, it is most unlikely that the individual will be selected for any special privileges such as scholarships, official travel, or material rewards, or that the person will be eligible for promotions in his or her place of work.

At this time, it is difficult to assess Cuba's present policies or practices with regard to those who wish to emigrate, because few Cubans are able to obtain visas from the countries to which they would like to emigrate. A few still are able to go to Venezuela; Costa Rica and Spain still accept Cubans for the purposes of family reunification. As for the United States, which has taken some 800,000 Cubans over the years since the revolution, the government will now accept only members of the immediate families of U.S. citizens—these by special waiver—and a limited number of Cuban applicants from third countries. Present U.S. policies derive from the consequences of the 1980 boat lift of 125,000 Cubans from the Cuban port of Mariel.

Travel Inside Cuba

Travel by Cubans inside of Cuba is free of restrictions. When persons are lodged for extended periods with family or friends, arrangements for ration cards may have to be made by the latter. Cubans make reservations at hotels or other lodgings through the Instituto Nacional de Turismo.

Cubans are not prohibited by law from changing their places of residence. Nevertheless, the real possibility of changing one's place of residence is limited by government control over housing and employment. Cubans who change their places of residence must register with the CDR's in the new locations.

Cuban Exiles

It is still difficult for Cubans who have declared themselves to be permanent exiles to change their minds and resume their lives as resident Cuban citizens. When people state their intentions to leave the island permanently, they give up their homes and jobs. Government permission to return carries official responsibility to house them and assist them in finding work. If a Cuban residing abroad as an exile requests to return, the decision is transmitted from the Cuban diplomatic office or consul where the request is filed to the Ministry of Foreign Relations and to the Ministry of Interior.

The outcome of this process depends largely on the circumstances under which a person left the island. For example, an individual who left in order to marry an Eastern European and live in the spouse's country usually will have no problem returning if he or she wishes to reside again in Cuba. A Cuban who immigrated to the United States during the 1960's and asks to return, at the very least, will experience considerable delay in obtaining such permission. Cubans claim to fear that Cubans residing in the United States may be used for purposes of espionage, and therefore check requests from such applicants very thoroughly. However, people in the latter category—especially if they left the country while still quite young or are elderly people with family in Cuba— have been able to resume their Cuban citizenship. The group which has encountered the greatest difficulty in obtaining permission to return to Cuba is the most recent group to leave, that is, those who left in the 1980 "boat lift," the so-called "Marielitos."

Cuban exiles with Cuban citizenship, either wishing to return to or to visit Cuba, apply for an ordinary passport at a consular office or other designated office of Cuban representation. These requests are determined by the Ministry of Foreign Relations and the Ministry of Interior, on the basis of information about the applicant and the reasons given for wishing to travel to or reside in Cuba. If the stated reason is to visit family members, the corresponding office of Inmigración y Extranjeria will verify the visit with a member of the named family over 18 years of age. Should the family fail to confirm the visit, the visa request may be denied. Should the family in question wish to invite the visitor to stay in their home, they may do so by formally agreeing to take responsibility for the visitor's food and lodgings during the stated time. Cubans abroad requesting a temporary visa must present their round-trip tickets, or a ticket to a third country outside of Cuba. Temporary visas are given, usually for three-month periods, but may be renewed.

Other Visitors

Individuals traveling to Cuba for reasons other than family visits normally are either the invited guests of an official Cuban organization (e.g. the Communist party, the Ministry of Foreign Relations, the Federation of Cuban Women) or travel as part of an authorized tourist group. In the latter case, the international travel agency organizing the trip works through the Instituto Nacional de Turismo to establish a Programa de Visita. In the past few years, the Cuban tourist office has been able to arrange for individual tourism as well as group travel. Individual tourists may arrive in Havana and then establish their itinerary. Tourists must follow previously established programs in so far as their travel schedules and places of lodging are concerned, but they may substitute scheduled events for other activities, such as visits to friends. As in the case of tourists, invited guests of government or official entities arrange specific travel programs with these entities, but within the parameters of these arrangements they may make use of their free time as they wish, in keeping with Cuban laws.

Foreigners visiting Cuba include invitees and tourists, above, as well as students, clergy, artists, entertainers, journalists and businessmen, who are classified generally as temporary residents. In all cases, the individuals must obtain visas (unless they come from countries with which Cuba has established a Convenio de Extensión de Visado), and they must present round-trip tickets or tickets to other countries (or, alternatively, deposit the equivalent funds). Cuban authorities hold the passports or other documents of these visitors during their stay in Cuba; only people invited by the Cuban Communist party are exempt from this rule.

Persons who come to Cuba and request political asylum or who are granted refugee status by Cuba while outside the country are also considered temporary residents by law. . . . The grant of political asylum or refugee status is, according to statute, a temporary one, and beneficiaries should state their formal intention to return to their own countries as soon as conditions permit. While in Cuba they are provided with places to live and are permitted to work. Refugees and political exiles are given a special document by the Ministry of Foreign Relations attesting to their status.

THE U.S. AND CUBA AND FREEDOM OF MOVEMENT

Historically, the movement of people between the United States and Cuba has been large, and also politically controversial, even prior to the Cuban Revolution. Before 1959, Americans flocked to the island for tourism and gambling and frequently for illicit transactions of various kinds; many Americans, moreover, resided in Cuba, as the owners of large and small rural and urban enterprises. Cubans from middle- and upper-class families, typically, were educated wholly or in part in the United States and they often established business connections with U.S. or U.S.-owned firms. Both these groups, the American owners of property in Cuba and the Cubans who were educated in and economically dependent upon the U.S., by and large, were hostile to the revolution, and opposed it actively. The Cubans in the latter group comprised the majority of the first wave of exiles from Cuba to the United States.

Since the fall of the Batista government, some 10 percent of the Cuban population has left the country, overwhelmingly in order to settle in the United States. Although the first to leave were, in the main, of middle- and upper-class origins, the emigration eventually encompassed all social groups. Between January 1959 and October 1980 over 800,000 Cubans entered the U.S. The peak years of Cuban-U.S. migration occurred from 1959 to the end of 1962, from 1965 to 1973, and in 1980. The first wave came on regularly scheduled air flights, until these were suspended at the time of the Missile Crisis in October 1962. In this first wave, Cuba lost a substantial portion of its better-educated and trained professionals. As of March 1961, approximately 125,000 Cubans were already in the U.S. Some 1,500 of these, trained and equipped by the U.S., participated in an attempt to invade Cuba in an April attack at the Bay of Pigs. The second major wave took place following a mass exodus of Cubans from Camarioca in 1965, which in many ways resembles the Mariel boat lift of 1980. By means of the so-called "freedom flights," U.S. planes, with the permission of the Cuban government, brought Cubans directly to the United States between 1965 and 1973. Again, a disproportionate number of the better-educated and trained members of Cuban society joined the outflow.

Between the end of the "freedom flights" and 1980, relatively few Cubans emigrated to the United States. A number of Cubans who were the immediate relatives of American citizens and who had not previously been able to obtain visas were permitted to leave. Additionally, a few thousand political prisoners were released in order to go into exile. This was a period of slightly improved relations between the two countries, during which the two governments signed an antihijacking agreement (in 1973), established limited diplomatic relations through interest sections which operated in both capitals (in 1977), and for the first time began to work out means of effecting orderly immigration procedures to facilitate family reunification.

Also during this seven-year period, as well, a group of Cubans in the U.S. initiated a direct dialogue with the Cuban government. The most significant outcome of this dialogue was an agreement on the Cuban side to permit nearly all of the U.S.-based exiles to visit the island in order to see their families and to greatly ease the restrictions on Cubans making family visits to the U.S. The family visits benefitted Cuba in easing tensions caused by divided families and in contributing substantial amounts of foreign exchange to the Cuban economy. The new arrangement reflected a recognition on the part of both the U.S. and the Cuban governments that while a majority of the exile community was still hostile to the Cuban Revolution, the hostility was not unanimous. Moreover, even among those still strongly opposed to the Cuban government, the majority did not necessarily oppose talks between the U.S. and Cuba to facilitate travel and family reunification.

The limited détente between the U.S. and Cuba essentially ended by late 1978 when Cuba's military involvement in Africa caused U.S. officials to reject any further steps toward improving relations. Nevertheless, during 1979 some

100,000 Cuban-Americans visited Cuba, in almost all cases for the first time since they had left.

Until 1980, the U.S. and Cuba continued to implement a prisoner release program they had agreed to during 1978. In December 1978, this prisoner release plan was announced as one of the accomplishments of the dialogue between the Cuban-American exiles and the Cuban government. In fact, it had been agreed to prior to the dialogue by the two governments, but, as relations with Cuba worsened again, the U.S. government apparently did not wish to acknowledge that it had been negotiating with the Cuban government. Under the prisoner release agreement, Cubans released a number of political prisoners so that they could leave the island and go to the U.S. The U.S., however, did not process and admit these political prisoners at the rate they had promised. Instead of taking about 400 a month as the Cubans had been led to expect, the U.S. processed no more than about 50 per month. The Cubans encouraged current and former political prisoners to accept the option of exile in the U.S., and were willing to facilitate this exit by releasing some prisoners well before their terms were complete if they could be processed for departure. As Fidel Castro acknowledged in a press conference with Cuban-American journalists on September 8, 1978: ". . . the process of adapting to society is not easy for people who have been sentenced to prison for counterrevolutionary crimes. There's a certain rejection of them, and it is more difficult to find them jobs."

Contacts between Cuban exiles and residents increased as Cuban restrictions on travel to and from the country by nationals were eased. Immigration regulations facilitated family visits for most Cubans, but at the same time they were designed to assure: 1) that certain Cubans whose loyalty was doubted would not use the temporary exit visas they were given in order to remain outside of the country; (2) that Cubans in exile who were considered to be security risks would not be allowed to return to the island; (3) that Cuban nationals wishing to leave the island permanently would not remove those belongings which the Cuban government believed should become State property; and (4) that Cubans whose service or work were considered of great importance to national development (e.g. Cubans of military age, doctors) should not leave permanently without having fulfilled certain obligations.

CONCLUSION

Immigration, like most other issues, has been affected by the fact that Cuban-United States relations are at their lowest point in more than a decade. The serious problems affecting the movement of people between the two countries do not occur to nearly the same degree with regard to the movement of people between Cuba and other countries. It is, however, between Cuba and the U.S. that most of the traffic takes place.

Cuba continues to limit and to tightly control the travel, and especially the emigration, of its citizens. Although most Cubans who are invited out of the country by family or by international entities of some kind do obtain the requisite permission to travel, there have been and continue to be some notable exceptions. Over the years many Cubans judged to be too critical of Cuban policies have had requests to travel denied, but when subsequently invited to other events overseas, considered by Cuban authorities to be important, they have been granted exit visas. The decision-making process in this area is arbitrary, but apparently not highly restrictive.

All Cubans do not have the right to leave and to return to their country. The right to leave has been abridged by formal and informal regulations against the departure of people in certain groups. The right to return has been denied to most Marielitos who might wish to go back, and is only sometimes approved for other Cubans who decide against continued exile.

With regard to the right to leave, it is prohibited for a young man of military age who has not completed his service to leave the country (and there have been cases reported when young men who had completed their military service were denied permission to leave, on grounds that they were of military age). It has been extremely difficult, even if it is not formally prohibited, for medical doctors and certain categories of technicians to emigrate, unless they are elderly, and considered to have few years of productive activity ahead of them. Yet, as Cuba now has trained a full generation of people in these categories, and seems to have sufficient numbers to send as advisors to a number of other countries, restrictions may diminish. (Or, alternatively, as material conditions improve, the demand among these groups to emigrate may diminish.)

Apart from Cuban restrictions on travel, other factors limit the ability of Cuban nationals to emigrate. Most important, migration is influenced by the receiving country's willingness to accept Cubans as immigrants or refugees. Since 1978, the Cuban government has facilitated the departure of political prisoners and former political prisoners through a prisoner release plan, which allows these people to go to the United States as refugees.

Skyline of Havana. Most of the buildings were constructed before 1959. The Havana Libre Hotel, formerly the Havana Hilton, is in the center.

José Martí, father of the Cuban Revolution.

Fidel Castro Ruz, president of the Council of State and Council of Ministers, commander in chief of the Cuban Armed Forces, and first secretary of the Cuban Communist party.

Top Left: Raúl Castro Ruz, first vice-president of the Council of State and Council of Ministers, minister of the Revolutionary Armed Forces, and second secretary of the Cuban Communist party.

Right: Carlos Rafael Rodríguez, vice-president of the Council of State and Council of Ministers, and member of the Political Bureau of the Cuban Communist party.

Bottom Left: Vilma Espín Guillois, president of the Federation of Cuban Women and member of the Political Bureau of the Cuban Communist party.

Top: Nonaligned Summit. The heads of state and foreign ministers of the 92 countries in the Nonaligned Movement met in Havana in 1979, and Fidel Castro served as chair of the movement from 1979 to 1983. Cuba hoped this position would enable it to unify the Third World and make it a stronger force in world politics.

Bottom: Ernesto "Che" Guevara, one of the leaders of the July 26th Movement until his departure in 1965, meeting with peasants in the early 1960s.

Clothing Store. In such a typical store in today's downtown Havana, the average Cuban buys rationed goods, as well as some that are sold at higher prices in unrestricted quantities. Though the variety has increased in the last decade, there is still a limited choice in comparison to capitalist countries.

Pioneers' March. A group of Pioneers—the youth organization in which students receive training in civic awareness and practical skills, and through which they undertake public service projects—march in downtown Havana in 1982 to honor the Congress of the Union of Communist Youth (the Young Communists).

Top: Rebuilding Old Havana. With assistance from UNESCO and Spain, the Cuban government has been renovating the section of Havana that dates from the 16th century.

Middle: Tropicana. The Tropicana night club, perhaps the most famous in Cuba because of its lavish productions, was available only to the wealthy before 1959. Though still expensive today, average Cubans frequent it, often with subsidies from their unions. The productions now incorporate Afro-Cuban themes and have toned down the overtly sexual character of the costumes and choreography.

Bottom: CDR Meeting. On nearly every block in urban areas, and throughout the countryside, local Committees for the Defense of the Revolution meet frequently, as the one pictured here in Havana. Intended initially to protect against counterrevolutionary activity, they operate today as disseminators of public health information, as informal family courts, and as organizers of block activities.

Top: Secondary School in the Countryside. Approximately half of the students from seventh grade on attend boarding schools in the countryside, where they work half the day on agricultural projects and devote half the day to traditional subjects. This school in Matanzas province produced grapefruits, oranges, and tangerines.

Middle: Housing Project. In Santiago the José Martí housing project—begun in the mid-1970s (and seen here in 1980)—houses 30,000 people, most of whom had lived in the slumlike neighborhood adjacent to the project.

Bottom: Fertilizer Plant. This modern, technologically sophisticated plant in Cienfuegos is indicative of the efforts to introduce new techniques for industrial development.

Top: Rural Family. This family of five (two of the children pictured are neighbors) lives in a four-room house about 20 miles from the Bay of Pigs. They built the house themselves, with materials supplied by the state, in a fashion common among peasants who work on collective farms.

Middle: Peasant Home. A typical four-room home in the countryside, this house was photographed in 1974 in Matanzas province.

Bottom: Day-Care Center. This center, in Santiago, is typical of the day-care facilities in the country. It takes in children from the age of 45 days old, and provides complete care for the entire day.

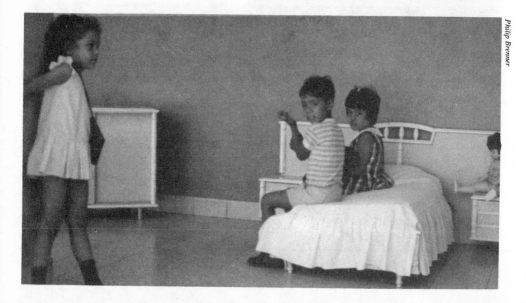

Granma

Top: Baseball. Baseball is the national sport. This photograph was taken during a game for the national championship.

Middle: Billboard. "Teaching is the finest and most beautiful thing in the world." Billboards are used to reproduce a key message from a historic leader, encourage civic virtue, honor a mass organization's activities, and reinforce revolutionary themes and goals.

Bottom: Island of Youth. Folksinger Silvio Rodríguez performs for students on the Island of Youth, where students from other countries study in schools. Rodríguez is part of the New Song movement, which regularly travels throughout the country.

Philip Brenner

ENSEÑAR ES LO MAS BELLO Y HERMOSO DEL MUNDO
JORNADA HOMENAJE AL EDUCADOR   JOSE MARTI
14 AL 22 DE DICIEMBRE

Granma

PART IV

Cuban Foreign Policy

Introduction

From the start, Cuban leaders attempted to endow the revolution with an internationalist spirit, and indeed, the victory in 1959 was due in part to the successful foreign policy of the July 26th Movement. Especially because Cuba is a small country, Cuban foreign policy cannot be segmented neatly from its domestic policy, and its relations with others have been essential to the way in which the revolution has unfolded.

The foremost concern evident in Cuban foreign policy is the security of the revolution, which is linked to, though is not identical with, economic development. Its roots in an ideology of proletarian internationalism provide Cuban foreign policy with an historical framework within which it orients immediate policy: Proletarian internationalism embodies a definition of progress (the decreasing exploitation of the South by the North), a theory of method (the common struggle to end relationships of dependency), and a moral imperative (support for those ideologically sympathetic forces that are engaged in struggle, whether they have state power or are attempting to seize state power).

As a small power, Cuba is severely limited in the way it can pursue these three concerns. Indeed, without the Soviet Union's military and economic assistance, the revolution would have been far different, if it had survived at all. Relations with the Soviet Union, then, have been the most important element of Cuba's foreign policy. Because of its importance to Cuba, the relationship with the Soviet Union raises questions—which we will address—about whether Cuba has replaced its prior dependence (and lack of effective sovereignty) on the United States with a similar dependence on the Soviet Union.

For the U.S. government, this is the central question about Cuba. If Cuba were nothing more than a surrogate for the projection of Soviet force—an often-repeated charge, rooted in the assumption that its alleged dependency necessitates its subservience—then the United States might have reason to be anxious about Cuba's relations with the Third World. In turn, U.S. anxiety becomes the principal source of Cuba's own insecurity, especially in light of U.S. efforts to overthrow and isolate the island.

Cuba acknowledges legitimate security concerns that the United States might have, such as the placement of a Soviet military base on Cuban territory (no Soviet base now exists there). But it perceives that its so-called threat to the United States turns as much on its relationship with the Third World as it does on its ties with the Soviet Union. Indeed, in both Africa and Latin America, Cuba and the United States have been on opposite sides of significant struggles. U.S. policy in Latin America for the last 30 years might even be characterized as a single-minded effort to have "no more Cubas." As a consequence, Cuba shapes its policy in the Third World partly in response to constraints imposed by the United States. Yet it would be more appropriate to describe the policy as emanating from Cuba's vision of progress in the Third World, which Cuban leaders see as ultimately helping to provide for the security and development of the Cuban Revolution.

The readings in this chapter elaborate the issues posed by Cuban foreign policy. Philip Brenner (Reading 29) describes the way in which decisions at the 1986 Third Communist Party Congress maintained the three-decade pattern of pragmatically attempting to secure the revolution and promote development, while fulfilling the Cuban sense of internationalism through its commitments to countries in Africa and Latin America.

Links between ideology and the strategic concerns of the revolution are clearly evident in the reading by Carlos Rafael Rodríguez (Reading 30), who provides the most cogent and authoritative description of the perspective that has guided Cuban foreign policy. Vice-President Rodríguez has had a significant role in directing Cuban foreign policy since 1959. He is one of the only senior members of the pre-1959 Cuban Communist party (known then as the Popular Socialist party) who joined the revolutionary government.

Without question, the Cuban military has been the most important institution affecting Cuban foreign policy. From the Cuban perspective, it has provided Cuba with the capability to deter an attack by the United States. From the perspective of other countries, particularly the United States, the Cuban military distinguishes Cuba from other states its size, and consequently generates concern. In Reading 31, Phyllis Greene Walker carefully describes the organization and various components of the military, and the way it functions in Cuban society.

Edward Gonzalez offers an alternative, and enduring, explanation for the nature of Cuban foreign policy (Reading 32). Instead of focusing on Cuban interests or ideology, he points to the founding fathers of the revolution, the groups of elites who have emerged and attached themselves to particular leaders, and the differences between the various leaders. These differences include varying perceptions of Cuba's interests.

The articles that examine Cuba's relationship with the Soviet Union address basic questions about whether Cuba has served as a Soviet proxy. Vice-President Rodríguez explains that the coincidence between Soviet and Cuban foreign policies should be expected, because they emanate from similar principles (Reading 33). Yet he emphasizes that each country retains its unique interpretation of these, in part because one is a small country and the other is a superpower.

From a different perspective, Robert Pastor reaches a similar conclusion about the similarity of their foreign policies (Reading 34). Outlining the history of their ties, he argues that the two no longer diverge in any substantial way and critiques prevailing metaphors for the relationship. He concludes that Cuba and the Soviet Union have a common set of interests and ideology, and that Cuba does act independently but within bounds established by the Soviet Union.

Yet the ties to the Soviet Union have generated costs. Several of these are discussed by Pamela Falk, in an excerpt (Reading 35) drawn from her detailed study of Cuban foreign policy.

Cuban policy has been affected perhaps as much by the other superpower, the United States. In Reading 36, Philip Brenner briefly describes the history of this mostly hostile relationship since 1959, and focuses on the 1980s. He elaborates the issues that divide the two countries, and observes that U.S. demands would require Cuba to alter itself fundamentally while none of Cuba's demands threaten fundamental U.S. interests.

Three events punctuate U.S.–Cuban history in the last thirty years. The first is the 1961 Bay of Pigs invasion, when U.S.-backed Cuban exiles attempted to overthrow the government by landing 1,500 guerrillas at the Bay of Pigs. In 1962 after the Soviets began to place ballistic missiles on the island, the Cuban missile crisis brought the United States and Soviet Union to the brink of nuclear confrontation. Finally, the 1980 Mariel exodus exacerbated tensions when 120,000 Cubans came to the United States in small boats over a four-month period. The first event is described in Reading 37, essentially from the Cuban perspective, by the late Herbert Matthews, whose reporting from Cuba for the *New York Times* in 1958 influenced America's perception of the revolutionaries and of the Batista dictatorship. Scott Armstrong and Philip Brenner focus on the danger of the missile crisis (Reading 38), and draw new lessons from that confrontation. Barry Sklar's analysis of the Mariel exodus (Reading 39) provides both solid details about the events and places it into a larger context of the increasing hostility between the United States and Cuba at the time.

Kenneth Skoug, Jr., who headed the Office of Cuban Affairs in the U.S. State Department from 1982 until mid-1988, outlines the official U.S. policy on Cuba in Reading 40. He emphasizes that it is Cuba's international behavior that principally concerns the United States, and that must change before the United States would be willing to normalize relations.

Where the United States and Cuba come into greatest conflict is in the Third World. Since 1959, Cuba has played a prominent role in Third World politics. It was the only Latin American country among the 25 founding members of the Nonaligned Movement (NAM) in 1961, and Fidel Castro (representing Cuba) was the chair of the Movement from 1979 to 1983. As chief of the U.S. Interests Section in Havana, Wayne Smith observed the 1979 NAM summit, and pointedly walked out of the meeting when Castro attacked the United States. Yet he carefully explains (Reading 41) that while Cuba's international political activities at times may serve Soviet interests, they first and foremost serve Cuba's interests. Cuba, he argues, does not act as a Soviet stalking horse in the Nonaligned Movement.

William LeoGrande's major study about Cuban policy in Africa, from which Reading 42 is drawn, describes the evolution and implementation of aid to two countries: Angola and Ethiopia. In both cases, Cuba acted along with the Soviet Union, yet with a significant measure of independence. As Leo-Grande's detailed analysis demonstrates, the benefits and costs—indeed, Cuba's calculus of interests—varied in each case and over time.

Cuba's relations with Latin America have been uneven, though today it considers good state-to-state relations with countries in the hemisphere to be an essential building block in its foreign policy. The way in which Cuba perceives its ties to the region are described by Rafael Hernández in Reading 43. He focuses on the changes in Latin America and the Third World that have brought the countries closer to Cuba and made all of the region akin to Cuba—as if they were all frontier states of the United States. In Reading 44, H. Michael Erisman describes the key period when Latin American countries began to reestablish ties to Cuba and reintegrate it into the hemispheric system. As his history explains, Cuba's relations with countries in the region reflected its nationalistic foreign policy.

One element of Cuba's activities in Central America is its nonmilitary aid. As Donna Rich observes (Reading 45), construction, education, and health programs, in general, receive far less notice than Cuba's military aid abroad. But they constitute as significant a part of Cuba's outreach to the Third World. She first describes the programs and then rounds out the foreign policy chapter by explaining how they emanate from the intersection of Cuba's geopolitical, economic, and ideological interests.

CHAPTER 10

Cuban Foreign Relations: An Overview

29. *Change and Continuity in Cuban Foreign Policy**

BY PHILIP BRENNER

Cuban foreign policy has been animated by two goals: the security and development of the revolution. Implementation of these objectives has been shaped by the nature of the threats against Cuba, and by the nature of the world economy. It has also been affected by the mix of Cuba's internationalist ideology and its characteristic pragmatism.

For Cubans, security and economic development are entwined notions, since they see the security of the revolution intimately linked to the strength of their economy. Their ability to achieve high health standards, universal literacy, decent housing, and so on—all of which strengthen the revolution, increase its legitimacy, and make it less susceptible to attack—is compromised by their difficulty in obtaining hard currency, and by indirect attacks, such as the U.S. economic embargo. Of course, the primary threat to their security would be a direct military attack, which would likely destroy the revolution. But their very fear of attack stifles development because it leads them to devote scarce resources to military preparedness.

These factors help to account for Cuba's relationship with the Soviet Union, a relationship that has preoccupied the United States. Without Soviet military assistance, Cuba would have been quite vulnerable to an invasion. Meanwhile, Soviet economic assistance has enabled Cuba to proceed with development

*This essay was written for this volume. Copyright 1988 by Philip Brenner.

plans. Moreover, the relationship with the Soviet Union brought Cuba into the socialist economic bloc, which gave her a set of international trading partners to replace those that vanished when U.S.-led Western nations closed their markets.

As with any ties, the links to the East have had effects on Cuban development. Cuba is dependent on imports for several essential goods, such as oil, and so it must be able to produce goods that, in effect, are used in exchange for the imports. Thus, like most small countries, outside markets affect Cuba's economic decisions. In its case, choices about which goods to produce are dominated by the "demand" of the socialist countries, because most of Cuba's foreign trade occurs with them. Close contact with the Eastern-bloc countries also has led Cuba to borrow economic models from them. Finally, and not surprisingly, because of the importance of these ties to Cuban security and development, Cuba also has constrained its international behavior at times to conform to the interests of the Soviet Union.

In a sense, then, Cuba's relations with both superpowers have influenced the course of the revolution. Yet, Cuba has maintained its own ideological perspective throughout. It is a vision of Third World solidarity, with an emphasis on socialist development. Cuba emphasizes its ties both to Africa—much of its population descends from slaves originating in Africa—and to Latin America. It has aid programs throughout both regions, where Cuban soldiers also have died in combat.

Internationalism in its foreign policy has taken many forms: support for guerrillas attempting to overthrow governments in Latin America, the deployment of troops in defense of governments in Africa, and the pursuit of Third World diplomatic initiatives through the Nonaligned Movement. Some of these activities have incurred significant costs, and have weakened Cuba's pursuit of security and development. Cuba's activities in Latin America, for example, led the Organization of American States to suspend its membership and endorse the U.S. embargo. Yet, Cuba perceives internationalism to be a framework that ultimately serves its two goals. If it can diversify its dependency, which would mean relying on Third World as well as industrialized nations, it is less likely to be submerged by the interests of either superpower. Furthermore, as a small country, it expects that it is more likely to find succor from other small countries with similar developmental perspectives than from advanced industrialized nations.

This ideology does not create a rigid, dogmatic set of formulas. Indeed, a hallmark of the Cuban Revolution is its pragmatism in pursuit of its two primary goals. For example, Cuba maintained good relations with Spain under the Franco dictatorship, because Franco did not follow the U.S. embargo. In Latin America, with the rise of left-leaning governments during the 1970s, Cuba largely abandoned its support of guerrillas and emphasized state-to-state relations.

The interplay of these factors can be seen in recent Cuban decisions. Most prominently, the Third Congress of the Cuban Communist Party (held in February and December 1986) focused on problems of economic efficiency, and linked this concern to its affirmation of a decision to integrate Cuba more fully into the socialist economic bloc, the Council for Mutual Economic Assistance (CMEA). It also approved plans to restructure Cuba's defense posture and simultaneously diminished the military's power within the Communist party. Finally, it reaffirmed existing commitments in Latin America and Africa.

INCREASING TIES TO THE SOCIALIST BLOC

Cuba had been trading with the Eastern European socialist countries since 1960, but until the 1980s, it had not coordinated its own economic plans fully with those of the CMEA countries. Once it did so, Cuba needed to improve its reliability as a supplier: Inefficiency had weakened Cuba's ability to meet production targets. Full integration into the CMEA meant that Cuba would plan its economy in accord with the socialist nations, and expect to depend on them for many of its imports.

Yet, the CMEA countries do not satisfy all of Cuba's needs, so Cuba also seeks to import some goods from the West, for which it needs internationally convertible ("hard") currency. Increased efficiency would also enable Cuba to export more to the West, earn more hard currency, and increase the rate at which it could substitute domestic goods for imports.

In announcing the decision to tie Cuba more tightly into the CMEA network, Castro said:

> Priority will be given to developing the machine and electronics industry, light industry, pharmaceuticals, biotechnology, and sugarcane by-products as important areas that will generate new exports. . . . Agricultural development will be stepped up . . . contributing to more exports of traditional agricultural products.[1]

In effect, the economic plan calls for Cuba to remain a supplier nation of raw materials under an international socialist division of labor. It would be expected to increase its sugar, citrus, tobacco, and nickel deliveries to CMEA countries, and to do so on a well-regulated schedule.

Cuba's international economic posture is reflected in part in the size of its external debt. Its balance of payments deficit with the West has been $500 million annually, and it owes Western banks $3.5 billion.[2] Yet, in contrast to other countries in the region, Cuba compares favorably. Latin American external debt is $400 billion. No Latin American country experienced as high a rate of growth, and in the same period the average gross domestic product for Latin America as a whole was virtually unchanged.[3]

Certainly, part of the stability of Cuba's growth can be attributed to Cuba's special relationship with the Soviet Union.[4] (See also Chapter 11.) By some accounts, Soviet price subsidies on Cuba's export of sugar and import of oil, along with direct economic assistance, amount to more than $4 billion annually.[5] While Cuba suffered along with other sugar-producing countries in Latin America when the world price dropped below four cents, it was reselling perhaps as much as two thirds of its Soviet oil shipments for a handsome profit. More than a third of Cuba's hard currency earnings were derived from the sale of oil in the mid-1980s.[6]

Here lay one source of its economic worries. As the price of oil on the international market dropped, Cuba needed to increase its export of other goods to the West in order to obtain hard currency. Trade with capitalist countries had declined from a high of 40.5 percent of all Cuban trade in 1975 to 15 percent in 1985. This problem required immediate attention, and so it dominated the Third Communist Party Congress.

It would be reasonable to expect that with even closer economic ties to the Soviet trading bloc, there will be some added Soviet influence on Cuban policies. Yet past practice suggests that Cuban foreign policy will not be a slave to Soviet whim. As Wayne Smith observes, Cuba

has its own interests and objectives—which may differ markedly from those of the Soviet Union—and within the parameters defined by its relationship with Moscow, it pursues its own agenda in its own way.[7]

To be sure, Cuba has acted against some of its own interests at the behest of its patron. Most prominently, when Cuba refused to condemn the 1979 Soviet invasion of Afghanistan, it lost credibility as a leader of the nonaligned countries, especially because Fidel Castro was president of the Movement at the time. But the notion that Cuba is a "proxy" state for the Soviet Union has been discredited by evidence of significant differences between the two countries.[8] In Angola, for example, Cuba differed with the Soviet Union over the backing of a threatened coup against Agostinho Neto. In Ethiopia, while Cuban troops fought under the Soviet Union's general command, the two countries differed over military involvement against the Eritrean rebels. (See also Reading 42.)

The relationship between Cuba and the Soviet Union is best characterized as two sovereign countries with compatible and often complementary interests. One indication of this is that Cuba has influenced Soviet foreign policy. It seems clear, now, that the Cubans convinced the Soviets to provide full support for the MPLA [Popular Movement for the Liberation of Angola] in Angola after Cuba had made its own commitments.[9] In Grenada, from 1979 to 1983, Cuba appears to have acted as a "broker" for the Grenadians, trying to secure assistance from a reticent Soviet Union.[10]

A continuing Cuban concern is the Soviet Union's still ambiguous commitment to defend Cuba. In a recent book on Cuban foreign policy, Michael Erisman observes:

As long as Moscow refuses to give Cuba an open, ironclad guarantee that it will respond to any U.S. attack on the island with whatever protective counterforce is necessary, the Fidelistas can never feel truly safe.[11]

Of course, the Soviet Union has provided Cuba with enormous military capabilities, including several versions of the MiG-23, the best Soviet tanks, surface-to-surface missiles, and an assortment of arms. From 1981 to 1985, moreover, the Soviet Union doubled the average annual tonnage of military equipment it sent to Cuba. (See also Reading 31.) However, the logistics of defending Cuba over a long distance, the reasonable Cuban skepticism about Soviet willingness to risk a wider war in the event of an attack, and the lack of an overt promise make Cuban leaders wary about relying wholly on Soviet defenses.

STRENGTHENING MILITARY PREPAREDNESS

Their worry, in part, led to changes in the structure of the Cuban military forces over the last five years, which were reflected in the second set of decisions at the party congress. The armed forces lost representation on the party's Central Committee, and its responsibility as the primary agent of the country's defense was diluted by the importance accorded to the recently expanded militia. This apparent change in the military's prominence could affect its influence in foreign policy decision-making.

The tradition of Cuban military involvement in the running of government dates back nearly to the start of the century. Since 1959 the Revolutionary Armed Forces (FAR) has been the most powerful organization in Cuba besides the Communist party.[12] The leaders of the guerrilla army, which the FAR replaced, became the leaders of the present regime. As in the guerrilla army, responsibilities often have overlapped between the military and civilian sectors.

In light of its power and prominence, therefore, the reduction in FAR representation from 50 to 34 members on the 225-person Central Committee is striking. At the end of the second party congress, 27 percent of the Central Committee were military officers; now it is 15 percent.[13] The loss of representation not only diminishes the military's power within this major policy-making body but it also reduces the military's aura of being the primary route to power for subsequent generations, thereby reducing its influence at all levels of the society.

The official explanation for the reduction has been that the party sought to increase the proportion of members from underrepresented sectors of society while it held the size of the Central Committee constant. (See also Reading 20.) Indeed, party leaders did want to signal to a new generation that the system was not closed, that there was place for both mobility and disagreement. Repeatedly, there had been talk of the need for "socialismo sin sociolismo," that is, socialism based on firmer ground than an old-boy network or personal relations. The most dramatic decision in this regard was the dismissal of Ramiro Valdés Menendez, the Interior Minister, who had been one of the founding fathers of the revolution in 1953.[14]

However, this rationale begs the question of why the military bore such a large brunt of the redistribution, or why maintaining a fixed Central Committee size took precedence over retaining FAR influence on the committee. A more likely explanation is that the party sought to reduce the military's role in national security and in civilian affairs. With probable resistance because of the military's diminished authority, the party undoubtedly needed to undermine the FAR's representation in order to effect its decision.

Indeed, it took extraordinary leverage for the party to develop a new institution—Territorial Troops Militia (MTT)—which now shares the FAR's essential responsibility for defending the island. This new mode of territorial defense, characterized as a "people in arms," envisions an invasion by the United States that would be countered by protracted warfare from citizen-guerrillas. The principal task of the regular army would be merely to provide sufficient time for the militia to mobilize.

There are now 1.5 million members of the MTT. It has light infantry weapons and combat equipment, receives periodic training, and accounts for an increasing portion of the military budget.[15]

President Castro described the change to editors of the *Washington Post* in 1985. "Before," he said, "war was the job of the army and the reserves, while the rest of the citizens did nothing more than watch what went on; today, it is the concern of every citizen."[16] He now heads an informal Council of Defense, accountable to the party, which would run military operations in the event of an attack.

Grenada confirmed a decision made in 1981 to abandon sole reliance on the FAR for Cuba's defense, and to complement it with the MTT. (See Reading 31.) While the FAR garnered respect for its Angolan and Ethiopian operations, there was condemnation of the military's inaction during the 1983 U.S. invasion of Grenada. Rag-tag Cuban construction workers, not the polished military advisors, resisted the U.S. Marines; the advisors surrendered quickly, and the officers in charge were disgraced upon their return to Cuba.

The 1981 decision to create the MTT was made because the Cubans believed that a U.S. invasion was a real possibility during the Reagan Administration. Moreover, a feeble Soviet leadership obsessed with the Polish crisis was not a source of strong support. Thus, in 1981 Cuba requested increased arms from the Soviet Union for the MTT, which accounts for much of the growth in shipments since then.[17] The Grenada invasion led Cuba to speed up development of the militia, because it enhanced fears that the military had grown complacent and that the FAR's concept of defense might not serve to deter an invasion.

Cuba has now developed what might be called the "Swiss" form of deterrence against invasion.[18] Were any country even to contemplate an attack, it would need to consider that the Cubans could have a force of armed people on their beaches larger than any likely landing party. In addition, the MTT enables Cuba to maintain military forces abroad without threatening the security of the island. The largest number of Cuban forces is in Africa.

AFRICA

Cuba has economic assistance programs and military advisors in seventeen African countries.[19] There are approximately 5,000 Cuban soldiers still in Ethiopia.[20] But its largest commitment remains to Angola, where an estimated 400,000 troops already have served and a force of 35,000 to 40,000 continues to provide support for the government.[21] The party congress approved a resolution that reasserted "Cuba's unbreakable solidarity with the Angolan revolution," and implied endorsement of a long-term Cuban presence there.[22]

Castro went even further in his closing speech, and for the first time linked the withdrawal of Cuban troops to the end of apartheid in South Africa. "There is," he said,

> a perfect and very just formula in Angola. If U.N. Resolution No. 435 is applied and if apartheid is suspended, on the following day, the Cuban troops begin their total withdrawal from Angola.[23]

Cuba and Angola had reached an agreement in November 1984 that specified the conditions to be met prior to Cuba's military departure. In addition to the implementation of U.N. Resolution 435 with respect to the independence of Namibia, it included the complete withdrawal of South African troops from Angola and suspension of aid to the UNITA guerrillas. At that point, under the agreement, Cuba would phase the removal of its troops, though Castro later suggested that up to 10,000 soldiers might remain to guard airports, the capital, and the Chevron/Gulf Oil operations in Cabinda. By 1988, however, Cuba agreed in principle to remove all of its troops from Angola, after negotiations between Angola and the United States indicated that the United States might cease funding the UNITA guerrillas and recognize Angola if Cuba withdrew its forces. This was consistent with Cuba's often-stated policy that it would maintain troops in Angola only as long as they were requested by the Angolan government.[24]

LATIN AMERICA

To say that Cuba has had an uneven relationship with countries in the hemisphere over the last 25 years would be at best understating the obvious. While it sought to be a leader and champion of Latin America, Cuba also became a pariah for its support of revolutionary movements. In the 1970s, however, Cuba emphasized the importance of state-to-state relations, as conditions in the hemisphere changed. Socialist or left governments gained power in major countries such as Chile, Peru, and Venezuela, and in smaller nations of the Caribbean basin. Cuba began to develop new links in the hemisphere, and by 1975 the Organization of American States voted to lift its embargo against Cuba and permit countries to renew economic and political relations.

This warming trend was disrupted at the start of the 1980s by four factors. First, Cuba's refusal to condemn the Soviet invasion of Afghanistan resurrected some ill will, especially among Latin American members of the Nonaligned Movement. Notably, Cuba did not receive strong hemispheric support in its bid for the Latin American seat on the U.N. Security Council, despite its chairmanship of the Nonaligned Movement. Second, Cuba antagonized Peru and Venezuela in its handling of embassy incidents that led to the 1980 Mariel exodus. (Relations with Venezuela had been tense already because of Venezuela's refusal to expedite prosecution of three terrorists involved in the 1976 bombing of a Cuban airliner that killed 73 people.) Third, the election of conservative governments in countries with which Cuba had begun to establish good relations—such as Colombia, Costa Rica, Jamaica, and St. Lucia—reversed these movements. Finally, the Reagan Administration made strong efforts to isolate Cuba.

For Cuba, the situation was untenable. Cuba placed a high value on good relations with Latin America, because it saw the area both as critical for its security and as an essential aspect of its internationalism. Therefore, Cuba made extraordinary efforts to regain the ground it had lost.

The turnaround started with the 1982 Malvinas/Falklands War, during which Cuba offered to provide military assistance to Argentina. By 1985, Argentina had surpassed Mexico as Cuba's largest trading partner in the region, and was supplying it with millions of dollars in new credits.[25] The emergence of new democracies also fueled the trend to warmer relations. Brazil, Uruguay, and Bolivia began to reestablish diplomatic and commercial contacts in 1984. Today, Cuba has full diplomatic relations with 15 countries in the hemisphere (including Canada and Mexico), and varying degrees of relations with ten others. In part, these countries played the Cuba card for domestic political purposes, as a way of providing a symbolic reward to the left. Relations with Cuba were also a means of demonstrating a country's independence from the United States.

One aspect of the outreach to Latin America has been Cuba's opening toward the Cuban Catholic church. It provides a potential bridge to Latin American countries, and repression of Catholics in Cuba had been one obstacle in the way of Cuba's rapprochement with the Catholic countries in the region. Notably, Castro lauded liberation theology in his Main Report to the Third Communist Party Congress. Two weeks after the February session of the party congress, almost 200 Catholic bishops, clergy and lay people held an unprecedented conference in Havana to discuss Christian life in Cuba.

Less successful have been Cuban moves to lead Latin America on the matter of foreign debt. What at first appeared to be a brilliant means of uniting Latin American countries around a common objective, Cuba's call for debt repudiation has since gained little ground. At a mid-1985 conference on the debt, there were no government officials of any Latin American nation, though the major debtors did send delegations.[26] In part, Latin American leaders pointed to Cuba's own unwillingness to repudiate its debt to Western banks, which it worked hard to reschedule several times in the 1980s. They also were reluctant to undercut the newly elected Peruvian president, Alan García, who had made resolution of the debt crisis his focus too. Paradoxically, while Cuba was denied approval for its strong stance, it gave added credibility to García's radical formulation by making the Peruvian's plan seem more moderate. Still, Castro recognized that the debt issue did not provide useful returns, and he did not dwell on it in his Main Report to the congress. He merely reiterated his call for the

> governments of the developed creditor countries [to] assume the debts of Third World countries, with their own banks, and that 12 percent of what is now invested in military expenditures be used to pay off the debts.[27]

However, there was no reticence in his support for the Nicaraguan government. Castro promised that "if they [the U.S.] increase the aid for the Somocist bands, we will do everything possible to step up our aid for the Nicaraguan people."[28] In his Main Report, he compared Nicaragua's revolution to Cuba's, and pointed to the aid rendered by Cuban "teachers, doctors, construction workers, technical personnel and—no need to hide it—military and security advisors." The congress followed suit with a resolution that "reiterates its full support for the FSLN [Sandinista National Liberation Front] and the Nicaraguan revolutionaries."[29] One U.S. official observed that the congress underscored the "central importance" Nicaragua holds for Cuba.

According to official Managua accounts, there are about 800 Cuban military personnel in Nicaragua, and probably more in light of the high-level Cuban commanders who have been resident there. In all, approximately 8,000 Cubans are providing economic and military assistance. But significantly, there is no Cuban commitment to fight by Nicaragua's side were it invaded, because that would expose Cuba itself to unacceptable risks of a wider war. This is one reason Cuba repeatedly endorsed the Contadora negotiations, and has expressed its willingness to abide by any treaty that would require the removal of all foreign militaries from Central America. Cuba also endorsed the Arias peace plan, approved by the Central American countries in August, 1987.

Writing in 1978, Jorge Domínguez observed that "the survival of revolutionary rule remains the foremost objective of their [Cuban] foreign policy."[30] Nothing has happened since then to contradict his conclusion, and the Third

Party Congress only adds further evidence to buttress it. Increased Cuban integration in the CMEA and the restructuring of the military are actions that reflect a search for security. It would be reasonable to associate Cuba's move toward the Eastern bloc in the last five years with the increased threat posed by the U.S. during that time.

While Cuba views the United States with apprehension—references to "Yankee imperialism" run throughout the party congress documents—it also has the capacity now to be flexible with respect to the United States. Notably, the party congress endorsed efforts to establish normal relations with the United States. Cuba's flexibility comes from its strength. It has achieved many developmental goals, especially with respect to health and education, and has less to fear in opening up to the United States. Its ties to the Soviet Union, while providing an imperfect security umbrella, continue to give Cuba the wherewithal to deter an invasion and to maintain steady economic growth. Replacement of the second tier of the Communist party's leadership and reforming the role of the military give Cuba a sense that the revolution has been institutionalized and will endure. Cuba's renewed links to Latin America, and outreach to the Catholic church, reflect a dynamism and pragmatism that could be applied to efforts at normalizing relations with the United States.

Cuba recognizes that as a developing country it cannot be economically independent. But when world economic conditions in the mid-1970s gave it some freedom to choose, Cuba opted to diversify its dependency between East and West. It has generally defined its security in terms of not being dependent on a sole source of sustenance. The pragmatic pursuit of such diversity to secure and develop the revolution, and to fulfill its sense of obligation to international socialist solidarity, is likely to mark the continuing pattern of Cuban foreign policy.

NOTES

1. Fidel Castro, "Main Report to the Third Congress of the Communist Party of Cuba," *Granma Weekly Review* (February 16, 1986), p. 9. Castro also exclaimed: "Equal importance is attached to ensuring our country's contribution to the Comprehensive Plan for Scientific and Technological Development up to the year 2000 recently adopted by the CMEA. . . ." (p. 8)

2. Roger Lowenstein, "Castro Looks to West for Help in Bolstering Sick Cuban Economy," *Wall Street Journal* (June 18, 1985), p. 1; Alfonso Chardy, "For Cuban economy, '85 was a very bad year," *Miami Herald* (January 26, 1986), p. 30A.

3. Andres Oppenheimer, "Latin exports to show 9% decline," *Miami Herald* (December 16, 1985), Business Monday section, p. 24; Inter-American Development Bank, *Economic and Social Progress in Latin America: 1985 Report* (Washington: Inter-American Development Bank, 1985), p. 388.

4. Cole Blasier, "Comecon in Cuban Development," in Cole Blasier and Carmelo Mesa-Lago, eds., *Cuba in the World,* (Pittsburgh: University of Pittsburgh Press, 1979).

5. The measurement of this subsidy is much in dispute among economists, and depends on calculations of what the Soviet Union and Cuba might obtain, respectively, for their products on the international market. For example, if the typically high "spot" market price for oil is used

as a basis for calculating how much less Cuba pays for oil from the Soviet Union than it would pay otherwise, the subsidy would appear larger than if lower, long-term contract prices are used.

6. Jose de Cordoba, "Nose dive in world oil prices puts Cuba economy over barrel," *Miami Herald* (April 12, 1986), p. 12A. Also, interview with Cuban official, 1986.

7. Wayne S. Smith, "The Cuba-Soviet Alliance," unpublished paper prepared for Johns Hopkins University-DISEU Conference (March 19–23, 1986, Havana, Cuba), p. 2. Similarly, Mark Katz contends, "Soviet and Cuban foreign policies have since the late 1960s served mainly to support each other." See, "The Soviet-Cuban Connection," *International Security* (Summer 1983), p. 101. Also, see Reading 34.

8. William M. LeoGrande, "Cuba," in Morris Blachman, William LeoGrande, and Kenneth Sharpe, eds., *Confronting Revolution* (New York: Pantheon, 1986), pp. 250–252.

9. M. Katz, "The Soviet-Cuban Connection," pp. 94–96; Jorge I. Domínguez, "Cuban Foreign Policy," *Foreign Affairs* (Fall, 1978), pp. 96–97.

10. Lourdes Meluza, "Cuba was 'broker' for Grenada in Soviet dealings, scholar says," *Miami Herald* (August 19, 1985), p. 1B.

11. H. Michael Erisman, *Cuba's International Relations* (Boulder, CO: Westview, 1985), p. 175. Also, see M. Katz, "The Soviet-Cuban Connection," p. 105.

12. For a good discussion of the military's role in foreign policy, see Jorge I. Domínguez, "The Armed Forces and Foreign Relations," in C. Blasier and C. Mesa-Lago, *Cuba in the World*.

13. In the 1980s their number actually increased to over 30 percent of the Central Committee. Phyllis Greene Walker, "National Security," in James Rudolph, ed., *Cuba: A Country Study,* U.S. Army Foreign Area Studies Handbook (Washington, DC: 1987), p. 247. In what was undoubtedly an attempt to console the FAR, General Abelardo Colome Ibarra was promoted to full member status on the Political Bureau.

14. A similar message was sent by the removal of hard-line Central Committee ideologist Antonio Pérez Herrero. See, Lourdes Meluza, "Castro has purged nine top officials, experts say," *Miami Herald* (July 23, 1985), p. 9A.

15. Juan del Aguila, "Political Developments in Cuba," *Current History,* January, 1986, pp. 14–15; "Main Report," *Granma Weekly Review* (February 16, 1986), p. 10.

16. "Entrevista con los periodistas del Washington Post," *Granma* (February 11, 1985), as quoted in Ignacio Ramonet, "Cuba: Renovation Dans La Revolution?" *Le Monde Diplomatique* (September 1985), p. 3. [Translation from the French by Philip Brenner.]

17. Ramonet, "Cuba: Renovation Dans La Revolution?" p. 2; also interviews with Cuban officials, 1986.

18. George Kennan provides an interesting theoretical discussion of this notion of deterrence, though without reference to Cuba, in "A New Philosophy of Defense," *New York Review of Books,* February 13, 1986, pp. 3–6.

19. Pamela S. Falk, "Cuba in Africa," *Foreign Affairs,* Vol. 65, No. 5 (Summer 1987), p. 1087.

20. Alfonso Chardy, "Cuban: Pullout from Angola is unlikely soon," *Miami Herald* (March 27, 1985), p. 18A.

21. P. S. Falk, "Cuba in Africa," p. 1084. Also see, Jim Hoagland, "Castro Outlines Goals in Africa," *Washington Post* (February 6, 1985), p. 1.

22. "PCC Foreign Policy Resolution," Havana Radio Rebelde Network (February 7, 1986); FBIS Daily Report Latin America (February 7, 1986), p. Q 72.

23. "Fidel Castro's Closing Speech," Havana International Service (February 8, 1986), FBIS Daily Report Latin America (February 10, 1986), p. Q 36.

24. J. Hoagland, "Castro Outlines Goals in Africa," p. 13; David B. Ottaway, "Cubans, Angolans Agree to Total Troop Withdrawal," *Washington Post,* February 2, 1988, p. A12.

25. Joseph B. Treaster, "Castro, Once Isolated, Forms New Bonds in South America," *New York Times* (May 19, 1985), p. 1. Also, see Mimi Whitefield, "New Latin democracies warm to Cuba," *Miami Herald* (March 23, 1985), p. 1; Boris Yopo H., "El reacercamiento de Cuba con America Latina," *Cono Sur* (Santiago de Chile) (January-March 1986), pp. 9–11.

26. Sam Dillon, "Castro vents frustration as debt parley fizzles," *Miami Herald* (July 30, 1985), p. 3A; Edward Cody, "Castro Takes Up Cause of Latin American Debtors," *Washington Post* (July 3, 1985), p. A19.

27. "Main Report," *Granma Weekly Review* (February 16, 1986), p. 19.

28. "Fidel Castro's Closing Speech," FBIS Daily Report Latin America (February 10, 1986), p. Q 36. Also, see Sam Dillon, "Cuba: We'll back Managua," *Miami Herald* (February 22, 1986), p. 1.

29. "Main Report," *Granma Weekly Review* (February 16, 1986), p. 18; "PCC Foreign Policy Resolution," FBIS Daily Report Latin America (February 7, 1986), p. Q 71.

30. J. I. Domínguez, "Cuban Foreign Policy," p. 84.

30. Strategic Foundations of Cuban Foreign Policy

BY CARLOS RAFAEL RODRÍGUEZ
Translation by ESTI (Cuban government service)

The international policy of the Cuban State is based on the Marxist conception that links historical development with class struggle. According to the theses we advocate, class struggle occurs both at the local level—within national societies—and internationally. As of 1917, and in increasing measure as the number of socialist countries has increased, class struggle on a world level has been evidenced in the essential historical contradiction that characterizes our times and that opposes capitalism and socialism as antagonistic systems.

Our Marxist conception of history sets down another premise: The historical trend of contemporary societies—that is, that the capitalist process in its imperialist stage and the contraposition of the capitalist and socialist systems —makes the world move towards socialism.

This affirmation often leads to the error of considering this trend as inexorable, automatic and fatal. Actually, it is not that the world necessarily *must* become socialist, come what may, as the outcome of a successive chain of historical events independent of man's will. This mechanical and linear inter-

*From *Cuba Socialista* (Havana), December, 1981, pp. 10–33. Edited for this volume. Vice-President Rodríguez is a member of the Political Bureau and the Secretariat of the Central Committee of the Communist Party of Cuba.—eds.

pretation of progress is alien to Marxism. What our materialist theory assumes is that imperialist capitalism creates, on the one hand, the *objective* conditions that make transition toward socialism *possible* and *necessary* as a consequence of the general crisis of the capitalist system; and, on the other, that this very crisis—operating through class struggle—creates, in turn, the *subjective* conditions for people's action (the action of social groups and classes) aimed at defeating capitalism on a world scale and establishing socialism as the dominant system to replace it.

For this *possibility* to become *reality,* there must be conscious action by the revolutionary social classes both domestically and internationally.[1]

This is the basis of our international positions. The Programmatic Platform and the Thesis "On International Policy" of the First Congress of the Communist Party of Cuba clearly stated that the Cuban Revolution's essential objective in this sphere was to contribute to the cause of socialism. The decision to subordinate—in the development of our foreign policy—"the interests of Cuba to the general interests of the struggle for socialism and communism, national liberation, the defeat of imperialism and the elimination of colonialism, neocolonialism and all forms of exploitation and discrimination of peoples and men . . ."[2] was categorically affirmed. This commitment calls for a simultaneous struggle for peace, an objective that in today's conditions, is inseparable from the struggle for socialism and communism. . . .

The fundamental strategic premise of our foreign policy, namely that history moves toward socialism, presupposes a permanent head-on struggle against imperialism and its many manifestations.

It should also be noted that this struggle is irreversible. The Marxist conception of history entails acceptance of the thesis that in order to go from capitalism to socialism a *revolutionary rupture* must occur. It would be unrealistic, antihistorical, to deny that many elements of capitalist society will pass on to the future socialist society. It must be stressed, however, that the *revolutionary rupture* must occur, even in the exceptional event that socialism is attained through peaceful means, even through parliamentarian channels.

But the fact that the contradiction between socialism and capitalism is unavoidable does not mean that it will have to be settled through an armed conflict. We Marxist-Leninists have always shunned the idea of global conflict as the path toward socialism. Cuban Communists consider that the contribution to the victory of socialism is therefore absolutely compatible—*we might even say necessarily compatible*—with peaceful coexistence. This is why, as was stated before, the struggle for peace—in its widely varying manifestations—is an essential element in the strategic objectives of our international policy.

But at the same time, we do not consider peaceful coexistence as a conciliatory compromise leading to immobility. Peaceful coexistence between the two antagonistic systems implies not only the continuation of the ideological struggle, but sustained class struggle as well, both locally and internationally. The

U.S. imperialists' idea of imposing their concept of peaceful coexistence between them and the Soviet Union as an agreement that would result in a
partitioning of "spheres of influence," or a compromise that would force the
peoples fighting for national independence and socialism to slacken or even
halt their struggle is totally unacceptable. These struggles in which imperialism is the main enemy—not only will continue, but they will become more and
more intensified.

Here another strategic premise of the Cuban Revolution's foreign policy
finds its place: internationalism.

It is Cuba's duty to exercise—and it always will—revolutionary proletarian
internationalism. This is one of its essential forms of contributing to the
historical victory of socialism over capitalism. It is not merely an act of
identification and sympathy. It is also a duty tied to our entire strategic
conception.

"Imperialism" is thus our historical enemy. But what do we understand by
"imperialism"? Of course, we are referring to the system as a whole. It is not
a matter of defeating only the U.S. imperialists and leaving imperialism intact
in the rest of the world. However, appropriate strategic consideration compels
us to clearly identify the true enemy we must overcome.

And the first thing that Leninism teaches us is that, although imperialism
is a *system,* this system is not a single, homogeneous entity, rather a set of not
only heterogeneous but essentially contradictory elements. . . .

The idea of making full use of inter-imperialist contradictions is present in
all of Lenin's works pertaining to that period. . . .

Examples of Lenin's masterly strategic and tactical use of the inevitable
contradictions within the imperialist system in favor of the survival of the new
socialist state would fill volumes.

From its inception, the Cuban Revolution, under the guidance of Comrade
Fidel Castro and the group of revolutionaries who rallied around him, and
later under the leadership of a Communist party whose main guide is Fidel,
has taken as the basis for its foreign policy the same strategic foundations put
forth by Lenin.

In the strictest loyalty to principles, without making concessions that would
be incompatible with them, the Cuban Revolution has always been able to
differentiate the positions taken toward it by the various big capitalist powers
and the diverse capitalist countries of average development.

Capitalists are capitalists and will always be capitalists. We are all too well
aware of that. But the interests and positions of the various sectors of international capitalism—as Lenin presumed six decades ago—remain unidentical.
Numerous explanations could be found for the fact that France—whose ideological position was so diametrically opposed to that of Fidel and the Cuban
Revolution—maintained a respectful position toward the Cuban Revolution
—though this in no way bridged the ideological gap—and defended sustained

economic cooperation and diplomatic ties with Cuba, despite the many, intense and overt pressures of U.S. imperialism.

The similar position adopted by General De Gaulle was more readily understandable and could be traced to his political and economic contradictions with the rulers of the United States, which had emerged in the very first days of the struggle against Nazism and fascism.

In the light of these positions adopted by Spain and France, Cuba found it less difficult to convince other, more die-hard capitalists such as the United Kingdom, Federal Germany, and Italy to establish relations that, though difficult and frequently interrupted, allowed us—together with Mexico's political stance and Canada's opening, also motivated by economic and political contradictions—to prevent the U.S. blockade against Cuba from becoming as generalized within the framework of the imperialist system as had been intended.

Most certainly, the essential premise to achieve this rupture was the fact that economic cooperation with the Soviet Union and other socialist countries broke the basis of the isolation the Americans intended to impose on us. Having the necessary political realism to understand how ineffectual the Yankees' economic offensive would turn out to be, their Western allies did not follow suit. The same could be said of Japan, for whom stable sugar supplies at appropriate prices were combined with the possibility of bringing its sales to Cuba up to heights never dreamed of by the Japanese exporters.

It is not a question of having the major European countries and Japan renounce their basic alliance with U.S. imperialism and cease to be the representatives of imperialism. This would be impossible as long as the forces of monopoly finance capital continue to exert the decisive influence they still have on all those countries. But what should be recorded in our analysis and what should be part of our strategy is an awareness of the contradictory conditions in which this basic alliance is now taking place.

All this has taught us that, even though we are fighting against imperialism as a whole, we don't have to—and as a matter of fact, we should not—take on all the imperialists simultaneously, nor deal equally with all capitalist governments.

This premise of our strategic repertoire is of enormous importance under present international conditions.

Once again our main enemy, U.S. imperialism, is threatening us in all fields: military, economic, and political. . . .

A mechanical attitude would lead us to consider that since close ties still exist between the United States and the ten member countries of the Organization for Economic Cooperation and Development (OECD), the members of the NATO military alliance, and the signatories of the Rio Treaty, they should all follow in Washington's footsteps against Cuba. If we did so, however, we would be forgetting that OECD, the European Economic Community, and even the North Atlantic Treaty do not even come close to eliminating the contradictions that exist among their members. It is therefore necessary and possible to differentiate among their attitudes and play on their differences. If we did not do so, we would be acting with the political extremism of adolescents.

We should not confine our examination to the different positions these countries have taken with regard to Cuba and Cuban politics. The contradictions are much broader and deeper.

Reagan's policy has failed to win over its major Western allies—with the exception of Mrs. Thatcher, who is ideologically akin to the new Yankee president and even surpasses him in certain manifestations of alienating neo-conservativism—to its arms buildup and dangerous nuclear escalation policy, of which its demented antagonism against Cuba is just a part. . . .

In the political and military sphere, the difference in situations—and, consequently, in objectives and methods for finding solutions—is ever greater between the United States and its Western and Asian allies.

First of all, there is a matter of preventing a "Euroshima,"—the nuclear immolation European leaders see with growing concern; the fact is that the U.S. "nuclear umbrella," with which Europe considered itself protected from the "threats" that some of them believed the Soviet Union posed or could pose, is becoming a myth. What is emerging as a threatening reality is the United States' attempt to immolate Europe in a nuclear confrontation provoked with the USSR, while the United States stays out of the atomic fire as a privileged and favored spectator. There is no other purpose behind its stubborn insistence on deploying atomic missiles in European territory and manufacturing neutron bombs for the same local arena. That is why Europe is reluctant to play the victim in this sinister game and is calling for talks with its Soviet neighbors before taking the final steps toward this new nuclear armament.

The same thing is happening with the Japanese. The experience of the World War II has shown the Japanese people—and their leaders, including the all-powerful economic sectors—that Japan has nothing to gain and very much indeed to lose if it persists in its determination to be a militarist and aggressive power. Over the past 40 years of peace, the Japanese have managed to place themselves at the head of the Western world in terms of industrial organization, technological inventiveness, and productive efficiency. To attain their economic objectives they no longer need—as they considered necessary after World War I—to accompany their goods with cruisers and occupation armies; rather, they have chosen to continue along the path of economic victories. The U.S. imperialists, on the other hand, are endeavoring to force them once again along the path of militarization and are urging them to take the first steps in that direction by accepting the role of gendarme in neighboring oceans so as once again to become later on a great allied power that will serve to supplement and offset Maoist China, whose erroneous foreign policy has been so beneficially used by Washington sectors. . . .

All this confirms the importance of our strategic conception in Cuban foreign policy making: not equating under the same sign and not combating on the same premise all capitalist governments in states that, in one way or another, are still part of the imperialist system as a whole. The careful analysis made in the Reports of the Central Committee to the First and Second Congresses shows that Cuba bases itself on a dynamic and differentiating appreciation of the various policies of capitalist states. The starting point of that analysis is the irrefutable consideration that Cuba desires to have normal relations with all the countries of the international community, including the United States itself.[3] And on the basis of this overall conception, Cuba works to further its relations with the developed capitalist countries as well, so as to make use of all the economic and technological possibilities they have to offer either bilaterally or multilaterally. Thus, we are contributing to breaking the Yankee blockade. Of course, we strive for these relations to be equitable and mutually beneficial, but we realize that equity and mutual benefit will never be complete so long as imperialist domination persists in international relations.

It goes without saying that the international policy derived from this strategic conception is not only independent but also totally our own. This means that although Cuba is never loath to subordinate its national interests to the interests of socialism as a universal aspiration, this does not and cannot mean subordinating our everyday international policy, with its own objectives and its own interests, to the policy of other socialist states. The confusion between these two assumptions—which bear some resemblance but are actually dissimilar—is what leads most of our enemies to waste their time disseminating the idea that Cuba imitates and follows the Soviet Union in its international projections. It is true that there is and will continue to be great correspondence between Soviet and Cuban foreign policies. The same could be said of the Cuban foreign policy and the Vietnamese, or the Bulgarian or that of the German Democratic Republic. This is due to the common status of the socialist countries and the fact that, on the basis of this status, we pursue identical historical objectives. But the dissimilar situations of the Soviet Union and Cuba necessarily lead to different approaches in their respective relations with the countries that form part of the world capitalist system.

Thus, the implementation of a differentiated strategy—as Lenin demanded —will be somewhat different for the Soviet Union and Cuba, although both socialist countries work on the basis of the same theoretical approach and identical assumptions.

In Cuban foreign policy making and development, we can never overlook these main strategic conceptions. We start from our essential course toward socialism. We base ourselves on the role of the struggle for peace and national independence with regard to this objective. We use the permanent and intractable contradictions among the main world imperialist centers, and we understand the evolution of history, which places within the government of states of an imperialist nature forces that aim to introduce essential changes in the societies of those countries.

To consider the international field of action with all these nuances and this historical accuracy is a basic and indefeasible principle for drawing up a correct foreign policy in keeping with the guidelines set forth by the two Congresses of the Communist Party of Cuba.

NOTES

¹ Of course, this "conscious action" is in turn conditioned by economic and social factors. In this sense, the will of the social classes and their members in exercising this "conscious action" has very little to do with the so-called "free will" extolled by individualist philosophers. As Marx pointed out in his earliest works, particularly the prologue to *A Contribution to the Critique of Political Economy,* it is not man's social conscience that determines his social existence, rather, just the opposite: It is his social existence that determines his conscience. Hence, the objective factors of contemporary social existence that favor the shift toward socialism exert a positive influence on and promote the actions of revolutionary social classes aimed at carrying out the tasks that will bring about the defeat of imperialism and the emergence of socialism throughout the world.

² *Programmatic Platform of the Communist Party of Cuba* (Havana: Department of Revolutionary Orientation of the Central Committee of the Communist Party of Cuba, 1976), pp. 120–21.

³ The grounds for developing such normal cooperation between the United States and Cuba are well known and need not be repeated here.

31. The Cuban Military*

BY PHYLLIS GREENE WALKER

In terms of sheer military might, the Cuban armed forces in early 1985 represented the second or third most powerful military force after the United States and, possibly, Brazil, in the Western Hemisphere. Cuba continued to spend more money per capita on its armed forces than any other Latin American nation. The country remained at the forefront of Latin America with respect to military manpower; it had the largest standing army in proportion to its population of any country in the hemisphere. The armed forces were equipped with the most technologically sophisticated weapons that its superpower ally, the Soviet Union, was willing to export, including MiG-23 supersonic fighters and Mi-24 attack helicopters. By 1985 Cuban relations with the Soviet Union were at the highest level of development in the history of the revolution.

The modern Cuban military officially traces its traditions back to the Ten Years' War (1868–78) and the struggle waged by the *mambises,* as the inde-

*From James Rudolph, ed., *Cuba: A Country Study* (Washington, D.C.: U.S. Department of the Army, 1987), pp. 227–283. Edited for this volume.

pendence fighters were called, to free themselves from Spanish colonial rule. The *mambises* were led by such heroic guerrilla leaders as Antonio Maceo and Máximo Gómez, a former Spanish army commander who trained and fought with the rebels.

The attack on Santiago de Cuba's Moncada Barracks on July 26, 1953, led by Fidel Castro, a lawyer and former University of Havana student leader and "action group" member, represented the first organized armed revolt against Batista. It was also the first military action by those who would provide the core leadership for the Rebel Army and, after its victory, the Revolutionary Armed Forces (Fuerzas Armadas Revolucionarias—FAR).

In mid-January 1959 the provisional revolutionary government suspended the law regulating the structure of the old military, permitting it legally to reorganize the new armed forces according to its needs. The constitution, which had prohibited capital punishment, was amended to allow for the execution of Batista's collaborators judged guilty of "war crimes." The often televised executions by firing squad of former Batista-era officials were supported by the majority of Cubans, who were eager to avenge the dictatorship's excesses, but the United States government viewed them with alarm and used them as a standard by which it judged the civility of the new government. However, Castro, the de facto leader of the revolutionary government, eventually recognized that the bloodletting could not continue if the leadership wished to end the spasmodic violence that had wracked the country for most of the past decade. After the retributive executions were halted, efforts to consolidate the revolutionary government's power began in earnest.

CONSTITUTIONAL PROVISIONS AND TREATY OBLIGATIONS

Article 64 of the 1976 Constitution of the Republic of Cuba establishes that "the defense of the socialist homeland is the greatest honor and the supreme duty of every Cuban citizen." Military service, incorporated under Article 64, is regulated by law. Treason against the nation is defined as "the most serious of crimes" and, accordingly, is "subject to the most severe of penalties." Also incorporated in the constitution is the right of all Cuban citizens to "reach any rank of the Revolutionary Armed Forces . . . in keeping with their merits and abilities."

Between the early years of the revolution and the mid-1980s, Cuba resisted entering multilateral or bilateral defense pacts and otherwise refused to enter into agreements that might limit its actions in the international arena. As Article 10 of the 1976 Constitution specifically stipulates the Republic of Cuba "rejects and considers as illegal and null all treaties, pacts and concessions which were signed in conditions of inequality, or which disregard or diminish [Cuban] sovereignty over any part of the national territory."

This position remained consistent with the actions of the Cuban leadership in the early years of the Revolution. In March 1960 Cuba withdrew from the 1947 Inter-American Treaty of Reciprocal Assistance (Rio Treaty), which provided for collective hemispheric defense against external aggressors. Five months later Castro terminated the United States Mutual Defense Assistance Program agreement signed by the Batista government in 1952. Cuban participation in the Organization of American States (OAS) was suspended in January 1962, when member states determined that the Cuban government's Marxist-Leninist ideology was "incompatible with the interests of the hemisphere."

THE REVOLUTIONARY ARMED FORCES AND THE GOVERNMENT

Throughout the first 26 years of the Cuban Revolution, distinguishing the responsibilities of civilian government officials from those of FAR personnel was often difficult. This was especially true during the 1960s as the government attempted to consolidate its power and organize popular support. The term coined by Professor Jorge I. Domínguez of Harvard University—the "civic soldier"—epitomized the nature of civil-military relations. The concept of the civic soldier represented the military men who ruled over large sectors of military and civilian life, who were held up as symbols to be emulated by all Cuban citizens, and who were the bearers of the tradition and ideology of the revolution. The fusion of civilian and military roles and duties at the national level was embodied in Castro, who, in addition to being the commander in chief of the FAR, was also the head of the nation's top decision-making bodies, including the Council of State, the Council of Ministers, and the Communist Party of Cuba (Partido Communista de Cuba—PCC). His brother Raúl, minister of the FAR, held the second highest position in these same bodies.

In the chaotic governmental reorganization efforts of 1959 and the early 1960s, the FAR served as an important repository of leadership and administrative expertise and, as the successor to the Rebel Army, represented the most powerful institutional body that had survived the overthrow of Batista. The involvement of the Cuban military in public administration dated back to the 1920s and served to legitimize the newly created FAR's participation in and control over governmental affairs. As the requirements of military specialization increased through the 1970s and as Cuban government officials independently developed expertise in public administration, the distinct responsibilities of the civilian and military sectors became somewhat more pronounced. Nevertheless, through the mid-1980s the highest levels within the Cuban government continued to be filled with former Rebel Army officers, many of whom, although not active-duty FAR officers, were regularly identified in the

Cuban media as "commanders of the revolution," using the honorific rank in addition to their governmental title.

Members of the Cuban armed forces were not only educated to become professionals in civilian and military affairs but were also among the vanguard of the PCC. In late 1970 nearly 70 percent of all military officers belonged to either the PCC or its youth wing, the Union of Young Communists (Unión de Jóvenes Comunistas—UJC). Of the PCC members holding military rank at that time, fully 69 percent were commissioned officers. By the time of delegate selection for the Third Congress of the PCC . . . however, foreign observers were arguing that civilian party cadre were attempting to reduce the influence of the FAR within the party organization.

After its founding in 1965, the PCC was organized most quickly within the armed forces. The PCC was organized at all commands within the FAR. Each of the three services—the army, air force, and navy—had its own political section. Political bureaus were organized at battalion or regimental levels, and political groups functioned at the level of company, "platoon and squad," battery, or squadron. Political units were organized from below, wherein party cell members did not report directly to the PCC but indirectly through higher-level units that ultimately reported to the armed forces' Central Political Directorate.

Membership in either the PCC or the UJC was considered a decisive factor in promoting an individual within the FAR. The FAR was considered by the PCC leadership to be an excellent agent for the political indoctrination of nonparty members. Instruction in Marxist-Leninist ideology by a PCC political officer who held rank in the FAR was included as a regular component of basic military training.

The responsibilities of the civic soldier also entailed carrying out the economic mission of the armed forces, which included the organization of civilian sectors of the economy along military lines. The economic role of the Cuban armed forces, like its influence in the PCC, was also larger than that of the Soviet or Chinese armed forces. It was not until after 1973, when increasing Soviet influence resulted in an emphasis on military professionalism and specialization, that the direct involvement of the armed forces in the state economy began to decline.

After the 1973 reorganization of the FAR, a number of production-related tasks previously assigned to the armed forces were turned over to civilians. Defense-related work assigned by government ministries to civilians employed in production or in the field of education, however, did not revert to the armed forces. At the same time, all productive labor came to be viewed not only as an economic contribution that enhanced national security but also as a social duty. The result was an increase in the FAR's influence over a civilian population that often found itself working for both nonmilitary and military ends, a situation that prevailed through the mid-1980s.

THE MINISTRY OF THE REVOLUTIONARY ARMED FORCES

The Ministry of the Revolutionary Armed Forces (Ministerio de las Fuerzas Armadas Revolucionarias—MINFAR) was created on October 16, 1959, to replace the Batista-era Ministry of Defense. At that time Raúl Castro was appointed minister of the FAR, a post he held into the mid-1980s. After a restructuring of the MINFAR's system of ranks in 1973, Raúl Castro held the rank of general of the army and Fidel Castro, that of commander in chief of the FAR. Also at the top of the MINFAR hierarchy in the mid-1980s were three first vice-ministers, all of whom held the rank of division general, and ten vice-ministers.

Between 1959 and the mid-1980s, the MINFAR consisted of three major services: the Revolutionary Army (Ejército Revolucionario—ER), the Antiaircraft Defense and Revolutionary Air Force (Defensa Antiaérea y Fuerza Aérea Revolucionaria—DAAFAR), and the Revolutionary Navy (Marina de Guerra Revolucionaria—MGR). In 1972 the DAAFAR and MGR had been established as separate services with their own commands. Various staff directorates augmented the MINFAR's organizational structure. . . .

There were varying estimates of the size of the FAR in early 1985. Data published by the London-based International Institute for Strategic Studies in September 1984 placed the size of the regular armed forces at 153,000, not including the 94,500 conscripts who were then completing their period of conscription, known as General Military Service. The regular ER, which included a proportion of the reserve troops on active duty, was composed of some 125,000 officers and soldiers. In addition, some 75,000 conscripts were assigned to the ER. The DAAFAR force strength was estimated at 16,000, complemented by approximately 11,000 conscripts. The MGR was made up of 12,000 personnel, including 350 naval infantry, plus some 8,500 conscripts.

United States Defense Intelligence Agency (DIA) estimates in early 1985 placed the size of the FAR at 162,000, broken down into 130,000 personnel in the ER, 18,500 in the DAAFAR, and 13,500 in the MGR. These figures did not include members of the combat-ready reserve forces, estimated at 135,000, who could be mobilized on as little as two to four hours' notice. Reserve forces were assigned to all three branches of the FAR, yet data regarding the reserves' distribution among them were unavailable.

Regular military forces were complemented in early 1985 by other organizations with paramilitary duties. The MINFAR's only official paramilitary organization was the Youth Labor Army (Ejército Juvenil de Trabajo—EJT), the size of which was estimated in mid-1984 at 100,000 and whose mission was primarily that of civic action. The Territorial Troops Militia (Milicia de Tropas Territoriales—MTT), created in mid-1980, was made up of some 1.2 million civilians in July 1984, according to Castro. Cuban officials stated that the MTT was established as a deterrent to the threat of a United States invasion. The Civil Defense forces, estimated to be composed of some 100,000 civilians, also complemented the nation's defense organization.

Although formal diplomatic relations were established by Cuba with the Soviet Union in May 1960, the consolidation of Cuban-Soviet amity did not occur until nearly a decade later. Between 1970 and 1985 improved relations between the Cuban and the Soviet governments proved critical in terms of the MINFAR's professionalization and the development of its military capabilities.

One of the first indications of the growing Soviet influence on the Cuban armed forces was the 1973 MINFAR reorganization. Increased emphasis was placed on professionalization and military discipline. The development of the MINFAR's technical capabilities also resulted from the decision to assign greater numbers of regular troops to exclusively military tasks. The system of military ranks—made up of varying grades within the single rank of "commander"—was restructured to conform to more universally accepted standards. The reorganization also resulted in a decrease in the size of the armed forces to some 120,000 personnel.

After 1975 Soviet support included the provision of airlifts and sealifts of Soviet equipment and supplies and Cuban troops to the MINFAR's Expeditionary Forces in Africa. The Soviets undertook an intensive force modernization program that increased both the level and the sophistication of the matériel it provided the MINFAR. During the late 1970s, as United States–Cuban relations again became hostile, the level and sophistication of the military equipment provided by the Soviets increased markedly.

By the early 1980s Cuba was receiving the most advanced military equipment that the Soviet Union was willing to export to any of its allies. This enabled the Cuban FAR to become one of the best educated, equipped, and disciplined of armed forces in the Western Hemisphere. Deliveries of military equipment and supplies increased markedly after 1981, the beginning of a new five-year economic planning cycle. Between 1981 and 1984, according to United States government sources, Cuba received an average of US $750 million a year in Soviet military assistance. During these four years Soviet merchant ships delivered an estimated 200,000 tons of military equipment in contrast to the 21,000-ton annual average over the previous ten years. The increased assistance was believed to include light weapons destined for the newly created MTT and equipment for increasing the mechanization, mobility, and armored capacities of the MINFAR ground forces. Soviet military assistance to Cuba traditionally included arms and equipment as well as technical training and advice with respect to Cuban military operations. Cuba relied on Soviet technical personnel for the maintenance and repair of much of the more sophisticated equipment in its inventory and for the petroleum, oil, and lubricants they require.

The continuing relations also allowed the Soviet Union to maintain a regu-

lar, peacetime presence in Cuba. Through the mid-1980s Soviet naval flotil-
las and reconnaissance and antisubmarine aircraft routinely paid visits to
Cuba and often carried out joint Soviet-Cuban maneuvers off the coasts of
Havana or Cienfuegos. As part of the naval ship visit program begun in
1969, about 24 naval task groups had visited Cuba by the end of 1984. The
largest electronic intelligence collection facility located outside the Soviet
Union was in operation at Lourdes on Cuba's northern coast near Havana,
monitoring the military and civilian communications of the United States as
well as of other countries, if desired. There was also considerable concern
among United States strategic planners in the mid-1980s that Cuba could be
used as a recovery and relaunch platform for the long-range TU-26 strategic
bomber. The island was a likely site for the refueling and resupply of nu-
clear-equipped Soviet submarines.

A Soviet military advisory group on the island, made up of some 2,500 to
2,800 personnel in early 1985, provided technical advice in support of the
MINFAR's more sophisticated weaponry. Some advisers were also believed
attached to Cuban ground units. A separate group, a ground forces brigade,
was believed to number between 2,600 to 3,000 troops. It was the "discovery"
of this force in August 1979 that raised United States concerns over the
possible stationing of Soviet combat forces on the island. It was later recognized that the formation had been known to have been on the island since at
least 1962 and did not have significant airlift or sealift capabilities that might
enable it to engage in combat outside of Cuba. Although the unit was not the
combat brigade it was initially believed to be, the administration of President
Jimmy Carter subsequently ordered an increase in surveillance of the island
and the establishment of the joint United States Forces Caribbean Command
at Key West, which in 1981 was upgraded to Commander, United States
Forces Caribbean. In 1982 the ground forces brigade consisted of one tank and
three motorized rifle battalions as well as various combat and support units.
Its likely mission was to provide security for Soviet personnel and key Soviet
facilities, such as the Lourdes monitoring complex, and to provide a symbol
of Soviet support. Brigade members may also have been involved in training
Cuban personnel in the use of sophisticated Soviet equipment, such as T-62
main battle tanks, BMP combat carriers, and ZSU-23-4 self-propelled antiaircraft guns, delivered in the late 1970s.

Under the provisions of the 1973 Law of General Military Service, all Cuban
males between the ages of 16 and 50 were required to perform a minimum of
three years' service in the active-duty military, the military reserve, or both.
Although compulsory military service had first been instituted by the Castro
government in 1963, the 1973 regulation expanded the kinds of military service
to be performed by conscripts. General Military Service options included being
drafted into either the paramilitary Youth Labor Army (Ejército Juvenil de
Trabajo—EJT) or the regular armed forces units or performing alternative

civilian social service at places and posts designated by the government. Women were exempt from obligatory service, yet were eligible to enlist in the armed forces after age 16. Those women with special training were eligible to be members of the reserve forces until age 40.

The Territorial Troops Militia

The Territorial Troops Militia (Milicia de Tropas Territoriales—MTT) was created by the Cuban government on May 1, 1980, under the command of the MINFAR. The commander of the MTT in early 1985 was Division General Raúl Menéndez Tomassevich, a MINFAR vice-minister, a title also held by the commanders of the FAR's three armed services. The first units of the MTT were established in eastern Cuba at a ceremony led by Castro on January 20, 1981, the same day—as Castro noted in his speech—that United States President Ronald Reagan took his oath of office. Within two years the size of the MTT had grown to 500,000, and in July 1983 Castro announced the decision to increase it to 1 million. By May 1984 the government revealed that this goal had been reached. On July 26, 1984—exactly a year after the decision to increase rapidly the force's size—Castro declared that the MTT, including its reserves, was 1.2 million strong.

The MTT rank and file were composed mainly of men above draft age who were not active members of the MINFAR reserve or Civil Defense forces, young men between ages 16 and 18, and women of all ages. Participation in the MTT was voluntary. Public consideration was given by Cuban officials in late 1984 to possibly lowering the age for MTT youth membership to include 15-year-olds. In late 1982 approximately 25 percent of MTT members were women, according to Castro.

According to Raúl Castro the MTT's wartime mission was to include fighting alongside, and providing replacements for, regular armed forces personnel; protecting strategic defense positions, such as bridges, highways, railroads, factories, and towns; and undertaking any other measures of harassment that might immobilize, wear out, and ultimately destroy an enemy invader. The 336-page *Basic Manual of the Territorial Troops Militia Member* outlined these objectives and described procedures to be followed in the event of an attack. Training of MTT units was usually carried out on weekends or in the evenings after work in order not to interfere with a worker's productivity or a student's studies. In addition to receiving field training in the handling and use of light weaponry, the militia members were taught military discipline.

The Cuban Military Abroad

Cuban military forces on active duty outside the country were divided into two groups: the Expeditionary Forces, which included personnel assigned to combat duty, and the Military Assistance Forces, which included personnel assigned to train and advise foreign military personnel. In early 1985 the two

Cuban Expeditionary Forces retained the status of independent armies and were assigned to Angola and Ethiopia. Should the Expeditionary Force be withdrawn from either of those locations, it is likely that its status as an army would be downgraded. In late 1984 one estimate placed the total number of Cuban military personnel abroad—including members of the Expeditionary Forces and the Military Assistance Forces—at some 70,000 officers and troops. By early 1985 there appeared to be no reason to assume that this figure, if correct, would decrease substantially.

The provision of military assistance—in terms of both training and the supply of matériel—to other Third World nations and revolutionary movements had been a feature of Cuba's foreign military policy since shortly after the 1959 revolutionary victory. The main justification for the presence of a Cuban military advisory mission in a given country was "internationalist solidarity." Much conflicting information existed with respect to the size of Cuba's foreign military involvement. To complicate matters further, in the mid-1980s the Cuban government was unwilling to discuss the activities of its foreign assistance missions beyond the tacit recognition that they provided military equipment and training.

One example of the kind and scale of possible involvement of Cuban military assistance personnel in a foreign country was cited in an account of the activities of the Cuban mission in the People's Democratic Republic of Yemen (South Yemen) in the late 1970s. After the attack in early 1979 by South Yemen on the Yemen Arab Republic (North Yemen) in a dispute over their mutual border, Cuban military personnel reportedly provided some artillery backup in addition to logistics and communications support. Cuban personnel were not believed to have crossed into North Yemen after the invading South Yemeni troops, however. By the end of the border war in mid-March 1979, Cuban pilots in MiG jets were reported to have been flying daily patrols over the Red Sea and the Gulf of Aden.

Almost all reports of Cuban military assistance personnel participating in foreign combat stated that those personnel involved were small in number and that they saw only limited combat. In the early 1960s some 400 Cuban tank troops were reportedly sent to Algeria to aid in its border conflict with Morocco. Small numbers of Cuban personnel were reportedly involved in guerrilla fighting in territory encompassing present-day Zaïre, Tanzania, and Guinea-Bissau.

The level and activities of Cuban military personnel in Nicaragua remained a hotly contested issue in late 1984 and early 1985. The International Institute for Strategic Studies placed the number of Cuban military and security personnel at 3,000 in *The Military Balance, 1984–1985,* a 2,000-man increase over what it had reported the previous year. The more recent figure coincided with the 2,500 to 3,500 estimate often used by the United States government in early 1985. In mid-March 1985 Nicaraguan President Daniel Ortega stated that there were exactly 786 Cuban military advisers in Nicaragua and that the total size of the Cuban presence, including civilian advisers, was below 1,500.

In March 1984 Cuba announced that it had reduced the number of military advisers in Nicaragua while increasing the military training given the civilian advisers, known as "internationalists." These internationalists were civilian volunteers in the fields of health, education, and construction, who, as part of the government-sponsored development assistance program, had received a minimum of a month's rudimentary military training that emphasized defensive tactics and included the handling of light weapons. It was believed that civilian internationalists sent abroad after training were routinely issued light arms for their defense. By 1985 as many as 5,000 civilian internationalists were believed to be working in Nicaragua.

Between 1984 and 1985 the Cuban government affirmed its willingness to withdraw all military and security personnel from Nicaragua in accord with the peace proposal drawn up by the so-called Contadora Group—composed of representatives from the governments of Mexico, Panama, Venezuela, and Colombia—as part of its efforts to remove all foreign forces from Central America.

32. Institutionalization, Political Elites, and Foreign Policies*

BY EDWARD GONZÁLEZ

INSTITUTIONALIZATION

The "institutionalization of the Cuban Revolution" since 1970 has been acclaimed by outside observers and the Cuban leadership alike as marking a new, decisive stage in Cuba's political order. Indeed, the Cuba of the late 1970s is strikingly different from the Cuba of a decade earlier. Institutionalization has brought about the depersonalization of governance, the strengthening of the party and governmental structures, and the greater efficacy and rationality of the economy. Additionally, the state and governmental system has undergone a major reorganization under the new socialist constitution, leading to the creation of new leadership posts and organs of representation, and culminating in islandwide elections in late 1976. Yet it is not only Cuba's domestic order that experienced major transformations: Cuba's foreign policies also were dramatically altered in the post-1970 period.

*From Cole Blasier and Carmelo Mesa-Lago, eds., *Cuba in the World* (Pittsburgh: University of Pittsburgh Press, 1979), pp. 3–36. Edited for this volume.

Institutionalization and Broadened Leadership

There are three major aspects of the institutionalization process that has altered the composition of the Cuban leadership since 1970.[1] The first is the depersonalization of governance—the delegation of effective decision-making powers from Fidel Castro and his immediate entourage to new and more technically qualified appointees and to governmental agencies that could now function in more regularized and orderly fashion without the interventions of the *líder máximo*. This step was initiated immediately after the 1970 harvest when some of Fidel's closest associates were replaced by new personnel drawn from more qualified civilian and military circles.

The second aspect involves two major administrative reorganizations. Carried out in November 1972, the first change established a new Executive Committee attached to the Council of Ministers, with seven deputy prime ministers to supervise and coordinate clusters of ministries engaged in related activities. This reorganization gave further impetus to the post-1970 tendency of appointing new personnel to leadership posts, with no less than four army majors—then the highest rank in the Revolutionary Armed Forces (FAR)—being appointed deputy prime ministers and another becoming a minister by the end of 1972. The second and more sweeping institutional change has occurred since February 1976, with the implementation of Cuba's new socialist constitution. As will be seen subsequently, it has led to the remodeling of Cuba's state and governmental structure similar to that of the Soviet Union, with a new National Assembly of People's Power, Council of State, and Council of Ministers being established in December 1976.

The third aspect of the institutionalization process concerns the Communist Party of Cuba (PCC): A stepped-up recruitment drive more than doubled its membership from 100,000 in 1970 to 202,807 in September 1975; new leadership was introduced at the highest levels through the expansion of the old six-man Secretariat to include five additional members in February 1973; and finally, a new Political Bureau, Secretariat, and Central Committee were unveiled at the party congress. In sum, the PCC was being transformed in Leninist fashion and accorded heightened political legitimacy as Cuba's ruling institution.[2]

Elite Coalitions and Reconcentrated Political Power

By the mid-1970s there existed a broader distribution and diversity of political elites in the Cuban leadership than at any time since the mid-1960s. The "old Communists" from the PSP were now included in the supreme organs of the party, state, and government. Carlos Rafael Rodríguez became the most prominent of the ex-PSP notables by virtue of his membership in the Political Bureau and Secretariat and his vice-presidency in both the Council of State and Council of Ministers. . . .

While a broadening of elite representation has occurred, this coalition building has thus led to a reconcentration of political power in the two Castro brothers and their following. They clearly dominate the key organs of the party, state, and government in terms of sheer membership numbers and control over the most sensitive or powerful ministries. But more than that, Fidel's position as the supreme *líder máximo* has now been institutionalized in his multiple roles as first secretary, president of both the Council of State and Council of Ministers, and commander-in-chief. As president of the Council of State, moreover, he is empowered not only to name the first vice-president, vice-presidents, and other members of the Council of Ministers, but also to replace them with substitutes.[3] Institutionalization has thus reconcentrated power even though it has also resulted in a broader distribution of political elites in the present leadership.

POLITICAL ELITES AND FOREIGN POLICIES

Fidel's successful coalition building, together with the favorable outcome of the institutionalization process, has affected Havana's foreign policy postures on several fronts. This strengthened power base at home has evidently emboldened Fidel to embark upon new foreign policy ventures toward Latin America, the Third World, and Washington since 1973. Additionally, the very diversity in the makeup of Cuba's new ruling coalition, along with Fidel's resurgence, now makes Cuba's foreign policies far more complex than was the case before or immediately after 1970.

Diversity and complexity do not necessarily mean that there is intense interelite conflict or an absence of consensus within the regime. On the contrary, the Cuban leadership of the 1970s appears to enjoy a basic agreement on such major foreign policy goals as maintaining Cuba's independence from the United States; assuring adequate levels of Soviet economic and military support while minimizing Cuba's client-state relationship; acquiring trade, advanced technology, and training from capitalist countries; and forging strong links with the Third World.[4] But different elites are likely to emphasize some goals over others or to favor a particular strategic line for the attainment of a goal. Accordingly, I shall argue below that three foreign policy tendencies emerged in Cuba after the early 1970s which generally reflect the basic policy interests, mentality, or organizational mission of the major elite actors within the new ruling coalition. Further, I will contend that two of these tendencies—those associated with Fidel, and with Raúl and the military—have now become predominant owing to the highly favorable outcomes of Cuba's military victory in Angola. The internal elite composition has affected foreign policy outcomes, but the success or failure of the latter has also had a major effect on the final balance of elite forces within the regime.

Foreign Policy Tendencies

Three foreign policy tendencies can be identified in the new ruling coalition. These are (1) the pragmatic economic tendency (Rodríguez), (2) the revolutionary political tendency (Fidel), and (3) the military mission tendency (Raúl-MINFAR).

The Pragmatic Economic Tendency. The impulse toward greater pragmatism on the economic, political, and diplomatic fronts reflects the new influence of the civilian technocratic and managerial elites. It also stems from the greater Soviet involvement in Cuban affairs since 1970 which, in turn, has reinforced the position of the more pragmatic leadership within Cuba. This group is led by Carlos Rafael Rodríguez, whose continued prominence was confirmed by his selection for the vice-presidency of both the Council of State and Council of Ministers in late 1976. His allies, as in the past, include Vice-President Osvaldo Dorticós, Foreign Trade Minister Marcelo Fernández, Sugar Industry Minister Marcos Lage, Hector Rodríguez as head of the State Committee for Economic Collaboration, as well as other specialists in charge of agencies dealing with technical, financial, or economic matters. These pragmatists, in turn, tend to find support among the "old Communists" from the PSP who have risen in influence within recent years. As befits their role specialization, the pragmatists attach highest importance to the primacy of economics. Consequently, they emphasize the need to promote Cuba's rapid and sustained economic development through rational methods of socialist planning, cost accounting, and financing at home, and by greater trade and technological ties with the advanced countries of the socialist and non-socialist worlds.

In this respect, the pragmatic leadership is painfully aware of Cuba's underdevelopment and its dependence on the more advanced countries for continuing modernization of her economy. In September 1974, for instance, Dorticós lamented Cuba's "scientific and technological poverty" which could be overcome only through the importation of what he termed capital-intensive "vanguard technology" for the modernization of Cuban agriculture and industry.[5] Similarly, Cuba had to expand its ties with advanced capitalist countries because, according to Rodríguez in early 1975, "a whole range of technologies is not yet available in the socialist camp."[6] Indeed, the cruel dilemma of global interdependence confronting Cuba and other underdeveloped countries was strikingly put forth by Rodríguez at the FAO World Food Conference in November 1974. Rising oil prices, he observed, threatened to plunge the capitalist countries into a catastrophic economic crisis which would confirm the Marxist prophecy regarding the ultimate collapse of capitalism. Nevertheless, Rodríguez flatly rejected the advisability of this development because such a catastrophe would involve "the risk of a prolonged period of backwardness for the peoples struggling for development. Therefore, we cannot declare ourselves in favor of such a doomsday solution to the economic and social contradictions. . . . This is why we are willing to work with all those who are trying to avert such a world economic crisis."[7]

The pragmatic tendency, therefore, proceeds from a set of economic assumptions and strategems that partially explains Cuba's foreign policies in recent years. These are that (1) Cuba remains economically and technologically underdeveloped; (2) this underdevelopment must be attacked by exploiting Cuba's economic and technological dependence on the more advanced socialist and capitalist countries; and (3) the resulting dependency can be eased in the short run by the diversification of Cuba's economic ties and in the long run by ultimately attaining higher levels of development. Since 1970, with respect to socialist countries, Cuba has gained admittance to COMECON (July 1972), signed new and highly favorable long-term economic agreements with the Soviet Union (December 1972), obtained a new trade, economic, and technical agreement for 1976–1980 with the Soviets (April 1975), and coordinated a new five-year plan with that of the Soviet Union for 1976–1980. But to balance this heightened dependence on the USSR, Rodríguez also began to negotiate new trade agreements, long-term credits, and investment contracts with numerous non-socialist countries after the early 1970s, when the booming sugar prices of 1974 and early 1975 greatly strengthened his negotiating position with western countries.[8] Rodríguez also appears to have been the driving force in seeking a new opening with the United States in hopes of securing elusive U.S. agricultural equipment, technology, and computer facilities, among other items.

The Revolutionary Political Tendency. The second tendency impels Cuba toward the return to more revolutionary postures in its foreign policies. This more combative line bears the personal stamp of Fidel and is backed by veteran Fidelista revolutionaries and close associates who occupy top leadership posts in the party, state, and government. It stems in large measure from Fidel's greatly strengthened political power base at home after 1973. But it also derives from his perception that détente between the superpowers offered Cuba heightened security and that U.S. imperialism was increasingly weak and defensive as evidenced by the war in Vietnam, Third World solidarity, and especially the international capitalist crisis of the mid-1970s. In Fidel's eyes, therefore, "capitalism and imperialism are living in a crisis hour. . . . For many, the capitalist world is on the brink of the most serious disaster it has confronted since the somber periods of the Great Depression of the '30s."[9] Both his success in gaining control over the institutionalization process and his perception of the shift in the global balance emboldened him to take more aggressive foreign policy postures on several fronts.

Fidel's assertive policy of confrontation and defiance is aimed at U.S. imperialism and, as such, it is reminiscent of the Fidelista line of the 1960s. But the old line also appears to have been tempered by realization of Cuba's continued underdevelopment and dependence and by concern that post-1970 economic recovery could be jeopardized by adventuristic policies. Thus, Fidel evidently has been inclined to apply his revolutionary line somewhat more selectively than in the 1960s in an effort to reconcile it with the island's economic, technological, and political needs. Hence, he apparently favored the development of closer ties with Western Europe and Latin America and overtures toward Washington in 1974–1975.

While Fidel is concerned with Cuba's underdevelopment and dependence, he is far more ideological and political than are the pragmatists. The imperialism of the United States is to be combated through active solidarity with the Third World and by espousing Latin America's unity and separateness from the United States. Hence his affirmation in September 1974: "The United States on one side and the peoples of Latin America and the Caribbean on the other side form two worlds as different as Europe and Africa: They do not belong in the same community."[10] Within Cuba, in the meantime, the purity of the revolution will be maintained by combating the foreign viruses of "ideological diversionism," represented by the non-Soviet Left, and "consumerism," represented by capitalist societies.

Above all, the Fidelista mentality is highly political in its world outlook and *modus operandi*: As in the past, Fidel is most concerned with disparities in power, and he is the master practitioner of leverage politics for redressing or reversing adverse power relationships. Unlike the pragmatists who emphasize economic strategies, Fidel employs leverage politics as the principal means by which his otherwise vulnerable, dependent island is to be made secure and great. Its extreme vulnerability to the United States, for example, is offset through long-standing protective and supportive ties with the Soviet Union. But more recently, Fidel sought to augment the island's limited power capabilities through closer association with the Third World. In particular, in September 1974, he called for the unity of the OPEC countries with the less developed world as the primary means by which to ease dependency and fundamentally alter the global balance in favor of the Third World: "If the petroleum countries stand united and firm, if they do not allow themselves to be intimidated by the threats of the United States, and if they seek the alliance of the remainder of the underdeveloped world, the industrialized capitalist countries will have to accept as inevitable the disappearance of the shameful and unjust terms of trade that they have imposed on our peoples."[11] Later he warned that "any playing around with imperialism by any Arab country is dangerous, because political opportunism cannot replace frank, open, and revolutionary diplomacy—and sometimes it leads to flagrant betrayal."[12] Even before the large-scale incursion into Angola, Cuba was extending military and economic assistance to Middle Eastern and African nations in an apparent attempt to solidify Cuba's Third World links and thereby augment its global influence.

Latin America provided another region in which Cuba could generate international leverage. In early 1975, Fidel observed that there were fundamental changes in Latin America toward "greater independence with respect to the United States, greater national awareness . . . and a greater understanding of what imperialism is and a willingness to confront that imperialism."[13] In fact, Cuba had already moved to capitalize on these trends through increased economic, political, and military relations with a number of countries. The Caribbean became the principal arena for considerable Cuban activity and the region in which Cuba began to emerge as a second-order power. Havana cultivated close ties with the regimes of Torrijos in Panama, Burnham in Guyana, and especially with the Manley government in Jamaica. There, the Cubans began training members of the prime minister's palace guard, stepped up Cuban economic and technical assistance, and otherwise cemented close political ties with the Manley government. Elsewhere, Cuba greatly improved its relations with Mexico, as demonstrated by President Echeverría's visit to Havana in August 1975, followed by Raúl Castro's return visit to Mexico City in September. Cuba had meanwhile reestablished diplomatic relations with Venezuela in 1974 and subsequently sought closer relations with the Andrés Pérez government as the latter became more assertively nationalist in its foreign policy postures. Further affirming its Caribbean presence, Cuba joined the Latin American Economic System (SELA), cosponsored by Mexico and Venezuela in October 1975, and became an active member of the Caribbean Multinational Shipping Enterprise (NAMUCAR). Finally, Cuba has provided active support for the Puerto Rican independence movement in recent years, culminating in the sponsorship of a proindependence conference in Havana in September 1975. Such support, in turn, could provide the Castro regime with additional leverage in the event of future negotiations with Washington. . . .

The Military Mission Tendency. The third foreign policy tendency is headed by Raúl Castro and other MINFAR officers and involves the external, professional role of the Cuban armed forces. To a large degree, this tendency also is a product of a more institutionalized order. Not only has the FAR emerged as a major political actor within the Cuban regime, as suggested by the results of the party congress and the makeup of the new Council of State and Council of Ministers, but the institutionalization process has strengthened the capacity of the civilian sector to carry out administrative and economic activities that were previously assigned to the Cuban army because of its higher level of professional competence, technical training, and organizational skills. The strengthening of the civilian sector, combined with lowered perceptions of external threat from the United States, meant that the Cuban army could be pared down to a highly professional standing force of about 120,000 and devote itself primarily to military tasks beginning in the early 1970s. In the process, the army has expanded its traditional military mission from one of

internal defense of the homeland, to a new external mission in support of
Cuba's foreign policy objectives. Indeed, the high levels of professionalization
and institutionalization attained by the army may have impelled it to search
out and identify new organizational missions abroad.[14]

In Latin America, the role of the FAR has been confined to the establishment of professional military-to-military relations with the friendly governments of Peru, Panama, Guyana, Trinidad and Tobago, Jamaica, and Mexico.
Even so, Havana held out the prospects of rendering conventional military
assistance to Latin American governments beginning in the early 1970s. To
military delegations from the above named countries, Fidel declared that "the
experiences of our armed forces are at the service of the progressive governments and peoples of this continent."[15] Meanwhile, Cuban military units were
already being sent overseas to the Middle East and Africa beginning in the
early 1970s.

During military exercises in November 1974, Fidel could proclaim with
some justification that the Cuban armed forces were at the service "of our sister
peoples of Latin America in their struggle against imperialism, and we are on
the side of the peoples who face up to imperialism in all parts of the world."[16]
The Cuban armed forces worked to improve their combat readiness and develop their offensive capabilities by engaging in new mobile defense operations
during military exercises in 1974 and 1975. As will be seen below, the end
result of the army's expanded military mission and capabilities was the embar-
cation of an estimated one thousand Cuban soldiers to Angola by mid-Septem-
ber 1975. Later, with the rapid buildup of the Cuban military presence to over
14,000 combat troops, the FAR became the decisive factor in the victory of
the Popular Movement for the Liberation of Angola (MPLA).

Policy Contradictions

The three foreign policy tendencies described above presented contradictions
in Cuban postures by the mid-1970s, and they imposed internal constraints on
policy initiatives as well. To be sure, the revolutionary and military mission
tendencies of Fidel and Raúl-MINFAR, respectively, tended to cohere and be
mutually supportive. Still, Fidel's line of heightened confrontation with imperialism could come in conflict with the organizational interests of the FAR
were the Cuban military to suffer serious reverses in one of its overseas operations. In any event, both stood in obvious contradiction to the pragmatic
tendency aimed at broadening Cuba's economic, technical, and political ties
with Western countries. As was illustrated by the so-called Carlos affair in
Paris in mid-1975, both these more militant foreign policy tendencies could
have undermined the Rodríguez line.[17] That they did not do so prior to Angola
was due in large measure to Havana's success in divorcing its revolutionary
and military postures in the Third World from its more pragmatic policies
toward Latin America, Japan, Western Europe, and Canada.

NOTES

1. On these and other post-1970 developments, see Carmelo Mesa-Lago, *Cuba in the 1970's: Pragmatism and Institutionalization* (Albuquerque, NM: University of New Mexico Press, 1974); Leon Gouré and Morris Rothenberg, *Soviet Penetration of Latin America* (Coral Gables, FL: Center for Advanced International Studies, University of Miami, 1975), pp. 19–80; and Edward Gonzalez, "Castro and Cuba's New Orthodoxy," *Problems of Communism* (January-February 1976), pp. 1–19. See also Nelson P. Valdés, "Revolution and Institutionalization in Cuba," *Cuban Studies* (January 1976), pp. 1–38; and Jorge I. Domínguez, "Institutionalization and Civil-Military Relations," Ibid., pp. 39–66.

2. Fidel himself had earlier underscored this transfer of political legitimacy to the PCC: "In the early years of the revolution, individuals played a decisive role, a role now carried out by the party. Men die, but the party is immortal." *Granma Weekly Review* (August 5, 1973), p. 5.

3. These powers are granted in the new Law on the Organization of Central State Administration, Articles 7–9. The text of the law is in *Granma Weekly Review* (December 19, 1976), pp. 9–12.

4. For a comprehensive analysis regarding these and other foreign policy issues, see Edward Gonzalez and David Ronfeldt, *Post-Revolutionary Cuba in a Changing World* (Santa Monica: Rand Corporation, December, 1975, R-1844-ISA), pp. 51–78. Much of the following discussion of elite-policy tendencies draws on this study.

5. *Granma* (September 14, 1974), pp. 2–3.

6. *Le Monde* (January 16, 1975), pp. 1, 4.

7. *Granma Weekly Review* (November 24, 1974), pp. 9–10.

8. For instance, in December 1974, Rodríguez obtained $900 million in Spanish credits; in January 1975, he visited Paris and obtained $350 million in credits; in March, Canada extended $155 million in credits; and in May, he secured an Anglo-Cuban cooperation agreement worth $580 million in British credits.

9. *Granma Weekly Review* (October 27, 1974), p. 3.

10. Ibid. (October 6, 1974), p. 3.

11. Ibid.

12. Ibid. (March 30, 1975), p. 3.

13. Interview with Mexican newsmen, Radio Havana, January 10, 1975.

14. See J. I. Domínguez, "Institutionalization," pp. 47–55, 61–62.

15. *Verde Olivo* (January 8, 1974), p. 6.

16. *Granma Weekly Review* (December 1, 1974), p. 7.

17. The French government expelled three Cuban diplomats from the Paris embassy in June 1975, accusing them of being Cuban intelligence (DGI) agents with ties to "Carlos," the notorious Venezuelan international terrorist, who had shot down three French security agents investigating a Palestinian terrorist ring.

CHAPTER 11

Cuba's Relations with the Soviet Union

33. Why We Have Points of Concurrence with the Soviet Union*

BY CARLOS RAFAEL RODRÍGUEZ
Translated by Eliana Loveluck

AREITO—Among certain circles in the United States, Cuba's foreign policy is considered to be dependent on the Soviet Union. Among others, it is believed not only that Cuba has its own foreign policy, but that this is very significant given its status as a small, non-oil-producing nation. What would you say are the points of concurrence between Cuban and Soviet foreign policy, and what would you consider to be the "tropical fruits" of the revolution's foreign policy?

C.R.R.—It is both natural and understandable to have points of concurrence or identification between Cuban and Soviet positions on basic contemporary foreign policy issues. Cuba and the Soviet Union are both socialist countries, and their leaders are inspired by the same Marxist-Leninist principles that guide their theoretical analyses. Therefore, it is not unusual that when examining the international situation and the economic causes in the current political crisis, both nations focus on these problems from the same perspective and explain them in similar fashion. Further, even if they carry out their analyses

*From Carlos Rafael Rodríguez, *Letra Con Filo* (Havana: Editorial Ciencas Sociales, 1983), Vol. 2, pp. 554–56. AREITO is a magazine edited and published by Cuban-Americans in the United States.

independently, they arrive at the same conclusions and emerge with similar proposals.

Some maintain that Cuba should hold a wide range of divergent positions from the Soviet Union's in order to demonstrate her independence. This is absurd. As socialists, both states adhere to a program which springs from the same principles. Among the objectives outlined in both the Cuban and Soviet constitutions are peace, disarmament, peaceful coexistence, the establishment of relationships based on mutual respect, and the independence of all nations of the world. It can be no other way. Does "independence" mean the acceptance of war as a way of resolving international disagreements, or the proclamation of an arms race while the Soviet Union defends disarmament?

The same problem arises with issues such as struggles for national liberation and development. Nobody should be surprised by the fact that while Cuba and the Soviet Union defend the rights of the peoples of Africa and the struggles for independence of Asian nations, imperialism is on the opposite side using new methods to maintain its economic and political domination over its colonial and neocolonial states.

Thus, because fundamental differences cannot exist between the foreign policies of Cuba and the Soviet Union, it is useless to look for them. Of course, Cuba's foreign policy is determined not only by general principles and theoretical guidelines, but also by very specific historical and geographic circumstances which sometimes mark its differences and its own pecularities. For example, among the "tropical fruits" of our foreign policy is the Cuban Revolution's militant position with respect to direct assistance for popular revolutionary movements in Latin America, movements which struggle against governments acting against international law. The example of Somoza is the most recent, but certainly not the only one. It can also be explained by Cuba's peculiar international position: Cuba is not a great power, and yet she has provided combative assistance and solidarity to countries like Ethiopia and Angola, which have requested Cuba's military presence in order to defend their national independence. If instead of a Cuban military presence there had been a Soviet military presence in these countries, the essence of the problem would have been the same. Logically, however, the international consequences would have been completely different.

The specificity of Cuba's foreign policy also appears internationally in such decisive problems as nuclear proliferation. The Soviet Union has been a leading actor in the Treaty Against Nuclear Proliferation. It can be understood that, as one of the main nuclear powers, the Soviet Union has an obligation to contribute to nuclear disarmament and a gradual reduction of the nuclear threat. Cuba views this issue from a different historical and geographical position. No one can think of Cuba as a nuclear threat. For that reason, when facing the Treaty Against Nuclear Proliferation and the Tlatelolco Treaty— put forth by Mexico with good intentions and a spirit which we share and support—Cuba has refused to sign either document. This is done as a form of protest against the fact that North American imperialism—the principal threat to Latin American peoples and the region—not only maintains but has expanded its nuclear base on territories over which it maintains a colonial domination.

Our independence cannot be based on a childish effort to differentiate ourselves from the Soviet Union's international positions much less to antagonize them. In his historical speech at the Fourth Summit Conference of the Nonaligned Movement in Algiers, Fidel Castro stated very clearly that Cubans are glad that one of the two modern superpowers is a socialist one. What would happen to developing nations were it not for the Soviet Union's military and economic prowess? Would Nicaragua have freed itself from Somoza if the present international correlation of power did not exist? Would the current Latin American repudiation of U.S. interventionist policy in Nicaragua have been possible in a world such as that which existed until a short time ago, where imperialist forces had a free reign?

Our foreign policy emanates out of our own decisions, it is based on our own analysis and its foundations are found in the principles we uphold. But one of its permanent elements is the consideration of the Soviet Union's historical role, and the fact that the USSR is our most important ally in the struggle for peace, national independence, and the socialism to which we aspire.

34. Cuba and the Soviet Union: Does Cuba Act Alone?*

BY ROBERT A. PASTOR

Imagine, for a moment, that the U.S. Air Force helped airlift 36,000 Colombian soldiers to fight in an African country. At the same time, the United States flew tanks, artillery, and other heavy military equipment directly to that country for use by the Colombians, whose wounded were evacuated to the United States for treatment. Two years later, about 12,000 Colombian soldiers would be airlifted to another African country by the United States to fight under the command of a U.S. general. And imagine that Colombia received more economic aid from the United States than did any other developing nation and that it received all its military equipment free.

Now imagine how the Cuban government would describe Colombia. Would

*From Barry B. Levine, ed., *The New Cuban Presence in the Caribbean* (Boulder, CO: Westview Press, 1983). Edited for this volume.

Cuban officials or scholars suggest that Colombia was an autonomous actor in international affairs or that it was leading the United States into Third World missions of liberation? Not likely. Even when Latin American governments rail against U.S. foreign policy in public and in private, Cuba has no compunction about referring to them as "puppets of U.S. imperialism." If one used Castro's own criterion of what constitutes a "puppet" or a "proxy," Cuba would qualify. No country in Latin America has so slavishly followed the international line of the United States in the 1970s as Cuba has that of the USSR. However, as Castro knows better than any American, the principal purpose of using words like "proxy" is propaganda—to force the target to defend its independence and to alter its policies.

This chapter will not use Castro's standard; rather its purpose is to analyze the extent to which one can view Cuban foreign policy as independent.

HISTORY: US–CUBA–USSR

... Three distinct phases in Cuban foreign policy, which correspond to changes in the Cuban-Soviet relationship, can be identified: (1) revolution by improvisation, 1959–1967; (2) revolution in due course, 1968–1975; and (3) revolution by professionalism, 1975 to the present.

Phase I: Revolution by Improvisation, 1959–1967

In the early 1960s, Castro and his Argentine comrade Ernesto "Che" Guevara pursued the elusive revolution through Bolivia, Guatemala, Colombia, Peru, and Venezuela. Their adventures stemmed initially not from devotion to the world communist movement but rather from a romantic Latin American tradition of revolution, a sense of social injustice, and a deep-seated animosity toward the United States. Their *foco* strategy was aimed at replicating their experience in Cuba, making revolution by a small, well-organized group. It was Leninism mixed with Latin American impatience and youthful exuberance.

This strategy stood in contrast to the methodical and deliberate approach of the Soviet-line Communist parties in Latin America, which had been working for decades to create the conditions whereby revolution would become possible. The Cuban Revolution caught them—and the Soviet Union—by surprise.[1]

Scholars differ on whether Castro was pushed into the waiting arms of the Soviet Union by an embittered and belligerent hegemone (the United States) or leaped on to the unsuspecting shoulders of the Soviets as the best means of centralizing his control. All agree, however, that this two-sided relationship was driven and shaped by an unconnected third corner—the United States—and that the consequence of the replacement of U.S. hegemony with that of the Soviet Union was the elimination of alternative sources of economic and political power within Cuba and the systematic consolidation of a bureau-cratic-militarized state.[2] The Soviets provided Castro with a legitimizing doc-trine, a protective security shield, and economic aid and support to withstand the U.S. embargo and to help the Cubans extend their influence.

In this improvisational period, the Cuban Revolution was something of a mixed blessing for the Soviet Union. On the one hand, it represented the first advance of communism since the Chinese Revolution, and as the ideological and strategic struggle with the People's Republic of China grew more serious, the Soviets were eager to have the Cubans associate with their line. On the other hand, although the Cubans electrified the romantic left in Latin America, they also confounded the traditional Communist parties. Castro did make a few attempts to enlist the support of Latin America's Communist parties, notably in a meeting of the Soviet Communist party and Latin American Communist parties in Havana at the end of 1964. But he and Guevara had little patience with the Communist parties, and in the cases of Venezuela, Colombia, and Guatemala, the Cubans were not averse to criticizing the Communists and supporting the guerrillas.[3]

The Communist parties feared that the revolutionaries—whom they called "leftist opportunists"—would provoke a harsh reaction and jeopardize all that they had sought to build. The Soviets urged the Cubans to be cautious and to work with the Communist parties rather than try to run over them, but the Cubans did not listen. "In the end," Cole Blasier concluded, "events proved Moscow and the orthodox Communists right."[4] Both the guerrillas and the Communist parties were crushed throughout Latin America, and in October 1967 Che Guevara was killed in Bolivia. To a great extent, Cuba's freewheeling period of fomenting revolution died with Che.

In 1967–1968, relations between the Soviet Union and Cuba reached the breaking point. The Soviets first used an orthodox group of the Cuban Com-munist party led by Aníbal Escalante to try either to preempt Castro or to persuade him to cease his support for the armed struggle in Latin America. When Castro crushed that group, the Soviets turned to more conventional leverage, reducing shipments of petroleum to Cuba, which was—and re-mains—dependent on the Soviets for 98 percent of its supplies. Simultaneously the Soviets announced additional exports of petroleum to Brazil and Chile, two enemies of Cuba.[5] As Cuba had closed its U.S. and China options, Castro had no choice but to accept Soviet direction.

Phase II: Revolution in Due Course, 1968–1975

Castro's endorsement of the Soviet invasion of Czechoslovakia in 1968 and the Brezhnev Doctrine, which asserted the right of the Soviet Union to define the limits of permissible behavior for Communist countries, signaled the end of the improvisational phase of Cuban foreign policy and the beginning of a more conventional approach. . . .

In this second phase, while adopting a foreign policy more compatible with that of the Soviet Union, Cuba also tightened its economic and political relationship, driven by the failure of the ten-million-ton harvest and the decline of the entire economy. In 1972 Fidel Castro visited Moscow twice to negotiate Cuban membership in the Soviet-bloc Council for Mutual Economic Assistance (COMECON) and to sign five agreements, which have been described as the "point of no return" for Cuban economic dependence on the USSR. Castro also pledged that Cuba would never accept "opportunism, neutralism, revisionism, liberalism, or capitalist ideological penetration"; in short, the Soviet Union could rely on Cuba.

Although Cuba did not retreat from supporting revolution abroad, it put away its trumpet and avoided antagonizing the Communist parties. After Che's death, Castro shifted his attention away from Latin America and more toward Africa, Asia, and the Middle East. Cuba had supported African liberation movements since the beginning of its revolution, but in this second phase Castro began investing personnel and resources in training and supporting the various liberation movements.

A major emphasis, however, was on reestablishing normal diplomatic relations with its neighbors and seeking leadership of the Nonaligned Movement (NAM). Latin American countries responded favorably to Cuba's expressed interest in peaceful relations, and by 1975, Argentina, Peru, Colombia, Venezuela, Panama, Costa Rica, and the four main English-speaking Caribbean nations—Jamaica, Barbados, Trinidad and Tobago, and Guyana—had all reestablished diplomatic relations. The United States also privately began to explore relations in 1975 and publicly played an important role in removing OAS sanctions. . . .

Phase III: A Coordinated, Professional Approach to Revolution

The third phase of Cuban foreign policy began in September 1975 with the massive Cuban military intervention in Angola. If the first phase represented Cuban pursuit of an objective—Communist revolution—shared by the Soviet Union by tactics that were not, and the second phase, Cuban acceptance of Soviet tactics, the third phase represented the culmination of the new and deeper relationship—a more coordinated and professional approach to extending communism to the Third World. In 1975 the First Congress of the Cuban Communist Party approved a platform that acknowledged the subordination of Cuban to Soviet foreign policy.

In September 1975 the first detachment of 1,000 Cuban soldiers arrived in Angola to fight on behalf of the Popular Movement for the Liberation of Angola (MPLA), one of three Angolan factions seeking power. There had been up to 100 Cuban advisers in Angola for at least a decade and roughly 250 since the spring of 1975, but the September intervention represented the first use of Cuban combat troops on a major scale. Cuban soldiers arrived by ship and by airplane from Cuba, but most of their equipment came directly from the Soviet Union and Eastern Europe. After the South African incursion on October 23, some 2,000–3,000 Cuban reinforcements were airlifted; they arrived before the Portuguese formally lowered their flag on November 11 and Angola ceased to be a colony.

By January 1976, there were 10,000–12,000 Cuban troops using increasingly sophisticated Soviet weaponry, and the Cuban-backed MPLA was firmly in charge of Luanda and much of the country. Castro would later admit that at the height of Cuban involvement in the spring of 1975 there were 36,000 Cuban troops in Angola.[6]

. . . Cuba exploited its success by broadening its diplomatic relations in Africa (from eight nations in 1972 to 31 after Angola), by deepening its relationships in the Caribbean among groups and governments that were sympathetic with the black African struggle against South Africa, and by being elected host to the sixth summit of the NAM to be held in September 1979, thereby becoming chairman for the following three-year period.

Cuba also earned significant new amounts of economic and military aid from the Soviet Union for the operation. On April 14, 1976, the Soviet Union signed a new five-year economic agreement with Cuba that more than doubled Soviet economic and technical aid. The Cuban military also profited, increasing its political power in Cuba (two generals were appointed to the Council of State) and gaining a new generation of sophisticated military equipment from the Soviets. . . .

Just as Cuba chose military involvement in Angola rather than normalization of relations with the Ford administration, so too did it choose its next military involvement—in Ethiopia—in January 1978 despite clear messages from the Carter administration that such an act would make further progress toward normalization impossible. The Ethiopian operation was the result of complete coordination with the Soviet Union, and 12,000 Cuban troops fought under the command of a Soviet general.

. . . In March 1979 a group of radicals called the New Jewel Movement (NJM) seized power in Grenada in the first undemocratic change of government in the English-speaking Caribbean and requested Cuban support. There is some evidence that the Cubans assured the NJM that if they were able to seize and hold power for a short time, the Cubans would soon come to their aid, as they did.

Cuba's approach toward Central America tended to favor armed struggle as the path to power because the region's politics were violent and because Castro felt he had some scores to settle against governments that had tried to overthrow him. Needless to say, Cuba observed political developments in Nicaragua in 1978–1979 with great interest, but it let Venezuela, Panama, and Costa Rica play the central role in helping the Sandinistas. Cuba stayed in the background, offering political and military advice to the military *comandantes* and supplying arms to the Sandinistas through a variety of means.

THE STRUCTURE OF THE CURRENT RELATIONSHIP

One of the major intellectual contributions of Marxism to social science is the concept that human or institutional behavior is shaped, and sometimes determined, by economic and political structures. Let us therefore examine the structure—specifically, the economic, political, military, and attitudinal bonds that currently tie Cuba to the Soviet Union and affect the day-to-day relationship.

The economic relationship between Cuba and the Soviet Union has evolved from a few project agreements in the early 1960s, to membership in COMECON in 1972, to two five-year economic plans (1976–1980 and 1981–1985), which further integrated Cuba into the Soviet economic system. From 1960 to 1979, Cuba received the equivalent of $16.6 billion in aid from the Soviet Union.[7] Of this, about 35 percent (or $5.7 billion) was loans provided as balance of payments support and development aid, and 65 percent (or $10.9 billion) was subsidized prices for sugar and nickel that the Soviet Union purchased from Cuba and reduced prices of petroleum that it sold to Cuba. . . .

The overall level of aid has quadrupled since 1974, partly in compensation for new Cuban activities in the world and partly because the world price of sugar has declined and that of oil has risen much more rapidly than Soviet prices. Soviet aid amounted to about $3 billion in 1978 and again in 1979, representing about one fourth of the Cuban gross national product in each year. In 1972, the USSR terminated interest charges on Cuba's debt and postponed initial repayment until 1986. Cuba's debt reached $2.6 billion in 1980, of which $1.6 billion is hard-currency debt to Western commercial banks.

There have been three enduring strains in Cuba's economic development in the last twenty years. First, the economy remains very dependent on the export of sugar—probably the only country in the world more dependent on a single crop in 1978 (83 percent of exports) than in 1958 (78 percent). Second, it remains strikingly dependent on a single trading partner. In 1959, 68 percent of Cuba's trade was with its nearest neighbor, the United States; twenty years later, 66 percent of its trade was with the Soviet Union. Third, it continues to suffer a chronic trade deficit, currently financed by the Soviet Union. . . .

The military relationship has drawn much closer since the intervention in Angola. Cubans fought under Soviet command in Ethiopia while Soviet pilots substituted for them in Cuba. Cuba is the only country receiving Soviet military equipment free of charge, and it has been receiving massive quantities of it. Most recently in 1981, according to the U.S. State Department, Cuba received some 66,000 tons of military equipment, including the most sophisticated jet fighters, transports, and naval vessels—three times more equipment than in any previous year since 1962.[8] The State Department estimates a total of about 40,000 Cuban soldiers in a dozen African nations and 1,800 to 2,000 military and security personnel in Nicaragua. Although Cuba is not a member of the Warsaw Pact, Cuban leaders routinely participate as observers in Warsaw Pact military maneuvers. Cuba provides facilities for port calls by Soviet submarines, a massive intelligence-collection facility, an air base to deploy Soviet reconnaissance aircraft, and training facilities for tropical warfare for a 2,600-man Soviet combat brigade.

The political relationship between the two governments has been shaped by personal relationships and by the Cuban Communist party, which Fidel Castro calls "the revolution's finest expression and guarantee." As dependence on the Soviet Union increased, the Cuban Communist party grew in importance and in numbers—doubling its membership from 1970 to 1975 and again from 1975 to 1980. . . .

Cuban dependence on the USSR for economic and military aid, support, and defense is staggering not just because of the magnitude of the aid and its importance to the Cuban economy, but also because Cuba lacks an alternative. As the Cuban government has no apparent interest in either ceasing its support for revolution or starting a new dependent relationship, a normal relationship with the United States is unlikely, even though popular attitudes in Cuba and elite attitudes in the United States might support bridging the chasm separating the two countries. The structure of the current relationship suggests that the Soviets will retain considerable power to compel Cuban foreign policy to remain within proscribed boundaries.

PROCESS: CUBAN-SOVIET INTERACTION

To understand the role of Cuban foreign policy in the Cuban-Soviet relationship, it is important to understand not only the structure and the boundaries of the relationship, but also the process of interaction.

During the last 20 years, the only public disagreement between Cuba and the Soviet Union was during the missile crisis, when the Soviets agreed to withdraw their missiles and permit international inspection in exchange for a U.S. pledge not to invade Cuba. Castro strongly condemned the Soviet decision. . . .

Cuba remains more eager than the Soviet Union to take risks, more willing to assist national liberation movements in any and all ways. . . . The Soviet Union . . . is naturally more reluctant about directly confronting the United States, more interested in maintaining its control of Eastern Europe, more protective of the international Communist movement, and more niggardly about providing foreign aid.

In those areas in which Cuban and Soviet objectives and tactics converge, such as in Angola, Ethiopia, and the Middle East, one could predict that the Cubans would encourage the Soviets to do a little more, a little quicker, while the Soviets would be more cautious and sensitive to the geopolitical implications of sending Cuban and/or Soviet soldiers into combat. In the case of Angola, for example, scholars who stress the independence of Cuban foreign policy have argued that the Cubans pressed the Soviets to undertake the operation rather than the other way around. That argument is plausible, for Castro is undoubtedly more predisposed to risking an adventure. Moreover, the risks would be greater for the superpower if the Cubans were defeated and the Soviets watched passively. But once it became clear that the South Africans would withdraw, that U.S. involvement would be minimal, if anything, and that no other foreign military involvement was likely, the massive Cuban intervention seemed an effective and relatively low-risk operation. It needs to be recognized, however, that the Cuban effort would never have reached the magnitude it did without Soviet consent and logistical support, so that the suggestion that the Cubans did not even consult the Soviets is unrealistic. Moreover, the Cuban effort could not have succeeded if the Soviets had opposed it, or even if they had not supported it. Cuban Vice-President Carlos Rafael Rodríguez admitted as much: "Cuba and Angola did not have all the technical means for their men to fight the racist South African army . . . without the USSR, imperialism would have defeated the Angolan people."[9]

In Central America and the Caribbean, the Soviets have probably given the Cubans the most room to maneuver because the Cubans clearly know both the actors and the political landscape better and also because Fidel Castro has tremendous personal influence over the region's revolutionaries, which the Soviet Union could never duplicate. Occasionally, the Soviets used the Cubans as intermediaries, such as in August 1981, when Cubans arranged a meeting in Panama between a senior Soviet Communist party functionary and Central American Communist party leaders to discuss strategy in the region.[10]

The Cubans probably lobbied the Soviets to give more aid to Nicaragua, Grenada, and while Manley was in power, Jamaica, but the Soviets are not eager to subsidize other governments, as it is hard to see how these governments could benefit the Soviet Union any more than Cuba already does. The Soviets have been burned in Egypt, Indonesia, Ghana, and Somalia and are understandably reluctant to bankroll other governments that have not yet committed themselves totally to communism. . . .

On Poland and Afghanistan, in which Soviet and Cuban interests diverged, the Soviets did not even bother to keep the Cubans informed. In 1979 one of Cuba's principal foreign policy goals was to assume the leadership of the Nonaligned Movement in fact as well as in name and to try to steer the movement toward a "natural alliance" with the Soviet Union. After the summit, Cuba sought a seat on the United Nations Security Council in its capacity as chairman of the NAM, but the majority of Latin American states balked and joined the United States, Western Europe, and a number of Asian governments to block Cuba's bid. After more than one hundred votes in which Cuba was often quite close to winning the seat, the Soviets invaded Afghanistan, and within days the Cubans recognized that their position in the NAM was undermined and withdrew.

It must have been painful for Castro, who had the leadership of the NAM and the Third World almost within his grasp, only to be deprived of it by his patron—particularly as the Soviets did not consult him prior to their intervention or brief him afterward. One month after it occurred Castro was still puzzled about what had happened and why the Soviets had done it.[11] But when the United Nations General Assembly moved to condemn the Soviet Union for the invasion, Castro did not need instructions from the Soviet Union; he knew what position to take.

In a convoluted speech somewhat reminiscent of Castro's endorsement of the Soviet invasion of Czechoslovakia in 1968, the Cuban ambassador to the United Nations voted with the Soviet Union, but instead of endorsing the invasion, he attacked U.S. imperialism. That was as near as Castro could bring himself to criticizing the Soviet action, which had cost him dearly. . . .

PARTNER, PROXY, PUPPET, OR PALADIN?

How should one characterize the relationship between Cuba and the Soviet Union? Since the Cuban involvement in Angola, three quite different U.S. administrations have referred to Cuba as a "proxy" of Soviet policy, but most academics reject that term. "Cuba is not the Soviet Union's proxy in Africa," wrote political scientist William LeoGrande; "the two are partners, and though the partnership is asymmetrical, it is reciprocal nonetheless."[12] Cole Blasier, a noted scholar on both Latin America and the Soviet Union, wrote: "Castro has shown time and again, most particularly in the 1960s, that he is not a Soviet puppet, but a formidable negotiator, and useful ally."[13] And finally, Edward González and RAND has suggested that Cuba is really a "paladin," which denotes Cuba's autonomy "and her value as a separate global actor."[14]

Castro, of course, insists on his independence. In an interview in April 1976 about whether in sending troops to Angola he acted on his own or at the command of the Soviet Union, Castro insisted: "Cuba made its decision completely on its own responsibility. The USSR . . . never requested that a single Cuban be sent to that country."[15] And in a typical response to a similar question by Dan Rather, on October 1, 1979, Castro threw the question back: "I am not going to respond to that ridiculous charge, but I will ask a question: Why, if we are a satellite country, is there so much attention paid to Cuba? And it is obvious that the U.S. government in the political field is paying practically more attention to Cuba than to the Soviet Union. So then we are unquestionably facing a strange case of a satellite." . . .

Cuba is neither a "puppet," a nation whose policies "are prompted and controlled" by the Soviets, nor a "partner" in the sense that denotes some rough form of equality. However, to the extent that a "partner" means "a player on the same side or team," as Cuba is with the Soviet Union, and with the understanding that the latter is the captain, the coach, and the owner of the team, the term could be considered more accurate. But this view suggests the Cubans do not call any plays themselves, which they clearly do; or that they would only accidentally go "off-sides," "clip," or "rough the kicker," which they clearly do on purpose and with considerable relish.

González's term "paladin" is clever if one identifies it with the "hired gun" of a popular television show. The dictionary definition, however, says that a "paladin" is "one of the twelve legendary knights of Charlemagne, therefore a determined advocate or defender of a noble cause." This does not appear to be what González had in mind, nor does it seem applicable. "Surrogate" or "proxy" means "one who is appointed to act for another; a deputy; a substitute," but this too is inadequate since it suggests that the Cubans are acting only in the Soviets' interests, whereas they are clearly acting in their own as well. It suggests that the two nations' foreign policies are virtually interchangeable, although the previous discussion on the evolution of Cuban foreign policy and the process of interaction with the Soviets makes it clear that the Soviet Union and Cuba have two foreign policies, not one. They share some important objectives—extending communism and containing the United States—but because of different national perspectives and interests, the leaders of the two nations do not see the world in identical ways nor do they approach it in the same way. Cuba might very well be more of a *demandeur* in its relationship with the Soviet Union, as the burden of maintaining international peace sits more lightly on Castro's shoulders than on those of the Soviet leadership, and because the Cubans are offering Soviet resources rather than their own.

The combination of Cuban manpower and Soviet resources has proved an effective tool for furthering the two nations' interests in the world. The Soviet Union cannot undertake the kinds of activities and operations in the Third World that the Cubans do routinely without provoking global tensions and perhaps a response from the United States or the People's Republic of China. The irony is that the United States is inhibited from confronting Cuba because Cuba is perceived as an independent, Third World nation struggling against the most powerful nation in the world.

The Cubans do make tactical foreign policy decisions themselves, but strategic decisions such as those that involve Cuban troops require Soviet consent. Scholars or policymakers are hard-pressed, however, to find an area in which Cuban and Soviet foreign policies have significantly diverged since 1968— certainly not in Angola, Ethiopia, Central America, the Caribbean, or the Nonaligned Movement. In areas where Cuban interests might lead them in a different direction—like Afghanistan, Poland, or China—the Cubans have dutifully supported the Soviet position.

It has been argued that Cuba is a small country with a big country's foreign policy. No other developing nation maintains more diplomatic missions, intelligence operatives, and military advisers and troops abroad than does Cuba, not even the oil-producing states that can afford it. The gap between its internal resources and its external capabilities is filled by the Soviet Union, not because of altruism, but because the Soviets are assured that what the Cubans do abroad will serve their purposes. That does not mean that the Soviet Union gives instructions—it generally does not have to, as was shown, for example, by the vote on Afghanistan. Soviet instructions are not necessary because Cuba is pursuing a set of interests that coincide with those of the Soviet Union. . . .

NOTES

1. Jerry Hough described the Soviet reaction to Castro's triumph as an "absolutely unexpected event"; their Institute of Latin America was first established in 1960. See Jerry F. Hough, "The Evolving Soviet Debate on Latin America," *Latin American Research Review,* Vol. 16, No. 1 (1981), p. 127.

2. On the thesis that the United States pushed the Cubans, see, for example, Maurice Zeitlin and Robert Scheer, *Cuba: Tragedy in Our Hemisphere,* (New York: Grove Press, 1963). For a brief but cogent discussion of the thesis that the Cubans were the pushers because "it was impossible to conduct a revolution in Cuba without a major confrontation with the U.S.," see Jorge I. Domínguez, *Cuba: Order and Revolution* (Cambridge, MA: Harvard University Press, 1978), pp. 137–49.

3. William E. Ratliff, *Castroism and Communism in Latin America, 1959–1976* (Washington, D.C.: American Enterprise Institute and Hoover Institution on War, Revolution and Peace, 1976), p. 27. Also see Cole Blasier, *Soviet Relations and Latin America in the 1970s* (Cambridge, MA: National Council for Soviet and East European Research, 1979), Part 4, pp. 8–20.

4. C. Blasier, *Soviet Relations with Latin America,* Part 4, p. 17.

5. J. I. Domínguez, *Cuba: Order and Revolution,* pp. 161–62.

6. Fidel Castro's admission was in his speech to the Council of Ministers at the National People's Government Assembly, December 27, 1979. For a good description and analysis of the Cuban involvement in Angola, see William M. LeoGrande, *Cuba's Policy in Africa, 1959–1980* (Berkeley: Univ. of California Institute of International Studies, 1980), Policy Papers in International Affairs, No. 13, pp. 13–34 [excerpted in this volume, Reading 42]; Nathaniel Davis, "The Angola Decision of 1975: A Personal Memoir," *Foreign Affairs,* Vol. 57, No. 1 (Fall 1978), pp. 109–24; and Edward González, "Institutionalism, Political Elites, and Foreign Policies," in Cole Blasier and Carmelo Mesa-Lago, eds., *Cuba in the World* (Pittsburgh: Univ. of Pittsburgh Press, 1979), pp. 23–33 [also excerpted in this volume, Reading 32].

7. This section on the economic relationship borrows heavily from the statistics in Lawrence H. Theriot, "Cuba Faces the Economic Relations of the 1980s," a study prepared by the U.S. Department of Commerce for the Joint Economic Committee of the Congress, March 22, 1982. Also see Cole Blasier, "COMECON in Cuban Development"; Carmelo Mesa-Lago, "The Economy and International Economic Relations"; and Jorge F. Perez Lopez, "Sugar and Petroleum in Cuba-Soviet Terms of Trade," in C. Blasier and C. Mesa-Lago, eds., *Cuba in the World,* pp. 169–98, pp. 225–56, and pp. 273–96.

8. For more details, see the interview with Alexander Haig, *New York Times* (February 8, 1982), p. A12. Carlos Rafael Rodríguez confirmed in a speech to the United Nations on June 16, 1982, that Cuba had "almost doubled" its military capability in 1981.

9. Cited in Nelson Valdés, "Revolutionary Solidarity in Angola," in C. Blasier and C. Mesa-Lago, eds., *Cuba in the World,* p. 105.

10. U.S. Department of State, Bureau of Public Affairs, "Cuba's Renewed Support of Violence in Latin America" (December 14, 1981), p. 3.

11. For a brief account of the meeting on January 17, 1980, between President Fidel Castro, Peter Tarnoff of the State Department, and the author, from which this observation and others came, see Jimmy Carter, *Keeping Faith: Memoirs of a President* (New York: Bantam Books, 1982), pp. 479–80.

12. W. M. LeoGrande, *Cuba's Policy in Africa,* p. 68.

13. C. Blasier, "The Soviet Union in the Cuban-American Conflict," in C. Blasier and C. Mesa-Lago, eds., *Cuba in the World,* p. 37.

14. E. González, "Institutionalism," p. 37.

15. Cited in N. Valdés, "Revolutionary Solidarity," p. 110.

35. The Cost of Cuba's Trade with Socialist Countries*

By Pamela S. Falk

Cuba's economy is a centrally planned stated-owned economy in which the "state organizes, directs, and controls the economic life of the nation."[1] Foreign trade, according to the Constitution, is "the exclusive function of the state" (Article 18). The Ministry of Foreign Trade was created in 1961 to be the only state agency authorized to conduct foreign trade.[2] All trade is conducted by the ministry through its 40 foreign trade enterprises, each responsible for a specific product. The central planning agency, the Junta Central de Planificación (JUCEPLAN), established in 1961, formulates the direction of long-range economic planning, and in 1970 it became the highest agency of Cuban economic policy.[3] Annual budgets of individual agencies and economic enterprises are submitted to JUCEPLAN. After conferring with members of the National Bank where it compiles Cuba's central budget, JUCEPLAN then submits a recommended budget to the Council of Ministers. The budget today is based on a system of cost accounting and calculated by computer and data collection systems introduced since 1970. Cuba's state bank, the National Bank of Cuba, in addition to aiding JUCEPLAN in the formulation of the annual budget, issues all currency and finances all imports. The Ministry of Foreign Trade (MINCEX) directs the movement of the enterprises such as CUBAZUCAR (sugar and sugar products); CUBAEXPORT (oil, cement, chemicals); CARIBEX (seafood);

*From Pamela S. Falk, *Cuban Foreign Policy* (Lexington, MA: Lexington Books, 1985), pp. 131–36.

CUBATOBACO (tobacco); CUBANIQUEL (nickel); and CUBARTE-SANIA (textile garments). Until 1975 the Cuban enterprises did not retain their earned income; nor did they fulfill cost-accounting and profitability measures. The new 1975 Economic Management System requires each enterprise to balance its budget. Since all elements of the economy are state owned, trade and specific commercial agreements rely heavily on Cuban government policies of (1) budgetary accountability, (2) profitability, (3) diversification of trade partners, and (4) domestic development.

As a result, the implementation of the Economic Management System (Sistema de Dirección Económica) also affects Cuba's foreign trade. Foreign trade in the 1970s, Cuba's choice of foreign trading partners, and the terms of foreign trade agreements have together had a forceful impact on Cuba's balance of payments, its ability to increase trade with different non-socialist nations, and its choice of domestic economic development programs. Ultimately they have been the most significant factors in the determination of the direction of the domestic economy. The Cuban economy must absorb the entire shock of its foreign trade arrangements. In sum, the levels of development indicate that Cuba's trade is as vulnerable on the international financial market as it was in prerevolutionary days. . . .

INTEGRATION IN THE CMEA

In January 1949 the Council for Mutual Economic Assistance (CMEA) was established in Moscow with the objectives of improving the economic development of socialist nations, exchanging technological and economic information, and counteracting the Marshall Plan assistance program from Western nations.[4] In 1969 the CMEA charter was written, and it listed the aims of the organization as follows: (1) to contribute to advanced economic and technical growth of member countries, (2) to achieve a higher level of industrialization in the less-developed countries of the organization, (3) to increase labor productivity through efficiency, and (4) to insure continual progress in the welfare of member states.[5]

A significant aspect of CMEA agreements is the link between foreign trade and national development plans which is implicit in its policy of "international socialist division of labor," which was adopted by CMEA members in June 1962. At that time, the organization enunciated the goals of *coordinated development* of the economies of member nations as well as a policy of specialization of their export products.

The trade policies most significant to Cuba's involvement in CMEA are those of integration and specialization. Planning of integration and specialization in CMEA countries is based on the principles of socialist development. This definition, which orients CMEA accords, applies several tenets of Marxist economic theory to policies of distribution. The realization of the Communist welfare state is a major objective of development based on the principle of "to each according to his needs, from each according to his ability." Each society, according to its resources and production capability, must achieve as high a rate of growth as possible with the maximum possible diversification of products. A second tenet applied in these socialist trade agreements is the law of planned proportional development. The application of a proportional development strategy requires an economy which is state owned and centrally planned and which follows a growth strategy which considers social as well as political and economic objectives. By definition, planned proportional development includes socially progressive programs such as education. This policy is sometimes referred to as unbalanced since it seeks, at times, to deemphasize rapid growth in certain sectors in favor of the policy of distribution and social reform. Finally, economic development along socialist lines requires the deemphasis of the importation of capital goods in order to emphasize self-sufficient production and reduce consumer product imports.

The CMEA policy of specialization derives from the simple trade maxim that concurrent expansion of trade within a region or alliance enables the region to expand trade and production at a faster rate than the domestic production in each member nation individually. This policy is established by eliminating overlapping and duplicate production among participant countries.[6] A 1960s study of intraregional coordination policies within CMEA illustrated that a 50 percent increase in production specialization would increase their labor productivity by 20 percent.[7] The result, CMEA planners insisted, would be mutual interdependence.[8]

The major problem with a policy of specialization in theory (and one which has been responsible for the lack of development within certain key sectors of Cuba's economy) is that it increases trade dependence. Among the beneficial effects of regional cooperation is the resultant increase in regional labor productivity and trade relations which are interdependent not dependent.

CMEA trade is organized on the basis of two types of trade agreements: first, trade protocols or annual accords which fix prices and quantities, and, second, middle-term (five-year) trade agreements.[9] Two international organizations that serve as extensions of CMEA trade organizations (and are tangentially important to Cuba's membership) are the two banks of the council: the International Investment Bank (IIB) and the International Bank for Economic Cooperation (IBEC).[10] Both banks were established to serve the member nations with intraregional trade: IBEC provides short-term capital credits in nontransferable currency, the transferable ruble; the IIB provides long-term capital for members and has an endowment of both transferable rubles as well as hard currency.[11]

In 1954 CMEA established the policy which linked *specialization* to the coordination of member countries' national economic plans.[12] A CMEA handbook, published in 1972, defined the policy of specialization as follows:

The idea of international division of labor, which is one form of social *division of labor,* is that countries should specialize in the production of particular goods for subsequent exchange. *Transcending national borders,* it has drawn all peoples into the process of social production.[13]

Although this process guarantees the most efficient use of natural, economic, and manpower resources, there are significant problems with the policy.

CMEA: TRADE POLICY

Since the 1960s, CMEA has adopted the principles of international socialist division of labor. In the early 1970s, CMEA had other serious economic problems. Among those were the following: (1) the Eastern bloc had a hard currency debt to the West, estimated at $45.8 billion* at the end of 1976; (2) global inflation and the international recession increased prices of imports to CMEA countries; (3) there was less demand since reduced aggregate growth in developed nations of the West had reduced imports; and (4) oil prices were higher with Eastern Europe paying $3 billion for oil supplies.[14]

Even more significant, the major problem within CMEA trade is the regulation of prices. In the past decade, CMEA has produced a market in which the prices paid for machinery and equipment are higher than the world market prices and the prices paid for primary products with the exception of sugar are lower.[15] Since Cuba's trade in 1974 was 52 percent with CMEA in addition to the fact that this trade was done as a semibarter negotiating process, the amount of convertible currency in Cuba was (and is) low. CMEA agreements or annual trade protocols establish the prices and volume of each nation's trade quotas with the council and are based on political considerations and foreign policy decisions in addition to economic factors.

Cuba's trade with the CMEA has accounted for a significant proportion of Cuba's foreign trade since its membership in 1972. Exports to CMEA countries tripled between 1973 and 1976, from $781 million to $2.3 billion in 1976. Imports from CMEA countries almost doubled during the same period, from $1.2 billion in 1973 to $2.2 billion in 1976. In 1974 after two years of trade under the CMEA agreements, Cuba's trade concentration with member nations of the CMEA and other socialist nations combined did not exceed Cuba's trade concentration with the United States in 1958. By 1976, however, Cuba's trade concentration with socialist nations was at approximately the equivalent to Cuba's prerevolutionary U.S. trade. At that time, Cuban exports of sugar to CMEA countries reached 64 percent of total sugar exports.

CMEA trade agreements offered Cuba additional subsidies to those that Cuba received from Soviet trade. Cuba joined CMEA because it provided incentives even greater than Cuban-Soviet trade had, with no reduction in

*[Currency rates are stated in U.S. dollars.—eds.]

Soviet assistance. In fact, Cuba entered the CMEA on terms far more favorable than all other nine members.

In December 1979 Fidel Castro emphasized the problems of CMEA trade when he addressed the National Assembly. Trade with CMEA member nations, he stated, is unable to provide Cuba with essential supplies. Wood, for example, was a product that Cuba needed, and it had an agreement to buy five hundred thousand cubic meters from the Soviet Union. The contract was not honored, however, and only three hundred thousand cubic meters were delivered, which had a severe impact on Cuba's troubled construction industry. A second socialist trade agreement for chickens was cancelled, thereby forcing Cuba to slaughter more cattle in order to fulfill domestic food needs. However, subsidies from the Soviet Union for sugar exports in December 1979 were 30 cents above the world market price (of 14 cents per pound). Oil sold below world market prices (of $25 to $30 a barrel).[16]

Subsidies by CMEA nations by 1980 were high, and in the short term Cuba could not find as favorable trade agreements on any other market. Although Cuba's domestic production has been low and domestic economic problems prevail, Cuba does not have the viable option of diversifying trade partners or reducing trade concentration in CMEA nations for the foreseeable future. Cuba's membership in CMEA offered Cuba, at a minimum, a continuation of subsidized sugar prices and favorable terms of trade on capital goods imports from the Soviet Union. The additional advantages included greater efficiency with less labor necessary as a result of the CMEA policies of labor division and plan coordination.

The significance of Cuba's export structure in the early 1970s has become more apparent since the close of the decade. Higher levels of productivity did occur in the late 1970s, and the volume of Cuban exports did not increase. Rather, Cuba's membership in the CMEA has resulted in a static policy of comparative advantage and expanded production in Cuba's single principal sector—sugar. Clearly, the costs of Cuba's membership in the CMEA have been and continue to be extremely high.

It is too simple an answer to point only to pressures from the Soviet Union for an understanding of Cuba's motivation to join the council. Cuba's debt to the Soviet Union in 1972 was high, but Cuba during this period had substantial economic and political assets to offer to both council member nations and the Soviet Union. First, Cuba's membership added political credibility to the organization. Second, and more important, Cuba's economy in 1972 was beginning to gain steadily—though slowly—and all indications were that the Cuban economy was in the beginning of a period of sustained growth. This prospect was evident in 1973, and it culminated in 1974 in high sugar prices, consequent high revenues, and a surplus balance of payments.

Cuba joined the CMEA in 1972 because the Soviet Union provided Cuba with strong incentives to do so. In addition, Cuba had options in the 1970s;

perhaps they were restricted relative to the economic prospects of a developed market nation. Nonetheless, Cuban economic planners and political leaders had a choice, and the promise of an economically sound future. As Cuba entered its third development decade, Cuban planners had a narrower range of options. According to the Cuban government, the economy has grown at an annual average of 4.7 percent during the last 25 years. However, other sources point to growth rates as low as -0.2 percent during the same period. The 1985 plan cited the growth of gross social product from 4.5 percent to 5 percent; a 3.5 percent increase in productivity; a 1.5 percent increase in wages; and maintenance of the present "standard of living."[17] At this point, with an infrastructure firmly tied to sugar production, and record world market inflation, Cuba has little choice but to retain the trade alliances which it made slightly more than a decade ago.

There had been several incentives for Cuba to enter the CMEA, including high subsidized prices for Cuban commodities, low prices for necessary capital goods and oil, and perhaps most significant, the promise of more efficient production through policies of coordinated planning. Membership, however, necessitated that Cuba emphasize production which required the least immediate investment—sugar. Cuban economic planners reluctantly acknowledge the fact that Cuba's trade with the CMEA encouraged Cuba's sugar production and trade.[18] The second term Cuba accepted was one which all member nations must accept—the *barter trade* based on nonconvertible currency, the result of which is the restriction of Cuba's trade partners due to a shortage of currency with which to trade on the open market.

TRADE WITH THE SOVIET UNION

In addition to Cuba's trade with the Soviet Union through CMEA agreements, Cuba and the Soviet Union maintain substantial separate commercial arrangements. A sign of increased Cuban-Soviet relations were the five Cuba-USSR 1972 Economic Agreements, signed on December 23, 1972. The first two agreements concern the repayment of Cuba's foreign debt and the establishment of credits. The first agreement, regarding Cuba's debt to the Soviet Union incurred from 1960 to 1973, postpones repayment of the credits which the Soviet Union granted to Cuba to compensate for an unfavorable balance of trade until 1 January 1986 (Article 1). Thereafter, they are to be paid over a period of 25 years (Article 2) with interest suspended (Article 3). The second agreement reschedules the debt incurred by Cuba to the Soviet Union for the years 1973, 1974, and 1975. It too is deferred until 1986 for a period of 25 years with no interest. [Editors' note: it has since been extended.] The third agreement specifies the commodities which would be exchanged in the 1973 to 1975 period by both countries. The most significant agreement, however, is the fourth agreement, concerning economic and technical cooperation during this three-year period. In Article 1 of this agreement the Soviet Union and Cuba agree to cooperate in the development of the textile, nickel, electric power, and oil-refining industries and to discuss such projects as mechanization of the sugar harvest, introduction of computers in the national economy, automobile repair plants, military training, and irrigation project cooperation.

The fifth agreement establishes a floor price of sugar at approximately 11 cents per pound and a floor price of nickel at approximately five thousand dollars per ton. This agreement is an attempt, according to Fidel Castro, "to create conditions to promote the production of sugar and nickel in Cuba and eliminate the influence of wavering world market prices."[19]

Soviet subsidies in the form of loans, credits, and commodity subsidies have been substantial. The Soviet Union assisted Cuba in the maintenance and modernization of Cuba's sugar industry.[20] Cuba's debt to the Soviet Union for military assistance totaled $1.7 billion for the 1981–83 period.[21] Economic support from the Soviets had risen to $13 million per day by 1983, or $4 billion a year in addition to $600 million annually in military assistance.[22]

An additional subsidy supplied by the Soviet Union in the mid-1980s was the increasing supply of fuel, which the Cuban government was permitted to export for hard currency, if domestic consumption was limited and surpluses were available.[23] By 1983, Soviet exports of oil to Cuba totaled 225,000 barrels daily.[24] In 1984, Cuba resold approximately two thirds of the total oil imported from the Soviet Union.[25]

NOTES

1. Article 16 of the Constitution defines the purposes and general direction of the Cuban economy: "The state organizes, directs, and controls the economic life of the nation in accordance with the *central plan of socioeconomic development* in whose elaboration and execution the workers of all the branches of the economy and of the other spheres of social life have an active and conscious participation. The development of the economy serves the purpose of strengthening the socialist system, cultural needs of the society and of the citizens and of promoting the flowering of human personality and serves the progress and the security of the country and the national capacity to fulfill the internationalist duties of our people." Pamela S. Falk, "Cuba, 1974–78," in Albert P. Blaustein and Gilbert H. Flanz, eds. *Constitutions of the Countries of the World,* (Dobbs Ferry, N.Y.: Oceana, 1979). Monograph.

2. Created by Act 964, 1961. Fidel Castro, "Report to the First Party Congress," Havana, December 1975.

3. Although JUCEPLAN was established in the early years of the revolution, its authority to institute economic plans was taken away in 1966, and its economic policy decentralized. Both its early plans of 1962 to 1966 and annual plans from 1965 to 1970 were reviewed but not instituted. See Jan Knippers Black *et al., Area Handbook for Cuba* (Washington, D.C.: Government Printing Office, 1976), p. 379.

4. Membership included the founding nations: Bulgaria, Czechoslovakia, Hungary, Poland, Rumania, and the Soviet Union. Present membership also includes: German Democratic Republic (1949), Mongolia (1962), Cuba (1972), and Vietnam (1949). Observer status countries include Yugoslavia and Finland. Albania was a former member (1949–62).

5. A study by Edward A. Hewett argued that the CMEA in the 1970s pursued a policy of rapid growth following more rigid policies of integration and specialization in order to achieve larger gains from trade. This policy of "static comparative advantage" of the less developed member nations was fought by the Rumanian government, which argued that the program was similar to capitalist trade patterns that resulted in long-term primary product economies in developing nations. Edward A. Hewett, "Cuba's Membership in the CMEA," in *Revolutionary Cuba in the World Arena,* ed. Martin Weinsten (Philadelphia, PA: ISHI, 1979), p. 62. See also Marie L. Lavigne, *The Socialist Economies of the Soviet Union and Europe,* translated by T.G. Waywell (White Plains, N.Y.: International Arts and Sciences, 1974).

6. Josef M.P. Van Brabant, *Essays on Planning, Trade and Integration in Eastern Europe* (Netherlands: Rotterdam University Press, 1974), pp. 43–63, 83–103.

7. Ibid., p. 270.

8. J. Van Brabant points to the fact that often the member nations develop a dual technology: sophisticated methods of production in key sectors (large capital-to-labor ratios), and they pay less attention to other sectors, which must be operated on the basis of old and existing technology (with low capital-to-labor ratios), Ibid., p. 47.

9. Specific terms of CMEA agreements are not often published. For a discussion of this problem see E.A. Hewett, "Cuba's Membership," p. 52.

10. See M.L. Lavigne, *Socialist Economies,* pp. 297–99, for an extensive discussion, and B. Poklad and E. Shevchenko, COMECON (Handbook) (Moscow: Novosti, 1973).

11. Funds for the IIB are from members and international financial institutions.

12. M.L. Lavigne, *Socialist Economies,* p. 303. The example that Lavigne gives is the 1957 specialization projects in Poland, which was to become the main supplier of coal in CMEA. In 1957 Poland cut back the coal supplies because of internal difficulties. This threatened the economic equilibrium in other countries, and the GDR and USSR could not adequately supplement supplies. In 1977 CMEA financed and opened the coal mines in Poland.

13. B. Poklad and E. Shevchenko, COMECON, p. 33.

14. Ibid.

15. E.A. Hewett, "Cuba's Membership." CMEA prices are calculated by the council and are supposed to be related to world market prices. In fact, they differ significantly with this example of the relative costs of machinery and primary products, one of the more blatant examples. It is common, Hewett argues, however, for trade agreements within CMEA to deviate from the agreed upon central prices. Ibid., p. 63.

16. Trade with the capitalist world at world market prices at the time of Fidel Castro's speech, he emphasized, would be catastrophic. His estimates, according to the report of revenues, were that seven million tons of sugar at world market prices would earn Cuba only $2 billion and purchase of oil at world market prices would cost $2.5 to $3.0 billion. *Latin American Weekly Report* (February 8, 1980), p. 3. See also Edward Hewett, *Foreign Trade in the Council for Mutual Economic Assistance* (Cambridge: Cambridge University Press, 1974).

17. F. Castro's figures were cited in a 1984 interview with *Newsweek* magazine, "Castro's Challenge to Reagan," interview with Patricia J. Sethi, *Newsweek* (January 9, 1984), pp. 38–41; Castro cited similar figures in the *Second Congress of the Communist Party of Cuba,* (Havana: Political Publishers, 1981). The Third International Round Table Discussion on Rural Development sponsored by the FAO Regional Office for Latin America and the Caribbean estimated an average annual growth of 3.4 percent from 1970 to 1981 and 4.2 percent between 1975 and 1976. In *Cuba Update* (January-February 1984), p. 5. U.S. government World Bank statistics showing the 1960 to 1978 per capita annual rate of growth as—1.2 percent. In *Cuba's Renewed Support for Violence in Latin America,* Special Report 90 (December 14, 1981), p. 3.

18. Interviews by the author with Felix Loaces and Alejandro Romero, Ministry of Foreign Commerce (MINCEX) Havana, January 25, 1979. See also Lawrence Theriot and Linda Droker, *Cuban Trade with the Industrialized West 1974–1979,* Office of East-West Planning, Department of Commerce (Washington, D.C.: Government Printing Office, May 1981); Lawrence Theriot and John Gibbon, *Cuban Trade with CMEA 1974–1979,* Office of East-West Planning, Department of Commerce (Washington, D.C.: Government Printing Office, April 1981).

19. Fidel Castro, *Granma* (January 14, 1973), pp. 2–3.

20. Lawrence Theriot, "U.S.-Cuba Trade: Question Mark?" *Commerce America* (April 24, 1978), p. 554. See also Lawrence Theriot and Linda Droker, *Cuban Trade with the Industrialized West 1974–1979,* Office of East-West Planning, Department of Commerce (Washington, D.C.: Government Printing Office, May 1981); L. Theriot and J. Gibbon, *Cuban Trade with CMEA 1974–1979.*

21. U.S., Department of Defense, *Soviet Military Power,* Washington, D.C., April 1984, p. 123.

22. *Financial Times* (London) (November 14, 1979), p. 7.

23. Cuban dependence on sugar export earnings ranges from 81 percent to 95 percent of its total export earnings. Sugar constituted at least 80 percent of Cuban exports prior to the revolution. According to Raúl León Torras, minister-president of Cuba's National Bank, "The crisis on the sugar market is as dramatic as at the worst moment of the Great Depression of the '30's." Cited in *Business Week* (September 20, 1982), p. 56–57.

24. National Bank of Cuba, *Economic Report* (Havana: 1985), p. 1.

25. National Bank of Cuba, *Economic Report* (Havana: National Bank of Cuba, February 1985), pp. 1–10; For an earlier assessment of Cuba's rescheduling of foreign debt with the banks, see Elaine Fuller, "Cuba Negotiates Rescheduling of Foreign Debt," *Cuba Update,* Vol. 5, No. 2 (March/June, 1984), pp. 5–6; *New York Times* (December 25, 1983), p. A12; *Wall Street Journal* (August 3, 1984), p. 20.

CHAPTER 12

Cuba's Relations with the United States

36. United States–Cuban Relations in the 1980s*

BY PHILIP BRENNER

"The United States never remembers and Latin America never forgets" is a well-known Latin American aphorism. It succinctly explains the depth of Cuban distrust about the United States and the continuing surprise North Americans manifest about Cuban behavior. Cuban national pride is fierce, and for the better part of a hundred years the United States undermined, disparaged, and ignored Cuban sovereignty.

To be sure, the United States has acted toward much of Latin America with an orientation that Abraham Lowenthal aptly characterizes as a "hegemonic presumption."[1] Cuba experienced the full brunt of the treatment, because the United States considered Cuba to be its "pearl of the Antilles" for the first half of the 20th century. In its vain attempt to recapture the glory-filled days of the 1950s, when U.S. power was beyond challenge, the Reagan Administration has focused on Cuba as a major obstacle.

Though there have been short periods of reduced tension between the two countries in the 1980s, relations in this decade often have been at their worst since the 1962 missile crisis. This was a marked contrast to the warming that occurred in the 1970s, and it might lead one to believe that the variation in relations could be explained by differences between the Carter and Reagan Administrations.

*This essay was written for this volume. Copyright 1988 by Philip Brenner.

While there is much veracity in such an explanation, it obscures the legacy which the Reagan Administration inherited from its predecessor, the continuity of U.S. policy since 1960, and the variation in Cuban behavior that contributed to the pattern of relations. All of these must be examined in evaluating whether the history of antagonism between the United States and Cuba is likely to endure long past the 1980s.

PRELUDE TO THE 1980s

By the early 1970s, several factors coalesced to counter the cold war between Cuba and the United States, which had developed after 1959. The Nixon Administration had fashioned détente with both the Soviet Union and China as its hallmark. Anti-Communism was less in vogue. At the same time, Cuba had abandoned its practice of supporting armed revolution in the hemisphere, and had begun to develop state-to-state relations with several Latin American countries.

The Vietnam War also had a multifaceted though indirect effect. It weakened the dominance of the U.S. in the Third World. In Latin America, leaders were more willing to risk independent positions, in part because they saw the U.S. consumed by its attention to Vietnam. In the United States, the war exploded the post-World War II consensus, which had included a common view in the executive and legislative branches about the proper role for the U.S. in the Third World. As fundamental questioning about that role began to grow, policy towards Cuba became a natural object of attention.

A movement to relax the hostility between Cuba and the U.S. first began in the U.S. Congress in 1971, and it gained force in the next three years.[2] In 1974 two senators and several congressional aides traveled to Cuba, with several representatives and more senators going the next year. Members perceived that U.S. policy toward Cuba was both hurting U.S. interests and undermining U.S. prestige with allies, especially those in Latin America. The United States appeared isolated, while the intent of the policy had been the reverse—to isolate Cuba. A growing number of Latin American countries were breaking the trade embargo and calling for a change in the Organization of American States' prohibition on trade. To several key members of Congress involved in foreign affairs it seemed clear that the policy made the United States look like an ogre, which reinforced an image harmful to U.S. interests in the region.[3]

While congresspeople acted independently, and with some courage in light of persistent anti-Cuban rhetoric from President Nixon, key officials in the executive branch signaled their support for the congressional activities. The U.S. signed an antihijacking treaty with Cuba in February 1973. In June 1974, during the waning days of President Nixon's tenure, Secretary of State Henry Kissinger gave approval for a trip to Cuba by Pat Holt, Senate Foreign

Relations Committee chief of staff. Holt had requested permission to travel there more than a year before.

At about this time Kissinger also named William Rogers as Assistant Secretary of State for Inter-American Affairs. Rogers had served on the Linowitz Commission, a private group composed largely of business leaders and former government officials that had advocated the normalization of relations with Cuba. By the end of 1974 he was meeting with Cuban United Nations diplomats to assess the possibilities for negotiations on normalization.

The U.S. also relaxed its position on the embargo against Cuba—albeit under pressure from Latin American countries. In 1974 it permitted third-country subsidiaries of U.S. corporations to trade with Cuba, and in 1975 it voted to lift the Organization of American States' embargo.

Though a sharp contrast from Nixon's antagonistic posture toward Cuba, these efforts of the Ford Administration to reduce tension were so tentative that they were quickly dashed by the war in Angola. By the fall of 1975, Kissinger had grown angry that Cuba was helping to thwart perceived U.S. interests there, and he ended talks between the two countries. Then, in October 1976, terrorists blew up a Cuban civilian airplane, killing the 73 passengers. Some of murderers had once been on the CIA payroll, and this led Cuba to abrogate the antihijacking agreement, because it included provisions on preventing terrorist attacks. Thus, Jimmy Carter inherited a hostile atmosphere with respect to Cuba when he took office three months later.

The Carter Administration moved quickly to reduce the tension.[4] (It was reinforced by several members of Congress, who resumed trips to Cuba in 1977 and introduced legislation to lift the bilateral U.S. embargo against Cuba.) U.N. Ambassador Andrew Young characterized the Cuban presence in Angola as a "stabilizing" influence. Assistant Secretary of State Terence Todman traveled to Cuba in April 1977 to sign a fishing and maritime boundary agreement. He also negotiated a changed status for the diplomatic missions that represented U.S. interests in Cuba and Cuban interests in the United States: U.S. and Cuban diplomats began to staff the missions, respectively, in September 1977. The U.S. also facilitated tourist travel by easing currency restrictions and permitting charter flights. This change led to a massive flow of exiles to Cuba for family visits in 1979, after the Cuban government agreed to such travel.

By then, however, the warming trend in relations had been reversed. As in the Ford Administration, U.S. and Cuban paths crossed in Africa, and the clash toppled the fragile structure that was being built toward normalization. Cuba and the United States took opposite sides in the war between Ethiopia and Somalia. (Officially, the U.S. opposed Somalia's 1977 invasion of the Ogaden region.) But with respect to Zaire, President Carter went out on a limb in 1978 when he accused Cuba of training and encouraging the Katangese rebels who invaded Shaba province. It was a limb from which he would not withdraw, though the Senate Foreign Relations Committee found that the

President's charges were overstated.[5] From then on, U.S.-Cuban relations grew increasingly tense.

For example, during the 1979 summit of the 92-nation Nonaligned Movement, which was held in Cuba, President Carter revealed the existence in Cuba of an alleged 3,000-person Soviet combat brigade. Though it turned out that the unit had been stationed in Cuba since the 1962 missile crisis, that it was not a combat brigade, and that the U.S. had long known about its presence, Carter insisted that the brigade posed a new threat to the United States. He ordered the creation of a military unit—the Caribbean Joint Task Force—on Key West to counter the danger.

To underscore the official view that Cuba was once again a major enemy of the United States, the President issued a policy statement, PD-52, which ordered national security agencies "to devise strategies for curbing Cuba's activities [in the Third World] and isolating it politically."[6] On top of these strains, the Mariel boatlift of April–May, 1980 fully returned U.S.-Cuban relations to the heights of tension they had been in earlier years. (See Reading 39.)

The Carter Administration thus bequeathed to the Reagan Administration a set of hostile relations with Cuba, and a public that had been fed anti-Cuban rhetoric for two years. The halting efforts toward normalization by Ford and Carter left another legacy as well—a sense among policymakers that U.S. policy toward Cuba had failed to achieve U.S. objectives because it had been insufficiently harsh. John Ferch, head of the U.S. Interests Section in Havana from 1982 to 1985, described the feeling in 1983 when he remarked that "there is no doubt that the moderation of the Carter Administration was interpreted in Cuba as a sign of weakness."[7]

THE REAGAN YEARS

It is not clear whether the Reagan Administration even noticed what it had inherited from the Carter Administration. Several members of the new government had advocated harsh measures against Cuba before taking office, and Cuba was a focal point of their anti-Communist crusade.[8] From the start they pursued a "get tough" policy and were joined by others who shared their perspective. As Wayne Smith observed in 1982,

The [Reagan] Administration began by excluding normalization of relations even as a distant objective. . . . Its initial position was that the United States would not even talk to the Cubans until they ceased all interventionist activities in Latin America and withdrew their troops from Africa. If they refused to do so, Washington would exclude no option, including a U.S. blockade or invasion of Cuba.[9]

Indeed, Secretary of State Alexander Haig established the orientation in a February 1981 declaration, saying that the United States must "deal with the immediate source of the problem [in El Salvador]—and that is Cuba."[10]

President Reagan himself was fond of describing Cuba as a threat to U.S.

access to Caribbean sea-lanes, "our lifeline to the outside world."[11] The Cuban "threat," which became a continuing theme of the administration, was underlined in a 1986 joint State/Defense Department report. It asserted succinctly:

> An important long-range goal of Soviet and Cuban leaders is to estrange the United States from what they hope will be an increasingly radicalized and Communist Latin America.[12]

This rhetoric defined the framework of policy toward Cuba, and shaped the nature of public debate. It was concomitant to specific actions that appeared to revive the full range of objectives sought by earlier administrations: to destablize and overthrow Cuba, and to contain and isolate Cuba internationally.

Destabilization: While few in the Reagan Administration believed the embargo would bring Cuba to its knees, as the Kennedy Administration had hoped, there was some expectation that it could influence political and social dynamics within Cuba to U.S. advantage. The 1979 influx of exile visitors to Cuba had distorted the carefully crafted system of distribution for scarce consumer goods, because each visitor brought gifts worth thousands of dollars. This contributed to the impetus for the Mariel boatlift in 1980. U.S. analysts saw that the demand for consumer goods was a point of vulnerability in Cuba.[13] This was a weakness that a tightened embargo might have exacerbated, by raising the cost of obtaining goods. If it forced the Cuban government to repress demands, the ensuing conflict might have cost it legitimacy; if it led Cuba to give more flexibility to small farmers, in the hope of producing more, that might give that class increased power; if the embargo encouraged the government to provide escape valves to relieve the pressure in lieu of consumer goods, such as increased press freedom, this might build greater internal pressure.

Radio Martí was also embraced by the Reagan Administration in 1981 as a means of exacerbating tensions within Cuba through propaganda broadcasts.* In its original form, it was to be identical to Radio Liberty and Radio Free Europe, and housed in their agency—the Board for International Broadcasting.**

There may be a fine line between attempting to generate internal pressure in a country for the purpose of improving conditions there—as the Reagan Administration claimed it intended to do with the embargo and Radio Martí—and trying to undermine a government with the hope of overthrowing it. Cuba perceived that the U.S. had crossed the line with the inauguration of Radio Martí. It reacted with the sort of rhetoric it had curtailed after

---

*It also served as a symbolic reward to the Cuban exile community, which had strongly supported Ronald Reagan's campaign.

**Congress forced the administration to alter the nature of the station and place it in the Voice of America. It began operation on May 20, 1985.

the early days of the Reagan Administration, when Fidel Castro exclaimed that "the group that constitutes the main nucleus of the current U.S. Administration is fascist."[14] Cuba also suspended an immigration agreement with the U.S. it had signed in December 1984, and announced it would no longer permit exiles to visit the country.[15] The agreement would have returned to Cuba 2,746 "undesirable" immigrants who had fled in the 1980 Mariel exodus (Reading 39), and enabled 20,000 Cubans to migrate to the United States annually.[16]

While Radio Martí was not likely to undermine the stability of the Cuban government—Cubans already received news broadcasts from the Voice of America and anti-Castro propaganda from Miami radio stations—it did represent an attack on Cuba and seemed to reflect a disposition toward overthrowing the government. Indeed, the official Cuban government statement linked it to the embargo and similar "threats and aggression of all kinds from the United States."[17] Such an interpretation was not unreasonable in light of the sustained anti-Castro propaganda by the Reagan Administration. If the Reagan Administration did want to attack Cuba militarily, it would need the public to believe that Cuba were worthy of being overthrown—both for its behavior toward its own people and because of the threat it represented to the United States.

When a giant characterizes a small state as an enemy, the small state has to be wary. It appears that this was the reaction that the Reagan Administration sought, as it attempted to keep Cuba "off balance." Naval exercises near the Cuban coast in 1982 and 1983, for example, served as graphic reminders that the United States has the capability of following through on its threats. Cuba responded by placing its forces in a state of full military mobilization and by holding practice civil defense drills. The U.S. invasion of Grenada in October 1983 sent a special shock throughout Cuba, because of its close ties with Grenada. Deputy Foreign Minister Ricardo Alarcon told the *Washington Post* that Cuba saw the Reagan Administration using the invasion as a basis for "intervention elsewhere."[18] The military actions appeared to coincide with administration statements about bringing the Central American war home to Cuba.

Isolation: As in the 1960s, the Reagan Administration too sought to make Cuba a pariah state. Speaking in December 1984 about U.S. policy, the director of the State Department's Office of Cuban Affairs said:

> For Cuba the way back from its present alienation from the political democracy which is advancing throughout the hemisphere will be long and arduous. Havana may someday realize that its own best interests would be served if it again joined the American mainstream.[19]

The effort to isolate Cuba went beyond rhetoric. The United States successfully blocked Cuban participation in an international development conference at Cancun, Mexico, in 1981—despite the fact that Cuba was head of the Nonaligned Movement. The U.S. also encouraged Latin American countries to break the ties they had developed with Cuba in the 1970s. Jamaica and Colombia, which had recently elected conservative governments and which were in great need of U.S. assistance, complied and broke relations in 1981. Costa Rica hinted it might do the same in 1983.

Finally, the Reagan Administration attempted to reduce Cuba's trade links to non-socialist countries, and to tighten the U.S. embargo. The U.S. threatened to confiscate any imported goods that contained Cuban nickel, and it pressured European allies not to renegotiate their outstanding loans, which Cuba had difficulty repaying, or to make new loans. As a symbol of the new vigilance, President Reagan revoked President Carter's order to permit tourist travel to Cuba. Relying on his authority under the Trading with the Enemy Act, he granted permission for travel only to scholars, journalists, and Cuban exiles who wished to see their families.[20] The travel ban had little practical effect. Its purported rationale was to deny hard currency to Cuba, but the largest number of U.S. citizens traveling to Cuba had been exiles who could continue to spend money there. Still it did underscore the U.S. determination to make the embargo more effective.[21]

During this period Cuba improved its relations with Latin American countries. This both disturbed the Reagan Administration and undermined its efforts to isolate Cuba. Cuba's hemispheric policies principally were born out of its interest in expanding ties in the region. They were not formulated as a reaction to U.S. policy, yet they countered some U.S. measures.

The most troublesome behavior for the United States was Cuban support for the Sandinista revolution. This emanated from a combination of ideological affinity, internationalism, and Cuba's defensive desire to secure the presence of a similarly oriented regime in the region. Cuba has provided Nicaragua with military advisors, teachers, health professionals, and technical assistance. It also encouraged the Soviet Union to provide assistance, substantial amounts of which began to arrive in 1984. The Reagan Administration relied on the Nicaraguan-Cuban relationship as a major reason for its war against Nicaragua.[22]

Cuba's Central America policy, though, comes closer to that of most Latin American countries than does U.S. Central America policy. To be sure, Cuba is the major hemispheric supporter of Nicaragua, and it has provided political support for the FDR/FMLN in El Salvador.[23] But significantly, it embraced the Contadora peace process and the 1987 Arias plan, and it has endorsed proposals for an international peacekeeping force in El Salvador and for international inspection in Nicaragua. Indeed, Cuba's Central American policies opened the possibility that Reagan Administration hostility toward Cuba could alienate the U.S. from Latin America. At a point when Latin Americans saw the United States as an enemy of diplomatic solutions to the wars in Central America, Cuba's accommodating stance highlighted the growing isolation of the United States in the hemisphere.

Similarly, Cuba's effort to rebuild ties with South American countries not only vitiated the Reagan Administration's attempts to isolate Cuba. It created another potential source of friction between the United States and countries in the hemisphere. The Organization of American States had suspended Cuba's membership in 1964, at a time when Cuba openly supported revolution in the region. But by the late 1970s Cuba had altered its policies, emphasized the importance of respectful state-to-state relations, and restored good relations with several countries. This trend was halted by 1979 and reversed in 1981 by U.S. pressure and the rise to power of conservative parties in Latin America. A return to the earlier trend began in 1982. This was facilitated by the U.S. support of the United Kingdom in the Falklands/Malvinas conflict; Cuba supported Argentina. Today, Cuba has full diplomatic relations with fifteen countries in the hemisphere, and varying degrees of relations with nine others.[24]

Relations between the United States and Cuba seem to be at an impasse today. In interviews, U.S. State Department officials say that they see little likelihood of any improvement.[25] They echo the earlier comments by Secretary of State George Shultz in response to Castro's remarks about the 1984 immigration agreement. The Cuban leader characterized the pact as a "constructive and positive" sign that could lead to negotiations in other areas of mutual interest. In contrast, Shultz called Castro's remarks "a lot of rhetoric." He added, "What we look for is some change in his behavior. And his behavior is to continue to try to export revolution all over the hemisphere."[26]

Cuban officials make a similar assessment about normalizing relations. In a February 1987 interview, Vice-President Carlos Rafael Rodríguez said that Cuba would be willing to "talk to the United States about anything," but that "the State Department only wants to negotiate minor issues—nothing of significance." He characterized U.S. demands as nothing more than the unacceptable requirement that "Cuba subordinate itself to the power of the United States."[27]

ISSUES IN CONTENTION BETWEEN THE U.S. AND CUBA

The "deep freeze," as journalist Julia Preston characterizes United States–Cuban relations today,[28] appears to emanate from U.S. hostility. Indeed, from a review of the bilateral and multilateral issues that each side emphasizes, it becomes clear that the U.S. position is one that precludes serious negotiations over major differences.

U.S. Demands

Kenneth Skoug, head of the State Department's Office of Cuban Affairs, has explained that "U.S. policy toward Cuba is shaped primarily by our perception of Cuban conduct in international affairs."[29] Three concerns dominate the U.S. agenda with respect to international issues—Cuba's relationship with the Soviet Union, Cuban support for both the Nicaraguan government and the FDR/FMLN in El Salvador, and the presence of Cuban troops in Angola.

1. *Relations with the Soviet Union*: The "bond" between the Soviet Union and Cuba, John Ferch said in 1983, "and the Soviet military and intelligence services in Cuba represent a considerable threat to the United States and its security."[30] This "special relationship with the Soviet Union," Skoug asserted in 1984, is "the first and most critical" concern for the United States in considering relations with Cuba. It is a relationship, he added, on which the Reagan Administration does not believe the U.S. can have much influence.[31]

Cuba has never acknowledged that the U.S. concern about the nature of the Soviet presence there is a legitimate issue. The 1962 agreement and the 1970 accord, under which the Soviet Union agreed not to place offensive weapons or base nuclear submarines in Cuba, were solely between the two superpowers. Cuba asserts its right as a sovereign nation to invite whatever forces are willing to come. For the United States, the issue is one of security. It was raised prominently in 1979, when President Carter claimed that the Soviets had placed a new combat brigade in Cuba. From time to time in the 1980s, unsubstantiated allegations have surfaced in Washington that Cuban MiGs have been reconfigured to make them capable of carrying nuclear weapons.

2. *Central America*: Administration officials regularly link their concerns about Central America to Soviet and Cuban activities in the area. In part, they argue, Soviet military assistance has given Cuba the wherewithal to provide alleged support for revolutionary struggles in the region. It also adds a global strategic dimension to the local conflicts, because Soviet bases in Central America, they say, could threaten the ability of the U.S. to respond appropriately to its international interests.[32] Cuba has contended that the conflicts in Central America can be settled only through multilateral negotiations such as the Contadora process, not as part of bilateral talks. It has agreed to abide by accords that result from regional peace processes, including the removal of any military forces.

3. *Angola*: Initially, President Carter acquiesced in the view that Cuban troops in Angola were a "stabilizing" influence, as Ambassador Andrew Young maintained, and that they had been sent to support the MPLA in 1975 only after South Africa invaded Angola, as veteran diplomat Wayne Smith reports.[33] They became a source of grievance after Carter's verbal altercation

with Castro over the invasion of Shaba province by rebels stationed in Angola. The Reagan Administration inherited this issue when it took office, and added a new twist. It endorsed the South African demand for the removal of Cuban troops from Angola as a precondition for the withdrawal of South African troops from Namibia. The U.S. argues that the Cuban presence in Angola is the sole stumbling block to an agreement on Namibian independence, despite South Africa's occupation of its neighbor in violation of U.N. Security Council Resolution 435.

Until its third Party Congress in February 1986, Cuba had said that it would be willing to call home its estimated 40,000-person force after South Africa withdrew from Namibia and ceased its logistical support for guerrillas in Angola.[34] Cuba and Angola had reached an agreement in November 1984 that specified the conditions to be met prior to Cuba's complete military departure. These apparently changed early in 1988, and may lead to the withdrawal of Cuban forces sooner than expected.[35]

Three enduring issues on the U.S. bilateral agenda are unsettled claims for expropriated property, Cuban support for Puerto Rican independence, and human rights.

1. *Unsettled Claims*: Since the break in relations between the two countries, the United States has advanced the claims of U.S. citizens who allege that the Cuban government expropriated their property without due compensation.[36] In 1972, the U.S. Foreign Claims Settlement Commission certified claims against Cuba of $1.85 billion, which totals over $5 billion today with accrued interest. The operative claim is probably smaller due to losses already covered by income tax deductions, insurance payments, and the de facto sale of claims to speculators. Cuba has said it would be willing to negotiate this issue, and it has repaid claimants from Canada, Switzerland, France, and Spain. But it also has counterclaims against the U.S. for the losses incurred during the covert war and as a consequence of the embargo.

2. *Puerto Rico*: As with the question of a Soviet military presence in Cuba, the Cuban government has never recognized that its support for the independence of Puerto Rico is a legitimate bilateral issue with the U.S. Cuba views its efforts in the U.N. Committee on Decolonization and at the summits of the Nonaligned Movement to be an international matter, because it argues that Puerto Rico is not a part of the United States.[37] Conversely, the United States claims Puerto Rico's status is an internal matter, especially in light of electoral outcomes that give little support to those who favor independence. It views Cuban initiation of pro-independence resolutions with hostility. In addition, though the evidence to support the charge is flimsy, there have been claims that Cuba has aided pro-independence guerrilla actions.[38] The U.S. has formally demanded that Cuba cease its support, in whatever form, of the independence movement.

3. *Human Rights*: Since the start of the Carter Administration, a demand for the improved protection of human rights in Cuba has been on the U.S. agenda. Release of political prisoners was the main focus of the demand in the 1970s.[39] In the Reagan Administration the demand has expanded to cover unsubstantiated allegations about violations that involve torture and unwarranted detention, as well as the denial of the freedoms of speech, religion, and the press. Cuba has denied charges of torture and contends that human rights is not an appropriate issue for discussion prior to normalization of relations. It also emphasizes that its conception of human rights differs from that of the United States, because Cuba gives highest priority to the right to health care, housing, and sufficient food for all its people.

Cuban Demands

Cuba has stated that it would be willing to negotiate its differences with the U.S. over international issues in the manner of normal sovereign states. It maintains that these matters are not appropriate for consideration as part of the discussions related to the process of normalizing relations. Cuba identifies its differences with the U.S. in terms of the roles of the two countries in Central America, the activities of each in Africa, proposals for Third World development, and each country's position in international forums. Its agenda of bilateral issues contains five items: Radio Martí, the economic embargo, terrorism and subversion, violation of Cuban airspace, and the naval base at Guantánamo.

1. *Radio Martí*: The Cuban government perceives the series of propaganda broadcasts on one AM and two shortwave bands, which constitute Radio Martí, as far more sinister than the mere distribution of "forbidden" information and ideas to its citizens. It considers Radio Martí to be an attack against its sovereignty and security. In part, this stems from Cuba's history with Radio Swan, which were CIA propaganda broadcasts used as a prelude to the Bay of Pigs invasion.[40] From the time it was officially proposed, Cuba has made clear its opposition to Radio Martí.

2. *Embargo*: In the 1960s Cuba viewed an end to the economic embargo a vital necessity. Today, it has more symbolic than practical significance. The Reagan Administration's efforts to tighten the embargo—by pressuring Western European creditors to deny new loans, and forbidding the purchase of products that contained Cuban nickel—did create the potential to harm the Cuban economy. And it was troublesome enough to warrant the creation of "dummy" corporations in third countries, which would enable Cuba to circumvent the trade barriers. But the embargo no longer denies essential goods to Cuba. Several Latin American countries have resumed trade with Cuba. Spare parts for pre-1961 machines are

still needed, but the major Cuban industries and their infrastructures are linked to products from socialist countries, Western Europe, and Japan. It might be less expensive to trade with the U.S. than these other countries, because of reduced transportation costs, but with powerful sugar and citrus lobbies operating if the embargo were lifted, Cuba would not be able to sell much to the U.S. and would probably try to avoid the likely imbalance resulting from a one-way trading relationship. Thus, Cuba has demanded an end to the embargo as a sign that the U.S. has abandoned the end for which the embargo was initiated—the destabilization and overthrow of the Cuban government.

3. *Terrorism*: When the United States officially ceased its "secret" war against Cuba following the missile crisis, it did not give up its secret army of exiles. Several continued to be paid by intelligence agencies, and others who had been trained and supported by the United States continued the war on their own.[41] In 1980 they had organized training camps in the U.S. with Nicaraguan exiles. While they have focused their energy on overthrowing the Nicaraguan government, Cuba can hardly be certain that they will not attack Cuba again. Indeed, in recent years some have penetrated into Cuba and destroyed facilities. Several are members of an international terrorist network that has assassinated Cuban diplomats, bombed Cuban diplomatic missions, and blown up a Cuban commercial airliner. In 1978 the FBI did share some information with Cuban authorities about the exile community. Cuba has asked the U.S. again to provide data to counter the terrorists and to cease any support for the terrorist activities.

4. *Violation of Airspace*: The United States began reconnaissance flights over Cuba in the summer of 1962, and triumphantly used photos from them in its U.N. presentation that condemned Soviet intrusion in the hemisphere. The flights continued for the next 15 years, ostensibly to monitor Soviet compliance with the 1962 agreement on the removal of missiles. As a gesture of good will, President Carter canceled all reconnaissance flights over Cuba in 1977. But he reinstituted them in September 1979, after the "discovery" of the Soviet brigade, and they continue today. There is little practical purpose for the flights because of the U.S. satellite surveillance capability, and so they serve as little more than symbols of the hostile posture that the U.S. maintained at the time of the missile crisis. For Cuba they also represent an infringement on its sovereignty.

5. *Guantánamo*: The U.S. naval base on the southeast coast of Cuba poses only a minor threat to its security and is an unreliable outpost for the United States given its location. The U.S. has highlighted it as a symbol of military might by holding occasional exercises from the base.[42] To Cuba it is also a reminder of the hated Platt Amendment and the periods of U.S. occupation. Cuban insistence that the U.S. has no right to hold any of its land for a military base also rests on its concern about national sovereignty.

CONCLUSION: TOWARD A NEW RELATIONSHIP?

The contrast is stark between the positions of Cuba and the United States. None of Cuba's demands threaten fundamental security interests of the United States, and all are amenable to compromise. On the other hand, the United States would have Cuba relinquish the security that the Soviet Union provides, and renounce basic principles that are articulated in its constitution. While there are some peripheral issues on which the two countries no doubt could have fruitful discussions, the U.S. stance precludes any meaningful negotiation on the question of normalizing relations. Without a change in the U.S. posture, then, there is little likelihood that there could be any movement toward a serious reduction in tension between the two countries.

Meanwhile, the United States's Cuba policy has failed to achieve any of its objectives. Not only has the Cuban regime weathered the U.S. attacks on it, it may even have been strengthened by them, as the government has rallied the Cuban people around it under the banner of nationalism. Efforts to isolate and contain Cuba have succeeded at various times in reducing Cuban contact with the West, but their ultimate purpose of destabilizing the government has been a failure.

The cost of this failed Cuba policy goes significantly beyond the opportunities lost to secure U.S. interests. The very framework of the policy—which poses Cuba as a threat to the viability of the United States—generates an immediate cost to the U.S. and holds out the potential of even greater stakes. If Reagan Administration rhetoric is taken seriously by allies, the United States would appear to be relatively complacent about an alleged menace to its survival. Though U.S. allies tend *not* to share the perception of Cuba as a threat to the United States, they might be concerned about U.S. credibility if they perceive that the U.S. officials actually believe their own propaganda about Cuba.

Perceptions based on such confusion can take on a life of their own and lead the U.S. to act irrationally. Elected officials, for example, tend to worry that they will be hurt at the polls if the U.S. seems impotent. Consequently, they have supported illegal actions against countries with close ties to Cuba—such as the Contra war against Nicaragua and the invasion of Grenada—largely to demonstrate their resolve against communism.

Ultimately, because the United States is a world power, U.S. behavior sets a tone for the world community. To the extent that its relationship with Cuba is a model of great-power/small-power interaction, the U.S. is encouraging a resort to force in international affairs. This is a cost the U.S. must avoid. With interests around the globe, it should seek to have diplomacy replace armed conflict. Otherwise, the United States is likely to be drawn into needless wars wherever it has interests at stake.

Such arguments alone are unlikely to influence U.S. policymakers to enter into negotiations with Cuba for normalization. But Cuba appears open to discussions with the U.S., and other factors may add weight to the arguments for a change in the U.S. stance. These might include pressures from Latin America, and the desire for a comprehensive resolution to the wars in Central America. Nearly three decades of antagonism between the United States and Cuba has generated an inertia that itself constrains discussions. It does not preclude the possibility of negotiations, but it becomes the prologue for them and establishes several of the issues that would be on the table.

NOTES

1. Abraham F. Lowenthal, "Ronald Reagan and Latin America: Coping with Hegemony in Decline," in Kenneth Oye, Robert Lieber, Donald Rothchild, eds., *Eagle Defiant* (Boston: Little Brown, 1983).

2. Philip Brenner, *The Limits and Possibilities of Congress* (New York: St. Martin's Press, 1983), pp. 45–52.

3. Ibid., pp. 52–63.

4. For an outstanding review of this period, see Wayne S. Smith, *The Closest of Enemies* (New York: W. W. Norton, 1987), especially Chaps. 4 and 5.

5. Bernard Gwertzman, "Carter's Case on Cuba Not Proved, Foreign Relations Chairman Says," *New York Times* (June 10, 1978), p. 1.

6. Barry Sklar, "Cuba: Normalization of Relations," Issue Brief #75030, U.S. Library of Congress (January 13, 1980), p. CRS-17.

7. John Ferch, "Cuban-American Relations: The U.S. Perspective." Paper presented at the International Roundtable: United States in the 1980s, Center for the Study of the Americas, Havana, March 16, 1983 [Spanish version; author's translation], p. 16.

8. Philip Brenner, "Waging Ideological War: Anti-Communism and U.S. Policy in Central America," *The Socialist Register* (1984), pp. 247–51.

9. Wayne S. Smith, "Dateline Havana: Myopic Diplomacy," *Foreign Policy*, No. 48 (Fall 1982), pp. 159–60. For good reviews of the first two years of administration policy, see William Leo-Grande, "Cuba Policy Recycled," *Foreign Policy*, No. 46 (Spring 1982), pp. 108–14; and Max Azicri, "Cuba and the United States: What Happened to Rapprochement?" in Barry Levine, ed., *The New Cuban Presence in the Caribbean* (Boulder, CO: Westview Press, 1983).

10. Jane Franklin, *Cuban Foreign Relations: A Chronology 1959–1982* (New York: Center for Cuban Studies, 1984), pp. 36–37.

11. "Text of Reagan Address on Central America," [April 27, 1983], Congressional Quarterly *Weekly Report* (April 30, 1983), p. 853.

12. U.S. Department of State and Department of Defense, "The Challenge to Democracy in Central America," (Washington, D.C.: Government Printing Office, June 1986), p. 13.

13. Cuba saw the same thing and, after 1980, significantly increased the availability of consumer goods. See Alfonso Chardy, "Open market lets resurgent Havana dress for success," *Miami Herald* (March 25, 1985), p. 1A; Medea Benjamin, *et al.*, *No Free Lunch: Food and Revolution in Cuba Today* (San Francisco: Institute for Food and Development Policy, 1984), Chap. 5.

14. Christopher Dickey, "Castro Blasts Reagan at Global Conference," *Washington Post* (September 16, 1981), p. 1A; Philip Brenner, "U.S.-Cuba: Tension Mounts," *CubaTimes* (Fall 1981), p. 1.

15. R. A. Zaldivar, "Castro retaliates for Radio Marti," *Miami Herald* (May 21, 1985), p. 1A.

16. The immigration agreement was restored on November 20, 1987. See Neil A. Lewis, "U.S. and Havana Agree to Restore Immigration Pact," *New York Times* (November 21, 1987), p. 1.

17. "Statement by the Government of Cuba," May 19, 1985, Cuban Interests Section, Washington, D.C.

18. Edward Cody, "Cuba, Reading a Warning in Grenada Invasion, Alters Tone," *International Herald Tribune* (March 23, 1984); also, "Around the Americas: Cubans stage practice for a U.S. invasion," *Miami Herald* (August 21, 1984), p. 8A.

19. Kenneth Skoug, "The United States and Cuba," *Current Policy* No. 646 (December 17, 1984), U.S. Department of State, Bureau of Public Affairs, p. 5. (Reading 40.)

20. Aaron Epstein, "Supreme Court says president can limit civilian travel to Cuba," *Miami Herald* (June 29, 1984), p. 1A. Also, M. Azicri, "Cuba and the United States," pp. 180–81.

21. The Reagan Administration became embroiled in an embarrassing domestic political squabble over efforts to deny hard currency to Cuba in 1986. It refused to permit entry to Cuban exiles who had paid large sums to travel to third countries before arriving in the U.S., but backed down after vociferous criticism from the Miami Cuban community.

22. U.S. Department of State and Department of Defense, *The Soviet-Cuban Connection in Central America and the Caribbean* (Washington, D.C.: Government Printing Office, March 1985), especially pp. 19–28.

23. In 1982, Fidel Castro acknowledged that Cuba had provided some arms and training for the guerrillas until 1980. See, Serwyn Bialer and Alfred Stepan, "Cuba, the U.S., and the Central American Mess," *New York Review of Books* (May 27, 1982), p. 5.

24. Joseph B. Treaster, "Castro, Once Isolated, Forms New Bonds in South America," *New York Times* (May 19, 1985), p. 1. The 15 countries are: Argentina, Bahamas, Barbados, Bolivia, Brazil, Canada, Ecuador, Guyana, Mexico, Nicaragua, Panama, Peru, St. Lucia, Trinidad and Tobago, and Uruguay.

25. Interviews conducted by the author in March and April, 1987.

26. Leonard Downie, Jr., and Karen DeYoung, "Cuban Leader Sees Positive Signs For Ties in Second Reagan Term," *Washington Post* (February 3, 1985), p. 1; "Around the Americas: Shultz dismisses Castro overtures, tells Managua to change behavior," *Miami Herald* (February 15, 1985), p. 22A. Also, see K. Skoug, "The United States and Cuba," p. 5; "Cuba's 'signals' for talks aren't valid, U.S. says," *Miami Herald* (January 31, 1985), p. 6A.

27. Interview with the author and Carmen Diana Deere and Robert Stark, February 16, 1987, in Havana.

28. Julia Preston, "Cuban-U.S. Ties Termed Worst in Decades," *Washington Post* (April 19, 1987), p. A19.

29. K. Skoug, "The United States and Cuba," p. 1. Also, see: Philip Brenner, "The Unchanging Agenda in U.S.-Cuban Relations," Paper presented at the Eleventh International Congress of the Latin American Studies Association, Mexico City (September 30, 1983), pp. 5–13.

30. J. Ferch, "Cuban-American Relations: The U.S. Perspective," p. 6.

31. K. Skoug, "The United States and Cuba," pp. 2, 3.

32. K. Skoug, "The United States and Cuba," p. 3; "The Soviet-Cuban Connection in Central America and the Caribbean," pp. 3–10, 41.

33. W.S. Smith, *The Closest of Enemies,* pp. 96–97. Also, see William LeoGrande, "Cuba's Policy in Africa," in this volume (Reading 42); Jorge Dominguez, "Cuban Foreign Policy," *Foreign Affairs* (Fall 1978), pp. 96–97.

34. Jim Hoagland, "Castro Outlines Goals in Africa," *Washington Post* (February 6, 1985), p. A13; Alfonso Chardy, "Cuban: Pullout from Angola is unlikely soon," *Miami Herald* (March 27, 1985), p. 18A.

35. J. Hoagland, "Castro Outlines Goals in Africa," p. A13; David B. Ottaway, "Angola Offers Removal Of All Cuban Troops," *Washington Post,* February 14, 1988, p. 32A; Howell Raines, "4 Powers Meet to Explore Ways to End Angola War," *New York Times,* May 4, 1988, p. A3.

36. Alfred L. Padula, Jr., "U.S. Business Squabbles Over Cuba," *The Nation* (October 22, 1977), pp. 390–93.

37. Austin Linsley, "U.S.-Cuban Relations: The Role of Puerto Rico," in Cole Blasier and Carmelo Mesa-Lago, eds., *Cuba in the World* (Pittsburgh: Univ. of Pittsburgh Press, 1979), pp. 122–23.

38. U.S. Senate, Committee on the Judiciary, "Terroristic Activity: The Cuban Connection in Puerto Rico; Castro's Hand in Puerto Rican and U.S. Terrorism: Hearings," 94th Cong., 1st Sess., July 30, 1975.

39. W.S. Smith, *The Closest of Enemies,* p. 102.

40. Peter Wyden, *Bay of Pigs* (New York: Simon and Shuster, 1979), pp. 22–23.

41. Saul Landau and John Dinges, *Assassination on Embassy Row* (New York: Pantheon, 1980), pp. 246–51; Al Burt, "Miami was rife with rumors of war," *Miami Herald* (December 11, 1983), p. 17M.

42. M. Azicri, "Cuba and the United States," p. 178; Carla Anne Robbins, *The Cuban Threat* (New York: McGraw-Hill, 1983), p. 244.

37. The Bay of Pigs*

By Herbert L. Matthews

It would be stupid to underestimate the danger that the communization and pro-Soviet policy of the Castro regime represented to the United States. After all, it did lead to the missile crisis.

From their beginnings as an independent nation, Americans have feared that a foreign power hostile to the United States could either annex Cuba or use her as a base from which to attack the mainland. The advent of Fidel Castro brought a Cuban regime independent of and hostile to the United States. Moreover, this regime identified itself with the United States' chief antagonist in world affairs—the Soviet Union. . . .

Put in oversimplified form, in 1960 Fidel Castro's room to maneuver had only two exits. Even granting that he was the one who slammed the normally used door in Uncle Sam's face, it was also true that the Yankee neighbor turned the key and bolted the lock. That left only the other door, which led eastward to the Communist world. . . .

*From Herbert L. Matthews, *Revolution in Cuba* (NY: Charles Scribners' Sons, 1976), pp. 190–206. Edited for this volume.

In his campaign speeches Kennedy was critical of Eisenhower and Nixon for having been pro-Batista and then "presiding over the Communization of Cuba." Kennedy called for sending an expeditionary force of "democratic" refugees to crush the "Communist enclave," although the exiles of that period were mainly ex-*Batistianos* and the Castroites not yet Communist.

Nixon brazenly condemned Kennedy's "dangerously irresponsible recommendations," although he himself had helped organize the exiles then being trained for the Cuban invasion. He evidently thought that this was still a secret. Nixon came out in one speech for a repetition of the Guatemalan operation of 1954, where, as he incorrectly stated, "a Communist dictator" was overthrown by "the Guatemalan people." . . .

Colonel Castillo Armas, a Guatemalan exile, gathered a band of less than a thousand men just inside the Honduran border. The United States armed them and gave them four planes and money. Starting on June 18, they managed to penetrate about ten miles into Guatemala, but bogged down. The effective job was done in Guatemala City, where the "pistol-packin' " United States ambassador, John Peurifoy, suborned the army leaders—who, anyway, were anti-leftist. They forced Arbenz to resign and depart on June 25.

Castillo Armas peacefully entered the capital in July, where he was duly elected President—and was murdered in 1958, leaving Guatemala as corrupt and with the same mass peasant poverty and tiny wealthy minority as of old—but safe for American strategy and business. . . . The successor to Castillo Armas was Miguel Ydígoras Fuentes, who provided the facilities for the Bay of Pigs invasion.

. . . From the spring of 1959 onward, the CIA did everything that it could to bring about the overthrow of the Castro government. Beginning in January 1960 at the latest, CIA planes from Florida, some with American pilots, were raiding Cuban fields with napalm-type bombs to burn the sugarcane. The Cubans claimed that four of the planes that crashed had American pilots. . . .

The former *New York Times* correspondent Tad Szulc wrote in an article for the February 1974 *Esquire* that President Kennedy spoke to him in November 1961 about being under pressure from intelligence advisers to have Castro assassinated.

What Fidel called "revolutionary bandits" were active through the spring and summer of 1960 in the Escambray, Maestra, and Cristal Sierras, especially the first-named. There were also underground groups, one of the most important at that time being the Movimiento de Rescate Revolucionario (Movement of Revolutionary Recovery, or MRR). It included a young Catholic professor, Manuel Artime. Money, supplies, arms, and transportation came from the CIA.

Justo Carillo, a distinguished banker and economist, headed a small underground group in Havana. The outfit that had become the largest and most important of all by 1961 was led by Manuel Ray, former minister of public works under Castro. This was the Movimiento Revolucionario del Pueblo (Revolutionary People's Movement, or MRP). Unfortunately for itself and for the exiles, "Manolo" Ray and the MRP were considered too radical by one of the main CIA organizers of the Bay of Pigs operation . . . , Frank Bender (or Droller), so the MRP got no American help. Their slogan was *Fidelismo sin Fidel* (Fidel's reforms without Fidel).

Castro did not feel able to concentrate on the dangerous Sierra de Escambray guerrilla bands for some time. He knew of the invasion plans, but apparently thought that the attack was coming in December 1960 or January 1961. In a speech on January 2 he told the Cuban people that Eisenhower was planning to attack before he left office on January 20 on the excuse that Cuba was constructing rocket pads on the island. On December 31, Foreign Minister Raúl Roa had called for a Security Council meeting on the subject. . . .

When the invasion did not materialize, Fidel cleared the Sierra de Escambray of most of the peasants living there. Some of them had been helping the guerrillas. Then he gathered and sent in the rural militia and Rebel Army forces, whom he had organized. They cleaned out the region with a few weeks' leeway to meet the Bay of Pigs invasion in April.

A CIA recommendation to arm and train Cuban exiles for guerrilla warfare had been made to Eisenhower on March 17, 1960. He agreed. From that day on, the United States was caught in an inexorable millrace; something had been started that could not be stopped.

John F. Kennedy, for his part, had committed himself in his electoral campaign to help the exiles and domestic Cuban opposition to overthrow Castro. He was caught in a trap that he himself had laid, and in this respect was as responsible for the fiasco as anybody. It was, therefore, no more than right that he should have taken the blame on himself.

The President-elect was briefed in mid-November 1960, and learned that the Pentagon and CIA were doing what he had recommended. He gave a keep-going signal, although, according to Theodore Sorensen, one of his White House assistants, he had "grave doubts." In fact, he still had them when the invasion time came around, but since every high official of the CIA and the Pentagon favored the invasion, Kennedy had hardly any support for his doubts. The whole American business community; the expropriated American companies; the overwhelming force of public opinion expressed in an almost unanimously hostile press; and by no means least, the uniquely intense and emotional anti-Communism of the American people and press—all these brought an enormous weight of pressure on Kennedy to do something.

Inexcusably, the President was misinformed and misled by the CIA, the Pentagon, and the Cuban exiles. It was also unfortunate for him that diplomatic relations had been broken, because the American Embassy in Havana had been better informed than the CIA. The only meaningful choice which the President had was whether or not to back the invasion force with American arms, men, and naval and air forces. When he decided against an American intervention, he doomed the invasion to virtually certain failure. . . .

On the verge of the invasion, the *New York Times* emasculated a dispatch from Miami by its correspondent Tad Szulc, leading President Kennedy later to say to Managing Editor Turner Catledge: "If you had printed more about the operation you would have saved us from a colossal mistake."

The arguments about secrecy and preserving American security were nonsense. As early as October 31, 1960, in an interview in the U.N. General Assembly, Cuban Foreign Minister Raúl Roa was able to give full and accurate details about the recruitment and training of the Cuban exiles (he called them "counterrevolutionaries and mercenaries"). He had the names and places where they were being trained in Florida and knew of the connivance of Guatemala and the fact that the preparations were being directed by the CIA. The information he used came from *Life,* the New York *Daily News,* and the Columbia Broadcasting Service. The Cubans, of course, also had their own intelligence information. . . .

The Bay of Pigs (Baia de Cochinos) is on the south coast of Cuba at the eastern edge of the extensive marsh known as the Ciénaga de Zapata. There is another marshland to the east. Access is limited to two good highways, one coming down from the north, the other going east to the large port of Cienfuegos. Just behind the latter road is a small but serviceable airfield. An established beachhead would have to be enlarged quickly and held firmly, for with the swamps on either side and the sea behind, there is no line of retreat.

The idea was to hold such a beachhead, fly in a "Provisional Government," which the United States would immediately recognize, and then back it strongly with arms, supplies, and advisers. A Cuban Revolutionary Council was formed, comprised of a quarrelsome, mutually suspicious political mixture of anti-Batista but pro-American, pro-establishment moderates headed by Dr. José Miró Cardona. They had no following in Cuba and would not have been welcomed under any circumstances, least of all as representing a Yankee-backed invasion. . . .

The Brigade 2506, as it called itself, was taken to Puerto Cabezas, Nicaragua. It sailed in six ships on April 14, 1961. President Luis Somoza, the Nicaraguan dictator, was there to cheer them on, jocularly urging them to bring him back some hairs plucked from Castro's beard.

While Fidel knew that the invasion was coming, he could not tell where it would strike. The Bay of Pigs was an obvious possibility, and he had it constantly patrolled. He had cannily dispersed and camouflaged his small air force. Some obsolete, unusable planes were put out conspicuously to fool the attackers and draw bombs. Early in the morning of April 15, 1961, Castro went to his military headquarters in Havana and ordered a nationwide alert.

Two U.S. B-26 bombers attacked at six in the morning, bombing four Cuban airfields. The planes had been disguised as Cuban by the CIA with Cuban Air Force markings. They did little damage.

Another B-26 bomber, with a pilot who had defected from the Cuban Air Force, flew from Nicaragua to Miami as a diversion, claiming that he had bombed some Cuban airfields. However, one of the two real bombers developed engine trouble and, being unable to return to Nicaragua, also had to land in Miami.

The deception was quickly pierced by American newspapermen, but not before Ambassador Adlai Stevenson at the United Nations and his assistant Harland Cleveland rejected Raúl Roa's complaint to the U.N., saying that the planes were from the Cuban Air Force. . . .

The invading force comprised about 1,500 men, divided into six battalions. The political chief was the right-winger Manuel Artime, who had made himself unpopular with many exiles but who was the favorite of Frank Bender of the CIA.

(An interesting sequel may be inserted here. Artime, with several other Bay of Pigs participants, was to figure in the Watergate case. The later-convicted conspirator E. Howard Hunt, Jr., was the CIA operator who supervised the planning and execution of the Bay of Pigs invasion with Frank Bender.) . . .

(Three other Cubans involved at the Bay of Pigs were arrested and convicted in the Watergate case with Hunt—Eugenio R. Martínez, Virgilio González, and Bernard L. Barker, who acted as the exiles' paymaster. In February 1972, Artime, by then the owner of a meat-exporting firm in Miami, organized the Miami Watergate Defense Relief Fund and collected $21,000, which was given to the convicted Watergate burglars.) . . .

The force anchored a half-mile offshore in four vessels. The first men to land were Americans, not Cubans—frogmen to mark the positions. Each ship had an American CIA "adviser." The choice of the landing site was the only unknown factor for the *Fidelistas.* Coral reefs (evidently the maps were faulty) destroyed or delayed several of the landing craft. Other boats had engine trouble. Supplies, reserve ammunition, and one of the battalions were still at sea when dawn came on April 17, but landings were finally made on both beaches of the Bay of Pigs. (The Cubans use the name of one of the two beaches, Playa Girón, for their official designation of the invasion.) . . .

The outcome of the battle itself was never in doubt. The one great question was whether President Kennedy would change his mind and authorize American air and sea support, which would have had to be followed by one more Caribbean intervention with U.S. Marines. The President wisely refused to yield to temptation or advice, including Richard Nixon's counsel, to go in. The United States would have had another Vietnam on its hands, or—who knows?—would have learned such a lesson in Cuba that Vietnam would not have happened. Besides, Kennedy was keeping in mind the possibility that if the United States moved on Cuba, the Russians might move on Berlin. . . .

The survivors, 1,180 out of 1,297 who landed, were rounded up and taken as prisoners to Havana. Castro announced casualties of only 87 (which on the tenth anniversary of the battle he raised to 149). Other witnesses gave losses ranging between 1,100 and 1,600. In the early stages of the battle, the Cuban infantry and militia losses must have been heavy. . . .

The prisoners were ransomed for medical supplies to the supposed value of $62 million. Fidel released them in time to go back to Florida for Christmas 1962, before the full ransom was paid.

38. *Putting Cuba and Crisis Back in the Cuban Missile Crisis**

BY SCOTT ARMSTRONG AND PHILIP BRENNER

For 25 years, the men who decide how and when America goes to war have found the Cuban missile crisis to be the principal model for crisis resolution. Now, despite a wave of revisionist revelations, the current generation of national-security managers find themselves repeating by rote Cuban missile crisis lessons that are not only incorrect but dangerously likely to turn the hidden errors of 1962 into very real terrors of the 1980s.

The traditional view has held that President John F. Kennedy's unblinking brinksmanship led to a successful resolution of the most dangerous superpower confrontation in history. Kennedy and his inner circle of ExCom (Executive Committee) advisers are credited with cleverly managing superior conventional and strategic force, circumventing normal bureaucratic channels, carefully weighing intelligence and the insights of specialists, building consensus among allies by keeping them posted on each new detail and—on the eve of a U.S. congressional election—disarming an unprecedented divisive partisan debate over foreign policy.

These celebrations of successful crisis management have now proved to be horribly myopic. Former ExCom members, as well as Soviet and Cuban officials, after analyzing newly available documents and insider details, acknowledge in retrospect that they were unaware of essential facts about their own forces and were fundamentally wrong about the opposing forces, and that the situation was beyond the control of any one of the leaders.

Former Defense Secretary Robert S. McNamara and his ExCom colleagues now acknowledge what they did not know at the time:

—That the U.S. missiles in Turkey whose dismantling provided the key component of the final U.S.-Soviet deal had—despite the fact that the United States had already considered them obsolete—only become operational in mid-October, 1962, at almost precisely the same time as the Soviet missiles in Cuba.

*From *Los Angeles Times,* November 1, 1987, Part V, p. 3.

—That without higher authorization the commander in chief of the Strategic Air Command elevated the alert level of all SAC units without customary encryption, causing the Soviets to prepare for a pending attack.

—That the extent of damage by U.S. depth charges to Soviet submarines forced to the surface during the blockade was much more serious than known at the time.

—That nuclear weapons were loaded aboard U.S. bombers in Europe during the crisis.

—That none of the ExCom members were aware that U-2 reconnaissance flights on the borders of the Soviet Union continued during the crisis until after one strayed accidentally into Soviet airspace the same day a U-2 was shot down over Cuba.

For their part, the Soviet officials now confirm that the Soviet Union had targeted Berlin, and that Cuba had plans to strike certain southern U.S. cities if U.S. forces invaded Cuba. The Soviets claim that because Kennedy made no prior private diplomatic overtures, his sudden announcement of a military blockade took them by surprise. They view his subsequent rejection of a secret Soviet request for a summit as provoking a world crisis that could have been handled quietly.

McNamara and his colleagues admit having believed Khrushchev's claims that nuclear warheads were already in Cuba and would be used against the United States on already deployed weapons were Kennedy to follow the advice of some advisers to stage a preemptive strike on the Cuban bases. Although American officials now claim they were wrong about the presence of nuclear weapons in Cuba, Soviet officials still insist that warheads were there and that they doubt Khrushchev could have prevented their use by Soviet troops in the case of such a strike.

Most important, it is only now that McNamara and others give credence to the Soviet motivations articulated at the time for putting missiles in Cuba. The Soviets have always claimed that they faced a rapidly growing U.S. nuclear arsenal of vast superiority, sufficient to render them vulnerable to being wiped out by a preemptive first strike.

American nuclear superiority was so complete—5,000 warheads to 300—that a massive first strike was in fact one of the five options available to the President under the U.S. nuclear war-targeting plan at the time. The approximately 40 intermediate-range missiles the Soviets were sending to Cuba would not have given them a first-strike capability. But it would have made the Soviet strategic deterrent credible.

The second Soviet reason and the primary Cuban justification, the prevention of an impending invasion of Cuba, was scoffed at by American officials in 1962. But McNamara and others on the ExCom assert that they were unaware of important covert operations against Castro during the 16 months after the April, 1961, Bay of Pigs invasion, which they acknowledge must have made a second invasion seem imminent.

The United States had mounted a sophisticated and sustained secret war against Cuba that involved weekly landings by Cuban exiles based in Florida. The exiles sabotaged Cuban factories, poisoned food supplies, destroyed transportation and communication facilities and sent aid to counterrevolutionaries in Cuba's Escambray range. Cuban officials at the time saw these activities and continuing assassination attempts against Castro as an effort to destabilize Cuba, softening it up for an invasion. The missiles offered Cuba a joint "tripwire" deterrent and a "doomsday" device in which a U.S. invasion would be an attack against a strategic Soviet outpost as well as the catalyst for an ultimate patriotic sacrifice.

Other aspects of the crisis as recently revealed would credit luck rather than skill in resolving it. On the morning of October 27, 1962, a U.S. U-2 reconnaissance plane was shot down over Cuba. Such overflights had confirmed the original missile emplacements and were used to monitor Soviet progress in readying the missiles and to determine whether they were being armed with nuclear warheads. Precisely this assurance enabled Kennedy to hold off the demands from hawks on the ExCom to make immediate air strikes against the installations.

Khrushchev had U.S. concern about the U-2 underscored by Attorney General Robert Kennedy's visit to Soviet Ambassador Anatoly Dobrynin on the afternoon of the 27th. Kennedy told the ambassador that unless the missiles were out in 48 hours, the United States would take action. He added ominously, though, that if another plane were shot down, the President would have to follow the wishes of his military advisers for an immediate retaliation. Less than 12 hours later Khrushchev ordered the installations to be dismantled.

Indeed, the Soviet premier could not count on controlling his military assets in Cuba. No command had been given from Moscow that the U-2 be shot down, and he did not know why it had been fired upon.

It now appears from U.S. intelligence decryption that Soviet troops there transmitted a report from Cuba that a "fire fight" had occurred in the vicinity of a Soviet surface-to-air missile (SAM) installation, and that some Soviet soldiers had been killed. Who killed them? Had some Cuban soldiers seized the SAM site and shot down the U-2? Both Soviet and Cuban officials deny this charge. Had Cuban counterrevolutionaries—who were well-armed and were fighting to overthrow the Castro regime—attacked the Soviets? No Soviet or Cuban official has offered this otherwise convenient explanation, and the true explanation remains unclear even today.

Immediately following the U-2 shoot-down, Castro ordered—without Soviet consultation—that his Cuban-controlled antiaircraft batteries should fire on any low-level reconnaissance flights over the island. Castro also refused to allow an international inspection of the missile installations after Khrushchev ordered them destroyed on October 28. Communications between Cuba and the Soviets were very bad during the crisis, and Cuba was not consulted during any of the negotiations between the United States and the Soviet Union.

Remarkably, while the ExCom members admit they failed to understand the importance of Cuba's perceptions about an American threat, they also note that no specialist in their midst had much knowledge about Cuba. U.S. officials had little sense about Cuba's potential for messing up their carefully crafted crisis management. And most startling, they now acknowledge that they had allowed themselves only limited access to expertise about the Soviet Union.

The Kennedy advisers who denied any hostile intention toward the Soviet Union or Cuba in 1962—and no evidence suggests otherwise—today understand why both countries would reasonably perceive that the United States was preparing to attack them and that the missiles were a serious attempt by the Soviets and the Cubans to improve crisis stability.

The new lessons of the Cuban missile crisis appear to be that no matter how brilliant, crisis managers cannot foresee all contingencies and know all the factors necessary to control events. More important, it was the U.S. threat of force before October and during the crucial 13 days that appears to have engendered and heightened the crisis. The lesson is not that superior force will resolve tensions.

Khrushchev's fear that the Soviet Union would lose a nuclear war led him into crisis, not away from it. He backed down as he recognized that events were swerving out of control and toward a nuclear holocaust. Similarly, Kennedy appears to have been ready to trade the missiles in Turkey publicly, despite political costs.

Today, as tension heightens in the Persian Gulf, it becomes imperative to draw the appropriate lessons from the Cuban missile crisis. Superpower threats to topple or coerce a frightened regime serve only to exacerbate underlying insecurities. Such threats lead to complex crises in which rational management does not guarantee survival. The missile crisis should have taught us to be more cautious with countries about which we know far too little.

39. Cuban Exodus 1980: The Context*

By Barry Sklar

The sudden migration of over 120,000 Cubans to the United States in 1980 was part of an intricate set of factors related to economic and political developments in Cuba, as well as a function of the steadily deteriorating U.S.-Cuba relationship. The current refugee situation has become an issue which not only

*From U.S. Congress, Joint Economic Committee, *The Political Economy of the Western Hemisphere: Selected Issues for U.S. Policy,* Prepared for the Subcommittee on International Trade, Finance and Security Economics of the Joint Economic Committee, 97th Cong. 1st Sess., September 18, 1981, pp. 100–116.

has serious implications for Cuba's domestic political and economic situation and for its system in general, but also has implications for U.S.-Cuba relations. The refugee issue, which began as a dispute between Cuba and the governments of Peru and Venezuela over political asylum, also affects Cuba's foreign policy in terms of its position in the Third World and its relations with its Latin American neighbors. Implications from the domestic U.S. perspective are especially serious as policymakers grapple with a myriad of problems related to immigration law and the effect internally of this latest influx of refugees. . . .

The spark for the so-called Mariel exodus came on April 1, 1980, when six Cubans, seeking political asylum, crashed through the gate of the Peruvian embassy in Havana; a Cuban policeman guarding the embassy was killed in an exchange of gunfire. This was the latest in a series of forcible entries into the embassies of Peru and Venezuela by Cubans seeking political asylum, which had become the source of a contentious diplomatic dispute between Cuba and the two governments. The Cuban government, earlier, had been especially incensed by the actions of the Peruvian government, which had ordered its ambassador to Havana to provide diplomatic protection for a group of Cubans he initially talked out of seeking asylum. The ambassador was subsequently recalled by Lima. After the April 1 incident, the Peruvian and Venezuelan governments demanded that the Cuban government grant safe-conduct passes to the 40 people who had sought refuge in the two embassies.

On April 4, President Castro denounced the "deceit and cowardice" of the Latin governments that, at the "bidding of the United States," participated in the diplomatic and economic boycott of Cuba. He specifically charged the embassies of Peru and Venezuela with providing protection for "common criminals, bums, and antisocial elements." His most significant statement that day, however, was the announcement that Cuba was withdrawing the guard from the Peruvian embassy.

As a result of what seems to have been a miscalculation by the Cuban government, upon receiving word that the guard had been withdrawn, Cubans in vast numbers flocked to the embassy. Within 72 hours, until the point when the Cuban government actively began to prevent people from approaching the embassy by erecting barricades in the Miramar neighborhood, 10,800 Cubans crowded onto the embassy grounds.

After some days, as health and sanitary conditions rapidly worsened, the Cuban government announced that all those in the embassy would be permitted to leave Cuba with the exception of those who had forcibly entered the grounds. On April 16, after Peru and other nations agreed to accept a certain number of refugees from the embassy, the first planeload left for Costa Rica, where they were to be transported to Peru. Other countries, including Spain, West Germany, Canada, and the United States agreed to take a share of the refugees. The United States said it would accept 3,500.

The Cuban government, however, angered by the anti-Cuban manner in which Costa Rican President Carazo greeted the first arrivals, stopped the flights after two days. The Cubans were also angry over Costa Rican plans to create a huge staging area for the refugees in San José. The Costa Rican government said the staging area was to facilitate the orderly dispersal of the refugees to the final country of destination, but, in Cuban eyes, it was a deliberate attempt to create anti-Cuban propaganda over refugee conditions.

The Cuban government cleared the way for what became an exodus of thousands to the United States on April 21, when it announced that evacuation of those who wanted to leave would be permitted by boats arriving from Florida. *Granma,* the official daily newspaper and organ of the Cuban Communist party, clarified the announcement by reporting on April 22 that the Cuban government would comply with requests from those bringing boats from Florida seeking to evacuate relatives in addition to refugees from the Peruvian embassy. According to *Granma* and to statements by Fidel Castro later, the Cuban government opened the exit gates to accommodate the requests of Cuban exile leaders who traveled to Havana to negotiate the arrangement.

These events notwithstanding, however, there are indications that the Cuban government . . . was interested in permitting emigration to the United States. Recent economic and political developments had an unsettling effect on Cuban life, and pressures on the government were definitely building within the population. In this period, quiet discussions between U.S. and Cuban officials in Washington and Havana focused on the application of the recently passed Refugee Act of 1980 to the question of permitting additional Cubans, principally released political prisoners, to emigrate to the United States. In these same discussions, Cuban officials expressed their government's anger over what they perceived as U.S. encouragement of illegal emigration from Cuba. Specific references were made to the warm reception and accommodation granted to those fleeing Cuba in hijacked ships in a rash of incidents since November 1979. These Cubans who left illegally were granted political asylum and given shelter in this country. The Cuban government felt that U.S. actions were in violation of the spirit of the antihijacking agreement to which the Cubans contend they still adhere, although it is not technically in effect. The Cubans felt also that U.S. actions were tantamount to U.S. encouragement of illegal emigration and increasingly were becoming anxious regarding its effects on the domestic situation in Cuba. . . .

Prior to the events of the spring of 1980, the most recent Cuban arrivals were 15,000 released political prisoners and their families who had come in the past year and a half. This release of 3,600 political prisoners by the Castro government came in response to efforts on the part of some leaders of the Cuban exile community at the end of 1978 to establish a closer relationship with Cuba. The

United States agreed to admit the political prisoners and their families under the parole authority of the attorney general.

The United States response in the early weeks of the spring 1980 exodus generally was unclear and uncertain.[1] Taken by surprise by Cuba's sudden lifting of the gates to emigration, the Carter Administration, in a short period of time, both encouraged and discouraged the exodus from Cuba. At the same time that President Carter declared that the U.S. government would welcome the refugees "with an open heart," authorities were seizing boats involved in the exodus. Meanwhile the Administration attempted to use the multilateral approach held in Costa Rica with other concerned nations. The United States, however, was unable to gain support other than the agreement to establish a three-nation commission which would attempt to deal with the Cuban government.

The influx of thousands of Cubans presented the United States with a series of dilemmas relating to recent U.S. immigration policy. The Refugee Act of 1980, recently enacted, established quotas for refugees that would be accepted from the various countries. The Act provided that applications for asylum would be considered on a case by case basis. The tremendous daily flow of people, however, made the law virtually inoperable. A further complicating factor was the apparent distinction being made between the newly arriving Cubans and the over 15,000 Haitian refugees in Florida. Before the Cuban refugee exodus began, the Administration ruled that the Haitians were economic, rather than political, refugees and therefore deportation proceedings were initiated. The willingness of the Administration to consider the Cubans as applicants for political asylum and to ignore economic considerations led to charges of "double standard" and discrimination by those who saw the Cuban and Haitian cases as similar. Perhaps the major complication, however, was the fact that U.S. public opinion generally was negative. It reflected concern with regard to the burdens this influx of people would have on the already strained U.S. economy.

THE EXODUS IN CONTEXT

The desire of tens of thousands to emigrate to the United States, arguably, is not particularly a Cuban phenomenon. Long lines of people applying for visas at U.S. embassy buildings and consulates in major Latin American cities are stark testimony to the reality of the "pull factors" attracting people to this country. The contrast of this nation's general affluence with Latin America's general poverty, the belief that opportunity awaits those who work for it, and the way of life within a democratic and open political system are major factors which draw people to try to migrate to the United States. A study done by the Kettering Foundation in the early 1970s found that one out of every three persons in Latin America wanted to migrate to the United States.[2] A recent State Department report stated that four million visa applications per year are received from people who want to immigrate to the United States.[3] In terms of actual numbers, Western Hemisphere immigration to the United States in the 1967–76 period showed an increase of 43.4 percent over the 1956–65 period. From 1967 to 1976, 1,507,434 people from Latin America, the Caribbean, and Canada migrated to this country.[4] In addition, INS and the Bureau of Census acknowledged that from three to six million people are in the United States as illegal aliens.

Those factors that draw immigrants to the United States played a large role in the Cuban exodus. Cuba's present social, economic, and political situation provides additional keys to understanding this latest wave of migration.

The collectivist philosophy of socialism has brought Cuba a way of life that has not been accepted by the nation's entire population. Government policies in the name of the common good have been responsible for education and public health systems which are ranked among the best in the developing world as evidenced by Cuba's very low rate of infant mortality, as only one example. Policies of equitable distribution of the nation's limited resources, on the one hand, while eliminating the extremes of rich and poor so prevalent throughout Latin America, have been undertaken at great individual sacrifice on the part of the Cuban people. The social and political system also requires a collectivist approach with its strong demand for mass participation at highly structured and organized government-sponsored activities which pervade all facets of Cuban life. A significant segment of the Cuban population, reacting against this style of life and to pressures and influences from within and outside the country, after 21 years chose to leave for the United States. The following is a discussion of the economic and political setting in Cuba which provided the context for the exodus of 1980.

Economic Situation

The Cuban economy was in a period of sharp decline. The projected growth rate for 1980 was 3 percent. This continued the decline begun in 1979 when the growth rate fell to 4.3 percent from the 1978 figure of 9.4 percent.[5] In per capita terms, the rate of growth fell from 8.2 percent in 1978 to 3.1 percent in 1979, and was projected to fall to 1.8 percent in 1980.[6] The sugar output was projected to fall to 6.5 million tons in 1981, from the 1979 production of 8 million tons. This limited foreign exchange earnings and slowed imports of badly needed raw materials and technology.[7]

Cuba's serious economic plight was acknowledged by the nation's leadership and had been known to the Cuban public since the fall of 1979 through a series of major addresses by officials, including Fidel and Raúl Castro. In these speeches, Cuban officials not only spoke of the acts of nature that severely damaged the island's economy but also addressed themselves to the problems created by the lack of raw materials and manufactured goods. In a speech much reported in the U.S. press (although made in a closed session of the National People's Government Assembly on December 27), Fidel Castro gave

a comprehensive account of the plight of the Cuban economy, referring to
shortages, the high cost of energy and other problems. References were made
to the problem of receiving goods from the Soviet Union and other socialist
countries that are not necessarily needed, such as TV sets, while such needed
items as towels, sheets, and other textiles are not received.

Raúl Castro, in a speech on December 4, spoke about unjustified absenteeism and lack of motivation among the workers and charged that many workers
deliberately worked at a slow pace so that production goals would not be
upgraded. . . .

The speeches and measures pronounced in this period conveyed another
important message that had particular relevance to the refugee situation that
occurred. The Cuban people were being told, very directly, that 21 years of
economic hardship would continue for some time in the future. Fidel Castro
in his December 21 speech said that Cuba was

> sailing in a sea of difficulties. We have been in this sea for some time and we will
> continue in this sea, sometimes more stormy and other times more calm, but the
> shore is far away. . . . We will march through a sea of difficulties; we will not be
> crossing it.[8]

The Cuban people were being told that the shortages that they have endured
would continue. They will have to work harder and more efficiently.[9] They
would have to continue to contend with the rationing of basic foodstuffs,
clothing, and other commodities. They will, therefore, have to continue to
limit themselves to the two pounds of meat per month, one and one half
pounds of chicken per month, two ounces of coffee every 15 days, four meters
of cloth per year, two packs of cigarettes per week, one pair of shoes, one pair
of trousers, one dress and two shirts per year. . . .

The visits to Cuba by thousands from the exile community in the United
States became a significant part of this economic setting. In 1979, 100,000
members of the *Comunidad* (as they are referred to in Cuba) visited families
and friends as part of the "dialogue" established by Fidel Castro and exile
community leaders. The motivation for the Cuban government to initiate the
"dialogue" was both political and economic. It was seen as an opportunity to
transform the exile community into an agent for, rather than against, normalization with the United States. The Castro government permitted the visits and
released 3,600 political prisoners. The "dialogue" created some good will and
needed foreign exchange. In 1979, visitors from the *Comunidad* spent $100,-
000,000. Whether or not the Castro government foresaw the ramification of
the exile visits, it is clear that they played a significant role in the exodus.

The stark contrast in American and Cuban lifestyles was evident every day
as members of the exile community and their Cuban friends and relatives
exchanged emotional greetings and farewells. The success stories of members
of the Cuban exile community in Miami told to their brethren in Cuba's cities,
towns, and rural villages were underscored by the photographs of the houses,

businesses, and cars, stylish quality clothing, expensive jewelry, calculators, tape recorders, and cameras. The exiles brought other symbols of affluence for their Cuban relatives and friends to see. A typical city scene in Havana of teenagers sporting Levis and T-shirts from Disneyworld and with slogans familiar to the United States such as "Better in the Bahamas," "Marlboro," and "Adidas" was evidence of the changes seen since the influx of the thousands of visitors from the exile community. It also created a strong demand for American goods brought in by the visitors, stimulating the black market where jeans sell for $125–$250 and shirts for $70. . . .

Political Situation

Cuba's highly structured and all-pervading political system, under 21 years of rule by Fidel Castro, has alienated a segment of the population. Loyalty to the regime is measured in terms of participation in government-sponsored mass organizations and programs. Those who choose not to participate in mass organizations like the Committees for the Defense of the Revolution, the Union of Communist Youth, and the Federation of Cuban Women have chosen not to be in the mainstream of Cuban life. They are less likely to accept the exhortations of the government for continued sacrifice in the name of the revolution. The majority of these people are considered to be "antisocials" by the government. While it is not possible to determine the actual loyalty of Cubans who are participants in the political system, those who have chosen to exclude themselves are more likely to represent dissatisfied elements of the population. Even among those who are considered participants, there are indications that there has been a diminishing of revolutionary zeal and fervent support of the government.

The somewhat unsettled situation in Cuba in 1979, much related to the economy as discussed above, had its effect on the political climate. Signs of unrest and discontent began to appear in December 1979 when anti-Castro posters and leaflets were reported to have been seen in Havana and a clandestine printing press reportedly was discovered. At this time, it was reported that 40 arrests were made, many of them being released political prisoners.[10]

It is conceivable that the presence, in the streets of Havana, of hundreds of released political prisoners was responsible for some of the unrest and tension present in this period before the exodus. Most of these former prisoners had been given their exit permits by the Cuban government and were waiting for processing by the U.S. Interests Section for entry into the United States. The Cuban government repeatedly pressed the United States to speed the processing; some officials believed that the United States deliberately was foot dragging in order to keep this discontented and disruptive element in Cuba as long as possible. Many of these former prisoners held menial jobs or were unable to obtain work because of their status. Some of the former prisoners were involved in an incident at the U.S. Interests Section on May 2 at the time of the exodus.[11]

In his December 27, 1979, speech before the National Assembly, Fidel Castro declared that there was going to be a crackdown against this growing "extremist" element. His appointment of Central Committee member and trusted associate Ramiro Valdés as Minister of Interior in January emphasized Castro's new hard line. The government security crackdown produced arrests for black marketeering, petty crimes, and other antisocial activity. This created some tension among those who look to the black market for foodstuffs and other commodities. According to some of the arriving refugees, those arrested for petty crimes were placed on "conditional liberty," which entails strict probation and loss of job and pension rights. Refugees also complained of the arbitrariness of the "Ley de Peligrosidad" (Law of Common Danger) by which the police made sweeping arrests for antisocial behavior. According to some accounts, many people had been arrested under this law for associating with antisocial elements even though it may have been in work surroundings. The presence of armed police and unarmed military (albeit in casual activity and seemingly off-duty status) is a phenomenon that was not seen in Havana by observers in the 1970s. . . .

Those Involved in the Exodus

Whereas earlier heavy migrations from Cuba brought to this country, first, political supporters of the Batista regime along with those from the business sector, and then those from the professional and skilled classes, this new influx seems to be composed of lower, semiskilled or unskilled working-class Cubans. Many of the refugees seem to be what the Cuban government considers the "antisocials." They are the nonsupportive, nonparticipative, antisystem elements, which include the vagrant, the petty criminal, the homosexual, and the prostitute. Many, however, are respectable family members who are students, lower-level government employees, truck drivers, restaurant workers, and laborers. In fact, there is some evidence that some of the new arrivals were formerly exemplary militant supporters of the Castro government who simply have lost faith in the power of the government to improve their economic plight.

Suspicions and charges on the part of U.S. officials that the Cuban government was taking advantage of the situation by emptying the nation's jails of common and hardened criminals began to be heard as individual men, more hardened and rougher in appearance than earlier arrivals, were placed on boats ahead of those from the Peruvian embassy and those with relatives in the United States. The White House on May 14, 1980, accused the Cuban government of taking hardened criminals out of prison and mental patients out of hospitals and forcing boat captains to take them to the United States. Many of the refugees say they were released from jail on the provision that they leave for the United States on boats from Mariel. . . .

The Cuban government has denied a deliberate policy of foisting Cuba's undesirables on the United States. *Granma,* on May 15, 1980, said that the antisocials were leaving voluntarily and that the government has not permitted the departure of persons involved in crimes or acts of bloodshed. The article also stated that mentally ill persons on the boatlift were probably there because they had been requested by relatives who arrived in Mariel to take them to the United States.

Official statistics from U.S. government sources indicate that the number of criminals and other undesirable elements is lower than originally reported in the media. Out of the total of 120,737 Cuban refugees, 1,656—a little more than 1 percent—are being held in Federal correctional institutions as "potentially excludable" under U.S. immigration law.[12]

One problem with determining the number of actual criminals is the fact that a certain percentage of this element has committed relatively minor crimes, such as purchasing an item on the black market. A further complication in determining the number of criminals is that, reportedly, many ordinary people are voluntarily professing that they are homosexuals, prostitutes, or otherwise have engaged in antisocial behavior, in order to receive exit papers from Cuban authorities.

It is significant that even the Cuban government, in a departure from its earlier position, seems to be accepting the fact that individuals other than antisocial *lumpen* (scum) and antigovernment "reactionaries" are making the decision to leave Cuba for the United States. A *Granma* editorial of May 19, 1980, related the phenomenon of emigration from underdeveloped countries to developed nations to the poverty that results from the unequal distribution of resources in the world. The government organ mentioned the large numbers of Mexicans, Haitians, and other Latin Americans who want to migrate to the United States because of economic conditions. *Granma* noted, significantly, that "It does not occur to anyone to call them dissidents." After making this point, however, the editorial charged the United States with the destabilization of Cuban life which promoted the mass exodus; and it reverted to the characterization of *lumpen* for those leaving Cuba. . . .

In the short-term domestic political context, the Cuban government was able to turn the events of the spring of 1980 into positive advantage. The decision to open the gates to all who desired to leave permitted the government to rid the country of that segment of the population that had not participated in the system as well as those who had been extremely unhappy under the regime. Mixed in among the political prisoners, the vagrants, and the other antisocials were the workers, students, and reportedly, even government and military personnel whose unhappiness created pressures on the Castro government. . . .

The *Granma* editorial of May 19, which may have been written by Fidel Castro himself (according to speculation that major *Granma* editorials on the exodus have been written by the Cuban president), also sent a message to the Carter Administration. It was made clear, in response to the announced desire of the United States government to discuss the emigration situation with the

Cuban government, that "We are ready to discuss and negotiate with the United States our problems and global relations, but not isolated and partial problems which interest only them and their strategy against Cuba." The Cubans believe that the question of emigration is inextricably related to the entire set of issues that comprise the U.S.-Cuba agenda.

NOTES

1. For an analysis of the Cuban situation as it related to U.S. immigration policy, see U.S. Library of Congress. Congressional Research Service. Refugees in the United States: The Cuban Emigration Crisis. Issue Brief No. 1B80063, by Charlotte Moore, May 16, 1980 (Washington, D.C., 1980).

2. *Washington Post* (May 8, 1980), p. A19.

3. *Washington Post* (May 28, 1980), p. A19.

4. U.S. Library of Congress. Congressional Research Service. U.S. Immigration Policy: The Western Hemisphere. Issue Brief No. IB 80-69, by Joyce Vialet, April 9, 1980 (Washington, D.C., 1980).

5. Telephone conversation with Carmelo Mesa-Lago, University of Pittsburgh. Data taken from his book, *The Economy of Socialist Cuba: A Two-Decade Appraisal* (Albuquerque, NM: Univ. of New Mexico Press, 1981).

6. Ibid.

7. *Business Week* (May 5, 1980), p. 80.

8. Fidel Castro. Speech before the National People's Government Assembly, December 27, 1979.

9. In March it was announced, for example, that the textile industry was being put on a full-time schedule to increase production and to create jobs. (Radio Havana, March 18, 1980.)

10. *Boston Globe* (April 11, 1980), p. 39.

11. The former prisoners and family members had been called to the Interests Section so that U.S. officials could respond to their increasing pressure to speed the processing procedure. While being addressed by the U.S. staff outside the entrance, they were attacked by Cubans who, according to some sources, were government security agents.

12. Cuba-Haiti Refugee Task Force, August 25, 1980.

40. The United States and Cuba*

BY KENNETH N. SKOUG, JR.

I appreciate very much the kind invitation of "Face-to-Face" to address you tonight on the subject of U.S.-Cuban relations.

*From United States Department of State, *Current Policy,* No. 646 (December 17, 1984). This address by Kenneth N. Skoug, Jr., Director of the Office of Cuban Affairs, was given before the "Face-to-Face" program of the Carnegie Endowment for International Peace, Washington, D.C., December 17, 1984.

A discussion of this subject appears timely at mid-passage of the Reagan Administration, a traditional time for stocktaking. It also comes three days after we completed an important agreement with Cuba on migration matters, about which I will say a few words later.

In his study of European relations in the period between the two world wars, E. H. Carr divided students of international politics into two groups. He called them—I believe without pejorative intent—utopians and realists. The utopians he described as primarily composed of intellectuals prone to emphasize idealistic considerations. By contrast, he placed diplomats and bureaucrats in the realist camp and said they liked to quote Machiavelli and Bacon.

To my knowledge Machiavelli never had much to say on the Cuban question. One of his more trenchant aphorisms for general reference, however, was that even enemies have "hidden bonds of interest." He was thinking in balance-of-power terms, counseling that one should not overly weaken a foe lest a third party gain too much in the process. We might wish, however, to inquire what kind of hidden bonds might exist between the United States and Cuba and whether they are conducive to positive or negative directions in our relationship.

Francis Bacon, who also passed in silence over the Cuban question, did recommend to his sovereign a policy of vigorous foreign involvement so that the domestic difficulties of the Stuart monarchy might be swallowed up in a wave of English patriotism. This concept, too, might have some relevance to the foreign policy of Cuba.

U.S. policy toward Cuba is shaped primarily by our perception of Cuban conduct in international affairs. Despite its size, it acts in world affairs in both a political and a military sense as a major power, with a large and well-equipped armed force—second largest in Latin America—and a history of a quarter century of foreign engagement. The Cuban Armed Forces are relatively rich in combat experience, almost all of it far from Cuban shores. Almost alone among Latin American states, Cuba involves itself intensively with the affairs of every state and virtually every political movement in the hemisphere and many even beyond. Havana is not merely aware of other states, but it knows about them in depth. It has a policy for each of them and for the region. It is one of the few states in Latin America with a sense of mission for the region as a whole, as well as a policy for Africa. Surely, there are few small states in modern history which have involved themselves voluntarily in so many and so disparate foreign policy questions, not as an object but as a subject.

Under the leadership of the past 26 years, Cuba has become a crusading country. This curious internationalism might well have the collateral effect of disarming or even coopting potential domestic critics, but it seems to stem from the fundamental sense of Havana's post-1959 leadership that Cuba alone is much too small a place for so much zeal. Small wonder that Fidel Castro told a recent visitor he regretted that Cuba does not have the natural resources of Brazil or an Argentina. But he has harnessed Cuba's impressive human resources to a foreign policy of engagement which is unique among small states.

Cuba, of course, claims to be a developing country. In recent meetings of the Council for Mutual Economic Assistance (CMEA), Cuba appeared in a role alongside Vietnam and Mongolia as the developing little brothers in a community where even the more industrialized brethren are not exactly success stories. In economic terms Cuba today is clearly properly classified as underdeveloped. But Cuba has and has had for a long time very high standards of health, sanitation, and education and had living standards in 1959 that rivaled some West European countries.

Dealing with Cubans, whether expatriates or nationals, one has the sense that while Cuba is now in an economic sense a developing country, in many other respects it remains an advanced society. Cuba was in 1959, in many respects, highly advanced. It has become paralyzed economically by mismanagement and particularly by a long-term commitment to produce sugar, a commodity decreasingly in demand on world markets and intended for a special market which can pay Cuba only in barter.

Cuba's place in international affairs seems shaped by three sets of associations. It would serve no purpose to lose sight of these underlying realities. The first and most critical is Cuba's special relationship with the Soviet Union. The second is its own revolutionary imperative, which stands apart from and is older than its ties to Moscow. The third is its self-image as a protagonist for a regional bloc in the hemisphere—"Nuestra America" in the much exploited term of José Martí—which would, to the extent possible, exclude the participation and influence of the United States. Through all three of these associations flows a strong hostility to the United States on the part of the Cuban leadership and a perceived need to be a leader of the so-called nonaligned in a way which is supportive of the Soviet Union and opposed to the United States.

CUBA'S DISTANT FRIEND

The Soviet-Cuban symbiosis owes its origin to Fidel Castro's assessment that his domestic and foreign policy would alienate Cuba's powerful neighbor, but that while Cuba's enemy was near, the enemy's own nemesis could redress the balance. While they may have since become close ideological kinsmen, for Cuba the USSR was first and foremost a guarantor behind whose protection Havana felt secure in pursuing with relative impunity the radical transformation of Cuban society and the foreign policy mission which its own leadership was determined to carry out.

Moscow was also from the outset a vital source of economic aid without whose help Cuba could not have taken the course that it did. For the USSR,

Cuba represented a windfall opportunity to introduce Soviet power and influence into the Western Hemisphere and to oblige the United States to address itself much more than in the recent past to the security of its own region. The new accord between Moscow and Havana also substantially increased the likelihood that future revolutions in the region would take on an East-West coloration, whatever their roots. Revolutionary Cuba thus provided the Soviet Union with a low-risk opportunity to alter the strategic balance.

Without reviewing the historic vicissitudes of the Cuban-Soviet relationship, most of which are well known to this audience, it is important to note that the fundamental elements which gave it birth have in no way lost their relevance. If anything, the contrary is true. In the 1970s the burden of this relationship on the Soviet Union grew as Cuba's economic dependence increased, but so did the value due to Cuba's unique capacity to advance objectives shared or favored by Moscow in Africa, Central America, and the Caribbean. The Cuban linchpin became more expensive, but it was still a bargain for Moscow. There is no sign that the Soviet Union is reassessing the value of Cuba or that the Cuban leadership has reconsidered the utility it derives from close alignment with the USSR.

Is Cuba a satellite or an ally? The Soviet Union has utilized its economic leverage over Cuba successfully in the past. The leverage is much stronger now due to the steady growth of Cuba's economic dependence, which in turn has come about through fundamental and probably irreversible economic decisions as well as the change in the terms of trade between the two countries. The enhanced value of oil and the shrunken outlook for sugar have given the transfer of commodities increasingly the character of aid. The Soviet Union now provides Cuba with the ruble equivalent of over $4 billion per year in assistance. But the recent summit meeting of the CMEA countries in Havana symbolized Cuba's status in that community and confirmed the island's economic future. No doubt as a matter of pride, Fidel Castro chafes at the notion of a subsidy, preferring to refer to the "just price" paid by the USSR for Cuba's sugar, but he knows all the same that Moscow does not pay the same "just price" for Brazil's sugar, and he knows that with Moscow's largesse come strings of steel.

While Cuba is increasingly dependent on the USSR and subject to Moscow's manipulation, it would be erroneous to regard it as merely a coerced Soviet satellite. In Eastern Europe there is an old joke which inquires why those states are always described as brothers of the USSR and not merely as friends. The answer is that you get to choose your friends. Although Cuba is now a little brother in a family that has only one big brother, Havana did choose this connection. The Cuban leadership presently has a similar world view as does the USSR. It is true that Cuba asserts that it is a nonaligned state, a fiction that is as much in Moscow's interest to maintain as it is in Havana's, but the fact is that Cuba gives full support to the Soviet Union in all major questions—whether it be the Soviet invasion of Afghanistan or any issue in the United Nations. The muscle which Cuba is able to apply in Third World forums is due not only to its own fervor but to the support of its strong friend, whom it terms the natural ally of the developing world. Cuba is, indeed, subject to Soviet pressure and control, but it does not have to be coerced to assail the United States at virtually every opportunity as the universal foe.

Is there a hidden bond of interest in this? Cuba uses its hostility toward the United States to obtain a volume of assistance from the Soviet Union that Moscow gives to no other country. At the same time, though, Cuba is falling progressively further behind many Latin American countries whose standards it once surpassed. From Cuba's point of view, some redress could be obtained if the United States' embargo were lifted. Since Moscow does not oppose Cuba's efforts in this direction, probably because the USSR would welcome a little burden-sharing, Cuba could probably trade on a limited basis with the United States as it now does with some Western countries, without offending Moscow. What it could not do and still retain Moscow's favor, however, is alter its fundamental commitment to give unswerving support to Soviet policy.

In this context it is sometimes suggested that the successful Nixon-Kissinger initiative toward China could be emulated with respect to Cuba by another conservative administration in the United States. This comparison, like similar ones suggesting that Cuba could become a Caribbean Yugoslavia, overlooks the underlying geopolitical reality as perceived by those who seized power in Cuba 26 years ago. In the case of China, it had expressed substantial concern long before 1968 for its security from a nearby and none-too-friendly Soviet Union. The invasion of Czechoslovakia, which Fidel Castro felt obliged in his own interest to endorse, evoked a very different response in Beijing, which recognized that Moscow was prepared to use force against another Communist country even if the victim denied any intent to leave the alliance or abandon "socialism." If China needed further persuasion, the battle on the Ussuri River in 1969 and the hints of Soviet surgical strikes against Lop Nor must have encouraged it to look to its own hidden bonds of interest with the United States. What followed was surely a creative act of diplomacy, but it was a diplomacy which rested on the firm bedrock of substantial mutuality of strategic interest.

One should not overload the circuit for diplomacy. In the case of Cuba, the USSR is far away. From Havana's point of view, indeed, it may be slightly too far. It has been Moscow's large-scale military assistance that has enabled Cuba to conduct a militantly anti-American foreign policy. Cuba says this relationship with the Soviet Union is not negotiable. Only if Havana itself were to reassess its own fundamental objectives and decide that its interests were not being well served by present policies would there be much room for creative diplomacy.

CUBA'S REVOLUTIONARY IMPERATIVE

Another basic consideration is Cuba's own revolutionary imperative, anchored in the 1976 Cuban constitution, which states that Cuba has the right and duty to support revolutionary and national liberation movements. Cuba is more sophisticated today in its approach to revolution than in the 1960s. Where once its zeal conflicted with Moscow's preference for caution, the Cubans must now balance revolutionary aspirations against hopes for influence with other Latin American governments. But these objectives—revolution and regional influence—are not necessarily self-contradictory. Cuban support for revolutionaries has been most effective when Havana was joined by non-Communist states in the region, as in the case of the Sandinista revolution in the late 1970s.

Nevertheless, the greater sophistication in the Cuban approach to stimulation and support of Latin American revolutionaries has not diluted the aboriginal combative spirit of the Castro regime. Havana knows very well who the revolutionaries are in Latin America, and it stays in close touch with developments. That touch means everything from scholarships, financial assistance, political advice, and radio broadcasting through the hemisphere to military training and support and the provision of arms. Cuba's approach to revolutionaries who are not in power is consistently to urge the formation of the widest possible alliance on the left, not excluding alienated persons in the moderate center, with the purpose of building a successful revolutionary force. Only after the attainment and consolidation of power may the revolution begin to eat its own children.

Fidel Castro has boasted that he had to tell the Soviet Union who the revolutionaries in Latin America are. He knows them, in part because they seek him out. Cuba is a mecca for Latin American revolutionaries and many a dissident Latin American politician. Those connections win Cuba influence even where prospects for revolution are either inauspicious on their own merits or to be played down on tactical grounds. By giving thumbs up, Fidel induced guerrillas in Colombia to spare the life of the brother of President Betancur. It could also have been thumbs down or no sign at all. This sort of influence is not lost on even those political leaders who have little sympathy for Cuba or for revolution.

Cuba can also orchestrate the use of revolutionaries for political ends, even if their objective prospects for success are relatively remote. The introduction of Cuban-trained revolutionary forces into Honduras does not stem from any internal conflict and might seem akin to the old *foco* approach. Apparently, it is intended primarily as a warning to Honduras not to oppose Cuba's friends on Honduras' southern and eastern borders.

The events in Grenada last year came as a shock to Havana. It saw the loss of a proto-Communist stronghold in the eastern Caribbean, the first direct military conflict between U.S. and Cuban forces, the surrender of many Cubans who had been expected to fight to the death, the unwillingness or inability of the Soviet Union to engage itself, the alignment of almost all the English-speaking Caribbean in favor of the action, the lack of any support in Grenada itself for the discredited regime, the overwhelming backing of the American public for the action, and, to add insult to injury, the expulsion of most of the Cuban presence from a promising situation in Suriname.

As a consequence, the Castro regime had little about which to cheer on the 25th anniversary of its seizure of power. It had to do some serious taking of stock. Out of this review there seems to have emerged, alongside a greater appreciation of the remoteness of Moscow from the Americas, a redoubled sense of self-reliance and a perceived need to stress Latin American solidarity as a means of safeguarding gains in Central America.

On August 30, 1984, looking on the bright side, the head of the America Department of the Communist Party Central Committee, Manuel Pineiro Losada, enunciated four reasons why Havana did not need to be pessimistic about prospects for Latin America.

First, he said, the Cuban revolution was stronger than ever.

Second, Somoza no longer ruled in Nicaragua.

Third, the oligarchy could not destroy the revolutionary movement in El Salvador.

Fourth, representative democracies in Latin America were rebelling against "imperalist domination."

What he seemed to be saying was that Cuba, if necessary by means of a people's war, is now strong enough alone to defy the United States, that the Nicaraguan regime would be able to consolidate itself, that the guerrillas in El Salvador could, at least, not be defeated, and that the United States cannot count on support from even democratic Latin American governments.

For the present, then, Cuba's revolutionary emphasis seems first to be centered on the defense of its own revolution, then on the consolidation of the Nicaraguan regime, and thirdly on a settlement in El Salvador which advances the prospects of the guerrillas for a share of power. Cuba sees Central America as the revolutionary cockpit where its energies must now be concentrated, while at the same time acknowledging that Cuban military forces could not be reinforced in case of combat. For the moment, at least, Cuba appears to be shaping its attitude toward other states in the hemisphere primarily on their stand on Nicaragua and El Salvador.

This more prudent tactical approach is, in part, a reaction to adverse developments. What are the hidden bonds of interest with the United States? Cuba does wish to avoid a major war in Central America where U.S. and Cuban soldiers might again come face to face. However, Havana has made clear that its support for revolution, like the Soviet alliance, is not for negotiation. It continues to support regimes or revolutionary movements patterned on the Cuban model. It is Cuba's striving, with Soviet support, to introduce Marxist-Leninist regimes throughout the hemisphere which still lies at the heart of our differences.

CUBA'S AMERICA

Aside from the revolutionary imperative, Cuba also seeks to build an anti-U.S. regional bloc of Latin American countries.

There is, at least potentially, a conflict between supporting Communist revolution in Latin America and the Caribbean and wanting to be accepted as a pillar of stability in the region. Cuba aspires to be accepted both as a revolutionary symbol and a leader among Latin American states. Bridging this gap in the face of historically based suspicions is no simple task for Cuba. However, historically or culturally based resentments against the United States in the region can be exploited by Cuba. Here again, criticism of the United States might be the common denominator which Havana would try to exploit in building Latin American regionalism.

Despite its emphasis on revolution, at least as a final goal, Cuba frequently appears to give priority to building a Latin American bloc. Its rush to support the Galtieri regime in Argentina is a case in point, where a chance to show Latin American solidarity against the United States weighed more for Havana than the regime's domestic policy. The current effort by Cuba to utilize the regional debt crisis is in the same spirit of putative regional alignment. If Cuba were to deemphasize violent revolution and political dictatorship in order to improve its status in the Latin American community, we might have some positive bond of interest. Even if this thrust were initially directed against the United States, we could hope that Cuba would eventually turn its human resources toward more positive objectives in the region.

Unfortunately, there is no present sign that Cuba, which allows no form of dissent at home, will be prepared to renounce its efforts to produce analogous regimes in the region.

The hard reality is that both Cuba's objective of promoting Marxist-Leninist type revolutions in Latin America and the Caribbean and its goal of creating subregional solidarity are linked to its desire to diminish American influence in the region.

DEALING WITH CUBA

The relationship between the United States and Cuba, especially with reference to Cuba's policies in third countries, has been essentially characterized by conflict. Unfortunately, this seems unlikely to change unless there is some fundamental reassessment in Havana of Cuba's need to act as a multiregional power in consonance with the Soviet Union.

There are some bonds of interest, however, which, while they cannot bridge the profound ideological and geopolitical gaps between us, at least allow for the solution of some important problems. While it would be an error not to try to resolve issues which seem susceptible to resolution, it would be unfounded to suppose that such efforts under current circumstances will lead to fundamental improvement in our relations. Such excessive expectations would only lead to frustration and could even undermine realistic efforts to resolve what can be resolved.

It is true that we have neither reconciled our differences with the Castro regime nor terminated its existence as a threat to U.S. interests and to those of friendly nations. We are not able to do the first because Castro's interests require an adversary relationship. Efforts to conciliate Cuba have coincided with some of the most active periods of Cuban-Soviet cooperation toward objectives inconsistent with U.S. interests. We could not do the second without direct use of military force against Cuba.

There still is room for some constructive diplomacy, however. The recently concluded agreement on migration is an important achievement on its merits and very much in the U.S. interest. It will also benefit Cuba, which would otherwise not have signed it. It is an example of a situation where we were able to find and exploit positive bonds of interest although the diplomatic process was enormously complicated by the history of the past quarter century.

The background of this problem is known to most of you. In order to relieve itself of domestic pressures, which in 1980 exploded into embarrassing diplomatic problems with Latin American states, the Cuban leadership turned to its favorite foe and opted to open its doors to a mass exodus to the United States. Among the 129,000 Cubans who came with the Mariel boatlift were several thousand criminals or mentally incompetent persons who have been a heavy burden on U.S. society and who were ineligible for lawful admission to the United States under U.S. immigration law.

A serious effort to negotiate their return to Cuba was made in the final weeks of the Carter Administration with the approval of the Reagan transition team. We offered Cuba, then, as in 1983 and 1984, the resumption of normal immigrant visa processing in the U.S. Interests Section in Havana and the resumption of a program under which expolitical prisoners and their families could come to the United States. These talks failed because Cuba would agree to consider the return of the so-called Mariel excludables only if they were returning voluntarily and only on a case-by-case basis.

It was obvious that those Cuban conditions would have frustrated any solution to the Mariel problem since hardly anyone wished to return to Cuba of his own volition. Thus the Mariel excludables continued to be a serious problem for state and local governments in the United States, for law enforcement agencies, and for the American public. The activities of this criminal element also gave an unmerited black eye to the overwhelming majority of Cubans who participated in the boatlift and, judging by public opinion polls, soured the attitude of many Americans toward refugees.

The pressures which the U.S. government applied to Cuba were to deny issuance of preference immigrant visas in Havana and to suspend the refugee program. Obviously, both of these caused hardships to innocent persons as well, but without them there would have been no solution to the problem. Conversely, Cuba's stand cost it seriously in terms of U.S. opinion, including many persons who might otherwise have been more favorably disposed toward Cuba.

We proposed in May 1983 that Cuba simply take back the Mariel excludables, in exchange for which we would have resumed normal processing of immigrant visas. Cuba responded negatively, but in the exchange of notes which followed, it did not rule out discussing the issue in a rather ill-defined framework of migration issues. The events in Grenada brought this initiative, temporarily, to a close. In March and again in May of the present year, we again proposed talks. Cuba ultimately agreed in principle to talk, but only after the U.S. elections.

Although we found it curious that Cuba would cite our election campaign as grounds for further delay in discussing this matter, we had to accept Havana's decision. We did plan to resume a limited refugee program, unilaterally, in Havana.

At this point we were consulted by Jesse Jackson's staff as to what issues he might raise while in Cuba. We mentioned Mariel and the question of long-term Cuban political prisoners. When we learned that Fidel Castro had agreed to earlier talks, we at once proposed an early date, and Cuba agreed.

These negotiations, although strictly limited to migration issues, were encumbered by mutual fears about intentions. In the end we achieved a result which is satisfying in all respects to the United States.

The main elements of the agreement are that some 2,700 common criminals will be returned to Cuba in an orderly and phased manner, that normal immigrant visa processing will resume at once in Havana, and that up to 3,000 expolitical prisoners and their families will come to the United States in the current fiscal year, with the expectation that this humanitarian program will continue in future years.

We were successful in this endeavor because our objectives were limited and realistic and we were prepared to offer the Cubans what they recognized was a reasonable bargain. The Cubans will be able to get one very large monkey off their backs. They will also make a lot of hard currency in the process through the charges they place on the emigration process.

Welcome as this agreement is, however, it should not be taken as indicating change in our resolve to deal firmly with Cuba's aggressive foreign policy. We do diplomacy a disservice if we exaggerate what it can accomplish. After all, Machiavelli never said that hidden bonds of interests alone would make enemies cease to be enemies. A good deal more is required.

We do not despair for the future of Cuba. A people of such enormous talents with their roots in the enlightening process of Western civilization cannot remain forever in the sway of a political doctrine which stifles human endeavor and creativity, fails to reward initiative, does not respect human rights, and forcibly excludes the population from the political process. If, in the meantime, Cuba has anything useful to tell us, or vice versa, the means of formal communication between our two governments exist and can be used. For Cuba the way back from its present alienation from the political democracy which is advancing throughout the hemisphere will be long and arduous. Havana may someday realize that its own best interests would be served if it again joined the American mainstream. In those circumstances there would be open and obvious bonds of interest between us.

A Cuba that wished to live in peace and harmony with its own citizens and with its neighbors in this increasingly free hemisphere would be welcomed back in the comity of American states. First must come the will. Then there could be a way.

CHAPTER 13

Cuba and the Third World

41. Castro's Cuba: Soviet Partner or Nonaligned?*

BY WAYNE S. SMITH

INTRODUCTION

There seems to be a misconception in the United States that because Cuba is a Marxist-Leninist state, it should not, by rights, be a member of the Nonaligned Movement (NAM). In fact, a country's system of government has no bearing on its membership. . . . The real question concerning Cuba's nonaligned credentials has to do with whether it has an independent foreign policy. . . . As Cuba looks out at the world, is it principally as Moscow's partner and ally, or principally as a nonaligned state that for tactical reasons must depend upon the Soviet Union for its survival?

The central purpose of this essay is to probe that question. In doing so, subsidiary questions must be raised. What, for example, would seem to be the natural milieu within which Cuban foreign policy can be most effectively articulated: the socialist world or the Third World? Is Castro first and foremost a Marxist-Leninist or a Third World nationalist? How have Cuba's relationships with the Soviet Union and with the NAM evolved? At its inception, what was the nature of the Cuban Revolution? Were its first steps instinctively toward Moscow and Marxism-Leninism or toward Third World nationalism of a Latin American strain?

*From Wayne S. Smith, *Castro's Cuba: Soviet Partner or Nonaligned?* (Washington, D.C.: Woodrow Wilson International Center for Scholars, Smithsonian Institution, 1984).

THE EARLY REVOLUTIONARY PERIOD: MONCADA TO FALL 1959

Whatever else Castro may have been when he came to power in January 1959, there is no credible evidence at all that he was a Marxist-Leninist;[1] and the deputy director of the Central Intelligence Agency (CIA), C. P. Cabell, confirmed this in testimony during November 1959. . . . As he came to power, moreover, Castro persistently denied that he had any links to the Communists, any sympathy with them, or any intention of adopting a Soviet model for Cuba.[2] During his April 1959 trip to the United States, for example, he stated categorically that he was not a Communist, and that he did not agree with the Communist system.[3]

If Castro did not see himself as a Marxist-Leninist and if the communization of Cuba was not, initially, his goal, what then did he see as his historical role and what were his principal objectives as he came to power?

First of all, while he of course had domestic goals (to bring about a social revolution in Cuba), they were only a means to an end; he needed a revolutionary base (in other words, a model of his own) if he was to project himself onto the larger international stage. Given Castro's ambition and ego, it is difficult to imagine that he would ever have been content to play exclusively on a small domestic stage. Even one of his most sympathetic chroniclers, Herbert Matthews, has noted that "there is also a Messiah complex. Fidel has all along felt himself to be a crusader, if not a saviour. He is out to achieve a second liberation of Latin America."[4]

This messianic vision is crucial to understanding Castro's actions in those early days. It was this that drove him. Foreign policy objectives outweighed all domestic goals and considerations. The centerpiece of his foreign ambitions was the "liberation of Latin America," a goal encapsulated by the slogan "The Andes will become the Sierra Maestra of South America." As Castro phrased it to José M. (Pepín) Bosch, the head of the Bacardi rum company, who accompanied the bearded leader to the United States in April 1959, he hoped to do nothing less than free Latin America from U.S. economic domination as Simón Bolívar more than a century earlier had freed it from Spanish political control.[5] He saw himself as a liberator and as the potential spiritual leader of a great new Latin American revolutionary bloc. The main enemy was U.S. economic imperialism, but as Castro assessed the power structure in most Latin American countries, most of the national governments represented *vendepatria* (or sellout) classes whose interests were closely linked to those of the United States. Thus in the other countries, as in Cuba, the first step in driving out U.S. influence was the overthrow of the national governments themselves. . . .

Castro saw himself principally as a Latin American nationalist; hemispheric liberation was his principal objective. His ambitions, however, were by no means limited to his hemisphere. He had been moved by the Bandung Conference of 1955, the first gathering of heads of state of the Afro-Asian countries, out of which grew the Nonaligned Movement.[6] The theme of unity among the developing countries in the face of imperialist exploitation touched a responsive chord in Castro. This made excellent sense to him. There was strength in numbers and in unity. If Latin American states could defend their interests better as a bloc than individually, could they not also have more weight on the world stage as part of a global association of developing countries?[7]

Even before he took power, then, Castro had an intense interest in playing a role within an association of Third World countries, and even before there was a Nonaligned Movement, the Cuban Revolution was identified with the broader Third World struggle. In his first speech before the U.N. General Assembly in September 1959, for example, Cuban Foreign Minister Raúl Roa indicated a nonaligned course for Cuba. It was time, he said, that the great powers left the small countries alone and stopped interfering in their internal affairs. The world, he went on, was dangerously divided between the two powerful blocs. By history and tradition, Cuba was part of the West. But for the first time Cuba was really free and would have an independent foreign policy. It no longer accepted the inevitability of choosing between capitalism and communism. There were now other paths and other solutions. Cuba's paths and solutions were those of the other Latin American states and of the peoples of Africa and Asia, as well as of Latin America.[8]

To give concrete form to the perceived need for tricontinental unity, Castro very early tried to promote an international conference of underdeveloped countries in Havana. It was never held, but the idea was one of the precursors of the present Group of 77. . . .

It should be emphasized that as the Cuban Revolution had been nationalist in content, so too was Castro's international vision fueled by nationalism. The other revolutions he hoped for would spring from the soul of Latin American nationalism. The great new revolutionary bloc he expected it to form would be anti-imperialist and anti-U.S. yes, but inspired by the thought of Simón Bolívar, José Martí and Rubén Darío, not of Marx or Lenin.

CASTRO THE NATIONALIST TURNS TO THE SOVIET UNION: 1959–61

If Castro initially had no intention of turning to the Soviet Union, why did he subsequently do so? What changed his mind?

To begin to answer those questions, we must understand that all along Castro had seen clearly that the pursuit of his objectives in Latin America was likely to carry him, in time, to a direct confrontation with U.S. power. He hoped to do no less than to impose sharp limitations on U.S. economic interests and to challenge U.S. political leadership in the area. The United States, he surmised, would not watch passively as he did so. Unless there were other restraining factors, sooner or later it would move against him.

Initially, Castro counted on a show of Latin American unity to provide that restraining factor. Cuba standing alone against the Colossus of the North was one thing. Cuba as the leader of an alliance of revolutionary states would be something else again. Cuban survival, then, was seen to depend on the near-term triumph of other revolutionary movements in Latin America. Castro had hinted at this in his January 21, 1959 speech, stating that the Cuban Revolution had to be defended not just for Cuba but as something that belonged to the whole continent. The same theme was seen also during a television appearance on March 6, 1959, in which he appealed for the support of the other Latin American peoples. How much he felt he needed it was seen clearly in his remark that "we are fully aware that in order to consolidate its victory, the Cuban Revolution needs the power of public opinion of these peoples."[9]

Time was of the essence. The new revolutionary regimes had to emerge quickly before the United States had time to react. In the euphoria of his own victory, Castro seems to have expected that other revolutions, inspired by his, would soon break out all over the continent. But he was wrong. The other revolutions did not occur. And, as we have seen, in those instances in which Castro tried to help them along, his efforts failed miserably. By the latter half of 1959, then, Castro was forced to reassess the situation. The Cuban Revolution might not be spark enough to ignite uprisings around the hemisphere. Nor, apparently, could one always produce an "instant guerrilla front" simply by landing a few Cubans. Native cadres would have to be trained, armed, and funded. Thus, the process would be longer than anticipated and would require much more in the way of effort and resources than Castro had originally estimated.

Meanwhile, the other Latin American governments and the United States were becoming increasingly concerned over Cuban efforts to foster other revolutions. The fifth meeting of American foreign ministers, held in Santiago in August 1959, took up, *inter alia,* the cause of tensions in the Caribbean. It did not mention Cuba, but it did strongly uphold the principle of nonintervention, and it directed the Inter-American Peace Committee to take steps to prevent one state from attempting to overthrow the government of another.

Castro could draw his own conclusions. With the Organization of American States (OAS) beginning to gear up to meet the challenge he planned to mount, and the Inter-American Peace Committee alert to future incursions, he faced a daunting situation. New Cuban efforts such as those against Panama and the Dominican Republic would almost certainly be detected and meet a strong reaction. Even clandestine support to insurgents might well be exposed. The odds were that in time the United States, working through the OAS, would build up a formidable case against Cuban intervention. It would then have a free hand to confront the Castro regime, and, as it would be acting in the name of the OAS, its actions would be cloaked with a convincing mantle of legality. As Castro must have assessed them, the prospects were bleak indeed. If he continued to pursue his objectives in Latin America, he would find himself face to face with the most powerful nation in the world, and he would stand alone. His choice, then, was one of giving up his foreign policy objectives, or of seeking a shield against U.S. power—at least until he could bring into being the other Latin American revolutionary governments of which he dreamed. In order for such a shield to be credible, the nation providing it had to be a powerful one. And to which of the world's powers could Castro turn with any hope that his request would be honored? Obviously, only to the Soviet Union. Only the Soviet Union had both the power and an intense interest in undercutting U.S. influence in the area. Castro's choice was obvious and he took it.

Exactly when Castro reached his decision is not clear. He probably had been mulling over the options since late summer. But whether the decision came in August, September, or October, by the late fall of 1959 it was obvious that a shift was in progress. . . . As Hugh Thomas has characterized this period of fall 1959–winter 1960, "the regime was now moving into a stage when preparations were being made for the complete realignment of her national and international posture."[10]

Eventually, this realignment led to a close relationship with the Soviet Union. The latter had extended almost immediate recognition to the Cuban revolutionary government when it came to power in January 1959, but the Cubans had not even bothered to respond. That oversight was now rectified. On May 7, 1960, Cuba and the USSR established diplomatic relations. By the summer of 1960, the Soviet Union was beginning to supply most of Cuba's petroleum needs. And when the United States cut Cuba's sugar quota in July 1960, Moscow eventually offered to take up the slack. More importantly, by late 1960, Cuba was receiving large quantities of weapons from Eastern Europe—principally from Czechoslovakia. As Castro had intended, the Soviet bloc became Cuba's principal backer and ally against a common foe, the United States.

It should be noted, however, that during the period from the fall of 1959 until April 1961, Castro saw the Soviets as allies but not as ideological soul mates. During all those months, there was nothing from Castro or any other senior member of the Cuban government to suggest that Cuba had opted for the Marxist-Leninist path. The Cuban Revolution was becoming more radical, yes. But as Guevara himself suggested at the time, it remained essentially left-wing nationalist in orientation.[11] As Castro probably saw it at the time, Moscow would assist him in his struggle against the imperialists in the same way it had earlier assisted Nasser in Egypt, or Sukarno in Indonesia. That assistance implied no change in his own objectives or the ideological makeup of his regime. In December 1959, for example, even after his decision to turn to the Soviets for help, Castro insisted that it was "an act against the interests of the Fatherland to describe the revolution as socialist."[12] . . .

CASTRO EMBRACES MARXISM-LENINISM

On April 16, 1961, however, Castro suddenly shifted his ground and declared, to the surprise of his followers, that the Cuban Revolution indeed *was* socialist.[13] What had happened to change his mind? Having maintained a non-communist position even while grasping for a Soviet shield against U.S. power, why did he now declare his movement to be Communist—and subsequently go on to describe himself as a convinced Marxist-Leninist?[14]

As Castro's need for a defensive umbrella had increased, so had his willingness to adopt any posture necessary to secure it. If the Soviets had indicated they could commit themselves to the defense only of socialist countries, and if the ideological imperative for that defense was operative only in the case of Marxist-Leninist states, very well; he would declare his movement to be Marxist-Leninist. It was not by accident that he did so on the very eve of the Bay of Pigs invasion. That an invasion was on the way, Castro knew. He doubtless expected to face the full impact of U.S. power—that marine divisions as well as Cuban exiles would shortly be landing on his beaches. The motive behind his identification with socialism, then, was transparent. He was in effect saying to the Soviets, "I am a good Marxist-Leninist just like you; if the Americans attack me, you must come to my defense."[15] Having once taken that step, all else flowed from it. Over the years, Castro did indeed transform Cuba into a full-fledged Marxist-Leninist state. . . .

CUBA'S INDEPENDENT POSITION IN THE NAM: 1961–68

Castro had publicly embraced Marxism-Leninism in order to enhance the possibility that the Soviets would indeed extend him a defensive shield. His purpose, however, was still to pursue his own objectives in his own way behind that shield. Even after April 16, 1961, neither his objectives nor the way he pursued them changed much at all. It was as though for expediency's sake he had accepted a Marxist-Leninist mantle but in fact had retained the attitudes and purposes of a radical nationalist. His eyes remained on revolution throughout Latin America and on its identification with the Third World. One could see this clearly even in so inflammatory a document as the Second Declaration of Havana, issued on February 4, 1962. As the First Declaration of Havana had been a response to the OAS meeting in San José, the second was a reaction to the OAS meeting of foreign ministers held in Punta del Este, Uruguay, in January 1962, at which Cuban membership in the OAS was suspended. Castro's response was immediate and vitriolic. Many, indeed, described it as virtually a declaration of war against the other governments of the hemisphere, as well as against the United States. Even though the latter was "insolently gathering its forces" to prevent it, he declared, hemispheric revolution was inevitable.[16] . . .

Nowhere in the declaration will one find any reference to Marxist-Leninist theory, any socialist exhortations, or suggestions that the Latin American revolution should take a socialist path. On the contrary, his was an appeal to all "patriotic Latin Americans." If the Yankee yoke was to be thrown off, Castro asserted, all, from old-line Marxists to sincere Catholics, would have to work together. . . .

Meanwhile, Castro continued to pursue a line within Third World fora independent of Soviet positions. He might now be a Marxist-Leninist, but in Castro's mind that obviously did not imply any acceptance of Moscow's discipline or leadership; rather, he thought, he could continue to go his own way.

Cuba was a founding member of a Nonaligned Movement, which emerged out of the Belgrade summit in August and September 1961. President Osvaldo Dorticós of Cuba attended that meeting and also the NAM's second summit, held in Cairo in October 1964. In neither did he suggest a natural alliance between the nonaligned and the socialist nations. He did (at Cairo) say the former were threatened not by the latter but rather by the imperialists. He did not go on, however, to suggest a community of interests and purpose between the two.[17] That was a thesis the Cubans were to take up only during the decade of the 1970s, and under very changed circumstances.

Dorticós did not even describe the Cuban case as resulting from East-West conflict. Cuba's revolutionary path had not been predetermined by Cold War tensions between the two great powers; rather, it was the product of a colonialist situation in which an imperial power, the United States, accustomed to imposing its will in Latin America, had been defied by Cuba. All else flowed from that.

Traditionally, the Soviets had behaved with great caution in Latin America, believing it to be a U.S. sphere of influence so close under U.S. guns as to preclude successful Soviet adventures. What was perceived by Moscow as U.S. failure of will at the Bay of Pigs tempted Soviet decision makers to conclude that the law of geographic determinism might no longer be operative. Perhaps, after all, adventures were possible, even in the Caribbean. It was this perception, more than anything else, that led the Soviets to introduce missiles in Cuba—and to think they could get away with it. U.S. resolve during the October 1962 crisis, however, demonstrated to the Soviets that they had been right the first time. When its interests and security were really challenged in the area, the United States would still go to the mat. Geographic determinism was not dead. Soviet caution returned and in the wake of the 1962 crisis, the two superpowers began to grope toward détente.

This suited Castro not at all. He was not in the least interested in accommodation with U.S. imperialism; rather, he was intent on driving it out of Latin America at the point of a gun. Not surprisingly, therefore, at the Cairo NAM

summit, the Cuban delegation denigrated the whole idea of détente. In Dorticós's words, there could be no peaceful coexistence that did not also include
the small countries. An accord strictly between the two superpowers was
unacceptable, he asserted. There could be no peaceful coexistence while simultaneously imperialist aggression continued against the small countries. It could
come about only if it made provision for the peace and independence of
embattled states such as Cyprus, the Congo, Vietnam, Cambodia, and, of
course, Cuba.[18] . . .

Although Ernesto "Che" Guevara, for example, was often described in the
U.S. media as an agent of international communism, he was in fact never under
Moscow's—and barely under Castro's—discipline. He had his own vision of
pure Marxism and his own ideas as to Moscow's ethical responsibility to
support national liberation groups. He did not hesitate to express these views,
even though they contradicted the Moscow line, and, indeed, were highly
offensive to the Soviet leadership. As time went on, Guevara's criticisms
became more rather than less pointed. . . .

Perhaps the culmination of Castro's efforts to assert his independence from
Moscow was seen in his January 1968 purge of the so-called microfaction from
the Cuban Communist party. Led by Anibal Escalante (the same Moscow-
lining member of the pre-Castro Communist apparatus who had been in
trouble with Castro in 1962 for "sectarianism"), the group was charged with
propaganda against the interests of the revolution and "undermining Cuba's
relations with other governments." Most were not only expelled from the party
but given prison sentences as well. Testimony against them included references
to their damaging conversations with representatives of the Soviet government—almost as if the Soviet Union were an enemy power (which, in a certain
sense, it was). It was reported, moreover, that "their arguments and positions
coincided with those adopted by the pseudo-revolutionaries [read, the orthodox Communist parties] and the CIA".[19]

Strong stuff indeed! An open schism between Havana and Moscow began
to appear almost inevitable, especially in view of the LASO (Latin American
Solidarity Organization) conference held in Havana in August 1967. This had
been an incendiary follow-up to the Tricontinent [conference held in 1966] and
was particularly galling to the Soviets. It may have confirmed to them that the
problem of their headstrong partner in Havana would not disappear. If Castro
was to be shut up, they would have to take the initiative in doing so.

CUBA AS A LOYAL SOVIET PARTNER IN THE NAM: 1968–79

Perhaps not surprisingly, however, the break never came. Unlike Yugoslavia
and Communist China, Cuba was not, on its own, a viable economic entity.
It needed a powerful patron. Moreover, it was located hard on the flank of the
most powerful country in the world, the United States, whose government was

even more bitterly hostile to Castro than to the Soviet Union or China. Without some sort of implied protection from the Soviet Union—however limited—Castro's chances even of survival would have been poor indeed. Castro had wished to maintain his separate line and identity, but it must have been clear to him all along that if push came to shove, he would have little choice but to accommodate Soviet concerns.

By January 1968, push had indeed come to shove. In Moscow's view, Castro has gone quite far enough. Cuba depended on Soviet petroleum shipments. This was the obvious place for the squeeze to begin, and begin it did. The Soviets informed their wayward Caribbean associates that they would not be able to meet Cuba's petroleum needs for 1968, and some shipments were held up.

Castro got the point. He saw that he had carried his quarrel with the Soviets about as far as he realistically could. The first indication that he was backing down came in a speech on August 23 in which he had been expected to condemn the Soviet invasion of Czechoslovakia. The Czech Communist party, after all, was only doing what Castro himself wished to do; chart its own course. There had already been indications of Cuban sympathy for its cause. On August 23, however, Castro reversed course. The new leadership in Czechoslovakia, he said, had used slogans with which Cuba sympathized, such as that of having the right to develop their own form of socialism. But the Czech leadership had also entered into a conspiracy with agents of the United States and West Germany. Socialism was endangered; a counterrevolutionary situation was developing. This, he asserted, the socialist camp had an absolute right to prevent.[20] In so saying, Castro endorsed the Brezhnev doctrine. . . .

Castro's shift doubtless resulted not only from Soviet pressure, but also from the painful recognition that after almost a decade of effort, armed struggle had failed as a tactic; it had not produced a single victory in Latin America. Che Guevara's defeat in Bolivia dramatized this failure and must have led to some soul-searching on Castro's part.

Other developments also encouraged him toward a revision of his original line. He had argued that in Latin America the only way to bring about a revolution was through the barrel of a rifle. He had also argued that the traditional armed forces had to be destroyed. In 1968, however, the Peruvian military took power and instituted a series of popular reforms, including the expropriation of the International Petroleum Company, an American subsidiary. In a speech on July 19, 1969, Castro had to admit that the Peruvian military seemed to be leading the country toward a true revolution, thus implicitly recognizing for the first time that both the tenets he had advanced so confidently were wrong. There were, after all, ways of making a revolution other than through the barrel of a rifle, and rather than having to be destroyed, the traditional armed forces themselves might in certain circumstances make that revolution.[21]

The success of popular front tactics was demonstrated to Castro again when Socialist party leader Salvador Allende, at the head of a progressive coalition, won the presidency in Chile.[22]

While Castro's tactics had gained nothing, Soviet popular front strategies and emphasis on state-to-state relations were paying off handsomely, as witnessed not only by the encouraging developments in Peru and Chile but also by the fact that in a very short space of time, Moscow had established diplomatic relations with Colombia, Venezuela, Bolivia, Ecuador, Costa Rica, and Guyana—as well as with Peru and Chile. As Castro surveyed the scene, he must have concluded that it was time to begin breaking out of his own diplomatic isolation in Latin America. This, then, was still another reason to mute earlier emphasis on armed struggle throughout the hemisphere. . . .

As Castro was thus forced by circumstances (some beyond his control, others of his own making) to play the role of loyal Soviet ally, this was reflected in Cuba's position within the NAM. At the 1964 Cairo summit, Cuba had followed a distinctly independent line. By the time the next NAM summit was held, at Lusaka in 1970, the Cubans were beginning to float the concept of a natural alliance between the socialist world and the nonaligned world. Speaking on September 27, 1970, Foreign Minister Raúl Roa, who headed the Cuban delegation, asserted that

> the socialist countries are the strongest of the anti-imperialist front. We cannot leave them out or isolate them if we expect to engage in battle with the imperialist countries led by the U.S.[23] . . .

Given Algeria's views and positions, the fact that the NAM's next summit was to be held in Algiers presaged a more radical outcome. . . .

At Algiers, Castro attended a NAM summit for the first time. He began his speech by asserting forthrightly that Cuba was a Marxist-Leninist country— something Cuban delegations had previously downplayed. He then gave effusive thanks for Soviet assistance to Cuba and reminded other countries that the Soviets had stood by them also.

Castro went on to emphasize that the principal enemy of the developing countries and emerging states was U.S. imperialism (certainly not a new thought for him). Only the closest alliance of all the progressive forces of the world, he declared, would give them the strength to defeat the imperialist enemy. Thus, he warned, "Any effort to pit the nonaligned countries against the socialist camp is profoundly counterrevolutionary and only and exclusively benefits imperialist interests."[24] . . .

Brezhnev himself backed up Castro's words with a message to the delegates at Algiers insisting that Moscow was their natural ally. The real division of the world, he insisted, was not between developed and underdeveloped countries; rather, it was between socialism and imperialism.[25] Push it though he did,

Castro could not sell the "natural alliance" idea at Algiers. Resistance to it was deeply ingrained. . . .

At Algiers, such influential nonaligned states as Yugoslavia, India, Tanzania, and Algeria insisted that nonalignment meant just that and that their movement could not endorse either one side or the other in the East-West equation. Algeria, for example, pushed for radical language (as suggested above), but the conference's draft resolutions, which it authored, criticized both East and West. Algeria and Libya, moreover, were the principal advocates at Algiers of the theory of "two imperialisms"—that is, they were the "echo" Castro had mentioned in his speech.

. . . Whatever his principal motives, whether he was responding more to Soviet needs or to his own interests, the results were the same. For the next six years, Cuba took an outspokenly pro-Soviet position in the NAM and pushed the benefits of a "natural alliance" for all they were worth.

At the fifth NAM summit, held in Sri Lanka in 1976, Havana was chosen as the site for the sixth NAM summit, to be held in September 1979. This was, of course, regarded as a victory for Cuba—and for the group of radical countries it headed in the NAM (such as Vietnam, Angola, and Ethiopia). Even so, strong resistance to the "natural alliance" concept continued. Indeed, Cuba's persistence in supporting it resulted in challenges to Havana's nonaligned credentials. Havana, some NAM members insinuated, was serving Soviet objectives rather than those of the NAM. . . .

ECONOMIC ISSUES

Cuba had long championed more equitable trade and financial arrangements for the developing countries. . . . As Castro's emphasis on armed struggle against the imperialists waned, his attention to economic development issues increased. Not all NAM members had agreed with his fiery rhetoric and export of revolutionary policies, but, he doubtless sensed, few would disagree with the thesis that the developed countries had not given their poorer brothers a fair shake and that the only way the latter might force them to do so was through a united front. Castro's greater attention to developmental issues coincided with a growing sense of urgency and frustration on the part of other NAM members. Hit by rising energy costs and uncertain prices for their own commodities, most faced an economic crisis of alarming proportions. Rather than advancing economically, they saw themselves slipping further and further behind the wealthy industrialized countries. Their reaction, not surprisingly, was to blame the latter for their predicament and to make increasingly militant demands on them. And as most of their trade and financial arrangements were with the industrialized countries of the West, their resentments were directed much more at them than against the socialist countries. This added to the movement's inherent imbalance stemming from the fact that the colonial yokes recently thrown off had been those of Western countries. Thus "anticolonial" attitudes and policies inevitably tended to be anti-Western in orientation.

The economic declaration of the Algiers summit had reflected the growing militancy of the nonaligned countries with respect to the question of developmental issues, and particularly to the responsibility of the capitalist countries for their impoverishment. This took on a new institutional form at the 1974 and 1975 special sessions of the U.N. General Assembly when the nonaligned delegates called for a new international economic order. Not only was this call repeated at the Sri Lanka summit in 1976, but the Western industrialized countries were condemned for their intransigent resistance to the new order. . . .

CUBAN INVOLVEMENT IN AFRICA

As the NAM moved toward the Havana summit, it seemed to many Western observers, and most especially to the Carter administration in Washington, that Cuban military intervention in the Angolan civil war of 1975 and in the Somali-Ethiopian war of 1977–78 was cause for a serious review of its nonaligned credentials. Few NAM members saw it that way, however. On the contrary, given that Cuba had had a close relationship with the Popular Movement for the Liberation of Angola (MPLA) for over a decade, its intervention on the latter's behalf was not perceived as strange or as a matter of responding to Soviet rather than Cuban interests. Further, since Cuban troops had been sent in to help the MPLA fight off the hated South Africans, their intervention was applauded by most NAM members, and most enthusiastically by black Africa. Rather than hurting Cuba's position in the NAM, the intervention in Angola probably enhanced it. Through it, Cuba was able to present itself as a strong, reliable partner to which other NAM members could turn in times of crisis. In a sense, by using Soviet logistical support as a substitute for a population and resource base, Cuba had been able to project its force and influence into a distant corner of the globe, almost as if it were a great power. Heady stuff indeed!

The Ethiopian case was somewhat different. Here, Cuban troops were used not against South Africans but against another nonaligned nation. Further, they were under the command of a Soviet general. At the same time, however, Ethiopia, to whose aid they had come, *was* the victim. It had been invaded by Somalia, and the invasion had been condemned by the Organization of African Unity. Thus, on balance, few NAM members felt Cuba's actions should be criticized—so long as it did not invade Somalia or involve itself in Addis Ababa's efforts to suppress the Eritrean secessionists. The Cubans refrained from both.[26]

The central point, in both the Angolan and Ethiopian cases, was that the

Cubans argued, and argued persuasively, that they were pursuing their own objectives and that the decisions to go to the assistance of the MPLA in Angola and the revolutionary government in Ethiopia were essentially Cuban decisions, not Soviet. The United States might reject these arguments, but in the Third World they were generally accepted.

THE HAVANA SUMMIT AND BEYOND: CUBA ADOPTS A MIDDLE WAY

Predictions that the radical countries would run away with the Havana summit were not borne out. Not only was the natural alliance thesis shelved, but the moderate states more than held their own on other questions as well. The two most contentious issues had to do with (1) seating a Cambodian delegation, and (2) expelling Egypt (because of its signature of the Camp David agreements). The radicals failed to win a clear victory in either case. . . .

That Castro's performance at the Havana summit reflected a significant shift in Cuba's foreign policy line was confirmed by his speech at the U.N. General Assembly a few days later. He began by saying that, while he had his differences with the United States, he had not come to criticize the host country; rather, he had come to express Cuba's deep concern over the economic crisis faced by the poor countries. He then picked up one of the key themes of his summit speech, reeling off statistics to illustrate the seriousness of the economic crisis faced by the developing nations. He repeated his calls for détente and a drastic reduction in armaments. The really crucial problems faced by the world, he suggested, were underdevelopment, hunger, depletion of the soil, and contamination of the air and water. Yet, rather than devoting resources to the solution of these problems, the great powers were spending ever increasing amounts on armaments. This had to stop.[27]

Although the implicit criticisms of Castro's U.N. speech were directed far more at the U.S. than at the USSR, it was nonetheless a different kind of speech for him, one in which he tried to put himself forward as a responsible spokesman for the legitimate developmental aspirations of the Third World. If he did not actually take a middle course (between Moscow and Washington) in the speech, it was at least couched in North-South rather than East-West terms.

If Castro had decided prior to the Havana summit that continued identification of his views and objectives with those of the Soviets was likely to yield diminishing returns, events in the wake of the summit doubtless led him to the conclusion that it would actually be counterproductive. When the Soviets invaded a founding member of the NAM, Afghanistan, in December 1979, for example (without, by the way, consulting or even informing the Cubans), it not only made a mockery of the idea that Moscow was the shield of the nonaligned countries but also sharply damaged Cuba's international position. Cuba had been on the verge of winning a seat on the UN Security

Council. In the wake of the Soviet invasion, it eventually lost to Colombia. Further, Cuba had obviously hoped to use its three-year chairmanship to solidify a preeminent leadership role. Rather than that, because of the Soviet invasion, it found itself constantly on the defensive. Having identified itself so closely with the USSR, it now had to pay the cost of that identification.

That these and other factors were having an impact on Cuban calculations was seen clearly in an authoritative article by Vice-President Carlos Rafael Rodríguez in *Cuba Socialista*, the theoretical journal of the Central Committee of the Cuban Communist party. Entitled "The Strategic Foundations of Cuban Foreign Policy," the article emphasized the divergence of Cuban and Soviet policy needs and objectives. [See Reading 30.—eds.] . . .

That indications of a more independent Cuban line reflected a significant policy change rather than a tactical shift was borne out by Castro's performance at the seventh NAM summit in New Delhi in March 1983. In vivid contrast to his speech a decade earlier in Algiers, a speech in which he had lauded the Soviet Union, described it as the protector of the Third World, and insisted that a natural alliance existed between the two, at New Delhi, Castro did not even refer to the Soviet Union.[28] Gone were any allusions to a natural alliance. The gains of the NAM were *not* said to have been made possible by the correlation of forces wrought by the Soviet Union; rather, Castro referred to them as gains achieved by the nonaligned nations themselves.

Castro then went on again to link peace and development. Without the one there could not be the other. "We have said that the struggle against war is for us, the members of the Nonaligned Movement, not only to oppose the global holocaust but also to defend our own immediate political interests. . . . Without peace—and we are certain of this—development is not possible, just as it is true that without development there can be no peace."[29]

Castro ended his speech with an impassioned call for peace, for development, for a strengthened United Nations, and a strong, more united Nonaligned Movement. There was no mention of the socialist countries and no repetition of earlier calls for the solidarity of all progressive forces (i.e., of nonaligned and socialist forces). . . .

Thus Castro's performance at New Delhi was essentially that of a Third World leader, not that of a Soviet partner. As in the 1960s, Cuba is again moving toward an independent line in the NAM. It is unlikely to articulate that line in the same way it did during the 1960s. The Cuban leaders are too weathered and pragmatic for that. They understand that they cannot afford to break with the Soviets, let alone provoke them to an open dispute. Hence, their more independent line is likely to be pursued discreetly and within such bounds that it will not be overly offensive to the Soviets. One will be able to deduce more from what they do *not* say than from what they do say. But efforts that tend to identify them overly with Soviet causes, such as the natural alliance thesis, are not likely to be resuscitated.

CONCLUSIONS

To understand Cuba's foreign policy, and most especially within the context of the NAM, one must analyze it on two levels of perception. At the first, one has its primordial objective, which, as with most states and individuals, is survival. It was to assure that survival that Castro initially turned to the Soviet Union and over the years took on Marxist-Leninist coloration. The hostile external environment that prompted his metamorphosis—and that of the Cuban Revolution—has not changed. On the contrary, under the Reagan Administration, U.S. hostility is almost pathological. Nor has Cuba been able to make itself economically independent. Hence, assuring its lifeline to the Soviet Union remains as much an imperative now as in the past.

The relationship with Moscow, moreover, has advantages beyond survival. Soviet arms have enabled Cuba to build itself into a military power. With Soviet support, it, more than any other Third World country, has been able to project its influence abroad. Castro is not likely to give up the tie that makes all that possible. Maintaining a viable relationship with Moscow will remain the first objective of Cuban foreign policy.

There is, however, a second layer to that policy. The Cuban Revolution was not initially Marxist-Leninist. It was a product of Third World nationalism. Castro has understood from the beginning, moreover, that the Third World, with its politics concentrated in the NAM (and the U.N.), is his natural milieu. It is there that he can best bring to bear his own special talents. Winning unquestioned and unchallenged leadership of the Third World has probably been his key foreign policy objective since he first came to power—an objective only overridden by the very needs of survival. In other words, pursuit of his objectives in the Third World must be conditioned by the needs of Castro's relationship with Moscow, on which that survival depends. On the other hand (and this is a delicious irony), had it not been for his international ambitions, his quest for Third World leadership, Castro would not have had to turn to the Soviet Union in the first place. Remember that it was precisely so that he could continue to pursue those objectives that he needed a shield against U.S. power, a shield provided (more or less) by the Soviet Union.

Castro's relationship with the Soviet Union has at times helped him achieve specific goals in the Third World; for example, Soviet support made it possible for him to play the role of savior to the MPLA in Angola. But in a far more basic way, the inherent contradiction between nonalignment and partnership with the Soviet Union remains as serious a complication as ever to his objectives on this second level of perception. During the 1960s he tried to handle the obvious contradiction simply by ignoring it. He became a Marxist-Leninist and accepted Soviet assistance, but he refused to recognize the restrictions that flowed from that; he tried to go his own independent way. In time, the Soviets made it clear that he could not, that there were parameters and that he would have to respect them.

Forced into line by Moscow, Castro tried to make the best of it by assuming the role of loyal partner and by pretending (to himself perhaps as much as to anyone else) that this was in the natural order of things. Did not the promotion of Soviet interests serve as well those of the nonaligned states, and vice versa, given that they had a common foe, U.S. imperialism? And as Moscow was the natural champion, defender, and ally of the impoverished nonaligned world, could one not be the enthusiastic partner of both?

By 1979, Castro could see that the answer to this question was no. Subsequent events (Afghanistan, Cancún, etc.) confirmed this beyond the shadow of a doubt. In the NAM, Cuba therefore began to eschew identification with the Soviet Union and to stress instead its Third World credentials and objectives. For the foreseeable future, it can be expected to continue to maximize its margin for maneuver and to take an increasingly independent line in the NAM.

It is interesting to note that Cuba's more independent line of the 1980s is almost the reverse of that of the 1960s. Then, Cuba's approach was an inflammatory one calling for all-out struggle against the imperialist foe. There was no place in Castro's vocabulary for the word *détente*. Now, it is the key word. After 25 years in power, Castro has few illusions left. He knows full well that when a revolution achieves power, it has only begun to face the staggering problems of development, that there is no certainty whatsoever it will succeed in solving them, and that it is likely to need capitalist technology, investments, and trade advantages if it is to do so. In the real world, revolutionary credentials alone do not create jobs or put bread on the table. Hence, rather than global confrontation, Castro is now urging détente between East and West so that the governments of the world can devote their attention and resources to development and conservation, the problems that haunt the world's future. . . .

NOTES

1. David D. Burks, *Cuba Under Castro,* Headline Series (New York: Foreign Policy Association, 1964), pp. 27–40.

2. Jules Dubois, *Fidel Castro* (New York: Bobbs-Merrill Co., 1959), pp. 372–74.

3. *Revolución* (April 20, 1959).

4. Herbert Matthews, *The Cuban Story* (New York: George Braziller, 1961), p. 191.

5. José M. (Pepín) Bosch in personal communication with the author, 1962.

6. Robert Mortimer, *The Third World Coalition in International Politics* (New York: Praeger, 1980).

7. Fidel Castro, Remarks on Afro-Asian–Latin American solidarity (conversation with a group of diplomats, including Wayne Smith, during a reception at the time of the Sixth NAM Summit in Havana).

8. *Revolución* (September 25, 1959).

9. Maurice Halperin, *Rise and Decline of Fidel Castro* (Berkeley & Los Angeles: Univ. of California Press, 1972), p. 25.

10. Philip Bonsal, *Cuba, Castro and the United States* (Pittsburgh: Univ. of Pittsburgh Press, 1972), pp. 92–133; also, see Hugh Thomas, *Cuba: Pursuit of Freedom* (New York: Harper & Row, 1971), p. 1254.

11. *Bohemia* (January 31, 1960).

12. Jacques Levesque, *The USSR and the Cuban Revolution* (New York: Praeger, 1978), p. 10.

13. *Revolución* (April 17, 1961).

14. *Revolución* (December 2, 1961).

15. For an excellent discussion of Castro's calculations, see J. Levesque, *The USSR and the Cuban Revolution,* pp. 20–38.

16. *Cuba Socialista* (March 1962), pp. 1–27.

17. *Cuba Socialista* (November 1964), pp. 8–20.

18. Ibid.

19. Quoted in Maurice Halperin, *The Taming of Fidel Castro* (Berkeley & Los Angeles: Univ. of California Press, 1981), p. 272; also see pp. 269–320.

20. *Granma* (August 25, 1968).

21. *Granma* (July 20, 1969).

22. See an interview with Fidel Castro in *Puro Chile* (August 4, 1970).

23. *Granma,* International Edition (September 27, 1970).

24. *Bulletin of the Cuban U.N. Association* (1978), p. 18.

25. Quoted in William M. LeoGrande, "Evolution of the Nonaligned Movement," *Problems of Communism* (January/February 1980), pp. 35–52.

26. For a full discussion of Cuban involvement in Ethiopia, see Nelson Valdés, "Cuba's Involvement in the Horn of Africa: The Ethiopian-Somali War and the Eritrean Conflict," in Carmelo Mesa-Lago and June S. Belkin, eds., *Cuba in Africa,* (Pittsburgh: Univ. of Pittsburgh Press, 1982), pp. 63–94.

27. *Granma* (October 13, 1979).

28. Fidel Castro, Speech in New Delhi (March 1983). Official text distributed by the Cuban Interests Section, Washington, D.C.

29. Ibid.

42. Cuba's Policy in Africa*

By William M. LeoGrande

. . . From the beginning, Cuba was drawn not only to the socialist camp, but also to progressive governments in the Third World—governments whose revolutionary experience paralleled Cuba's. In Africa, Cuba quickly developed

*From William M. LeoGrande, *Cuba's Policy in Africa, 1959–1980* (Berkeley: Institute of International Studies, University of California, 1980, passim. Edited for this volume.

very close relations with two such governments: Kwame Nkrumah's Ghana and Ben Bella's Algeria. The first Cuban military mission in Africa was established in Ghana in 1961; it was maintained until Nkrumah's ouster in 1966.[1] As early as 1960, Cuba provided military and medical supplies to the Algerian National Liberation Front (FLN), and after Algeria gained its independence in 1962, a Cuban military mission was established there which remained until the overthrow of Ben Bella in 1965. When the Algerian-Moroccan border war erupted in 1963, Cuba came to Algeria's aid with both arms and a battalion of combat troops—the first deployment of regular Cuban troops abroad.

The principal point of reference in the history of Cuba's involvement in Africa is Ernesto "Che" Guevara's extended tour of the continent in 1964–1965. Guevara visited virtually every "progressive" country . . . i.e., all those which had comprised the Casablanca Group prior to the inauguration of the Organization of African Unity: Algeria, Ghana, Guinea, Mali, and the United Arab Republic. He stopped in Algiers three times—once to deliver a stinging attack on Soviet trade policy to the Afro-Asian Peoples' Solidarity Organization.[2] His overall objective on this trip was to counter the USSR's withdrawal from involvement in sub-Saharan Africa by enlisting Ben Bella's support for the formation of a union of Third World nations.[3] . . .

In Congo-Brazzaville in 1964, Guevara met with leaders of the major nationalist movements in the Portuguese colonies. Within a year Cuba began providing arms and instructions for the Movimiento Popular de Libertação de Angola (MPLA), the Partido Africano da Independencia da Guiné e Cabo Verde (PAIGC), and the Frente de Libertação de Mozambique (FRELIMO).

In 1965 and 1966, Cuba's two closest friends in Africa—Ben Bella and Nkrumah—were both deposed by coups d'état. By demonstrating the vulnerability of progressive governments to military coup, these events prompted a new departure in Cuba's African policy. Cuba began providing fairly large military missions to friendly governments—missions intended not only to provide military training, but also to act as palace guards protecting those governments from their own military institutions.[4] . . .

Though Cuba's presence in Africa during the 1960s was modest, the basic direction of Cuban policy emerged quite clearly. Its overall objectives were to promote national liberation movements (by providing them with Cuban arms and advisors) and to help defend existing progressive movements (by furnishing Cuban military missions). When no backers were found for Guevara's proposal for a Third World anti-imperialist front, Cuba pursued its policy objectives unilaterally.

Cuban policy toward Africa was internationalist in that its motivation was essentially ideological. Cuba had little to gain economically or strategically by promoting revolution in Africa. Ideologically, however, Cuba has always taken the principle of international solidarity very seriously—no doubt because the survival of the Cuban revolution itself has been so dependent upon international assistance. Thus Cuban activism in Africa was motivated not by hopes of direct tangible benefits for Cuba, but rather by hopes of advancing the cause of socialism and establishing the principle of proletarian internationalism as a key ingredient of the foreign policies of *all* socialist countries. During the 1960s Cuba provided assistance to guerrillas in Senegal, Malawi, Mali, and Eritrea as well as to the nationalist movements in the Portuguese colonies.[5]

Ironically, Soviet policy toward Africa in the late 1960s was undergoing a transformation in precisely the opposite direction. In the late 1950s and early 1960s, Soviet African policy had also had a strong ideological component. Military and economic assistance was channeled to "revolutionary democrats" who showed evidence of pursuing progressive domestic and foreign policies (e.g., Guinea, Ghana, Mali, Morocco, UAR, Algeria), but the fall of Ben Bella and Nkrumah, coming in the wake of the defeat of the Soviet-supported rebellion in the Congo in 1964, shattered this policy. After 1966 the Soviets saw little prospect of any true revolutionary transformations in Africa, and Soviet policy was reformulated around geopolitical rather than ideological considerations. . . . As Cuban involvement was growing, based on a faith in the revolutionary potential of the continent, the Soviets' interest was waning precisely because they had lost that faith.

CUBAN INVOLVEMENT IN ANGOLA, 1965–1979

Cuba's first contact with the MPLA came in the early 1960s, and its military assistance program to the MPLA dates from 1965. Che Guevara conferred with MPLA President Agostinho Neto in Congo-Brazzaville during Guevara's 1965 diplomatic tour; later that year, when Guevara's guerrilla force withdrew from its abortive effort to overthrow Tshombe's government in Congo-Leopoldville (Zaire), part of it remained in Congo-Brazzaville to establish training camps for the MPLA.[6]

From this point onward, Cuban support for the MPLA was uninterrupted. The MPLA participated as the Angolan delegation to the Tri-Continental Conference held in Havana in 1966, and President Neto along with MPLA Military Commander Endo visited Cuba that same year. Shortly thereafter, MPLA students and guerrilla recruits began arriving in Cuba for education and military training.[7]

Cuba's early preference for the MPLA over its rivals—Holden Roberto's Frente Nacional de Libertação de Angola (FNLA) and later Jonas Savimbi's União Nacional para a Independência Total de Angola (UNITA)—was primarily ideological. Not only was the MPLA the oldest liberation movement in Angola, but it was also by far the most ideologically sophisticated; founded in 1956, it appears to have been directly descended from the merger of the Angolan Communist party with several radical nationalist groups. From the outset the MPLA has adhered to a staunchly anti-imperialist, multiracialist, and pro-socialist ideological position, and it has pursued a strategy of political organization primarily among the *mestiço* and black urban working class of Luanda.[8]

In contrast the FNLA, which was descended from the União das Populações de Angola (UPA), began as a rural, tribally based separatist movement of the Bakongo people in northern Angola. Though it abandoned its separatist aspirations in 1958, the FNLA never escaped an essentially tribalist orientation. To the extent that the FNLA exhibited an ideology, it was a rudimentary appeal to racialism (anti-white, anti-*mestiço*, tribalist, and anti-Communist). Not surprisingly, the FNLA's strategy for ending Portuguese rule varied sharply from the MPLA's. While the MPLA emphasized political education and mobilization, the FNLA's approach was essentially military.[9] Moreover, Roberto refused to cooperate with the MPLA in any sort of unified front, going so far as to execute MPLA guerrillas who attempted to set up operations in northern Angola. From the late 1960s on, fighting between the two groups was endemic.[10]

Founded in 1966 by Savimbi, a former FNLA member, UNITA was also based predominantly upon a tribal group—the Ovimbundu peoples in the rural south. Though Savimbi initially propounded a Maoist theory of self-reliance, he has proven adept at shifting ideological ground in pursuit of outside aid. . . . Like the FNLA, UNITA relied mainly upon a primitive ideological mixture of racialism and tribal populism.[11]

The Cubans had more than ideological reasons for believing that an MPLA government would be a good deal more progressive than one dominated by either of its rivals. The MPLA drew almost all of its foreign support from the socialist bloc and from the former members of the progressive Casablanca Group within the OAU—the countries with which Cuba felt the closest kinship. . . . The FNLA, on the other hand, received almost all of its aid from pro-Western Zaire. After the assassination of Patrice Lumumba in 1961, Cuba regarded the succession of Zairean governments as all more or less reactionary puppets of imperialism. The Cubans accused both Roberto and his patron Mobutu of having CIA connections long before it became publicly known that Roberto had been put on a CIA retainer in 1962.[12] Cuba also accused Mobutu of hiring Cuban exiles to train FNLA recruits in Zaire.[13]

While Cuban aid to the MPLA was consistent and uninterrupted, Soviet aid was halted twice—once in 1963–64 (before Cuban aid began) and again in 1972. The first interruption in Soviet support followed a diplomatic debacle suffered by the MPLA in the OAU in October 1963: the OAU's African Liberation Committee granted recognition to the FNLA's Revolutionary Government of Angola in Exile, largely because of the MPLA's military weakness. A year later the OAU adopted a new position favoring unity between the FNLA and MPLA (thus granting the MPLA tacit if not official recognition), and Soviet aid resumed.[14]

In 1972–73 the Portuguese army launched a series of major offensives in Angola which resulted in severe military setbacks for the MPLA. These defeats exacerbated political divisions within the movement, leading to a number of defections. . . . With the MPLA in military retreat and political disarray, Soviet aid began to decline in 1972 and by early 1974 had been halted altogether.

When the Armed Forces Movement overthrew the Caetano regime in Portugal, in April 1974, Soviet and Cuban policies in Africa were not only operating under different assumptions, but in the case of Angola were at odds. Two developments during the summer of 1974 brought Cuban and Soviet policies toward Angola into harmony. The first was the arrival in June of Chinese arms and military instructors for the FNLA; the second was a decision by the United States in July to begin shipping arms to the FNLA through Zaire.[15] In November, just six months after it had been cut off, Soviet aid to the MPLA resumed. . . .

Under OAU pressure, Neto, Roberto, and Savimbi met in Portugal in January 1975 to negotiate a peaceful transition to independence. The resulting Alvor Agreements established a tripartite transitional government, called for a single national army, and set November 11, 1975, as the date for Angolan independence. The uneasy peace established at Alvor was short-lived, as the conflict between the three liberation movements rapidly became internationalized.

Immediately after Alvor, the U.S. "40 Committee"* authorized (at the urging of the CIA) an increase in covert aid to the FNLA. Given the FNLA's long commitment to a military solution in Angola, its military superiority, and its history of opposition to cooperation with the MPLA, such an increase in U.S. aid could only have had the effect of undermining the FNLA's adherence to the Alvor Agreements. Indeed, in March 1975, bolstered by new shipments of U.S. arms, the FNLA launched an attack on MPLA offices in Luanda and expelled the MPLA from the northern territories under FNLA control. Later that month, the conflict was further internationalized when 1,200 regular troops from Zaire entered Angola to fight alongside the FNLA. These reinforcements gave the combined forces of the FNLA/Zaire and UNITA a four-to-one advantage over the MPLA.[16]

The MPLA responded to this escalation of fighting by seeking additional aid from both the USSR and Cuba. The Soviets quickly stepped up their flow of arms, and after a meeting between Neto and Cuban Comandante Flavio Bravo in May, Cuba agreed to provide several hundred instructors to open four military training camps for MPLA recruits. According to most accounts, 230 Cuban instructors arrived in Angola in June.[17]

. . . In early July, after expelling FNLA troops from Luanda, the MPLA launched a campaign to gain control of Angola's provincial capitals before

*A crisis-management committee of the senior policymakers charged with overseeing covert operations.

November 11. . . . It appeared that November 11 would bring an independent Angola with an MPLA government.

The precarious position of the pro-Western forces catalyzed a new escalation of international intervention. Both the FNLA and UNITA turned to South Africa for assistance, while their backers—Zaire and Zambia—appealed to the United States. Both the United States and South Africa responded positively in at least partial conjunction with one another.[18] On July 17 the U.S. "40 Committee" authorized a massive expansion of arms aid to both the FNLA and UNITA, as well as a program of covert action by the CIA. "Operation Feature," as the covert program was called, included the recruitment of mercenaries, the use of CIA personnel as military advisors in both Zaire and northern Angola, and $32 million in armaments (worth approximately $65 million after adjusting for the normal undervaluation of such stocks).[19] . . . As fighting in the north intensified, South African troops crossed the Namibian border on August 9 and took up positions a few miles inside Angola at the Cunene River hydroelectric project. Shortly thereafter, South Africa opened training bases for both the FNLA and UNITA in Namibia and southern Angola.[20]

These escalations once again led the MPLA to ask its allies for additional aid, including military advisors. An MPLA delegation to Moscow in August found the Soviets unwilling to provide more than arms, but the Cubans proved to be more responsive. A military delegation . . . visited Luanda in late August, and several hundred additional Cuban troops left for Angola shortly thereafter.[21]

At this point, Cuban-Soviet coordination in Angola was still relatively limited. Each country continued to follow its historic policy of aiding the MPLA, and the level of aid provided by each had been growing gradually since early 1975. The policies of both were essentially reactive: Each increase in aid came at the request of the MPLA in response to escalations by the MPLA's opponents—domestic and foreign. Through the summer of 1975, Cuba and the USSR appeared to be making independent decisions about their aid to the MPLA; as the compatibility of these decisions became clear, greater coordination was established. . . .

Probably as a consequence of its allies' inability to gain the upper hand on the battlefield, South Africa intervened directly in the Angolan civil war on October 23. Under the code name "Operation Zulu," some five thousand South African troops launched an armored assault from Namibia. It moved rapidly up the coast, covering five hundred kilometers in just over a week. Faced with a suddenly desperate military situation, the MPLA on November 4 asked for Cuban troops to help defend Luanda; on November 5, Cuba agreed. One battalion was airlifted immediately to Angola with the objective of holding Luanda until reinforcements could arrive. This first combat unit landed on November 8 as additional troops left Cuba by sea.[22]

Militarily, Cuba's troops made the difference. From November 1975 to

March 1976, between 18,000 and 36,000 Cubans arrived in Angola. By mid-December the South African advance in the south had been halted, and the MPLA-Cuban forces had gone over to the offensive against the FNLA-Zairean forces on the northern front. When the U.S. Congress prohibited further U.S. aid to the FNLA or UNITA, South Africa withdrew its troops to the border, charging that the United States had defaulted on its pledge to provide whatever military assistance was required to defeat the MPLA. Without the South Africans, UNITA quickly disintegrated as a fighting force. By early February, Cuba and the MPLA were able to concentrate their forces in the north, and within a few weeks the FNLA was in full retreat across the border, seeking refuge in Zaire. The collapse of UNITA and the FNLA was so rapid that by mid-March Castro and Neto were able to agree to a schedule for Cuban troop withdrawals.

Diplomatically, South Africa's troops made the difference. Any residual African support for the MPLA's opponents or for a negotiated settlement of the war was quickly erased by the South African intervention. On January 22 the OAU condemned South Africa while pointedly refusing to condemn Cuba or the USSR. On February 11 it admitted the People's Republic of Angola (PRA) to membership, thereby recognizing the legitimacy of the MPLA government. . . .

It is almost certain that Cuba's decision to commit large numbers of troops in regular combat units was an independent one—not one directed by the Soviet Union. Though it represented a qualitative escalation of Cuban military assistance, it was nevertheless in line with Cuba's decade-long policy toward Angola. Moreover, it was also wholly consistent with Cuba's well-established policy of giving military aid to progressive African liberation movements generally—a policy which arose in the mid-1960s not from Soviet urging but at a time when Cuba perceived a weakening of Soviet willingness to live up to the principles of proletarian internationalism. In addition, Cuba's intervention in Angola fit the basic criterion Cuban policymakers had apparently employed in making previous commitments of regular troops in Algeria (1963) and Syria (1973): the MPLA was a friendly progressive movement (in Cuba's view, the only legitimate claimant to govern Angola) beset by direct imperialist intervention which threatened its survival.

Cuba has denied from the outset that the decision to intervene in Angola was taken at Soviet behest.[23] . . . Gabriel García-Márquez, in his quasi-official account of Cuba's role in Angola, goes so far as to say that the Soviet Union was not even consulted until the decision to intervene had been made. Soviet sources have confirmed that the Cuban decision was an independent one, and in early 1976 even Secretary of State Henry Kissinger voiced his opinion to that effect.[24]

Indeed, the USSR was probably hesitant to make a major commitment in Angola for fear of provoking a confrontation with the West in an area of low strategic priority for the Soviets—a confrontation which might well have had reverberations in policy areas of much greater strategic importance (e.g., detente, strategic arms limitation, and Sino-Western relations). In any event, the Soviet involvement proceeded much more cautiously than the Cuban involvement. In August 1975 the USSR refused the MPLA's request for military advisors, and though several hundred were finally dispatched to Luanda in November, the Soviet role remained primarily that of arms supplier.[25] It was the Cubans who, along with MPLA commanders, planned the conduct of the war. Even Soviet logistical support for the Cuban intervention seems to have had its limits. Though the rapid deployment of Cuban troops in November was critical for the MPLA's survival, the Cubans came to Angola by means of converted freighters and obsolete commercial airplanes. The USSR's willingness to provide air transport for the Cubans was equivocal. The Soviets flew Cuban troops to the staging areas in Congo-Brazzaville during early December, but suspended the flights after a U.S. protest. The flights resumed after the U.S. Congress prohibited U.S. involvement in the war, but stopped again after a second U.S. protest. They resumed once more in January 1976, and continued for several weeks after U.S. diplomatic pressure had successfully denied the Cuban planes landing rights in several countries, making the continued use of Cuban commercial air transport impossible.[26]

The evidence indicates that, through the summer of 1975, Cuba and the USSR decided independently to expand their assistance programs to the MPLA as the civil war became increasingly internationalized. As the compatibility of their policies became clear, the Cubans and Soviets began coordinating their actions. They did *not* hatch a plot to intervene in Angola as an opening move in a joint offensive against Western influence in Africa. On the contrary, increases in Cuban and Soviet aid were essentially reactive. The West, especially the United States, initiated the internationalization of the Angolan conflict by escalating its aid to the FNLA in hopes of promoting a military solution that would deprive the MPLA of any effective role in the coalition government outlined at Alvor. In view of both Cuba's and the USSR's history of support for the MPLA, U.S. actions virtually guaranteed a concomitant increase in Cuban and Soviet involvement, thus transforming the local conflict into an East-West confrontation. Indeed U.S. intelligence analysts predicted as much.[27] The most grievous failing of U.S. policy was that the United States provoked such a confrontation in a situation where, due to the weakness of its local allies and its inevitable association with South Africa, it could not possibly win.

Next to the MPLA's victory, Cuba's greatest benefit from Angola was in its relations with the Soviet Union. The compatibility of Cuban and Soviet policy in Angola, and the fact that Cuban involvement was the key to that policy's success, served to further cement the good relations Cuba has enjoyed with the USSR since the early 1970s. Since 1975 Soviet economic and military assistance to Cuba has expanded, and the military stocks supplied to Cuba have been of increasing sophistication—the delivery of MiG-23s being the most publicized example.[28]

While Cuba's actions in Angola strengthened its relationship with the USSR, they also served to expand the parameters of Cuban independence vis-à-vis its principal ally. By greatly extending Cuban influence and prestige in Africa, Angola made Cuba a more valuable spokesman for socialism among the nonaligned nations. Cuba's advocacy of socialism as the only possible solution to underdevelopment is in itself politically and ideologically valuable to the USSR. Cuba has argued that nonalignment does not mean neutrality toward imperialism or neo-imperialism, and has maintained that the socialist camp led by the USSR is the Third World's natural ally.[29] In addition, Cuba has aggressively attacked Chinese influence in the nonaligned movement by denouncing China's "three worlds" theory and its condemnation of Soviet "social imperialism" and "hegemonism." Reducing Western and Chinese influence are two of the USSR's principal objectives in its policy toward the Third World, and Cuba is proving to be an indispensable ally for achieving both these goals. This gives the Soviet Union the first truly positive benefit it has derived from its relationship with Cuba, and makes any deterioration of that relationship more costly to the Soviets. This, in turn, increases Cuba's latitude for independent action and strengthens its bilateral bargaining position with the USSR.

Through cooperation, Cuba and the USSR were both able to achieve policy objectives which neither could have achieved alone. Cuba could not have quickly deployed a heavily equipped force to Angola without Soviet arms shipments—and eventually, Soviet transport—while the USSR could not have undertaken a direct combat role without risking confrontation with the United States, a deterioration of détente, and charges of Soviet imperialism. The Cuban-Soviet partnership in Angola was a perfect example of a positive-sum game. Their policy objectives, though not identical, were not in conflict, and were attainable only through cooperative action. Thus their operational policies, which evolved independently, became increasingly coordinated as the Angolan civil war intensified.

Not surprisingly, Cuba paid the greatest price for the Angolan intervention in its relations with the United States. One of the principal goals of Cuban foreign policy since 1972 has been to normalize relations with the United States in order to diminish the U.S. military threat to Cuba (thus reducing its dependence on the Soviet "nuclear umbrella") and to further diversify Cuban foreign trade (thus reducing Cuba's economic dependence on the USSR). In the years immediately prior to the Angolan civil war, substantial progress had been made toward normalization, but the Cuban intervention in Angola abruptly halted that process. . . .

On the whole, from the Cuban perspective, the intervention in Angola was a great success. The costs were minimal and the benefits were substantial. This alone is perhaps enough to explain why the Cubans decided to repeat that intervention in Ethiopia.

CUBAN INVOLVEMENT IN ETHIOPIA, 1977–1979

The context of Cuba's decision to undertake a second major troop commitment in Ethiopia differed significantly from the Angolan context. In Angola, Cuba came to the aid of a movement it had been supporting for a decade, a movement beset by external enemies of a clearly "imperialist" character—Zaire, South Africa, and the United States. In Ethiopia, Cuba came to the aid of a relatively new government with which Cuba had no historical relationship. Moreover, Cuban troops were entering into combat against troops of a nominally Marxist-Leninist Somalia which had *itself* been a recipient of Cuban military aid less than two months prior to Cuba's intervention in support of Ethiopia.

The character of Cuban-Soviet cooperation in Ethiopia was also significantly different from what it had been in Angola. Rather than evolving independent policies and eventually developing a measure of cooperation as they had in Angola, Cuba and the Soviet Union closely coordinated their military aid to Ethiopia from the outset, with the USSR playing a much more prominent role than it had in Angola. In Ethiopia the ideological lines of the conflict were much less clearly drawn and the geopolitical dimension of the conflict loomed much larger. Cuba was thus much more vulnerable to the charge of acting as a Soviet proxy. . . .

The Ethiopian revolution began in February 1974 when Emperor Haile Selassie's troops refused to move against urban strikers and demonstrators. By April the military had created an alternative center of governmental power— the Coordinating Committee for the Peaceful Solution of Present Problems (later the Coordinating Committee of the Armed Forces, Police, and Ground Forces)—and in September the emperor was deposed. The armed forces then formed a Provisional Military Administrative Government (the Dergue) headed by a Provisional Military Administrative Council (PMAC).

Having disposed of Haile Selassie, the Dergue's military commanders quickly discovered that they were by no means in agreement as to how the revolution should proceed. In November, the PMAC's moderate chairman, Aman Mikael Andom, and 59 other officers were arrested and executed, purportedly for plotting a counterrevolutionary coup with U.S. assistance. The purge of Andom's group was a victory for the Dergue's left; within a month, the PMAC, now headed by Terefe Bante, announced its intention to build a socialist Ethiopia. Over the next year the Dergue nationalized most of the Ethiopian economy. The Dergue produced its first formal program in April 1976. Entitled the "Program of the National Democratic Revolution," it called for Ethiopia to "lay a strong foundation for the transition to socialism." It also included a policy position on self-determination and regional autonomy, followed in May by a nine-point policy statement aimed at a peaceful solution of the war with Eritrea.[30] The Eritrean policy proposal led to another high-level purge: In July, Major Sissy Habte, chairman of the PMAC's Foreign Affairs Committee, was executed along with a number of others for opposing the policy.

A critical turning point in the Ethiopian revolution was reached on February 3, 1977, when a PMAC meeting deteriorated into a shootout between Terefe Bante's supporters and a more radical faction led by Mengistu Haile-Mariam. Terefe was killed, his supporters were executed, and Mengistu became the PMAC's chairman.[31] The radicals' victory resulted in a sharp reorientation of Ethiopia's international position.

In addition to its own internal divisions, the Dergue faced seemingly insurmountable security problems in 1977. In the urban areas, especially Addis Ababa and Asmara, the ultra-left student-based Ethiopian People's Revolutionary Party (EPRP) was carrying out a full-scale campaign of assassination aimed at Dergue officials. In the Ogaden region the Western Somali Liberation Front (WSLF), with aid from Somalia, had taken advantage of the government's precarious position to escalate its war of secession. In Eritrea the Dergue faced armed opposition from the conservative Ethiopian Democratic Party (EDP) aided by Sudan, the Islamic Eritrean Liberation Front (ELF) aided by Sudan, Egypt, and Saudi Arabia, and the Marxist Eritrean People's Liberation Front (EPLF).

As the Ethiopian revolution moved to the left in 1976 and 1977, geopolitical alignments in the Horn of Africa were reshuffled with startling speed. Ethiopia, which had been one of the West's staunchest allies under Haile Selassie, began to move toward the USSR. The Soviet Union, which had tried with varying degrees of success to cultivate influence in Somalia and Sudan as a counterweight to U.S. influence in Selassie's Ethiopia, now sought to establish closer ties with the Dergue. Ethiopia was receptive to these overtures, both for ideological reasons and because the United States had begun slowing its arms deliveries to Ethiopia—ostensibly on human rights grounds, but more likely because of the radicalization of the revolution. Beset on all sides by enemies, the Dergue turned to the USSR for military aid in December 1976, and four months later Ethiopia severed its military relations with the United States by expelling the U.S. military mission.[32]

Somalia was particularly upset by these developments. Somalia was, after all, a self-proclaimed Marxist-Leninist state whose army was trained and equipped by the USSR. To see the Soviets suddenly begin sending military aid to a traditional Somali enemy was very disturbing, especially since Soviet arms deliveries to Somalia began to slow down—no doubt because Somalia's President Maxamed Siad Barre continued to aid the WSLF in its attempt to dismember Ethiopia at the same time the USSR was trying to improve relations with the Dergue.[33]

Somalia's disaffection with the USSR prompted renewed efforts by Sudan, Egypt (both former recipients of Soviet aid), and Saudi Arabia to wean Somalia away from the Soviet camp. They warned the Somalis of Soviet infidelity, appealed to their Islamic heritage, and enticed them with Saudi petrodollars.[34] Having been ousted from Ethiopia in April 1977, the United States joined this campaign in July by offering to supply Somalia with "defensive weapons"—an offer that was later quietly withdrawn after regular Somali troops entered the Ogaden. The geopolitical realignment in the Horn of Africa was completed in November 1977, however, when the Somalis expelled their Soviet military advisors and severed diplomatic relations with Cuba.[35] . . .

Cuban involvement in the Horn of Africa was minimal before 1976. In 1974 it had sent several dozen military technicians to Somalia, and in 1976 this contingent was reinforced by several hundred men as part of Cuba's expanded presence in Africa following the Angolan civil war.[36] As the Dergue moved to the left in 1976–77, Cuba came to regard the Ethiopian revolution as genuine—largely because a number of the Dergue's policies bore a striking resemblance to policies of the Cuban revolution's early years (e.g., agrarian and urban reforms, nationalizations, creation of a popular militia, and creation of the Kebele—an urban block organization reminiscent of Cuba's Committees for the Defense of the Revolution).[37]

Cuba became directly involved in the conflict between Ethiopia and Somalia in March 1977 when, during his trip to Africa, Castro acted as mediator at a summit meeting between Mengistu and Siad Barre in South Yemen. Castro proposed the creation of an anti-imperialist federation composed of South Yemen, Ethiopia, Somalia, an autonomous Ogaden, and an autonomous Eritrea. Siad Barre maintained that such a federation could be discussed only after the Ogaden was granted independence; Mengistu rejected this condition. The summit ended inconclusively, but (according to Cuban accounts) with a Somali pledge to refrain from military intervention in the Ogaden pending further negotiations.[38] Shortly thereafter Soviet President Nikolai Podgorny, also on a diplomatic tour of Africa, engaged in shuttle diplomacy between Addis Ababa and Mogadishu in an attempt to promote essentially the same solution, but also without success.

At the end of his African tour, Castro made an unscheduled visit to Moscow just after Podgorny's return. While the joint Cuban-Soviet communique following Castro's visit pledged continued Cuban and Soviet aid to southern African guerrillas,[39] the situation in the Horn was almost certainly the principal topic of the consultations. . . . From March 1977 onward, Cuban and Soviet policies were closely coordinated.

The Cuban military buildup in Ethiopia proceeded in two stages: (1) the dispatch of military advisors beginning in May 1977 after several thousand heavily armed WSLF guerrillas entered the Ogaden from Somalia, and (2) the deployment of regular combat troops in January 1978 after Somalia broke off diplomatic relations with Cuba in November 1977.

The first major escalation of the Ogaden conflict came on May 25, when three- to six thousand WSLF guerrillas entered the Ogaden from Somalia. Somalia's decision to intensify the war was probably a response to the increased Soviet arms shipments to Ethiopia following the Dergue's ouster of the U.S. military mission in February. The Ethiopian army would require some time to switch its arms inventories from U.S. to Soviet hardware. If the Ogaden issue was to be settled militarily, the optimum time for a war (from Somalia's perspective) was during this interim—i.e., before the Ethiopians stockpiled Soviet arms and learned how to use them.

The Soviets responded to the guerrilla invasion by renewing their diplomatic drive for the federation solution and by offering Somalia increased aid if it would cease hostilities. The Saudis countered with an offer to expand their aid to Somalia twelvefold to $350 million if Siad Barre would break with Moscow. In June, as fighting in the Ogaden raged, an army of the conservative EDP entered Eritrea from Sudan under cover of artillery support from Sudanese troops massed on the border. At this point the number of Cuban military advisors in Ethiopia was only fifty.[40]

The Dergue's military position deteriorated rapidly in July. In an effort to bolster the Saudis' attempts to entice Siad Barre away from Moscow, Secretary of State [Cyrus] Vance suggested on July 1 that the United States might be willing to provide arms to Somalia. Two weeks later, 40 thousand regular Somali troops invaded the Ogaden, and in less than two weeks they had captured 112 towns and 85 percent of the region. The Soviet Union and Cuba responded by increasing their aid to Ethiopia; the Western nations, on the other hand, turned a blind eye to the invasion. Then, on July 26, the United States reiterated its interest in providing Somalia with "defensive arms" so long as they were not used in the Ogaden, and the next day Britain followed with an arms offer of its own—without the caveat about using them for defense only. The Somalis interpreted these offers as sub rosa support for their invasion, but when Somalia's intervention became too obvious to ignore, the United States withdrew its offer of arms and pressed its allies to do the same. Somalia apparently felt that U.S. hesitancy could be overcome if Somalia broke decisively with the Soviets and Cubans. On November 13 Somalia severed diplomatic relations with Cuba and expelled the Soviet military mission, which proved to be a grave miscalculation by Siad Barre. The Western nations still refused to come to his aid, and the expulsions served only to clear the way for a full Soviet-Cuban commitment to Ethiopia, which followed directly.

In January 1978 Raúl Castro traveled secretly to Addis Ababa and then to Moscow to coordinate the planned escalation of aid.[41] Over the next three months, the Cuban presence expanded from four hundred advisors to 17 thousand regular troops. . . . As noted earlier, not only were the increases in Cuban and Soviet aid to Ethiopia closely coordinated from the outset, but there was a much greater degree of cooperation than there had been in Angola. In Ethiopia, Cuban troops arrived not in converted freighters but in Soviet troop transports. Soviet military advisors numbered over a thousand, and they played a central role in planning and commanding the Ogaden campaign.[42] In Angola the role of Soviet personnel had been only marginal. Soviet-Cuban cooperation in Ethiopia was so close, in fact, that Soviet pilots were apparently assigned air defense duty in Cuba to ease the shortage of Cuban pilots, many of whom were flying combat missions in the Ogaden.[43] The Somalis, short on supplies, proved to be no match for the Cubans. Using standard Soviet assault tactics, a Cuban-Ethiopian force captured the key city of Jijiga in early March, and the Somalis fell back across the border.[44]

The West never came to Somalia's aid, and the United States even went so far as to block the transfer of U.S. arms to Somalia from Egypt and Saudi Arabia. Western neutrality was based upon the fact that Somalia was the clear aggressor in its attempt to incorporate the Ogaden into a "Greater Somalia," and thus was violating a cardinal principle of African politics: the permanence of existing borders. Most of Africa, including the key states of Nigeria and Kenya (against whom the Somalis also had territorial claims) supported Ethiopia, despite their distaste for the Dergue. The United States repeatedly warned, however, that it would reassess its policy of neutrality if Ethiopia carried the war into Somalia. Cuba, Ethiopia, and the USSR all gave assurances that this would not happen, and it did not.[45]

The extensive nature of Cuban-Soviet coordination in the Ogaden campaign was due primarily to the strength of the Soviet commitment in Ethiopia. Unlike in Angola, the USSR transported Cuban troops, put hundreds of advisors on the ground, and joined in tactical and strategic military planning. While some might attribute this difference in Soviet behavior to the weakness of the U.S. response in Angola, it is more likely that it stemmed directly from the priorities of Soviet foreign policy. The Horn of Africa's strategic location is such that it is of "inherent importance" to the USSR. While Soviet interest in sub-Saharan Africa declined in the late 1960s, interest in the Horn remained high. Thus, while Angola was in a low priority area as far as the USSR was concerned, Ethiopia was in a high priority area. . . .

Cuban motivations are less easily deciphered, but several factors probably contributed to Cuba's decision to become involved. Castro believed the Ethiopian revolution was moving in a genuinely socialist direction, and was thus attracted to the Mengistu government long before Cuba became militarily involved in the Ogaden conflict. He probably felt that, with the Dergue moving to the left, Ethiopia's and Somalia's common ideology would enable them to overcome old conflicts and enmities. His March 1977 summit meeting with Mengistu and Siad Barre was obviously intended to facilitate such a rapprochement. When Somalia resorted to force and then broke relations with Cuba, the Cuban leadership naturally held the Somalis responsible for the "fratricidal conflict" that ensued. The Cubans may also have seen Siad Barre's acceptance of Saudi petrodollars as evidence that Somalia was going the way of Egypt and China—i.e., sacrificing ideological principle for a pot of Western gold. Finally, their success in Angola may well have encouraged both Cuba and the USSR to attempt to duplicate it in Ethiopia. Given the geopolitical importance of the Horn for the USSR, the Soviets probably encouraged the Cuban involvement there, just as Cuba apparently encouraged the Soviet involvement in Angola. The Soviets could not, however, have forced a major Cuban troop commitment if the Cuban leadership had been opposed to it.

In any event, it should be noted that both Cuba and the USSR tried mightily to prevent the Ogaden war. Their military involvement was the result of their diplomatic failure. . . .

Once the Somalis had been expelled from the Ogaden, the Mengistu government turned its attention to the Eritrean insurgency. Mengistu's preferred strategy was to complete the consolidation of his regime by eliminating the Eritrean guerrillas militarily; to accomplish this he required the support of the Cubans and Soviets. This posed political problems for Cuba and the Soviet Union, both of whom had supported and provided material aid to the Eritreans in the late 1960s and early 1970s when they were fighting Haile Selassie. The Eritreans also had the backing of several radical Arab states with whom Cuba and the USSR sought to maintain cordial relations. Moreover, with some 16 years of guerrilla experience and wide popular support, the Eritrean insurgents promised to be a formidable military foe.

Historically, the Eritreans' greatest weakness has been internal conflicts. In 1970 the Marxist Eritrean People's Liberation Front (EPLF) split from the pro-Islamic Eritrean Liberation Front (ELF), and the rival movements spent much of the subsequent decade fighting one another. In July 1977, however, when Somalia invaded the Ogaden, the ELF and EPLF signed an agreement, at Sudanese urging, to coordinate their operations. By January 1978 the two movements controlled 90 percent of Eritrea's territory and population and held the provincial capital of Asmara under siege.

In March 1978, when the Ogaden war had just concluded, the Soviet Union appeared willing to risk the political opprobrium that would accompany its support of an Ethiopian offensive in Eritrea. The Soviets described the Eritrean insurgency in the same sort of language being used by Mengistu—e.g., the Eritreans were in league with "imperialist designs" against the Ethiopian revolution, and the insurgency was "a plot serving foreign interests."[46] The Cubans, however, were already on record as opposing a military solution to the conflict. In February, Cuban Vice-President Carlos Rafael Rodríguez called for a "political solution," arguing that Eritrea was an "internal problem" of Ethiopia.[47] Given Cuba's policy of sending combat troops abroad only to protect a friendly government from external threat, the definition of Eritrea as an internal problem was tantamount to a Cuban refusal to assist Mengistu in his plans to crush the rebellion militarily. . . .

The Mengistu government, however, was intractable. Mengistu traveled to Havana in April 1978, where he denounced the Eritreans as "secessionists," "reactionaries," and "agents of imperialism." He promised to "eliminate" them, and called upon the Cubans to help him in that endeavor. Castro reiterated the Cuban position that Eritrea was an internal matter of Ethiopia that ought to be settled peacefully,[48] but Mengistu was not persuaded. When Dergue Vice-Chairman Col. Atnafu Abate returned from a tour of Eritrea in late 1977, recommending a political settlement, he was executed as a CIA agent. Finally, in July 1978, while Cuba and the USSR were still trying to promote negotiations, the Ethiopian army launched a major offensive in Eritrea.

In December the six-month-old Ethiopian offensive gained a major victory with the recapture of Keren—the Eritrean city which had been the headquarters of the liberation forces. This by no means ended the war, however, as both the ELF and ELPF announced a return to their earlier strategy of "protracted people's war."[49]

Cuban and Soviet military personnel continue to refrain from any direct involvement in the Eritrean fighting, though obviously their training and arming of Ethiopian forces, as well as the Cuban security role in the Ogaden, is essential for enabling the Ethiopians to conduct the Eritrean war. The likelihood of any more extensive Cuban or Soviet role in Eritrea is remote, unless there is some direct foreign intervenion on the Eritreans' behalf—from Sudan, for example.

Eritrea provides an interesting context for examining not only Soviet-Cuban cooperation but also Cuba's relations with a host country. Though both Cuba and the Soviet Union obviously remain committed to the security of the Ethiopian revolutionary government, all three parties appear to have their own policy preferences with regard to Eritrea. Whatever the mutual dependencies of the three, none has surrendered its autonomy; yet precisely because of their dependencies, each is constrained to follow a policy which is less than optimal for it. The Dergue would clearly prefer to defeat the Eritreans militarily, making no political concessions whatever; but for lack of Cuban and Soviet support, it cannot. Initially at least, the Soviets seemed to prefer a military solution as well, but Cuban resistance prevented them from acting on their preference. The Cubans have consistently made clear their desire to see a negotiated settlement; while they seem to have enlisted Soviet support for this solution, the Dergue has been unyielding. Ironically, Cuban troops in the Ogaden enable the Dergue to pursue a policy in Eritrea which the Cubans oppose. . . .

On balance, intervention in Ethiopia proved to be a good deal more costly to Cuba than its intervention in Angola. While the introduction of Cuban troops prevented Somalia from seizing the Ogaden—an eventuality which would probably have caused the fall of the Mengistu government—it by no means solved the Dergue's overall security problems. The Dergue continues to be plagued with internal divisions (much more so than the MPLA). . . .

Diplomatically, Cuba paid an immediate price for its Ethiopian intervention with its expulsion from Somalia. The principal Cuban (and Soviet) objective of building good relations with Ethiopia while maintaining good relations with Somalia was lost when their attempts to promote a negotiated settlement in the Ogaden failed. The Cuban intervention has also entailed wider diplomatic costs. In Angola, despite U.S. attempts to brand the Cubans as Soviet "mercenaries," most nonaligned nations viewed the Cuban decision to intervene as both independent and principled. Thus, the respect Cuba gained by demonstrating its military potency was not blemished by a belief that it was projecting its power abroad in pursuit of narrow national interests (either Soviet or Cuban). In Ethiopia, however, the diplomatic equation was more complex and the outcome for Cuba less positive. The harshness of the Dergue's internal policies (e.g., frequent executions of dissident Dergue members and the waging of a "red terror" against the EPRP) made the Ethiopian government unpopular internationally. In addition, the Soviet Union's readiness to replace the United States as Ethiopia's patron, even at the expense of its friendship with Somalia, struck many observers as crass geopolitical jockeying. Cuba's willingness to cooperate closely with the USSR to preserve the Dergue, forsaking both Somalia and the Eritreans in the process, gave credence to the argument that Cuban policy was being set in Moscow. In short, while Angola increased respect for both Cuba's power and its motives, Ethiopia added little to the former while detracting considerably from the latter. The suspicions about Soviet motives in Africa harbored by many nonaligned countries tended to be generalized to Cuba.

Little of this sentiment was publicly expressed in Africa, however. The Cuban-Soviet intervention received tacit support from the OAU, and even from such pro-Western nations as Kenya, Zambia, and Nigeria. This was due to the ability of Cuba and the USSR to justify their intervention as a defense of established borders—a near-sacred principle in African politics. Nevertheless, the changed perception of Cuban motives surfaced in the summer of 1978 in both the OAU and at the Belgrade meeting of foreign ministers of the nonaligned nations. In the OAU, Nigerian head of state Olusegum Obasanjo thanked Cuba for its aid to Africa, but warned the Cubans not to overstay their welcome in Africa lest they be regarded as the instruments of a new imperialism.[50] Cuba's Ethiopian intervention also occasioned heated debate at Belgrade, where President Tito charged that Cuban intervention served the interests of Soviet expansion, and Egypt sought to organize a boycott of the

Sixth Nonaligned Summit scheduled for Havana. Cuba prevailed in this debate (a resolution implicitly critical of Cuba's actions was rejected and the Havana site for the summit was reaffirmed), but its very occurrence demonstrated that Cuba's diplomatic position had eroded.[51]

As in the case of Angola, Cuba's intervention in Ethiopia derailed the process of normalizing U.S.-Cuban relations. When the Carter administration took office in 1977, the normalization process which had been interrupted by Angola was resumed. The Carter administration lifted the ban on U.S. tourism in Cuba, halted intelligence overflights of the island, successfully negotiated a fishing treaty with Cuba, and finally agreed to an exchange of diplomatic Interests Sections.[52] The intention to proceed with full normalization was clear on both sides, but Cuba's intervention in Ethiopia halted the process completely. . . .

If Ethiopia made the United States suspicious of Cuban intentions in Africa, the effect it had on the U.S. perception of Soviet intentions was much greater: Ethiopia, along with other purported Soviet political gains (or U.S. losses) in South Yemen, Afghanistan (1978), Kampuchea, and Iran, catalyzed a major debate over the shape of "post-Vietnam" U.S. foreign policy. At issue was how the United States should respond to perceived "challenges," given the recognition that U.S. power to influence foreign events is not unlimited. One of the main elements in this debate was Cuban-Soviet cooperation in Africa, particularly in Ethiopia.[53] . . .

In the late 1960s, Cuban and Soviet policies toward Africa stood in marked contrast to one another. Cuba was pursuing a militant though limited policy based upon its ideological attraction to progressive regimes (e.g., Algeria, Ghana, Guinea) and national liberation movements (e.g., MPLA, PAIGC, FRELIMO); the USSR was reorienting its policy away from ideological considerations toward more geopolitical ones. As a result, Cuba was openly critical of Soviet behavior.

In the 1970s, as the direct threat to Cuba's security offered by the United States receded, Cuba began to place increasing emphasis on expanding its influence in the Third World. An expansion of Cuban military aid to Africa was one manifestation of that policy, and when Cuba's longtime friend in Angola—the MPLA—was faced with major external threats, Cuba came to its aid with military advisors and later with regular combat troops. This policy was compatible with a Soviet decision made at about the same time to provide the MPLA with heavy weapons, and after the summer of 1975, Cuban and Soviet aid to Angola became increasingly coordinated despite Soviet reluctance to become deeply involved in an area it regarded as being of little geopolitical significance.

In Ethiopia, Cuban-Soviet cooperation developed sooner and was far more extensive than in Angola. Both nations sought to achieve a negotiated settlement to create an anti-imperialist federation in the Horn, and from at least

March 1977 onward, this aim was pursued jointly. When their diplomatic efforts collapsed, Cuba and the USSR cooperated in providing extensive military aid to Ethiopia.

The evolution of Cuba's African policy demonstrates quite clearly that its interventions in Angola and Ethiopia were logical extensions of Cuba's historic policy of providing international assistance to progressive forces abroad. Cuban policies have evolved independently, and despite their compatibility and increasing coordination with Soviet policies, they are different both in concept and application. Cuba is not the Soviet Union's proxy in Africa; the two are partners, and though the partnership is asymmetrical, it is reciprocal nonetheless. Through cooperation, each partner is able to attain policy objectives which neither could attain if acting alone.

NOTES

1. For an excellent summary of the Cuban military assistance programs in Africa prior to Angola, see William J. Durch, *The Cuban Military in Africa and the Middle East,* Professional Paper No. 201 (Arlington, VA: Center for Naval Analysis, 1977). Also see Nelson Valdés, "Revolutionary Solidarity in Angola," in *Cuba in the World,* ed. Cole Blasier and Carmelo Mesa-Lago (Pittsburgh: Univ. of Pittsburgh Press, 1979), pp. 87–118.

2. Ernesto "Che" Guevara, *Che: Selected Works of Ernesto Guevara,* ed. Rolando E. Bonachea and Nelson P. Valdés (Cambridge, MA: MIT Press, 1969), pp. 350–62.

3. Ibid., "Introduction," p. 25–27.

4. Also, see W. J. Durch, *The Cuban Military in Africa,* p. 20.

5. N. Valdés, "Revolutionary Solidarity in Angola," p. 95.

6. W. J. Durch, *The Cuban Military in Africa,* pp. 27–31.

7. Gabriel García Márquez, "Operation Carlotta," *New Left Review* (February-April 1977), pp. 101–02; Danny Schecter, "The Havana-Luanda Connection," *Cuba Review,* Vol. 6, No. 1 (March 1976), pp. 5–13; and John A. Marcum, *The Angolan Revolution: Exile Politics and Guerrilla Warfare, 1962–1976* (Cambridge, MA: MIT Press, 1978), pp. 224–25.

8. Richard Gibson, *African Liberation Movements* (New York: Oxford University Press, 1972), pp. 208–17; J. A. Marcum, *The Angolan Revolution,* passim.

9. R. Gibson, *African Liberation Movements,* pp. 276–77.

10. J. A. Marcum, *The Angolan Revolution,* pp. 185–240; R. Gibson, *African Liberation Movements,* pp. 222–23.

11. J. A. Marcum, *The Angolan Revolution,* pp. 162–67, 193–95, and 276–77.

12. *New York Times* (September 25, 1975).

13. W. J. Durch, *The Cuban Military,* pp. 63n. and 105.

14. Ibid., pp. 171–72. For a history of Soviet-MPLA relations, see Christopher Stevens, "The Soviet Union and Angola," *African Affairs,* Vol. 75, No. 229 (April 1976), pp. 137–51.

15. Basil Davidson, *et al., Southern Africa: The New Politics of Revolution* (New York: Penguin, 1976), pp. 85–86; John Stockwell, *In Search of Enemies: A CIA Story* (New York: W. W. Norton, 1978), p. 55.

16. Seymour Hersh, *New York Times* (December 19, 1975), p. 1; J. A. Marcum, *The Angolan Revolution,* pp. 257–59; and N. Valdés, "Revolutionary Solidarity in Angola," p. 9.

17. For example, see J. A. Marcum, *The Angolan Revolution,* p. 273; and W. J. Durch, *The Cuban Military,* pp. 41–42. But G. García Márquez reports that the first delegation of instructors arrived in early October, "Operation Carlotta," p. 124.

18. J. A. Marcum, *The Angolan Revolution,* pp. 262, 271.

19. Ibid.; J. Stockwell, *In Search of Enemies,* pp. 19–23, 46.

20. J. A. Marcum *The Angolan Revolution,* pp. 266–69.

21. Ibid., p. 443 n257.

22. G. García Márquez, "Operation Carlotta," pp. 127–28, 136. However, J. A. Marcum in correspondence with the author estimates that as many as 1,500 Cubans were in Angola in October.

23. Fidel Castro, "Angola: African Guam," *Granma Weekly Review* (April 18, 1976).

24. Gabriel García Márquez reported this comment from a Soviet official: "We did not twist their arms. The Cubans wanted to go in. . . . They are more radical than we are." *New York Times* (February 5, 1976), p. 128. Henry Kissinger's views are reported in the same article.

25. C. Stevens, "The Soviet Union and Angola," pp. 143–45. On the factors involved in the Soviet decision to intervene, see Jiri Valenta, "The Soviet-Cuban Intervention in Angola, 1975," *Studies in Comparative Communism,* Vol. 11, Nos. 1–2 (Spring-Summer 1978), pp. 19ff.

26. C. Stevens, op. cit.; W. J. Durch, *The Cuban Military,* pp. 48–49.

27. *Washington Post* (April 10, 1977).

28. U.S. House of Representatives, Committee on International Relations, Subcommittee on Inter-American Affairs, *Impact of Cuban-Soviet Ties in Western Hemisphere,* Testimony from the Defense Intelligence Agency (March 14, 15, and April 5, 12, 1978) (Washington, D.C.: Government Printing Office, 1978), pp. 2–3. Also see *New York Times* (November 17, 1978); *Washington Post* (November 18, 1978).

29. See especially, Fidel Castro, Speech to the Nonaligned Conference in Algiers, *Granma Weekly Review* (September 16, 1973), p. 12. For a discussion of Cuba's role in the Nonaligned Movement, see William M. LeoGrande, "The Evolution of the Nonaligned Movement," *Problems of Communism* (January–February 1980).

30. Raúl Valdés Vivo, *Ethiopia's Revolution* (New York: International Publishers, 1978), pp. 102–106.

31. Ibid.

32. *New York Times* (November 14, 1977).

33. Ibid.; *Washington Post* (May 26, 1977).

34. *New York Times* (March 13, 1977).

35. Ibid. (November 14, 1977).

36. Ibid. (April 5, 1976).

37. For example, see R. Valdés Vivo, *Ethiopia's Revolution;* Fidel Castro's interview in *Afrique-Asie* (March 29, 1967); Miguel F. Rosa, "Para Defender la Revolución Etiope," *Verde Olivo,* Vol. 13 (1977), pp. 18–21.

38. Fidel Castro, Speech of March 18, 1978, *Granma Weekly Review* (March 19, 1978).

39. *New York Times* (March 13, 1977); *Washington Post* (March 18, 1977).

40. *Washington Post* (May 26, 1977); *New York Times* (June 21, 1977).

41. *Washington Post* (January 13, and February 2, 1978).

42. *Newsweek* (March 13, 1978); *New York Times* (February 8, 1978).

43. *New York Times* (February 14, 1978).

44. *Washington Post* (April 1, 1978).

45. *New York Times* (February 11 and 14, 1978); *Washington Post* (November 18, 1977); *International Bulletin* (January 30, 1978).

46. *Pravda* (Moscow) (March 15, 1978).

47. *The Observer* (London) (February 27, 1978).

48. See the speeches by Fidel Castro and Mengistu Haile-Mariam reported in *Granma Weekly Review* (May 7, 1978).

49. *New York Times* (December 1, 1978).

50. Ibid. (July 20, 1978).

51. Ibid. (June 11, and July 26, 1978).

52. Carmelo Mesa-Lago and Sandra Miller, "Chronology of U.S.-Cuban Rapprochement: 1977," *Cuban Studies,* Vol. 8, No. 1 (January 1978), pp. 36–43.

53. Donald S. Zagoria, "Into the Breach: New Soviet Alliances in the Third World," and Robert Legvold, "The Super Rivals: Conflict in the Third World," *Foreign Affairs* Vol. 57, No. 4 (Spring 1979), pp. 733–54 and pp. 755–78.

43. *Cuba: The Frontier of Latin America**

BY RAFAEL HERNÁNDEZ

From the start, the Cuban Revolution asserted a profound critique of the prevailing Inter-American system, particularly with respect to the pull exerted on it by the United States. Cuba defended the idea of Latin American unity against the North, and supported anti-imperialist and national liberation movements in the region which opposed those forces aligned with the United States.

In the 1960s, the major regional organizations bowed to U.S. pressure and expelled Cuba from their ranks. The United States characterized Cuba as a Soviet proxy in the Western Hemisphere, which was an aspect of its ideological anti-Communist crusade, and which made policy toward Cuba an object of its policy toward the Soviet Union. However, Cuba has become an entrenched concern for the United States over the last 25 years apart from the Soviet Union, because of the hegemonic interests of the United States and the impact of regional factors on these interests.

Contrary to the trend of the 1960s, Cuba has expanded its ties with Western Hemispheric countries, and today has diplomatic relations with 15 countries in the region, including Canada.[1] Of even greater significance, Cuba now shares with Latin America a number of common interests in opposi-

*This essay was written for this volume. Copyright 1988 by Rafael Hernández.

tion to the United States, in the spheres of economics, politics and national security.

The Central American crisis illustrates this commonality. Latin American countries do not perceive the crisis as the consequence of the "export of the Castro revolution," which is how the U.S. describes problems in the Caribbean Basin. Moreover, Cuba shares in the Latin American consensus, which holds that sincere negotiations are the route to peace in the region. This implies compromises by all parties. President Fidel Castro has maintained that self-determination in Central America means each country should be able to choose its own system—whether it be capitalist, socialist, or mixed—without foreign interference.[2]

To be sure, Cuba regards the struggle for liberation in Central America as a continuation of its own liberation struggle. But it does not expect social transformations in Latin America to follow the Cuban model.[3] It is the United States that maintains the view that "other Cubas" are in the making in the hemisphere.

While U.S. hostility toward Nicaragua, and toward negotiations in general, remains unabated, Cuba will maintain its right to assist Central American revolutionaries. While this help is mainly of a civilian nature, Cuba would be willing to relinquish its right in the framework of a comprehensive agreement, under which the United States would pledge to abide by the principles of Contadora. Even without an agreement, Cuba has declared that it could not participate actively in the defense of Nicaragua or in support of the FMLN [in El Salvador] if there were a U.S. invasion in Central America.[4]

Cuba also shares with the countries of the Caribbean Basin a geopolitical space, which the United States has defined as vital for its national security. This has resulted in the greatest concentration of all U.S. military bases, the permanent patrolling by U.S. warships, and nearly constant U.S. military maneuvers. It suggests that any relations with "extracontinental" powers are a source of concern for the United States.

The militarization of the Caribbean Basin is a problem for all of the neighbors in the subregion. But this problem is not limited only to Central America and the Caribbean islands. The Malvinas/Falklands war, the failure of the proposed South Atlantic Treaty Organization, and the rebirth of representative democratic systems in Latin America once again raise the issue of Latin American national security in terms other than the narrow context of Pan Americanism. It is clear that national security interests are not identical in all parts of the hemisphere. The North and South perceive in different ways the problems of "extrahemispheric enemies" and the "threat to hemispheric security." Latin Americans do not define national security in terms of the Soviet Union, but instead by the ways in which they can limit United States national security projections.

Latin Americans are developing a new attitude toward security, which replaces the much touted and manipulated concept of Pan American national security. It is an attitude based on the primary interests shared by Latin American countries, which emanate from their proximity and need for political cooperation. It manifests itself around concrete problems: ocean passes, exploitation of energy resources, diversification in the sources of military supplies, cooperation with nonhemispheric enterprises, access to new markets in other regions—in countries which are not allied to the United States. While this security agenda—which Cuba has in common with Latin America—does not appear in the countries' official foreign policy declarations, it is already a reality for many of them.

Cuba is also on common ground with Latin America in the search for economic integration and new development formulas. The shared goals include: improvement in the terms of trade and competitiveness in the world market; the diversification of markets for nontraditional products; the promotion of multilateral cooperation, especially in terms of South-South relations; a solution to the acute problem of foreign debt. In spite of the economic blockade, and the advantages Cuba derives from its integration into the [Eastern bloc's] Council for Mutual Economic Assistance (CMEA), Cuba is still linked to the economies of the Western countries, and increasingly to those in Latin America. Its trade and financial relations with the relatively more developed countries, such as Mexico and Argentina, have continued to grow. The prospect of establishing major economic agreements with Brazil seems promising. Economic cooperation with Peru, Guyana and Nicaragua has been growing.

Last, the countries of the region have challenged traditional pan-Americanism by adopting the Third World agenda. With the political tactics used to address the problems mentioned earlier, Latin American countries have cast a doubt on the Inter-American system itself. The process of democratization has included on its agenda the matters of self-determination and the diversification of Latin American international relations with all countries of the world. All of these changes have produced, as a by-product, a new stand vis-à-vis the United States.

Cuban foreign policy today converges with this differentiated Latin American political environment. Indeed, the presence of Cuba as an active member of the Latin American community—outside the framework of the classical institutions of the Inter-American system—is consistent with the pluralistic and democratic characteristics of the actual community rather than the ideological dogmatism of traditional Monroeism. There is now a greater diversity in the political systems of Latin America and the Caribbean than at the time when Cuba was expelled from the Organization of American States. As a result, there are two options before the region: to restore Pan Americanism, or to articulate a new Inter-American system. These offer the possibility for a decisive hemispheric watershed, which would mean that Latin America would share in the isolationism of the United States or that there would be a new coexistence which allowed for diversification. In contrast to the 1960s, this time Cuba is not forcing the countries to make a choice.

The closer bonds between Cuba and Latin America reflect a shift in U.S.–Latin American relations. The whole region now is moving toward the U.S. frontier. This movement has not occurred because of the Cuban Revolution, but is a result of the dynamics enveloping Latin America, the Third World, and even the United States through the way it projects itself in the world. The enormity of this change means that the United States cannot effectively "manage" it merely by using the expedient of negating Cuba.

Relations between Cuba and the United States historically have reflected the tensions, perceptions, and problems existing between the two poles of the hemisphere. The U.S. attitude toward Cuba has been shaped by the way it perceives the situation in Latin America. This was evident from the growing hostility toward Cuba in the face of the Central American crisis. A modification in U.S. policy toward Cuba, therefore, will be related to the implementation of an alternative U.S. policy toward Latin America. In this regard, U.S. policy implicitly recognizes the reality of the close ties between Cuba and the countries of the hemisphere.

NOTES

1. The countries are: Argentina, Bahamas, Barbados, Bolivia, Brazil, Canada, Ecuador, Guyana, Mexico, Nicaragua, Panama, Peru, St. Lucia, Trinidad and Tobago, and Uruguay.

2. Fidel Castro, Interview with U.S. journalists, *Granma* (July 28, 1983), p. 3.

3. Press conference with Fidel Castro and Patricia Sethi, *Bohemia* (February 6, 1984).

4. Fidel Castro, Speech at the Opening Session of the 10th Congress of the World Federation of Trade Unions, *Granma* (February 11, 1982), p. 3.

44. Cuba and the Americas: 1972–1979*

BY H. MICHAEL ERISMAN

As Havana entered its initial globalist phase, it heavily stressed that it considered itself first and foremost a Latin American nation and that it intended to play a major role in hemispheric affairs. As Castro put it in a July 1972 speech, "We are in this hemisphere, on this side of the Atlantic. We are Latin Americans. . . . We think that one day we will be politically and economically integrated with the rest of the peoples of Latin America."[1] Accordingly,

*From H. Michael Erisman, *Cuba's International Relations: The Anatomy of a Nationalistic Foreign Policy* (Boulder, CO: Westview Press, 1985), pp. 45–50, 68–91.

Havana launched an offensive that proceeded rather smoothly and successfully to reclaim what it felt to be Cuba's rightful place in the hemispheric family.

From 1972 to 1975 Cuba established diplomatic relations with the following Latin American and Caribbean countries: Barbados, Trinidad and Tobago, Guyana, Jamaica, and Peru in 1972; Argentina, 1973; Venezuela, 1974; and Colombia, 1975. Mexico, of course, had never severed its ties with Havana, and Chile under Salvador Allende restored relations in 1970. This new respectability led to growing sentiment to lift the sanctions imposed by the OAS on Castro's government in the 1960s. Peru first proposed this move in 1972, and it was finally approved in 1975. The Fidelistas' reaction was somewhat ambivalent, reflecting the cross-pressures of pragmatic nationalism and intransigent anti-imperialism operative in their foreign policy. On the one hand, they very much welcomed the opportunity to expand their political and especially their economic contacts with their neighbors, for such diversification was indispensable to their aim of avoiding great-power dependency. On the other hand, they continued to revile the OAS as a tool of U.S. colonialism and refused to reactivate their membership, calling instead for the creation of a purely Latin American organization that would exclude the United States.

Although shunning the OAS, Havana became increasingly attracted to various hemispheric functionalist associations, particularly ones such as SELA (the Latin American Economic System) that forbid U.S. participation, or that seemed to have potential as vehicles through which Latin countries could achieve greater unity and thus confront Washington more effectively. As they were created, Cuba joined the Latin American Energy Organization (OLADE, 1973); the Latin American and Caribbean Sugar Exporting Group (GEPLACEA, 1974); and the Caribbean Multinational Shipping Company (NAMACUR), the Caribbean Committee of Development and Cooperation (CCDC), and SELA, all founded in 1975. Cuba was not the driving force behind the formation of any of these groups, but as a charter member it strongly supported all of them and was especially enthusiastic about SELA because, says Steven Reed, "From the beginning, SELA's purpose has been to attempt to solve Latin American economic problems collectively and to reduce Latin American economic dependence on the United States; the organization can be interpreted as an important challenge to U.S. economic interests and influence in the hemisphere."[2] Ideally, Havana hoped to use SELA and its counterparts to wean the hemispheric nations away from their traditional "special relationship" with Washington and then draw them into the mainstream of nonaligned affairs, thereby furthering Cuba's emerging aspirations for a major leadership role in the Third World.

Indeed, it was in the realm of Third World politics that Cuba's incipient globalism became most evident, its higher profile in the Nonaligned Movement and its expanded presence in Africa setting the pace. By opening these new fronts along with its initiatives in Latin America, Havana graphically demonstrated that it was becoming committed to a vigorously proactive foreign policy on a worldwide scale. . . .

By 1975, Cuba's Third World position was stronger than ever. It had preserved its standing as a leader in radical circles and also achieved greater respectability in the eyes of nonaligned moderates. Accordingly, Cuba was chosen as the coordinator for all agenda items concerning national liberation movements at a February 1975 meeting of developing states in Dakar, was selected a member of the working group of the U.N. Special Committee on Decolonization in February 1975, and in March 1975 hosted the Third Ministerial Meeting of the Nonaligned Movement's Coordinating Bureau. The stage was set for Havana to proceed to a new plateau in its globalist activities. It would do so in Angola, short-circuiting in the process what appeared to be the first significant movement toward the normalization of U.S.-Cuban relations in many years. . . .

Although ignored by many observers, U.S. officials being perhaps the worst offenders, the intensification of Cuba's globalism was quite compatible with the nationalistic dimension of its foreign policy. This was especially evident as its Third World hemispheric scenario unfolded. Havana's initiatives in Africa, for example, clearly had the potential to further its long-standing yearning to maximize its autonomy and its international leverage, particularly in its dealings with the United States and the USSR. Indeed, as Wolf Grabendorff has pointed out,

Cuba's greatest expectation [was] the possibility of gaining a *two-folded bargaining power* from its African involvement. On the one hand, it could enhance its position vis-à-vis the hegemonic USSR, since the Soviet Union is probably well aware of the fact that the military, organizational, and developmental achievements of Cuba could serve antithetical interests in the Third World. On the other hand, Cuba could also gain bargaining power vis-à-vis the United States. Its African card could become a useful trump in overcoming problems and resuming diplomatic relations with the United States.[3]

Such nationalistic aspirations were, however, restrained by the fact that the Fidelistas' ambitious military internationalism inevitably demanded some Soviet logistical support, and by Havana's aspirations to function as a link between the socialist bloc and the Third World, which required it to advocate some controversial pro-Soviet notions such as the natural ally thesis. This Moscow connection, which was reinforced by the island's need for the Kremlin's economic help and security guarantees, worried the more moderate nonaligned states and thus limited Cuba's influence with them. Castro, of course, insisted that his troops would never be used for aggressive purposes in the service of Soviet expansionism. For instance, in a major speech following the Angolan victory, he pledged that "No Latin American country, whatever its social system, will have anything to fear from the Armed Forces of Cuba. It is our most profound conviction that each people must be free to build their own destiny; each people and only the people of each country must and will make their own revolution. The Government of Cuba has never thought of taking revolution to any nation of this hemisphere with the arms of its military units."[4] . . .

The Western Hemisphere was initially not a major arena for Cuban globalism during 1975–1979. This was partially due to Havana's preoccupation with African affairs and its drive for leadership of the Nonaligned Movement. Equally important, however, was its belief, nurtured by the failure of Fidelista radicalism in the 1960s and the 1973 destruction of Salvador Allende's experiment at leading Chile down the peaceful road to socialism, that the region's leftist potential was for the time being limited. Accordingly, Cuba's Latin American initiatives throughout much of this period were rather cautious, consisting mostly of low-profile attempts to normalize relations with most hemispheric governments and to wean them away from a "special relationship" with Washington by encouraging and capitalizing on Latin nationalism. Exemplifying this thinking, Castro declared in his main report to the Cuban Communist Party's First Congress (December 1976) that

> Latin America is not yet on the eve of the kind of overall changes that lead, as happened in Cuba, to sudden socialist transformations. It is clear that such changes are not impossible in some of the Latin American countries, but the determining factor in our America is, above all, a general consciousness—not only among the working class and the peoples, but also at key levels in some of the governments—that the conflict of interests between Latin America as a whole (and each of our countries separately) and the policy of Yankee imperialism cannot be resolved through sellouts or conciliations but requires joint resistance, which is already being formed.
>
> . . . While the masses of Latin America's workers and peasants continue their struggle, governments are appearing which in some cases are inspired by political concepts that lead to socialist aspirations and in other cases are guided by a clear anti-imperialist idea and by the defense of their countries' natural resources and economies in a purely nationalistic context. As a whole, these concepts and policies are the groundwork for widespread Latin American unity to resist and defeat the imperialist policy and will inevitably contribute to profound social transformations urgently needed by Latin America.[5]

In short, Havana was at this juncture giving the mobilization of anti-American sentiment a higher priority than the struggle for socialism. Its strategy was based on the assumption that the defeat of U.S. imperialism through undermining the country's traditionally great influence in, if not hegemony over, the hemisphere was a *necessary precondition* for leftist revolutions to succeed in Latin America.

The Cubans' prudence was well illustrated by their attitude toward the Omar Torrijos regime in Panama. While strongly supporting Panama's demand that the Canal be returned and lauding Torrijos as the prototype of a new breed of progressive, independent-minded Latin military officers, Havana was careful to avoid even the appearance of embracing him as an ideological fellow traveler or attempting to prod him into more militant policies. Instead, Castro praised his commitment to patient negotiations rather than violent confrontation with Washington on the Canal issue and counseled others to do likewise. Thus Havana, once the bastion of inflexible leftist radicalism, reached a genuine accommodation with the mainstream of pragmatic hemispheric nationalism.

Until 1979, the only Latin American government besides Mexico toward which Cuba seemed to display any serious ideological affinity was Michael Manley's regime in Jamaica. Although a democratic socialist rather than a Marxist-Leninist, Manley, who had become prime minister in 1972, nevertheless moved steadily closer to Havana following his 1976 reelection landslide. Not only did his foreign policy take on a more radically nonaligned coloration, but he also displayed growing interest in the Cuban economic model. The Fidelistas responded enthusiastically, extending substantial moral and material support in an attempt to encourage Jamaica's leftist proclivities. During a highly successful Jamaican tour (October 16–21, 1977), Castro stressed at every step his country's eagerness to help the beleaguered island economically, promising buses for Cuban-built schools, tractors for sugar cooperatives, prefabricated housing plants for construction workers, and doctors, teachers, or technicians wherever they were needed. His pledge at a rally in Montego Bay was typical.

> We are willing to bring to Jamaica all our experience in agriculture, cattle raising, public health, education, economic development, fishing, sports—in everything we can. Our universities are open to you, our research centers, hospitals, technological institutes—we shall never keep a secret from you. Anything that might be useful to us, we are willing to offer to you.[6]

Eventually, however, Cuba became more optimistic about the Caribbean Basin's revolutionary potential. The catalyst for this reassessment was events in Nicaragua, where the left-wing Sandinista National Liberation Front (FSLN) was waging an increasingly effective war against the venerable Somoza dynasty, Washington's oldest, most trusted ally in Central America.

> The uprisings in Nicaragua's cities in September 1978, even though they failed to unseat Somoza, were so massive that they persuaded the Cubans to reassess their opinion of Nicaragua's revolutionary potential. Cuba's leaders seemed to conclude that they had underestimated the strength of the left in the northern tier of Central America (Nicaragua, El Salvador, Honduras, and Guatemala). In late 1978 Cuba began once again to provide material aid to guerrilla movements in those countries. The Sandinistas were the first beneficiaries of this new policy.[7]

Along with other Caribbean Basin governments, such as Costa Rica, Venezuela, Panama, and Mexico, that also desired Somoza's overthrow, Havana stepped up its support to the Nicaraguan insurgents, increasing its training and advisory activities, supplying some military equipment while also helping in establishing wider contacts within the international arms market, and playing a role in organizing the brigade of Latin American volunteers that fought beside the rebels in 1979. Although the Fidelistas maintained a much lower profile than other regional sympathizers in furnishing direct military and related aid to the Sandinistas—its moderation apparently motivated by Havana's determination not to provide a pretext for large-scale U.S. intervention in Somoza's defense—the extralegal assistance aspect of Cuban globalism had nevertheless been significantly rejuvenated in Central America. The Cubans hoped that the leftist tide that had been stymied in the 1960s would once again surge through the region.

This optimism was rewarded in March 1979 when, in a dramatic departure from the Commonwealth Caribbean's tradition of parliamentary democracy, a group of young rebels led by Maurice Bishop staged a successful uprising in Grenada and began implementing their brand of socialism on the small island. Although Havana played no role in Bishop's coup, it quickly demonstrated its solidarity with the new government by providing arms, security advisers, doctors, and a fishing trawler. Cuba also agreed to pay one-half the cost of a new $50 million airport, to be built by Cubans.[8]

Shortly thereafter, Nicaragua also veered sharply leftward, with the Sandinista-led insurgents finally driving Somoza from power on July 19, 1979.[9] As the triumphant guerrillas consolidated their control and began to implement their revolutionary program, Havana warmly embraced the new regime. A delegation of the FSLN's top leadership was given a tumultuous welcome when it arrived on the island for the 1979 July 26th anniversary festivities, which quickly turned into a celebration of the Sandinista victory and Cuban-Nicaraguan friendship. By year's end Havana had dispatched approximately 50 military advisers and 2,000 civilian workers (mostly doctors and teachers) to assist Managua in rebuilding the shattered country.[10]

Despite the euphoria generated by these developments, the Fidelistas' approach to aiding leftists was now much more circumspect than it had been in the 1960s. Cuba still encouraged and helped radical elements, but in a prudent manner designed to minimize the potential political and economic risks both to itself and to its ideological brethren. It repeatedly cautioned them against moving too far too fast in attempting to make their revolutions. Havana also sought to reassure the hemispheric community that it was not systematically exporting Fidelismo or interfering in the affairs of other states. This concern was evident in Castro's comments comparing the Cuban and Nicaraguan experiences:

they themselves [the Sandinistas] will by no means say that the two revolutions are exactly alike. They are both profound revolutions, alike in many ways and in many ways different, as all true revolutions must be.

This is important for our people, important also for world opinion. Each country has its own road, its own problems, its own style, methods, and objectives. We have our own; they have theirs. We did things one way, our way; they will do things their way.[11]

As the 1970s ended, Havana, drawing upon its traditions of both Fidelista radicalism and normalization diplomacy, was pursuing a basically two-pronged hemispheric policy, especially in the Caribbean Basin. Cuba's policy involved (1) providing firm, but low-keyed support for revolutionary groups, including some engaged in guerrilla wars; and (2) encouraging nationalism, which in turn could help to generate an atmosphere conducive to closer links between the island and its neighbors. Castro apparently hoped to use anti-Americanism to bind these two threads together and thereby forge a radical left/progressive nationalist coalition in Latin America. This scenario would be consistent with Havana's larger global strategy of cultivating new political and economic partners as alternatives to potential dependency on a superpower.

NOTES

1. Fidel Castro, "Speech on the Nineteenth Anniversary of the Attack on the Moncada Garrison," *Granma Weekly Review* (August 6, 1972), p. 5.

2. Steven L. Reed, "Participation in Multinational Organizations and Programs in the Hemisphere," in Cole Blasier and Carmelo Mesa-Lago, eds., *Cuba in the World,* (Pittsburgh: Univ. of Pittsburgh Press, 1979), p. 300. Read the entire article, pp. 297–312, for an excellent overview of Cuba's participation in hemispheric functional organizations.

3. Wolf Grabendorff, "Cuba's Involvement in Africa: An Interpretation of Objectives, Reactions, and Limitations," *Journal of Interamerican Studies and World Affairs,* Vol. 22, No. 1 (February 1980), p. 24. Emphasis in original.

4. Fidel Castro, *Angola: African Giron* (Havana: Editorial Ciencias Sociales, 1976), p. 24. Note, however, that he only rules out the deployment of *regular* Cuban forces against Latin governments, thus leaving open the possibility of providing various forms of assistance to revolutionary groups short of combat units. Also, he includes only *black* countries in his African reassurances, which implies that the Cuban military could be used against the white minority government in the Namibian-South African struggles.

5. Fidel Castro, "Main Report to the First Congress of the Cuban Communist Party," *Granma Weekly Review* (January 4, 1976), p. 10.

6. *Facts on File,* Vol. 37, No. 1932 (November 19, 1977), p. 884.

7. William M. LeoGrande, "The Dilemmas of Cuban Policy in the Third World" (Typescript), p. 18. LeoGrande cites as the source of this evaluation a May 1979 CIA report on Cuban activity in Central America.

8. Maurice Bishop's growing Cuban connection, which included the establishment of diplomatic relations on April 16, 1979, generated considerable anxiety in the United States. Washington was especially incensed when in January 1980 Grenada voted with Cuba against a resolution in the UN General Assembly condemning the Soviet intervention in Afghanistan. Henceforth, the

United States considered Grenada firmly in the Cuban-Soviet orbit. Examples of U.S. concern about Cuba's influence in Grenada can be found in "Storm Warnings," *Newsweek* (August 27, 1979), pp. 31–34; "Serpent in Caribbean's Island Paradises," *U.S. News and World Report* (May 19, 1980), pp. 25–26; and Richard Buel, "Grenada: Cold War in a Hot Country," *National Review,* Vol. 32 (November 14, 1980).

9. Among the best of the many studies analyzing the Nicaraguan revolution are "Crisis in Nicaragua," *NACLA Report on the Americas* Vol. 12, No. 6 (November-December 1978), pp. 2–42; Thomas Walker, ed., *Nicaragua in Revolution* (New York: Praeger Special Studies, 1981); and John A. Booth, *The End and the Beginning: The Nicaraguan Revolution* (Boulder, CO: Westview Press, 1982).

10. H. Michael Erisman, "Colossus Challenged: U.S. Caribbean Policy in the 1980s," in H. Michael Erisman and John D. Martz, eds., *Colossus Challenged: The Struggle for Caribbean Influence* (Boulder, CO: Westview Press, 1982), p. 4. Details about the Cuban presence in Nicaragua at this time were vague. U.S. Department of State, Bureau of Public Affairs, Current Policy no. 167 (April 17, 1980), "Cuban-Soviet Impact on the Western Hemisphere," p. 2, stated that in late 1979 the Cuban aid mission in Nicaragua numbered at least 2,000 and included about 200 military-security advisers, a minimum of 1,200 teachers, and several hundred developmental assistance personnel.

11. Fidel Castro, "26th of July Speech," *Granma Weekly Review* (August 5, 1979), p. 2.

45. Cuban Internationalism: A Humanitarian Foreign Policy*

BY DONNA RICH

It has been said that Cuba is a little country with a big foreign policy, and nowhere is this more true than in regard to Cuba's foreign economic and humanitarian assistance programs. While much has been written about Cuba's military assistance program abroad, little attention has been paid to its civilian assistance programs. These programs, however, are an extremely important aspect of Cuban foreign policy, and have been a key factor in building Cuba's prominence in the Third World.

Cuba's Third World assistance programs responded to Cuban interests in three general areas: ideology, geopolitics and economics. The notion of proletarian internationalism evolved through the 1960s and 1970s to become a central theme that unites the various objectives of Cuban foreign policy. H. Michael Erisman has defined proletarian internationalism to be a "commitment to help one's ideological brethren in other countries to seize power and consolidate their regimes."[1] One can find roots of proletarian internationalism in Marx's appeal for international class solidarity ("Workers of the world unite"). Cuban foreign policy, however, has traditionally reflected the ideas of

*This essay was written for this volume. Copyright 1988 by Donna Rich.

Jose Martí and Ernesto "Che" Guevara more than Marx. Both of these national heroes hailed internationalism and have led Cuban policymakers to look outward and extend Cuban support to revolutionary movements and progressive governments worldwide.

In addition to well-known military assistance, Cuba has consistently provided humanitarian assistance. While civilian programs were limited at first, there has been a significant growth in Cuba's export of skilled labor primarily because in the past ten years Cuba has had a surplus of labor. These civilian programs are the result of two principal factors: First, due to the U.S. trade embargo, Cuba has suffered from a lack of hard currency that led it to focus its aid in the form of personnel and not money. Second, the revolution has emphasized education and personal development, which has contributed to the emergence of a large skilled labor force.[2] This excess of skilled labor has enabled Cuba to pursue the ambitious humanitarian assistance programs.

In the second half of the 1970s there was a sharp increase in Cuban economic assistance programs to friendly governments including Angola, Vietnam, Ethiopia, Jamaica, Grenada, and Nicaragua. Smaller programs were instituted in a wider range of nations. Cuba sends specialists abroad in agriculture, fishing, sugar refining, mining, transportation, cattle raising, irrigation, industry, construction, and economic and physical planning.[3] Civilian assistance programs have also been developed in the field of social services—especially health and education.

Cuba has programs in 37 different countries in Africa, Asia, and Latin America, and by the mid 1980s there were more than 20,000 civilians abroad.[4] An examination of the major aid recipients suggests that Marxist-Leninist control of the state is not the main criterion for being an aid recipient. A country that has an anti-imperialist, nonaligned foreign policy combined with a progressive, socialist-oriented internal policy would more accurately fit the profile of a typical recipient of Cuban aid. In fact, these criteria conform with the Resolution on International Policy of the First Congress of the Cuban Communist Party, which points out that Cuba willingly accepts indigenous forms of socialism with the primary goal being the defeat of imperialism and the elimination of colonialism.[5]

Construction is the largest component of the humanitarian assistance program. It was provided for the first time in Peru, in 1971, following a major earthquake. Cuban construction workers built six rural children's and maternity hospitals for the military government. In 1974–75, 900 Cuban construction workers went to Vietnam to work on projects ranging from hospitals to highways. By 1979, three percent of Cuba's construction workers were actively involved in overseas programs. There were 1,900 construction workers alone in Angola.[6] In Grenada, perhaps the most famous of the construction projects, Cuban workers helped to construct the international airport.

Cuba's second largest civilian assistance program is in education. This is a twofold program: Cuban educators go abroad and teach, and students from

Third World countries come to study in Cuba on the Isle of Youth. The number of Cuban teachers in foreign countries has climbed steadily. In 1979 there were 2,300 teachers abroad, more than half of whom were in Nicaragua; in 1980, 3,500 teachers, comprising 2 percent of all Cuban instructors were abroad; and by 1982 over 4,500 Cuban teachers were abroad in 20 different countries.[7] They have taught literacy as well as engineering, agriculture, and middle-level industry; adult education is especially emphasized.[8]

The third major component of Cuba's civilian assistance programs is the field of health care. Between 7 and 13 percent of all Cuban doctors have worked abroad, and they make up 50 percent of Cuba's overseas health workers. Eckstein reports that by 1983, there were 3,000 Cuban doctors in 26 countries.[9]

The Isle of Youth is recognized worldwide for its innovative approach to educational assistance. The concept of schools-in-the-countryside is based on an idea of José Martí who said "ideally, we should not speak of schools at all, but rather we should speak of schools as workshops for real life: in the morning the pen, but in the afternoon, the plow."[10] The Cubans use the Isle of Youth as a type of giant boarding school for foreign students to study as well as help in the island's agricultural development. (The Isle of Youth produces citrus fruit for export.)

By 1985, there were 12,000 foreign students from 11 countries studying and working on the island. The countries include: Nicaragua, Democratic Yemen, Ethiopia, Mozambique, Angola, Namibia, Ghana, the Congo, Saharawi Republic, Guinea Bisseau, Sao Tome and Principe. The students are selected by their own governments and range in age from 12 to 20. There are 24 schools of at least 300 students each; each country has its own school. Some countries have more than one school, and there are several Cuban schools as well. Each school costs the Cuban government $1.2 million pesos, which go to food, lodging, education, medical care, pocket money and travel expenses for all the students.[11] The Cubans also support nationals from each of the represented countries to teach the language, history, geography, and literary background of the country. Cuban instructors teach subjects such as Spanish, math, and sciences. The foreigners are permitted to maintain their own cultural and religious practices, and church services are available.[12]

Foreign students may enroll in military training courses identical to the program that Cuban students may take, which involves theoretical training as well as shooting practice.[13]

Foreign students are taught vocational skills that will be useful to them upon their return home; only a small percentage are allowed to stay and go on to higher education in Cuban universities. This is primarily because the Cuban government has not yet developed sufficient resources for all those who would like to stay and continue their studies. There are currently about 1,000 foreign students in Cuban institutions of higher learning.[14]

While Cuba does not benefit immediately from this program, it is probable that the long-run rate of return is positive. As Fidel Castro summed it up: "The strength of ideas and the spirit of cooperation generated by internationalism is much more powerful than all the tanks, battleships, aircraft carriers, bombers, strategic missiles and deadly weapons."[15]

REASONS BEHIND INTERNATIONALISM

Why has Cuba, a Third World country itself still struggling with underdevelopment, devoted so many of its resources to overseas commitments? Cuba's civilian assistance programs are responses to Cuban interests in three general categories: economics, geopolitics, and ideology.

Economic Gains

Humanitarian assistance programs produce limited economic benefits for Cuba. While Cuba did receive some benefits from its Third world trading partners, there were no immediate financial benefits from the major aid recipients during the 1970s.

Africa accounted for only 3 percent of Cuban exports and less than 1 percent of her imports.[16] While the majority of the Third World recipients of Cuban aid do not produce exportable goods needed by Cuba and most of them share Cuba's shortage of hard currency, there are other kinds of rewards that Cuba can expect. Angola, for example, allows Cuba to enjoy fishing rights in its waters, and more importantly, Angola is an oil-exporting nation. Currently, there are no oil agreements between the two countries, but Angola is a potential supplier of Cuba's future oil needs. The Third World, including the financially strong trading partners, supply a total of 4 to 7 percent of all Cuban trade.[17]

Some say that economic benefits to Cuban overseas programs come from increased Soviet aid, but Eckstein points out that Soviet financial aid did not improve markedly in the 1970s after Cuba increased activity in Angola and Ethiopia. Through history, the Soviets have responded by increasing aid during periods of tense security situations in Cuba; Cuba has not been "rewarded" for its international assistance.[18] Yet some of Cuba's overseas programs might be seen as joint undertakings with the Soviet Union, in which the Soviet Union provides material assistance and Cuba provides personnel.

Cuban humanitarian programs incur some domestic opportunity costs. Construction, for example, the most lucrative foreign exchange generator, sends Cuba's best workers abroad to compete for foreign building assignments, while Cuba needs construction workers at home. In fact, the domestic economic growth rate declined in the late 1970s when Cuban overseas involvement expanded. There were, however, other factors that also contributed to the economic decline, such as the severe drop in sugar prices and the OPEC price hikes.[19]

Thus, Cuban humanitarian assistance programs are not inspired by domestic material considerations. There is important economic return from civilians who go abroad as a result of trade agreements with financially strong Third World countries. The civilian aid programs may prove to be financially lucrative in the long run if the Third World aid recipients become economically stable or if barter arrangements can be made. At the present, however, there is little evidence to suggest that Cuba chooses her aid recipients on the basis of their ability to pay. On the contrary, high opportunity costs and relatively low economic return suggest that Cuban aid programs to date may be net detractors from the Cuban economy.

Geopolitics

Though economic reasons for Cuban internationalism may be an increasingly important aspect of Cuban foreign assistance programs in the future, economic reasons are far from the sole motivation. Cuban civilians abroad help to guarantee long-run friendly relations with Third World allies. Because much of Cuban assistance is either free or low cost, aid recipients find Cuba to be an outstanding donor, and bilateral political relations are enhanced. The new Third World relations also strengthen Cuba's prestige, contribute to its role as a world power, and fulfill Fidel Castro's desire to be a world leader.

Cuba's expanding role in the Third World also has interesting implications for its relations with the U.S. and the Soviet Union. Cuba's civilian assistance programs affect its position with Western capitalist countries in two rather polar ways. As Cuba's development methods are well received and successful, western nations—especially the United States—are forced into defensive positions of either matching Cuban assistance or attacking it. For example, one recommendation of the Kissinger Commission was to increase the number of foreign scholarships awarded to Central Americans. It actually calls for literacy campaigns without crediting Nicaragua or Cuba for theirs.[20]

On the other hand, Cuban assistance programs abroad also serve Cuban relations with the West as foreign exchange earnings from some Cuban aid programs increase Cuba's ability to trade with capitalist countries. Cuba's trade imbalance with the West is eased and doors are opened to broader trade relations.

There have been numerous accusations that Cuba acts as a Soviet surrogate around the world. While Cuba certainly cooperates with the Soviet Union in many areas, there is little evidence to suggest that Cuban aid programs are dictated in Moscow. In fact, civilian assistance programs have reduced Cuban dependence on the Soviet Union. Philip Brenner has pointed out (Reading 29), "the logistics of defending Cuba over long distance, the reasonable Cuban skepticism about Soviet willingness to risk a wider war in the event of an attack and the lack of an overt promise make Cuban leaders wary about relying wholly on Soviet defenses." Thus, while Cuba must still depend heavily on

Soviet support, Cuban policymakers seek a nonaligned position that links Cuba to the Third World in an attempt to improve their national security position.

Cuban military and civilian assistance to Angola illustrates Cuban policymakers pursuing Cuban objectives: Cuban prestige in Africa skyrocketed and Cuba's position in the Nonaligned Movement climbed following Cuban aid to the MPLA. This has assisted Castro in his quest for Third World recognition. Additionally, furthering the cause of socialism in the Third World deepens Cuban–Third World relations because of shared ideology, and this will eventually lead Cuba to be less dependent on the Soviet Union. In the future this could serve to increase Cuban security as Cuba will have numerous friends in the Third World.

Thus, in return for Cuba's socialist internationalism, Cuba receives several geopolitical benefits: international recognition, Third World leadership, less dependence on a single source of support, and improved national security. While economic and geopolitical reasons explain some of the reasons behind Cuban assistance programs, ideological reasons are probably the most important catalyst behind the aid.

Ideology

As previously mentioned, internationalism is a fundamental principle of Marxist-Leninist ideology. More significant in many ways than Marx to the Cubans is Che Guevara who believed "proletarian internationalism is a duty, but it is also a revolutionary need."[21] The Cubans have come to believe that internationalism is a moral and revolutionary duty, a matter of principle and consciousness. Because Cuba's own postrevolutionary development depended to a great extent on international socialist support, today Cubans are taught that just as they once depended on others, they are now in a position to help. The great emphasis on the principles of internationalism that is instilled in every Cuban has produced a great deal of popular support in Cuba for civilian overseas programs. Fidel Castro points out: "What would have become of our revolution and our country without internationalism? How much have we done for others compared to what others have done for us in so many fields?" International assistance allows Cubans to "settle their debt with humanity."[22] Cubans who volunteer to go abroad demonstrate commitment to humanitarian and patriotic concerns and in some cases receive political and economic return as well. There is a prestige value to being an internationalist. It is not uncommon that civilian returnees receive favored positions or salary increases as a by-product of their services abroad. But, because there is no guarantee of improved position, it is doubtful that material incentives are the reason that Cubans volunteer to go abroad.[23]

Cubans pride themselves on reaching the most distant locations in the Third World, and setting up assistance programs where there has been no previous development.[24] The Cubans have proven to be more tolerant of uncomfortable living conditions than their western or Soviet counterparts. They have a remarkable record of mixing with the nationals without much cultural conflict as often occurs with more ethnocentric Soviet and U.S. advisors. Africans can easily identify with black and mulatto Cubans facilitating Cuban integration into the host society. The greater trust that is developed improves the chance of successful outcome of development projects.

Cubans also learn a great amount about their own situation from trips abroad. The Cuban government today is worried that Cuban youth will lose their revolutionary commitment because they have not had to experience struggle. Civilians who go abroad to serve in assistance programs are introduced to Third World poverty for the first time. This has the important effect of making them appreciate the gains of their own revolution.[25]

CONCLUSION

It first appears somewhat paradoxical that a small island country, struggling itself to survive, is significantly investing in foreign assistance programs. On further examination, however, it is evident that Cuba has reaped important benefits from its humanitarian assistance programs; so much so, in fact, that the world's greatest superpower is taking note and, on occasion, implementing some of Cuba's tactics itself. Cuba's commitment to humanitarian assistance goes far deeper than economic gain. When Cuba's Third World trading partners are separated from its Third World aid receivers, the economic return on pure aid is not in Cuba's immediate favor. In fact, the economic benefits enjoyed by Cuba from its Third World trading partners account for such a small percentage of the Cuban trade balance that even this hardly warrants such vigorous assistance programs.

As Castro struggles to reduce Cuba's isolation, improve its position as a world power, and further his personal ambitions as a world leader, proletarian internationalism has worked to his benefit. Third World nations praise Cuba's generosity and guarantee long-run friendly relations. Furthermore, as Cuba pursues a nonaligned foreign policy, her dependence on the Soviet Union decreases. Less dependence on a distant ally and increased links to the Third World enhance Cuba's national security position.

While geopolitical advances are important, motivation to participate in Cuba's humanitarian assistance programs is drawn from a strong ideological commitment to the principles of socialist internationalism and Cuban nationalism. This ideological commitment works not only as a motivator for participation, but also as an important return from these programs. While economic gain is likely only in the future, and Third World recognition is difficult to quantify, tens of thousands of Cubans have participated in civilian assistance programs abroad and have returned with increased awareness of the advances of the Cuban Revolution. This often translates into increased revolutionary commitment, undoubtedly the most essential ingredient for the future survival of the Cuban Revolution. Thus, the most concrete motivation behind Cuban humanitarian assistance programs, and the greatest benefit to Cuban society as a result of the programs is ideology. It is, however, doubtful that ideology alone would constitute Cuba's strong socialist internationalism, and thus economic and geopolitical motivations enhance ideological motivations to produce a serious commitment to foreign assistance.

NOTES

1. H. Michael Erisman, *Cuba's International Relations: The Anatomy of a Nationalistic Foreign Policy* (Boulder, CO: Westview Press), p. 7.

2. Susan Eckstein, "Structural and Ideological Issues of Cuba's Overseas Programs," *Politics and Society* (1982), p. 212. All of the above paragraphs come from this source.

3. Susan Eckstein, "Cuban Internationalism" in Sandor Halebsky and John Kirk, eds., *Cuba: 25 Years of Revolution* (New York: Praeger Publishers, 1985), p. 374.

4. Ibid., p. 374; *New York Times* (June 23, 1983), p. 2.

5. S. Eckstein, "Cuban Internationalism," p. 375.

6. S. Eckstein, "Structural and Ideological Issues," p. 96.

7. S. Eckstein, "Cuban Internationalism," p. 374, and "Structural and Ideological Issues," p. 98; "Los Maestros Cubanos: Un Vivo Ejemplo de Internacionalismo Proletario," *Granma,* Cuban Edition (November 20, 1985), p. 2.

8. *Granma Weekly Review* (July 19, 1981), pp. 2, 3.

9. S. Eckstein, "Cuban Internationalism," p. 96. Also see speech given by President Fidel Castro at ceremony to found the Carlos J. Finlay Medical Sciences Detachment, *Granma* (March 28, 1982), p. 8, for 1980 data.

10. Jonathon Kozol, *Children of the Revolution* (New York: Delacorte Press, 1978), pp. 125–126.

11. *Granma Weekly Review* (March 10, 1985), pp. 8, 9.

12. Much of this information comes from a personal visit by the author to the Isle of Youth in November of 1984. Numerous Nicaraguan and Mozambican students were interviewed. The Nicaraguan students said that they attended church. Also see *The New York Times* (October 4, 1982), Section 6, p. 32.

13. *Granma Weekly Review* (March 10, 1985), pp. 8, 9.

14. *The New York Times* (October 4, 1982), p. 32. Those who are permitted to stay are integrated into the Cuban system. This author interviewed a Jamaican woman who was studying on full scholarship provided by the Cubans at the University of Havana in December 1984.

15. *Granma Weekly Review* (March 10, 1985), pp. 8, 9.

16. S. Eckstein, "Structural and Ideological Issues," p. 197. Main aid receivers: Angola, Ethiopia, Nicaragua; Main Third World trading partners: Algeria, Egypt, the Sudan.

17. William M. LeoGrande, "Foreign Policy: The Limits of Success", in Jorge I. Domínguez, ed., *Cuba: Internal Order and International Affairs* (Beverly Hills, CA: Sage Publications, 1982), p. 178.

18. S. Eckstein, "Cuban Internationalism," p. 379, and "Structural and Ideological Issues," p. 108.

19. S. Eckstein, "Cuban Internationalism," p. 381.

20. While the U.S. action was primarily meant to compete with the Soviet Union, Cuba's activities in education have been of concern to U.S. policymakers as well. In a tour through Central America made by this author in 1985, one of the most common concerns voiced by pro-American educators is that many Central Americans went to study in Cuba where they were impressed by the Cuban system. There were requests that the U.S. meet the Cuban challenge and provide adequate education and ideological ammunition so that they could counter students returning from Cuba.

21. Ernesto "Che" Guevara, "Man and Socialism in Cuba," in Bertram Silverman, *Man and Socialism in Cuba: The Great Debate,* (New York: Atheneum, 1971), p. 353.

22. Fidel Castro, Speech, *Granma Weekly Review* (April 16, 1982), p. 3.

23. In interviews with Cuban teachers in Nicaragua in August 1985, this author found that those who volunteered in Nicaragua actually accepted a pay cut. Though their room and board was covered, spending money allowed them just enough for occasional bus rides into Managua. The incentive was almost entirely ideological. Interview with Karen Wald in Washington D.C., November 20, 1986.

24. Interview with Cuban internationalists in Cuba who had been to Mozambique and Angola, November 1984.

25. Interviews with Cubans in Nicaragua, August 1985. They related their first encounters with poverty upon their arrival in Managua and a new profound commitment to their own revolution and to their work as internationalists.

PART V

Daily Life and Culture

Introduction

Cuban revolutionary leaders always have acted on the basis of the belief that what is "personal" is also "political." They consciously structured the basic institutions of daily life—which affected how people obtain food, where they live, and their recreation—to make such activities consistent with revolutionary ideals of equality and the "new Cuban man." For example, for many years the market did not distribute scarce commodities such as refrigerators. Instead, people would vote in their work centers for the most deserving recipients, based on need and performance at work.

The revolutionary government also sought to discourage the sort of mass migration to cities that characterizes most of Latin America. One purpose of the effort was to plan the island's internal development. Another was to diminish the social and economic inequality between rural and urban workers. A third purpose was to raise the low social esteem that had been attached to rural work, in contrast to urban jobs. This purpose reflected the dream of developing "new Cubans," who would applaud mental and physical work equally, who would engage themselves in activities to their full potential, and whose energies were directed toward social as well as personal improvement.

There has also been an attempt to engender interpersonal relations consistent with the political goals of the revolution, including the end of racism and sexism. Legal statutes and consciousness-raising campaigns toward this end affected every institution, from the family to the government. They also led to great resistance, demonstrating the inability of "rational" plans to anticipate all human responses.

This combination of progress and resistance was evident perhaps most graphically in the development of Cuban arts during the last 30 years. The government sought to overcome the island's colonial heritage by promoting a distinctively Cuban culture and a Cuban national identity through the arts and by expanding participation in the creation and consumption of art. These efforts sparked an outpouring of creativity. Whereas in 1959, Cuba had been perhaps best known artistically for the cha-cha, and only one or two of its writers were known off the island, today it has internationally acclaimed filmmakers, dancers, poets, folksingers, and painters whose work is varied and highly stylized. While there is censorship in Cuba, artistic works do not seem uniform or rigid. But several artists did not feel comfortable with the revolution, especially in the 1960s when restrictions on artistic expression were severe. The Cuban Revolution thus promoted artistic activity and also drove some of the best artists away from the country.

A pattern of simultaneous progressive and regressive change characterizes much of the revolution and makes it susceptible to half-baked caricatures. One North American critic, for example, reported that his first impression of Havana on a mid-1970s visit was its shabbiness. Others miss the opulence and *joie de vivre* of the 1950s. In contrast, some visitors have emphasized the still active street life in Havana, the decisions to direct scarce resources, such as paint, to the countryside instead of the old cities, and the broad distribution of amenities available previously only to the elite.

Both pictures are somewhat accurate, though they cannot be neatly joined at the edges to develop a whole. Few Cubans, for example, would champion a return to the prerevolutionary culture that excluded most of them, yet many embrace fashions of the 1950s, such as the grand *quince* party for their teenage daughters or Guy Lombardo-style music in nightclubs. Average Cubans are proud of the rural development throughout the island, and city dwellers even pay attention to mundane agricultural statistics on milk or sugar production. But they also complain about potholes in the city, and they do not glorify the lack of paint. They hold out the refurbishing of Havana as a goal for the future.

The future now dominates the Cuban spirit in unprecedented ways, and this may be the most telling effect of the revolution on daily life. Cubans have a sense of purpose. Most visitors report that there continues to be a national feeling of vitality, as if average people are part of a great experiment in constructing a new society. To be sure, some people feel left out of the movement, and others do not like its direction (although the direction has not been determined definitely). But most Cubans sense that they are developing a true national identity in which they do not merely mimic the mores of a dominant Spanish or U.S. culture.

This collective effort also gives Cubans a sense of personal dignity uncommon in Third World countries. It undergirds an outlook that does not obscure the inequities and injustices that plague the revolutionary society, and that nurtures a hope that these will be alleviated by the Cubans themselves.

These readings illustrate and explain how the transformation of Cuba has affected the Cuban spirit: in daily life, health and education, problems of sexism and racism, culture, and the arts.

Susan Eckstein, in "The Debourgeoisement of Cuban Cities" (Reading 46), compares the political geography of Cuba to other Latin American countries and the forces that have distorted their urban and rural development. By consciously promoting growth in the countryside through a variety of incentives, Cuba not only has avoided the horrors of shantytowns that dot the decaying urban landscape of the region, but has also provided for a greater integration of the disparate parts of the country.

Seemingly apolitical activities such as sports can also embody political values as described by Raudol Ruiz Aguilera, in "The Cuban Sports Program" (Reading 47). He explains that Cuban sports are intended to encourage participation and collective values and to discourage individualism and personal gain.

It is perhaps through social services that the Cuban Revolution has made the greatest impact on the life of every Cuban. From rural polyclinics to the renowned high-tech medical center in Havana, Cuba's far-flung medical system has become the envy of many developing nations. As Robert N. Ubell describes in his survey of health care (Reading 48), Cuba "has emerged in such good health that its medical statistics rival those in the industrialized world."

The equally remarkable advances in education are outlined by Marvin Leiner (Reading 49). Leiner's article reveals a government resolved about the importance of education and a society enmeshed in educating itself. More than one third of all Cubans are enrolled in school—in day care, primary, secondary, higher, vocational, or adult education. Leiner documents both the achievements of the Cuban educational system, especially the improvement in literacy, and the ongoing dilemmas, such as the reproduction of inequality.

Most accounts characterize Cuba in 1958 as more sexist and less racist than the United States at the time. Cuba shared a "macho" culture with other Latin American countries in which women were second-class citizens. Blacks in Cuba also suffered severe discrimination, but lighter-skinned blacks (mulattoes) were somewhat integrated into the society. Indeed, Fulgencio Batista was a mulatto, though during the time of his elected presidency, in the early 1940s, he was denied admission to the exclusive Havana Yacht Club because of his color. Today, Cuba has made great strides to overcome sexism and racism, juridically and in practice, though both discriminations are still evident.

In Reading 50, Max Azicri describes the changes in women's lives since 1959. The Federation of Cuban Women (FMC) is the principal mass organization, he explains, that provides an institutional mechanism through which women can help to balance conflicting roles and responsibilities. He also examines the links between Cuban women's education and their position in the labor force, and critically assesses the disparity between Cuban goals for women's equality and the current status of women.

Lourdes Casal was a Cuban exile whose life was sadly cut short by illness at a point when her scholarship was beginning to influence much that was being written about Cuba. The reason for this impact is evident in two articles reprinted here: "Race Relations in Contemporary Cuba" (Reading 51) and "Cultural Policy and Writers in Cuba" (Reading 54). In the first article, she explains that the accomplishments of the Cuban Revolution with respect to race cannot be assessed accurately without an adequate account of race relations before the revolution. Much of the literature about race in prerevolutionary Cuba, she observes, has understated the extent to which there was discrimination, violence against blacks, and a pervasive antiblack culture. As a consequence, the achievements of greater equality, an end to any overt discrimination or violence, and the promotion of Afro-Cuban culture appear less significant than they are in fact. In Reading 54, Dr. Casal details how government policy often shifted between 1959 and 1971, and served both to restrain writers and to encourage the production of writing forms uncommon before 1959.

Sandra Levinson's tour d'horizon of Cuban arts, "Talking About Cuban Culture: A Reporter's Notebook," provides details about the great advancements made in music, mass media, plastic arts, dance, theater, and literature (Reading 52). She provides a framework for understanding these changes by explaining the duality with which Cuban leaders approached the arts. On the one hand, they believed both that free expression was integral to a fully developed cultural environment and that cultural expression would not be readily susceptible to control. On the other hand, they wanted to use culture as a way of generating and sustaining revolutionary ideals and of denigrating values of the old order.

Cuban film has reflected this dualism, while it has acquired international acclaim for its quality. Pat Aufderheide, in "Cuba Vision: Three Decades of Cuban Film" (Reading 53), demonstrates how Cuban cinema has evolved through three distinct periods, and has come to define a style of its own.

Folksinger Silvio Rodríguez and poet-novelist Pablo Armando Fernández are celebrated Cuban artists whose works reflect the dynamic of creative expression linked to Cuban revolutionary values. Rodríguez's song, "When I Say Future," (Reading 55) is one of those in the repertoire of the new Cuban troubadours (nueva trova). Fernández's poem "From Man to Death" (Reading 56) was written in 1959. It was the last "story" in a seven-part "poetic re-creation" of Cuban history that began with Columbus and ended with the struggle against Batista. The poem takes its scenes and quotations from the diaries that Raúl Castro and Camilo Cienfuegos wrote during the fighting in 1957 and 1958.

CHAPTER 14

Daily Life

46. *The Debourgeoisement of Cuban Cities**

BY SUSAN ECKSTEIN

There now is a vast literature on urbanization in the capitalist countries of Latin America. The way that Latin American economies have been integrated into the world economy has shaped how the continent has been urbanized. The major cities have grown much faster than the population at large, and as they have increased, so too have regional disparities and the number of ill-housed and ill-fed city folk. Poor migrants and their children have not been able to secure jobs enabling them to earn a decent living. While the dominant cultural ethos of the cities continues to be set by the upper class, most of the populace is caught up in a "petty capitalist" type of existence. Must Latin American cities necessarily develop in this fashion? This chapter describes how conditions in cities and the importance of cities have changed in Cuba since the 1959 Castro-led revolution to see whether Latin American cities develop differently under socialism than under capitalism.

While vestiges of Cuba's capitalist past persist, we will see that Cuban cities have been debourgeoisified since the revolution, to the extent that they now differ from other modern Western cities in important ways: market forces, private profit, property interests, consumerism, and competitive individualism no longer dominate urban life to the extent that they did before 1959. Although initially petty bourgeois property and privileges were protected by the revolutionary leadership, at the expense of large-scale domestic

*From Irving Louis Horowitz, ed., *Cuban Communism,* 3rd Edition (Brunswick, N.J.: Transaction Books, 1981). Edited for this volume.

and foreign capital, and although initially the "masses" were given access to bourgeois and petty bourgeois culture which they previously had been denied, since the 1960s the Cuban government has tended to use its power to transform the class structure, to equalize income, to democratize access to material goods, housing, and social services, and to proletarianize the dominant cultural ethos. It also has used its power to correct demographic and economic regional imbalances created during the capitalist epoch. These changes are documented below. We will see that many of the characteristics generally assumed to be basic attributes of modern cities and inherent consequences of urbanization and economic development in the Third World prove to be linked with capitalist but not necessarily with socialist development.

DEMOGRAPHIC AND INVESTMENT DECENTRALIZATION

Before the revolution Cuba was highly urbanized, and Havana was the principal city. As documented below, Havana was the most populated urban center. There was widespread poverty in the city, but social and economic conditions tended to be better there than in the rest of the country. The Castro government reduced regional imbalances, especially during the first decade of the revolution. . . .

The proportion of the total population living in Havana has remained relatively constant since World War II, but the city has come to house an increasingly smaller proportion of the country's urban population. Havana has expanded less rapidly than other major Cuban cities, a trend that began already before the revolution: In 1943, 1953, and 1958 the city was, respectively, 1.59, 1.54, and 1.50 times larger than the combined size of the next 12 largest cities.[1] Secondary cities, and Santiago in particular, have grown in importance since the revolution.

In order to create a more regionally balanced society the revolutionary government constructed new communities, stabilized former communities with mobile populations (bateyes), and "urbanized" the countryside.[2] It concentrated formerly dispersed people in small towns and then provided them with electricity, sanitary installations, furniture, social services, and employment. . . .

Under Castro, Cuba has constructed more cities and rural towns than any other Latin American country. Between 1959 and 1962 alone 83 new towns, with an average population of 300–500, were founded: 27 in Oriente, 17 each in Havana and Las Villas, 9 in Pinar del Rio, 8 in Camagüey, and 5 in Matanzas.[3] By 1971, 246 new settlements had been built, about half with more than 40 dwelling units. Most of the settlements are connected with work centers: with sugar and cattle farms, and, to a lesser extent, with other agricultural, mineral, and textile centers.[4] . . .

In designing the new communities the Cuban leadership has been inspired both by Western and socialist sources. The Soviet Union has constructed well-serviced "urbanized" communities, including "agrocities," around centers of production. However, Cuba has not sponsored large industrial colonization projects as did the Soviet Union initially after its revolution.[5] . . . The Cuban government has been somewhat constricted in its planning options by the country's capitalist heritage. While only two countries—Bolivia and Haiti, both of which are much less economically developed than Cuba—had lower urban growth rates between 1960 and 1970 than did Cuba,[6] Cuba remains one of the most urban countries in Latin America. Since Castro assumed power, the country has dropped from the fourth to the fifth most-urban Latin American nation. Furthermore, Havana still is the most populated city in Cuba, and it contains a somewhat higher percentage of the total national population in the postrevolutionary period than it did before.[7] Thus, the Cuban experience suggests that demographic regional imbalances are not easily corrected after a socialist transformation.

Cuba probably would be much more urbanized and the population of Havana much larger had the government not intervened to counter the forces that generally contribute to urbanization. The government, for one, now restricts geographic mobility by controlling access to jobs and housing. It also has improved conditions in the countryside, making migration less attractive. Agricultural workers no longer are faced with seasonal unemployment as they were in the capitalist epoch. The income gap between agricultural and other workers has diminished, as agricultural wages have increased more than wages in other sectors of the economy (see Table 1). Social services have expanded more rapidly in the countryside than in cities.

Rural-urban imbalances diminished more during the first than the second decade of the revolution, however. During the 1960s, for example, the number of schools, pupils graduated, and students receiving scholarships increased more rapidly in the countryside than in the cities (see Table 2). By contrast, according to available statistics, schooling increased at a more or less equal pace in urban and rural areas in the 1970s. Similarly, hospital facilities expanded more rapidly in the countryside than in cities during the first decade of the revolution (see Table 3). While there were 67 general urban hospitals with 3,264 beds but only 3 general rural hospitals with 10 beds in 1958, by 1969, 82 urban and 47 rural hospitals functioned with 18,382 and 1,160 beds, respectively. The number of hospitals in rural areas increased more rapidly than in urban areas in the late 1960s and early 1970s and the government did open medical dispensaries in rural areas beginning in the late 1960s. Yet the rate of expansion of hospital bed facilities in cities has been greater than in the countryside since the early 1960s: The ratio of rural to urban beds decreased from 1 to 32 in 1958 to 1 to 11 in 1962, and then increased to 1 to 16 in 1969 and 1 to 18 in 1975. Furthermore, in the 1970s the mean wage in agriculture

Table 1: *Mean Salary Within State Sectors*

	1962	1966	1971	1975
Agriculture	954	1059	1323	1543
Industry	1941	2063	1463	1693
Construction	1700	1803	1693	1883
Transportation	2227	2336	1800	1945
Communication	1983	1937	1556	1675
Commerce	1360	1502	1299	1469
Service	1704	1721	1332	1458
Other	1100	1884	1162	—
National	1547	1601	1407	1638

% Increase

	1966–62	1971–66	1975–71
Agriculture	11.0	24.9	16.6
Industry	6.3	−29.1	15.7
Construction	6.1	−6.1	11.2
Transportation	4.9	−22.9	8.1
Communication	−2.3	−19.7	7.6
Commerce	10.4	−13.5	13.1
Service	1.0	−22.6	9.5
Other	71.3	−38.3	—
National	3.5	−12.1	16.4

Sources: *Boletín Estadístico de Cuba, 1970* (Havana: JUCEPLAN, 1972), p. 36; *Anuario Estadístico de Cuba, 1974* (Havana: JUCEPLAN, 1974), p. 41; *Boletín Estadístico de Cuba* (Havana: JUCEPLAN, 1978), as cited by Claes Brundenius, "Measuring Income Distribution in Pre- and Post-Revolutionary Cuba," *Cuban Studies,* Vol. 9, No. 2 (July 1979), p. 33.

continued to rise, but not at the same rate as in the late 1960s, and not as rapidly as in other sectors of the economy.[8] Thus, the rural-urban income gap still is narrowing, although at a slower pace than it did during the first decade of the revolution. We shall see below that Castro's second decade of governance tends to be more urban biased than the first in other ways as well.

The Castro government initially favored the provinces in economic as well as social investments. Before 1959 Havana generated over half the value of industrial production, or three fourths of the value if sugar is excluded, and 90 percent of the country's imports entered Havana's port. To offset the economic concentration the Castro regime during its first ten years of rule located new industries near natural resources, and it developed provincial ports, especially in Nuevitas and Cienfuegos, thereby reducing the importance of Havana as a center of trade. . . . The Castro government may have corrected

Table 2: *Rate of Increase in Urban and Rural Elementary Schooling, 1962–75*

	% increase number schools		% increase teachers		% increase matriculated students	
	urban	rural	urban	rural	urban	rural
1962/3–1966/7	.5	6.0	27.3	9.6	18.7	4.8
1966/7–1970/1	−1.5	6.5	36.6	40.9	26.7	15.1
1970/1–1974/5	8.5	1.1	28.3	28.3	17.1	13.2
	% increase promoted students		% increase students graduated		% increase scholarship students	
	urban	rural	urban	rural	urban	rural
1962/3–1966/7	47.8	58.0	60.8	120.6	71.7	385.6
1966/7–1970/1	19.4	7.7	12.2	58.1	4.1	156.5
1970/1–1974/5	54.3	64.0	130.0	134.9	−33.0	6.4

Source: Calculated from *La Economía Cubana, 1975* (Havana, n.d.), p. 208.

regional imbalances partly for political reasons. It invested heavily in Oriente Province where the rebel army had been strongest. The government has promoted especially large industrial programs in the Nicaro-Moa area in the north and in Santiago in the south.[9] The government also developed tourism and port facilities in Santiago, and a new city with a projected population of 130,000 in Levissa. However, by the second decade of the revolution the government once again turned its attention to Havana.[10] In 1969 Fidel announced that new industries would be located in the capital because the city had good port facilities, infrastructure to support the new industries, a concentrated con-

Table 3: *Percent Increase in Rural and Urban Medical Facilities, 1962–75*

	% increase hospital beds		% increase hospitals		% increase rural dispensaries
	urban	rural	urban	rural	
1962–67	37.8	42.2	55.1	7.3	—
1967–71	30.0	6.5	10.5	15.9	101.7
1971–75	25.6	−10.8	7.1	13.7	−5.8

Sources: *1962 data:* Calculated from C. Paul Roberts and Mukhtar Hamour, eds., *Cuba 1968: Supplement to the Statistical Abstract of Latin America* (Los Angeles: Latin American Center, Univ. of California, 1970), p. 109.

1967–75 data: Calculated from *La Economía Cubana, 1975*, p. 232.

sumer market, an abundant supply of labor (especially of skilled domestic labor and foreign technicians), and a disciplined and experienced labor force.[11] Supposedly, Havana no longer was parasitic. The government now claimed that it was "realistic" and "technically rational" to concentrate resources in Havana, even though the "realism" conflicted with the government's previously declared "maximum of ruralism" policy. As the regime's emphasis shifted, engineers and administrators were sent to the Soviet Union to learn industrial and managerial skills, and Cuba received Soviet aid to develop Havana. The two countries collaborated in the expansion and modernization of the city's port facilities and in the construction of steelworks, auto repair, thermoelectric, and other industrial plants.[12]. . . .

Not only has the Castro government attempted to halt the urbanization trend of the prerevolutionary period, it also has initiated new housing concepts. While initially guided by petty bourgeois ideas, it has gradually come to be guided by more proletarian considerations.

At the inception of the new regime, Castro argued that each rural and urban family should have decent housing and the right to own their own home or apartment: Just as each rural family should be able to own its own tract of land, so too should each urban family have the right to own property. Fidel first articulated this idea in his 1953 Moncada defense.[13]. . . .

Since there was a housing deficit at the time that Castro took power and since the revolutionary government did not expand the housing supply sufficiently so that each family could acquire its own home, it also concerned itself with the living conditions of tenants. A law passed during Castro's first year in power lowered rents by 30–50 percent; tenants who previously paid least received the largest reduction. The Urban Reform Law, enacted in October 1960, further improved conditions for tenants.[14] It allowed tenants to acquire the housing they inhabited through monthly payments equal to the rent they had been paying, over five to 20 years. The law also set a rent ceiling of no more than 10 percent of family income. Subsequent legislation relieved residents of run-down tenements who had paid 60 monthly payments of rental obligations: however, they were requested to pay six to seven pesos a month to the government to help pay for the new housing they would subsequently receive. In 1971 the government exempted families who earned no more than 25 pesos a month from rent payments, provided that they were good workers with no "social parasites" in their family.[15]

The government, in addition, protected small urban property owners. For one, rents in owner-occupied buildings with apartment units that rented for less than 150 pesos a month in 1959 were not lowered. Second, homeowners benefited from tax exemptions.[16] Third, as previously noted, the Castro government initially subsidized private home construction. However, the revolutionary regime limits the amount landlords can collect in rent and it regulates inheritance. When an owner of a building dies, the next of kin do not necessarily inherit the property. The persons who reside in the home at the time of the death are entitled to continue living there.

At the same time that the new government protected petty bourgeois property interests it restricted the economic base of large property owners. Laws passed in 1959 forced the sale of vacant land and regulated the sale and use of land. The government also ended urban and suburban land speculation, proscribed leasing, regulated purchase and sales agreements, called for expropriation without compensation of all tenement buildings, and cancelled all mortgages and loans.

The Castro government also modified the architecture of cities. Initially it promoted social, not socialist architecture, and it drew on a variety of architectural techniques and concepts. It built schools, medical facilities, and other social service centers.[17] Inspired by the elan of the revolution, the Havana art school, Cubanacán, broke with prerevolutionary architectural canons. It was modern and innovative in design, but elitist in conceptualization and costly. After assuming power the government also built two large housing developments in the capital—East Havana and El Cotorro—that were costly and premised still on Western middle-class design ideas. El Cotorro was built to house industrial workers in the southeast of the city, in order to reduce workers' travel time and to ease congestion. East Havana was constructed for urban poor on land assembled for speculative purposes before the revolution. Foreign architects, including Skidmore, Owings and Merrill, Oscar Niemeyer, and José Luis Sert, had been approached to build luxury housing on the property. Situated on a beautiful site overlooking the Havana bay, the project contains 1,500 dwelling units, and it includes diverse social and urban services. Many of the original poor families were unaccustomed to apartment living, abused the buildings, and ultimately moved away. The more educated families who replaced them seem to find the area an attractive place to live. Since the project proved to be expensive, the government never completed its plan to build 100,000 dwelling units there.[18]

By the mid-1960s the government emphasized practical, functional, and more economical projects. For one, it turned to new low-cost production techniques, such as the panel system NOVA (later renamed Sandino).

The first large-scale prefabricated housing development in a major city, known as José Martí, was constructed in Santiago in 1967 to rehouse urban slum dwellers. The housing units were produced at a plant donated by the Soviet Union, and the design of the project draws on a French-inspired Soviet system. The area is subdivided into districts with day-care centers and food stores, and into subdistricts with primary schools, commercial centers, and meeting space for mass organizations. Serving the entire community are theaters, polyclinics, outdoor televisions, and a dental clinic. The community includes one- to four-room apartments in four-story high dwellings. It was designed to house 40,000 people, one sixth of the city's population. Resident families pay 10 percent of their income as rent, and an additional 2 percent to amortize furniture costs. Local groups associated with the Committees for the Defense of the Revolution (CDR), a mass organization, help maintain the area.[19]

Construction of large prefabricated apartments expanded especially in the 1970s, but unlike earlier housing, this was built by workers with no formal training in building trades. In 1974 workers built 40,000 new units. That year marked the first time that more units were built than required to keep pace with population growth.[20] The housing makes minimal use of professional architects and construction workers. The Department of Social Construction (DESA), with its professional staff, organizes and supervises construction at the building sites, and assumes responsibility for the construction of community facilities. The apartments are built by brigades of 33 to 35 workers who are released from their ordinary work commitments for one and one-half to two years. The brigade members continue to be paid by their work center, and the housing that they construct belongs to the work center. When the units are completed the workers collectively decide who, on the basis of need and work performance, should get to live in the apartments. As Fidel proclaimed, "In the case of two workers with equal need, the one with the greatest sense of social responsibility and merit should have priority."[21] Accordingly, access to housing depends on work performance and politics, not, as in capitalist economies, mainly on income.

The microbrigade-built housing constitutes further evidence that the government once again is investing in Havana. The most impressive project is Alamar, on the outskirts of the capital. Begun in 1971 on land that had been held for speculative purposes before the revolution, upon completion it is expected to house some 130,000 people. It is to have 32 day-care centers, 18 semiboarding schools, 6 theaters, sports and health facilities, and new industries.[22] The original housing design has been modified over the years, in response to criticisms raised by the first residents. As a result, the newer buildings include balconies and service patios. As in the José Martí development in Santiago, CDR units oversee the upkeep of this housing. They have organized residents to paint and clean the buildings and to landscape the area.

This prefab housing contrasts with the mushrooming number of poorly serviced, illegally formed squatter settlements in other Latin American metropolises. Squatter settlements have proliferated in the capitalist countries, partly because the formal housing market has not expanded sufficiently to provide inexpensive homes for the rapidly growing population. Because the Castro government regulates the supply of low-cost housing and access to the housing, the conditions which have given rise to shantytowns in the rest of Latin America no longer exist in Cuba.

The post-1959 Cuban regime has not only introduced new housing concepts, new construction techniques, and new construction strategies. It also has improved conditions for the poorest socioeconomic stratum, in ways that other Latin American regimes have not. . . .

Also, neighborhoods possibly are less income-stratified than in the pre-Castro epoch. The prerevolutionary upper and middle classes continue to live in their old spacious homes, but some of the housing left vacant by exiles has been passed on to workers. Furthermore, workers of varying skill and education levels live together in the new microbrigade-built apartments.

In sum, urban property relations and the usage of urban property have been debourgeoisified, under the direction of the state. The Castro government has changed the architecture of Cuban cities, construction strategies and techniques, and urban living conditions.

THE EMBOURGEOISEMENT AND SUBSEQUENT DEBOURGEOISEMENT OF LEISURE-TIME ACTIVITIES AND CONSUMERISM

The cultural life of Cuban cities has in many respects changed since the revolution. As in other dimensions of urban life, so too with culture: The revolutionary government's initial politics were petty bourgeois in inspiration, but subsequently they became more proletarian.

Prerevolutionary Havana was known for its nightclubs, gambling, and prostitution. Gambling and prostitution now are outlawed, although neither has been entirely eradicated. Nightclubs and cabarets continue to operate, but access to them has been democratized as entertainment costs have been lowered; the same holds for dance, music, and the theater. Thus, the excitement of the old Havana has vanished, but all Havana residents can now enjoy the leisure-time activities that do exist.

The revolutionary government, however, has not only democratized access to culture. It also has inspired cultural activities which are innovative in content and technique. Workers, as well as professional artists, now produce shows. In addition, the traditional relationship between artist, artwork, and audience has been altered as the public has been encouraged to partake in performances; in the past, audiences were passive spectators.

Patterns of material consumption have also changed since the revolution. They now are much less income-determined. For one, rationing, introduced in 1962, guarantees all Cubans, regardless of their wealth, equal access to basic necessities. Secondly, while some nonessentials can be purchased by anyone willing to pay, others are allocated through work centers on the basis of merit, politics, and need. Third, the microbrigade-built housing is alloted on the basis of merit, politics, and need and comes equipped with furniture, including television sets. Cubans still covet material goods, but the basis of consumption has changed. . . .

Cuban cities no longer are plagued by the "disorganization" so characteristic of cities in capitalist societies. Cuban streets are clean and safe, and rarely populated by drunkards. Furthermore, as previously noted, neither prostitution nor gambling is as pervasive as in the Batista epoch. The mass organizations have contributed to the social and cultural transformation of neighborhoods. The CDRs, for instance, organize civil guards to patrol streets at night, assume responsibility for the cleanliness and beautification of neighborhoods, sponsor community festivities and political discussion groups, and integrate families into school programs. . . .

CONCLUSION

The Cuban experience demonstrates how urban growth and developments within cities vary with social and productive forces. In the process of socializing the economy, the Castro government has transformed the urban class structure and modified how goods and services are distributed among socioeconomic groups. It also has attempted to introduce a new set of norms, values, and attitudes to govern urban life.

Once the state ceased to depend on capital to stimulate production it could deploy resources to reduce inequities. It has allocated goods and services more equitably among regions; eliminated private manipulation of the housing market; democratized access to leisure activities, consumer goods, and housing; made merit and need, as well as income, bases for consumption; and proletarianized the production and content of cultural activities. . . .

Over the years the national leadership has modified its policies, as social and economic conditions have changed. The government has been flexible and nondogmatic in its approach to socialism. For example, when state bureaucracies proved insufficiently responsive to the concerns of the populace, the government reprivatized part of the service sector.

While the class structure and culture of Cuban cities have been debourgeoisified since the Castro-led revolution, the development of Cuban cities continues to be constricted by the way the country was integrated into the capitalist world economy historically. The island remains economically underdeveloped and poorly industrialized.

NOTES

1. Maruja Acosta and Jorge Hardoy, *Reforma Urbana en Cuba Revolucionaria* (Caracas: Síntesis Dosmil, 1971), p. 97.

2. The Cuban government changed its census definition of urban as it provided communities with facilities and services historically found only in areas with large population concentrations. Prior to the revolution all areas with 2,000 or more inhabitants were classified as urban. By 1970 the definition included, in addition, communities with 500 or more inhabitants which also had four or more of the following characteristics: electric lighting, paved streets, running water, a sewage system, medical facilities, a school. *Boletín Estadístico* (Cuba, 1970), p. 20.

3. M. Acosta and J. Hardoy, *Reforma Urbana*, p. 52.

4. Tony Schuman, "Housing: A Challenge Met," *Cuba Review,* Vol. 5 (March 1975), p 8.

5. I base my discussion of Russian and Chinese urbanization and community development on Manuel Castels, *La Question Urbaine* (Paris: François Maspero, 1972), pp. 93–94. The governments of Eastern Europe apparently regulate city size, develop new and old cities around the neighborhood unit concept, provide urban dwellers with well-serviced housing, and integrate city planning with economic and regional planning. On urban developments in Eastern Europe, see Z. Pioro, M. Savic, and J.C. Fischer, "Socialist City Planning: A Reexamination," in Paul Meadows and Ephraim Muzruchi, eds., *Urbanism, Urbanization and Change: Comparative Perspectives* (Reading, MA: Addison-Wesley, 1969), pp. 553–65.

6. *Economic Bulletin for Latin America #18,* (1973), p. 109.

7. C. Paul Roberts and Mukhtar Hamour, eds., Cuba 1968: *Supplement to the Statistical Abstract of Latin America* (Los Angeles: Latin American Center, Univ. of California, 1970), p. 19. The demographic primacy of Havana peaked in 1963. The city increased its share of the total population from 20 percent in 1943 to 21 percent in 1953 and 1958, and then to 22 percent in 1963. Afterwards, its share of the population gradually declined. Also see M. Acosta and J. Hardoy, *Reforma Urbana,* pp. 60–61.

8. The definition of economic sectors changed in the 1970s. Since 1971 economic sectors apparently have been defined according to administrative principles, whereas they formerly had been defined in terms of production. Thus, as of 1971 the agricultural sector includes people on the payroll of the Agricultural Ministry, whether or not they engage in agricultural work. The change in classification probably accounts for some of the increase in average earnings reported in agriculture.

9. Jorge Hardoy, "Spacial Structure and Society in Revolutionary Cuba," in David Barkin and Nita Manitzas, eds., *Cuba: The Logic of the Revolution* (Andover, MA: Warner Modular Publications, 1973), p. 10.

10. Jean-Pierre Garnier, *Une Ville, Une Révolution: La Havana* (Paris: Editions Anthropos, 1973), especially Part III.

11. *Granma Weekly Review* (February 17, 1975), p. 7.

12. Ibid., p. 11.

13. Fidel Castro, *History Will Absolve Me* (London: Grossman, 1969), p. 52. [Reading 3.]

14. For a detailed discussion of the Urban Reform Law, and antecedent laws, see M. Acosta and J. Hardoy, *Reforma Urbana,* and *Urban Reform Law* (New York: Center for Cuban Studies, n.d.).

15. *Granma Weekly Review* (January 17, 1971), p. 8.

16. M. Acosta and J. Hardoy, *Reforma Urbana,* p. 132; T. Schuman, "Housing: A Challenge Met," p. 5.

17. For an excellent discussion of the history of architecture and the architectural profession in Castro's Cuba, see Roberto Segre, *Cuba, Arquitectura de la Revolución* (Barcelona: Editorial Gustavo Gili, 1970). The book contains photographs of contemporary Cuban architecture.

18. Ibid., p. 111.

19. In at least some of the new housing, development delegates of the Federation of Cuban Women (FMC) and the Communist party also work with resident families. See *Granma Weekly Review* (June 7, 1970), pp. 5–6.

20. *Granma Weekly Review* (December 28, 1975), p. 6.

21. Ibid. (April 25, 1971), pp. 2–3.

22. T. Schuman, "Housing: A Challenge Met," p. 14.

47. The Cuban Sports Program*

BY RAUDOL RUIZ AGUILERA

At the triumph of the revolution in Cuba there were athletes, but no sports. . . . The sports life of the country was circumscribed by two classic phenomena.

Firstly, the development of championships among the large clubs, called the Big Five or Big Six, which were organized by the private schools and the Amateur Athletic Union of Cuba. . . . The regulations of the Cuban AAU (Amateur Athletic Union) denied the participation of blacks—racism being a part of this first phenomenon.

Secondly, there was professionalism. Since North American college baseball and football were not as developed then and basketball had not yet reached the professionalism it has today, professional baseball and boxing were the two biggest of North American sports commercialism. With the force of that professionalism, Cuban baseball and boxing turned out great stars, like Kid Chocolate and Gavilan, and professional ball players who still play on U.S. major league teams.

The athletes in track and field, who were poor and mostly black, had to resort to that form of sports because they could not afford any other.

. . . Other sports, like fencing, were exclusive and accessible only to the ruling class. . . . Some athletes emerged as a natural consequence of Cuban traditions, the potential of Cubans, and through personal vocation, effort, sacrifice and being hungry and discriminated against. That's why we say we had athletes, but no sports.

. . . Our schools did not really have physical education for children. Given 600,000 children without schools, 10,000 teachers without jobs, a million illiterates, and a million unemployed, one can analyze quickly the situation and know that sports did not exist as a system.

Recreation, say the modern sociologists, is a natural result of the existence of free time, the famous "leisure time." But in the context of more than a million illiterates and more than a million men and women unemployed, we did not call it "free time," but "dead time"; time without work, time without the possibility to live, time to hope that the harvest would come soon to supply a few possibilities, and a few pesos. What was recreation then? It was the recreation of the ruling class.

. . . From 1959 until 1961, we gathered a group of comrades in the sports

*From *Cuba Review,* Vol. 7, No. 22 (June 1977), pp. 10–20 (New York: Cuba Resource Center). Edited for this volume.

field and to us fell the honor of founding the National Institute of Sports, Physical Education and Recreation (INDER). In setting it up, we formulated new criteria for a state apparatus of sports, physical education and recreation. We started from primarily revolutionary criteria, which today we can say were Marxist criteria. In that moment, however, we knew very little about Marxism. Today, looking back on what we did, we launched a whole dialectical process that was truly just. . . .

In a way we wanted everyone to have the conditions of life that the children of the ruling class had. This forced us to think that what we wanted was for all children to have physical education as a part of an integrated education. We wanted every citizen to have the right to recreation. We wanted sports to cease being a formal performance to line some people's pockets, to be a way to educate the people and create a new generation. Theoretically, this sounds good, but putting it in practice with the weight of our inherited problems, our shortcomings, our ignorance, was not easy.

We . . . experimented with sports to try to find a method that would permit mass participation in sports, to give everyone the opportunity to practice and play sports. At the same time, we wanted competition, the climax of sports, to have an ideological foundation while serving as a process of collective, accelerated development.

. . . INDER was . . . among the new institutions created by Law 936 in 1961. Initially, it has the powers to direct, orient, and plan the development of sports, physical education, and recreation as an integrated whole. Law 936 states that this institution is to promote and stimulate the participation of the masses in this development process through the creation of Voluntary Sports Councils. These councils, created in workplaces, schools, and peasant areas, are composed of people who have a talent for sports and want to contribute something to and work in sports. . . .

INDER sets national policy for the development of physical education in schools and directs student programs in cooperation with the Ministry of Education that implements them at every level from day-care centers to the university. Over the last 16 years, we've had results in young people's development and growth, functional capacity, habits and sports culture. . . .

In statistical terms we reach all the basic secondary schools, all the vocational schools, university preparatory institutes, technological institutes and universities. That is not the case for primary schools. In the cities physical education is offered to about 60 percent of the elementary schoolchildren. In the countryside, in the peasant areas, it is definitely worse; only 10 percent of the children have physical education. This is one of the serious problems we are trying to solve. Since the primary school population, between 6 and 12 years of age, is very large, there aren't enough facilities, equipment, or instructors.

. . . Even when enough instructors graduate, the pace of construction is inadequate; many schools don't have the proper sports facilities. In the old schools, in old Havana for example, where there aren't even any sidewalks, it is pretty difficult to have physical education.

In sports at present, we statistically have a participation of 4.7 million a year. This does not mean 4.7 million individuals, because one person might participate in three sports and, of course, each time he plays during the year it is counted. . . .

. . . Though we do not have the final results of statistical surveys yet, we believe that there are about 1.5 million people between the ages of 10 and 40 participating in sports. This is a respectable figure for a population which isn't quite 10 million.

SPORTS AND POLITICS

. . . Bourgeois theoreticians say that politics has nothing to do with sports. We take a totally contrary view. Politics is an instrument to serve sports, to make sports humanized and educational, to make sports the right of every citizen. Independent of whether a citizen has medals or not, the most important thing is that all the people can take part in sports and improve their health.

With that concept, we tried to find a system of participation. The majority of sports systems have many sports clubs participating at a given level. Let's say New York City has a municipal basketball championship with 30 teams. They all compete by some formula, by simple elimination, by double elimination, by "round robin" or whatever. But in the end there is a champion, only one wins. Then there are 29 remaining teams in New York City which are left behind defeated and frustrated. A valuable group of players doesn't continue playing because only one team represents New York and goes on to compete in other championships.

We began to think over this problem of elimination formulas in team sports. In order for every single good player to be able to develop his potential, we decided to make a selection of the athletes from amongst the losing teams. At the municipal level, then, the competition begins with the teams from schools, factories, military bases and peasant areas. All these teams go to the national convocation of the championship for baseball or soccer or whatever. When the competition is over, let's say, the Salvador Allende Basic Secondary School is the winner. But there may have been nine other teams participating. So a selection is made among the players of the remaining nine teams, which then takes the name of the municipality. If the competition were in Marianao, for example, it would be called Marianao. Then they move to the provincial competition, the two teams, the champions and the selection.

This way of conducting competitions guarantees development of individual athletes with potential, but for us that isn't what is most important; what is important is the ideological factor.

Because of the thorough imperialist exploitation, our country inherited incredible atomization of classes, a violent class struggle. It was necessary that sports serve to aid the disappearance of these irreconcilable class positions. When the students, soldiers, workers, and peasants who played in the nine teams that lost become part of the selection team, we achieve an extraordinary degree of integration.

. . . The athlete then sees that the province is no more than a political-administrative division of the country in the interest of development. He begins to realize that the entire country is his territory, that its traditions, ideology, and principles are his. Therefore, when the athlete goes abroad to compete, he competes for powerful reasons. People don't understand this, the force of ideology is much more powerful than any steroid or artificial drug that is given to an athlete.

PYRAMID OF SPORTS EXCELLENCE

The national organization of sports looks like a pyramid and its base is the permanent source of mass participation in sports, that is, the more than two million children who participate in school. At the primary school level there are special sports facilities where a trainer is present. Teachers recommend certain students for the special sports facilities on the basis of a selection test using specific criteria related to the particular sport. These children continue at their same school, and care is taken that they participate in all the normal school activities so as not to isolate them. They may go to a special sports facility or simply have a different physical education schedule at the same school's facility. All the elementary schoolchildren from the special sports facilities are tested, and the best go on to the intermediate level, the specialized sports secondary schools called Escuelas de Iniciacion Deportiva Escolar (EIDE). We have seven EIDE's, one in each of the six provinces, two in Oriente. One day we hope to have 14, one in each province. [Ed. Note: In 1976 Cuba reorganized its provinces from six to 14.]

This school is the initiation to sports. While there is academic study and physical education, there is also a training schedule. With observation and without pressing the youngster, we seek athletic achievement. . . .

At the top of the pyramid is an advanced school, Escuela Superior de Perfeccionamiento Atletico (Advanced School for Athletic Perfection) or ESPA, for highly specialized sports training. . . .

ESPA is a single national school. This system is based on the movement from mass participation toward expertise, a process of development which an athlete must undergo scientifically. It is never less than six years or more than ten, depending on the sport. . . .

We do not aspire to have athletes like robots, or athletes who represent our country at the cost of their own alienation. We want men and women who represent this nation, who can relate to other people educated in the revolutionary process, who are capable of feeling the revolution as a natural feeling not as something imposed, and who are capable of defining the revolution as a result of their own feelings. Moreover, they must acquire a cultural level which allows them to understand and evaluate what goes on in the world and be able to identify clearly its ideological framework. Further, they must have sufficient sophistication to recognize their own efforts and to value them. They should be able to converse with the trainers, doctors, psychologists and not be just on the receiving end of orders. Only in this manner can we really obtain the kind of athlete who is revolutionary.

CHAPTER 15

Social Services

48. Twenty-five Years of Cuban Health Care*

BY ROBERT N. UBELL

When Cuban guerrilla bands fought in remote mountain villages more than a quarter of a century ago, one of their first promises was to provide Cubans with medical care equal to any in the world. Today, on the eve of the silver anniversary of the "triumph of the revolution," even Cuba's detractors admit that the new government has made good on that commitment. Although in certain respects Cuba's revolutionaries started with a nation somewhat less medically deprived than other Third World countries, Cubans still suffered the punishment of poverty and neglect. Now the island has emerged in such good health that its medical statistics rival those in the industrialized world. [See Appendix B, Part III.] The cruel irony of the achievement is that now, like the advanced industrialized countries, Cuba is faced with cancer, heart disease, and stroke as the three leading causes of death.[1]

Today, life expectancy in Cuba is close to that in the United States. And since the 1970s, the nation's infant mortality rate has been reduced by more than half—from 38.0 to 17.3 per 1,000 live births. In the United States[2] the rate is 11.2, but among black Americans it is 21.1. By the mid-1970s, polio had been entirely eliminated in Cuba. The last death caused by diphtheria occurred more than a decade ago. Cases of tuberculosis were down to well under 100 by last year. Nearly 5,000 cases of tuberculosis were reported annually just before the revolution; today, deaths from the disease have all but disappeared.

*From *New England Journal of Medicine*, Vol. 309, No. 23 (December 8, 1983), pp. 1468–72.

Deaths from other infectious diseases, including malaria and gastroenteritis, which were leading causes of mortality before the revolution, are negligible.[3]

The new government provides medical care for all Cubans at no charge. The bill for these services comes to more than 15 percent of the nation's gross national product. The figure is 10 percent in the United States and 8 percent in Canada.[4] By most standards, Cuba is enormously generous in its health care.

The country's entire health-care system is run by the Ministry of Public Health [Ministerio de Salud Pública], a vast bureaucracy that not only employs all the island's doctors and other health-care workers but also runs its clinics, hospitals, nursing homes, and other services. The Ministry's arm also stretches across Cuba's medical, nursing, and allied technical schools. Everything associated with medicine, including the pharmaceutical industry, local pharmacies, and druggists, falls under the Ministry's authority.

POLYCLINICS

Cuba's system is comparable in some ways to the Czech model on which it was initially based but differs in its attempts to decentralize a far-flung bureaucracy.[5] The most prominent feature of this effort is the local polyclinic. However, even though the aim is to permit more autonomy, in fact, the 397 polyclinics on the island are largely cut from the same mold. All are headed by a physician-director, and all deliver a fairly standard core of services, planned at the top by the Ministry.

The physician-dominated system has come up against patient dissatisfaction, and doctors have responded by meeting certain community demands. For example, the patient is no longer seen by whatever physician happens to be on duty but is treated by his or her own doctor, who is responsible for all families within a defined neighborhood. The doctor is usually familiar with the patient's medical history and family. What's more, patients need no longer wait while their clinical records are retrieved from a central file. Instead, physicians can easily locate the records on open shelves in consulting rooms.

Polyclinics are the principal facilities for ambulatory care.[6] They were first launched as a nationwide primary health-care system in 1965, just six years after the revolution. Earlier, Cubans either had been treated by private physicians or had participated in *mutualista* medical-care associations, a Cuban variant of health-maintenance organizations.[7] Much of the population (and particularly Cubans living in the countryside) received almost no medical attention. Some people relied on *curanderos* (traditional healers).

Staffed by young, Cuban-trained doctors, nurses, and other personnel, the island's polyclinics provide treatment in both rural and urban settings. Typically, an urban clinic serves 20,000 to 30,000 people, but in remote areas as few as 7,500 people may be served. Each clinic has a team of community medical workers who offer routine care. At Polyclinic Plaza, for example, a three-story structure in a mixed working-class-professional neighborhood in

Havana, nine internists, a half-dozen pediatricians, several obstetrician-gynecologists, a group of psychologists, and an ophthalmologist are on duty. Some clinics also offer dentistry. The facilities are open to the public from 9:00 in the morning until late in the afternoon. Most doctors and nurses go out into the community after lunch, making team house calls, visiting patients at risk on a nondemand basis, and surveying local health conditions.

In the pediatric department of Polyclinic Plaza, located on the ground floor, the children appear to feel at home as they dash in and out of the waiting room, which is open to the street. Surprisingly, neither the staff nor the mothers, who chat while waiting to be called, seem to mind the noise or the frisky playroom atmosphere. Healthy babies under one year of age are scheduled to be seen by their pediatrician twice a month, and at least once in the first year, the doctor, often accompanied by a nurse, visits the baby at home. From 2 to 5 years, the child comes to the clinic twice a year; from 6 to 15 years (the age at which the family doctor assumes responsibility), the child is more likely to be seen by the school doctor or the physician associated with the day-care center.[8] Pediatric visits in 1982 averaged 2.8 per patient per year, up from 1.2 per year just before the revolution.[9]

No appointments are required, and some patients may wait for an hour or more, especially during busy morning hours, before being called. Others are taken soon after they arrive. As in the National Health Service in England, patients must first see their family physician, who provides general treatment and refers them to appropriate specialists or arranges for hospitalization. According to official figures, from 1967 to 1982, the average number of patient visits to doctors' offices increased from three to five per year.[10] Workers do not receive wages for time taken off from their jobs to obtain routine care at a polyclinic. But if illness keeps them off their jobs for more than three days, they receive 50 percent of their salary.

In need of a fresh coat of paint, Polyclinic Plaza does not appear institutional by U.S. standards; it looks more like a community center than a neighborhood health-care facility. Patients are seen in small, simply furnished consulting and examining rooms by doctors who are generally in their early 30s. A nurse usually stands by at each examination. Of the dozen or so physicians on duty during my visit to Polyclinic Plaza, all were women (except for one male internist), and most were black. The presence of large numbers of black physicians—and notably, black women doctors—throughout the Cuban medical-care system is striking to a U.S. observer.

HOSPITALS

In 1959 there were 58 hospitals in Cuba, most of which were either proprietary or religious.[11] Approximately 60 percent of all hospital beds were in Havana. To redress the imbalance and fulfill a promise to bring medical care to remote parts of the country, the revolutionary government has constructed many facilities elsewhere on the island. Although the number of beds in Havana has remained fairly stable over the past 25 years, the percentages have been reversed; now 40 percent of Cuba's hospital beds are in Havana and 60 percent are in rural areas and other cities and towns. Moreover, the total number of beds has nearly doubled, from 28,563 in 1959 to 47,327 at the end of 1983.[12]

Today, when polyclinic doctors advise further treatment outside the community, they send their patients to one of 256 hospitals located throughout the country.[13] More than a third of these medical facilities are general hospitals in cities and larger towns. Some 50 others are rural hospitals in villages and outlying regions. National medical institutes carry out highly specialized procedures, such as kidney transplantations and some heart operations. Provincial hospitals provide a good deal of the tertiary care in the country. Regional and municipal hospitals offer secondary care, including routine surgery.[14] Children are sent to separate pediatric facilities, and almost all newborns (98.9 percent) are delivered in maternity hospitals. Cuba also has a wide range of hospitals offering other kinds of specialized care, including cardiology, ophthalmology, and psychiatry, among others. As in the United Kingdom, in Cuba the general practitioner entrusts the care of a patient to specialists the moment the patient enters the hospital. According to one observer,[15] the treatment offered in Cuban hospitals is not unlike that found in Britain.

At the Joaquin M. Albarran Hospital, one of 14 teaching facilities attached to Havana's medical school, a staff of 1,000, including 160 physicians, 160 nurses, 200 technicians, and 50 administrators, serves a community of 86,000 in a region with six polyclinics. Built as a private-care hospital just before the revolution and located not far from Havana's giant sports complex, Albarran is a modest place in the style of local U.S. hospitals of the 1950s. It is a general hospital and offers no pediatric, maternity, or psychiatric care. With seven X-ray machines (largely of German make) and other fairly up-to-date instruments, including equipment for ultrasonic diagnosis, endoscopy, and automated blood chemical analysis (practically all Japanese), the hospital performs all clinical tests in its own laboratories. CAT scanning, however, is performed elsewhere. Albarran orders equipment from the provincial arm of the Ministry. "We have no problem getting what we need," reported Enrique Filgueiras, the hospital's physician-director, "but often what we receive depends on the U.S. embargo and our economic conditions."

Although most of the drugs (83 percent) used in Cuba are manufactured by its own pharmaceutical industry, certain substances remain in short supply. The shortage is related in part to the U.S. embargo, since a few key drugs are available primarily in the United States. Filgueiras claimed, however, that the government takes extraordinary steps to secure the needed pharmaceuticals elsewhere. The USSR and Eastern Europe contribute some drugs, and others come from Sweden, Mexico, Spain, and other Western European countries.

The U.S. embargo has also damaged Cuba's medical-literature resources. Current issues of many periodicals are unavailable, and physicians and research workers complain bitterly about the lack of up-to-date literature.

Albarran's 531 beds are constantly filled, reported one administrator, and its emergency service handles about 400 to 450 patients a day, mostly for acute respiratory conditions (notably, asthma and pneumonia). Six hundred people pass through the hospital's outpatient clinics each day. The emergency-room and outpatient departments are overcrowded, despite the availability of treatment at neighborhood polyclinics. One observer commented that many Cubans believe the "real doctors" are found in hospitals. Still, as one hospital official explained, a possible reason that outpatient waiting rooms tend to be jammed is that people show up hours before their scheduled appointments—a complaint frequently voiced by hospital administrators elsewhere.

Each ward at Albarran Hospital contains seven beds in a clean, open, well-lighted room. Patients lounge on beds or in chairs, chatting in a friendly, communal atmosphere. No privacy is offered; there are no curtains to draw around the beds. Doctors see patients in examining rooms off the ward. A color television set is available for patients on each floor.

The families of patients in intensive care are given reports by physicians at appointed hours three times a day, and a day-and-night telephone service also reports on patient status. Patients on regular wards may be attended by one family member 24 hours a day—a practice that was introduced in 1978 in adult-care hospitals throughout Cuba. The hospitals provide free meals for these visitors. Round-the-clock visiting was first offered to parents of children in pediatric hospitals in 1969.

At adult-care hospitals like Albarran, the average stay is ten to 14 days for general treatment and eight to ten days for surgery. Costs at Albarran run from $35 to $40 per patient-day, but it is unclear whether physicians' salaries and plant costs are included in these figures. The hospital's annual budget is estimated at about $5 million a year.

NEW CENTRAL HOSPITAL

The most spectacular medical center in Cuba is the recently completed Hermanos Almejeiras Hospital, a 24-story tower in central Havana overlooking the bay. Many visitors from abroad are surprised that such a facility exists in a country still struggling to provide essential services to its people. It stands as a striking symbol of Cuba's zeal for high-technology medicine. The nine hundred-bed national-care center is the first major hospital to be built in the capital since the revolution; it was under construction for 10 years.

The Hermanos Almejeiras Hospital has a staff of 2,500 serving a population of more than a quarter of a million. The center's sleek public areas and halls, sheathed from floor to ceiling in local, pale-colored marble, and its gleaming modern facilities present an imposing face. The hospital is well equipped with high-powered diagnostic tools from all over the world; the latest and most sophisticated equipment is mostly from Japan.

The $45-million center, designed for postgraduate work, offers 36 specialties, primarily in six areas: advanced heart, brain, and reconstructive surgery, gastroenterology, psychiatry, and nuclear medicine. Five of the center's 25 operating rooms are used for microsurgery. The hospital is completely automated and houses two main-frame computers and 32 display units; it is also equipped with the island's second CAT scanner.

MEDICAL EDUCATION

Most students enter medical school at about 18 years of age, right after they complete secondary school, without passing through four years of liberal arts college, as students do in the United States. No examination is required to gain admission, but students must have achieved a 92 percent grade average in high school. "Grades are not the only criteria for entrance," noted Manuel Peña, chief of research at Havana's medical school. "You must also want to be a doctor. You must have the right moral characteristics for a medical career, and you must have revolutionary feeling."

Students who do not succeed in achieving satisfactory high school grades but who still wish to become a doctor can pursue studies in an allied health profession; if they succeed and pass special entrance examinations, they too are admitted to medical school. Some 5 percent of each class enter through this door. Because of the enormous demand on the medical schools, Peña predicted that "perhaps an examination will come yet," even for secondary school students with high marks.

"Women are invading the medical school," Peña observed, reporting that 52 percent of the students now enrolled at Havana's medical school are women. This represents the continuation of a steady increase that began in the early days after the revolution. Unlike women in the Soviet Union, who practiced medicine in large numbers even before the Bolshevik Revolution, Cuban women were largely excluded from medicine under Batista and earlier. From 1728, when it was founded, until 1959, the medical school at the University of Havana graduated only 496 women physicians.[16] Today, women account for 38 percent of all registered doctors in Cuba, but more than half of them practice general medicine, with few found in the specialties. For example, only 3.5 percent of women doctors are obstetricians, and only 1.8 percent practice psychiatry.[17] Remarkably, the revolutionary government has offered women unprecedented opportunities for participation in medicine, but as is sadly true in the rest of the world, in Cuba the top ranks of the profession are occupied mostly by men, who also predominate at the Ministry. . . .

Large numbers of foreign students, principally from other Latin American countries, Arab nations, and Africa, are enrolled in Cuban medical schools. At Havana's medical school, some 200 of the 2,800 students come from abroad. In all, there are 1,743 foreign medical students in Cuba. Cuban and foreign students alike receive free medical education; some are offered stipends.

Cuban medical school graduates no longer take the Hippocratic oath. Instead, they promise to abide by new revolutionary principles: renunciation of private practice and agreement to serve in rural areas, to practice in the name of the people, to promote preventive medicine and human welfare, to strive for scientific excellence and political devotion, to encourage proletarian internationalism, and to defend the Cuban Revolution.[18] All graduates, upon earning their degrees, are required to perform rural service, practicing community medicine in the countryside. Soon after the revolution, young doctors were sent to the mountains and to the farms for 14 months. But as the number of physicians increased, so did the period of rural duty. In 1968 it was increased to two years, and the current three-year period of service was introduced in 1974.

After completing their rural duty, physicians have several options: perform a residency in one of 38 specialties, pursue internal or general medicine without additional training, or (a new option) complete a three-year stint in a teaching hospital in order to practice "family" medicine in a polyclinic. Future plans call for all doctors (including those who wish to practice internal medicine) to enter a residency program before they specialize. Werner discovered that "Despite [the] universal status and increased exposure of medical students to community medicine, after their . . . compulsory rural service, 80% of doctors still apply for residencies in some branch of highly specialized, hospital-centered curative care."[19]

Although most U.S. doctors would find the Cuban system strange, many would feel at home in Cuba, where doctors enjoy considerable prestige and have wide latitude in making most decisions about patient care and medical policy. Several attempts have been made to give the people a larger share in public-health decision making. Community and women's organizations, such as the Committees for the Defense of the Revolution and the Federation of Cuban Women, participate in local policy making. But in the end, the doctor remains the key authority. Cuban rhetoric appeals to doctors to embrace egalitarian principles, but Cuban physicians find themselves in a conspicuously well-paid, elite profession. Salaries for Cuban doctors range from as little as $250 a month for residents to as much as $718 for full professors. The professors who are at the highest levels of their profession are among the highest paid of all Cubans, often receiving salaries equal to or exceeding those paid to government ministers. The average salary for all Cuban workers is about $200 per month.

CLINICAL RESEARCH

Students who wish to follow a research track do not receive a sixth year of hospital training. Instead, they return to medical school, where they take advanced courses in physical and biological sciences. At the end of the sixth year, they receive their medical degrees along with the other students, but they do not perform rural service. Instead, they complete at least one more year of advanced study at school. Many continue for two or three more years.

Clinical and biomedical research is performed by eager young physicians and scientists, many of whom have gone abroad for postgraduate work at top foreign laboratories, not only in the Soviet Union and Eastern Europe but at leading centers in Canada, Scandinavia, and other Western European countries.

The Basic Science Institute, where Peña is research director, is housed in the Higher Institute of Medical Sciences, Havana's medical school. In 1962 the faculty moved into its present quarters, a Stanford-like campus on the grounds of a former wealthy Catholic girls' school in a lush Havana suburb. New dormitories, a computer center, and other modern buildings circle the older, classical structures.

New avenues of research at the medical school are now funded by the "Biological Front," a high-level, policy-making body formed just two years ago. Created to speed up focused research, the Front provides new laboratories with direct government support, short-circuiting red tape. Cuba's new Center for Biological Research, another laboratory not far from the medical school, where production and purification of interferon are under way, was the first facility to be placed under the Front's umbrella last year. The Center has performed several promising, although modest, clinical trials with alpha interferon.[20] A number of other laboratories perform biomedical research; prominent among them is the National Center for Scientific Research, where recombinant-DNA studies are just beginning.

Pilot studies to detect sickle-cell anemia have revealed a relatively high incidence of the disorder among Cubans. Nearly 4 percent of all Cubans (and as much as 7 percent of the population in the eastern provinces) are at risk. "Many Cubans are of mixed races," noted Peña. "It is almost impossible to judge who is white and who is black," so all will be screened. Thus far, genetic screening has been limited to research-level trials and is generally available only in a few provinces. But early next year, Peña reported, detection services for neural-tube defects and sickle-cell anemia, as well as for Down's syndrome and phenylketonuria, will be introduced nationwide. Apart from genetics, Havana's medical-school research concentrates on perinatal growth and development, arterial hypertension, obesity, and immunology (mainly, studies of hepatitis B).

"MEDICAL POWER"

Cuba is creating large armies of young doctors. Some 17,300 students are currently enrolled at its 17 medical schools and four medical colleges. Since 1959, Cuba has trained approximately 16,000 doctors—nearly three times the number that were practicing the day the guerrilla army marched into Havana.[21] At that time, there were 6,300 physicians in the country, but almost half of them fled the island in the first five years after the revolution. Last year alone, Cuba produced just under 1,100 doctors. Sergio del Valle, the minister of public health, reports that this year Cuba expects to add over 2,500 more as part of a new policy aimed at training large numbers of physicians in the next decades. "By 1985, we expect to graduate 3,000 and then increase continuously. Between 1983 and the year 2000, we expect to train 50,000 doctors," del Valle predicted. Today, Cuba claims more than 17 doctors per 10,000 inhabitants, or one for every 750 people, as compared with one for every 540 people in the United States and one for every 1,750 people in Brazil (one of the more developed countries in the Americas).[22]

Many new graduates are headed for foreign service, following contingents that have served in the Third World since 1963, when the first medical brigades arrived in Algeria.[23] Today, 3,044 Cuban health workers, including 1,743 physicians, serve abroad. In Angola, for example, there are 847 Cuban doctors, nurses, and other health personnel. Cuban physicians are also stationed in 26 other countries, including Nicaragua, Vietnam, and Ethiopia.

Dispatched for one to two years and often working under hardship, young Cuban doctors commonly provide routine community health care to people with few or no other medical resources. In some countries, Cuban physicians represent a large fraction of the medical work force. Most nations receive the medical aid at no cost; a few, however, pay for it. Cuban doctors abroad receive wages comparable to those earned by local doctors, and their families receive the full salary the doctors would have been paid had they remained on the island. Cubans also provide training, biomedical research, and other services overseas. In South Yemen, for instance, they have helped the new government establish its first medical school.

Having been successful at home, Cuba is clearly on the road to exploiting its medical triumphs internationally. Fidel Castro sees the next phase as one in which his country will emerge as a "world medical power." What this slogan means in practice is not entirely clear. Certainly, Cuba believes that it can set an example for the rest of the developing world. The big surprise may come when Cuba turns its health services to its own economic advantage. The government's massive investment in what at first glance seems to be an essentially nonproductive endeavor may be a platform from which to take the next leap. Having instituted health-care measures equal to those in many industrialized nations, Cuba may now be able to focus its attention on putting its people to work more productively and creatively. A nation hobbled by disease and poverty cannot accomplish much. And in the long run, Cuba may be able to export more than its doctors and nurses. Its medical-support industries (pharmaceuticals, computers, and other services) may follow sugar into the world market in the next decades.

Cuba has engineered a national medical apparatus that is the envy of many developing nations. For some of these nations, it is not Boston, Massachusetts, but Havana, Cuba, that is the center of the medical world. At a recent international health-care conference (Health for All, held in Havana July 1 to 10, 1983), delegates from the Third World responded enthusiastically to accounts of Cuba's successful endeavors in health care. Still, many remained puzzled over how to implement similar strategies in their own countries. Obviously, Cuba made the fundamental choice years ago not to rely on paramedical care. Unimpressed with "barefoot doctors," Cuba has systematically supported the far more expensive route of training and equipping Western-style physicians. Many health officials from developing nations doubt that they could implement a similar system of capital-intensive, physician-dominated, high-technology medicine without the sustained and heavy contributions Cuba receives from the USSR. Yet they recognize that the promise of high-quality health care in Cuba has been kept not merely with the aid of Soviet rubles and oil but with the island's own political and social will.

"The commitment to health of this country's leadership is truly remarkable," said Halfdan Mahler, director-general of the World Health Organization, speaking in Havana in early July. "As for Cuba's self-reliance in health matters . . . it has become legendary."[24] Mahler's assessment echoes the reports of dramatic reversals in Cuban medical care that have been widely and prominently published in scholarly periodicals outside Cuba. In the United States, much of this news has been received with skepticism or, worse, has been ignored. But in view of recent events in Central America and the Caribbean, this may be the right moment to recognize what Cuba has achieved.

NOTES

1. *Informe Anual 1982* (Havana: Minisiterio de Salud Pública, 1983), pp. 18–55.

2. H. M. Smith, "Castro's Medicine," *MD,* Vol. 27 (1983), pp. 144–63.

3. *Informe Anual 1982,* pp. 18–55.

4. H. M. Smith, "Castro's Medicine," pp. 144–63.

5. R. S. Danielson, *Cuban Medicine* (New Brunswick, NJ: Transaction Books, 1979), pp. 127–63.

6. R. S. Danielson, "The Cuban Health Area and Polyclinic: Organizational Focus in an Emerging System," *Inquiry,* Vol. 12 (1975), July Supplement, pp. 86–102.

7. R. S. Danielson, *Cuban Medicine,* p. 127–63.

8. M. Leiner and R. Ubell, *Children Are the Revolution: Day Care in Cuba* (New York: Viking Press, 1974), pp. 119–44.

9. *Informe Anual 1982*, pp. 18–55.

10. Ibid., pp. 18–55.

11. P. Orris, *The Sociology of Health and Medical Care: Citizen Involvement in Cuba, 1959–1980*, Report No. 81 (Chicago: Red Feather Institute for Advanced Studies in Sociology, 1980), pp. 1–40.

12. *Health for All: 25 Years of Cuban Experience* (Havana: Ministerio de Salud Pública, July 1983), pp. 16–18.

13. *Informe Anual 1982*, pp. 18–55.

14. D. Campos-Outcalt and E. Janoff, "Health Care in Modern Cuba," *West Journal of Medicine*, Vol. 132 (1980), pp. 265–71.

15. V. Navarro, "Health, Health Services, and Health Planning in Cuba," *International Journal of Health Services*, Vol. 2 (1972), pp. 397–432.

16. R. S. Danielson, *Cuban Medicine*, pp. 127–63.

17. *Información Estadística*, No. 4 (Havana: Ministerio de Salud Pública, June 1983), pp. 1–15.

18. D. Campos-Outcalt and E. Janoff, "Health Care in Modern Cuba," pp. 265–71.

19. D. Werner, *Health Care in Cuba Today: A Model Service or a Means of Social Control—or Both* (Palo Alto, CA: Hesperian Foundation, 1978), pp. 1–38.

20. R. Ubell, "Cuba Launches Interferon Lab," *Bio/Technology*, Vol. 1 (1983), pp. 343–44.

21. P. Orris, *The Sociology of Health and Medical Care*, pp. 1–40.

22. H. M. Smith, "Castro's Medicine," pp. 144–63.

23. P. H. Grundy and P. P. Budetti, "The Distribution and Supply of Cuban Medical Personnel in Third World Countries," *American Journal of Public Health*, Vol. 70 (1980), pp. 717–19.

24. Ministerio de Salud Publica, *Health for All: 25 Years of Cuban Experience* (Havana: Ministerio de Salud Pública, 1983), pp. 16–18.

49. *Cuba's Schools: 25 Years Later**

By Marvin Leiner

After my first visit to Cuba in 1968–69, I reported that "throughout Cuba, in the city streets and alongside rural roads, banners proclaim education as one of the most important themes of the Revolution." I recognized that slogans like "The path up from underdevelopment is education" or "The school plan is your responsibility" were not simply propagandistic platitudes but rather reflected the high priority given to education there.[1]

Now 25 years after its revolution, Cuba's highest flag is still the banner of education. More than one-third of the people—3.5 million—including nearly all children between the ages of 6 and 12, are enrolled in school. The number of teachers committed to the educational enterprise is a source of national

*From Sandor Halebsky and John M. Kirk, eds., *Cuba: Twenty-five Years of Revolution, 1959–1984* (New York: Praeger Publishers, 1985), pp. 27–44. Edited for this volume.

pride. During the 1982–83 school year Cuba had approximately 250,000 teachers and professors, more than 83,000 in the primary schools, more than 94,000 in the secondary schools, almost 8,600 in special education, approximately 25,000 in adult education, and nearly 12,500 in university centers. The present teaching population is approximately 11 times higher than before the revolution with 130,000 having been added to the teaching force since the early 1970s.[2]

EDUCATION IN PREREVOLUTIONARY CUBA

During the 1950s, just before the revolution, only about one half of the island's primary-school age children were enrolled in school. In poor communities, especially in rural areas, enrollment was even lower. Lowry Nelson, in his study of rural Cuba, noted: "In some places there are school buildings, but no teachers; in other places there are teachers, but no school buildings. There has been no systematic plan of school-building construction for rural areas. . . ." He concluded that "little if any progress has been made since 1907 in providing school opportunities for the nation's children."[3]

A 1951 World Bank report documenting administrative waste, inefficiency, and corruption in the schools explains that historically "A teacher in Cuba was a government official, with life tenure on full salary, whether teaching or not." It found that outright purchases of appointments occurred and quoted a former education minister, who characterized his ministry as "an opprobrium," "a shame," and "a dangerous menace to the Cuban nation." The report recognized the decline in "the quality and morale of the teaching and supervisory force" and noted the public's lack of confidence in its public schools.[4] . . .

NATIONAL GOALS AND EDUCATIONAL CHANGE

Once the revolutionary leadership assumed power, Cuba's education was set on an altogether different path. The new objectives sought to halt stagnation and give education highest priority—not merely in state planning but also in practice—by providing large budgets for school construction, program development, teacher training, and the national mobilization to eliminate illiteracy.

At the end of the new Cuban road, schooling was to be made available to all, especially the poor living in rural areas. In addition, education was reoriented to help achieve national goals: "to replace the rigid class structure of capitalist Cuba with a classless and egalitarian society; to eliminate sexism and racism; to end the city's economic and cultural domination over the countryside."[5]

What's more, education came to be regarded as a tool for promoting development through the training of a skilled and technically proficient population and for drastically altering the traditionally hostile attitudes toward science, technology, and modern agricultural methods. With education of the masses as one of its top priorities, Cuba nationalized all schools, reorganized its school system, and embarked on its extraordinary Literacy Campaign. The changes initiated in 1959—which continue even today—are unique in the history of world education.

The Literacy Campaign is considered by a number of scholars to be a major achievement of the early stages of the Cuban Revolution, representing a "large-scale government effort to advance the level of education and break down the psychological barriers to participation by adults in efforts to educate them."[6]

Literacy is a word with various definitions—both historically and currently. It is important, therefore, to note the achieved literacy level in 1961: "From a technical point of view, the campaign was one of providing a first grade level of reading and writing."[7] The achievement of a first-grade level for 96.1 percent of the population was the highest in Latin America and among the highest in the world. For the next decade, adult education classes throughout the island followed up the literacy campaign to win the "Battle for the Sixth Grade." From 1962–63 through 1973–74 more than one half million adults completed sixth-grade adult education programs.[8] . . .

QUANTITATIVE ACHIEVEMENTS

Jorge I. Domínguez, noted scholar on contemporary Cuba, suggests that "because the middle third of the twentieth century witnessed educational stagnation in literacy and school enrollment, the quantitative achievements of the revolutionary government are truly impressive."[9] Some of these quantitative changes, that is, the numbers of students, schools, and teachers, are illustrated in the Table on p. 448. These would not have been possible without a huge investment in education—the budget increasing steadily from 12 pesos per person in 1959 to 137 pesos per person in 1980.[10]

A major indicator of social and educational change is the percentage of children in school. Whereas a little over one half of Cuba's children were enrolled in school in 1956, virtually all children aged 6 to 12 go to school today. The secondary school population has also increased dramatically. Today, more than 84 percent of the 13–16 year olds are enrolled in secondary schools, a figure 13 times higher than that for 1958–59.

. . . In 1959 there were only three university centers in the country, and all were located in provincial capitals. Humanities (23 percent) and economics (29 percent) were the dominant disciplines. Few students came from the working class or peasant families.

In contrast, there are now 40 university centers with a student population 14 times greater, a curriculum embracing 150 different specialties and a large

Enrollment, Schools, and Teachers in Cuba
1958–59 and 1982–83

	1958–59			1982–83		
Type of Education	Number of Students	Number of Schools	Number of Teachers	Number of Students	Number of Schools	Number of Teachers
Day care				80,575	839	17,688
Kindergarten	91,700			118,072*		5,258*
Elementary	625,717	7,567	17,355	1,363,078	11,215	83,358
Secondary	88,135	80	4,571	1,116,930	1,915	94,193
Special				37,058	352	8,576
Adult				392,945	1,418	25,376
Youth				19,663	143	2,165
Higher education	2,063	6		200,000	40	12,433
Others	3,730	28	669	2,303		393
TOTAL	811,345		22,595	3,330,624		249,440

*Note that kindergarten programs are offered in elementary schools and day-care centers.

Blank spaces indicate that data were not available. "Youth" includes special programs for 13–16 year olds who are behind normal grade level. "Others" include foreigners taking special courses.

Source: *Suplemento al Resumen del Trabajo del MINED,* 1982–1983 (Havana: Ministry of Education, 1983).

number of blacks and women in all specializations, ranging from medicine to the agricultural sciences. Women are 46 percent of the total university population. In 1983 Cuba ranked twentieth of 142 countries in the world—ahead of major Latin American countries such as Argentina, Brazil, Chile, Mexico, Colombia, and Venezuela—in percentage of women enlisted in university programs.[11] About 50 percent of the current student body works, and higher education is not only tuition-free, but students also receive support in the form of lodging, board, and stipends.

Even while recognizing Cuba's giant steps in higher education, the real drama has been elsewhere—in day care, primary, and secondary education, and adult education. Day-care centers, known as *círculos infantiles,* are open to children from 45 days old up to age 6 (through kindergarten), although many of the nurseries I visited had few children less than one year old. From extensive interviews with day-care leaders and staff, I learned that their goal was to educate the "whole child." Specifically, they wanted to provide a strong basis for later growth in reading, mathematics, and science. At the same time these centers insist upon three nutritionally balanced meals a day, emphasize health care, and are much concerned with cleanliness.

These *círculos,* under the direction of the Federation of Cuban Women, permit mothers to enter the country's work force and provide them with their first real opportunity to further their education. In 1983, 839 day-care centers existed with an enrollment of 93,200 and a staff of almost 17,000.[12]

THE "PERFECCIONAMIENTO"—A PLAN FOR IMPROVING SCHOOLING IN CUBA (1976–1981)

In 1976, after 17 years of experience under the new policies, Cubans started to restructure their school system. The "Plan for Improving Schooling" had its roots in the National Congress of Education and Culture held in Havana, April 23–30, 1971. Among the 3,106 recommendations proposed by teacher delegates were suggestions for changes in curriculum, more efficient organization of the school system and use of time, improvement of teacher training, and development of new textbooks and materials. According to a five-year *Perfeccionamiento* (1976–1981) plan, the educational system would offer 12 instead of 13 years of schooling for all children. More classroom hours would be demanded, however. Under the new plan, the nation guaranteed to all its children one year of kindergarten. There were 107,700 enrolled kindergarten students in 1983–1984, although the universalization of kindergarten education has not yet been realized.

The revamped elementary school program now offers two stages—grades 1–4 in self-contained classrooms (cycle 1), grades 5–6 (cycle 2) offering "special subjects." In the first cycle, children stay with the same teacher for all four years. Cycle 2, more conventional in nature, is followed by three years of junior high and three of senior high school.[13] Compulsory education through grade 9 has been discussed but has not yet been put into effect. Currently, a sixth-grade education is compulsory.

The first elementary school cycle is expected to provide "solid training in the mother tongue and mathematics." Schools at that level aim at helping children develop "skills and habits necessary for independent work." What's more, they hope to "inculcate a love for study and to contribute to the ideological and integral formation of the pupils."[14]

Cuban educators argue that the self-contained, same-teacher organization of cycle 1 enables the teacher to support and know the young child. They claim that the resulting continuity of instruction and the strong, supportive base better equip the children for the more demanding and specialized studies to follow.

Cuban educators have placed strong emphasis on mathematical proficiency and on mathematics/science foundations in the curriculum. Consequently, in elementary school and high school all children are required to study biology, physics, chemistry, and mathematics. In a recent interview (1983) José R. Fernández, minister of education, told me that "There is no doubt that mathematics, physics, chemistry, and biology form the basis for development in today's world." . . .

Except for offering students two hours per week in senior high school, Cuban educational leadership does not advocate "electives" in the curriculum.

They reason that curriculum designs and "requirements" are determined by consideration of "quality education" and the nation's modern developmental needs.

Cuba is beginning to reap the benefits of their 25 years of educational strategy, and has become one giant school through heavy budget commitments and public and social will. In an article titled "Cuba's Great Leap," in the English science journal, *Nature,* a member of a 1983 U.S. science delegation to Cuba reports that "Cuba's leap into twentieth-century science and engineering in only one generation has hurtled the island in most fields far beyond its Latin American neighbors." This is not restricted to such areas as health care, cattle breeding, and world leadership in sugarcane by-product research. Cubans have now pushed "into more sophisticated terrain—computers, interferon, tissue culture and biotechnology."[15]

Cuba has also become a "medical power," "creating large armies of young doctors." In 1959 there were 6,300 doctors in Cuba; half of them left the island by 1964. In 25 years Cuba has trained 16,000 physicians. There are presently over 17,000 medical students enrolled in 17 medical schools and four medical colleges. . . .

RURAL FOCUS: LA ESCUELA-EN-EL-CAMPO

For prerevolutionary Cuba, no less than for the rest of Latin America, the rural sector was the most economically depressed and the most educationally neglected. Consequently, the Cubans have attempted to change the educational landscape in the countryside. Flying in an airplane over rural areas, one sees many instances of a Cuban educational innovation dotting the rural fields and hills, *la escuela-en-el-campo* ("the school-in-the-countryside"). This uniquely Cuban adventure grows out of a major investment of its national resources and its efforts in education.

The first school in the countryside was built in 1971. Today, there are 384 junior high and 183 senior high schools of this type. They are seen as "the model of the future school."[16] Each *escuela-en-el-campo* costs approximately $1.7 million to build and houses 500 to 600 students with equal numbers of boys and girls. Each new rural school offers not only classrooms, laboratories, library, and recreational areas for students and teachers but also has its own dormitories, a dining room, and a kitchen.

A large fraction of Cuba's youth is now educated in these countryside schools—37 percent in junior high and 47 percent in senior high. The annual cost of maintaining each school is reported to be approximately $572,000. From 1975 to 1980, enrollment in junior high countryside schools increased from 277,000 to 478,000, an extraordinary jump. José R. Fernández, minister of education, summarized the admission policy as follows: "These schools are for all students, but those who pass the sixth grade and don't have a secondary school near where they live are given priority."[17]

The schools set aside one half of the day for academics and one half for work. The early evening, from 5:30 to 7:30 P.M., is devoted to individual and group study time. The students attending a school of this type work on the school farm (citrus, tobacco, or other cash crops) and, in this way, contribute about 600,000 pesos per year to support school development and maintenance. All schools-in-the-countryside are boarding schools: Both students and faculty sleep in dormitories. Transportation to and from home on weekends and for summer vacation is provided by the school.

Although work/study programs exist in other socialist and capitalist countries, the Cuban boarding school, which is located in rural areas and offered as *the* national model for secondary school education, is unique. The Cubans see this model as consistent both with Cuban historic roots and Marxist philosophy. Fidel Castro has said that the *escuela-en-el-campo* "unites fundamental ideas from two great thinkers: Marx and Martí. Both conceived of a school tied to work, a center where youth are educated for life . . . this school responds to conceptions about pedagogy, realities, necessities . . . consistent with the development of man—connected to productive and creative work."[18]

For developing nations, and advanced countries as well, Cuba's *campo* program raises a number of significant issues. The boarding school, designed to accommodate adolescents, must be considered in the light of what we know about development during these years when children are filled with energy and idealism. What effect do these adult-supervised, away-from-home environments have on them? What are the consequences of a peer-group living arrangement for both self-help and collective aims? What opportunities are available for extended study, cooperation, health, hygiene, and nutrition?

SOME PROBLEMS AND DILEMMAS

Even while the record of educational progress is impressive in many ways, particularly in view of Cuba's developmental status, certain problems persist: a shortage of fully trained teachers, an emphasis on achievement testing as the gauge of progress, the problem of dropouts and holdovers, the emergence of special schools for scientifically and technically gifted students in a society dedicated to egalitarianism, and an apparent overemphasis on political considerations in the selection of educational leaders. I will discuss these briefly.

Teacher Quality

The rapid expansion of opportunity after the revolution and the consequent explosion in student enrollment caused an enormous demand for teachers. The commitment to expansion combined with the exodus of middle-class professionals resulted in a shortage of trained personnel. But since the revolution had promised to push ahead, the new government felt it had no choice; it was forced to make concessions. The quality of Cuba's new teachers would be modest, but at least there would be teachers.

For example, when *círculos infantiles* were first opened, they were led by *asistentes,* that is, teachers having at least a sixth-grade education. In 1971, the *Instituto de Infancia* established the *Escuela de Educadoras* to prepare day-care teachers with a minimum ninth-grade education and training in the arts, physical and social sciences, and language skills important for preschool children.[19]

I first visited the national elementary school teacher-training facility, located in the mountains of Oriente Province, during the 1960s. This was a time when Cuban policy proclaimed that if the revolution in education was to occur, teacher training should take place in rugged, isolated, rural conditions. Students would then be prepared for the toughest assignments.

In the 1970s, I interviewed both leaders and classroom teachers about this policy and found many critical of it, claiming that it had adversely affected teacher recruitment and the quality of teacher training. Fidel Castro, in his report to the First Congress of the Communist Party, acknowledged that the regime had made "a major mistake in education during the 1960s" by adopting this policy. "We were slow in realizing that the system was unrealistic," Castro said, "and that for a time it affected the availability of graduate teachers."[20]

In the early 1970s, teacher training was decentralized, and teacher-training centers began to emerge all over the island. In 1983 there were 21 teacher-training facilities with an approximate enrollment of 48,025 students. The five-year program consists of academic subjects, psychology, pedagogy, and intensive field practice.

The dramatic increase in secondary school enrollment generated opportunities for staffing classrooms using a variety of creative approaches. I personally observed classes taught by veteran teachers as well as by paraprofessionals and "monitors," that is, outstanding students who taught selected classes under the guidance of an experienced teacher. Other untrained classroom aides came from the "pedagogical detachment," a group of dedicated 18 and 19 year olds. Still others were trainees, enrolled in pedagogical institutes, who taught during the day and attended teacher-training classes in the evening. In one school-in-the-countryside which I visited in 1979, 40 out of 60 teachers were licensed, and the remaining 20 were still in training.

Recognizing that certain dislocations would result from using an unevenly trained teaching force, the country chose nonetheless to expand education. In visits to classes, I found many teachers who dynamically and effectively used a variety of materials and children's experiences in their work. In other cases, I observed boring lessons in which the in-service teacher or trainee rigidly held to the text in dull question/response style. Too often a "blue book syndrome," the copying of teacher-dictated notes in little blue notebooks, dominated the student/teacher interaction.

Aware of these problems, educators organized a massive in-service training program which operates during the academic year and for one month in the summer. While all students are on holiday during July and August, the teachers attend workshops during one-half of this period, giving them one month for vacation.

Elite Schools in an Egalitarian Society

A persistent dilemma is raised in Cuba by the existence of special or elite high schools, designed to develop scientific and technical talent, in the midst of the call for equality. In 1969, there was only one such school; now there are similar schools in each of the provinces. Students are chosen on the basis of scholastic achievement.

In 1980–81 a new elite school, The School for Exact Sciences, opened to develop talented students in mathematics, chemistry, and physics. Students are selected by a national competitive examination on which they demonstrate their ability in mathematics and chemistry or mathematics and physics. There are currently 150 students enrolled in the school, 50 in each of the three major areas. While the students are expected to carry out the usual maintenance and cleanup responsibilities, they do not participate in the countryside program. This school structure is an exception to the countryside model in Cuban secondary education.

Intelligence testing and ability grouping are *not* used in Cuba's elementary and secondary schools. One teacher explained that such "segregation within the school would contradict socialist principles of our society." Exceptions are the special scientific high schools just mentioned. According to the Cubans, these special enclaves in each province are dictated by national necessity, the need for a scientific cadre. On a visit to the Lenin School I discovered through interviews with students and faculty that textbooks in use there were the same as those used elsewhere in the nation, but the quality of teaching and equipment were superior. This contradiction persists into the 1980s.

Curriculum Change

Shortages of textbooks, poor quality of old texts when available, and lack of supplementary aids and materials plagued a school system which was expanding rapidly in every city and rural community. Serious and important changes in curriculum and materials have been made to improve the quality of instruction. For example, Cuba now produces its own modern audiovisual materials. These include large, "come apart" models of cows and human bodies for primary school science lessons and a variety of concrete materials for modern mathematics. With the help of East German consultants, Cuba has introduced a high quality, well-organized, modern mathematics program for grades 1–12.

Over the past decade I have witnessed a carefully orchestrated curriculum change. There has been a tremendous investment in the production and distribution of new textbooks at every grade level. Teams of gifted Cuban teachers, in consultation with experts from abroad, have prepared new materials and courses of study appropriate for the country's needs.

Testing Emphasis

In the "battle for quality" in Cuban education, the focus is now on how well the schools are doing on their exams (on a quarterly basis and especially on the final) and the "percentage of promotion," starting especially in grade 5. Students, faculty, principals, and parents cite examination and promotion data as evidence of achievement. For senior high school graduates, entrance to the university is determined by one's scholastic average.

The pressure on students to succeed on exams has caused some unfortunate disruptions. Evidence of fraud and cheating has been acknowledged publicly by Fidel Castro on a number of occasions.[21] In my own opinion, the heavy emphasis on tests as a measure of student and teacher worth often leads to stultification of both teacher and student, with critical thinking and creativity supplanted by rote learning.

Educational Leadership

While selection of school principals is governed by various criteria, it appears that the principal's "political history," that is, dedication to the revolution, is still a crucial factor. While this might pay off in terms of conscientiousness and long hours of service, it does not of itself ensure educational leaders who stimulate instructional improvements.

The problems of Cuban schools, especially the issues of the quality of instruction and the implementation of curriculum change, have been publicly acknowledged and discussed by teachers and educational leaders. Minister Fernández recently noted that "a whole driving force of new ideas" has of necessity come up against traditional teaching ideas. . . .

> It should be realized that the improved system entails a profound change in the content of curricula and that this in turn demands greater teaching qualifications. . . . Moreover, there was the well-known explosion in enrollment in intermediate education, which forced us to open hundreds of schools almost simultaneously. Problems that have had to be tackled on the way were finding new teachers, new school principals and administrators, and seeing that they further improve their qualifications.[22]

When asked what Cuban educational priorities for 1981–1985 would be, Fernández replied that the main task is to continue to improve the quality of teaching and education, primarily through staff training. Overall, he reported,

> We will struggle to improve schooling for students between the ages of 13 and 16; to introduce morning and afternoon sessions in primary schools; to improve our work in vocational training and professional guidance; to give added impetus to physical education, sports and cultural activities; to expand and improve special education; to apply the principles of contemporary educational concepts;

to see to it that all intermediate education teachers get their diploma and primary school teachers improve their education level.[23]

CUBA'S SCHOOLS AND LATIN AMERICA

To appreciate Cuba's dilemmas and achievements, we must keep in mind the status of children in the rest of Latin America. A recent study reported that "most young children in Latin America are profoundly affected by poverty, both physically and emotionally. More than 50 percent suffer from the effects of protein deficiency. Nutritional anemia affects 10 to 20 percent of them directly. Malnourished children exhibit apathy and reduced responsiveness in the environment, irritability, withdrawal, and an inability to carry out tasks."[24] But even if these children were offered early childhood education, two additional conditions must be met: "secondary education must be available to those who finish primary school and jobs must become available."[25] Obviously political and economic realities make it unlikely that this will happen in the near future in much of Latin America.

In the case of Cuba, we have the one Latin American country that has overcome the lockstep of school failure, the absence of educational opportunity, and poverty. Cuba has gone a long way toward fulfilling the educational needs of children at all school levels and has adopted broad measures to provide sound health care and proper nutrition, indispensable ingredients in a comprehensive effort to achieve victory over a history of neglect. . . .

NOTES

1. Marvin Leiner, "Cuba's Schools, Ten Years Later," *Saturday Review* (October 17, 1970), p. 59.

2. Office of the Vice-Minister of Education, Ministry of Education, Cuba, 1984.

3. Nelson Lowry, *Rural Cuba* (New York: Octagon Books, 1970), pp. 236, 239.

4. International Bank for Reconstruction and Development, *Report on Cuba* (Baltimore: Johns Hopkins Press, 1951), pp. 404, 425, 434.

5. Samuel Bowles, "Cuban Education and the Revolutionary Ideology," *Harvard Educational Review*, Vol. 41 (November 1971), pp. 41, 474.

6. Jorge I. Domínguez, *Cuba: Order and Revolution* (Cambridge: Harvard University Press, 1978), p. 165.

7. Anna Lorenzetto and Karel Neys, *Methods and Means Utilized in Cuba to Eliminate Illiteracy*, UNESCO Report (Havana: Ministry of Education, 1965), p. 72.

8. Azucena Plasencia, *"Montaña Adentro: La Batalla del Sexto Grado,"* *Bohemia*, Vol. 67 (March 7, 1975), p. 35.

9. J.I. Domínguez, *Order and Revolution*, p. 167.

10. Fidel Castro, *Granma Weekly Review* (September 21, 1980), p. 3.

11. Ruth Leger Sivard, *World Military and Social Expenditures, 1983: An Annual Report on World Priorities* (Washington, D.C.: World Priorities, 1983), p. 36.

12. For further discussion of day care in Cuba (history, goals, organization and curriculum) see Marvin Leiner, *Children Are the Revolution: Day Care in Cuba* (New York: Penguin Books, 1978). Also see *Educación en Cuba: Regional Conference of Ministers and Education, December 4–13,* Mexico, UNESCO (Havana: Empresa Impresoras Gráficas, MINED, 1979), pp. 12–18, and *Suplemento Al Resumen del Trabajo Anual del MINED, 1982–1983* (Havana: Ministry of Education, 1983).

13. Max Figueroa, "Improvement of the Educational System: On a Thesis of the First Congress of the Party," *Granma Weekly Review* (June 29, 1975), p. 4.

14. Cuba, Ministry of Education, *Cuba: Organización de la Educación. Report of the Republic of Cuba to the 26th International Conference on Public Education* (Havana: Empresa Impresoras Gráficas, MINED, 1977), p. 122.

15. Robert Ubell, "Cuba's Great Leap," *Nature* (April 28, 1983), p. 745.

16. *Suplemento Al Resumen del Trabajo Anual del MINED, 1982–83,*

17. Jesús Abascal López, interview with José R. Fernández, Vice-President of the Council of Ministers and Minister of Education, *Granma Weekly Review* (November 16, 1980), p. 2.

18. Fidel Castro, "La Escuela en el Campo," *Educación,* Año 1, April/June 1971, p. 13.

19. See M. Leiner, *Children Are the Revolution,* Introduction, p. 1 and Chapter 2, "The Paraprofessional Solution," pp. 33–50.

20. Fidel Castro, *Report of the Central Committee of the CPC to the First Congress* (Havana: Department of the Revolutionary Orientation of the Central Committee of the Communist Party of Cuba, 1977), p. 173.

21. Fidel Castro, "Speech delivered on 4 September 1978 for opening of the 1978–79 School Year," *Granma Weekly Review* (September 17, 1978), pp. 2, 4.

22. J. A. López, interview with J. R. Fernández, p. 2.

23. J. A. López, p. 4.

24. Robert Halpern, "Early Childhood Program in Latin America," *Harvard Educational Review,* Vol. 50 (November 1980), pp. 484–85.

25. Ibid., p. 485.

CHAPTER 16

Racism and Sexism

50. Women's Development Through Revolutionary Mobilization*

BY MAX AZICRI

The women's movement in Cuba poses some thought-provoking questions to feminists, ideologues, and scholars in other quarters. This is particularly so if the Cuban revolutionary experience is examined according to feminist notions cherished in Western societies: concepts which sustain the ideology defining the nature, and supporting the objectives, of the women's movement. Seemingly, the Cubans characterize themselves as rejecting values (in their own women's liberation ideology) such as status-seeking and achievement orientation or some kind of hard-core individualism: "The liberation of women, then, has come to have quite different meaning in Cuba than in the United States . . . to mean the act of being freed from bourgeois, capitalistic domination."[1]

Rather than fighting the government for recognition of their demands, Cuban women have struggled for their emancipation, and scored substantive gains, within the parameters of a socialist society whose goals are actually prescribed by an almost all-male leadership. Consequently, the regime supports the Federation of Cuban Women and its work by encouraging, requesting, and/or inducing women to comply with modernizing policies which have been decided by the government. However, operating within the context of the revolution's egalitarian and collectivistic values, the government also allows and expects rank-and-file participation in the decision-making process. Up to this point, the women's movement under the revolution represents a mixed

*From *International Journal of Women's Studies,* Vol. 2, No. 1 (1981). Edited for this volume.

record of achievements and shortcomings, characterizing a highly commendable but not quite fully satisfactory attempt by the regime to solve the "woman problem" in Cuban society.

THE FEDERATION OF CUBAN WOMEN

Central to this struggle for modernization has been the Federation of Cuban Women (*Federación de Mujeres Cubanas* or FMC, also known as the Federation), which as a national mass organization has worked as a catalyst for women's liberation within the framework of mobilization-based participatory politics established by the regime. Also, the FMC became the social and political structure that made possible the release of latent female energy, making women not only accessible to governmental mobilization but available for active political participation and collective revolutionary action. All of this newly experienced political and social activism allowed women to become effective partners in the building process of a socialist state under the revolution.

In short, the well-recognized participation of women in the revolutionary process was carefully designed upon lines of societal mobilization which were either directed, manipulated, or at least influenced from above by the government—similar in style and substance to those mobilizational directives drawn up for different population groups since the revolution came to power in 1959.[2] Supported by the militancy of the Federation and its members (the *federadas*), the government seeks to free women from traditional sex-typed roles and to provide them with new choices entailing a wide range of alternatives for changing their traditional lifestyles.

This process of social change has been pursued using a variety of policies which include open access to education to a degree never seen before, and the breaking down of sexist occupational barriers (with some noteworthy exceptions) by massive incorporation of women into the labor force. Most importantly, by attempting needed changes in the usually male-dominated nuclear family structure—especially since the enactment of the Family Code in 1975—the regime sought to eradicate the most pervasive of all values shared by Cuban males: *machismo*. This Cuban variety of a more universal syndrome of male chauvinism was highly visible in prerevolutionary days and to a lesser degree it still exists today, in spite of all the changes that have taken place regarding a woman's place in revolutionary Cuba.

Political and Social Objectives of the Women's Movement

A delegation of 77 women who traveled to Santiago, Chile, in November 1959 to attend the First Latin American Congress of Women constituted the original nucleus of activists who organized the women's movement in Cuba under the revolution. A short time later on August 23, 1960, the Federation of Cuban

Women was finally organized with a membership of approximately 17,000 within a few months. This had the effect of bringing together the already existent women's groups into a unified revolutionary mass organization.

According to Vilma Espín, Federation organizer, founder and only president throughout all these years, the long-term objectives of the new organization at the outset were not completely clear or fully understood by the women. Interestingly enough, it was the President of the Council of State, Fidel Castro, who asked her in 1959 to organize and become the head of the women's federation at a time when Espín had no thought of a women's movement under the revolutionary government. In her own words: "I asked precisely why do we have to have a women's organization? I had never been discriminated against. I had my career as a chemical engineer. I never suffered, I never had any difficulty."[3]

Espín's upper-class family background, which allowed her some time in the United States taking courses at MIT, could explain her attitude at the time—"I was very poorly read in politics," she acknowledges. "But Fidel was different. He was much more prepared than any of us. He had read revolutionary materials. I was only beginning to be a revolutionary."[4] Her political naiveté during those early years of the revolutionary government stood in contrast to her legitimate credentials earned earlier during the insurrectionary struggle against the regime of Fulgencio Batista; she had been in charge of coordinating the underground activities of the 26 of July Movement in Oriente Province. Later, after joining Major Raúl Castro's forces in the second Front "Frank Pais" in northern Oriente, Espín stayed with them permanently at Raúl's request; she was "high on the wanted list by that time."[5] Presently, besides presiding over the FMC, Espín is a member of the Central Committee of the Cuban Communist Party; she is also married to Raúl Castro—Fidel's brother—who is First Vice President of the Council of State and the Council of Ministers, Minister of the Revolutionary Armed Forces, and Second Secretary of the Political Bureau and Deputy Chairman of the Secretariat of the Cuban Communist Party.

THE FMC'S FOUNDING YEARS

In retrospect, looking back to the early years of the Federation, Espín could thoughtfully comment that "while the revolution presented a new opportunity with workers' and peasants' power guaranteeing the elimination of inequalities on the basis of sex . . . [on the other hand] we also knew that women in Cuba were not ready for the tasks that awaited them in a new society." The complexity of this political and social reality became clearer as the work proceeded.

As indicated earlier, an important characteristic of the women's movement in Cuba is that it was conceived as a social structure that would only attain its own identity by becoming an integral part of the national revolutionary process. Seemingly, it has been a matter of official policy all along that women would achieve their liberation by becoming active cadres of the revolution, enjoying their newly acquired status of social equality by integrating themselves into the revolutionary process. Properly speaking, under the revolution it has never been an independent movement seeking the liberation of women in the same terms as in a pluralistic political system where different and opposing interest groups compete with one another for the government's attention and favors. The FMC has been characterized as a mass organization directed from above, with women's goals pursued only when they coincide with those of the government and coming always after national goals and priorities have been set by the regime.[6]

On this particular account, it is Espín again who makes clear the organic nature of the Federation, working as an integrating social force operating in a revolutionary context:

> From the first days of our organization we could see that the objectives we pursued were not oriented to gain partial revindications for women alone, but to unify them, and to mobilize them, so we could constitute a powerful force that could defend, support and fight for the revolution, which had by then defined its populist and anti-imperialistic character.[7]

The women's movement was never seen by FMC and government leaders as a process whereby the articulation of demands on behalf of a specific population group could eventually challenge the regime, demanding the satisfaction of needs and aspirations contrary to or in spite of national policies. Thus, not by confrontation with the revolutionary government, but by mobilizing and incorporating women in the tasks of modernizing the country, the Federation sought to satisfy the specific goals of the women and the common goals of the nation. It was quite clear that social equality could only be achieved in Cuba by revolutionary involvement and action.

Institutional Analysis of a Women's Mass Organization

In its first two years, the FMC had laid the foundations of the roles women would play in the revolution. Starting with such simple tasks as dressmaking courses and followed by first aid courses and the establishment of children's circles, women were later mobilized for all kinds of work. By 1961, the *federadas* had emerged victorious from two different and difficult undertakings. First, women participated at the time of the Bay of Pigs invasion on April 17th in the defense of the revolution, enrolling in the Women's Militia organized through the Federation—this later became a branch of the defense establishment and women were organized through their work place.

Secondly, women participated in the Literacy Campaign, a major national mobilization effort of the revolution. It was at the First National Congress (1962) however, that the statutes of the organization were established and major programs were either accelerated or initiated; programs such as the Women's Improvement Plan, the Schools for Directors of Children's Circles, the Ana Betancourt School for Peasant Girls, and the Schools for Children's Circle Workers.

Part of the success story of the Federation is the growth of its national membership. By 1974 the *federadas* represented more than 54 percent of Cuban women 14 years and older. Two years later, the FMC had reached more than two million members (in only 16 years it had increased more than 127 times its original membership). In 1978, its total membership included 2,248,000 *federadas* representing over 80 percent of all women old enough to become members.[8]

Women responded positively to the twofold functions performed by the FMC. Its downward flow of communication of policies and programs, representing the regime's concerns, alerts women to governmental decisions and to what is expected of them in the national revolutionary effort. The second function of the FMC, articulating and integrating women's aspirations within the revolutionary process, provides the *federadas* with a sense of new status and new identity. Due in part to the Federation's efforts, new positions were opened to women which had hitherto been reserved for men. . . .

The Federation follows a complex pyramidal network in its organizational structure. Under the office of the president of the FMC are six levels: national, provincial, municipal, block, and delegation; all headed by general secretaries. The seventh level is made up of the rank and file *federadas* who are in direct contact with the people. The national level is made up of eight committees— production, finance and transport, education, social work, ideological orientation, organization, day care, and external relations—which function under supervision of the secretary. The provincial level repeats the same secretarial arrangements with the exception of the offices of external relations and ideological orientation, which are combined in one committee. At the regional level there are the same committees with the exception of finance and transport and organization, which are unified into one office. The municipal, block and delegation levels have almost the same structure as the regional level, lacking only the day-care center committee. The structure of the Federation is designed to simplify the lower administrative levels, while upper level committees include more offices and functions.[9] Basically, however, the responsibilities and concerns of each Secretariat remain the same throughout the FMC structure. Obviously, as the geographic area becomes larger, coordination within the Federation and with government ministries, agricultural plans, etc., becomes a major part of the administration.

The secretary of the organization carries out vital and diverse functions for the Federation; recruiting new members, collecting dues, reminding the *federadas* of their meetings and deciding on the agenda for discussion. While a delegation represents the membership at the neighborhood level, several delegations form a block (the immediate higher echelon) with several blocks constituting a municipality, and so on. Below the municipal level all secretaries are volunteers. Starting with the municipal secretary, however, they become full-time paid cadres of the FMC. All the secretaries, as well as the general secretary, are elected by the membership. The delegations are also responsible for nominating candidates who, in their estimation, have the leadership ability to hold positions of responsibility at all levels.

All in all, this structural organization has allowed the Federation to become a major force in the political and social life of the revolution, and to incorporate women into the overall mobilization of the population by the regime. Both in Cuba and abroad, however, there have been complaints and serious dissatisfaction regarding the Federation's performance and organizational characteristics. "A generational gap," "avoidance of thorny issues," and "out of step with the rank and file" are some of the criticisms leveled at the FMC, particularly by its younger members. According to a Cuba watcher, the Federation's magazine, *Mujeres* (Women), even though it publishes articles dealing with women in agriculture (or in their performance of military duties) and once published an illustrated article about a woman who "photographed the birth of her own baby (astounding for a Latin country)," dedicates a substantial part of each issue to reinforcing traditional female roles and concerns. . . . The institutional ability of the Federation to respond positively to these criticisms may decide not only the future of the organization but in many ways the future of the women's movement in Cuba as well.

Women's Social Equality and Education

For the leaders of the revolution, underdevelopment and illiteracy were more than related evils; they were different phases of the same problem. According to Castro, "Only a revolution is capable of totally changing the educational scene, and the social scene."[10] Not surprisingly, the Campaign Against Illiteracy (1961) developed into the first major national mobilization effort by the revolution. It was also the first ongoing countrywide mobilization campaign in which the Federation participated. As a result of that historical event many important steps were taken in the advancement of women in the nation: not only because by the end of 1961, 56 percent of the 707,000 new literates were women, but also because some were able to participate as *brigadistas* (brigade members) in the *Populars,* Conrado Benítez, or Workers Brigades, and teach other fellow Cubans to read and write—thereby reducing the illiteracy rate from 23 percent to 3.7 percent.

Before the revolution, women in Cuba had a literacy rate of 78.8 percent, which gave them a lower level of illiteracy than men (21 percent for women and 26 percent for men). These figures, however, were not representative of the rural areas where illiteracy for women was much higher than in the cities.

At the time of the 1953 census, "one third of ten-year-old girls were not in school . . . and only 1 in 100 women over 25 had any university education."[11] Still, "more females than males over the age of ten received some schooling (77 percent compared with 73 percent respectively), and a higher percentage of women attended primary school (72 percent compared with 67 percent of the men), probably because males were removed from school to work in agriculture."[12] In higher education women were underrepresented. This may explain the low rate of professional women since before 1959 more men than women received some secondary education—2.4 percent compared to 16 percent respectively—and 1.6 percent of the males compared to 0.8 percent of the females received some university education.[13]

Parallel to the governmental educational programs were those sponsored by or entrusted to the FMC and tailored specifically to meet women's needs. "Family reading circles" (*círculos familiares de lectura*) were designed for those women who remained illiterate after the 1961 literacy campaign; about 2,000 of these "reading circles" were established by 1968. At the same time, courses in health care and personal hygiene offered by the Federation had an enrollment of about 700,000 women in the late 1960s. Crash courses to prepare women to enter the labor force covered a wide variety of subjects such as agricultural techniques (gardening and tractor operation), clerical skills (typing and stenography), handicrafts, cooking, and physical education. Also under the administration of the Federation were teacher-training programs such as the Conrado Benítez Revolutionary Teachers' School as well as student scholarship programs.

The impact of women's participation in education has not been limited to special or remedial and vocational training. The overall increment in women's education has been phenomenal under the revolution; by 1967 the rate of female students was already 49 percent at the primary level and 55 percent in junior high school. Almost half of the university students today are female. Women represent 50 percent of the students in medicine, 30 percent in engineering, 90 percent in education, 60 percent in biochemistry and biology, 22.7 percent in technology, and 35 percent in agricultural studies. Moreover, women are now being instructed to become officers of the revolutionary armed forces at the Military Technical Institute.[14]

In the field of education the FMC has performed a variety of functions, implementing governmental policies, initiating or adapting programs to their own reality, and above all working as a mass organization responsible for enlisting women in the comprehensive educational programs offered by the regime. All in all, it seems that a more alert, educated and assertive woman is the product of these educational programs and of the social and political activism brought about by the FMC and its mobilization campaigns. In this sense, education has been instrumental in maximizing social equality in Cuba, thus contributing to the modernization of women.

Liberation through the Labor Force

For the revolutionary government, the ultimate mobilization effort by the Federation has been the incorporation of women into the labor force. Getting women out of the home to join men in the workplace was made the real test of social equality for the women's movement. In this sense, the prevailing Cuban outlook has been that "women do not have just a right to work, but an obligation to society to engage in 'socialist productive labor.'" Castro has been rather explicit on this subject:

> ... the whole question of women's liberation, of full equality of rights for women and the integration of women into society is to a great extent determined by their incorporation into production. This is because the more women are incorporated into work ... so will the way to their liberation become easier and more clearly defined.[15]

Women had, of course, worked in Cuba before the revolution. In fact, the experience of Cuban women in the labor force antedates the twentieth century. In the nineteenth century, however, it was work characterized by a tradition rooted in slavery. Long after slavery was abolished in 1880,[16] the demographic characteristics of working women had strong racist connotations. Toward the end of the nineteenth century women in the labor force were mostly black and poor—74.4 percent in 1899 of the total female work force—and they were limited to working as maids and/or laundresses.

During the first quarter of the present century, and particularly during the 1920s, white women started to move into salaried work at an increased rate, due largely to the generalized conditions of deprivation in the country. Still, as late as 1907 black women represented 64.9 percent of all females in the labor force. Working women were brought into salaried work only out of necessity, and their living conditions remained at the same poverty level even when holding a salaried job. Another important characteristic of this early period was that women would stay on the job until old age due to the lack of any social security which could provide a retirement pension.[17]

In the late twenties there was a rapid decline in the number of women working due to the international economic crisis of the period which severely affected the Cuban economy. The lowest point was reached in 1931 when women represented only 5.9 percent of the labor force. Throughout all these years, even though there was some small diversification of occupational activities, domestic work was still overwhelmingly predominant. The number of women in the labor force had increased to 10.2 percent by 1943, 11.6 percent by 1953, and reached its highest point under the revolution with 15.9 percent by 1970 and 25.7 percent by 1974.[18]

At the time of the 1953 census, the women's share of the economically active population was a clear indication of the difficulties they faced when entering the labor force. It was also conclusive evidence of how the lines were drawn to safeguard a man's domain from any woman's interference. For women, first of all, there was domestic service; 89 percent of the workers in this area were women. Secondly, in clerical work 53 percent of the women were typists. In other fields women accounted for only 5 percent in administration and management, 1 percent in agriculture and fishing, and 2 percent in mining and quarrying. At the same time, women as artisans and factory workers were doing somewhat better with 15 percent.[19]

In the professional fields women were largely represented in teaching (82 percent), social work (45 percent), and pharmacy (34 percent). In other professions their ratio was much lower; 13 percent in medicine, 7 percent in law and the judiciary, and 5 percent in engineering. Women had a low rate in the medical and legal professions in spite of the fact that these two occupations represented 12 and 9 percent, respectively, of the total number of professionals in the country.[20] This kind of participation of women in the labor force— limited in the number of occupational fields as well as in their share of the total economically active population—was still in existence long after the Constitution of 1940 declared illegal the practice of occupational discrimination on the basis of sex, and made it mandatory that there should be equal pay for equal work.

QUANTITATIVE AND QUALITATIVE CHANGES

Between 1953 and 1974, before and after the revolution, there was an increase of 14.1 percent in the number of women workers on a salaried basis in the total national labor force—by 1974 a total of 604,589 women had joined the economically active population. Yet, more significant were the changes which provided women with a wide range of occupational choices. For example, in 1953 domestic work represented more than a fourth of the total female labor force, but by 1970 this occupational bias had practically disappeared.[21]

Another significant difference in the conditions of working women before and after the revolution can be seen in their distribution among various age categories. While in 1953 women ten to fourteen years old represented 10.9 percent of the female labor force, this age group was almost nonexistent by 1970. The real increase of women in the labor force under the revolution was among those between the ages of 21 and 44; the group between 20 and 24 holding the highest rate with 25.3 percent. It was for this age group that the revolutionary policies of encouraging women to join the labor force had its greatest impact.

The six economic sectors with the highest rate of employed women in 1974 were social services (where women had a slight majority with 50.7 percent), communications (40.5 percent), commerce (39.2 percent), industry (21.5 percent), agriculture (11 percent), transportation (8.3 percent), and construction

(6.8 percent). In the area of social services women were particularly active in the 40 to 54 age group (41.2 percent), followed by the ages between 20 and 39 (34.5 percent), and reaching the lowest level in ages under 20 (21.9 percent). This sector included, among others, the fields of education and public health—the former being a field traditionally dominated by women, a trend that has continued under the revolution. In industry, the areas with the highest rate of working women in 1970 were textiles, beverages, tobacco, chemicals, food, and graphic arts—most of which represent a departure from those occupational areas which were open to women before the revolution.[22]

CONTRADICTORY LABOR POLICIES FOR WOMEN

The 1976 Constitution has provided some legal foundations regarding women's incorporation into the labor force that could be termed sexist in ideology even if not in intent. For example, Article 43 of the new Socialist constitution states that "In order to assure the exercise of . . . [women's] rights and especially the incorporation of women into the socially organized work, the state sees to it that they are given jobs in keeping with their physical makeup. . . ." This constitutional provision is supportive of a resolution enacted in 1976 by the Ministry of Labor which ". . . prohibits women from occupying nearly 300 jobs. [And] it is contended that the measure was taken in the best interest of women's health." It has been suggested that the motivation behind such a policy is ". . . to free jobs occupied or which could be occupied by women so that those men who have been rationalized (transferred) out of their jobs can be once again employed."[23]

The 1976 Ministry of Labor Resolution interpreted in a way inimical to women a decision (Resolution 6.2) approved by the Thirteenth Congress of the Confederation of Cuban Workers (CTC) held November 11–15, 1973. The CTC Resolution 6.2 put an end to two resolutions from the 1960s (Resolutions 47 and 48) whose often contradictory stipulations were creating confusion and problems. Resolution 47 established "the freezing of many jobs as they are vacated . . . reserving those jobs for women workers" while Resolution 48 "prohibited women from taking certain jobs . . . considered harmful to their health." At the time, the policy orientation taken by the Thirteenth Congress of the CTC was that women's qualifications should be improved in all areas so they would not be excluded from any line of work because they were less prepared than men. Still, it accepted the notion that ". . . this does not mean that there are no jobs from which, in the interests of health, it is necessary to exclude women."[24]

The 1976 Resolution has served to clarify for the time being the confusion created by these contradictory resolutions regarding women's participation in the labor force. Unfortunately, however, some of the policies decided upon by the regime have interpreted Cuba's social and labor realities in a way which is inimical to the best interests and aspirations of the *federadas,* at least to the extent that women are free to join the labor force in all kinds of occupations is concerned. Nevertheless, this situation has provided a positive impetus to the political dynamics of the women's movement in Cuba, in spite of its obvious negative features in terms of effective social equality for women. That is, the stance taken by the *federadas* at the leadership and rank and file levels has been one of invigorating activism, voicing rather assertively their opposition and dislike for these official policies.

WOMEN'S POLITICAL PARTICIPATION

Today, 18 years after its inception, the Federation of Cuban Women enjoys a prominent position in Cuban society which has been repeatedly recognized by the government and the population at large. The importance of the political role played by the Federation has been acknowledged on different occasions; President Castro in his well-known address to the First Congress of the Cuban Communist Party in December 1975 gave a positive evaluation of the contributions made by the *federadas* and their mass organization to the revolution. The FMC also received recognition in the present phase of institutionalizing the revolution—particularly in Article 7 of the 1976 Socialist Constitution, which by defining the role played by the Federation as well as other mass organizations in revolutionary Cuba signifies not only its importance but also its permanence.

On the occasion of the Federation's Second National Congress in 1974, Espín provided some insight on the achievements and shortcomings of the movement, especially in the area of social and political roles allocated to women. According to her, "total incorporation of women in the political, social and economic life of the country in conditions of equality with men has not been achieved in its entirety."[25] The implications present in Espín's statement raise questions regarding the feasibility, despite the government's commitment to pursue that goal, of real emancipation for women in the near future. The tradition of female subordination and male superiority present in the cultural, social and political institutions inherited by the revolution has demonstrated a strong tendency to survive, lingering on in spite of the many changes that have taken place under the revolution and even before—such as the progressive statutes included in the 1940 Constitution and the social reform policies enacted during the 1940s and 1950s.

The political mobilization of women has been pursued by the revolutionary government within the context of societal mobilization which has affected different population groups. More specifically, women's mobilization has taken place at different levels of participation. Women have been mobilized as part of groups such as workers, youths, peasants, and the population in general. They have also been equally involved in pursuing political action by themselves under the leadership of the FMC. In spite of the involvement by women in mobilization campaigns sponsored by different mass organizations and/or the government, the centrality of the Federation for women's political activism is an ever-present feature of life in Cuba today.

THE FAMILY CODE

The Family Code, a revolutionary law toward which the FMC and its leadership had been working for a long time, was designed by the regime to counter traditional attitudes rooted in cultural values, held by both females and males, which inhibit the acceptance of equality in practice as well as in theory. The law went into effect on March 8, 1975—International Women's Day of the International Women's Year. The occasion was celebrated with a ceremony in which Espín, as the national representative of all women, received a copy of the final draft of the Family Code from Blas Roca, who as chairperson of the Commission of Juridical Studies of the Communist party was responsible for the final drafting of this legislation after considering all the numerous changes suggested by women and men across the country. This initial step in the collectivization of household chores within the family was taken in response to the serious problem of the double shift encountered by women when they joined the labor force. Moreover, a significant breakdown of the traditional family had occurred under the revolution. Divorces had soared at least tenfold: "from 2,500 in 1958 to 25,000 in 1970—50 percent of the new Cuban marriages end in divorce."[26] Evidently the nuclear family as it existed in prerevolutionary days was not functioning well. This was in part due to the fact that the revolution had substantially eroded the traditional dichotomy of women's "la casa" (the home) and men's "la calle" (the street), as well as the legitimacy of other traditional values and those social institutions used to reinforce the allocation of sex-related roles.

Much attention and controversy was centered on Section I of Chapter II of the Family Code, which covered the "rights and duties between husband and wife." Article 24—the first of the section—defines the institution of marriage as one of full equality for both partners. In theory, establishing the foundations of the family in accordance with revolutionary egalitarianism, the code strengthens the central core of the nuclear family by demanding from husband and wife loyalty, consideration, respect, and mutual help.

The care of the family and the upbringing of the children has been entrusted by this code to both partners while specifically requesting that they guide their children "according to principles of socialist morality" and insisting that both parents participate and cooperate in the running of the home. Also, both are responsible for the family's well being "according to his or her ability and financial status." Finally, the famous and much discussed issue of husbands being legally bound under the Family Code to share half of the house workload with wives was legislated in less precise or ominous words than the wording included in earlier versions of the law. Its intent, however, remained the same: ". . . if one of them (husband or wife) only contributes by working at home and caring for the children, the other partner must contribute to this support alone, *without prejudice to his duty of cooperating in the above mentioned work and care.*"

The question remains, however, of why Cuban policymakers chose to perpetuate the nuclear family, which has been identified by some as an institution necessarily unequal to women and characteristic of capitalistic societies, rather than allowing the family to disappear—"to wither away"—along with so many other traditional features of prerevolutionary life. Not withstanding the merits of this argument, it is important to examine the structural nature of the new Cuban family or at least of the type of family expected to emerge.

The new family unit is basically a social institution conceived within the canons of the revolution's value system. The new model of family life has been defined and redefined by behavioral patterns emerging from a seemingly everlasting process of social change. While on the one hand the more traditional notion of family unit and identity has been preserved (as a matter of fact, it has been reinforced considerably), on the other a new structure whereby both partners can live and function on an equal basis is also provided. Although the expectation is that all members of the family—wife, husband and children—will be able to enjoy the active and participatory life of revolutionary Cuba. Therefore the ever-increasing number of day-care centers, *círculos infantiles* (children's circles), workers' dining halls, and especially the new provisions of the Family Code regarding the division of house workload are intended to free women from responsibility for household chores which only perpetuate their traditional roles. In that sense, the revolution's goal is that the objective social conditions (the needed infrastructure) will eventually be matched by the subjective individual conditions (attitudes and lifestyles).

CONCLUSION

The women's movement in Cuba under the revolution has developed as a major social experience with extraordinary significance both within and without the country. The modernization of women followed certain processes which were partly originated by prevailing national conditions and past history as well as by those contextual characteristics identifiable more directly with the politics of mobilization of the revolution.

The establishment, growth, and performance of the FMC as an institution that in a revolutionary context has played the major role in modernizing a specific population group offers valuable insights into the dynamics of social change in revolutionary Cuba, particularly with respect to the characteristics of mass organizations and the role they play in the revolutionary system. At a more general level, however, the problems faced by the women's movement in Cuba are also indicative of the complex modernization problems faced by most developing nations.

Since the early sixties, the creation of the FMC institutional structure as well as the phenomenal growth in the number of *federadas* allowed the Federation to successfully penetrate society and to mobilize women. This structural growth and development rapidly increased the efficiency and capabilities of the Federation as a mass organization. It was able to pursue the satisfaction of women's goals, articulating their needs to the government, and also to mobilize women, extracting higher levels of service and production from the *federadas* for the national development effort. That specific women's issues have been incorporated into national policies and programs is an indication not only of the responsiveness of revolutionary policy-making but also of the work performed by the FMC in bringing women's issues to the regime's attention.

Not withstanding these concrete pluses, there appear to be serious problems within the Federation which need attention and may indicate future changes in the institution itself. A younger generation of women will bring new dimensions to the women's movement. Issues will be faced that have been overlooked or that did not seem important enough to the present leadership of the FMC. This could be a natural outcome for a revolution that built a socialist society and provided a new cultural system with egalitarian and collectivistic values which not only justified the liberation of women, but practically made it a necessary national goal.

NOTES

1. Oscar Lewis *et al., Four Women Living the Revolution—An Oral History of Contemporary Cuba* (Urbana, IL: Univ. of Illinois Press, 1977), p. x.

2. Max Azicri, "A Study of the Structure of Exercising Power in Cuba: Mobilization and Governing Strategies (1959–1968)," Unpublished doctoral diss., University of Southern California (1975).

3. Sally Quinn, "Vilma Espín: First Lady of the Revolution," *The Washington Post* (March 26, 1977), B1, B3.

4. Ibid., B3.

5. Margaret Randall, *Cuban Women Now* (Toronto: The Women's Press, 1974), pp. 298–99.

6. Susan Kaufman-Purcell, "Modernizing Women for a Modern Society: The Cuban Case," in Ann Pescatello, ed., *Female and Male in Latin America—Essays,* (Pittsburgh: University of Pittsburgh Press, 1973), pp. 259, 257–71.

7. Vilma Espín, "La Mujer Como Parte Activa de Nuestra Sociedad," *Cuba Internacional,* special issue (November 1974), 70.

8. Nancy Robinson Calvet, "The Role of Women in Cuba's History," *Granma Weekly Review,* (January 15, 1978), 12.

9. Heidi Steffens. "FMC at the Grass-roots," *Cuba Review,* Vol. 4, No. 2 (1974), pp. 25–26; and Gladys Castaño, "Una Vez Más Cumpliremos," *Mujeres,* Vol. 16 (1976), pp. 12–13.

10. *Revolución* (September 7, 1961), p. 6, as cited in Richard R. Fagen, *The Transformation of Political Culture in Cuba* (Stanford: Stanford University Press, 1969), p. 35.

11. Carollee Benglesdorf and Alice Hageman, "Emerging from Underdevelopment: Women and Work." *Cuba Review,* Vol. 4, No. 2 (1974), pp. 4, 3–12; and S. Kaufman-Purcell, "Modernizing Women," pp. 260–61.

12. Ibid., p. 260.

13. Ibid., p. 261.

14. Max Azicri, "Cuba: The Women's Revolution Within a Revolution," in Patrick A. Kyle, ed., *Integrating the Neglected Majority—Government Responses to Demands for New Sex-Roles* (Brunswick, OH: King's Court Communications, 1976), pp. 77–78; and S. Kaufman-Purcell, "Modernizing Women," p. 266.

15. *Granma Weekly Review* (December 15, 1974), 3.

16. Franklin W. Knight, *Slave Society in Cuba During the Nineteenth Century* (Madison: Univ. of Wisconsin Press, 1970), p. 177; and Verena Martínez Alier, *Marriage, Class and Colour in Nineteenth Century Cuba—A Study of Racial Attitudes and Sexual Values in a Slave Society* (London: Cambridge Univ. Press, 1974), pp. 4–5, 33–34.

17. "Aspectos Demográficos de la Fuerza Laboral Femenina en Cuba," *Junta Central de Planificación,* Departamento de Demografía, Cuba (September 1975), pp. 5–6.

18. Ibid., 6, 52–54; and Wyat Mac Gaffey and Clifford R. Barnett, *Cuba, Its People, Its Society, Its Culture* (New Haven: HRAF Press, 1962), p. 344.

19. Ibid., pp. 343–44.

20. Ibid.

21. "Aspectos Demográficos," pp. 5, 9.

22. Ibid., pp. 3–6.

23. Marifeli Pérez-Stable, "The Emancipation of Cuban Women," paper presented at the Institute of Cuban Studies Conference on Women and Change: Comparative Perspectives with Emphasis on the Cuban Case, Boston, Mass. May 1977, pp. 9–10.

24. "CTC Resolutions," *Cuba Review,* Vol. 4, No. 2 (1974), p. 18.

25. V. Espín, "La Mujer," Ibid. p. 70.

26. H. Steffens, "A Woman's Place," Ibid. p. 29.

51. Race Relations in Contemporary Cuba*

BY LOURDES CASAL

It is the purpose of this report to attempt to draw a coherent picture of the status of blacks in pre- and post-revolutionary Cuba and an analysis of the changes which have transpired since the Revolution. Both tasks are rather difficult and fraught with perils. First of all, the descriptive task is hard, given the scarcity of systematic studies about the status of blacks in post-revolution-

*From Anani Dzidzienyo and Lourdes Casal, *The Position of Blacks in Brazilian and Cuban Society,* Minority Rights Group Report No. 7 (London: Minority Rights Group, 1979), pp. 11–27. Edited for this volume.

ary Cuba and the lack of appropriate attitudinal surveys. The task of comparing the present position of blacks with the pre-revolutionary society is even
harder, because the paucity of contemporary "hard" data is more than
matched by the lack of reliable, serious studies of race relations in pre-1959
Cuba. . . .

Particularly because of the paucity of data, it is easy to distort the "baseline"
information about the status of blacks in pre-revolutionary society. Without
an adequate description of this "baseline," it is not possible to make a fair
judgment of how the status of blacks has changed since the Revolution. It is
my opinion that, given the characteristics of the pre-revolutionary system of
race relations, the level of oppression of Cuba's blacks and the barriers to their
mobility have traditionally been minimized. They have been minimized in the
literature about race relations coming from liberal academicians in the U.S.
(i.e., Nelson Amaro and Carmelo Mesa-Lago's essay in *Revolutionary Change
in Cuba*[1]) but they were also minimized in Cuba's dominant ideology before
the Revolution. These beliefs, about the non-problematic nature of race relations in Cuba, affected both white and black in pre-1959 Cuban society. They
are part of the baseline description of race relations in Cuba which I will have
to outline later. A position which understates the level of oppression of blacks
in pre-revolutionary society will, automatically, tend to minimize the changes
brought about by the Revolution. . . .

RACE RELATIONS IN PRE-REVOLUTIONARY CUBA

As a young black Cuban, many things puzzled me about the complicated set
of rules governing relations between the races in my country and particularly
about the codes which regulated communications on race relations. I still
remember how I listened, wide-eyed and nauseated, to the stories—always
whispered, always told as when one is revealing unspeakable secrets—about
the horrors committed against my family and other blacks during the racial
war of 1912. A grand-uncle of mine was assassinated, supposedly by orders
of Monteagudo, the rural guard officer who terrorized blacks throughout the
island. Chills went down my spine when I heard stories about blacks being
hunted day and night; and black men being hung by their genitals from the
lamp posts in the central plazas of small Cuban towns.

The stories terrified me, not only because of their violence, but because my
history books said nothing about these incidents. The racial war of 1912, in
which thousands of blacks lost their lives was, at best, a line or a footnote in
the books. And even then, it was dealt with condescendingly. Typically, it was
referred to as *"la guerrita del' 12"* (the little war of 1912), as if it had been
a minor, quasi-farcical episode which could be dismissed or ignored. And yet,
thousands of blacks, both rebels and civilians, had died in war actions, race
riots and massacres.

The stories terrified me even more, because they conflicted with the *"no hay problema, aquí no ha pasado nada"* ("there's no problem; nothing has really happened") attitude about race relations which was communicated to me, even by my family. The horrifying stories were not to be told. Only on two or three occasions I managed to cajole some member of my family into talking about these things. In general, they seemed to share with the rest of Cuba in some sort of gentleman's agreement: not to speak "disagreeable" things concerning race. I could not understand. It seemed aberrant to me, that memories which were still alive in participants and witnesses, even in victims and relatives of victims, could have been so completely obliterated from the collective consciousness, so completely erased from everyday discourse and from history books. . . .

To understand Cuba's pre-revolutionary pattern of race relations it is necessary to survey (however briefly) the history of the Republic. The history of Cuba is so deeply interwoven with the history of black Cubans that one cannot be told without the other (in spite of the efforts of white bourgeois historians). Cuba's late independence and the development of annexationist and reformist ideologies in the nineteenth century seem to be linked to the "black scare," the spectre of another Haiti which afflicted the Cuban bourgeoisie and which was skillfully nurtured by Spain. Race relations during the Republic were deeply affected by the legacy of slavery (the legal abolition of which did not come in Cuba until 1886). In spite of the fact that a large percentage of the Cuban liberation army was black, black Cubans did not achieve the desired equality with their achievement of independence from Spain. The Cuban Republic soon betrayed the egalitarian ideology of José Martí, who had been the architect of the independence struggle. The long tradition of prejudice and the proximity of the abolition of slavery, to which we must add the further negative impact of U.S. influence and practical domination during the early years of the Republic, led to discriminatory practices which belied the formal equality guaranteed by the Constitution of 1901. Thus, restrictive statements in the Constitution about the franchise effectively limited the rights of blacks to vote. . . .

The Liberation Army was not considered by the U.S. occupation forces as an appropriate basis for the army of the young Republic. Thus, the Liberation Army was disbanded and the weapons of the old fighters bought for a few *pesos.* In the meantime, the Havana police and the rural guard were developed, strictly with white personnel.[2]

The black fighters of the Liberation Army were thus excluded from important administrative appointments (on the alleged basis that they did not have the necessary educational qualifications) and from appointments in the developing military establishment. A general in the Liberation Army, Quintin Banderas, was offered a position as postman by the Estrada Palma administration and in general, the first administration of the Cuban Republic was marred by discriminatory practices in employment and other areas. Even black congressmen were the targets of offensive practices by the administration. Thus, A. Poveda Ferrer and Generoso Campos Marquetti, elected members of the House of Representatives of the young Republic, received invitations to a reception at the Presidential Palace which excluded their wives. They returned the invitations and the incident was one of many which incensed blacks during the Estrada Palma administration.[3]

Exclusion from the governmental payroll was a serious handicap in a country devastated by war and affected by serious unemployment. Blacks attempted to gain access to employment by fighting for power within the structures of the existing parties and by 1908 through the organization of an association of black voters which became the *Partido de los Independientes de Color.*[4] However, the Morúa Amendments to the Electoral Reform Law of 1910 closed the doors of legality to the organization of parties along race lines and eventually led the *Independientes* to take arms against the José Miguel Gómez Administration. The ensuing racial war, still insufficiently studied, led to a nationwide extermination of blacks of quasi-genocidal proportions.[5]

The black Cuban community never recovered from the heavy losses inflicted upon its most race-conscious male leadership. Since the *Independientes* were hunted down during the war and its aftermath, no other political organization of blacks emerged in the neo-colonial Republic.[6] As Domínguez has pointed out, "the ethnic cleavage . . . was not reflected in the party system, and the parties were alike in opposing black affirmations of identity as well as in courting their votes."[7]

In spite of a few leading black politicians, black representation in elected offices remained at a dismal low throughout the Republic. Domínguez has estimated black proportion in the House of Representatives, as of the mid-20s, as less than 5 percent; with no blacks represented in the Senate.[8] During the 1933 Revolution against Machado, when Cuban radicalism tasted power for the first time during the first Grau Administration, a *Ley de Nacionalizacion del Trabajo* was passed by the radical wing of the Administration led by Antonia Guiteras. The law established that all industrial, commercial or service enterprises had to employ at least 50 percent of Cuban natives among its personnel. Although the law did not have an explicit racial intent, it had a great impact upon the structure of employment opportunities for blacks.

Arredondo describes occupational discrimination on the eve of the promulgation of the Law as follows:

> Blacks could not be tramway conductors, salesmen in any department or ten cent stores, railroad conductors or employees of commercial establishments or foreign enterprises. They found the doors closed to jobs as nurses, typesetters, hat makers, etc. Even in industries such as tobacco, the best paid jobs were closed to blacks. For him, the only jobs open were the most brutal jobs—such as dockworkers—and the most menial positions such as shoeshine boy, newspaper sales . . . , etc.[9]

Batista's domination of Cuban political life brought certain changes to Cuba's blacks: The former sergeant was obviously mulatto and regardless of his betrayal of the 1933 Revolution, his willingness to become a tool of the U.S. interests in the island and his many crimes, particularly in his later (1952) administration, Batista accomplished—wittingly or unwittingly—certain tasks of revolutionary importance. For example, the rank-and-file army rebellion against the officialdom which he eventually came to lead (and his assault upon the resisting officers which had taken refuge at the Hotel Nacional), effectively liquidated the army elite and opened the doors for a significant process of mobility within the army ranks which led to the promotion of many blacks to officer status. . . .

RACE RELATIONS ON THE EVE OF THE REVOLUTION

According to the last pre-revolutionary census—the 1953 Census—blacks and mulattoes represented 26.9 percent of the Cuban population. . . . Racial distribution varied from province to province, with the greatest concentration of blacks in recent censuses occurring in Oriente Province. . . . [On the basis of 1919 and 1943 census information, it is clear] that blacks were seriously underrepresented in Banks, Commerce, and Professions, while they were over-represented in Construction and Personal and Domestic Services. Thus, the 1943 Census provides clear indication of race discrimination manifested in occupational distribution differentials.

There were significant differences in the participation rate of black and white women in the labor force. While only 9.6 percent of all white Cuban women aged 13 or over were employed; 11.6 percent of all "colored" women aged 13 or over were thus classified.[10] "Colored" includes blacks, mulattoes, and Asiatics. Unfortunately no comparison with the 1953 Census is possible, given the lack of occupational breakdown by race in the last pre-revolutionary census. However, it is possible to compare the 1943 figures with those corresponding to the 1919 Census. Thus, some tentative conclusions can be drawn about the changes in black occupational status during that intercensus period.

Black participation in construction and manufacturing was maintained at high levels but there was a significant decline in the Agriculture, Fishing and Livestock category and moderate progress in black participation in Transportation and Communications, Banks and Financial Institutions and Professional Services (although in all these categories the black participation index even by 1943 remained below 100). Thus, the 1919–1943 intercensus period witnessed some improvement in black access to certain occupational categories but no dramatic changes in pattern (with the exception of the changes in the Mining category). In other words, in spite of quantitative changes, the same categories which found blacks underrepresented in 1919 found them underrepresented in 1943. . . .

Race differentials in income were also found in the 1943 Census data; although only two thirds of the labor force answered the income question, the available data show . . . blacks were more likely than whites to be found at the lowest income levels. The 1943 Census also provided information concerning "colored" and white unemployment in different occupational categories, and although given the problems of pre-revolutionary Cuban economy there were high rates of unemployment for both races, the available 1943 data suggest that the average "colored" unemployment rate was higher than the average white unemployment rate with significant differentials appearing in major areas of employment such as the sugar industry and government.[11] The 1943 Census data on education by race was limited to information on literacy rates (this was more than offered by the 1953 Census which did not provide any). A black-white differential in literacy rates was also in evidence, with roughly 73 percent of all whites age 10 and older being able to read while only 67.4 percent of all "colored" in a comparable age bracket could do so.[12] . . .

Most quantitative indicators suggest a gradual improvement in the status of blacks, but a rather slow one, with significant differentials obtaining in all categories up until the eve of the Revolution. However, gradual improvement in certain quantitative indicators for blacks does not necessarily mean that their position, with respect to whites, was improving; that is to say, the gap between the races was closing. Thus, Domínguez has reviewed data from physical anthropological surveys made between 1900 and 1964; changes in average height can be considered as indirect indicators of living standards. The findings suggest that

Although the improvement in living standard benefited all all three racial categories surveyed, both sexes, and all age groups tested, it was shared unequally: whites profited the most, and, as a result, the gap in life changes between whites and blacks widened considerably.[13]

As no formal studies of racial attitudes were conducted in pre-revolutionary society, it is not possible to complement the above discussion of indicators with information about the prevalence and forms of prejudice except from anecdotal records and other observers' reports. The latter usually agree in presenting a complex picture. There was undeniable racial discrimination, but frequently it was difficult to separate purely racial discrimination from discrimination on socioeconomic grounds. There was widespread prejudice, especially among the middle and upper sectors but not exclusively within them. Discrimination was more severe in certain regions, such as Camagüey, than in Havana. Patterns of social discrimination along racial lines were more clear-cut in small towns and cities in the countryside than in larger cities, except in Havana, where there were many private clubs and the beaches controlled by them. Also, the most prestigious private schools had exclusionary practices.

In general, the prevalence of prejudice and the patterns of institutionalized and non-institutionalized prejudice are described as less severe and blatant than in the U.S. However, it must be pointed out that white writers (the overwhelming majority) usually tend to present a far rosier picture of race relations during Republican times than black writers. . . .

Race was only one element in the determination of status in pre-revolutionary Cuba. Further, as Booth has emphasized, the existence of a relatively large "free colored" population since colonial times may have been a factor in avoiding a wide dichotomous division of the society.[14] Other factors to be considered are the process of "mulattoization" provoked by the scarcity of white women since colonial times, the significant role of blacks in the Cuban Liberation Army, and the role assigned to racial unity and integration by the most important leaders of the Cuban independence struggle such as José Martí (white) and Antonio Maceo (black).

It is not surprising, then, that black Cubans, even before the 1959 Revolution, would tend to see their problems in class rather than primarily racial terms. Thus, David Grillo Sáez, a black journalist who authored a book on *The Problem of Black Cubans (El Problema del Negro Cubano)* in 1953, sees the solution to the "problem of black Cubans" in a change in the status of all oppressed groups and social classes, since the problem is seen as basically a class problem. . . .[15]

However, it is the opinion of this writer that Cuban home-grown racism, with the "improvements" added to it by the strong U.S. penetration during Republican times, was more virulent and insidious than most writers on the issue have been willing to admit. The normative system of values at the core of the definition of nationhood was egalitarian, and integrationist but the practices were blatantly racist. . . .

In Havana, upper-class social clubs excluded blacks and mulattoes systematically. (Even Batista, during his term as President of the Republic [1940–1944], was blackballed at the Havana Yacht Club, the most exclusive of the upper-class clubs.) These clubs controlled private beaches in Havana which, therefore, excluded blacks. Middle-class clubs, especially those organized around professional associations, admitted those blacks who belonged to the respective professional associations. In Cuban small towns and provincial capitals, segregation was rigidly enforced in formal social life and in the patterns of informal association related to courtship, etc., such as the *paseos,* parks and other gathering places for young people. However, the most far-reaching structure of segregation was again not purely race-based. Instead it divided the Cuban population along class lines. I am talking about the school systems. Public schools in pre-revolutionary Cuba were integrated but the upper- and middle-income sectors massively abandoned the public school system during the 1933–1958 period. Thus, by 1958, no less than 120,000 grade school students and roughly 15,000 high school students attended *private schools*–approximately 14 percent and 29 percent of the total number of students enrolled at the respective levels. The private school system was predominantly, although not totally, white. Elite schools practised racial discrimination but it was hardly necessary: Very few blacks could afford the high tuition costs and other expenses.

Finally, it must be pointed out that during the years of the second Batista dictatorship (1952–1958), there was a concerted attempt to divorce the black masses from the revolutionary struggle and to divert its energies towards the development of facilities for blacks. In the words of José F. Carneado: ". . . there was an attempt to neutralize and to attract the black population towards the tyranny through the bastardly propaganda . . . that the struggle being fought in Cuba was 'white stuff.' "[16]

But the campaign was only partially successful. When the rebel forces entered Havana during the first week of 1959, blacks were represented at all levels—from the officialdom to the rank and file. In Havana, they met racial exclusivism and incidents at the Havana Hilton and other facilities were reported.[17] The revolutionary government would confront the issue head on.

RACE RELATIONS SINCE THE REVOLUTION

Masferrer and Mesa Lago have boldly stated that "after the Revolution, a picture of black suffering caused by discrimination was painted that exaggerated the degree of actual prejudice existing on the island."[18] Indeed, it must have seemed an exaggeration to them who minimized the degree of racial oppression in pre-revolutionary Cuba. However, if we take a less sanguine view of racial discrimination in Cuba before 1959, the changes—immediately after the revolutionaries took power—were clear-cut and definite. Fidel Castro, in a very early speech after the rebels had defeated Batista (March 1959), denounced racial discrimination in the most sweeping terms ever heard in Cuba from a political leader holding major office. The speech was unambiguous and tough. It recognized that "people's mentality is not yet revolutionary enough. People's mentality is still conditioned by many prejudices and beliefs from the past. . . ."[19] And then Castro proceeded (against the traditional conspiracy of silence about racial matters so deeply ingrained in the Cuban dominant ideology), to tell the truth, which hit Cuban society like a bombshell.

> One of the battles which we must prioritize more and more every day . . . is the battle to end racial discrimination at the work place. . . . There are two types of racial discrimination: One is the discrimination in recreation centers or cultural centers; the other, which is the worst and the first one which we must fight, is racial discrimination in jobs.

Thus, he finally addressed the issue which had irked black veterans of the Liberation Army during the first years of the Republic; the issue which had moved Estenoz and Ivonet to organize the *Partido de los Independientes de Color* and, ultimately, to the uprising of 1912; the issue which had motivated more frequently black protests and resentments until 1958: the unwritten barriers which prevented blacks from full equality of access to employment opportunities and which condemned them to the most menial and worst paid jobs; or to unemployment. But Fidel did not stop there. He attacked the best taboo:

> There is discrimination at recreation centres. Why? Because blacks and whites were educated apart. At the public grade school, blacks and whites are together. At the public grade school, blacks and whites learn to live together, like brothers. And if they are together at the public school, they are later together at the recreation centres and at all places.

The speech had a tremendously popular impact because of the sections of it which had dealt with the discrimination issue. . . .

It can be unhesitatingly affirmed that racial discrimination has been solidly eradicated from Cuban society. Nobody is barred access to jobs, education, social facilities of any kind, etc., for reasons of their skin color. The egalitarian and redistributive measures enacted by the revolutionary government have benefitted blacks as the most oppressed sector of the society in the pre-revolutionary social system. This does not imply that all forms of prejudice have been banned or that the consciousness of all the people has been thoroughly transformed. Privately, many white Cubans—even solid revolutionaries—employ the old racist language. The difference is that there is a tremendous cost in expressing such prejudiced opinions publicly. Also, the social system does not permit that these private opinions become translated into systematic discriminatory practices.[20]

Even if that bastion of white inviolability (the rate of interracial marriages) is considered, all the persons—white and black—which I informally interviewed in Cuba in 1978 agree that the frequency of interracial marriage has increased markedly since the Revolution and particularly in the last seven or eight years. There are no published statistics on interracial marriages, but the visible changes in terms of frequency of interracial couples seen strolling in Havana streets this summer of 1978 are remarkable. Booth already reported an increase in mixed couples as of 1975. This is a matter of considerable importance because it is the "most foolproof index of qualitative change in a colour-class system".[21] Personal observations by this author during visits to Cuba in 1976, 1977 and 1978, and opinions expressed by many Cubans interviewed, strongly suggest that mixed marriages—particularly of the black male-white female variety—are noticeably more frequent. Interracial couples do not tend to provoke the intense stares which they used to.

Attitudes towards interracial marriages, among Cuban youth, at least, had been found as relatively positive already in a survey of attitudes in Cuban students in 1962.[22] Nearly 60 percent (57.9 percent) of the young people interviewed by Torroella in 1962 said that they could marry someone of another race, while only 27.3 percent said that they would not, with the balance doubtful or not answering. Of course, interpretation of this survey result is made difficult by the lack of comparable data obtained in Cuba before the Revolution, or at a later point after 1962. However, 60 percent of pro-interracial marriage responses seems a high degree of positive responses, at least at the verbal level, suggesting an egalitarian normative system in the youth interviewed.

Evidence gathered by Geoffrey Fox in his dissertation, where he interviewed Cuban emigrés recently arrived in Chicago (both black and white) suggests another dimension to the changes brought about by the Revolution.[23] Some workers accused the Revolution of fostering racism. Upon investigation of what they exactly meant by that, it resulted that they felt the revolutionary leadership talked too much about race (violating the taboo which normally prevailed about the issue in polite Cuban society); that it had made blacks "uppity" (in Spanish *"le habia dedo ala a los negros"*) and that now blacks oppressed whites. Even black emigré workers felt embarrassed by having their race spoken about so much. Concerning Fox's study, it must be kept in mind that he interviewed only emigré workers, which by definition are examples of disaffection with respect to the Revolution, the changes brought about by it, etc. Maurice Zeitlin's study of industrial workers in Cuba as of 1962 provides a balancing picture. From Zeitlin's data it is very clear that black industrial workers (80 percent), even more than white industrial workers (67 percent) in his example, expressed support for the Revolution.[24] In Zeitlin's study, "many of the workers alluded spontaneously to the question of negro-white relations." Black workers frequently referred to the impact of the Revolution on race relations[25] in spite of the fact that the interview schedule did not contain any question about this issue.[25] Their comments referred to post-revolutionary equality of opportunity, the black Cuban freedom of access to all social facilities, their improvement in living conditions, etc.

IMPACT OF GENERAL REDISTRIBUTIVE MEASURES

There is clear consensus on the fact that the early redistributive measures of the Revolution (the two Agrarian Reform Laws, the Urban Reform Law, etc.) improved the status of blacks in particular, as they were overrepresented in the lowest sectors of the population. Revolutionary measures tending to equalize access to health and educational facilities (developing a massive public health system with preventive emphasis, elimination of private schools, expansion and improvement of the state school system, expansion of higher education and school facilities associated with the work place) have had special impact upon blacks. However, the Cuban Revolutionary Government has been criticized because they have not enacted policies of "positive discrimination" or "affirmative action" to offset the residual differences in life chances, access to elite schools or top level appointments which are the legacy of hundreds of years of oppression and discrimination.

The Cuban Revolutionary Government's position has been clear on this issue. They see "positive discrimination" measures as contrary to the egalitarian goals of the Revolution insofar as they tend to make the color of the skin an issue. They have practised some form of "positive discrimination" in terms of providing special facilities (i.e., rural communities) or programs (scholarships, etc.) to all members of a formerly disadvantaged group, but these examples have always involved all members of a formerly oppressed group, regardless of race. . . .

However, it could still be argued that unless some compensatory measures are taken, black Cuban children are going to find it very hard to compete, given the heritage of oppression. Domínguez, after reviewing published public health surveys before and after the Revolution, has concluded that racial inequality in public health remains a feature in Cuban life and that "Cuban blacks and mulattoes are demonstrably poorer; because they are poorer, they are more likely than whites to become sick. This was true before the Revolution, and it is still true in the 1970s."[26] However, his conclusions are based on an alleged high incidence of disease among blacks, particularly among what he calls "diseases of poverty." The evidence, however, is not strong enough to support his conclusions. In the first place, what seems well established is an *under*representation of blacks in some of what Domínguez calls "diseases of affluence" (heart attacks, cancer, etc.). With respect to the so-called "diseases of poverty," most of the evidence presented by Domínguez refers to pre-revolutionary surveys. Only two of those (burns on children and tuberculosis) deal with "diseases of poverty" according to his definition. The second problem is that many of the surveys deal with small samples and the representativeness and reliability of their results are highly questionable. . . .

The most far-reaching (in terms of development of racial equality) measure taken by the revolutionary government was probably the elimination of private schools. On the eve of the Revolution, roughly 15 percent of the Cuban grade school children and 30 percent of the high school students attended private schools, which were primarily white. The crisis of the state school system, its lack of resources for effectively carrying out its teaching mission, its poor reputation, had led to a proliferation of private schools where the children of the bourgeoisie (and the middle sectors which could afford them) were educated with little contact with the black masses and other oppressed sectors of the population. This segregation of the elite had far-reaching consequences as it made difficult the development of social networks across racial lines.

The private school system disappeared in Cuba by 1961. Since then, a totally integrated school system has developed. Nevertheless, it cannot be said that the long heritage of segregation and the impact of differential social chances have been completely erased. Visitors (particularly black American visitors, highly sensitive to these issues) notice underrepresentation of blacks in high-powered schools (such as the Lenin Vocational School, where a grade school average of 98 percent plus is a prerequisite for admission) and overrepresentation of blacks at the INDER (National Sports Institute) schools. However, the revolutionary government has already taken certain measures (i.e., the demand for a geographical distribution quota in admissions to the Lenin school) which, although they are not specifically directed at achieving racial balance, will have an undeniable effect in preventing these schools from becoming enclaves of the Havana elite. The whole thing must be placed into perspective; these high-powered schools serve a very small number of students, comparatively speaking. The bulk of Cuban students attend completely integrated schools where the races effectively mingle—from day-care centers to post-graduate education.

Other visible changes since the Revolution have occurred in the housing patterns. No clear-cut and rigid housing discrimination patterns existed in pre-revolutionary Cuba but blacks in Havana, for example, tended to be concentrated in dilapidated areas in the central city (Los Sitios, Jesús Maria, Atarés), the less desirable working class districts of Marianao and La Lisa, plus in the shantytowns such as "Llega y Pon." The Revolution brought an immediate reduction in rents (50 percent) and eventually ownership of the houses was granted to the former tenants. Thus, more blacks own their houses in Cuba than in any other country in the world. Yet the housing situation is very difficult for blacks and whites alike in contemporary Cuba because of the low priority given so far to construction of new houses—particularly in Havana—and because of the limited resources allocated to maintenance until now. . . .

An indicator of the changes in race relations transpiring since the Revolution is the accelerated process of "mulattoization" of Cuba. Publications to date of the data of the 1970 Cuban Census—the only post-revolutionary Census—have not included any breakdowns of the population according to race.[27] . . . However, in spite of the absence of published information on the racial breakdown of the Cuban population as of 1970, it is possible to speculate on the nature of the changes. It is my estimate that the percentage of "non-whites" in the Cuban population should have increased from 26.9 percent in the 1953 Census to a figure no less than 40 percent in 1970, and segregation of the races (i.e., separate social clubs, separate "walking routes" in the parks of Cuban small towns, the elimination of private schools, etc.) have meant increased opportunities for mingling of the races, which has accelerated the process of "mulattoization" of Cuba. . . .

BLACKS IN DECISION-MAKING STRUCTURES

Domínguez has estimated that the proportion of blacks in the 1965 Central Committee of the Cuban Communist Party was 9 percent, which in his view does not represent any improvement over the roughly 9 percent representation of blacks in "comparable" pre-revolutionary structures such as the House of Representatives and Senate, as of 1943.[28] However, the general thrust of the post-1970 changes has been in the direction of broadening the top decision-making echelons and clear structures and functional differentiations. A new analysis of black participation in the top level structures is in order. These structures are not any more just the Political Bureau at the Party level and the Cabinet at the Government level. Within the Party, the Political Bureau, the Secretariat, the Central Committee and the Control Commission would have to be analyzed. Within the State apparatus, one must look at the composition of the National Assembly and particularly the Council of State. Within the Government, the composition of the Council of Ministers should be analyzed. The national leadership of the mass organizations, such as CDRs, labor unions, FMC, FEEM, FEU, Pioneers, etc., would also have to be considered. This study is yet to be done. However, one must challenge the view which would judge black political participation in the revolutionary government just in terms of these top structures.

Inevitably, the top structures are more likely than not to reflect historical differentials as well as particular factors (such as the Batista propaganda which tended to identify the struggle going on during 1952–1958 as a "white man's problem"). Not even the worst critics of the Cuban régime have been able to present any evidence to the effect that blacks, because of their being black, have been excluded from decision-making positions. Blacks were well represented in the leadership of the PSP (Old Communist Party). Such blacks are still well represented in the revolutionary régime (Lázaro Peña led the unions until his death; Blas Roca has been a key figure in the institutionalization process and he is now the President of the National Assembly; other blacks, such as Severo Aguirre, are members of the Council of State). Given the fact that the top leadership in the Cuban régime still reflects the composition of the anti-Batista leadership, its racial makeup reflects historical factors. . . .

However, since the mid-sixties and with the institutionalization process and its concomitant broadening of the decision-making structures, there seems to have occurred a significant increase in black representation. However, a quantitative study is yet to be conducted. But looking just below the top echelons, at the intermediate levels of various structures, from the party to the army, would reveal a massive incorporation of blacks into the basic revolutionary institutions. Hard evidence is still to be collected, though. The above statement is based on informal observations which would require substantiation by other means.

An as yet unpublished study by Casal on the ethnic composition of the National Assembly, conducted during the last ordinary period of sessions (December 1978) shows combined black and mulatto representation in the National Assembly at approximately 36 percent, a fourfold increase with respect to the level of black and mulatto representation in equivalent elected structures before the Revolution. . . .

AFRO-CUBAN RELIGION AND CULTURE

Carlos More has decried Cuban government's practices with respect to Afro-Cuban culture and religion, which he claims are relegated to the level of folklore and not accorded the proper respect and importance. A major problem in More's perspective, as well as in the other expatriate and foreign black writers of the Revolution, is the tendency to apply to the Cuban context formulations derived from the black experience in other contexts, particularly the U.S. But as Sutherland points out "while similarities between the black Cuban and Afro-American experience existed, there must also be great differences."[29]

The major difference is that black Cubans cannot really be considered a national minority. The Cuban Communists, having committed that mistake once, when in 1934 they defined the black problem in Cuba as a national question and they proposed black self-determination in the so-called "black belt" of Oriente Province, have been very much aware of avoiding such a pitfall again.

Cuban culture, which has slowly been evolving during several centuries, is undoubtedly Afro-Hispanic. In spite of the efforts of the white dominant classes, in spite of their resistance, black cultural elements are integrated into Cuban music, Cuban popular lore (including proverbs and sayings), Cuban plastic arts, poetry, etc., in such fashion that, without their component of black heritage, they would not be what they are; they would not be *Cuban.* And this must not be seen as the result of an assimilationist option, but rather as the consequence of a true *mestizaje,* of the complex interactions of two powerful cultural traditions. Even black religious and fraternal groups had, during the Republic, gradually accepted whites within their ranks (i.e., the Abakúa secret brotherhood, as well as the most widespread of the syncretic religions, the Cuban version of the Yoruba religion, *santeria*). . . .

Cuba today has established the structural basis for full equality and total integration. Furthermore, the concept of the Cuban as basically Afro-Hispanic (with some Chinese elements thrown in) is taking root in the national consciousness (José Martí, Fernando Ortiz, and Fidel Castro would be building stones in the development of this consciousness). It was Fidel Castro's role to be the first Cuban white ruler to recognize openly the *mulatto* character of Cuban culture and nationhood. When in his speech of 19 April 1976 he quietly asserted "We are a Latin African people," Fidel was making history. . . .

Given the normal *decalage* between structural transformations and transformations at the level of consciousness *(conciencia);* given the lack of historical precedent for a truly integrated, *mulatto* culture; there is still some road to travel in the way to a society where the last vestiges of centuries of oppression and ideologies of racial division and superiority are finally eliminated. But of all the countries in the world it is Cuba, under socialism, where this appears as a historical possibility in the foreseeable future.

NOTES

1. Nelson Amaro and Carmelo Mesa-Lago, "Inequality and Classes," in *Revolutionary Change in Cuba,* ed. by Carmelo Mesa-Lago (Pittsburgh: University of Pittsburgh Press, 1971), pp. 341–74.

2. For a history of the Cuban armed forces during the Republic, see Louis A. Perez, *Army Politics in the Cuban Republic 1902–1958* (Pittsburgh: University of Pittsburgh Press, 1976).

3. Serafín Portunondo Linares, *Los Independientes de Color* (La Habana: Publicaciones del Ministerio de Educación, Dirección de Cultura, 1950), p. 15.

4. Ibid., p. 19.

5. For a general discussion of racial problems in the early Republic as they affected political life, see Thomas T. Orum, "The Politics of Color: The Racial Dimension of Cuban Politics During the Early Republican Years, 1900–1912," unpublished Ph.D. dissertation, Department of History, New York University, 1975.

6. David Booth, "Cuba, Color and the Revolution," *Science and Society,* 11, 2 (Summer 1976), p. 148.

7. Jorge Domínguez, *Cuba: Order and Revolution* (Cambridge, MA: The Belknap Press of Harvard University Press, 1978), p. 49.

8. Ibid.

9. Alberto Arredondo, *El Negro en Cuba* (Havana: Editorial "Alfa," 1939) pp. 146–47.

10. Centro de Estudios Demográficos, *La Población de Cuba* (La Habana: Edit. de Ciencias Sociales, 1976), pp. 105–6.

11. Ibid., p. 106.

12. Computed from Ibid., pp. 926 and 930.

13. J. Domínguez, *Cuba: Order and Revolution,* pp. 75–76 and Appendix B, pp. 515–20.

14. D. Booth, "Cuba, Color and Revolution," p. 318.

15. David Grillo Sáez, *El problema del Negro Cubano* (La Habana: n.p., 1953).

16. Jose F. Carneado, "La discriminación racial en Cuba no volvera jamas," *Cuba Socialista,* Year 2, No. 5 (January 1962), p. 62.

17. Cf. D. Booth, "Cuba, Color and Revolution," p. 155.

18. Marianne Masferrer and Carmelo Mesa-Lago, "The Gradual Integration of the Black in Cuba: Under the Colony, the Republic and the Revolution," in *Slavery and Race Relations in Latin America,* ed. by Robert Brent Toplin (Westport, CT: Greenwood Press, 1974), p. 373.

19. All quotations translated by the author from Fidel Castro, "Discurso del 22 marzo de 1959," *Revolución* (March 23, 1959), pp. 24–27.

20. Booth recognizes: ". . . in the climate prevailing since 1959, state-employed managers and functionaries have been unable to practice open racial discrimination" (D. Booth, "Cuba, Color and Revolution," p. 158).

21. Ibid., p. 165.

22. Gustavo Toroella, *Estudio de la juventud cubana* (La Habana: Comisión Nacional Cubane de la UNESCO, 1963), pp. 105–06. See also J. Domínguez, *Cuba: Order and Revolution,* p. 484.

23. Geoffrey E. Fox, "Working Class Emigrés from Cuba: A Study of Counterrevolutionary Consciousness," unpublished Ph.D. dissertation, Northwestern University, 1975, p. 101–18. See also "Cuban Workers in Exile," *Transaction,* 8, 11 (September 1971), pp. 21–30.

24. Maurice Zeitlin, *Revolutionary Politics and the Cuban Working Class* (Princeton: Princeton University Press, 1967), p. 77.

25. Ibid., pp. 75–76. Actually, all of Chapter 3 in Zeitlin's book is devoted to "Race Relations and Politics," pp. 66–68 and contains important material of relevance to the questions discussed here.

26. J. Domínguez, *Cuba: Order and Revolution,* p. 256.

27. However, the basic form employed by enumerators, included a question (No. 5) about color of the skin and four categories to be checked: white, black, mulatto and yellow. See Republica de Cuba, Juceplan, *Censo de Población y Viviendas 1970* (La Habana: Edicion Orbe, 1975); Centro de Estudios Demográficos, *La Población de Cuba* (La Habana: Edit. de Ciencias Sociales, 1976).

28. J. Domínguez, *Cuba: Order and Revolution,* p. 226.

29. For a highly nuanced picture, where many different black Cuban voices are allowed to speak, see Elizabeth Sutherland's *The Youngest Revolution: A Personal Report on Cuba* (New York: Dial Press, 1969), p. 155.

CHAPTER 17

Culture

52. Talking About Cuban Culture: A Reporter's Notebook*

BY SANDRA LEVINSON

Cuban cultural life and cultural policy appear at the periphery of every discussion about Cuban socialism—with good reason, for the changes in Cuban culture have mirrored changes in the Cuban revolution itself. The subject of culture is also caught up in the dynamic of U.S.–Cuban relations, as some intellecutals and embittered exiled artists regularly fan the flames of anti-communism by proclaiming that under Cuban socialism there is no freedom for the artist.

The complex interaction of these factors contribute to the difficulty in understanding how revolutionary culture has developed in Cuba. It is especially difficult for North Americans. Building a revolutionary culture means encouraging artists, writers, filmmakers, photographers, actors, and dancers to be as creative as they can be. At the same time, it implies that artists are accountable to their society, an implication that is alien to a capitalist, individualistic social system such as ours. Most artists and intellectuals in Cuba not only accept this responsibility, but consider it a part of their art. . . .

Reynaldo González is a Cuban writer of novels, essays and *testimonios,* that special genre in Cuba which enables a writer to fictionalize true events. He is 47, and despite the blue eyes and blond hair, pure *cubano,* born in Camagüey to parents who were both union activists. His father was killed in the middle

*This essay was written for this volume. Copyright 1988 by Sandra Levinson.

of a strike during Batista's reign, and his mother died of cancer shortly after being incarcerated for her political activities.

Since 1969, Reynaldo has answered my many questions with great patience, yet he always insists that I look at things from his, from Cuba's, perspective. "It's hard for you North Americans to understand what it means to make a revolution," he says, "and we've had to do it with you, our close neighbors, trying to stop us at every turn."

Reynaldo and I are sitting in his book-lined study in Havana on a recent sunny afternoon. A cassette of *Good Old America* with songs of the 1950s provides an incongruous background to our conversation. I ask him about freedom in Cuba, freedom for the artist.

> Look, I don't know of any country where that sublime goal of "freedom of expression" is totally fulfilled. True freedom of expression supposes the possibility of changing that which is criticized. When you bring up freedom, you start from the possibility of reaching catharsis, expressing a feeling, shouting complaints, pointing out defects, but often you only achieve the shout, the complaint, the catharsis. Nothing is changed. In that sense, what you have is the mirage of freedom. I don't believe in that.

He paused, reflecting, and then said,

> It's true that in Cuba we don't have opposition papers. I couldn't publish a novel which tried to subvert the revolutionary order and which consequently could be used by an enemy constantly fighting my country. I can't make a cult of drug addiction or express a public hosanna to hallucinogens. I live in a different political situation than you. . . . The circumstances in which the Cuban revolutionary process took place, the fragility of a past of dependent democracy and its subsequent lack of traditions, all of this led to a specific exercise of freedom in a process that was for the first time breaking the limits of a rightist dictatorship.

The fact that Cuban socialism provides people with their basic needs means that energy can be used creatively to a remarkable degree. First-time visitors to Cuba often comment that "It seems that everyone you meet in Cuba writes poetry, sings, dances, paints, acts or plays an instrument!" Although that's an exaggeration, it is true that Cuba's cultural institutions and activities occupy a disproportionately large space in a country of ten million.

Cuba today has 2,000 libraries and 250 museums; before 1959, it had 100 libraries and six museums. It prints 50 million books each year as compared to fewer than one million before the revolution, and all are sold below cost or distributed gratis. The film industry, which didn't exist before the revolution, now produces about ten feature films a year and 50 "shorts," sponsors an annual Latin American Film and Video Festival and in late 1986 opened a major film school for the Third World under the direction of Argentine filmmaker Fernando Birri. There are festivals of theater, jazz, ballet, guitar, popular music, and modern dance, as well as seminars and conferences on literature and art, the Havana Biennial (of Third World art), and the prestigious Casa de las Americas literary awards.

More than 200 *casas de cultura,* in neighborhoods throughout the island, offer workshops in dance, theater, art and music. Professionals train at the Instituto Superior del Arte at Cubanacán (on grounds once belonging to the Havana Country Club), and graduates are assured salaried jobs in their professions. There are lithographic and ceramics workshops; amateur arts groups in almost all workplaces and art, literary and music brigades for young professionals, and a *casa de fotografía* with teaching and darkroom facilities and large galleries. . . . The recording industry exports Cuban music worldwide, some of it even crosses the blockaded borders of the United States.

The diversity of Cuban culture is impressive. It is common now for classic and traditional art forms to coexist with the modern and experimental. In dance, the National Ballet Company, directed by Prima Ballerina Alicia Alonso; the Ballet of Camagüey, directed by ex-husband Fernando Alonso, the Modern Dance Company, and the Conjunto Folklórico Nacional, among others, live happily with the rumba, the cha-cha, the *merengue,* and rock of the clubs and the break dancing of the streets.

The National Art Museum exhibits works of Cuba's contemporary giants—Wifredo Lam, René Portocarrero, Mariano Rodríguez, Servando Cabrera Moreno and Raúl Martínez—alongside the Afro-Caribbean primitivist art of Manuel Mendive, Nelson Dominguez' lush tropical foliage and Tomás Sánchez' exquisite landscapes. More recently, the permanent collection has found itself sharing space with the family and neighborhood kitsch of Rubén Torres Llorca, Magdalena Campos' erotic suggestions of Afro-Cuban visual elements, and the installations of Flavio Garciandía and José Bedia, as well as with Roberto Fabelo's lovely drawings and Gustavo Pérez' sophisticated prints. Political and film poster art flourish, as do erotic paintings and sculptures by art students at Cubanacán, home of the university-level art school.

Theater ranges from the serious contemporary works and classics presented by the Teatro Estudio to the audience-participation pieces of the Teatro Escambray in the mountains, the street theater and "teatro de relaciones" in Santiago de Cuba, popular musical theater in Old Havana and experimental groups in factories and other work places.

Films (see Reading 53) range from the intellectual *Memories of Underdevelopment* by Tomás Gutiérrez Alea, to the comedic *House for Swap* by Juan Carlos Tabío or made-for-television romance and real life serials. There is the elegant poetry of Eliseo Diego, Cintio Vitier and Fina García Marrúz, the Afro-Cuban rhythms in the poetry of Cuba's national poet, Nicolás Guillén, and that of factory worker-poet Eloy Machado; the poetic explorations of the intimate and the revolutionary by Nancy Morejón and Pablo Armando Fernández (Reading 56); the testimonial novels of Miguel Barnet and Reynaldo González, the poetry and espionage novels of Luis Rogelio Nogueras.

The *nueva trova* (see Reading 55) music, born in the 1960s, exists happily with a musical panorama which includes symphony and *charanga* orchestras, the guitar classics of Leo Brouwer, the traditional dance rhythms of Orquesta Aragón, the Afro-jazz of Irakere, the pop *songo, son* and *merengue* of Los Van Van, the *decimas* of the countryside, the *soneros* of the clubs and even U.S. popular music, ever-present on radio and television. Photography encompasses the studio portrait photography of Osvaldo Salas, the vibrant street scenes of Mavito and Marucha, the men at work of Ivan Cañas, the experiments of Cuenca and Gory, the testimonial photographs of Korda and Corrales and the tinted works of Raúl Martínez.

Cuba is a cultural festival, and the revolutionary process gives the art a special grace and intelligence, its own distinct flavor. *El proceso,* the revolutionary process, is central to understanding Cuban culture. *El proceso* means that nothing is carved in stone—what works today just won't do tomorrow. Ideas change, institutions change, and even socialists and communists change. Policies of the mid-1960s to early 1970s do not define cultural policy today. Fifteen years ago many writers and artists were frozen out of Cuban cultural life. Some were gay, and suffered from prejudice. Others were seen as insufficiently serious about their responsibilities within the revolution. There were also those who became the object of a bureaucrat's dislike. Today, Cuban cultural life flourishes in a context where it is accepted that artists are "different," and that their very difference enriches Cuban society.

The government policy which compelled writers like Guillermo Cabrera Infante, Heberto Padilla, Reynaldo Arenas and others to leave Cuba belongs to the past. Much of the change stems from the birth of the Ministry of Culture in 1976 and the appointment of Armando Hart Dávalos to head the ministry. Before 1976, Cuban cultural policy was shaped by people at the Consejo Nacional de Cultura who seemed to care more for the revolution in the abstract than for revolutionary culture in practice. Many of their decisions reflected a belief that culture can be defined and used by the revolution, rather than that the revolution can feed artistic life, and that art in turn can give to the revolutionary process enlightenment and beauty.

The process of developing a modern revolutionary culture began with the successful 1961 literacy campaign, which meant that Cuba could construct cultural life on a literate base. The campaign to insure a sixth-grade education was followed by one to guarantee a ninth-grade education to all. The fruits of the literacy campaign and the free educational system, which assure a reading and writing public, are dramatically visible in Cuba's publishing industry, which is today one of the largest in Latin America.

Among the many publishing houses are two devoted to Cuban authors,

Letras Cubanas and UNEAC (The Cuban Artists and Writers Union); one dedicated to the social sciences; one specializing in translations and international classics, Arte y literatura; Editorial Abril, which publishes books and magazines for the young; Editorial Gente Nueva, for children and adolescents; Editorial José Martí, the foreign language publishing house; Editorial Orbe, which specializes in miscellaneous writing which can't be easily categorized; Ciencias técnicas, which publishes everything from pamphlets on gardening to histories of inventions, and the University of Havana. Casa de las Américas, a cultural institution devoted to Central and South America and the Caribbean, publishes books, magazines, pamphlets and recordings. A number of provincial publishers devote themselves to reviving traditions specific to the most remote regions of the country through books, pamphlets, and periodicals. In addition, there is a publishing house devoted to huge editions of textbooks, which are distributed free to those who fill the hundreds of schools throughout the country.

José Rodríguez Feo is a literary critic and translator who has the distinction of being the only Harvard graduate still living in Cuba. His family owned a large sugar mill in Oriente Province and, like many children of the rich in prerevolutionary Cuba, he went to U.S. schools.

"Before the revolution," he observed,

> I financed two important literary magazines, *Orígenes* and *Ciclón*. I know from my own experience as a writer and publisher the fate of anyone who wanted to be a writer in Cuba before—the lack of opportunity, the impossibility of having your work published, the total indifference of my own class and the previous government and its politicians to art and culture. I've seen how different everything is now compared to the miserable lives my writer friends led here before 1959, the recognition and help given writers and artists in the new Cuba. How couldn't I then feel for the revolution? Could any person of sensibility and intelligence be blind to the changes?

Nancy Morejón is a poet and essayist, who speaks French and English almost as fluently as her Cuban Spanish. She is the only child of a militant dock worker and his textile worker wife. In 1962, when only 17, she entered the University of Havana to study French. She has published many books of poetry and written about Nicolás Guillén, with whom she worked for many years, and has also written (with Carmen Gonce) *Lengua de pájaro,* a sociological essay about the Nicaro nickel mines and the people who work them. Today she directs the Caribbean program at Casa de las Américas.

Guillén wrote that Nancy's poetry is as black as her skin, and that it is also Cuban "with roots so deep they emerge on the other side of the planet." Friend and fellow writer Miguel Barnet says that "For Nancy, the revolution is not merely an option; it is a tangible essence."

I ask Nancy if her life would have been different without the revolution. "I wouldn't have created anything," she answered.

> I don't think that anyone would have developed my intelligence, detected my abilities. The revolution put at my command everything from the book they gave me to the book they published for me. . . . When I entered the university in 1962, the year of the October [Missile] Crisis, I entered an essentially political, revolutionary world—I was on guard duty during the October Crisis, and it was the first time I'd ever slept outside my own home; life itself was at stake. My first two books of poetry were published during my first two years at the university. . . .
>
> *Lengua de pájaro* is a sociohistorical monograph, completely different from my poetry, and for me this book is a way of contributing to the revolutionary culture of my country, expressing a reality which can't always be expressed through poetry. Much of my poetry is very personal and intimate, about my life and my family, but I can extend that intimacy to the more political, too, as in my poems about Grenada, which I wrote after the invasion. I met a young girl in my neighborhood the other day who came up to me and recited one of the Grenada poems. It was thrilling.

Nancy's remarks remind me of something Ambrosio Fornet wrote: "The poet understands that he must become, among other things, a master communicator . . . so that the poem he writes in silence today will be repeated by people in the streets tomorrow."

There is some justification for saying that Cuba is a land of poets: Between 1959 and 1984, Cuba published 2,644 literature titles by Cuban authors (exclusive of children's literature) and 844, or nearly 32 percent, were poetry. However, there has been a notable shift in emphasis in the years since the Ministry of Culture was established in 1976. Between 1977 and 1984, there have been more novels and short stories published and many fewer works of theory and biography. Whereas between 1959 and 1976, poetry represented 36 percent of the country's literary output (686 titles), short stories 15 percent (284 titles) and novels 11.5 percent (220 titles), between 1977 and 1984, poetry dropped to 21 percent (158 titles) and the short story and novel genres rose to 21.4 percent (160 titles) and 20.7 percent (155 titles) respectively.

Literary criticism has risen somewhat, from 6 percent (111 titles) in the earlier period to 9 percent (70 titles) in the latter. The biggest drops can be seen in the theoretical essays and biography: Between 1959 and 1976, there were 90 essay titles published, 4.7 percent of the total, and only five titles published 1977–84, or 0.7 percent; 100 titles of biography were published 1959–76, 5.2 percent, and in the later period only 11 or 1.5 percent.

The changes indicate that younger writers have found a voice, and that their creative output has displaced the earlier more "political" works of biography and Marxist theory. Criticism is becoming an important part of Cuban cultural life—not only have the number of published books of criticism increased, but literary and artistic criticism appears regularly in daily newspapers and in newsmagazines as well as in cultural magazines, and much of it is sharply pointed.

At the beginning of the revolution, a literary supplement of the newspaper *Revolución, Lunes de Revolución,* offered Cuban readers an avant garde literature meant for an intellectual elite. It was as though Cuban intellectuals were looking to western Europe to define their artistic aspirations. Cuban writer Edmundo Desnoes, who now lives in New York, confirms this early attitude:

> Ambrosio Fornet and I were asked to be editors of the new publishing house, and we agreed to do so only if we began by publishing Joyce, Kafka and Proust. Today, that wouldn't be my priority. What does someone with a sixth grade education really understand about Kafka, and what does Kafka really have to say to a young person in a revolutionary society? But the revolution published them; in a certain sense it was more tolerant than we were. Today I would think it much more important to create a kind of literature in which people can see themselves, that expresses the society and their lives; to paint about Cuba as Michaelangelo painted about the Renaissance, in a humanistic way, or to write as Shakespeare wrote about power.

Lunes ceased publication in less than two years, a victim of the belief among some government leaders that "elitist" writing was not a priority of the revolution.

Literature has been the art form most affected by the revolution and its cultural policies. The "Padilla case" in 1971 deeply affected Cuban writers and unleashed a storm of criticism from foreign intellectuals (See Reading 54). Poet Heberto Padilla was arrested, held in custody for 38 days, and then made a public pseudo-confession in which he condemned several of his fellow writers for the alleged crime of unbounded "egoism" and "vanity" to which he had just confessed. In the next nine years he was unable to publish any work (though he lived well in a large house in Havana), and he emigrated in 1980. In fact his "crime" appears to have been that he actively encouraged foreign intellectuals to criticize Cuba harshly, and that he saw himself as a privileged citizen who did not need to heed ordinary limits. The episode was an unfortunate way to teach a revolutionary lesson, that with the liberating circumstances of revolutionary transformation comes revolutionary responsibility.

In this regard, Desnoes says,

> If you believe in revolution, you must go through the torture of reshaping yourself. Most people never question their values, but it is the responsibility of the intellectual to question his values. At the beginning in Cuba our values were

sympathetic to socialism but had bourgeois roots. I think that what was destroyed in 1971 with the Padilla case was the bourgeois idea that the artist is the conscience of society. Perhaps these bourgeois ideas were destroyed with unnecessary violence and with other methods, more writers might have understood, but it does seem that people don't really understand without a complete overhaul of the system.

The years following the Padilla case were difficult for writers. Many of Cuba's best-known writers today were not published at all in the early 1970s. But the fear that the Padilla case would mean cultural "Stalinism" proved groundless, and current cultural policy has been formulated with the active participation of many of the very artists and writers once shunned by the government.

Cuban plastic arts have received international acclaim, perhaps because the question of abstract/modernist art versus "socialist realism" has never been an issue. Fidel Castro underscored this early in the revolution when he said, "Our enemies are capitalists and imperialists, not abstract art."

Several of Cuba's best artists were part of the "Group of Eleven" who had fought the Cuban art establishment before the revolution, in an attempt to make abstract art legitimate. Yet one of them, Raúl Martínez, found that after the revolution abstraction was not the language with which he wanted to communicate. In an interview he said,

> I wanted to paint so that I could communicate my feelings about the revolution very directly to everyone, not just to a knowledgeable elite. I began to experiment with what you call pop art, in large extravagant paintings of our revolutionary heroes and of ordinary people. Often I used photographs I'd taken of friends as the basis for my paintings. They have strong colors, lots of people and lush foliage, and I think they say something very directly about our revolution.

Martínez' multiple images of José Martí and Fidel Castro, and his murals of ordinary people, found their way not only into the galleries and museums, but also became backdrops to C.D.R. block parties.

Cuban poster art firmly established itself as an exciting communicator of revolutionary messages by the early 1960s. Posters made for every film and cultural event, as well as those commemorating revolutionary historical dates, health, ecology, and voluntary work campaigns, attest to what Eva Cockcroft refers to as a "stylistic diversity and a frank eclecticism which borrowed freely from the capitalist as well as the socialist world." Many of the best known posters—for example, Martinez's poster for *Lucia*—were produced for ICAIC, the film institute.

Against a background of pure yellow, a purple rose thrusts itself upward on a green stem, framed by shiny green leaves. From one of its two thorns falls a single drop of red blood. The bleeding rose is the most recognized graphic image to come out of revolutionary Cuba. It is emblazoned on T-shirts, record and book jackets, and political pamphlets the world over. It made its debut in 1967 as a poster for the first festival of "canción protesta" at Varadero Beach.

Artist Alfredo Rostgaard, when asked why he chose a bleeding rose, says, "I wanted to show both the beauty and pain of making a revolution. And that, after all, is what protest music is all about—making beautiful music about the world's pain."

Music is central to Cuba's cultural life, and its traditional forms—from the charanga and the *danzón* to the *son* and the cha-cha-cha and the rural *decima*—are as popular in revolutionary Cuba as before. There are also dozens of new musical groups, many of which, like Los Van Van and Irakere, two of the most popular jazz-salsa groups, combine modern and traditional forms of Cuban music.

Most revolutionary, however, was the birth of the *nueva trova* movement in the 1960s. Spearheaded by two young musician-composers, Silvio Rodríguez (Reading 55) and Pablo Milanés, both form and content of the new music were at first rejected by the music establishment and by musicologists, who said that the *nueva trova* "has nothing to do with Cuba; it could have been written anywhere." The songs spoke to the difficulties, as well as triumphs, of a society in transformation. . . . Under the wing of ICAIC, *nueva trova* musicians became part of the Grupo Experimentación Sonora that provided the music for most Cuban movies. Silvio and Pablo, joined by Sara González, Noel Nicola, Amaury Perez, Grupo Moncada, Grupo Manguaré and others, became leaders of a new song movement whose influence today stretches throughout the Americas.

In a 1986 television documentary, Silvio talked about freedom for the artist in Cuba. "I've always thought that to be an artist," Silvio remarked, "you must first be a human being." He continued:

> When you take up your guitar to play or your pen to write, or you dance or paint, you defend the option you chose as a person first. That was my case—I was with the revolution first and then I started to write songs, and, of course, they were songs in support of the revolution. Maybe they weren't revolutionary songs, because being a true revolutionary in art is very difficult. . . . We always believed that we were doing revolutionary art, because it was committed and self-critical. It wasn't accommodating or apologetic, but an art that served the revolution because it looked at our defects and sang to the best of what we could be.

Sergio Corrieri, actor *(Memories of Underdevelopment),* founder and director of the Escambray Theater and now the Central Committee's *responsable* for Cuban culture, was being interviewed by a U.S. journalist for an article that later was not published. The writer wanted to know why the spectacular shows at the Tropicana nightclub still existed in revolutionary Cuba. "There's nothing very revolutionary about dancing girls in scanty fifties' costumes," she commented. "Isn't the Tropicana an anachronism in socialist Cuba?"

Corrieri smiled indulgently. "Well, you may be right," he said.

> But that's something sophisticated people like you think about—and there are many people here too who think that way. They'd like us to rid ourselves of all vestiges of our prerevolutionary past, just as we put an end to the beauty contests at carnival time. But the Tropicana was always the fanciest nightclub, where only people with money could go. And now, when ordinary workers who never saw the inside of a nightclub can afford the Tropicana show, it doesn't seem right to us that they shouldn't have the chance. In fact, the Tropicana show has changed a lot, incorporating traditional African dances and ballet, comic routines that criticize and comment on daily life. I don't find the Tropicana objectionable, it's really quite beautiful, and it's very very Cuban.

Begun by Corrieri in 1969, the Escambray Theater is a good example of the concerted effort to build a society of participants, not merely culture consumers. Corrieri says that one factor in his decision to take theater people from Havana into the Escambray Mountains was the soul-searching engendered by his role in *Memories of Underdevelopment.* In the movie, he plays a middle-class, would-be writer who remains always at the fringes of the revolution, observing the changes but unable to participate.

The Escambray Mountains cover an area of Cuba which had been the site, in the mid-sixties, of greatest resistance to the revolution. Swept by missionaries from Brooklyn in the 1950s, the area included many Jehovah's Witnesses who refused military service. Aided and abetted by exiled mercenaries, the almost all-white population of the Escambray fought a last-ditch series of battles against the revolutionary government, in what Cubans call *la lucha contra los bandidos.* After their military defeat, many Escambray residents continued verbal battle against anything new—they argued against secondary schools in the countryside which would educate their children better but with less parental control; they disagreed with moves to collectivize inefficient farming in the area, and the Jehovah's Witnesses refused to participate in any collective social action they deemed in conflict with their religious beliefs.

The Escambray Theater was based on a radical idea: Plays would be written about the problems in the area as defined by those who lived there, and the plays would include audiences as actors in the play. This sociopolitical theater was put on in the open squares of small towns throughout the mountains. The plays reflected people's concerns about the revolutionary changes and were often written without endings, thus allowing the audience itself to act out the endings. If a play included a scene with a workers' assembly, the audience became that assembly. People vented their frustrations and anger in public, and the plays provided a rational context within which to discuss the problems.

Within months, University of Havana sociologists were following the Escambray Theater troupe, interviewing townspeople to see if their attitudes and ideas were changing. They were, and the Escambray Theater is now an essential part of the fabric of mountain life.

The dramatic advances in culture cannot be separated from Cuba's humanist inheritance that the revolution did not reject, but rather revived and values. (It is significant that Cuba's highest cultural award bears the name of a thin and angry, brilliant clergyman, Félix Varela.) Nor can the advances be separated from the revolutionary transformation itself. The arts in Cuba are inextricably linked to the social, political, and economic changes that have occurred in the past 27 years.

One cannot understand the growth of the publishing industry without knowing about the literacy campaign, nor understand the proliferation of amateur groups in the countryside while ignoring the creation of agricultural cooperatives. The U.S. blockade has subjected Cuba to an uninformed evaluation of its cultural reality.

This is not to say that Cuba can be compared to the cultural metropolises. As Reynaldo tells me,

> Such comparison is absurd and unfair, because Cuba is a blockaded, underdeveloped, and attacked island. You must compare us with Colombia, Ecuador, Venezuela, Costa Rica, Puerto Rico, to territories in the same area which have been subjected to similar historic conditions. The blockade has been one of the most difficult problems to overcome in the cultural field because it's prevented information from coming into Cuba, and an art which is isolated from its natural context—and that of Cuba is Latin America, the world in which our island is located both geographically and spiritually—can't be the same as the art of a culture that breathes freely.

The North American who can leave prejudice, the consumer mentality, and anticommunism behind, can appreciate cultural life in Cuba as a vibrant, exciting, different reality worthy of respect, one whose advances have occurred in the context of building socialism with enormous difficulties, not least of which is proximity to a powerful enemy.

Writer Alejo Carpentier, after surveying the visual art and poetry of Latin America and finding it subject to "an abominable folkloric realism," urged his compatriots to look deeply into universal culture, and into the culture of their own island, and to express "the magical, the singular, the directly poetic." Cuba today is well on the way to fulfilling Carpentier's hope for a cultural future uniquely Cuban.

53. Cuba Vision: Three Decades of Cuban Film*

BY PAT AUFDERHEIDE

"Cuban cinema was born without original sin," novelist-screenwriter Manuel Pereira likes to say. He doesn't mean there was no film in Cuba before the 1959 revolution—you could get a commercial made, or a home movie of your kid's christening, or crank out a porno quickie. You could even film events people would just as soon not have recorded, and use the film as blackmail. But cinema as a national industry began with the revolution, and its tensions and textures are those of life in socialist Cuba.

In March 1959, when the Cuban Institute for the Art and Industry of Cinema (ICAIC) was founded, filmmakers found the richest possible dramatic material right outside their doors. ICAIC launched its film work with brilliant, punchy, controversial documentaries. During the 1960s, filmmakers built on experience with fiction features incorporating documentary styles; films such as *Memories of Underdevelopment, The Other Francisco,* and *Lucia* became the darlings of international festivals as well as box office hits at home. For a while, it looked like Cubans were developing not only a film industry but a film language.

And then Cuban film disappeared from international sight for years. Actually, it went "into development," as they say in Hollywood. On the 25th anniversary of ICAIC in 1984, founding fathers such as Tomás Gutiérrez Alea, Santiago Alvarez and Humberto Solas finished long-standing feature projects for the occasion, and a new generation of feature directors has emerged.

This burst of production is rooted in the same soil as Cuban film's two earlier phases—the great rolling social changes that in Cuba go under one handy rubric: "The Revolution." The themes of recent films address the questions of a maturing society. Gutiérrez Alea's *Up to a Certain Point* puts filmmakers on the spot, in a film about making a movie. The director's focus on a woman worker (played by Marta Ibarra, Gutiérrez Alea's wife and a leading actress) raises questions not only about the role of the intellectual but the pervasive *machismo* of Cuban life. Manuel Octavio Gómez' musical *Patakin,* packed with ironic references both to Hollywood tradition and to clunky social realist

*This essay was written for this volume. Copyright 1988 by Pat Aufderheide. An earlier version of this article appeared in *In These Times* (April 4–10, 1984).

aesthetics, draws characters based on Afro-Cuban folklore—once disparaged by Cuban officialdom as "marginal." *The Tables Turned,* by new-generation director Rolando Díaz, turns gender and generation conflict into comedy, with a tale of two pairs of lovers. Here, it is the kids who are scandalized by their folks falling in love, and it is the women who bring the young man to a sense of his responsibilities. And in the wry domestic comedy *House for Swap,* young director Juan Carlos Tabio turns Cuba's chronic housing shortage into a hilarious sketch of rising expectations. A mother tries to fulfill her bourgeois dreams for her daughter—a "good-provider" husband who knows how to "beat the system," and a nice home to go with him—while the daughter, raised up in the revolution, has pinned her heart on the revolutionary hero. Undaunted, Mom spends the movie swapping houses (since sales are forbidden but exchanges encouraged), and the multi-family exchange takes us on a living-room tour of Cuban society. "I wanted to show the clash between old and new that we're still living through," says Tabio. "My style is comic, but comedy is a serious thing."

Situation comedy is a late-breaking phenomenon in Cuban cinema. Such works as Gutiérrez Alea's *Death of a Bureaucrat, The Twelve Chairs,* and *The Survivors* have employed a mordant ironic humor, and Alvarez's documentary essays regularly use mockery and ridicule. But just as the beaches once occupied by patrols warding off invasion are now packed on weekends with sunburned kids and picnicking families, so the stark drama of earlier films is ceding to the more intimate conflicts of daily life.

You can see it in documentaries as well as in fiction. (ICAIC only produces a handful of features every year, but makes a newsreel to be shown in theaters every week, and about 30 to 40 documentaries annually.) With wit and humor, documentaries are addressing the quality of life—sexual equality, for instance, mandated by law in 1975 and ever since a hot topic of public discussion. Rolando Díaz' half-hour *Controversia* records a debate among rural husbands and wives over domestic sex roles. As their comments reveal long-standing and unresolved problems, Díaz intercuts images of a macho horseman entering an idyllic glade heroically. As comments sharpen, the horse gets ever more skittish, until finally horse with rider turns tail and runs.

Another documentary, *El Piropo,* suggests that macho ideals are not so easily banished. The highly popular short made by Luiz Bernaza celebrates the custom of *piropos,* the sexual salvos men offer women on the street. A stuffy, scholarly narrator interviews passersby, and his little lectures are punctuated with cheesecake visuals and ooh-la-la remarks. In one way, the film stands as evidence of artistic freedom, with its leering visual style.

Filmic wit and humor does not have to have an obvious relation to social issues. For instance, the short cartoons that often precede features in theaters, many of them by master animator Juan Padron, are worlds inhabited by hapless vampires, comic drunks, and quixotic creatures from outer space.

But even in animation you can find close ties with the real, such as around the issue of sex roles. Originally the popular character Elpidio Valdés was a lone hero. "But the young girls in the Pioneers [scoutlike youth groups] complained—after all, 70 percent of the Pioneer leaders are girls," says Padrón. "So now Elpidio has a companion, María Silvia, who does everything he does." And Padrón's 1986 feature, *Vampires in Havana,* has a political bite, as the boy-vampire hero wars against international gangsters for control of the vampire cure-all Vampisol.

The lighter touch in films is only one evidence of the way films are exploring a deepening complexity in the social process. Pastor Vega, director of *Portrait of Teresa,* has now made *La Habanera,* an intimate drama in which love and heartbreak come to a psychiatrist when she finds evidence that her husband is having an affair. "I don't mix fiction and documentary directly— I want to explore what happens inside people's homes and consciences," says Vega, who nonetheless, along with the rest of the founding ICAIC filmmakers, traces his aesthetic origins to the powerful example of Italian neorealists. "You can't film the hearts of men with a candid camera. . . . The things that most influence daily life are the unconscious ones—the neorealists knew that." And filmmaker Humberto Solas, having completed a luxurious drama of political double-dealing set in decadent old Havana (*A Successful Man*), in 1987 embarked on a project that refers to a subject long under wraps in Cuban culture: homosexuality, as seen in a family drama, one of whose characters is homosexual.

From the start, Cuban filmmakers set out to make not simply movies, but to create art engaged in a revolutionary process. "In 1959," says Gutiérrez Alea, "we were thrown into the middle of a tremendous social change. Before 1959, we had tried everything to make movies and couldn't, no matter what we did. I had studied in Italy, but I had never made a film. And then suddenly—we could do anything. We had to invent our own cinema."

The Italian neorealists provided inspiration, and not only because some Cuban filmmakers had made the pilgrimage to the Italy of Open City and some Italian filmmakers traveled to the new Cuba. As Gutiérrez Alea told film scholar Julianne Burton in *Cineaste,* Italian neorealist experiments showed that "reality perceived by the camera in and of itself conveyed a situation full of contradictions; the act of documenting that historical moment could not, in fact, avoid bringing them to the forefront." But Cuban filmmakers were in search of expressions that could be authentic Cuban art.

Necessity provided inspiration. "The very difficulties we had with getting equipment, with having to get films out quickly, it was all a stimulus to invent a style," says the "father" of Cuban documentaries, Santiago Alvarez. Efficiency, availability, and urgency all went into the style that Alvarez put his stamp on—newsreels and shots using the scantiest possible narration, powerful and shocking montages, provocative cartoons, snippets from magazines and newspapers, bold title cards and animation. The newsreels, which typically developed a nine-minute essay through images, did not just deliver information but raised a new voice. Alvarez' own documentaries, including the sharply denunciatory *LBJ* and the brief exposé of American racism *Now*, were path-breaking efforts to engage—and enrage—the audience.

Conflict over the definition of a revolutionary art also shaped ICAIC in the early years. During the tense days following the Bay of Pigs invasion, painter Saba Cabrera Infante and cinematographer Orlando Jiminez Leál, part of the liberal intellectual group around the publications *Lunes de Revolución* and *Bohemia,* attempted to screen their 15-minute visual poem on Cuban nightlife, *P.M.* To ICAIC officials, who refused to license the film for exhibition, it looked like a paean to the decadence of the old regime. Then-ICAIC head Alfredo Guevara later told film scholar Michael Chanan (whose sober account balances different sources in his book *The Cuban Image*), "I reacted to the film as an offended revolutionary. Today I would manage a thing like that better."

The incident opened up the debate over intellectual freedom and responsibility, and resulted in a speech by Fidel Castro, in which he set the ground rules for the future by saying, "Inside the revolution, everything; outside the revolution, nothing." The incident marked the end of an "uncommitted" sphere for cinema.

It didn't, however, put an end to the question of *how* filmmakers were to produce a revolutionary art. ICAIC also confronted pressure from the zealously orthodox, which Guevara confronted directly in the 1962 First National Cultural Congress. He asserted the independence of ICAIC from sectarian "theoretical propaganda and pseudo-cultural phraseology," which was generating a "wave of bad taste . . . in no way inherent in socialist development." ICAIC even had to defend (successfully), in 1964, the right of Cuban audiences to watch Federico Fellini's *La Dolce Vita,* against an editorial condemning it as unwholesome in the Communist party newspaper *Hoy.*

The search for a revolutionary cinema reflected the process of social change. ICAIC's first feature, produced in 1960, was a three-episode compilation film, *Historias de la Revolución,* directed by Tomás Gutiérrez Alea. Each episode told a drama of the revolutionary war, in ways that reflect respect for Italian neorealism, understanding of the conventions of the international war movie genre, and also limited conditions of production. Audiences cheerfully overlooked technical flaws to watch their story on screen.

Each success brought new expectations. As filmmakers launched feature projects in a variety of styles, one tendency was notable: the interweaving of fictional narrative with documentary technique. Perhaps the most challenging example of a fiction-documentary mix, part of Phase Two of Cuban cinema, was *One Way or Another,* whose director Sara Gómez died of asthma before the film's editing was complete. An idealistic social worker tries to teach kids from an underclass where African folklore traditions are maintained in a hermetic and macho environment. She falls in love with a local man who is struggling to break out of the neighborhood's defensive insularity. The film starkly juxtaposes three film styles: survey shots of street scenes and construction, overlaid with cool narration; a traditional fiction love story; and vérité-style workplace scenes (some real, some staged). *One Way or Another* is a ruthlessly honest view of the pain and struggle involved in changing relationships—personal and social. "I think Sara was the one who most intensively used the language of documentary in fiction," says Marisol Trujillo, one of the few women filmmakers. "Unfortunately, her death stopped some projects in progress, and we're still waiting for someone to pick up her flag."

That moment may be arriving, since Cuban cinema is burgeoning with experiments. Not only are documentary styles surfacing in fiction, but fiction is becoming part of documentary. One example is *Story of a Scandal,* which is almost entirely reconstructed and re-enacted. Filmmaker Miguel Torres, a protegé of Alvarez who was a child when the 1949 "scandal" occurred, had been fascinated by the public uproar caused when a U.S. Marine scaled a statue of national hero José Martí and urinated on it. Torres wanted to re-create that moment in a movie that "would have been made by the ideal documentary filmmaker—someone in the right place at the right time with the right equipment."

If Cuban filmmakers are creating, as they claim, a new language, it is not for the pleasure of hearing themselves talk. As Gutiérrez Alea says, "The most important thing to realize is not just that there is a new Cuban cinema, but there is a new spectator as well." Similarly, filmmaker Julio García Espinosa argued in a 1969 essay called "For an Imperfect Cinema" that filmmakers had to transcend the traditional division between an artistic elite and a passive mass audience. These days he says, "We still need to develop a cinema that has a direct relationship with the popular class. But I think we have seen some fundamental change—we have spectators who are richer and more complex than before the revolution, and they are pushing us."

Cuban audiences are cinema sophisticates, especially in the younger generation, according to Juan Padrón, who has now watched the reactions of children to his films for more than a decade. "These days kids understand flashback, special effects, ellipsis much quicker than they did ten years ago," he says, although he says there are still big differences in reaction between the urban and the rural audiences.

Havana is full of film buffs. On any evening there are long lines for city-center cinemas. A steady flow of mothers with children, dating couples and adolescents keeps neighborhood movie houses busy. French comedies, Hungarian dramas, Mexican tearjerkers, Russian hits, kung-fu "actioners," the latest Cannes winners, and "golden oldies" from all over offer a plethora of choices. (ICAIC buys approximately 120 films from abroad every year for theatrical release.) Cubans love the kind of movie that rakes it in all over the world, and they are partial to traditional Latin American box office hits like sentimental Mexican movies.

How do Cuban filmmakers explain popular taste for lowest-common-denominator movies? Gutiérrez Alea says:

> Look, these films use fail-safe techniques of spectacle, like the circus does. There will always be an appeal in spectacle, and there's no need to throw it away. We'll also always be conditioned by the taste for Hollywood. But we have also learned how to make and to see other kinds of movies. Filmmakers can't move faster than the audience. That's what happened to Godard. His analytical cinema attracted me, but the public didn't get it. You have to include in your considerations what the known cinematic language is.

The Cuban spectator has plenty of opportunity to learn about cinema. Movies are also shown on television—sometimes even the latest American releases, which are lifted off satellite transmissions to cable channels. In rural areas some of the "mobil movie houses" that in the 1960s brought films to peasants who had never even seen an electric light (an experience caught in Octavio Cortázar's documentary *For the First Time*) still operate, now in the hands of the local government, or Poder Popular. ICAIC has also been upgrading sound and projection quality in regional theaters, and improving distribution outside major cities.

Critical and background material on film is as near as the newsstand. There are no fan magazines, but ICAIC has its own periodical, *Cine Cubano*, with interviews, essays and production information. Daily papers—four in Havana alone—carry reviews and film news, some of it with all the depth of a typical movie review in a North American daily. Reviews of Cuban films demonstrate that it is possible to pan a locally produced film, but the level of analysis generally stays in the safety zone of the politically correct.

More important in terms of providing a critical perspective on film viewing is television, where films are often presented in a kind of *Masterpiece Theater* format. The *Historia de Cine* series offers background information on the historical importance of the classic film shown that week. The weekly *Cinemateca* show runs two or three films with a similar theme back-to-back, afterwards comparing and contrasting them.

One of the most popular shows on TV is *24 Frames a Second*, a socialist version of Siskel and Ebert's *At the Movies*. The host is film critic Enrique Colina, who describes current films, shows clips and discusses their history and structure. "I don't tell people whether a film is good or bad," he says. "My job is to demystify movies, to show that film is a form of expression with a style and a point of view, as well as being a commodity."

Cuban features, which automatically get a two-week extendable run, are usually box office hits, with some exceptions and the occasional runaway success, like Pastor Vega's *Portrait of Teresa*. But the film that was the apple of ICAIC's eye for several years was one the public detested. *Cecilia* was supposed to be *the* Cuban epic movie of the Cuban classic 19th-century romantic novel, *Cecilia Valdés.* Most of ICAIC's feature film resources for more than a year were poured into the making of this one film. Humberto Solas, a turbulently passionate stylist and one of ICAIC's old guard, reinterpreted the novel in a romantic visual style that hinted at twisted morbid motivations among the central characters. It set off a nationwide debate on the difference between the book and the film. Some insiders saw *Cecilia* as the cost of the old-boy system operating among the small group of buddies that made up ICAIC's old directorial guard.

Cubans may measure their movies against their books, but they do not measure them against Hollywood's attractions. "Our movies reflect our social realities; they have to," one practical-minded engineering student told me. "This is a poor country, so we have to use what's in front of us for our sets. We can't afford to go around smashing up our cars like you do—we need them."

Film production reflects social conditions as much as do the subject, style, or reception of films. ICAIC has a management structure, but all the executives are either directors or producers, and the desk at which the buck stops— that of the vice-minister of culture—now belongs to filmmaker Julio García Espinosa.

Directors come up with ideas for a movie, and since other government branches have their own filmmaking divisions, ICAIC is free to choose all its own subjects. Directors often write their own scripts, too, which accounts for a relatively minor role for scriptwriters in Cuban film. ICAIC has boosted its priority on developing scripts, partly as a result of the scriptwriters' pressure. At an annual production meeting within each division (such as features, documentary, and newsreels) ICAIC members decide on priorities for new projects, budgets, and deadlines. The filmmaking union, organized vertically to include everyone from the truckdrivers to the directors, shares in the planning and scheduling. Once a project is established, the director is responsible for bringing in the film on time and on budget; the whole cast and crew will win or lose accordingly, since their salaries are fixed to the estimated schedule.

On the set of *Permuta,* veteran producer Sergio San Pedro explained how he designs a production schedule. "We all sit down together—the director, producer, cinematographer, production designer, and editor—and hash out the logic of the movie, what we want it to accomplish. Then I go away for a few days and let the different opinions percolate and come back with a production plan to discuss." Some directors use elaborate storyboards, while others, like Solas, go in with nothing more formal than a strong personal vision. Their production teams are usually composed of friends with a sympathy for the director's personal and aesthetic style.

San Pedro is not troubled by ironclad union regulations, but he is carefully watched by union representatives at every stage in production. There have been times when the union took ICAIC to court for grievances or for not enforcing new legislation. It has sometimes called special meetings when productions have become delayed or otherwise expensive. After the allocation of massive resources for *Cecilia,* the union exacted a commitment for a broadly dispersed budget for the following years. Union representative and documentary filmmaker Rebeca Chávez says, "We have a friendly relationship. It's based on the fact that everyone more than anything else wants to keep on making movies."

Love of making movies seems to pervade ICAIC. But Cuban filmmakers are beginning to chafe under the endless round of improvisation which poverty and the U.S. embargo impose. There is a chronic shortage of film stock. Juan Padrón notes that it took three years to complete a recent *Elpidio Valdés* feature, working with only two animators and one painter. Even then, he says, "we did it by killing ourselves with work." And in the documentary division, montage artist Santiago Alvarez is back to clipping out old magazines, since the last video news service ICAIC received, Viesnews, has been cancelled. As he tinkered with battered lenses on set, cinematographer Livio Delgado said, "Sure, we can be inventive, but you cannot use defect as effect all your life. You need good brushes to paint."

This new phase brings new challenges, and modifications in the old boy, old workshop approach. ICAIC is building up a backlog of scripts, to create a pool of possible projects as production heats up. Its archives in the Cinemateca are being reorganized as well.

Some film work is being done with a closer eye for the international market. About half of ICAIC's documentaries have a musical subject these days, in an attempt to generate foreign exchange with sure-fire sellers. "European TV buys a lot of documentaries," says Pastor Vega. "They demand an authentic tone, and of course that's our special area of excellence."

As Cuban film grows in complexity, so does the movement in which it plays a leading, and sometimes defining role: the "New Latin American Cinema," the independent and critical filmic voices of Latin American cultures. ICAIC, and the Ministry of Culture, have always invested heavily in hemispheric film cooperation, in hopes for a Latin America–wide revolutionary cinema. In 1979, ICAIC launched the Festival of New Latin American Cinema, which has become the most important mechanism for marketing Latin American films worldwide. Filmmakers from all over the continent have long used Cuban postproduction facilities. It was in Cuba that *Battle of Chile,* the documentary masterpiece chronicling the rise and fall of the Allendé government, was finally finished. The 1983 Oscar nominee *Alsino and the Condor* was a Cuban coproduction with Mexico, Costa Rica, and Nicaragua. In 1985 the continentwide Committee of Latin American Filmmakers—with which Cuban artists have been deeply involved—created a foundation dedicated to promoting film projects. A new international film school, launched in 1986, draws aspiring filmmakers from all over Latin America in small training teams; the school is headed by celebrated Argentine filmmaker Fernando Birri.

In three decades Cuban cinema has developed from a handful of eager amateurs making slapdash newsreels to a national industry and an international pacesetter in cinematic style. As Julio García Espinosa says, "On the face of it, it might seem like a luxury for a poor country to develop its own cinema." But Santiago Alvarez explains with typical emphatic gestures, "We have an urgent battle to wage against underdevelopment: to provide not just meals but culture for everyone."

54. Cultural Policy and Writers in Cuba*

BY LOURDES CASAL

Before 1959, there was little attempt by the state to control literary production, but, rather than a virtue, this was the result of government indifference to this type of activity. Some indirect influences were exerted, however, through the granting of government sinecures to a very limited number of writers who often were characterized by their mediocrity.

After 1959, with the dramatic increase of state sponsorship of literary activities and the Revolution's concern for politics, several techniques of control had been developed by the government. The elimination of royalties has been a key element in the government strategy since all authors had to be employed by or be dependent on the state in order to survive. [Authors now receive small royalties.—eds.]

Withholding of publication and the thematic restriction of literary contests (see the next section) have been other methods used in an attempt to manipulate intellectual life.[1] At another level, the curtailment of trips abroad and the quality and influence of the jobs awarded to a writer (or lack of jobs) have been important elements of the carrot-and-stick system.[2]

Writers accused of serious "deviations" (e.g., homosexuality in 1966) or those who have attempted to leave the country (e.g., Luis Agüero) were sent to labor camps to be reeducated. More serious political sins (as suspected association with counterrevolutionaries or foreign agents) have led to imprisonment (see the next section). However, these methods have not been constantly or consistently used. As will be mentioned later, there have been different stages in the evolution of the relationship between the writers and the

*From Lourdes Casal, "Literature and Society," in Carmelo Mesa-Lago, ed., *Revolutionary Change in Cuba* (Pittsburgh: Univ. of Pittsburgh Press, 1971), pp. 457–69. Edited for this volume.

government, and it is only since 1968 that more stringent controls have been applied.

THE ROLE OF THE WRITER AND THE FUNCTION OF LITERATURE IN SOCIETY

Any presentation of the panorama of the first ten years of the Revolution as a paradise of freedom for writers and artists is false. However, it is also false to maintain a negative view of the impact of the Revolution on literature and culture in general.[3]

It is obvious that "freedom of expression" does not exist in Cuba. In the words of a Puerto Rican social scientist sympathetic to the Revolution: "If we apply to Cuba the criteria about freedom of expression which prevail in capitalist countries, there is no doubt that, in that sense, freedom of expression does not exist there. But then, the Revolutionary Government has never claimed for itself the title of representative democracy."[4] However, it is also obvious that, given the scope and variety of the works that have been produced, there has been considerable leeway given to literary expression during the first ten years of the Revolution.

Initially there was a "honeymoon" period in which many writers who had been living abroad during the fifties returned to Cuba. There were many signs of effervescence and vitality during this period: Casa de las Américas was organized, *Lunes de Revolución* started publication, the Cuban Institute of Cinema Arts (ICAIC) was founded, and the Imprenta Nacional initiated its activities. This early period came to a close during the second half of 1961 with the *P.M.* affair and the demise of *Lunes de Revolución.*

The banning of *P.M.,* a film on Havana's nightlife, triggered a crisis that had been brewing since 1960. This crisis was induced by the intolerance of dogmatic elements . . . and their mistrust of *Lunes de Revolución,* which sponsored the television program on which the film was seen, and its director, Guillermo Cabrera Infante. The crisis was also fueled by existing rivalries between the leadership of the Cuban Institute of Cinema Arts, in particular, its director Alfredo Guevara, and the leadership of *Lunes de Revolución,* particularly Cabrera Infante. . . .

In June 1961, the *Lunes de Revolución* group, plus most Cuban writers and intellectuals, were invited to a series of meetings at the National Library. At these meetings, the leaders of the Popular Socialist party (PSP), particularly Edith García Buchaca, accused the *Lunes de Revolución* group of fostering division within the revolutionary camp and not being truly socialist. The confrontation was long and heated and Fidel Castro himself had to appear on June 30, 1961, to end the debate. Castro's speech established the outlines of the government's cultural policy for the following years.[5] Until 1968, at least, this policy was characterized by tolerance toward all forms of artistic expression as long as there was a basic acceptance and support of the revolution.

However, this confrontation provoked a restructuring of the literary establishment: *Lunes de Revolución* was closed, the showing of the film *P.M.* was forbidden, Antón Arrufat, director of the magazine *Casa de las Américas,* was dismissed, a convention of writers was called, and the Cuban National Union of Writers and Artists (UNEAC) was established.

In the following years, the underlying tension between cultural bureaucrats and most of the Cuban writers and artists was manifested in different ways, as in the controversy between socialist realism (or at least a strong populist line) and didacticism (which most of the writers violently opposed). Ernesto "Che" Guevara, writing in 1965, accused most writers and artists of not being authentic revolutionaries because of their bourgeois and petit bourgeois origins. But he also rejected simple-minded attempts at dirigibility and expressed his belief that a new type of writer would eventually appear: "The revolutionaries which will intone the songs of the New Man with the legitimate voice of the people shall come."[6]

During the second half of 1965, a new crisis developed. In an attempt to rehabilitate antisocial elements (e.g., people who did not work, homosexuals), militarily organized labor camps were created (UMAP—*Unidades Militares de Ayuda a la Producción*). Large numbers of Cuban writers and artists were sent to those camps, and some institutions (e.g., Havana University) were purged. *Paradiso,* José Lezama Lima's novel with its obvious homosexual references, almost did not get published. The resultant international uproar, the counterproductive effects of the camps, and the intervention of the UNEAC led to the eventual elimination of the labor camps, although the political-cultural scene remained very tense.

Toward the end of 1967, a debate over *Pasión de Urbino,* a novel by Lisandro Otero (a high-ranking cultural official) began in *El Caimán Barbudo.* Heberto Padilla sent a letter that debunked Otero's novel and praised Guillermo Cabrera Infante's *Tres tristes tigres.* This controversy ended with the resignation of the editorial board of *El Caimán Barbudo,* Padilla's loss of his job and the withdrawal of his permission to travel to Italy. In August 1968, an interview with Cabrera Infante was printed in the Argentinian magazine *Primera Plana.*[7] Although Cabrera Infante had been living abroad with no ties to the Cuban government since 1965, it was in this 1968 interview that he, for the first time, publicly attacked the revolution and denounced the condition of the writers within Cuba. This left Padilla in the dangerous position of having been on the side of a now public "traitor to the Revolution."[8]

When Padilla was awarded the 1968 UNEAC prize for his book of critical poems, *Fuera del juego,* and Antón Arrufat was awarded the theater prize for his play, *Los siete contra Tebas,* by an international jury, UNEAC officials strongly criticized the decision. Although the decision of the jury was respected and the books published, the editions were printed with the political disclaimer of UNEAC. A series of articles published in the magazine of the armed forces, *Verde Olivo,* under the pseudonym of Leopoldo Avila strongly criticized Padilla and Arrufat.[9] But more than a criticism of the two individual writers, the articles were an indication of a new offensive on the cultural front.[10]

UNEAC's stance and government criticism manifested by Avila's articles reflected a cultural policy established by a declaration of principles approved at the October 1968 Congress of Writers and Artists held in Cienfuegos. The declaration stated that "the writer must contribute to the Revolution through his work and this involves conceiving of literature as a means of struggle, a weapon against weaknesses and problems which, directly or indirectly, could hinder this advance."[11]

In order to prevent writers who did not fulfill their obligations to the Revolution from receiving contest prizes in the future, Haydeé Santamaría, director of the inter-American cultural agency Casa de las Américas, suggested that the juries for future UNEAC contests should consist only of Cuban authors. The advice was heeded during the 1969 contest, and the awards were predictably safe.[12] Nicolás Guillén, president of UNEAC, in his speech during the award ceremony reminded all that "these contests have taken place during an era of acute political crisis, one from which creative intelligence cannot—or rather, should not—consider to keep itself divorced. . . . Cuban writers and artists have the same responsibilities as our soldiers, with respect to the defense of the nation. . . . He who does not [fulfill his duty] regardless of his position, will receive the most severe revolutionary punishment for his fault."[13]

Guillén's speech came in the aftermath of the expulsion from UNEAC of José Lorenzo Fuentes, a winner of the 1967 annual literature contest with his novel *Viento de enero.* Fuentes was expelled from the UNEAC on September 22, 1969, because of his alleged involvement with H. Carrillo Colón, accused by the Cubans of being a CIA agent employed by the Mexican embassy in Havana. Carrillo Colón was supposedly in charge of penetrating intellectual circles and fostering defections. The expulsion decision was accompanied by an appeal by UNEAC's executive board, which addressed itself "to all Cuban writers and artists exhorting them to increase revolutionary vigilance, to avoid all forms of weakness and liberalism, and to denounce all attempts at ideological penetration and counterrevolutionary activity, faithful to the principle which gave birth to the Writers' Union: to defend the Revolution is to defend Culture."[14]

In general, then, there has been a new emphasis on an attempt to stimulate authors to produce works that are revolutionary in content: One aspect of this effort has been the nomination of more militant juries for the various literary contests; another aspect has been the thematic manipulation of the contests. For example, Haydeé Santamaría announced during the ceremonies in which the 1969 juries were installed that future juries would favor Latin Americans residing in their own countries instead of Latin Americans residing in Europe.[15] The 1969 David Award, established by UNEAC for unpublished writers, had markedly militant juries, mostly composed of party members: Portuondo, Guillén, Félix Pita Rodríguez, César Leante, Luis Marré and Raúl Luis. The short-story prize was awarded in 1969 to Hugo Chinea, also a member of the party.[16]

Perhaps it is not accidental that in the 1969 Casa de las Américas contest, none of the awards went to Cubans. Two of the chosen works dealt specifically with the guerrilla experience: *Los fundadores del alba,* a novel by Bolivian writer Renato Prada Oropeza, and *Perú 1965: una experiencia guerrillera,* an essay by the then jailed Peruvian guerrilla leader Héctor Béjar Rivera. Furthermore, the 1970 Casa de las Américas contests added a new category, "Testimony," restricted to books offering firsthand documentation of the present Latin American reality.[17] One of the objectives of the revolutionary armed forces contests is to stimulate the production of "works useful to the effort of constructing socialism in our country."[18] As another example of this trend, Nicolás Guillén, in a speech given during the 1969 David Award ceremonies, announced that the 1970 award "will be limited to works on a single theme . . . all the works must deal with the decisive effort of our country, of all of us, in the agricultural tasks."[19]

This new policy of revolutionary vigilance became even more evident when the director of Casa de las Américas withdrew an invitation to Nicanor Parra, a Chilean socialist poet, to be a juror of the 1970 Casa de las Américas contest because he had attended a reception at the White House.[20] Haydeé Santamaría, during the ceremonies in which the literary contest juries were installed, said: "This year we will be able to say that the awards have grown much greater and much more revolutionary, because there are only two roads open to us: the revolutionary and the nonrevolutionary one. . . . Casa de las Américas has the right and the duty to make the awards more revolutionary."[21] Practically all 1970 awards were granted to authors of "revolutionary" works, for example, the Uruguayans María Ester Gilio, for *La guerrilla tupamara,* and Carlos María Gutiérrez, for *Diario del cuartel* (both writing on the guerrilla in their country); and the Cubans Miguel Cossío, for *Sacchario* (a novel on the revolution and the sugar crop) and Víctor Casaús, for *Girón en la memoria* (on the Bay of Pigs invasion).[22]

In 1971, the above-mentioned trends became stronger, and the overall cultural policy of the Revolution hardened even further. On March 20, 1971, Heberto Padilla . . . was jailed, and then released 37 days later. Before his release, Padilla signed a long statement of self-criticism which he personally delivered at a meeting of the UNEAC, where he exhorted other writers present (among them Pablo A. Fernández, César López, Manuel Díaz Martínez, and Padilla's wife, Belkis Cuza) to follow his example. This new "Padilla affair" provoked a strong international reaction. A large group of European and Latin

American intellectuals (among them, Jean-Paul Sartre, Hans-Magnus Enzensberger, Gabriel García Márquez, Octavio Paz, Carlos Fuentes, and Mario Vargas Llosa) addressed a letter to Fidel Castro on April 9, 1971, expressing concern about Padilla's imprisonment. A second letter, dated May 20, protested Padilla's confession, pointing out the similarity of these proceedings with the worst moments of the Stalinist era.[23]

The Declaration of the First National Congress on Education and Culture and Castro's speech during the closing session of the Congress on April 30, 1971, further emphasized the new hard line on cultural affairs: (a) the primacy of political and ideological factors in staffing universities, mass media, and artistic institutions, (b) the barring of homosexuals from these institutions, (c) tighter controls on literary contests to assure that judges, authors, and topics are truly revolutionary, (d) more control on subjects of publication, giving higher priority to textbooks than to literary works, (e) the elimination of foreign tendencies in cultural affairs in order to wipe out "cultural imperialism," and (f) a violent attack against the "pseudoleftist bourgeois intellectuals" from abroad who had dared to criticize the revolution on the Padilla issue.[24]

CONCLUSIONS

Three generations of Cuban writers are active in literature with varying degrees of output and influence. The prerevolutionary generation, which became well known in the 1940s, . . . has possibly produced the finest literary work, but seems to be declining in terms of output and influence. The first generation of the revolution constitutes a generational transition; its members began to work (and a few of them to publish) in the 1950s, but came to maturity and became known after the revolutionary take-over. This is the most influential group (at least in 1959–1970), although the group has split apart, with some of its members choosing exile. The second generation of the revolution is composed of young writers born in the 1940s who began to publish mainly in the second half of the 1960s, challenging the dominant first generation. They have been involved in several literary-political controversies and the volume and quality of their literary work is rapidly increasing.

The predominant literary genre in prerevolutionary Cuba was poetry, followed by the short story and the novel. Under the revolution, an opposite trend can be observed: The largest increase of literary output has taken the form of the novel, followed by the short story, whereas poetry is just maintaining (or perhaps slightly increasing) the prerevolutionary volume. Thematically, literature has not reflected much of an interest in the revolutionary process itself, but rather in criticizing the prerevolutionary society (with some simplistic views), in glorifying the insurrectional struggle, or in using escapist fictional themes. A few short stories and novels, but mainly poems, have reflected a concern for current problems and conflicts or have appraised revolutionary changes. Many of these works tend to be propagandistic in nature and of poor literary quality.

The Revolution has substantially increased publishing facilities, both for books and magazines, has established well-funded and prestigious contests, and has subsidized most writers. On the other hand, the abolition of royalties, the nationalization of publishing houses and newspapers, the abolition of some journals, the organization of UNEAC under government auspices, and the integration of all publishing activities into the state agency Instituto del Libro have made the writer totally dependent on the state. The state has used this power to manipulate the writers by granting or withholding publication, using (temporarily) labor camps against some of them, hiring and dismissing them from state jobs, and pressuring them by criticism and appraisal through communications media. This process has not been exempt from tension and conflict, as the several controversies and polemics among the writers testify. In 1961, the official policy of the government vis-à-vis the writers was defined by Castro, and until 1968 there was relative tolerance toward those who accepted the revolution.

To stimulate the creation of literature concerned with the problems of a revolutionary society, the state has exerted pressure through various channels (e.g., granting of awards, exhortations). In spite of these efforts, until the turn of the 1960s the content of literary work had failed to become markedly militant.

As the first decade of the revolution came to an end, there was evidence of a strict tightening of controls, an emphasis not only on revolutionary loyalty, but also on revolutionary themes and concerns, and a concerted attempt to direct intellectual life toward a greater militancy.

NOTES

1. Fausto Masó's novel *La sangre de los buenos* received a mention in the Casa de las Américas contest. It was never published because he left the country. Other examples of withholding of publication among authors still in Cuba include the delayed publication of Rafael Alcides, *Contracastro;* and Reynaldo Arenas, *El mundo alucinante.* See Claude Couffon, "Reinaldo Arenas," *Le Monde* (March 22, 1969), supplement.

2. For example, Heberto Padilla lost his job with *Granma* after his involvement in the 1968 controversy with Lisandro Otero in *El Caimán Barbudo.* His planned trip to Italy was also cancelled.

3. Examples are Carlos Ripoll, "Coacción y creación en la literatura cubana actual," *Zona Franca,* Vol. 5 (October 1968), pp. 38–41; F. Masó, "Literatura y revolución en Cuba," *Mundo Nuevo* (February 1969), pp. 50–54; and Federico Hasse (pseudonym), "Filiberto o el último compilador," *Mundo Nuevo* (April 1970), pp. 63–74.

4. Manuel Maldonado-Denis, "Documentos de un viaje a Cuba en 1967," *Caribbean Studies,* Vol. 7 (January 1968), p. 17, trans. by this author.

5. Fidel Castro, *Palabras a los Intelectuales* (Montevideo, Comité de Intelectuales Artistas de Apoyo a la Revolución Cubana, 1961).

6. Ernesto Guevara, "El socialismo y el hombre en Cuba," in *Obra Revolucionaria* (Mexico, 1967), p. 636.

7. Tomás Martínez, "América: los novelistas exiliados," *Primera Plana* (July 30–August 5, 1968), pp. 40–50.

8. See Heberto Padilla, "Respuesta a Cabrera Infante," *Primera Plana* (December 24–30, 1968), pp. 88–89; Cabrera Infante, "La confundida lengua del poeta," ibid. (January 14–20, 1969), pp. 64–65.

9. Leopoldo Avila, "Las respuestas de Caín," *Verde Olivo* (November 3, 1968), pp. 17–18; "Las provocaciones de Padilla," ibid. (November 10, 1968), pp. 17–18; "Antón se va a la guerra," ibid. (November 17, 1968), pp. 16–18; "Sobre algunas corrientes de la crítica y la literatura en Cuba," ibid. (November 24, 1968), pp. 14–18; and "El pueblo es el forjador, defensor y sostén de la cultura," ibid. (December 3, 1968), pp. 16–17.

10. See I. S., "Cuba: ¿Fin de una tregua?," *Mundo Nuevo* (February 1969), pp. 80–84; *Times Literary Supplement* (January 5, 1969), p. 464. For comprehensive summaries of the controversy, see *Carte Segrete* (April–June 1969), pp. 230–39; and Gabriel Coulthard, "Cuban Literature and Politics," *Caribbean Monthly Bulletin*, Vol. 6 (March 1969), pp. 5–8.

11. *Granma Weekly Review* (October 27, 1968), p. 8.

12. For the composition of the juries, comments on the prizes, etc., see *Cuba International*, Vol. 2 (February 1970), pp. 36–39.

13. Nicolás Guillén, "Speech delivered at the awarding of prizes to winners of the Annual Literature Contest," *Granma Weekly Review* (December 7, 1969), p. 9.

14. *Bohemia* (October 3, 1969), supplement, p. 9, trans. by this author.

15. Ibid. (January 24, 1969), pp. 44–49.

16. Ibid. (August 1, 1969), p. 54.

17. *Granma Weekly Review* (March 8, 1970), p. 11.

18. *Bohemia* (August 8, 1969), p. 62.

19. Ibid. (August 1, 1969), p. 54.

20. Radio Habana-Cuba broadcast, May 13 and 28, 1970, and *Granma* (June 13, 1970).

21. *Granma Weekly Review* (July 5, 1970), p. 4.

22. *Granma Weekly Review* (July 26, 1970), p. 1.

23. Padilla's statement of self-criticism was released by the Cuban press agency, *Prensa Latina,* in Paris. Excerpts were published in *Le Monde* (April 29, 1971). The texts of the intellectuals' letters were published in *Le Monde* (April 9 and May 20, 1971). For more details see Marcel Niedergang, "Le poète Heberto Padilla à été libéré a La Havane," and Juan Arcocha, "Le poète et le commissaire," *Le Monde* (April 29, 1971), p. 2; and José Yglesias, "A Cuban Poet in Trouble," *New York Review of Books* (June 3, 1971), pp. 3–8.

24. See *Granma Weekly Review* (May 9, 1971). Practically the whole issue is devoted to the Congress.

55. *When I Say Future**

WORDS AND MUSIC BY SILVIO RODRÍGUEZ

Instruments; guitar, "tres," bass, flute, piano, percussion.

I invite you to believe me when I say future.
If you don't believe my words, believe the brilliance
of a gesture
believe in my body
believe in my toughening hands.

I invite you to believe me when I say future.
If you don't believe in my eyes
believe in the anguish of a shout
believe in the earth
believe in the rain
believe in the sap
There are twenty thousand new seeds
in the valley overnight
There are desperate faces
there are men and their women.

Our shackles are already broken
there's patience and more where that came from. . . .

There's a country of stone in ruins
beneath another country made out of bread
there's a mother walking
arm in arm with her clan.

Our shackles are already broken
there's patience and more where that came from. . . .

Right now there are four kids
smiling on a beach
and in the back room of a bullet
there's a soldier who hasn't had any sleep
and that same girl
alters her skirt once again.
Yes, everything from a child
to a hemline's important.

Our shackles are already broken
there's patience and more where that came from. . . .

I invite you to believe me when I say future.

*From Victor Casaus and Louis Rogelio Nogueras, eds., *Silvio: Que Levante La Mano, La Guitara* (Havana: Editorial Letras Cubanas, 1984), pp. 97–98.

Cuando Digo Futuro

LETRA Y MÚSICA PER SILVIO RODRÍGUEZ

Instrumentos: guitarra, tres, contrabajo, flauta, piano, percusión.

Te convido a creerme cuando digo futuro,
si no crees mis palabras, cree en el brillo
de un gesto,
cree en mi cuerpo,
cree en mis manos que se acaban.
Te convido a creerme cuando digo futuro,
si no crees en mis ojos,
cree en la angustia de un grito,
cree en la tierra,
cree en la lluvia,
cree en la savia.
Hay veinte mil nuevas semillas
en el valle desde ayer,
hay rostros de desesperados,
hay el hombre y su mujer.
Los hierros se fundieron ya
hay la paciencia y queda más.
Hay un país de roca en ruinas
baja otro país de pan;
hay una madre que camina
codo a codo con su clan.
Los hierros se fundieron ya
hay la paciencia y queda más.
Hay cuatro niños, ahora mismo,
sonriendo en una playa
y en la trastienda de una bala,
un militar que no ha dormido.
Y aquella misma muchachita
vuelve a recortar su saya
sí, es importante desde un niño
hasta el largo de un vestido.
Los hierros se fundieron ya
hay la paciencia y queda más
yo te convido a creerme cuando digo futuro.

56. From Man to Death*

BY PABLO ARMANDO FERNÁNDEZ   *Translated by Keith Ellis*

I

Look, I am re-creating everything
in times of hunger and blindness.
Who is he that scatters like sand or ashes the
    old beliefs?
    ". . . we have walked without a single night's rest,
    forty days."
That is precisely how history begins.
    ". . . for fifteen days we walked in water and mud."
They said that history was wasteland
without owner, an empty house, but for us
it means eating eleven times on a thirty-day journey,
for us traps and the enemy troops,
the Lituabo River, the Cantarrana bridge, ambushes,
    bursts and volleys of gunfire.
The 7th of September just before midnight,
the villages of Cuatro Compañeros and hills of Forestal,
the Trinidad estate three kilometres from the La Yegua
    River,
all this for us to stand firm and not surrender,
to writhe between death and victory,
to find joy in death or in victory.
It is to lift the dead when they fall and mark
the spot with endless love.
Not a single rose have we seen this whole day.
The sea smelling like fruit.
The overflowing river stopped us and that night we felt
the ardors of love,
woman as a necessity and food also.
We have learned that freedom is not a promise,
that it is not a discreet word, that neither orators

From Pablo Armando Fernández, *Toda La Poesia* (Havana: Ediciones R, 1961), pp. 57–65.

De Hombre a Muerte

POR PABLO ARMANDO FERNÁNDEZ

I

He aquí, yo hago nuevas todas las cosas
en tiempos de hambre y de ceguera.
¿Quién es aquel que esparce como arena o ceniza
    las viejas creencias?
    ". . . hemos caminado sin descansar una sola
    noche, cuarenta jornadas".
Precisamente así empieza la historia.
    ". . . durante quince días marchamos con el agua
    y el lodo"
Dijeron que la historia era un baldío
sin dueño, una casa vacía, pero para nosotros
es comer once veces en treinta días de viaje,
para nosotros las celadas y la tropa enemiga,
el río Lituabo, el puente de Cantarrana, emboscadas,
    ráfagas y descargas de fusilería.
Los días 7 de septiembre antes de media noche,
los poblados de Cuatro Compañeros y montes de
    Forestal,
la finca Trinidad a tres kilómetros del río La Yegua,
para nosotros es estar y no rendirnos,
debatirse entre la muerte y la victoria,
regocijarnos con la muerte y regocijarnos con la victoria.
Es recoger los muertos donde caen y marcar
con amor el lugar para siempre.
No hemos visto una rosa en toda la jornada.
En el olfato el mar como una fruta.
El río desbordado nos detuvo y esa noche sentimos
los ardores del amor,
la mujer como una necesidad y la comida también.
Hemos aprendido que la libertad no es una promesa,
que no es una palabra discreta, que ni los oradores

nor priests nor judges
can give it to the people.
    "The only night in forty we can rest."
Thus history is made with hunger and fatigue, in danger.
Between death and victory,
hearing the tremors of death.

II

Freedom, image of love that lives for more than itself,
freedom, you are not unknown to us, one is free
in the mountains. Here
    ". . . woods and meals are scarce"
but the dialogue is ours, one is free where one fights.
Many days are at the disposal of your love,
we have slept among your words.
We all want to crown you,
we want to be your chosen ones.
Sometimes we don't know where you are.
A thousand images of you are confused
with our single image.
You radiate light from a bird,
you inundate the plain.
We the dead of a coming day
love your visions—messages
that return from the dead—.
Doors, infinite thresholds . . .
Freedom, your alert eyes
are the closed eyes;
your arm raised high
are the fallen arms.
Your lips were made for song
Your look was made for company.
Only in you are mysteries of continuity revealed.
Speak to us of little things,
of the places frequented by people
—we know that you have lived in the ages
of darkness and silence—, let us speak . . .

    seven Garant rifles

no one told us what wisdom was.

ni los sacerdotes ni los juristas
pueden dársela al pueblo.
"La única noche que descansamos en cuarenta días."
Así se hace la historia con hambre y sueño, en el peligro.
Entre la muerte y la victoria,
oyendo los temblores de la muerte.

II

Libertad, imagen del amor que no vive para sí solamente,
libertad, no te desconocemos, se es libre
en la montaña. Aquí
    ". . . escasean los bosques y la comida"
pero el diálogo es nuestro, se es libre donde se pelea.
Hay muchos días para entregarlos a tu amor,
hemos dormido entre tu voz.
Todos queremos coronarte,
queremos ser tus elegidos.
A veces, no sabemos dónde estás.
Mil imágenes tuyas se confunden
con nuestra sola imagen.
Irradias desde el pájaro la luz,
inundas la llanura.
Muertos del día que vendrá
amamos tus visiones—mensajes
que vuelven de los muertos—.
Puertas, umbrales infinitos . . .
Libertad, tu ojo despierto
son los ojos cerrados;
tu brazo en alto
son los brazos caídos.
Tus labios se hicieron para el canto.
Tu mirada se hizo para la compañía.
Sólo en ti se revelan los misterios de la continuidad.
Háblanos de las cosas minúsculas,
de los lugares que frecuenta el hombre
—sabemos que has vivido en las edades
de la tiniebla y el silencio—, hablemos . . .

    siete rifles Garand

nadie nos dijo qué era la sabiduría.

four Springfields

Disciplined and courageous.

two 45 calibre hand machine guns

Today we have hardly eaten.

one M-1 rifle

Someone is praying for the pursued.
Someone is praying for the pursuers.

three 44 calibre Winchesters

Generations that are to come

a 12 calibre automatic shotgun

Our future hands.

22 calibre automatic rifles

The loud bangs of war,
the massacre of war.

History is not an ownerless wasteland.

Freedom,
speak to us of your many lovers
while in Mayari Arriba,
on the flat land, some remain.
Our hands
win a Thompson machine gun,
five Springfields
and some small arms.
Freedom
—not of the tiger or the bird—
but of people:
win us over for yesterday, for tomorrow,
win us over today.
We are your faithful lovers
Amid the loud bangs
and flashes
we can hear all that trembles within you:
your heart beats,
here among burnt pine trees and blood.
In your nakedness you are everywhere
and you sleep in the shade of ruins.

cuatro Springfield

Disciplinados y valientes.

dos ametralladoras de mano calibre 45

Hoy hemos comido poco.

una carabina M-1

Alguien está rogando por los perseguidos.
Alguien está rogando por los perseguidores.

tres Winchester calibre 44

Generaciones que son para la vida.

una escopeta automática calibre 12

Nuestras manos futuras.

rifles automáticos calibre 22

Los estampidos de la guerra
la masacre de la guerra.

La historia no es un baldío sin dueño.

Libertad,
háblanos de tus muchos amadores
mientras en Mayarí Arriba,
sobre el campo tendido, quedan algunos.
Nuestras manos
ganan una ametralladora Thompson,
cinco Springfield
y algunas armas cortas.
Libertad
—no del tigre o el pájaro—
la del hombre:
gánanos para ayer, para mañana
gánanos hoy.
Somos tus fieles amadores.
Entre los estampidos
y los fogonazos
oímos todo lo que en ti tiembla:
late tu corazón,
aquí entre pinos quemados y sangre.
Desnuda estás en todas partes
y duermes a la sombra de las ruinas.

We stop when we reach you.
You alone are destiny.

III

Men become old and die.
Who could be scared of death?
Those who anticipate it
in their daily tasks
are made dead by Death.
Men die
without this one
having had anything to do
with that one;
without them having shared any sadness.
Who could be scared of death?
The mountain shrouded in air
forgotten thousands of years ago.

> ". . . at seven in the morning
> a reconnaissance aircraft appeared."

The enemy detests my love.
Out in the rain my darling asking me
when we will see each other again.
Those men who never were in combat
who have not fought lovingly
who haven't walked away forever from crosses
do not know war.
We are not going to die.
We will be old when the time for old age comes.
We will be old to
recount and make speeches and sleep.

> ". . . at 11:30 A.M.
> six trucks passed
> full of soldiers"

Those birds will be
forever singing in my memory.
Now he will be sharpening his machete on the stone
and she will be picking up empty cups
—I hated to leave—
How submissive the bridge's posture.

En ti nos detuvimos.
Sólo tú eres destino.

III

Los hombres se hacen viejos y mueren.
¿A quién se le querrá atemorizar con la muerte?
Los que se le anticipan
en su oficio
son muertos de la Muerte.
Los hombres mueren
sin que haya tenido aquél
trato con éste;
sin que hayan compartido la tristeza.
¿A quién se le querrá atemorizar con la muerte?
La montaña llena de un aire
olvidado hace miles de años.

   ". . . a las 7 de la mañana apareció
     una avioneta de reconocimiento."

El enemigo detesta mi amor.
Expuestos a la lluvia preguntándome cuándo
    volveremos
a vernos, mi niña.
Esos hombres que nunca estuvieron en combate
que no han peleado con amor
que no dejaron para siempre las cruces
no conocen la guerra.
No vamos a morir.
Seremos viejos en el tiempo de la vejez.
Seremos viejos para
contar y orar y dormir.

   ". . . a las 11 y media de la mañana
    cruzaron seis camiones
    cargados de soldados"

Esos pájaros se quedarán
para siempre cantando en la memoria.
Ahora él estará afilando en la piedra su machete
y ella estará recogiendo las tazas vacías
—no quiso despedirme—
La postura sumisa del puente.

In the darkness the earth seemed to burn.
We want love, we want to live.
We have all the sadness,
(I will dance with you my love)
the clothing stinks of drenched animals smells of sad things.
(I will dance with you my love)
The machine guns do not understand
they do not comprehend this happiness

> ". . . at about four in the afternoon
> heavy gunfire was heard
> some four or five kilometres away."

All the verdure of that branch and the flower
that will bloom and my blood
are crying out for you to be here.
We want to live with sadness, with farewells,
with all our memories.
We want to live in happiness.
I love you

> ". . . at 7 o'clock sharp we
> set off."

En la oscuridad la tierra parece arder.
Queremos amor queremos vivir.
Tenemos toda la tristeza,
(bailaré contigo amor mío)
la ropa huele a animal mojado huele a las cosas tristes.
(Bailaré contigo amor mío)
Las ametralladoras no comprenden
no saben por qué es esta alegría

> "... a las 4 de la tarde aproximadamente
> se escuchó un nutrido tiroteo como a cuatro
> o cinco kilómetros."

Todo el verdor de esa rama y la flor
que vendrá y mi sangre
están gritando por que vengas.
Queremos vivir con la tristeza, con los adioses,
con todos los recuerdos.
Queremos vivir con la alegría.
Yo te amo

> "... a las 7 en punto nos pusimos
> en marcha."

APPENDIX A:

Chronology of Major Events

1895

15 April: Cuba's second war of independence began.

19 May: José Martí, poet and father of the Cuban independence movement, was killed in combat against the Spanish. (Reading 1)

1898

15 February: The U.S. battleship "Maine" exploded in Havana harbor.

25 April: The United States declared war on Spain. The Spanish-American war lasted three months and ended with a U.S. military occupation of Cuba.

1901

28 May: At U.S. insistence, the Platt Amendment was added to the Cuban constitution. It limited Cuban sovereignty in dealings with other countries and gave the United States the right to intervene in Cuba at will. (Reading 6)

1933

12 August: The dictatorship of Gerardo Machado was overthrown by the "Revolution of '33." (Reading 5)

1934

16 January: At the instigation of U.S. Ambassador Sumner Welles, Dr. Ramón Grau San Martín, President of the Revolutionary Government, was forced out of office by the military, headed by Fulgencio Batista.

29 May: The Platt Amendment was abrogated.

1952

10 March: Batista overthrew the government of Carlos Prío Socorrás.

1953

26 July: Led by Fidel Castro, 134 rebels attacked Moncada barracks in Santiago, marking the start of the insurrection against Batista. Most were killed or captured. At his trial, Castro gave his famous speech, "History Will Absolve Me." (Reading 5)

1959

1–2 January: Batista fled and Rebel Army troops under Ernesto "Che" Guevara entered Havana, marking the triumph of the revolution.

16 February: Fidel Castro, Commander of the Rebel Army, replaced Miró Cardona as Prime Minister of the Revolutionary Government.

15–26 April: Castro traveled to the United States at the invitation of the Association of Newspaper Editors and met with Vice-President Richard Nixon, who later in the year urged that the U.S. begin planning a paramilitary covert operation to oust Castro.

17 May: The first Agrarian Reform Law was promulgated, nationalizing about one third of the arable land in Cuba. Compensation for the property of U.S. citizens affected by the law became a major point of controversy in U.S.-Cuban relations.

1960

4–13 February: Soviet Foreign Minister Anastas Mikoyan visited Cuba and signed trade and aid agreements.

17 March: President Eisenhower gave approval for the CIA to begin planning the Bay of Pigs invasion.

8 May: Cuba and the Soviet Union established diplomatic relations.

7 June: U.S. oil companies, at the urging of the Department of State, refused to refine Soviet crude oil at their Cuban refineries. Cuba nationalized the refineries.

6 July: The United States suspended the Cuban sugar quota, effectively cutting off 80 percent of Cuban exports to the United States.

10 July: The Soviet Union agreed to buy Cuban sugar refused by the United States.

6 August: In retaliation for the U.S. suspension of the sugar quota, Cuba nationalized U.S. private investment on the island worth approximately $1 billion.

28 August: The United States imposed an economic embargo against trade with Cuba.

14 October: The Cuban government nationalized all large commercial and industrial enterprises.

1961

3 January: The United States broke relations with Cuba.

16 April: At the funeral for victims of bombing attacks on the eve of the Bay of Pigs invasion, Castro declared that the Cuban Revolution was socialist.

17–19 April: A CIA-sponsored invasion force of 1,200 exiles landed at the Bay of Pigs (Playa Girón) and was defeated within 72 hours. (Reading 37)

2 September: Cuba was the only Latin American state represented at the founding conference of the Movement of Nonaligned Nations.

2 December: Castro declared, "I am a Marxist-Leninist and I shall be one to the end of my life."

1962

22–31 January: The Organization of American States (OAS) launched the Alliance for Progress and suspended Cuba's membership.

4 February: Castro responded to Cuba's suspension from the OAS with the Second Declaration of Havana, calling upon the people of Latin America to rise up against imperialism and declaring, "The duty of a revolutionary is to make the revolution."

16–28 October: Intermediate Range Ballistic Missiles placed in Cuba by the Soviet Union triggered the Cuban Missile Crisis, the worst superpower confrontation of the nuclear era. The crisis ended when the Soviet Union agreed, without consulting Cuba, to withdraw the missiles in exchange for a U.S. pledge not to attack the island. (Reading 38)

1964

26 July: The Organization of American States adopted mandatory sanctions against Cuba, requiring all members to sever diplomatic and trade relations. Only Mexico refused to comply.

1965

1 April: Ernesto "Che" Guevara resigned his Cuban citizenship and left to wage armed struggle in Africa and Latin America.

3 October: The new Communist Party of Cuba was inaugurated.

1966

3–15 January: The first Tricontinental Congress met in Havana and formed the Organization of Solidarity with the Peoples of Africa, Asia and Latin America (OPSAAAL). Delegates from 27 Latin American countries created the Latin American Solidarity Organization (OLAS).

1967

13 March: Castro criticized the Soviet-bloc nations for maintaining diplomatic and commercial relations with "oligarchic" governments in Latin America.

9 October: Che Guevara was killed by U.S.-trained Bolivian rangers in the village of Vallegrande.

1968

2 January: The Cuban government introduced gasoline rationing due to a cutback in deliveries from the Soviet Union. Castro declared that "the dignity of the revolution demanded that Cubans refrain from begging for additional supplies from the Soviet Union."

28 January: Anibal Escalante and eight other members of the former Popular Socialist party (the Cuban Communist party before 1959) were expelled from the Communist party for "microfactionalist activities."

13 March: Castro launched the "revolutionary offensive," which immediately nationalized 55,000 small businesses and led to state control of nearly all trades and services.

23 August: Castro called the Warsaw Pact invasion of Czechoslovakia on August 21 a "drastic and painful measure" but a "bitter necessity," declaring that it "saved" socialism in Czechoslovakia.

1969

26 July: Castro announced the start of a campaign to produce ten million tons of sugar in the next harvest, requiring the transfer of many economic resources to the sugar sector of the economy.

December: The first contingent of the Venceremos Brigade, a group of volunteer workers from the United States, arrived in Cuba to work on the sugar harvest.

1970

19 May: Castro announced the sugar harvest had failed to reach its goal of ten million tons. However, the 8.5 million tons harvested was the largest in Cuban history. (Reading 12)

25 September: The United States warned the Soviet Union to discontinue construction of a nuclear submarine base in Cienfuegos, Cuba, based on the Kennedy-Khrushchev understanding that concluded the 1962 missile crisis. The Soviet Union subsequently halted construction of the base and reaffirmed the 1962 agreement.

1971

20 March: Poet Heberto Padilla was arrested and detained for 39 days for political differences with the government. (Reading 54)

20 October: Cuba became the 95th member of the Group of 77, a United Nations caucus of Third World countries.

10 November: Castro arrived in Chile for a three-week visit, his first to a Latin American country since 1959.

1972

3 May: Castro began a 63-day tour of Africa, Eastern Europe, and the Soviet Union.

11 July: Cuba joined the Council of Mutual Economic Assistance (CMEA), the economic organization of the Soviet Union, East European socialist countries, and Mongolia.

19 November: Castro accepted a U.S. proposal to begin formal negotiations over the problem of airline hijackings.

1973

15 February: The United States and Cuba signed an antihijacking agreement.

15 November: The 13th Congress of the Cuban Labor Confederation tied wages to productivity in an effort to improve efficiency.

1974

28 January: Soviet leader Leonid Brezhnev began a week-long visit to Cuba, along with a team of economic specialists. It was the first visit to Cuba by a head of the Soviet Communist party.

30 June: Matanzas Province held elections for delegates to the newly established organs of "Peoples Power." The Matanzas experiment was followed by the establishment nationwide of elected government assemblies at the local, provincial and national levels. (Reading 22)

September: U.S. Senators Claiborne Pell (D-Rhode Island) and Jacob Javits (R-New York) visited Cuba—the first U.S. elected officials to visit the island since the break in diplomatic relations.

November: U.S. and Cuban officials secretly met in New York to discuss possible areas for negotiations between the two countries.

1975

14 February: The Council of Ministers enacted The Family Code, a law that defined relations between husband and wife and parents and children.

29 July: A majority of the OAS, including the United States, voted to lift mandatory diplomatic and economic sanctions against Cuba. The United States, however, opted to maintain its bilateral embargo.

21 August: The United States announced that it would allow foreign subsidiaries of U.S. companies to sell products in Cuba, and that it would no longer penalize other nations for trade with Cuba.

5 November: At the request of the newly inaugurated Angolan government, Cuba sent a large contingent of troops to help the Angolans repel an invasion by South African forces launched on October 23.

17–22 December: The First Congress of the Communist Party of Cuba was held in Havana. It adopted party statutes, a programmatic platform, and approved the draft constitution. (Reading 18)

1976

15 February: Cubans approved a new constitution by referendum. It established elected assemblies and institutionalized the Communist party as "the superior force in society."

5 April: Secretary of State Henry Kissinger asserted that there is no possibility of United States relations with Cuba while Cuba has troops in Africa.

6 October: A bomb on a Cubana Airlines plane exploded after take-off from Barbados, killing all 73 people aboard. Luis Posada Carriles, a Cuban exile and former employee of the U.S. Central Intelligence Agency, was arrested in Venezuela and charged with responsibility for the terrorist act. In retaliation, Cuba suspended the antihijacking agreement with the United States.

1977

March: President Jimmy Carter lifted the ban on travel to Cuba by U.S. citizens.

16 March: During a wide-ranging trip to Africa, Castro attempted unsuccessfully to mediate the conflict between Ethiopia and Somalia over possession of the Ogaden region.

27 April: The United States and Cuba signed an accord on fishing rights.

25 May: The U.S. State Department warned that the recent deployment of Cuban military advisors in Ethiopia could "impede the improvement of [U.S.-Cuban] relations."

1 September: The United States and Cuba begin to staff their Interests Sections within the Swiss and Czechoslovak embassies respectively with their own diplomats.

5 November: Somalia expelled all Soviet advisors and broke diplomatic relations with Cuba, citing the presence of Cuban and Soviet advisors in Ethiopia.

Mid-December: Cuban combat troops began to arrive in Ethiopia, eventually totaling nearly 20,000.

1978

19 May: The U.S. charged that Cuban troops in Angola were involved in training and encouraging the Katangese rebels in Zaire's Shaba province. President Carter repeated the charges on May 25, but on June 9 the Senate Foreign Relations Committee found that the evidence for the charges was "inconclusive."

21 October: In an attempt at reconciliation with the Cuban-American community, Cuba released 46 prisoners and ex-prisoners who then flew to the United States. This followed the formation of the Committee of 75, a group of Cuban Americans that had helped to negotiate prisoners' release.

1979

1 January: Cuban-Americans are permitted to visit their families in Cuba. More than 100,000 visited Cuba during the coming year.

14 April: The new government of Grenada established diplomatic relations with Cuba, and subsequently developed close economie and political ties.

26 July: The annual celebration to commemorate the 1953 attack on the Moncada barricade was dedicated to the triumph of the Nicaragua Revolution on July 19.

30 August: As delegates to the sixth summit of the Nonaligned Movement gathered in Havana, the United States charged that a new 3,000-troop Soviet combat brigade had been discovered in Cuba. Cuba and the Soviet Union asserted that the brigade was a training group that had been stationed in Cuba since 1962.

3–9 September: The sixth summit of the Nonaligned Movement met in Havana. Castro was elected chair of the movement and served until 1982. (Reading 41)

1 October: President Carter announced several responses to the Soviet combat brigade in Cuba, including the establishment of a U.S. military headquarters in Key West, Florida, and expanded military maneuvers in the Caribbean.

1 November: A new penal code took effect, replacing the 1936 criminal code. (Reading 23)

1980

11 January: In a major governmental reorganization, President Fidel Castro assumed responsibility for overseeing the Ministries of Defense, Interior, Public Health, and Culture.

12 March: Cubans began work on a new international airport in Grenada, which became an object of concern for U.S.

March: Private "farmers markets" opened. Individual producers or cooperatives were able sell any excess over their contracted production level and new products for which they had not contracted. There was no control on prices.

1 April: Twelve people seeking asylum used a minibus to crash through the gates of the Peruvian Embassy in Havana. The Cuban government then removed guards from the embassy, and Peru announced that its embassy grounds would be open for anyone who wished to enter. 7,000 people did so.

21 April: Cuba announced that anyone wishing to leave the country could be picked up at the port of Mariel. By September 26, when the port was closed, 120,000 had left the country, most going to the United States. Approximately 1 percent were people released from prisons and mental institutions. (Reading 39)

2 May: Three hundred eighty-nine former political prisoners took refuge in the United States Interests Section in Havana, after a fight broke out between demonstrators and former prisoners waiting for visas to be processed.

17–20 December: Second Congress of Cuban Communist Party ratified a five-year plan which projected a 5 percent growth rate, and called for increased efficiency. The Main Report attributed the failure to achieve the 6 percent rate anticipated in 1975 to a dramatic increase in interest rates on foreign capital, and diseases that affected sugar and tobacco crops.

1981

20 January: The Territorial Troop Militia was launched at a ceremony in Granma Province. By 1985 it would have 1.5 million members, composed of people who are in neither the regular or reserve forces. (Reading 31)

18 February: U.S. Secretary of State Alexander Haig told NATO representatives that the United States has "to deal with the immediate source of the problem [in El Salvador]—and that is Cuba."

30 October: The U.S. Navy began four weeks of exercises in the Caribbean. Pentagon officials on November 6 said that the maneuvers were expected to send a message to Cuba.

31 October: Cuba mobilized its reserves and went on full alert in preparation for an anticipated U.S. invasion.

23 November: Cuban Vice-President Carlos Rafael Rodríguez met secretly with Secretary Haig in Mexico. No agreements were reached.

1982

10 April: Following Cuban offers of aid to Argentina in the Malvinas/Falklands conflict, the Cuban ambassador to Argentina returned to Buenos Aires after a long absence.

19 April: The U.S. Treasury Department—in a move proclaimed to tighten the embargo against Cuba—announced the reimposition of restrictions on travel to Cuba. (Reading 36)

16 June: Vice-President Rodríguez told the U.N. that Cuba had almost doubled its military strength since 1981 in response to the aggressiveness of the Reagan Administration.

1983

1 March: Cuba signed an agreement with 13 creditor nations to reschedule its $810 million foreign debt due between September 1, 1982 and December 31, 1983.

24 July: Castro, in a letter to the Contadora Group (Mexico, Panama, Colombia, and Venezuela), declared that Cuba would cooperate with any negotiated solution toward peace.

22 October: In the wake of the assassination of Grenadian Prime Minister Maurice Bishop, Cuba denied a request from Grenada to assist it militarily in the face of an impending U.S. attack.

25 October: The U.S. invaded Grenada with 8,800 troops, occupied the island, and established a provisional government. Of the 784 Cubans on the island, 636 were construction workers and 43 were military personnel. The U.S. captured 642 Cubans, killed 24, and wounded 57.

1984

19 March: Cuba and Angola outlined conditions under which Cuba would withdraw its troops, including removal of all South African forces from Namibia and implementation of U.N. Security Council Resolution 435.

14 May: The U.S. Department of Defense reported that it would spend $43 million to refurbish Guantanamo Naval Base.

28 June: U.S. Supreme Court ruled that the Treasury Department can impose restrictions on U.S. citizens that have the effect of banning travel to Cuba.

29 June: Presidential candidate Jesse Jackson left Cuba after a series of meetings that resulted in the release of 26 prisoners, further openings for the church in Cuba, and the assent by Cuba to open talks on immigration issues with the United States.

14 December: The United States and Cuba reached agreement on an immigration program under which Cuba would repatriate 2,746 "excludables" who had arrived during the Mariel exodus, and the United States would permit the immigration of 20,000 Cubans annually.

1985

1 January: A new housing law took effect under which occupants of rental property (house or apartment rented from the state) are permitted to purchase and ultimately sell their dwellings.

24 January: Five U.S. Catholic Church leaders met with Castro and high Cuban officials. This followed the opening earlier in the month of the Office of Religious Affairs, which signaled warmer relations between the Cuban government and church. (Reading 24)

19 May: The United States initiated propaganda broadcasts to Cuba over Radio Martí. In response, Cuba suspended the five-month-old immigration and repatriation agreement with the United States.

3 August: A five-day conference in Havana on foreign debt concluded with a call for a basic restructuring of the relationship between debtor and creditor nations. Twelve hundred delegates from 37 hemispheric countries attended the conference.

4 October: President Reagan issued a proclamation that banned travel to the United States by Cuban government or Communist party officials or their representatives, which effectively barred most students, scholars, and artists as well as officials.

1986

7 February: The Third Congress of the Cuban Communist Party ratified proposals to coordinate Cuba's economic plans more closely with the Council for Mutual Economic Assistance, to improve economic efficiency, to increase representation in the party hierarchy and the party itself by women, workers and other underrepresented sectors. (Readings 19, 20 and 29)

17 February: The Cuban Catholic Church hosted an international conference about the Church in Cuba, attended by bishops from most Latin American countries, and the United States, and a Vatican representative.

18 May: Private farmers' markets were closed, in response to reports that the program had begun to create a class of wealthy dealers.

14 June: The new housing law was modified to end the rapid rise in prices. Unregulated sales between individuals were suspended, with sales to occur only at a "legal" price. (Reading 16)

26 December: Castro announced budget cuts that reduced the amount of sugar available for public consumption, the number of children sent to schools in the countryside, the monthly ration of kerosene, and increased electricity rates, bus fares, and some parallel market prices.

1987

11 March: The United Nations Human Rights Commission voted down a U.S. resolution that harshly criticized Cuba for alleged human rights violations. Only one of the eight Latin American nations on the commission voted with the United States.

6 July: Cuban television began a seven-part documentary with dramatic on-the-scene footage that detailed espionage activities by U.S. officials stationed in the United States Interests Section (diplomatic mission) in Havana.

15 July: In retaliation for the Cuban television series, the United States expelled two Cuban diplomats stationed at the Cuban Interests Section in Washington.

13 August: Castro endorsed the Central American (Arias) peace plan approved on August 7 in Guatemala by the leaders of the five affected countries.

20 November: The United States and Cuba restored the immigration agreement that Cuba had cancelled in 1985.

1988

January 29: U.S. and Cuban representatives met for the first time to discuss the war in Angola. The United States previously had refused to attend any meeting about Angola with Cubans present. In May, a four-country parley (the United States, Cuba, Angola, and South Africa) began negotiations over the war.

February–March: A delegation of U.S. human rights leaders inspected Cuban prisons as part of an exchange agreement under which a Cuban delegation would later inspect U.S. prison facilities. The U.S. group reported that conditions in the prisons were generally no worse than those in U.S. prisons, that there is no evidence of systematic abuses, and that some practices such as conjugal visits are more humane than those in the United States.

March 10: The United Nations Human Rights Commission agreed to accept a Cuban invitation for a Commission delegation to visit the island, after the United States withdrew its proposed resolution to condemn alleged human rights violations in Cuba.

April 21: John Cardinal O'Connor, Archbishop of New York, met with Fidel Castro in Havana. It was the first visit by a Roman Catholic cardinal to Cuba since 1959. The Cuban leader agreed to grant visas to nuns who want to serve in Cuba.

APPENDIX B:

Basic Statistics on Cuba

I. POPULATION AND LAND (1985)

Population

10 million: 67% urban, 30% rural
Capital: Havana, 2 million
Ethnic divisions: 51% mulatto; 37% white; 11% black; 1% Chinese
Language: Spanish
Literacy rate: 90–95%[3]
Labor force: 3 million; agriculture, 30%; services, 20%; industry, 20%; construction, 11%; commerce, 10%; government, 5%[1,3]

Area

44,200 square miles; 14 provinces, 169 municipalities[2]

II. ECONOMY

General

Peso: $.76 (1988)[6]
Current account deficit (hard currency): $108 million[6]
Debt (to West): $3.4 billion (1984); $750 million due 1985

Debt (to Soviet Union): $22 billion[8]
Reserves: (1984) $179 million[6]
GNP: $15 billion; per capita, $1,534; real growth rate 1.4%.[3]
Agriculture: sugar, tobacco, rice, potatoes, citrus, coffee
Fishing[2]
Industries: sugar milling, petroleum refining, food and tobacco processing, textiles, chemicals, metals, cement. *Exports:* $6 billion (f.o.b.);[2] sugar, nickel, shellfish, citrus, rum, tobacco

Economic Structure*

Macroeconomic Indicators	1981	1982	1983	1984	1985
GSP in producer prices[a]	22.5[b]	23.1[b]	24.3	26.1	. . .
Real GSP growth %	13.9	2.5	5.2	7.4	4.8
Population mn	9.7	9.8	9.9	10.0	10.1[d]
Convertible currency:					
exports fob mn pesos	1,406	1,358	1,234	1,136	1,244
imports fob mn pesos	1,121	734	793	1,063	1,177
current account mn pesos	51	265	263	−212	−140
Reserves minus gold mn pesos	. . .	. . .	318.7	249.3	335.1
Total external debt mn pesos	3,167	2,669	2,790	2,989	3,258
Exchange rate (av) pesos per $	. . .	0.85	0.87	0.90	0.92
August 8, 1986 0.87 pesos per $					

Principal Imports 1984[c]

	pesos mn
Intermediate goods	794.5[b]
Capital goods	300.0[b]
Consumer goods	82.5[b]
Total	1,177

Origins of GSP 1985

	% of total
Agriculture & forestry	13.4
Industry	45.3
Construction	8.7
Transport & communications	7.8
Trade	24.1
Total incl others	100.0

Principal Exports 1985[c]

	pesos mn
Fuel (re-exports)	526.9
Sugar	171.2

	pesos mn
Seafood products	91.0[b]
Tobacco products	98.3[b]
Nickel	39.0[b]
Coffee	20.9[b]
Total incl others	1,244

*Main Destinations of Exports
1985*

	% of total
Socialist countries	88.8
Nonsocialist countries	11.2

Main Origins of Imports 1985

	% of total
Socialist countries	84.0
Nonsocialist countries	16.0

*Source: *Quarterly Economic Review of Cuba, Dominican Republic, Haiti, Puerto Rico,* No. 3 (London: The Economist Intelligence Unit, 1986).

[a]At 1983 constant prices Gross Social Product (GSP) is the Cuban equivalent to Gross Domestic Product, the measure of goods and services.

[b]EIU estimate

[c]Convertible currency

[d]Estimate

Trade*

Trade with Major Noncommunist Trading Partners[a]   MN $

Imports from Cuba	Monthly Averages Jan.–Dec.				Jan.–Mar.	
	1982	1983	1984	1985	1985	1986
Spain	9.18	7.81	7.31	10.31	10.65	9.16
Japan	9.30	7.60	6.40	7.70	9.10	10.90
Netherlands	3.94	7.51	4.96	5.41	8.69	5.63
France	4.70	4.80	2.90	3.20	1.50	2.00
Italy	3.60	3.10	3.90	3.20	5.50	4.30[c]
Canada[b]	6.41	3.81	4.03	2.67	2.35	4.34
West Germany	2.70	2.50	1.00	1.70	1.80	1.50
Finland	2.09	1.24	0.42	1.24	0.85	2.30[c]
United Kingdom	2.60	1.80	1.50	0.80	0.80	0.60
Switzerland	0.58	0.47	0.49	0.49	0.47	0.60
Portugal	3.65	0.53	0.59	0.37	0.56	. . .
Belgium/Luxembourg	0.81	1.07	0.54	0.17	0.19	0.19

Exports to Cuba	Monthly Averages Jan.–Dec.				Jan.–Mar.	
	1982	1983	1984	1985	1985	1986
Japan	10.50	8.70	20.80	25.30	25.40	34.70
Spain	8.98	7.52	14.93	24.11	17.06	25.39
Canada	21.95	24.54	21.73	20.17	26.86	27.74
France	4.70	8.30	8.50	8.90	10.10	6.90
West Germany	5.40	5.40	6.60	8.80	9.10	14.70
United Kingdom	9.50	5.80	7.20	6.40	5.80	7.09
Italy	3.20	2.50	6.10	5.20	4.60	4.30[c]
Netherlands	4.84	3.29	3.24	2.57	3.82	3.20
Sweden	1.65	1.42	2.51	2.59	2.13	2.64
Belgium/Luxembourg	1.29	1.16	1.02	2.26	2.00	3.21[c]
Switzerland	1.46	2.22	1.99	2.23	0.95	3.17
Ireland	2.13	2.19	2.10	—	—	—

*Source: *Quarterly Economic Review of Cuba,* No. 3 (London: The Economist Intelligence Unit, 1986).

[a]Exports, fob; imports, cif.
[b]Imports, fob
[c]January–February

Trade with Communist Countries   MN $[a]

	Exports to Cuba				Imports from Cuba			
	1981	1982	1983	1984	1981	1982	1983	1984
USSR	3,811	4,309	4,574	4,623	2,845	3,736	3,628	4,275
Bulgaria	190	206	223	. . .	193	172	194	. . .
Czechoslovakia	146	214	195	. . .	97	125	123	. . .
Poland	60	53	53	41	41	33	32	28
Hungary	51	71	64	74	73	60	12	18
Romania	180	—	140	. . .	89	—	80	. . .
Total of above	4,438	4,853	5,249	. . .	3,338	4,126	4,069	. . .

[a]Converted by commercial conversion factors which correspond, in general, to official exchange rates (mainly par values) established with the IMF.

USSR Trade with Cuba[a]   **MN Roubles**

	Jan.–Dec.	
Exports, fob (including re-exports)	*1983*	*1984*
Machinery & transport equipment of which:	969.9	1,028.7
tractors & agric. machinery	123.0	124.0
motor lorries	50.9	53.6
passenger cars & parts	42.7	40.1
other motor vehicles & garage equip.	77.6	73.3
aircraft & parts	60.1	94.1
Petroleum & products	1,184.5	1,324.8
Rolled ferrous products	96.9	98.2
Fertilizers & agricultural pest control preps.	55.8	53.8
Wood & paper & manufactures	116.7	129.2
Raw cotton	38.5	56.4
Grain (excluding groats)	138.8	155.5
Flour	36.5	39.0
Meat & milk products, animal fats, eggs of which:	47.2	48.9
meat products	27.1	28.9
Vegetable oils, edible	26.0	26.4
Domestic appliances, clocks & cameras	69.7	82.3
Total, including other items		
mn roubles	3,399.9	3,752.2
mn $	4,456.0	4,398.8
Imports, fob		
Metal ores & concentrates	196.6	166.2
Sugar	2,408.3	3,209.3
Total, including other items		
mn roubles	2,693.3	3,463.9
mn $	3,529.9	4,060.8

NB: Commodity totals are additions of items in the trade accounts and may be incomplete.
[a]Noncommercial rate: end 1983 0.763 roubles = $1.00; end 1984 0.853 roubles = $1.00.

Exports of Sugar from Cuba   '000 Tons

| | 1982 | 1983 | 1984 | 1985 | Jan–Mar | |
					1985	1986
USSR	4,426	3,315	3,650	3,709	1,814	1,940
Czechoslovakia	135	145	226	134	99	106
Japan	295	355	231	511	77	90
East Germany	213	281	279	277	131	89
Algeria	208	99	41	81	7	76
China	915	772	705	680	211	71
Bulgaria	278	331	360	400	120	64
Egypt	190	231	138	182	40	38
Canada	160	190	241	152	26	36
Libya	45	90	44	113	57	34
Iraq	134	158	113	130	40	27
Finland	39	65	39	76	15	13
Malaysia	26	60	39	52	26	13
Syrian Arab Republic	109	109	133	63	—	11
Angola	53	41	46	51	23	11
Poland	—	—	—	134	—	—
Venezuela	—	—	—	123	—	—
India	—	—	41	108	—	—
Tunisia	—	12	27	76	26	—
Romania	90	221	272	63	63	—
Vietnam	24	77	37	3	—	—
Peru	—	25	54	—	—	—
Total, including others	7,734	6,792	7,017	7,209	2,815	2,662

Cuban Central Budget *

1986 Approved	*Millions of Dollars*
Total revenue	12,018.2

Expenditures	
Production	3,958.1
Housing and community services	787.9
Education and public health	2,626.5
Other sociocultural and scientific activities	1,964.5
Administration of the organs of People's Power, the courts, the Attorney General's Office, and other organs and agencies of the state	650.5

1986 Approved	*Millions of Dollars*
Defense and internal order	1,307.1
Other activities	309.7
Reserve	392.6
Total Expenditures	11,996.9
Surplus	21.3

*Source: *Quarterly Economic Review of Cuba,* "Dominican Republic, Haiti, Puerto Rico," No. 3 (London: The Economist Intelligence Unit, 1986); Banco Nacional de Cuba.

III. HEALTH INDICATORS

	Year	*Number*
Demographic Indicators		
Estimated mid-year population (in thousands)	1986	10,200
Population density (inhabitants per km²)	1982	88.8
Annual growth rate (%)	1982	9.7
Percentage of population under 15 years of age	1982	28.6
Percentage of population 65 years of age and over	1982	7.9
Percentage of urban population (as nationally defined)	1982	69.7
Percentage of population in localities of 20,000 inhabitants and over	1981	47.9
Percentage of population in localities of less than 2,000 inhabitants	1981	33.9
Birth rate (live births/1,000 inhabitants)	1986	16.3
Mortality rate (deaths/1,000 inhabitants)	1986	6.2
Fertility rate (per 1,000 women 15–49 years of age)	1982	63.6
State of Health Indicators		
Life expectancy at birth	1986	74.5
Infant mortality rate (per 1,000 live births)	1986	13.6
Rate of maternal deaths (per 1,000 live births)	1983	0.3
Death rate 1–4 years (per 1,000 children 1–4 years)	1983	0.8

	Year	*Number*
Percentage of newborn with weight under 2,500 grams	1983	8.5
Percentage of deaths due to:		
•Infectious and parasitic diseases (001–139)	1983	2.0
•Tumors (140–239)	1983	19.1
•Heart diseases (390–429)	1983	29.1
•Motor vehicle traffic accidents (E810–819)	1983	2.9
•Signs, symptoms and ill-defined morbose states (780–799)	1982	0.3

Health Services Coverage Indicators

	Year	*Number*
Percentage of children under 1 year immunized against:		
•Diphtheria	1983	81.5
•Poliomyelitis	1983	93.6
•Measles	1983	70.9
•Tetanus	1983	81.5
•Whooping Cough	1983	81.5
•Tuberculosis	1983	96.3
Number of consultations per inhabitant	1983	5.2
Number of discharges per 100 inhabitants	1983	14.6[a]
Number of beds per 1,000 inhabitants	1983	6.1[b]

Human Resources Indicators

	Year	*Number*
Physicians per 10,000 inhabitants	1986	25.5
Dentists per 10,000 inhabitants	1983	4.4
Nurses and auxiliaries per 10,000 inhabitants	1986	48.3

*Source: *Pan-American Health Organization/World Health Organization Program Budget 1984* (Washington, D.C.: PAHO, 1984), p. 419.

[a]Admissions.

[b]Includes private sector beds.

IV. GENERAL EDUCATION INDICATORS*

Subject	1958/59	1985/86
Schools	7,679	13,815
primary		10,477
intermediate		1,266
technical		632
upper level		35
Teachers	22,798	231,806
Students Registered	811,345	2,832,800
(of them, women)		1,386,265
Graduates	26,693	787,486
(of them women)		340,951
primary		218,800
intermediate		204,600
technical		81,000
upper level		26,000
Scholarships		597,622

*Source: *Anuario Estadistico de Cuba 1985* (Havana: Comite Estatal de Estadisticas, 1985), p. 483.

SOURCES

1. Committee on Population and Demography, *Fertility Determinants in Cuba,* Report #26, by Paula E. Hollerbach and Sergio Díaz Briquets (Washington, D.C.: National Academy Press, 1983).

2. Republic of Cuba, Junta Central de Planificación (JUCEPLAN), *Anuario Estadístico de Cuba,* 1981 (Havana: Comité Estatal de Estadísticas, 1981).

3. Central Intelligence Agency, *The World Factbook* (Washington, D.C.: U.S. Government Printing Office, April 1984).

4. U.S. Department of State, "Background Notes: Cuba" (Washington, D.C.: U.S. Government Printing Office, April 1983).

5. Arthur S. Banks and William Overstreet, eds., *Political Handbook of the World: 1982–1983.* (New York: McGraw-Hill, 1983).

6. National Bank of Cuba, "Economic Report" (Havana: National Bank of Cuba, February 1985).

7. Economic Commission on Latin America and the Caribbean, "Preliminary Overview of the Latin American Economy during 1984." New York: United Nations/CEPAL, #409/410, January 1985, Tables 2,3.

8. Clyde H. Farnsworth, "Cuban Report Is Candid on Economic Burdens," *New York Times* (June 5, 1985), p. D1.

APPENDIX C:

Suggestions for Further Reading

Aguilar, Luis. E. *Cuba 1933*. Ithaca, NY: Cornell University Press, 1972.

Benjamin, Jules Robert. *The U.S. and Cuba; Hegemony and Dependent Development, 1880–1934*. Pittsburgh: University of Pittsburgh Press, 1976.

Benjamin, Medea, J. Collins, and M. Scott. *No Free Lunch: Food and Revolution in Cuba Today*. San Francisco: Institute for Food and Development Policy, 1984.

Bernard, Robert M. *The Theory of Moral Incentives in Cuba*. Tuscaloosa, AL: University of Alabama Press, 1971.

Betto, Frei. *Fidel and Religion*. New York: Simon and Schuster, 1987.

Blasier, Cole, and Carmelo Mesa-Lago, eds. *Cuba in the World*. Pittsburgh: University of Pittsburgh Press, 1979.

Bonachea, R., and Nelson Valdés, eds. *Revolutionary Struggle, The Selected Works of Fidel Castro*. Cambridge, MA: MIT Press, 1972.

——————, eds. *Che: Selected Works of Ernesto Che Guevara*. Cambridge, MA: MIT Press, 1969.

——————, eds. *Cuba in Revolution*. New York: Anchor Books, 1972.

Bonsal, Philip W. *Cuba, Castro and the United States*. Pittsburgh: University of Pittsburgh Press, 1971.

Boorstein, Edward. *The Economic Transformation of Cuba*. New York: Modern Reader, 1968.

Brenner, Philip. *The Limits and Possibilities of Congress*. New York: St. Martin's Press, 1983.

547

—————. *From Confrontation to Negotiation: U.S. Relations with Cuba.* Boulder, CO: Westview Press, 1988.

Brudenius, Claes. *Revolutionary Cuba: The Challenge of Economic Growth with Equity.* Boulder, CO: Westview Press, 1964.

Castro, Fidel. *Fidel Castro Speeches: Cuba's Internationalist Foreign Policy, 1975–1980.* Ed. by Michael Taber. New York: Pathfinder Press, 1981. Vol. I.

—————. *Fidel Castro Speeches: Our Power Is That of the Working People.* Ed. by Michael Taber. New York: Pathfinder Press, 1983. Vol. II.

—————. *Fidel Castro Speeches 1984–85: War and Crisis in the Americas.* Ed. by Michael Taber. New York: Pathfinder Press, 1985. Vol. III.

—————. *History Will Absolve Me.* London: Jonathan Cape, Ltd., 1967.

—————. *Nothing Can Stop the Course of History.* New York: Pathfinder Press, 1986. Interview by Jeffrey M. Elliot and Mervyn M. Dymally.

—————. *The World Economic and Social Crisis.* Havana: Council of State Publishing Office, 1983.

Danielson, Ross. *Cuban Medicine.* New Brunswick, NJ: Transaction Press, 1979.

Debray, Regis. *Revolution in the Revolution.* New York: Monthly Review Press, 1967.

del Aguila, Juan M. *Cuba: Dilemmas of a Revolution.* Boulder, CO: Westview Press, 1984.

Díaz-Brisquets, Sergio. *The Health Revolution in Cuba.* Austin, TX: University of Texas Press, 1983.

Dinerstein, Herbert. *The Making of a Missile Crisis, October 1962.* Baltimore: Johns Hopkins University Press, 1976.

Domínguez, Jorge. *Cuba: Order and Revolution.* Cambridge, MA: Harvard University Press, 1978.

—————, ed., *Cuba: Internal and International Affairs.* Beverly Hills, CA: Sage Publications, 1982.

Dorschner, John, and Roberto Fabrico. *The Winds of December.* New York: Coward, McCann, and Georghegan, 1980.

Draper, Theodore. *Castro's Revolution, Myths and Realities.* New York: Praeger, 1962.

—————. *Castroism, Theory and Practice.* New York: Praeger, 1965.

Dubois, Jules. *Fidel Castro: Rebel Liberator or Dictator?* Indianapolis, IN: Bobbs-Merrill, 1959.

Dumont, Rene. *Cuba: Socialism and Development.* 2nd ed. New York: Grove Press, 1970.

—————. *Is Cuba Socialist?* New York: Viking Press, 1974.

Duncan, W. Raymond. *The Soviet Union and Cuba: Interests and Influence.* New York: Praeger, 1985.

Erisman, H. Michael. *Cuba's International Relations.* Boulder, CO: Westview Press, 1985.

Fagen, Richard. *The Transformation of Political Culture in Cuba.* Stanford, CA: Stanford University Press, 1969.

Falk, Pamela. *Cuban Foreign Policy.* Lexington, MA: Lexington Books, 1986.

Foner, Philip. *A History of Cuba and Its Relations with the United States.* Two volumes. New York: International Publishers, 1962 and 1963.

Franklin, Jane. *Cuban Foreign Relations: A Chronology: 1959–1982.* New York: Center for Cuban Studies, 1984.

Franqui, Carlos. *Diary of the Cuban Revolution.* New York: Viking, 1976.

————. *Family Portrait with Fidel.* 2nd ed. New York: Random House, 1984.

Fuentes, Norberto. *Nos Impusieron La Violencia.* Havana: Editorial Letras Cúbanas, 1986.

Gerassi, John. *Venceremos: The Speeches and Writings of Ernesto Che Guevara.* New York: Simon and Schuster, 1968.

————. *Fidel Castro.* Garden City, NY: Doubleday and Co., 1973.

Gonzalez, Edward. *Cuba Under Castro: The Limits of Charisma.* Boston: Houghton Mifflin, 1974.

Goodsell, James Nelson, ed. *Fidel Castro's Personal Revolution in Cuba: 1959–1973.* New York: Alfred A. Knopf, Inc. 1975.

Guevara, Ernesto "Che." *The Diary of Che Guevera.* Ed. by Robert Scheer. New York: Bantam, 1968.

Halebsky, S., and J. M. Kirk, eds. *Cuba: Twenty-five Years of Revolution 1959–1964.* New York: Praeger, 1985.

Halperin, Maurice. *The Rise and Decline of Fidel Castro.* Berkeley, CA: University of California Press, 1972.

————. *The Taming of Fidel Castro.* Berkeley, CA: University of California Press, 1981.

Harnecker, Marta. *Cuba: Dictatorship or Democracy?* Westport, CT: Lawrence Hill and Co., 1975.

Hinckle, Warren, and William Turner. *The Fish Is Red: The Story of the Secret War Against Castro.* New York: Harper and Row, 1981.

Horowitz, I. L. *Cuban Communism.* 6th ed. New Brunswick, NJ: Transaction Inc., 1987.

Huberman, Leo, and Paul Sweezy. *Socialism in Cuba.* New York: Monthly Review Press, 1970.

————. *Cuba: Anatomy of a Revolution.* New York: Monthly Review Press, 1962.

Jackson, D. Bruce. *Castro, the Kremlin, and Communism in Latin America.* Baltimore: Johns Hopkins University Press, 1969.

Johnson, Haynes. *The Bay of Pigs.* New York: W. W. Norton, 1964.

Karol, K. S. *Guerrillas in Power: The Course of the Cuban Revolution.* New York: Wang and Hill, 1970.

Kennedy, Robert F. *Thirteen Days.* New York: W. W. Norton, 1969.

Kenner, M., and J. Petras, eds. *Fidel Castro Speaks.* New York: Grove Press, 1969.

Knight, Franklin. *Slave Society in Cuba During the Nineteenth Century.* Madison, WI: University of Wisconsin Press, 1978.

Kozol, Jonathan. *Children of the Revolution: A Yankee Teacher in the Cuban Schools.* New York: Delacorte Press, 1978.

LeoGrande, William M. *Cuba's Policy in Africa, 1959–1980.* Berkeley, CA: Institute for International Studies, 1980.

Levesque, Jacques. *The USSR and the Cuban Revolution: Soviet Ideological and Strategical Perspectives.* New York: Praeger, 1978.

Levine, Barry, ed. *The New Cuban Presence in the Caribbean.* Boulder, CO: Westview Press, 1983.

Lewis, Oscar, Ruth M. Lewis, and Susan M. Rigdon. *Four Men: Living the Revolution.* Urbana, IL: University of Illinois Press, 1977.

—————. *Four Women: Living the Revolution.* Urbana, IL: University of Illinois Press, 1977.

—————. *Neighbors: Living the Revolution.* Urbana, IL: University of Illinois Press, 1978.

Lockwood, Lee, *Castro's Cuba, Cuba's Fidel.* New York: Vintage Books, 1969.

MacDonald, Theodore. *Making a New People: Education in Revolutionary Cuba.* Vancouver, Can.: New Star Books, 1985.

MacEwan, Arthur. *Revolution and Economic Development in Cuba.* New York & London: The Macmillan Press, 1981.

Mankiewicz, Frank, and Kirby Jones. *With Fidel: A Portrait of Castro and Cuba.* Chicago: Playboy Press, 1975.

Martí, José. *Inside the Monster: Writings on the United States and American Imperialism.* Ed. by Philip Foner. New York: Monthly Review Press, 1975.

—————. *Nuestra America.* Ed. by Philip Foner. New York: Monthly Review Press, 1977.

Matthews, Herbert L. *Revolution in Cuba.* New York: Charles Scribner's Sons, 1975.

Menton, Seymour. *Prose Fiction of the Cuban Revolution.* Austin, TX: University of Texas Press, 1975.

Mesa-Lago, Carmelo. *Cuba in the 1970s: Pragmatism and Institutionalization.* Albuquerque, NM: University of New Mexico Press, 1978.

—————, ed. *Revolutionary Change in Cuba.* Pittsburgh: University of Pittsburgh Press, 1971.

—————. *The Economy of Socialist Cuba.* Albuquerque, NM: University of New Mexico Press, 1981.

Moreno Fraginals, Manuel. *El Ingenio.* La Havana: Museo Numismático de Cuba, 1964.

Nelson, Lowry. *Rural Cuba,* reprint. New York: Octagon Books, 1970.

O'Conner, James. *The Origins of Socialism in Cuba.* Ithaca, NY: Cornell University Press, 1970.

Perez, Louis. *Cuba Between Empires, 1878–1902.* Pittsburgh: University of Pittsburgh Press, 1978.

——————. *Army Politics in Cuba, 1898–1958.* Pittsburgh: University of Pittsburgh Press, 1975.

Phillips, R. Hart. *The Cuban Dilemma.* New York: Ivan Obolensky, Inc., 1962.

Randall, Margaret. *Cuban Women Now.* Toronto: The Women's Press, 1974.

——————. *Women in Cuba: Twenty Years Later.* New York: Smyrna Press, 1981.

Ratliff, William. *Castroism and Communism in Latin America, 1959–1976.* Washington, D.C.: American Enterprise Institute, 1976.

Reckord, Barry. *Does Fidel Eat More Than Your Father?* New York: Praeger, 1971.

Ritter, Archibald, R.M. *The Economic Development of Revolutionary Cuba: Strategy and Performance.* New York: Praeger, 1974.

Robbins, Carla Anne. *The Cuban Threat.* New York: McGraw Hill, 1982.

Rodríguez, Carlos Rafael, *Letra con Filo.* Two Volumes. Havana: Editorial de Ciencias Sociales, 1983.

Silverman, Bertram, ed. *Man and Socialism in Cuba: The Great Debate.* New York: Atheneum, 1971.

Smith Robert F. *The United States and Cuba: Business and Diplomacy, 1917–1960.* New Haven, CT: Yale University Press, 1960.

——————. *Background to Revolution: The Development of Modern Cuba.* New York: Alfred A. Knopf, Inc., 1966.

Smith, Wayne S. *The Closest of Enemies.* New York: W. W. Norton and Co., 1987.

Suarez, Andres. *Cuba, Castroism and Communism, 1959–1966.* Cambridge, MA: MIT Press, 1967.

Suchlicki, Jaime, ed. *Cuba, Castro and Revolution.* Coral Gables, FL: University of Miami Press, 1972.

Szulc, Tad. *Fidel.* New York: William Morrow and Company, 1986.

Thomas, Hugh. *Cuba: The Pursuit of Freedom.* New York: Harper and Row, 1971.

Valdés, Nelson P., and Edwin Lieuwen. *The Cuban Revolution.* Albuquerque, NM: University of New Mexico Press, 1971.

Wald, Karen. *Children of Che.* Palo Alto, CA: Ramparts Press, 1978.

Weinstein, Martin, ed. *Revolutionary Cuba in the World Arena.* Philadelphia: Institute for Study of Human Resources, 1979.

Welch, Richard E. *Response to Revolution: The United States and the Cuban Revolution, 1959–1961.* Chapel Hill, NC: University of North Carolina Press, 1985.

Peter Wyden. *The Bay of Pigs.* New York: Simon and Schuster, 1979.

Yglesias, Jose. *In the Fist of the Revolution: Life in a Cuban Country Town.* New York: Vintage, 1969.

Zeitlin, Maurice. *Revolutionary Politics and the Cuban Working Class.* New York: Harper and Row, 1970.

Zimbalist, Andrew. *Cuba's Socialist Economy Toward the 1990's.* Boulder, CO: Lynne Reiner Publishers, 1987.

Further Sources of Information

Amistad. Canadian Cuba Friendship Association. Liz Hill, Editor, CCFA. P.O. Box 326, Station L., N6E 472, Toronto, Canada.

AREITO, P.O. Box 441403, Miami, FL, 33144.

Cuba Update. Center for Cuban Studies Newsletter. 123 W. 23rd St., New York, NY, 10011.

Cuba Business. BCM Cuba, London WCIN 3XX, England.

Cuba Sí. Britain Cuba Resource Center, c/o Carila, 29 Islington Park St., London NI, England.

Cuban Studies/Estudios Cubanos. Center for Latin American Studies, University Center for International Studies, University of Pittsburgh, Pittsburgh, PA, 15260.

Granma Weekly Review (official organ of the Central Committee of the Communist Party of Cuba). Apartado Postal 6260, Havana 6, Cuba, C.P. 10699.

Problems of Communism. Superintendent of Documents, U.S. Government Printing Office, Washington, DC, 20402.

About the Editors

PHILIP BRENNER is associate professor of international relations at The American University in Washington, D.C. where he teaches foreign policy in the Washington Semester Program. He is the author of *From Confrontation to Negotiation: U.S. Relations with Cuba* (1988) and *The Limits and Possibilities of Congress* (1983), and his articles have appeared in journals and newspapers. Dr. Brenner is on the Advisory Board of the National Security Archive and is a member of the National Council on United States–Cuban Relations.

WILLIAM M. LEOGRANDE is associate professor of political science at The American University, where he served as Director of the Political Science Program from 1980 to 1982. He is the author of *Cuba's Policy in Africa* (1980) and co-author of *Confronting Revolution: Security Through Diplomacy in Central America* (1986), and his articles have appeared in *Foreign Affairs, Foreign Policy, The New York Times,* and other journals and newspapers. Dr. Leo-Grande was a Council on Foreign Relations Fellow in 1982–83, during which time he worked with the Democratic Policy Committee in the U.S. Senate.

DONNA RICH is a research analyst for the Cuba Policy Project at Johns Hopkins University School of Advanced International Studies (SAIS). She is a Ph.D. candidate at SAIS, where she received her M.A. Ms. Rich was a guest scholar at the University of Havana in 1984, and was an analyst at the National Security Archive where she developed a document set on the Cuban missile crisis. She has published articles on both Cuba and Mexico.

DANIEL SIEGEL is associate fellow at the Institute for Policy Studies. He was director of public education on the Contragate project at the Christic Institute. He was coeditor of *In Contempt of Congress: The Reagan Record on Central America* (1987) and coauthor of *Outcast Among Allies: The International Costs of Reagan's War Against Nicaragua* (1985). His articles have appeared in several newspapers and magazines including the *Los Angeles Times, Boston Globe, Newsday,* and *Des Moines Register.*

About the Contributors

LUIS E. AGUILAR is professor of political science at Georgetown University and a frequent contributor to newspapers and magazines.

Scott Armstrong is Executive Director of the National Security Archive. A former reporter for the *Washington Post,* he is the co-author of *The Chronology* (1987) and *The Brethren* (1979).

PAT AUFDERHEIDE is senior editor of *In These Times* and writes frequently about culture and film in magazines and newspapers.

MAX AZICRI is professor of political science at Edinboro University of Pennsylvania, and is the author of *Cuba: Politics, Economics, and Society* (1988).

MEDEA BENJAMIN works at the Institute for Food and Development Policy, a nonprofit public education and documentation center in San Francisco.

ROBIN BLACKBURN is the editor of *New Left Review* (London). He is the author of *The Overthrow of Colonial Slavery: 1776–1848* (1988).

CLAES BRUNDENIUS is a research fellow at the Research Policy Institute of the University of Lund, Sweden, and author of *Economic Growth, Basic Needs, and Income Distribution in Revolutionary Cuba* (1981).

LOURDES CASAL (1939–1981) was professor of psychology at Rutgers University and author of numerous scholarly articles and poems about Cuba. She was a founder of *Areito,* and was a member of the Committee of 75, which initiated a "dialogue" between Cubans living in the United States and Cuba.

FIDEL CASTRO RUZ is President of the Republic of Cuba, Commander-in-Chief of the Revolutionary Armed Forces, and First Secretary of the Communist Party of Cuba.

JOSEPH COLLINS is cofounder of the Institute for Food and Development Policy and author of *What Difference Could a Revolution Make? Food and Farming in the New Nicaragua* (1985).

MARGARET E. CRAHAN is Luce Professor of Religion, Power, and Politics at Occidental College and editor of *Human Rights and Basic Needs in the Americas* (1982).

JORGE I. DOMÍNGUEZ is professor of government at Harvard University and author of *Cuba: Order and Revolution* (1978).

SUSAN ECKSTEIN is professor of sociology at Boston University, and has written widely on Cuba. She is currently writing a book on the political economy of the Cuban revolution.

H. MICHAEL ERISMAN is professor of political science and chair of the department at Indiana State University in Terre Haute. He is the editor of *The Caribbean Challenge: U.S. Policy in a Volatile Region* (1984).

DEBRA EVENSON is a professor in the DePaul University College of Law, and is a specialist on the Cuban legal system. She is on the board of the Center for Cuban Studies.

PATRICIA WEISS FAGEN is currently Information Officer for the United Nations High Commissioner for Refugees (UNHCR). She was previously Staff Associate at the Refugee Policy Group in Washington, D. C., during which time she wrote the article excerpted in this volume.

RICHARD FAGEN is Gildred Professor of Latin American Studies at Stanford University and is the author of *The Political Transformation of Cuba* (1969) and *Forging Peace: The Challenge of Central America* (1987).

PAMELA S. FALK is associate director of the Institute of Latin American and Iberian Studies at Columbia University and author of *Superpower Conflict in Angola: A Case Study* (1987).

PABLO ARMANDO FERNANDEZ is editor of the newsletter of the Cuban National Union of Writers and Artists (UNEAC). He is the author of *Los Niños Se Despiden* (1968) which won first prize in the Casa de las Américas competition.

CARLOS FRANQUI was the editor of *Revolución* in the early 1960s, and is author of *Family Portrait with Fidel* (1984). He lives in Spain.

EDWARD GONZÁLEZ is a professor of political science at UCLA, and author of *Cuba Under Castro: The Limits of Charisma* (1974).

ERNESTO "CHE" GUEVARA was born in Argentina in 1928 and joined Fidel Castro's guerrilla army in Mexico in 1955. He was one of the leaders of the revolutionary government until 1965, when he left Cuba to carry on armed struggle first in Africa and later in Bolivia. He was captured and killed by the Bolivian army in 1967.

RAFAEL HERNÁNDÉZ is deputy director of the Center for Studies on the Americas (CEA) in Havana, where he specializes on North America.

LEO HUBERMAN (1903–1968) was an editor of *Monthly Review* and coauthor of *Socialism in Cuba* (1969).

SAUL LANDAU is a Fellow at the Institute for Policy Studies and is producer-director of the documentary film "The Uncompromising Revolution" (1988).

WASSILY LEONTIEF is professor of economics at New York University. He received the Nobel Prize for Economics in 1973.

MARVIN LEINER is professor of education at Queen's College, City University of New York, and is the author of *Children are the Revolution: Day Care in Cuba* (1978).

SANDRA LEVINSON founded and is executive director of the Center for Cuban Studies in New York, where she is editor of *Cuba Update*.

JOSÉ MARTÍ is one of the founding fathers of the Cuban Revolution. Born in Havana in 1853, he was exiled from Cuba in 1871 for political activities, and then lived for the most part in the United States where he worked as a journalist. He organized the Cuban Revolutionary Party in 1892 and returned to Cuba in February 1895, where he was killed in a battle three months later.

HERBERT L. MATTHEWS (1900–1978) was a reporter for *The New York Times* and covered Latin American affairs. He was the author of *Fidel Castro* (1969).

CARMELO MESA-LAGO is a professor of economics at the University of Pittsburgh and author of *Cuba in the 1970s: Pragmatism and Institutionalization* (1978).

ROBERT PASTOR is professor of political science at Emory University and author of *Condemned to Repetition* (1987).

MARIFELI PEREZ-STABLE is associate professor of politics at the State University of New York College of Old Westbury and has written widely on workers and trade unions in Cuba.

CARLOS RAFAEL RODRÍGUEZ, Vice-President of Cuba, is a member of the Political Bureau of the Communist party of Cuba. He was a senior official of the prerevolutionary Communist party (the Popular Socialist party) who joined Castro's rebel army, and has been a leading figure in the revolutionary government since 1962.

SILVIO RODRÍGUEZ is a writer-folksinger in Cuba who helped to found the Grupo de Experiment Sonora. His albums include "Unicornio" and "Mujeres."

RAUDOL RUIZ AGUILERA is a founder and official of the National Institute of Sports, Physical Education, and Recreation (INDER) in Cuba.

MICHAEL SCOTT is Director of Overseas Development Programs for Oxfam America, an international nonprofit aid and development organization.

BARRY SKLAR is a senior staff member of the Senate Foreign Relations Committee and formerly was Latin American analyst with the Library of Congress's Congressional Research Service.

KENNETH N. SKOUG is Deputy Chief of Mission in the U.S. Embassy in Buenos Aires, Argentina. From 1983 to 1988 he was Director of the Office of Cuban Affairs in the U.S. State Department.

PAUL SWEEZY is an editor of *Monthly Review,* author of *The Theory of Capitalist Development* (1942), and coauthor of *Socialism in Cuba.*

ROBERT N. UBELL is an editor and publisher. He was the editor of *The Sciences* and the U.S. publisher of *Nature.*

NELSON P. VALDÉS is professor of sociology at the University of New Mexico, Albuquerque, and Director of the Latin America Data Base.

PHYLLIS GREENE WALKER is working on her doctorate in government at Georgetown University. She writes on the role of the military in Latin America and has published several studies on the subject.

ANDREW ZIMBALIST is professor of economics at Smith College and editor of *Cuba's Socialist Economy Toward the 1990s* (1988).

Index